The School
in American Society

SECOND EDITION

The SCHOOL
in AMERICAN
SOCIETY

Second Edition

Ralph L. Pounds

James R. Bryner

The Macmillan Company, New York
Collier-Macmillan Limited, London

Preface

Tʜᴇ ᴏᴄᴄᴀsɪᴏɴ of the publication of a revised edition of this book gives the authors an opportunity to review the purposes for the writing of such a book and the purposes for offering a college course for which the book becomes one of the important resources. Courses for students in the field of education that will acquaint them with the trends and current characteristics of American social order are widely taught throughout the United States. In contrast to the situation at the time of the first edition, materials for such classes now are widely available. In our own classes, we have found the materials contained in this text to be effective. Many other schools throughout the country continue to find them satisfactory. Because of the contemporaneous nature of much of the material used for illustrations, it seemed advisable to prepare a new edition at this time.

The basic topics and problems used in this text were selected from among those that contemporary scholars indicate as being the major problems faced by our society. The aptness of these selections has been verified through examination of topics treated by writers and teachers in educational sociology and social foundations of education at major institutions. Many of the ways of setting forth, in clear but non-technical language, certain of the problems drawn from economics and other of the social sciences were developed in connection with the classes at the University of Cincinnati. Both of the authors have presented their materials to class groups and have secured informal and formal criticism from the students. Rough drafts of all chapters have been reviewed by authorities.

This text in social foundations of education focuses on the general structure and problems of American society, with emphasis placed on the role of the school in guiding children and youth to analyze and select from alternative solutions to the problems. The authors (and, they hope, the readers) are, figuratively speaking, standing on the doorway of the school, surveying the current cultural scene. A salient characteristic of the present culture is that we are in a state of rapid change. This book primarily is concerned with the important *trends* in that culture and their implications for the school.

Chapter 1 sets forth the importance of the rapidly growing field of social foundations of education and suggests problem areas in education to which this field of study may make significant contributions. Specific educational questions are listed. Complete, detailed answers to these questions may not be found in the book. Although some directions toward solutions are indicated in Part IV, it is felt that only continuous study of society by teachers and administrators can develop dynamic theories of curriculum and methodology for sound educational decision-making. If static solutions had seemed feasible, the authors would have given the answers without need for indicating to the student the background in social trends and problems from which the solutions might be derived.

The authors encountered less difficulty in finding definitive answers to the questions "What is the nature of present social trends?" and "What is the nature of current educational problems?" than they encountered in suggesting searching for alternative solutions to the problems. Educational philosophers represent many different viewpoints, which, utilizing the material presented in this book, will arrive at quite different answers. Some of these philosophic viewpoints not only interpret differently the sociological research on which curriculum construction is founded but also reject much of the psychological research that structures present methodology.

The authors have attempted to present without bias the conflicting philosophic viewpoints as to the goals of the school. They have attempted to utilize both sociological and psychological research in formulating guidelines to the role of the school, both in curricular content and in pedagogical methodology. The reader will probably be able to determine, in general, the viewpoint of the authors with respect to the alternative points of view set up in Chapter 15. It is likely that the authors are individual in their views and may disagree partially with each other as do most other persons who are creative in their thinking. The authors find themselves more in agreement with the experimentalist point of view as it is set forth in Chapter 15 than with any other. It is likely that they will find themselves in disagreement with some experimentalists; and on some matters they may agree more closely with other viewpoints. This means that they, like many other persons attempting to find answers to these problems, are somewhat eclectic in their approach.

The primary responsibility for writing certain chapters was allocated between the two authors. Dr. Bryner, the junior author, had the responsibility for Chapters 6, 7, and 9. Chapters 14 and 16 were first drafted by Dr. Pounds; but both authors participated in the final organization and wording of these critical chapters. All other chapters were the original responsibility of Dr. Pounds. The very careful and critical reading and rewriting of many parts of the manuscript by both authors, however, means that the total book is the product of both.

The new edition of the book, although following the same format that has been so successful in the earlier edition, does attempt to bring the information up to date, to condense so far as feasible all background material, to expand practical suggestions for the teacher, and to re-examine the entire text for clarity. The whole of Chapter 10 represents a new set of problems in a new field, the problem of depressed areas. This has become very important in recent years as private and public groups have become concerned about the problems of the culturally disadvantaged.

Attention of the reader is called to the carefully correlated list of books and films found at the end of each chapter.

The authors wish to express their appreciation to the students who helped to establish the problems and to provide trial groups for trying out most of the materials of this book. They acknowledge indebtedness to the pioneer thinking and research of Harris, Ross, Snedden, Gillette, Dollar, Warner, Davis, Havighurst, Quillen, and others in the field of educational sociology for many of the ideas presented in this book as the thinking of the authors. The junior author is especially indebted to Dean I. James Quillen, Professor Paul R. Hanna, and Professor Oliver E. Byrd of Stanford University, to graduate assistant June Jentz of the University of Cincinnati, and to Dr. Gerald A. Foster of the Atterbury Job Corps Center. The senior author is especially indebted to some of his students for preparing materials for certain of the chapters. He is especially indebted to Mrs. Rebecca Pittenger, who prepared a first draft of materials for the new chapter, "Problems of Depressed Areas," and who also helped in the editing of the new materials in his particular chapters. However, the responsibility for the final work is that of the authors, and the above persons are not to be held responsible for any errors or inaccuracies.

The authors also wish to acknowledge the materials that have been taken from numerous copyrighted sources. Recognition of permission granted by copyright holders is given at the appropriate places throughout the book.

R. L. P.
J. R. B.

Cincinnati

Contents

List of Illustrations

List of Tables

Part I. *The Relation of School to Society*

I N PART I the writers have addressed themselves to the general relationship of school to society. In the first chapter, which serves as an orientation to the entire book, the importance of society both to individual development and to the development of institutions is indicated. Stress is placed upon the reasons why teachers, administrators, and other persons interested in schools should know and understand social trends and their implications for the school.

After this early orientation in Chapter 1, materials are selected from the social sciences, primarily from anthropology and social history, concerning the way in which human society has evolved. The process of becoming "human" is discussed, as well as the several stages of human development and the over-all significant characteristics that serve to mark these stages. In the final chapter of Part I, attention is focused directly upon the school as it has been related to the society in which it is found. Examples are taken from various stages in the development of schools in order to indicate how the schools at different times in the past have been related to their societies.

Chapter 1. *Individual and Institutional Development in a Changing Culture*

THE PERIOD in which we are living has been variously described as an age of crisis, an age of anxiety, and an age of uncertainty.[1] Although many eras that have preceded ours have been described in similar terms, and justly so, the problems of today, by comparison, are much more grave than those of previous times, for several reasons: (1) They are more acute. (2) They are more complex. (3) They are more far-reaching in their inclusiveness of many peoples. Failure to meet the challenge of these problems, obviously, may have much more disastrous consequences for the entire world than were possible in any previous period. Fortunately, the knowledge and the facilities needed for solving these problems are more adequate than ever before. The major question, however, is: How can society—and education in particular—use the available knowledge and facilities to solve these problems?

THE PURPOSE OF THIS BOOK

It is the purpose of this book to set forth in some detail the nature of the present social order and in its proper perspective, and to show implications for the school.

Although attention is directed primarily toward society, the viewpoint is that of the professional educator. The educator is standing on the "porch of the school," so to speak, looking out at the culture. The viewpoint is that of someone familiar with the nature and problems of education. The focus is on those aspects of the *culture* that have particular significance for education. As the purposes of the school become more

[1] Clarence A. Glasrud (ed.), *The Age of Anxiety* (Boston: Houghton, 1960).

3

inclusive, it becomes obvious that all major social problems come within such focus. Specific implications for school practices are frequently drawn. Those who are to teach and to administer schools in this era need to know and to understand the prevailing social trends if they are to educate citizens and to equip them with the competencies needed to solve our major cultural problems.

IMPORTANCE OF AN UNDERSTANDING OF SOCIETY FOR EDUCATIONAL DECISION MAKING

It is assumed by the writers that an understanding of the nature of society is essential for teachers and administrators who must make decisions concerning education in this rapidly changing world. Such understanding is important regardless of the particular philosophical framework that may be used. These philosophical choices are outlined in considerable detail in Chapter 15. To some extent, one's understanding of social changes and of changes in our knowledge concerning the nature of the world may affect one's choice of a frame of reference. However, even if all held points of view maintaining that the main job of the school was to pass on certain fundamental, unchanging principles, certainly an understanding of the society in which we live would affect the way in which each of us might apply those principles. Further, certain other values and principles that are subordinate to the "unchanging" ones may change as our cultures change. To these points of view in which value choices, recommendations for curriculum, and other decisions depend upon the nature of the changing culture in which the school is found, it is crucial that the teachers and administrators understand the nature of the culture.

Following are examples of questions that demand of teachers and administrators more knowledge about their society:

1. What implications does the nature of present society have in developing the content of the curricular experiences that we have in school?
2. To what extent does the changing nature of our society (an ever accelerating change) affect the emphasis in our curriculum upon subject-matter skills as against the process of getting knowledge?
3. To what extent does the fact that the world in which the boys and girls now in school *will* live during their adult life will be very different from the world in which we *now* live affect the way in which we teach them problem-solving techniques while in school?
4. To what extent does the problem of changing values in a changing culture place a renewed emphasis upon the development and clarification of values as a part of the school's job?
5. To what extent does the urgency of some of the social problems arising out of social change place responsibility on the school to

take leadership in helping our society change its institutions to meet these problems?

6. To what extent does some of the knowledge arising out of recent developments in the social sciences have implications for the quality of experiences in the school and for the teaching methods used?

7. What is the effect of the changing life expectancy on the length of time to be spent in full-time schooling?

8. What is the effect of the increase in life expectancy on the amount of the energies of the school that should be devoted to adult education?

9. What is the effect of the increasing specialization of our culture on the diversity of the kinds of educational programs that should be devised?

10. What is the effect of the increasing specialization upon the kind of general-education program we should have?

11. What is the effect of automation on the kinds of vocational program and general-education program our schools should have?

12. What is the effect of automation on the amount and kind of leisure-time activities, and what are its implications for the school?

13. What are the implications for the school of the necessity to teach "readiness to use unknown ways to solve unknown problems" (to use Margaret Mead's phrase)?[2]

THE GENERAL NATURE OF THE PRESENT SOCIAL ORDER

We shall now set forth some of the major, general characteristics of the contemporary social order.

One of the first things that strikes the observer is the tremendous diversity within cultures, even within one country like the United States. In our country, predominantly one language is spoken, there are enormous facilities for the circulation of ideas, and there is a heavy mobility of population, yet there is still great diversity. This heterogeneity may be attributed to many things. The seeking of freedom on American shores by many of our forefathers served to set, in many areas, the patterns that have continued until today. The absence of an established church and the complete separation of church and state have served to encourage religious freedom and diversity. Hence there are more than 250 religious denominations in the United States.[3] One of the most important factors contributing to variability in our culture is the fact that the encouragement of diversity is one of the fundamental principles of our democracy. "Unity in diversity" might well be a statement of one of our democratic goals.

[2] Margaret Mead, *The School in American Culture* (Cambridge: Harvard University Press, 1951), p. 40.

[3] Most available reference is the current issue of *The World Almanac*. This does not count many minor movements and numerous unaffiliated congregational churches.

The proliferation of occupations that came about through the specializations necessitated by a complex culture is the source of another set of factors differentiating our ways of life. The *Occupational Outlook Handbook* listed about 700 different kinds of occupations and thousands of job definitions in 1964.[4] Each occupation carries with it a set of mores, including ways of thinking and a set of values. Each person lives in a subcultural occupational minority, even though he may be otherwise in a community majority group.

There are also differences of national origin (the effects of which usually fade out in the third generation), regional differences, and differences due to social status. The cultural effects of social status will be discussed fully in Chapter 9. In spite of the relative homogeneity of American civilization, there is great diversity according to geographical residence. The patterns range from those of the Maine fisherman to the many urban subgroups, as in New York City; from the Michigan "upper peninsula" to the resort culture of Florida; from the southern culture of the state of Georgia to the many subcultures of the state of Washington; from the culture of Texas to that of California; from the cow country of Montana to the wheat fields of the Dakotas.

To these complexities within our one country may be added those between countries, and with the continual change in all modern cultures there ensues a kaleidoscopic variety that defies any attempt at complete description, or even a broad interpretation made with any assurance.

RAPIDITY OF SOCIAL CHANGE

Social change apparently is an inevitable accompaniment of human society. Even in those societies in which change is discouraged and that consequently remain almost static for hundreds of years, there is a slow cultural drift. In times of catastrophe, however, even previously static societies in some cases have changed rather rapidly in order to adjust to the changed conditions. A changing society is not a new thing; however, the rate of change does vary markedly from time to time throughout human history. The culture of primitive man did continue for thousands of years with very little change—usually until change was forced from the outside. The Oriental type of civilization that eventually emerged out of an amalgamation of many cultures remained for long periods of time at a fairly constant level of development and with relatively unchanging mores.

In Western civilization with its idea of progress, although founded on different bases at different periods and partially eclipsed during the Middle Ages, there has been a great deal of conscious change. Many times this change was deliberately brought about by dissatisfaction with conditions

---

4 W. William Wirtz, *Occupational Outlook Handbook* (Washington, D.C.: Govt. Printing Office, 1964). Published every two years.

often evolving out of ferment from previous changes. With the advent of the scientific method and of the democratic forms of government, bonds were loosed, which gave rise to many events that fostered change. With every change that occurred, new potentialities for change emerged. It is said that the director of the Patent Office early in the nineteenth century resigned because he felt that his job was about done, because one million patents had been issued. However, each patent was a possible source of stimulation for new patents. Each advance is the basis for several new ideas toward other advances or changes. The wheel, the steam engine, and the vacuum tube—each was the start of a whole series of branching avenues of discoveries. Thus the rate of change has been accelerating. It is "exponential" in rate of growth. The rate of change may be compared to a snowball, which "the larger it grows, the faster it grows."

It used to be said that George Washington would have been more at home in ancient Greece than in modern America. The age of the automobile, radio, television, jet plane, and A- and H-bombs may well cause us to say the same now of William McKinley, who died in 1901.

The following first-hand description of the actual changes that have occurred within the lifetime of a middle-aged individual even in a rural community is illustrative of the previous statements:[5]

I remember Mamma and the house where I was born. This house stood just off the village pike in the middle of a very large yard and was surrounded by many large trees and many outbuildings. Papa bought this house soon after my oldest sister was born, and my three other sisters, one brother, and I were born and grew up here. The house was of a long rambling style, much like the ranch style house of today, with the parlor (where we entertained special guests) in "front," and the very large kitchen at the "back." In between was the company dining room, a large hall, where we ate in the summer, and the "family" room, where we sat around the grate fire on winter evenings. On the right side of this grate was the stone churn—the cream must turn to make butter. In front of the fire my mother placed the quilt. By putting a table leaf across the quilting frames and setting the kerosene lamp on this leaf she could quilt late into the night. Mamma had little time to quilt in the daytime—there were too many other things to be done. My brother sat on the left side of the hearth in a rocker—the man was always given preference in our family—while I sat under the quilt on the floor.

I do not remember Papa very well because God took him away when I was only six years old. Papa was sick for a long time, but he did not go to the hospital. Few people in our village ever went to the hospital. Dr. Jacobs drove his horse and buggy seven miles from the city to see him. Mamma nursed him, and when he became very ill, the good neighbors came and sat up all night. They also cut wood for us to burn on the grate. They milked our cows, fed the

[5] This statement was prepared by a graduate student of one of the authors from her own experience. Permission has been granted for it to be used without identifying names. Names given are fictitious.

pigs and cattle, and cared for the sheep. We didn't pay them. Neighbors always helped each other in their hour of need. We would help them when they became ill just as they had helped us. Papa was buried in our family burial lot on Grandma's farm. . . . Mamma said, "Jimmy was a good man—as men go." But she had a living to make and a family to raise and there was just one thing to do—go to work and do it. We never heard of "public welfare," and how could anyone make a living for five children in the city—especially when their only skill was sewing? My mother had worked as a seamstress before she married. She didn't go to college, not even to high school. She went to eighth grade, third part arithmetic. That was as far as you could go where she lived. When I worked buttonholes in a dress in a college sewing class, the teacher said they were excellent and gave me an A. Mamma said, "I wouldn't give you an F, they look like pig eyes instead of buttonholes." . . .

On Saturday we drove Miss Nancy, our buggy mare, into the city with the marketing. The marketing was butter, milk, and perhaps some chickens. We sold the eggs to the village store. With the egg money we bought flour, sugar, coffee, and kerosene. We didn't need many things from the grocery. We always had a good garden. This supplied us with fresh vegetables during the summer, and we canned enough vegetables for the winter months. We also canned peaches, pears, and grapes from the orchard, and blackberries from the woods. The potatoes and apples were stored in the cellar or "milk house" as we called it. The cabbages were buried deep in the ground so they wouldn't freeze. We grew most of our meat, too. We had fried chicken in the summer. When they became too large to fry, we stewed them and made dressing and dumplings to eat with them. Just about Thanksgiving time we butchered three or four hogs in the barn lot. We hired men to help butcher, but Mamma always cooked the lard in the black iron laundry kettles in the back yard. We cured the hams and sacked the sausage. This supplied us with pork and shortening for the entire year. We always ate the shoulders and middlings and saved some of the hams to sell. This was money in the bank, and everyone in our community who was "somebody" had money in the bank. The account grew ever larger, never smaller. This money that we saved had to take care of Mamma when she was old. When autumn came everyone wanted fresh meat to eat. So the farmers organized a beef club. This club met in our big barn lot every Friday, butchered a beef, and divided it among the members of the club.

On Sunday we wore our best clothes and went to the one-room country church. We had our Sunday school classes in the different corners of the church, and two Sundays in the month the pastor drove to our village and preached. Since we lived close to the church, it seemed to me that he always came home with us for dinner, especially in the winter when the roads got muddy and he couldn't get to the homes of many church members. We liked to have the pastor come. We put on the best white tablecloth and used the best silver and dishes. If he stayed all night, he slept in the parlor on the cleanest, fattest featherbed we had and under the best counterpane on the place—one that had been woven on the loom by Grandma.

When the pastor preached, he talked about man and his relation to God more than he talked about man's relation to man. He preached about the things we should not do rather than the things we should do. It seemed to me there were few things left to do. I was almost grown before I realized that "the old-time religion" was just something to preach about and wasn't really too different from the new religion. After singing "When the Roll is Called up Yonder" or "Blest Be the Tie," we stood outside the church and talked for a long time. This was about the only time we had to be *social* with our friends and neighbors. This was where most of the young people in our community learned not to be afraid of the dark!

Miss Nancy and Miss Mary had both been married in the church. They had beautiful white gowns. My sister, Susan Ann, was the flower girl at each wedding. When Susan Ann was twenty-one, she married at home in our parlor. The house was decorated with roses from our own rosebushes, and our pastor performed the marriage ceremony. All the guests said Susan Ann was a beautiful bride. She wore a hat with two plumes on it, and she had made her own wedding dress. Secretly, too, she had embroidered all her underclothes. Thirty-eight years and fourteen children later, her wedding band was removed for the first time since Robert put it there on their wedding day. It was removed after her death and given to her youngest daughter. Hazel and Lila were married in Tennessee during the "elopement era." Mamma thought "mighty little of it" —but, then, everyone was eloping. . . .

The forty to fifty families who make up this village lived very much the same way our family lived. Practically every farmer owned his farm of 150 to 250 acres. Most families were large enough to operate the farm in a gainful manner without hiring help; however, many families helped each other by "swapping" work. The social life centered around the church and school with a few "nice" parties sometimes. Nice parties did not include dancing and card playing. Most of the young people finished high school, found a mate in the village, married and "settled down" in the village to farm as their parents had done. A few young people, mostly girls, were ambitious and went to college in the nearby city. The idea of girls doing public work was slowly gaining consideration; and, since the teachers college was only seven miles away, many girls (twelve or fifteen) became teachers. The Lord "called" two of the young men to become ministers. Three girls went to the capital, twenty-five miles away, and took a business course. Practically all of the boys stayed home on the farm. In fact, many of them did not finish high school. Most people were interested in living the "good life" and carrying on their work on the farm. For many, many years the community boasted it had never had but one divorce. Some drinking was done, but this was just boys sowing their "wild oats"—they would settle down when they married.

Very slowly a few changes were being made in the community. Mr. Gibbs had had a telephone in the store for a long time. A telephone was needed in the store. When we needed to call Granny, we paid him a dime to let us use the phone. After a few years, eight of us formed a party line and each got a phone. Soon everyone who lived in the immediate village had a phone, but few families whose homes were on the mud roads had them. Mr. Gibbs bought the first car in our community. Mamma said he could afford it. He ran the post office and Uncle Sam paid him. Then the two churches, the school, and Mr. Gibbs got Delco light plants.

The farmers used to go to the city trading on "Court Day," but now they went every Thursday to the stock sales. They began to feel the need for cars to get there more quickly. With the purchase of cars, the mud roads had to be made into pikes. We got a car in our family when my brother was sixteen. Few women in the community were driving cars yet. Their place was in the home.

Sunday school rooms had been added to the churches and school buses now took the children to and from school.

In the summer of 1941, when I went home for a vacation, the old house I had lived in was torn down and Mamma was building a new and much smaller house—just large enough to care for the family that was left. The Rural Electrification Project had just been organized and everyone was discussing and organizing to have electricity put in their home. Mamma said we couldn't afford all these fancy new things, but it would be nice to have lights in the barn—she didn't care a thing about having them in the house. But other people were getting lights, so we got them too. A full-size basement was built under the new house, but Mamma wouldn't consider having a furnace put in. My brother insisted on having the bathroom built in the house, but Mamma could not see the necessity for installing the fixtures at that time.

By 1949 the farmers were buying tractors to farm with. Practically every farmer had a tractor by this time. Those who did not have them hired his neighbor to plow and help with his farm. There was only one hay-baler and one sheep-shearer in the community. The other farmers found it saved time and money to hire their hay baled and their sheep sheared. They were talking about hybrid corn, tobacco allotments, and more crop rotation. The farmers were going to the stock sales much more than formerly. Trading, buying, and selling was a much greater part of every farmer's life than it had been a few years before.

When electricity went into the homes, the women of the community immediately got electric irons, then electric churns. The next year's turkey crop was saved to buy an electric washing machine. Those who didn't have a washer in two years had suddenly found the old way of doing laundry just too back-breaking, so they bargained with a cousin and many families washed together until they could afford a washer. Refrigerators were the next "necessities." They reasoned with themselves how much food they could save with a refrigerator. When I was home in 1945, there were just a few electric stoves. Since that time practically every housewife in the community has an electric stove. Of course, some of the older people, like Mamma, have two stoves in the kitchen and often can be found cooking on both of them at the same time. Very few of the older people have invested in toasters and waffle irons. Their men folks still must have hot biscuits for breakfast and hot cornbread for dinner (noontime meal) so they have little need for these appliances. The younger families had just as soon eat toast for breakfast and they enjoy waffles in the evening sometimes, so they are investing in the smaller appliances as well as the larger ones.

Electric appliances and new ideas from the Homemakers Club have made the life of the farm wife much easier. The tractor and other farm equipment has left the farmer with "time on his hands." For this reason many of the older men in the community are buying more farm land to tend. In addition to these aids most of the people who can find a room in their old houses are having bathrooms put in. The newer homes are built with bathroom, furnace, and other conveniences just as homes in the city. As yet, there are very few food freezers, but each summer when I go home I find one or two more. They are no more expensive than keeping a frozen food locker in the city, they say. Many young people who finish high school are renting an apartment in the city and finding work at "Avon" or "The Factory." Those who continue to live in the village are building small homes on an acre or two of land and driving into the city to work. Most of the boys and girls are getting a job immediately after completing high school. College is too long and too expensive. Anyway, then can earn $40 or $50 a week with a high school education. Getting help on the farm or renting to a tenant is almost impossible. The older people, like Mamma, cannot adjust to this fast-changing life. Their children are too busy to care for them. When they are ill, they go to the hospital or to a nursing home. It is hard for them to understand young people who have land and don't raise a garden, who have barns and don't keep a cow, who buy all their clothes ready made, and who go to all the movies. Mamma says with all these conveniences they are always complaining about being tired and never have time for a thing.

Several years ago the people in each church said they needed a full-time pastor. So they built new personages with every modern convenience and hired a pastor to live on the field. Then the churches became too small and old-fashioned. Last year the Baptist Church spent $22,000 remodeling their church. The church now has its own baptistry, electric kitchen, and nursery. The nursery is equipped with a button system to summon the mother from the main auditorium when needed without disturbing the audience. Chimes that call the people to church each Sunday morning are quite an attraction in the community. The church music shows little improvement. Interest in church work is very keen. The young people have Daily Vacation Bible Schools and go to camp in the summer. Though little reading is done by the people themselves, they usually hire a graduate of a theological seminary for their pastor. Sermons are centering more around present-day living and world affairs. On the whole, it seems that the religious life of the community has kept pace with the changes in technology.

. . . I should say the educational life of the community has lagged far behind the religious and technological growth. This has perhaps been due to lack of interest on the part of the parents. In many respects, the teachers have done an amazing amount of work and good in the community. Their salaries have been much too meager for them to afford much additional training.

The one thing that has changed very little, if any, in this community is the "brand of politics." Feeling runs very high around election time, not only among the men, but also among the women. The big issue is not whether the candidate is a good man for the position, but how strong a Democrat or Republican is he. If politics were traced in most families, it would be found that at least 95 per cent of the people have the same politics their father, grandfather, and great-grandfather had. When "Ike" was nominated for President, all work was laid aside and many people in the village went to the homes where there were televisions (two in the village) to see and hear. The Democrats knew we would all starve to death when Ike became President, and the Republicans thought the Roosevelts would "bust the country" before they could get them out. . . .

Yes, the village is changing slowly, and with the change tension seems to be growing. As Mamma says, "With all of their conveniences and easy ways of doing things, they just race here and there—never time for a thing." Her grandchildren don't have time to eat a meal with her any more. In fact, the grandchildren all live in the city. They drive out to the village church on Sunday. The younger people prefer an easier job to having a large bank account. They buy things it would seem they can't afford. Their feeling of responsibility toward the older people is there, but their work prevents their getting around to help them often. And the older people won't leave their homes to live with the children. They still must take care of their farms. The younger people have a very great responsibility toward their immediate, small families. This is especially noticeable in the care and time that the fathers give the children. Their concept of moral values is still very high and many "recreations" are frowned on. They want their children to be educated, but they still feel that education means the three R's. Education is still for one thing, to help one make a better salary and live in an easier manner.

For the most part, I should say that the people in this community are a happy, contented group. They are interested in making money, having things, and doing things. But beyond this they have a set of values that are deeper and more enriching to them as individuals and as a group than money values.

COMPARISONS OF PRESENT SOCIAL CHANGE WITH THE PAST

Aside from the rapidity and increasing acceleration of social change in the present era, there are several characteristics that distinguish the present changes from those of the past. In the first place, changes in the past tended to be either in the nature of a gradual cultural drift or in the form of a sudden "jump" due to catastrophic causes. In the past, life was lived on a precarious basis. Anything that upset the status quo necessitated major readjustments. Many of these catastrophes were caused by war and were followed by conquest and virtual or actual enslavement. Others were caused by failures of food supply or by epidemics and were widespread in effect. In modern times, man has achieved greater physical security, has gained more ability to make adjustment to changes in physical environment, and is more able to change deliberately the physical environment in order to meet his needs.

Secondly, the changes that have come about in Western civilization to produce the modern period were the result of man's increasing ability to understand and to control his physical environment. Each new invention or other form of change brought a host of changes, widely spread through an increasingly complex and interrelated society. For example, the invention of gunpowder and the gun, while brought about for the purposes of advantage in fighting, was an important factor in the downfall of the feudal system, since the common footman with a gun was more than equal to the knight on horseback. The invention of the power loom and use of steam power destroyed the home craftsman because capital became necessary to purchase the required machinery. Man became a wage earner rather than a craftsman. The threat of unemployment arose because of these changes in economic conditions.

In the third place, the increasing complexity and speed of communications make events in one part of the world affect the other parts. The specialization of the productive process makes one part of the country intricately dependent on the others. The economic system, instead of being self-adjusting, may tend to run away in booms or "busts." Further, some parts of the culture tend to change more rapidly than others, thus throwing the parts out of relationship to each other. Each new change in society, instead of calling for a simple remedy which then serves until a new problem arises, calls for a type of remedy that itself is productive of further maladjustments.

A CONCEPT OF CULTURAL LAG

It is the differential in rates of change in the different parts of an interdependent society that gives rise to the phenomena known as "cultural lag." Usually changes in the material aspects of culture come first, followed by lags in institutional changes and in the ideas underlying those changes. Man seems to accept material changes more readily than institutional changes and seems to resist strenuously changes in fundamental ideological conceptions.

Some authorities have discarded at least partially the concept of cultural lag and speak of societal breakdown as due to disarticulation—a lack of fitting together of parts. It would seem, however, that the concept of cultural lag still has great usefulness in describing these phenomena.

The amount of social lag or "disjointedness" of a culture varies, of course, with the amount of social change. If there is very little or no social change, obviously the lag, if it exists, is small. In times when social change was the result of a single force (which, when once applied, subsided as a force toward change), the lag quickly was reduced as the society readjusted to the relatively static new conditions following the initial impact. In Western civilization there has been a rather consistent change owing to new events occurring largely within the society. These continuously have brought about changes in certain parts of society and hence a lack of adjustment with other parts that did not change. As Western society has entered the period of rapid social change, where each new change has set off a whole chain of other events, this lag has become acute.

In the era of relatively slow but constant change in the late medieval and early modern periods, the lag between the material culture and the ideological and institutional culture, although not great in absolute amount, was greater in point of time. As people became more consciously aware of change and as ideas of progress developed, persons were able to adjust more quickly in point of time to many of these changes. However, the changes came with increasing rapidity and, even though the lag in time was much less, the absolute lag was still as great or greater in many cases. For example a lag in time of two hundred years from the fifth to the tenth centuries might be a less "absolute" lag than fifty years in the nineteenth century.

Some of the important changes of the late modern period (from 1500 on) had implications that ran quite deeply into ideological concepts that had become almost permanent fixtures in the basic ideas of people. These fundamental changes were resisted in certain areas because they challenged concepts to which man wished to cling at all cost. For example, the findings of modern science starting with the discoveries of Copernicus have challenged the basic assumptions of philosophy concerning the ultimate nature of the universe, and in some cases have caused man to cling to outworn institutional patterns because these patterns help him protect his cherished ideas against change. In some cases the institutions themselves by their structure tend to prevent adjustment to the social changes. Institutions, developed to meet certain needs under given conditions, tended to be rigid in structure and partially to thwart man when the need for change was obvious.

The individual is a product of the society in which he is born. If that society changes greatly during the lifetime of the individual, he may find it difficult to accept change even on superficial levels—not to speak of fundamental changes in his thinking.

The effect of cultural lag of various kinds may be seen in such phenomena as poverty and want amidst the potential plenty that modern technology is capable of bringing forth. Another example is the political lag in many overlapping governments surrounding large cities and the inability of suburban areas to merge their differences and join with the central area in an efficient governmental unit or in a well-planned set of coordinated subunits. Also, the resolving of differences between countries by war is resort to a barbarian practice that probably has no longer a rational justification for either the victor or the conquered.

The Contributions of the Social Sciences to the Understanding of Man's Relation to Society

The modern social sciences, such as history, sociology, psychology, anthropology, economics, and political science, have developed rapidly in the last few decades, using techniques adapted from the earlier developed physical and life sciences. It is perhaps inherent in the nature of the various fields of study that mathematics should develop first, the physical sciences next, then the life sciences, and finally the social sciences. The sciences still lag, to some extent, in the same order as their development.

The scientific method of arriving at the facts and of applying those facts is used in the social sciences just as in the other areas. However, there are many difficulties:

The Problem of Maintaining Objectivity

Our own preferences and backgrounds cause us to see and to interpret phenomena in ways that agree with our previous convictions. The scientist who knew in advance whether he was measuring a Negro or a white brain in a study of brain capacity thought that he honestly found that the Negro brain was less developed. However, when the work was checked by another without the labels, no differences could be found.[6] We are not prejudiced about the properties of a metal. We are frequently prejudiced about matters relating to race, religion, and nationality.

The Problem of Formulating Useful Generalizations

The behavior of living creatures is so complex, the actions of humans so exceedingly complex, that it is difficult to make any type of generalization that will hold for most (or even many) cases or situations. Persons acquainted with the "laws" and formulas of the natural sciences are disappointed with the necessarily guarded and qualified generalizations of the social sciences. Many persons do not realize that in modern Einsteinian science the generalizations from physics and chemistry are also considered to be only approximations. They are man-made generalizations of what usually happens in ordinary circumstances. Although it is extremely probable that the phenomenon will happen as it is predicted in the generalization, the whole quantum mechanics is on a probability basis; and furthermore, most laws are not even practically accurate except within certain limits. This places the physical sciences on exactly the same basis as the social sciences except that the probabilities are so much higher because the physical sciences deal with so many greater numbers of the basic elements concerned, namely usually atoms or electrons or their equivalent.

The Problem of Prediction

Many factors enter into the direction in which a society (or group) may move, one of which may be the influence of the prediction itself. It is extremely difficult to make any kind of prediction that will hold reasonably true over any extended period of time. At times, minor factors, difficult to measure, occur at opportune (or inopportune) times to make marked differences in outcomes. For example, if you are predicting something that will happen to the group, and the group is sensitive to the prediction, the sensitivity may affect the outcome. For example, if the National Safety Council should predict that the number of accidents over a certain holiday weekend would be alarmingly great, the size of the number predicted to be killed, if announced, might scare many persons into driv-

[6] John Biesanz and Mavis Biesanz, *Modern Society*, 2d ed. (Englewood Cliffs, N.J.: Prentice-Hall, 1959), p. 164.

ing more safely. The actual numbers would then not be so great as had been predicted on the basis of factors available at the time of prediction.

Difficulty in Experimentation

People are not guinea pigs. As social scientists and educators, we are not able to manipulate our subject matter as the natural scientists do. Because we cannot always manipulate our human subjects, we must manipulate our data by using statistical factorial analysis methods. This is not as good, however, as if we could design the experiments and then manipulate our subjects in whatever way was best for checking the effect of the factors involved in the experiment.

Difficulty in Use of Terms

The social scientist must use the common language, but he must define his terms carefully. Consequently he quite often employs the same words as those used by the layman, but in quite different senses. This causes a lack of clarity in communication when results, conclusions, or implications are announced.

The Role of Values in Conclusions

Many kinds of data have significance only in terms of values of the culture, and these may be in conflict or changing. Consequently, two persons using the same data may arrive at quite different conclusions or generalizations. Numerous examples of this differentiation could be related. In particular, in the area of social studies—let us take, specifically, economics—conclusions on the part of persons whose political philosophies are based on contrasting sets of values they hope to realize by means of a particular kind of social order may be quite different. For example, the viewpoint of the late Senator Robert A. Taft and that of the labor leader Walter Reuther, in the period following World War II, were completely at opposite poles even though both were very well acquainted with economic "facts" of the situation, and were well aware of the so-called "laws of economics." Each, however, had a different conception of the values to be achieved by the economic system. This led to quite different conclusions with regard to the same facts in their possession.

In spite of these difficulties, social sciences have made great strides, and there is a growing body of widely accepted knowledge in all of these sciences. The use of field studies, case studies, and statistical methods, coupled with the new techniques of "action research," has served to broaden the scope of study and to enable conclusions to be better applied. Bringing together conclusions from the various sciences to the solution of a problem has led to improved results.

Students of society have observed that a culture falls into three or more fairly distinct elements. Different parts of the culture affect its members differently. The first are the *universals*—those common customs, attitudes, and beliefs shared by almost all members of a cultural group, such as a common language or a common belief in democracy. The second can be termed the *specialties*—those elements of culture shared by persons of certain classes, localities, or occupations. The third may be called *alternatives*—characteristics shared by certain individuals but not common to all or even to the other members of the subgroup. Closely related to these "alternatives" are *individual peculiarities*. Examples of the two last mentioned include religion (in American culture), politics, and food habits.[7]

Subcultures exist even in a culture as relatively homogeneous as that of the United States, and they often tend to determine one's ways of behaving. Examples are minority groups, occupations, and so on.[8] A given individual may have membership in several of these subgroups, each partially influencing his behavior.

Further understanding of the nature of culture may be given by the definition of certain terms. Societal cultures, or group habits, may be classified as *mores, folkways,* and *technicways*.[9] The *mores* are those aspects of culture to which all individuals are expected to conform. The mores are supported by the strongest of sanctions, in contrast to the folkways, which are desired but not compulsory. Violation of the mores are immoral acts in the broadest sense of the term. In our society, monogamous marriage, right of private property, and prohibitions against murder, rape, or incest are part of our mores. *Folkways* are customs that persons are expected to follow, but violations do not involve serious consequences. Taking off your hat when addressing a lady is a folkway, but failure to follow it is not immoral. Merrill and Eldredge add the term *technicways* to designate those new ways of behavior that have been developed and accepted as ways of adjustment to new technology.[10] An illustration would be new "dating" behavior because of the use of automobiles.

Every culture has a hierarchy of values that provide its motivation and drive. Whatever the source of these values may be said by myth or tradition to be, they have arisen in almost all cases out of the past experiences and traditions of the group. The myths, quite often based originally upon facts but then greatly elaborated, tend to undergird the value symbols of the group. All of these together lead to a conception or picture of the universe and of nature and of the place of man in that universe.

Lawrence K. Frank,[11] in his analysis of this aspect of man's development, indicates that different groups of men probably developed independently and gradually a body of concepts about all men in areas such

[7] Cf. Robert Bierstadt, *The Social Order* (New York: McGraw-Hill, 1957), pp. 220–243.

[8] Robert Bierstadt, *ibid.,* pp. 243–254.

[9] See Frances E. Merrill and H. Wentworth Eldredge, *Society and Culture,* Third Edition (Englewood Cliffs, N.J.: Prentice-Hall, 1965), pp. 32–33.

[10] *Ibid.*

[11] Paraphrased from Lawrence K. Frank, *Nature and Human Nature: Man's New Image of Himself* (New Brunswick, N.J.: Rutgers University Press, 1951), pp. 83–85.

as the nature of the universe; the place of man in the universe; the place of the individual within the group; and human nature and conduct. As each of the groups expressed these in more complicated form, they became our four basic concepts of religion, philosophy, law, and culture. These incorporate the myths and folklore as well as the arts. Since these developed independently, each group differs in its expression of its several assumptions about the universe. In every case, however, the conceptions in the four different areas are interrelated and are, relatively speaking, well integrated into one body of ideas.

Frank summarizes this:

In brief, acting upon these basic assumptions and guided by these beliefs, man has created his symbolic, cultural worlds of meanings and values which, like a screen or pattern, he has interposed between, or imposed upon nature and himself so that he sees everything, thinks about everything, acts toward everything and every person, including himself, largely in terms of these self-created and self-imposed meanings and purposes.

Thus man's cultural world is a man-made creation, another dimension of the environment, selectively established and interpreted from among the many possibilities and perpetuated by man himself. It is part of nature because it was created by man and does not exist as anything superhuman or supernatural. But it is different from the rest of nature, just as a machine is different: a machine never existed until man invented it, but it is natural in the sense that the machine is a new, selected arrangement, combination and sequence of processes that never before were brought together and operated for that purpose.[12]

THE APPROACH OF THIS BOOK

The authors have operated on the assumption that in order to understand the questions posed earlier in this chapter and other related questions, it is necessary to have a full understanding of the nature of society and of at least part of the vast knowledge concerning man and the world that has been formulated by the social sciences in the last few years.

The book has been organized into four parts. In Part I, "The Relation of School to Society," we have set forth in Chapter 1 an orientation to the importance of society to individual development and to the institutions that man has created in order to help him in solving his problems. Then follows Chapter 2, in which we have brought together materials from anthropology and other sources indicating how human society has evolved and how man the animal has become human. In Chapter 3 we have indicated the historical relationship of schools to their societies, giving numerous examples from the history of education to cite how the school has tended to reflect the culture in which it is found.

[12] Frank, *Nature and Human Nature, op. cit.*, p. 85.

In Part II, "Social and Economic Trends in America," we have set forth an overview of the social economic trends of America. In Chapter 4 is found an overview of American social trends, first in chronological and topical order for the entire period, then a summary of the social trends that seem to be those that are in process at the present time. Chapter 5 is given over to a discussion of the trends in the technological and economic realm. An attempt is made to acquaint the person who is not a student of economics with important facts about our industrial and economic system that anyone should know as a basis for understanding the many kinds of problems that face our society.

In Part III, "Problems Facing the Individual in Modern American Society," we have several chapters taking up a selection of the kinds of problems that modern American society faces: problems confronting members of a family; problems of mental hygiene in a period of rapid social change; problems of crime and delinquency; problems caused by intergroup relations, including the social class structure as found in America; problems of depressed areas; problems arising out of population trends; problems related to the nature of representative government, including problems of communication, propaganda, and public opinion; problems arising from the nature of the interdependent world of the present time. Although this list of problems is far from exhaustive, it is hoped that it will be enough to acquaint the student with the kind of problems so that some meaning will be given to the final clarification and summary in Part IV.

Part IV, "The Role of the School in Modern America," is a final summation of the role of the school in modern America. In the first of the three chapters in this section an attempt is made to clarify the central democratic values of our culture and the nature of the group process in our culture (group dynamics). In Chapter 15 is found a careful analysis of alternative viewpoints with respect to the schools and social change. In the final chapter (Chapter 16) the authors have summarized the main findings of the other chapters. The attempt is made to portray the role of the leader in a democratic situation and to give an indication of how his efforts can be directed toward helping the school to play an appropriate and effective role in this period of social change. The authors have surveyed the possibilities of the "foreseeable" future in our society and have indicated, in part, implications for school practices as they see them.

SELECTED BIBLIOGRAPHY

ALLEN, FRANCIS R., and others. *Technology and Social Change.* New York: Appleton-Century-Crofts, 1957. Pp. xi + 524.

AMERICAN ASSEMBLY, *Goals for Americans: Programs of Action for the Sixties.* The Report of the President's Commission on National Goals. New York: The American Assembly, Columbia University, 1960. Pp. xii + 372.

20   *The School in American Society*

Bonner, Thomas Neville, and others. *The Contemporary World: The Social Sciences in Historical Perspective.* Englewood Cliffs, N.J.: Prentice-Hall, 1960. Pp. xiii + 594.

Bierstedt, Robert, and others. *Sociology and Contemporary Education.* New York: Random House, 1964. Pp. xviii + 138.

Biesanz, John and Mavis Biesanz. *Modern Society: An Introduction to Social Change,* Third Edition. Englewood Cliffs, N.J.: Prentice-Hall, 1964. Pp. xiv + 718.

Butts, R. Freeman. *A Cultural History of Education,* Second Edition, Chapters X, XIV, XVI. New York: McGraw-Hill, 1955. Pp. xii + 645.

————, and Lawrence Cremin. *A History of Education in American Culture,* Chapters 1, 5, 9, 13. New York: Holt, Rinehart & Winston, 1953. Pp. 628.

Chinoy, Ely. *Society: An Introduction to Sociology.* New York: Random House, 1962. Pp. 404.

Foster, George M. *Traditional Cultures and the Impact of Technological Change.* New York: Harper & Row, 1962. Pp. xiii + 292.

Glasrud, Clarence A. (ed.). *The Age of Anxiety.* Boston: Houghton Mifflin, 1960. Pp. 219.

Gross, Carl H., Stanley P. Wronski, and John W. Hanson (eds.). *School and Society: Readings in the Social and Philosophical Foundations of Education.* Boston: Heath, 1962. Pp. 666.

Hodgkinson, Harold L. *Education in Social and Cultural Perspectives.* Englewood Cliffs, N.J.: Prentice-Hall, 1962. Pp. ix + 243.

Holton, Gerald (ed.). *Science and Culture: A Study of Cohesive and Disjunctive Forces.* Boston: Houghton Mifflin, 1965, Pp. iii + 348.

Kallenbach, W. Warren and Harold M. Hodges, Jr. (eds.). *Education and Society.* Columbus, Ohio: Merrill, 1963. Pp. xvi + 474.

Kerber, August, and Wilfred Smith (eds.). *Educational Issues in a Changing Society.* Detroit: Wayne State University Press, 1962. Pp. 477.

Kluckholm, Clyde. *Mirror for Man: The Relationship of Anthropology to Modern Life.* New York: Whittlesey House, 1949. Pp. xi + 313.

Kuhn, Alfred. *The Study of Society: An Unified Approach.* Homewood, Ill.: Irwin, 1963. Pp. xviii + 810. A detailed, theoretical analysis across disciplinary lines of the human society in its entirety.

Lerner, Daniel (ed.). *The Human Meaning of the Social Sciences.* New York: Harcourt, Brace & World, 1959. Pp. 317.

Manis, Jerome G., and others (eds.). *Man and Society.* New York: Macmillan, 1960. Pp. xx + 784.

Mead, Margaret. *The School in American Culture.* Cambridge, Mass.: Harvard University Press, 1951. Pp. 48.

Montagu, Ashley. *The Humanization of Man.* New York: Harcourt, Brace, & World, 1962. Pp. 319.

Stoodley, B. H. (ed.). *Society and Self.* New York: Free Press of Glencoe, 1962. Pp. 713.

Westby-Gibson, Dorothy. *Social Perspectives on Education: The Society, The Student, The School.* New York: Wiley, 1965. Pp. xvii + 481.

SELECTED FILMS

American Farmer (Ford Motor Co.) 28 min
> An intimate and beautifully photographed story of a modern farmer and the changes wrought in his life because of mechanization and scientific farming.

The American Road (Ford Motor Co.) 25 min
> An excellent film in the change of American culture brought about by changing technology, particularly changes in transportation.

Our Changing Family Life (McGraw-Hill) 22 min
> The change from the farm family of 1880 to the urban family of today.

Chapter 2. *The Evolution of Human Society*

WE HAVE SEEN the importance of society and its institutions in determining the ways of behavior of man and the relationship, in general, of social structure and social mores to various human institutions. It now becomes important to focus our attention more minutely on the origins and development of human society. The development of group mores and the ways in which changes in them came about are important elements in understanding modern-day man. The problems involved in the conflicts of mores in changing and in interrelated and interdependent societies have pertinence for our later discussion of the role of the school. It is necessary to explore in detail the effects on and the implications for social institutions of the social changes and the changed conception of the nature of society and of man, as provided mainly by the science of social (or cultural) anthropology. This will provide a basis for an understanding of the various topics and problems to be taken up later.

SOCIAL MORES AND THE STAGES IN MAN'S DEVELOPMENT

Social Mores: The Resultant of Circumstance and Adaptation

Numerous attempts have been made in all ages to explain the differences in the customs or mores of groups. Among the attempts of groups themselves to justify their unique customs or ways of doing, particularly when they feared a breakdown by threatened change from within or without, is that of recourse to various supernatural sources. Whether legitimately or not, peoples have attributed to direct or indirect contacts with deities or spirits, great or small, mores ranging from legal codes such as that of Hammurabi or the Mosaic law to food and marriage taboos and customs. Another approach attempts to justify the "superior" way of life of one's own group by reference to its superior racial inheritance, as did the Nazis.

Many of these explanations will not stand scrutiny. The modern study[1] of races, or even a casual reading of history, cannot support a "race" theory. Modern students of race agree that inherited differences in abilities or characteristics among races cannot account for "superior" modes of living. The record of man's experiences does indicate that the strong faith of a people in a supernatural source of their mode of life has often not withstood the ravages of time.

It seems evident to most students of the nature of man that the basic inherited structure of man and his potentialities has remained reasonably constant since the time of first modern man, Cro-Magnon, 20,000 to 50,000 years ago, and that reasons for cultural changes must be looked for elsewhere. The viewpoint to be set forth in this chapter will be at variance with many other theories of history that have been promulgated.

In the first place, the evidence of biology seems to indicate that the species *Homo sapiens* (that of modern man) secures by inheritance many fewer preformed behavior patterns than do other animals. In a later discussion of the social insects, such as the ant and the bee, we shall show that their social behavior is largely a function of inherited neural structure, mostly in the nature of reflexes. Man apparently inherits a much more plastic nervous system, which enables him to absorb the culture in which he is born and to add to it. In the study of hundreds of primitive human groups that have survived to the present day, anthropologists have uncovered many patterns of social organization, some of which were more successful than others—at least as measured by modern standards of living. However, the success or lack of success of a pattern does not seem to indicate that the intrinsic nature of man is any more adaptable to one pattern than to others. Mead's study shows that in the various types of cultural organizations (individualistic, competitive, and cooperative) there are records of successes and failures and of problems and difficulties, fairly randomly distributed.[2]

It would seem that different mores are really accidents of history. In nonliterate societies each separate group (usually the tribe) needed to solve its basic problems of food and shelter. In time, it stumbled on ways of so doing that at least provided a minimal solution to each problem. Many other mores probably were added accidentally, even though they

---

[1] Montagu Ashley, *Race, Science, and Humanity* (New York: Van Nostrand, 1963). This is only one of many references on this subject.

[2] Margaret Mead (ed.), *Cooperation and Competition Among Primitive Peoples* (New York: McGraw-Hill, 1937).

were not particularly functional, but through ingrained habit these soon gained the same status as those customs necessary to maintain existence.[3] This problem of the fixity of group mores, once they are established, is important enough to be looked at more fully later. Suffice it to say at this point that the type of mores established by a group, the changing of these mores, and the raising of the level of living, seem to be a result of a concatenation (or accidental coming together) of circumstances—including, of course, favorable geographic factors—not the result of inherited superiority or inferiority or of the favor of the gods.[4]

The Stages in Man's Development

Students of human culture have used different methods of marking of the various stages of man's development for the purpose of description, for example: the hunting and fishing stage, the pastoral stage, etc.; or the Old Stone Age, the New Stone Age, and the Bronze Age. For the purposes of our discussion here, it seems to be more functional to describe the various stages in terms of the internal structures of the society with respect to adaptability to change or progress.[5]

Under this latter approach, the stages would be (1) the primitive or nonliterate[6] stage; (2) a stage called "Oriental" because of its historical prevalence in the oriental part of the world; and (3) a stage called "Occidental" or "Western,"[7] again because it has been most evident in the Western area. To these might be added (4) a modern stage, which may be in its early phases now.

In the nonliterate stage, man has made an adaptation to his environment on a minimal level; particularly, he lacks a written language. Although the standards of food and shelter may be very meager (or may be fairly adequate in the kindlier environments), each group has become accustomed to its ways and tends to resist change, especially sudden innovations from within or without. Often this fear of change may be due to the fact that the initial effect of such innovations may well be quite un-

[3] See a humorous parody on the stubbornness of man's adherence to custom using paleolithic man as an example in Harold Benjamin, *The Sabre-tooth Curriculum* (New York: McGraw-Hill, 1939).

[4] Cf. Arnold J. Toynbee, *A Study of History* (New York: Oxford University Press, 1947), pp. 567–589.

Also see J. G. De Beus, *The Future of the West* (New York: Harper & Row, 1953) for a criticism of Toynbee and Spengler.

[5] Cf. James Mulhern, *A History of Education: A Social Interpretation*, Second Edition (New York: Ronald Press, 1959), pp. 10–21.

[6] The term "nonliterate" is apparently now preferred by scholars to either "primitive" or "preliterate."

[7] It must be emphasized that the use of the convenient terms "Oriental" and "Occidental," primarily because of accidental geographical reasons, do not imply and differences in the biological potential of the peoples. The definitions of these terms, to follow in this section, are cultural and sociological rather than geographical, biological, or racial.

settling. Sometimes a change may lead to disastrous results in terms of the stability of the group and its ability to meet its minimal needs. Thus, although some innovations might be of great value to the group, it hesitates to permit experimentation. Consequently individualism as to new methods of behaving is discouraged except within prescribed patterns such as personal bravery in battle or skill in hunting and fishing.

At the Oriental level, man has raised considerably his standard of living and has a written language and a literature. Usually the civilization covers a considerable geographic territory. Quite often it is accompanied by a highly developed art and other expressional forms, such as a complicated ritualistic religion based on a rather complete mythology. Once having achieved this level—by processes to be described later in this chapter—these civilizations resist further change by various methods, such as ancestor worship or powerful religious taboos. Examples of this stage were the early Egyptian civilization and various other ancient civilizations of the "Fertile Crescent," the sweep of productive land running east and south from Palestine through the Tigris-Euphrates Valley to the Persian Gulf. Such civilizations tended to remain constant for a great number of years (as did the Chinese) on a relatively high level or plateau unless changed by strong impact from an outside force.

In the Occidental-type civilization, a relatively high level of culture has been developed and definite mores have been established. The idea of progress or change has enough prevalence that individuals are somewhat free to experiment. At times, an Occidental-type civilization may succeed in almost eliminating innovations; again, it may change rapidly. In most cases, it is able to solve its crises by developing a mode of operation that enables it to adapt itself to the new change without complete disintegration or conquest from without. However, there seems to be present in all Occidental civilizations a fear of change, a hangover of the thinking of the nonliterate and Oriental stages (transmitted by culture, not heredity, of course) that is constantly at war with progress.

It may be that there is emerging, or that there will emerge in the future, a type of civilization in which, because of man's increasing knowledge of himself and of his environment and the institutions he has created, he will deliberately set out to create the kind of society he desires. After he carefully clarifies his values and tests them in the light of their consequences, he will make full utilization of available knowledge and of procedures involving the scientific method in its broadest implication. He will further utilize the scientific method in bringing about changes in his institutions, or even of his values if necessary, in the light of any new conditions brought about by social changes. This stage might be classified as the "modern stage."

Having reviewed briefly the stages in development, we shall now examine them in more detail.

MAN IN THE NONLITERATE STAGE

General Characteristics of Nonliterate Man

In spite of some political theories holding that, at some time in his existence, man the individualist agreed with a group of his fellow men by a compact to work together for mutual ends (the "social compact" theory[8]), it is now generally agreed that man probably has always been in association with his fellows. The evolution of human society starts, then, at least as far back as the first modern man, Cro-Magnon, who had approximately the same biological structure (including brain and nervous system) as contemporary man. All men from Cro-Magnon on, including the various modern races, belong to the same species, *Homo sapiens*. The date of Cro-Magnon man has usually been placed from 20,000 to 50,000 B.C.; however, earlier species of man are known to have been on earth nearly two million years ago. Cultural remains have been found as far back as 1,750,000 years. These dates are established by geological methods.[9] On geological and other evidence, the earth is generally believed to have been in existence for two billion years.[10] Life has existed for over one billion years. The first mammals appeared over 150 million years ago.[11] Man is thus a later comer. The earliest know inscription appears to have been in Sumeria and is dated around 3300 B.C. This places the historic period as beginning at least over 5,000 years ago.

Let us now look at the nonliterate period, which includes all men from approximately 25,000 B.C. to 3300 B.C. and many groups and tribes up to almost the present day. There is no evidence that early man of the *Homo sapiens* variety ever lived other than in groups. More details about the development of social institutions in primitive or nonliterate man will be given in the next section.

Certain characteristics are common to almost all groups of men in the nonliterate stage, even though the amount of variability in many aspects of cultural mores is great.

[8] Held in various forms by Hobbes, Locke, and Rousseau, among others. Cf. Harold J. Laski, "Social Contract," in Edwin R. Seligman (ed.), *Encyclopedia of the Social Sciences* (New York: Macmillan, 1934), Vol. XIV, pp. 127–131.

[9] Harry L. Shapiro (ed.), *Man, Culture, and Society* (New York: Oxford University Press, 1960), p. 21. This reference cites with approval the work of Leakey whose recent discoveries, announced in 1961, establishes the age of Zinjanthropus, bones of an early species of man, by means of the potassium-argon method.

[10] Cf. Fred Hoyle, *The Nature of the Universe* (New York: Harper, 1950) p. 11. Hoyle sets the origin of the earth at 2500 million years ago on the basis of astronomical evidence.

[11] Cf. any standard reference on geology. The newer methods of radioactive measurement of time give a relatively accurate chronology of geologic formations, which in turn date the fossil life contained therein. The oldest geologic rock accurately determined by radioactive methods is 1850 million years old. It is north of Leningrad in the U.S.S.R. The earlier Carbon 14 method is now considered not as accurate for earlier dates as is the potassium-argon method. See Harry L. Shapiro (ed.), *Man, Culture, and Society* (New York: Oxford University Press, 1960), p. 21.

Early man had solved his problem of living on a very precarious basis. He did not understand the nature of his physical environment nor the causal relationships that lay behind his successful attempts to provide for his minimal needs on a meager basis. In general, he was fearful of change. This may have been a result of experiences from time to time when individuals who attempted to innovate did upset the working relations and thus the meager adjustment of the tribe.

Nonliterate man, of course, operated in accord with ordinary causal relationships with respect to familiar things that, by trial and error, he learned could be controlled. In such activities as the felling of trees or the making of tools he acted in accord with causal relationships with much the same attitude that modern man would use and take. However, nonliterate man, understanding so little about the forces that operated in the world about, attributed much more to the "supernatural" than does contemporary man.

Whatever the reasons for the original mores may have been (including the necessity for a primitive technology), as time went on man forgot and tended to ascribe reasons that in most cases would not be verifiable by the use of scientific technique. Knowing himself as a creature that apparently could freely choose to do this and not do that, he tended to ascribe such freedom and personality to all other objects, animate or inanimate. This gave rise almost universally to a theory about the nature of his environment, the two different aspects of which are called respectively animism or animatism.[12] Either or both of these might be present in a given group.

In the one form, *animism*, nonliterate man extended to inanimate objects the concepts formed as the result of his experience with animate objects: a stone, like a person, possessed feelings of love or resentment and the power to act on its feeling, just as his fellow men, himself, and other animals apparently did. Animism thus places a spirit in each inanimate object. The object can then be controlled by cajoling, pleading, worship, or other means of manipulation. The extension of the generalization of the spirit in a tree to the spirit of the trees (as in Druid worship) comes later. A complicated system such as the Greek and Roman pantheon, including gods of love, harvest, and so on, is a much later generalization. The extension of this concept to the abstract—but, in some cases, personal—God of the more modern monotheism is probably a later development; although vague concepts, such as the Manitou of some American Indian tribes, seem to have been of this general nature.

The other aspect of supernaturalism, *animatism*, seems to have been an extension of man's effort to control familiar objects by utilizing a supernatural science that can best be termed magic. Man tried to control the forces in a supernatural cause-and-effect relationship by means of certain

[12] Ruth Benedict, "Religion," in Franz Boas (ed.), *General Anthropology* (New York: Heath, 1944), Chapter XVI; especially pp. 628–847.

rituals or formulas that probably had at some time appeared (by coincidence) to work and thus became a part of his thinking and action. Incantations, sorcery, and divination were a part of the magic, the use of which was quite prevalent in nonliterate man and persisted late into the Christian period of civilized man. Failure of the method usually was ascribed to errors in the procedure rather than in the conception back of it. Skeptics existed, but they were usually merely skeptical of certain persons' power to use the ritual or of a particular formula used.

The use of taboo to control the behavior of individuals in the group is also an aspect of dealing with the supernatural. Since the supernatural is power, it is dangerous. Whatever the actual origin of the taboo, such as a food taboo originating either in a coincidental or causally related sickness or death following eating, such origins in most cases have been forgotten. The reasons ascribed are almost entirely either the appeasement of a spirit or the avoidance of danger from the supernatural power involved.

Nonliterate man, living as he did in a world of precarious existence, got his security through his fixed mores, his myths to explain religious rites, the superiority of his group to others, and taboos of various kinds to enforce conformity. In many cases, primitive tribes lived with little change for thousands of years. The breakdown of mores, sometimes through forces originating inside the tribe but more usually due to crises from outside the group, will be described in a later section. It is sufficient to say, at this point, that the fear of change has been held by some students of modern society to lie back of opposition to change in such matters as public sanitation, vaccination, or fluoridation. The resistance, culturally inherited from the time that nonliterate man feared change as a threat to his security in a precarious world, may be a basis for some of the unreasoned conservatism found in modern culture.

Some cultural change existed at all times, even in those tribes that had the strongest antipathy toward change. This cultural drift in language, culture, social customs and institutions, and technology, while so slow as to be unnoticed in a generation, seems to have been universally present at all times in man's history and prehistory. "Nothing is constant but change."

Social Institutions in Man's Nonliterate Stage

Before looking at social institutions of nonliterate man, let us look at examples of social structure, cooperation, and even, by analogy, cultural institutions among the other animals.

The one-celled animal or plant does not exemplify any social behavior or even sensitivity to similar plants or animals. All multicellular animals or plants do represent a type of social adaptation or cooperation, from the simplest coelenterate to the complex dinosaur, bird, or man. In the simpler forms such cooperation is carried out with practically no differentiation in function, as in the jellyfish, where any of the group of cells may act as both mouth and anal opening and thus have both food-taking and excretory functions.

At a slightly higher level, such animals as the sponge have adapted by living as separate entities but in a cooperative relationship. Higher still, animals such as wolves or wild cattle cooperate by grazing or preying in groups for mutual protection or for more successful hunting.

The group of animals below man that appears to have the most highly socialized structure is composed of the ants, bees, and similar species. Here we have a highly developed social structure with a differentiation of work among individuals. Examples among species of ants are: specialized workers with a special anatomy for fighting; other ants for use as storage bins; and some with large jaws to crack hard-shelled seeds.[13]

In these cases, all the social structure is by biological inheritance, which is preserved by successful survival and the consequent continuation of the species. There is no evidence of culture in the sense of the successful adaptations of one generation being passed on by language or imitation to the next. In some species, all possibilities of such is prevented by the survival of the fertilized queen only, as in certain ants, or of the egg only in other insects. All such "social cooperation" is biologically produced and transmitted through inherited neural structures by the same well-known evolutionary procedures that have produced other physical structures.

A study of man has revealed the presence of the necessity for cultural adaptation. While the helplessness of the infant is a characteristic that the humans share with many of the other species, necessitating care in the early period, even the simplest adaptation of man to his environment seems to be culturally rather than biologically achieved. In other words, successful adaptation for humans is largely a result of a process of learning rather than merely a process of maturation, as it is in the other animals that are helpless at birth.

A comparison of man with the ape and other hominoid animals would seem to point up a great number of essential elements of difference. Animals of hominoid type can learn to solve problems of stacking boxes, can fit sticks together in the manner of a fishing pole, can play machines like slot machines in ways that seem much like those of humans. Animals, including the various hominoid species, are able to respond to language cues of various kinds and do have a sort of crude communication system using sounds.

In none of the animals that have been studied by anatomists in the speech center—that is, the portion of the brain that handles speech in man—is developed so much as it is in man. Man is the only primate that has a brain sufficiently well-developed to invent and to use language in the

---

[13] See A. L. Kroeber, *Anthropology*, Revised Edition (New York: Harcourt, Brace, and World, 1948), p. 35.

sense of developing abstract concepts.[14] There is a difference between responding to cues or symbols in a concrete situation and being able to communicate in an abstract situation. Someone has said that when the mother bear is able to come back from a foraging trip and explain to the cub bears exactly how to travel in order to find the honey tree without any other demonstration than the sounds the mother bear emits, then we can assume that the bears have invented language and have learned to use it for communication.

Man's ability to form a culture, therefore, depends on his higher ability to invent and use tools, and his ability to invent and use a conceptual language in solving his problems. The development of language, particularly, allows him to communicate experiences toward the further solution of new problems. These powers enable him eventually not only to adapt himself better to his environment, but to adapt the environment to his needs.

Although little can be known of the early development of the two most ancient and primary institutions, the family and that other basically most face-to-face group, the tribe, the study of contemporary primitive peoples at differing stages in development does give us some clues. The human family unit, probably frequently polygamous in early primitive man, seems to be based on the sexual drive and the attractiveness of the female, coupled with her accessibility to sexual advances in times other than the oestrual period. It is also based on the necessity for the protection of the immature young, a necessity that man shares with many animals that also have a protofamily group with or without the presence of the male.

The tribe, consisting of persons usually related by blood, was probably developed for mutual protection and better success in food-getting. The social relationships between individuals in these groups and individuals outside of these groups are carefully prescribed in most societies. Even the most individualistic societies, in which food-getting and other activities are neither competitive nor cooperative, still may carefully define relations between individuals on a basis of complicated social groupings.

Although social institutions are relatively simple individualistic societies and in those societies whose technology is still at the gathering or hunting and fishing stage, they usually become progressively more complex in the harvesting (without planting) stage and among those who practice agriculture. In the case of the harvesters, access to the area of the food plant, grown without agriculture but still seasonal and needing storage as surplus, may be carefully controlled and allocated to various tribes or sub-tribal groups. In the agriculture stage, property is usually more precisely defined, although it is not always individually owned, nor are the products of the individual's work necessarily used by that individual and his family

---

[14] Francis E. Merrill and H. Wentworth Eldredge, *Society and Culture*, Third Edition (Englewood Cliffs, N.J.: Prentice-Hall, 1965), pp. 61–62.

and kin alone.[15] Many variations and patterns, all of which determine the nature of the social institutions, are found. Some of these variations are discussed later in this chapter in the section on cooperation and competition.

Variations in Social Structure of Nonliterate Societies

Wide variations exist in the social structure and actions of the various primitive tribes. Many of these variations have existed down to the modern day and can be studied minutely. These studies of relatively simple nonliterate tribes may throw light on modern social problems. The examples used will be drawn largely from relations in the institution of the family. The section that follows will discuss in detail variations with respect to economic structuring, and will take up cooperative, competitive, and individualistic societies.

The family as a face-to-face unit may vary from the married adults and their children to the patriarchal or matriarchal family with several generations of descendants. The family may be polygamous in either of the two forms: *polygyny*, the marriage of one man to more than one woman; or *polyandry*, the marriage of one woman to more than one man. There is also one other form, very rare, the marriage of several women to several men. Polyandry is much more rare than polygyny.

Polygyny (frequently miscalled polygamy) is quite prevalent among nonliterate people and exists, or did exist, to some extent among relatively high civilized groups such as the early Hebrews (Solomon) and the Mohammedans. Research among polygynous societies has failed to reveal the existence to any greater extent than in a monogamous society of widespread jealousy patterns or bickerings due to unfaithfulness of husband or wife and attention toward others of the opposite sex.[16]

Attitudes toward sex both within and without marriage vary widely. Only three groups reported in the literature, the New England Puritans, the Ashanti, and the Timne (the latter two from West Africa) seemed to taboo sex relations even within marriage except for procreation.[17]

The nonliterate tribes in general seem not to taboo sexual relations before marriage and not to restrict them so completely to husbands and wives after marriage as in the Western world. (In this respect, the Western world has been far from absolute in practice, particularly in Europe where a double standard with respect to prostitution persists.) It would be incorrect to say that nonliterate peoples are promiscuous with respect to sex relations, since all such relations are subjected to numerous controls and

[15] See the discussion of the Tanala on pages 36–37 for a documented case of the changes in social structure that followed a change in the technology of food-getting.

[16] Cf. Gladys A. Reichard, "Social Life," in Boas, *op. cit.*, Chapter IX; especially pp. 409–426, 430–440.

[17] George P. Murdock, *Social Structure* (New York: Macmillan, 1949), p. 263.

taboos. For example, the incest taboo is practically universal in all societies, even in those in which sex relations are fairly free before marriage.

The extension of permissive sex relations beyond husband and wife follows a careful pattern, but one that varies from society to society. The most common practice is the extension to the sisters of the wife and to the brothers of the husband. Extremely rare are such practices as the hospitality of wife-lending to guests and the game of "putting out the light" in the multifamily home of the Ammassilik Eskimos.[18]

Economic functions, status, and taboos are usually sharply differentiated between the sexes, and there is a wide range of variation as to the status of women. The attitude toward women, the burden of work placed upon them, and their part in making important family, clan, or tribe decisions vary widely, although, in general, women have a lower status than that of the male. In cases where the women have real power, it is usually exercised "behind the throne," so to speak—that is, through the male.

This discussion of the variability of social institutions is not presented with the idea of emphasizing a complete relativity of choice as to alternatives, with one alternative being as good as the other. Certainly the results from anthropological study indicate that institutions, though extremely variable as between societies, do have relationship in a given society to the prevailing value systems and to the other institutions of the particular society, even though they are apparently not in any sense preferable one to another on the basis of innate or inherent psychological or personality factors. Persons within Western civilization have tended overwhelmingly, as a result of attitudes developed out of their historical experience, to prefer complete monogamy after marriage as their ideal, even though this ideal is often violated. Indeed, a thoroughly rational study might well establish that this choice is fully justified in the present state of civilization and in relation to the other values desired in the culture.

Cooperation and Competition in Nonliterate Man

Margaret Mead[19] has made a comparative study of the prevalent characteristics of a sample of thirteen nonliterate (primitive) societies in order to discover, if possible, any pattern of related factors favoring one society over another and some measure of the comparative success of these societies. The thirteen groups, after careful analysis and study, were divided into three classifications: competitive, cooperative, and individualistic. The classification is based upon strong trends in the society rather than upon an exclusive trend. Competition, for example, does not mean to refer to societies in which the individuals are in complete conflict, nor

---

[18] Jeanette Mirsky, "The Eskimo of Greenland," in Margaret Mead (ed.), *Cooperation and Competition Among Primitive Peoples* (New York: McGraw-Hill, 1937), Chapter II; pp. 51–86.
[19] Margaret Mead (ed.), *Cooperation and Competition Among Primitive Peoples*, pp. 458–511.

does cooperation mean complete solidarity. In many cooperative societies, competition as a motivation for increasing contribution to the group may be present, although the results of the competition are widely shared.

A summary of important character and personality traits as related to these forms of culture as compiled from Mead has been made by Kroeber.[20] It is interesting to note that this summary shows no basic causal relationship or pattern behind the particular predominant characteristics of a culture. For example, cooperative societies may arise in geographic areas in which competitive societies are more prevalent, and vice versa. The traits are widely scattered among the different cooperative or competitive types.

Mead's study indicates that there is a plasticity about the adaptability by a group to a general cultural trait that parallels the plasticity of an individual. It has been established by psychologists that any normal newborn baby will take on almost completely the characteristics common to the society in which it is reared. This study tends to show that the range of possible successful societies is also quite variable in pattern. The argument that "human nature cannot change" or that "people are born that way" cannot be used to promote or to oppose any given social change that seems desirable on other grounds. This statement, of course, does not mean that a society, once having developed its mores or ways of doing, will of its own accord or by outside pressure change easily without some internal disturbance. Neither does it indicate that an economic system may be changed without a major or minor change in ideology or primary motivational characteristics of the society. It probably does indicate that a society might —in the light of a rational approach to problems of adjusting itself to a rapidly changing technology—develop a system compatible with that technology. It can do this without doing any violence to any basic drives or forces due to inherent personality characteristics of the individual or to any kind of inherent "natural social structure." For example, man apparently is not born acquisitive; he may acquire this characteristic from his surrounding culture.

Education of Nonliterate Man

Neither the school as an institution nor education as a function of society developed separately from other aspects and institutions of nonliterate man. Except for the fact that the family appears in all early human groups and that the separate offices of tribal government usually developed early, on the whole there was little separativeness about any of the institutions, customs, or ways of doing of nonliterate man. Life was fairly well integrated. Abstractions, specialization, and compartmentalization of life are results of more highly developed society.

The education of the child came about naturally in his participation in

[20] A. L. Kroeber, *Anthropology*, p. 596.

family and group life. The purpose of education, had it been formulated, would have been to induct the young child into the ways of doing, thinking, and believing—the folkways and mores—of the group. In other words, conformity was taught. The method was imitation, learning by doing. However, in the "activity program" of nonliterate man, creativity was not encouraged. The child was expected to learn well to do things in the ways they had been done. Although in many groups, both competitive and cooperative, he was encouraged toward individual excellence, there was little permissiveness in experimentation with new techniques. Such new techniques as did evolve seem to have come about by unconscious drift, rather than by conscious effort toward improvement.

In almost all tribes there was no differentiation among persons responsible for teaching. Parents, other adults, and older children all participated in the effort to help the child grow into an adult. The ideology of the primitive group was instilled through conversation about such things as spirits and taboos, through storytelling of tribal myths, and through religious ceremonies. Most primitives were fairly indulgent with their children; however, the mores of the group seem always to have been thoroughly ingrained into those children by the time of adolescence.

The first vocation to become fairly sharply differentiated among nonliterate people was that of medicine man or priest, who came to have exclusive knowledge concerning religious rites and exorcisings. These religious persons may be said to be the ones who first considered it a function of their office to play any special part in the education of the young. Many of the primitive groups had complicated rites at the onset of puberty, which tended to intellectualize the process and emotionally to dispose the youth toward complete acceptance of the folkways and of his role as an adult. The school as an institution seems to have appeared only after the development of writing and reading skills. Since the priests were generally the most literate group in this, the dawning period of the civilized era, these schools were usually closely tied to religious institutions and religious leaders. While the schools of Greece and Rome represented a more secular approach, education and religion usually have been very closely related in most cultures even to the present time.

The education of nonliterate peoples was a tremendously successful process in accomplishing its goal of conformity to folkways. Since the society was practically united in respect to allegiance to its folkways and mores, and the child was imbued with them, he could do little else but be molded in conformity with the patterns of the tribe. A point worth mentioning here is that the method must always be considered together with the goal. In the primitive tribe, the complete activity approach—total participation in life situations—was used to develop a child who would be in complete conformity to the culture. There was little attention to creativity or to individual differences.

The Breakdown of Fixed Mores

It has been seen that, once a group has developed a certain type of culture, it tends to resist change in that culture. This is probably due in part to fear of the unknown based on uncertainty of knowledge of the environment. It is also due to the fact that the adults of the group who largely determine what mores are to be inculcated have fairly fixed habits. However, unless changes did occur, man would still be at a primitive level. Some groups improved technologically, achieved better standards of living, a written language, and a creative art, before others. Some of these changes came about very slowly by a kind of cultural drift without any awareness of sudden change by the group.

Numerous reasons have been given to account for these changes and for the variation among groups with respect to the time of arriving at various levels of civilization. Among the reasons that have been advanced are divine help, superior racial inheritance, and geographical conditions. The first two can be ruled out, inasmuch as modern biology and anthropology do not disclose racial differences sufficient to account for the progress, and most of the gods and myths have long since been discarded. Certainly favorable geographical conditions were helpful. The early Oriental-type civilizations developed in relatively fertile regions in the southern part of the North Temperate Zone. However, not all groups in this zone developed at the same time, and most of them developed and then faded away.

Our discussion has made apparent that the reasons for progress are multiple and involve much in the way of fortuitous circumstances or coincidences. The speed and type of the changes varied among the groups because of differences of internal social structure with respect to permissiveness toward slow cultural change of the drift type, which permitted changes to be in some groups and to proceed along different lines and different groups. However, the large breaks with past mores or folkways were brought about by events most of which might be considered disasters: drought, threatened famine, pestilence, fire, earthquake, war, and conquest. All served to *force* the group to move or change its ways. In many cases, contacts with other groups led to adaptions of superior practices from either group, sometimes peacefully. Sometimes the conquerors subdued the conquered but preserved the better part of their culture. Sometimes as a result of these cataclysms, but sometimes independently of them, new inventions occurred. When these inventions met a need or answered a problem for the group, they would be accepted by it. No one knows how many inventions "before their time" were rejected by the group.

When some of the groups had developed sufficient technology to permit considerable travel for trade or for conquest, some of the groups subjugated other groups in wide areas, thus facilitating diffusion of cultural practices from many different groups. This stimulated further contact with other groups, not only permitting cultural diffusions and accretions but also probably further stimulating inventions and the acceptance of improved technologies and other folkways.

The following example of the Tanala tribe faced with a necessity for change in technology and the influence of those changes on other folkways illustrates many of the points already made.[21]

The Tanala were a tribe of people living in the hills of western Madagascar. Up to about two hundred years ago, the economics of their life had been largely based on the cultivation of dry rice by a special method involving the cutting and burning of the trees off the land. In that particular territory, this gave a good crop the first year; and, by allowing the land to lie fallow, it would produce another crop about five to ten years later. Then the land had to be abandoned until a new growth of jungle had appeared—from twenty to twenty-five years as a minimum. This use of the land over great periods of time caused a particular village to move around considerably. The village tribe, as a whole, held the territory within which they moved from place to place. Any of the products of the forest that were taken out would belong to the person who took them. However, the land was owned by the tribe in general, and individuals or families were assigned in a given year to a certain amount. Since there was no sale for surplus crops, there was no drive for one family to obtain more land than the other.

The idea of cultivating wet rice came in from the outside and gradually spread through the group. In this case, by planting the rice in wet places, they could raise the crops continuously on the ground. They could even raise it the year around. They had had an idea of personal property before, but not personal land rights. However, the family to whom the land was assigned, having cultivated it from year to year, considered it to be their land. Some of the families came to own more land and to hire the others. There developed a class of landholders and others. Furthermore, the people began to settle down permanently and form little villages. Then there developed the threat of some of the groups attacking others in order to get more land. Consequently the villages began to fortify themselves with impregnable fortifications. Very complicated arrangements in regard to the use of the land and of property came about.

The total tribal organization of the Tanala had been very democratic with very little formal government of any kind. However, under the new system with permanent land tenure and with villages, one of the Tanala classes established domination over the others and declared itself royal and established a king. It will be thus noted that the Tanala civilization that eventually emerged after two hundred years was quite different from the one before. However, at the basis of this was merely a change in the economic system under which they operated. The type of economic system determined eventually the kind of government and the climate of life. Also, a careful study of the group indicated that during the period of change, there was considerable disintegration. There was at times a considerable lag behind the change of institutions, with

21 This account is paraphrased from the presentation found in Ralph Linton, *The Study of Man* (New York: Appleton, 1936), pp. 348–354.

problems that go along with such lag. Finally, however, the tribe made a new adjustment on the basis of the new economic system. Although of a quite different cultural type than the other, it was fairly satisfactory, and the bulk of its members were adequately fed and clothed.

Out of a process of invention, by diffusion through contacts with others, and through social changes within, the first cultures that might be termed civilizations finally emerged at around 5000 B.C. This stage in development can be measured by the development of a written language, by means of which there appears a recorded culture usually diffused over a fairly wide area.

CHARACTERISTICS OF ORIENTAL CIVILIZATION

The ancient civilizations that eventually achieved a written language and literature and developed cultures that were extended over fairly wide areas include the Chinese, Hindu, Egyptian, Babylonian, Assyrian, Persian, and Hebrew. Some of these, notably the Chinese, maintained an almost unbroken and unchanged type and level of culture into modern times. Others continued with marked changes but still maintained their essentially "Oriental" character.

As set forth earlier in this chapter, the characteristics of the Oriental-type civilization are essentially those of a well-integrated culture of a relatively high level but with a tendency to resist change in the manner of primitive cultures. All of the civilizations listed above, in their ancient form, except possibly the Hebrew, meet the requirements of the definition.

The pattern of emerging civilization of this type seems to have been that of conquest and unification by one tribe of a group of closely related tribes. In the case of Egypt this apparently came about by conquest, with the resultant unification forced from the outside by the Syrians. The period of cessation of intertribal hostility and the cross-fertilization of cultures after the conquest apparently led in many cases to the consolidation of the cultures, resulting in esthetic, literary, and technological achievements. The development of a written language, and thus the more effective passing on of the cultural heritage, enabled many of these civilizations to exist with little change for long periods of time. Some of these, such as Egypt, had periods of ebb and flow marked by new conquests. Others rose and fell, to be eclipsed or absorbed into a new civilization by their conquerors. This occurred frequently in the Mesopotamian region. In spite of the fundamentally static conditions of these civilizations, a great number of their contributions, later absorbed by Western civilization, can be listed. Among them are: astronomy, surveying, systems of time, the alphabet, legal codes, more advanced ethical and religious thinking, and advances in architecture.

CHARACTERISTICS OF EARLY AND MODERN WESTERN CIVILIZATION

It has been necessary to go into considerable detail to describe the nonliterate peoples, even though it has not been as important to describe the Oriental stage so fully. We shall now describe in somewhat greater detail the characteristics of Western civilization, since this is the general climate under which American society has grown. Western, or Occidental, civilization has been characterized by the concept of the acceptance of change. It has been centered on the ideal of bringing about continual improvements within the culture, even though at different times the basis upon which the improvements were to be made were different. In medieval days they were based upon the otherworldly religious concepts of the Church. In the age of enlightenment, the basis was reason or the rational process. In the modern age, it is the scientific method and the ideals of democracy. Even in those periods when change had been somewhat held down because of fixity of social structure, such as in the feudal stage, there were always areas in which progress was taking place; so Western civilization never developed the static quality of Oriental-type civilization.

Early Western Civilization

The conquering of the tribes in the Attic (Greek) peninsula (some with a relatively high civilization) by various Aryan tribes calling themselves Hellenes appears at first to have followed much the same pattern as the earlier Oriental civilizations. However, a group of independent city-states was founded, and the Greeks not only absorbed readily the earlier civilizations but then proceeded to improve upon them. The priestly caste did not play as predominant a role as in most Oriental civilizations. While the majority of the Greeks believed in the familiar pantheon of gods, these gods were never taken very seriously, and a primarily secular state developed. As Greek civilization advanced to its great heights in the fifth century B.C., there was much questioning of religious ideas as well as a prevalent desire to change political and social forms from time to time. It is well to note that this was the product of a peculiar and probably accidental set of conditions that developed in the culture rather than of a particularly superior Greek inherited ability. Neither the earlier nonliterate Greeks nor the Greeks of the modern period show a marked tendency toward mental or other abilities above that of other peoples.

The conquest of the Greeks by the related Macedonians and the later conquest of the then known world by Alexander the Great led to a diffusion of Greek culture and an absorption by the Greeks and others of many elements from the peoples conquered. The eventual conquest of the Greeks by the Romans, and the continuation of the *Pax Romana* that followed, thoroughly insured the spread of Greek culture and thought throughout the Mediterranean region. While the weakening and eventual downfall of the Roman state gave rise to the Teutonic invasion from the north and to a temporary eclipse of learning and Greek culture, they were never totally lost. The incorrectly named period of the "Dark Ages" was not totally so. The questioning and scholarly pursuits in the early universities of the twelfth and thirteenth centuries led the way to the renaissance of Greek culture and traditions starting in the twelfth century and perhaps culminating in the fifteenth.

Modern Western Civilization

Finally, an upsurge of freedom and individualism led to a breakdown of the feudal type of society that had developed during the Middle Ages and to a weakening of the control of the universal church. There emerged, one after another, the three elements that may be said to distinguish modern civilization in the Euro-American or Western scene:

1. The discovery and widespread application of the scientific method.
   Although there were scientists before the gradual development of the scientific method in the fifteenth and sixteenth centuries (leading to Bacon's *Novum Organum*, 1620), there seems to have been little understanding or even recognition of the possibility of the use of the scientific method of experimentation resulting in tested knowledge. Aristotle, one of the most prolific scientists of all time, was primarily a classifier of observed facts. He did not use or understand the experimental method of science. He made many errors because of this. The commonly given example of these errors is his principle that all bodies fall at speeds proportional to their weights. This seemed rationally or logically true, and he never thought of testing it. Galileo put this to an experimental test with the dramatic experiment at the leaning tower of Pisa and disproved the principle in a striking vindication of scientific method.[22] While this scientific experimental method, usually called Newtonian science, and its assumptions as to the nature of the universe, have had to be reinterpreted and expanded by Einsteinian science in recent years, it is this earlier version that has been followed predominantly, and it is to this method that the great achievements of modern scientists are almost entirely to be attributed.
2. The use of the scientific method to approach the solution of technological problems involved in the production of the necessities for life—the beginnings of the age of abundance.
   The rapid growth in man's ability to feed, clothe, and shelter himself by the application of the scientific method to his technological problems is so much greater than that of previous periods in man's development that this fact must be set forth as a differentiating char-

---

[22] Neglecting friction, all bodies fall at the same speed if dropped from the same height.

acteristic of modern times. As far as technology is concerned, in the industrialized countries of the West this can be the age of abundance. This situation is in contrast to that in most of the present nonindustrialized societies of the earth and in practically all of the previous ones. The lack of abundance leads, on one hand, to privileges for a few within a class-caste society (which includes in many cases slaves or peons) and, on the other hand, to war for economic purposes—to take wealth from other groups. A particular solution to the problem of supplying the necessities of life in turn causes new problems. For example, we in America have an economy of abundance with economic institutions largely geared to an economy of scarcity. War is now uneconomic for us, since its waging causes a greater economic loss than can ever be gained by victory.

3. The widespread acceptance of the democratic philosophy and the set of values and the way of life it implies.

While democracy as a form of government goes back well before the modern era—Greece having consciously developed it first—it has found complete and widespread acceptance only in modern times. Even in some primitive tribes there was participation of the members in the election of chiefs and in other decisions. The ancient Greek democracy was a pure democracy in the sense in that all citizens participated in the making of laws as well as in the election of officials to carry them out. However, the Greek citizenry was only a part of the population, which included many slaves with few or no rights and with no participation in government. The modern concept of and belief in democracy are so widespread that, with the exception of the brief advent of fascism, practically the entire world professes to be attaining it. Even Russia and its satellites loudly vaunt the superior virtues of their economic democracy and their "people's republics" as opposed to our "bourgeois capitalistic democracy." In spite of Russia's attacks on Western democracy, there is probably more democracy in the world now than fifty years ago, measured by any one of a number of objective criteria, such as number of voters, diffusion of economic benefits, emancipation of women, and relations within institutions such as the family.

By and large, in the Western world, democracy has come to mean much more than just general suffrage and representative government. It has given more rights to individuals and to minority groups in nongovernmental relations. It has affected philosophy in that it has challenged authorities who refuse to allow their philosophic bases to be examined. To some persons democracy has become a complete philosophy—a way of life. To many it seems to mean a more equitable distribution of goods and services. It appears to have been the most dynamic force of the last century.

THE INDIVIDUAL AS A PRODUCT OF HIS SOCIETY

Against the brief survey of the development of modern society, it is possible to examine with more understanding the relation of the individual to his society and the social institutions that affect his development.

Man differs from the other animals in several ways. Of major significance are his long period of infancy, the plasticity of his nervous system, and his consequent greater ability to absorb the culture in which he is born. Men born and raised apart from humans and human society, the feral humans for example, do not take on any of the behavior patterns of modern man. On the other hand, an infant born and raised in any society, primitive or modern, backward or advanced, has taken on, at least by the age of six, the folkways and mores (including the value systems) of the culture in which he was born. We are not born Americans; we become Americans by absorbing the culture of America in early childhood.

Awareness of the dependence of the individual on society for his very "humanness," as well as for the distinguishing characteristics of those humans of his culture, has been developed out of recent psychological study. This point of view is in opposition to earlier ideas, such as those of Rousseau, that assumed the development of preformed patterns from within. It is also different from the ideas of the biological determinists who, noting the inheritance of structurally based behavior characteristics of other animals, posit the same in man.

INSTITUTIONS, SOCIETY, AND SOCIAL CHANGE

The Nature of Institutions in a Changing Civilization

Returning now to the main story of the evolution of human society, we look at the role that institutions play. At the various stages in societal evolution, man has developed institutions to care for different aspects of his life as needs arise. In the broad sense, language, writing, property rights, and even fire, may be considered institutions. Institutions may be defined broadly as agreed-upon ways of behaving in given life situations; or more narrowly, as a framework of organization that a group may take when its members consciously join together to work for a certain purpose. For the moment, however, we refer to more structural-type institutions, such as the family, the tribal organization, religious groups, and the school.

These institutions are developed in a particular time in a particular culture and are structured in consistency with the folkways and mores of that culture. Change then comes about in that culture, gradually or rapidly. Individuals may change because they are born into the environment of the changed culture. Quite often, however, institutions are slow to change because they are not reborn in each generation. Sometimes their structure is such as to resist change or at least to assist the conservative individuals in that culture who are opposed to the changes that have occurred (or that ought to occur to be consistent with the new needs of the culture). Institutions thus contribute to the cultural lag that so often is characteristic of changing societies, particularly those that are changing rapidly.

The Institutional Arrangements in Society

The institutional arrangements of even the primitive (nonliterate) societies were complicated. While the institutions in many cases were not too clearly defined (except the family), the relationships in many areas where institutions did not exist were clearly defined.

The family is apparently the oldest of all institutions. The relationships among the members of the family, the kin included in the family concept, and the relationship with those outside are strictly prescribed in all cultures. These arrangements are so variable that the conclusion must of necessity be reached that they are probably the result of chance rather than of any inherited tendency toward a particular kind of relationship. Regardless of the particular nature of these arrangements, they are usually very well defined and exert great force on the behavior pattern of the family members.

Another institution is that involved in the system for obtaining a living. The arrangements in this case may vary from a simple society with very little specialization to complex economic systems such as are found in modern industrialized countries, with an intricate system of exchange and an extremely high degree of specialization. By the end of early childhood, the value systems and ways of behaving in whatever economic system is predominant in a given culture are usually absorbed along with other mores.

The institution of government includes the ways that people work together to promote the aims of their society, and its patterns are also extremely variable. The democratic form has emerged only recently. Government, among the institutions of society, has become more important as society has become more complex. It has absorbed many of the functions formerly performed by other institutions, including the family and even religious institutions.

The early beginnings of institutions of religion go back far in human history. The effort of man to understand the fundamental nature of the world and to come to terms with it has been ever present. Concepts and ways of behavior associated with religion are particularly resistant to change. For example, older pagan beliefs bitterly resisted the later monotheistic ideas. Ideas that became associated with monotheism, such as the Ptolemaic conception of the universe, were stubbornly held for a long time before succumbing to the onslaught of man's knowledge gained by science.

Man's self-expression through activity (play) and creativity (art) has also been institutionalized. The total number of institutions in which modern man may participate is very great, and their structural arrangements are very complex. Too, the institutions are often in conflict with each other. This conflict is present even in periods of relatively slow change, even when not fully recognized by the individual, because of the complex nature of these institutions. He may conform in compartmentalized fashion to varying value systems set up by the many institutions in which he may at different times play a part, without recognizing the conflict.

Institutions as Affected by Social Change

Institutional arrangements are developed at a particular time to meet particular needs for a particular phase of man's life. Man's nervous system may permit him to adapt readily at times when the need for change is great, but institutional forces usually seem to resist strenuously demands for changes that threaten radically to affect the institution. While institutions give to society a stability and are the means whereby the individual finds security (as do his early family relationships, for example), they also seem to slow down adjustments made necessary by social change. Institutions grip the loyalty of man, narrow his vision, render him at times unable to see the reason for changes, and, even if he does see them, slow down his effort to bring them about.

Institutions as Means to Ends in Society

One of the basic ideals held in common in all the major world religions and in political democracy is the fundamental respect for the individual personality—a belief in the importance of the well-being of the individual. All institutions should serve to that end. This is well stated in a publication of the Educational Policies Commission:[23]

If the individual personality is supreme, institutional arrangements are the servants of mankind.

Domestic, cultural, and political institutions are not in themselves suitable objects of veneration, except insofar as they contribute to the moral and spiritual values of human life. The family as an institution contributes to social stability and provides protection for the young. A family which is linked by affection rather than merely by authority affords a training ground for wholesome human relations. Similarly, schools and other institutions justify their existence as they contribute to the growth, happiness, and well-being of individuals. Governments, too, as stated by the Declaration of Independence, are instituted among men to promote their inalienable rights. Social institutions, then, are means of serving people. They are never more important than people. Man was not made for the Sabbath. While institutions should not be changed for trivial or transitory reasons, they should be subject to adjustments according to the needs and values of the individuals who function in them.

[23] From N.E.A., Education Policies Commission, *Moral and Spiritual Values in the Public Schools*, pp. 21–22. Copyright, 1951, National Education Association. Reprinted by permission.

That social institutions resist change is well known. One of the major functions of education is to encourage a continuing appraisal of the suitability of existing institutions to the current and prospective needs of the people. Of course, the schools of a totalitarian state are powerless to perform a function of this kind. In our country, however, the schools neglect a proper duty if they fail to provide the knowledge, skill and attitudes whereby public intelligence can function wisely to keep social institutions in line with moral and spiritual values. The schools should, indeed, go further to develop in all young people a strong sense of responsibility for community well-being and a willingness to devote themselves unselfishly to it.

Individual and Group Frustrations Due to Conflicts in Changing Culture

A large cultural area such as the United States is not really one cultural group, even though there are some characteristics that Americans may have in common that serve to distinguish them from members of other groups. There are wide differences in the mores of group living in the hills of Kentucky, the open spaces of Arizona, the small towns of Ohio, and the great metropolitan areas such as New York. One of the factors of cultural change in America has been the change from an agricultural to an industrial civilization, from rural to urban. Moreover, this has occurred so rapidly that many people now living in cities were raised in a rural community or small town with rural mores. The mobility of population, the lack of face-to-face relations with other members of his group, and the fragmented view of culture available to the typical present-day American have lessened the ability of the individual to adapt to the changed culture; but the major factor in the cultural confusions of the typical person has been the rapidity of cultural change. His idea structure has developed in one culture; he lives in another. He is usually unable (or unwilling) to operate according to his earlier idea system, and on the other hand he is unable to change in order to adapt completely to the new. Consequently he is frustrated. Even at best, the tempo of the modern industrial society places a strain on those who sophisticatedly develop a modern urban point of view. Another conflict comes from the different generations. Where the parents make adjustment to the new society by becoming inured to the changing parts of it and maintaining their older ideas or standards successfully without inner conflict, the new generation changes and then finds itself in conflict with the old and with institutions that have not made the corresponding change. The institutional structure resists change, and it may be largely controlled by those who cling to old ideas.

The very real frustration due to the conflict between an ideology of a childhood no longer entirely adapted to the present, and between various aspects or institutions of a culture that lag behind other aspects of the culture, in turn causes further individual and institutional conflicts and further maladjustment in our culture.

The School and Society

The School as a Social Institution

In Chapter 3 there is set forth a detailed description of the evolving relationship of schools to their societies throughout the historic period. At this point, an over-all portrayal of the school as an institution is presented.

The school as an institution evolved out of the educational function of the primitive tribe, the family, and the religious institutions. Although in Greece, and to some extent also in Rome, the school was secularized, by and large the school was closely related to religious institutions until the recent secularizing influences that produced separation of church and state also produced a school free of religious sectarianism. In England and Germany a cooperative relationship exists between the state and the church in educational enterprises, whereas in America the school has become completely secular.

As the state took over from the family and the church the strictly non-religious functions of education, certain problems arose. How shall the schools be governed? What shall the school do about controversies in our society? Shall the school teach in accordance with the majority point of view, just as it is expected that the majority policies will be carried out elsewhere in government?

Out of the thinking gropingly done on this problem, there have emerged certain principles that serve, by and large, officially and unofficially to determine school policy in the United States. The *de facto* operation of the school is in the hands of local lay boards elected for school purposes independent of other political controversy in a given community. The schools at first tended to limit education to literacy and to character traits that were agreed upon as desirable in our society. When the pressure of social events, such as the depression of 1930, forced upon the school consideration of controversial social issues, they were slowly admitted—with the proviso that the school, as such, would not take sides but would present the facts and arguments on the many sides of the issues to be explored.

The concept of the school as unique among governmental institutions has been slow to emerge. Some educational philosophers (as in Mexico) have come to think of the school as a fourth branch of government—the educational branch added to the executive, judicial, and legislative. Charles A. Beard explored this issue in a brochure written for the Educational Policies Commission of the N.E.A., *The Unique Function of Education in a Democracy*. He lists five major reasons for the school to be considered as unique and independent:

1. Scientific Instruction Is Independent of Politics.
2. The Humanities Have Their Independent Imperatives.
3. The Teaching of Controversial Questions Calls for Judicial Prerogatives.

4. Preparation for Citizenship Transcends All Partisan Limits.
5. To Education Are Entrusted Enduring Interests and Values.[24]

The Lag Between the School and Society

In Chapter 3 we shall explore, among other generalizations in the history of the school, the following two, apparently conflicting: one, schools tend to reflect the cultures in which they are found; two, in changing cultures, they tend to lag behind rather than to lead the culture. At this point, it is sufficient to point out the nature and extent of the lag.

In Chapter 15 we shall note conflicting ideas among educational philosophers as to the importance of this fact. Indeed, some of the philosophers, humanists, who are most concerned about this lag, would agree entirely with Beard's assumption in the preceding section. Some individuals in another group, the social realists who are concerned about narrowing the lag, are not so concerned about the independence of the schools from other political institutions.

The lag of the school behind society is no greater than that of many other institutions. Some of the reasons for the lag lie in the institutional character of the school. Other reasons will be explored later. Two of the most striking historical examples of lag are (1) the persistence of autocratic administrator-teacher relationships and teacher-pupil relationships long after the development of the democratic society; (2) the persistence of memoriter devices long after the certainty of psychological research that such learnings were quickly forgotten and could not as readily be transferred to new situations.

In general, the social (or cultural) lag of the school may be discussed under three headings:

(1) ADMINISTRATIVE—ORGANIZATION, BUILDINGS, AND EQUIPMENT. The slow change in administrative organization as some schools have developed better ways and the slow adaptation of buildings and equipment to newer design are very evident. Mort and Cornell made a study[25] of changes concerning which there is now no controversy, and they estimated that from fifteen to thirty-five years elapse from the beginning to the point where there is 95 per cent adoption of new school administrative and organizational methods.

(2) CURRICULUM AND METHODS. The bringing of textbook items up to date when new scientific facts are discovered is hindered by the amount of time it takes to get the items into a textbook and the text adopted by the schools. From ten to fifteen years may elapse. New curriculum organization based on modern educational research may be delayed still

24 Charles A. Beard, *The Unique Function of Education in a Democracy* (Washington, D.C.: National Education Association, 1938).
25 Paul R. Mort and Frances G. Cornell, *Adaptability of Public School Systems* (New York: Bureau of Publications, Teachers College, Columbia University, 1938).

longer due to inertia or to overt, open opposition of teachers, administrators, and the public.

(3) METHODS AND TEACHER-PUPIL RELATIONS. The introduction of newer methods based on modern psychological research or on broadened purposes for education is delayed very much due to the time lapse between the teacher's education and his years of service, due to the lack of opportunity for teachers to keep abreast, and again to opposition by some teachers, administrators, and the public.

SUMMARY

This chapter has presented a survey of man's evolutionary development in relation to his culture. We have identified man's relationship to other animals and his development as a social creature largely influenced by his environment. We have traced his development through the three stages of civilization: the nonliterate, the Oriental, and the Western. We have indicated the importance of man's development to institutions and of institutions to man's development. We have related these developments to the school. We have also indicated some of the problems that arise out of the lack of adjustment between changes, in the culture in general, and in man's institutions and ideologies.

In spite of the complexity of this analysis and the problems that it poses, there is perhaps room for optimism. In the early part of this chapter, it was indicated that we might be in the early phases of what might be called a new level of civilization—called, for want of a better term, modern civilization. In this level it may be discovered that man had secured through science—physical, biological, and social—a sufficient understanding of the world, of himself, and of human relationships that he might be able to produce a type of educated individual and of reconstructed social institution adaptable for the solution of the problems of each age and for the guidance and the direction of social change in directions most beneficial to himself. The role of the school in such a society is to maintain objective and unbiased presentation of truth, and development of scientific attitudes and democratic values in youth.

SELECTED BIBLIOGRAPHY

ALLEE, W. C. *The Social Life of Animals*, Revised Edition. Boston: Beacon Press, 1958. Pp. 233. "An interpretation, with human implication, of one of the most significant biological developments of recent years: The role of basic cooperative processes among living beings."

BARNOUW, VICTOR. *Culture and Personality*. Homewood, Ill.: Dorsey Press, 1963. Pp. xi + 410.

BENEDICT, RUTH. *Race, Science, and Politics*, Revised Edition. New York: Viking Press, 1943. Pp. xii + 273. Contains a good popular summary of what biologists and anthropologists know about race. Reprints several statements from learned groups on the race problem.

BRAMELD, THEODORE. *Cultural Foundations of Education: An Interdisciplinary Exploration.* New York: Harper & Row, 1957. Pp. xxi + 330. "A systematic examination of the theoretical foundations of education in their cultural setting."

BUTTS, R. FREEMAN. *A Cultural History of Western Education*, Second Edition. Pp. 2–8. New York: McGraw-Hill, 1955. Pp. xii + 615.

CAMIEN, LAITEN LESTER. *Education: The Process and Social Institution.* New York: Vantage, 1964. Pp. 165.

DOBZHANSKY, THEODORE. *The Biological Basis for Human Freedom.* New York: Colliers, 1956. Pp. vi + 139.

————. *Mankind Evolving: The Evolution of the Human Species.* New Haven: Yale University Press, 1962. Pp. xiii + 381.

EISELEY, LOREN. *The Immense Journey.* New York: Vintage Books, 1957. Pp. 210. A story of man's evolution and progress from an anthropological and naturalist point of view.

GARN, STANLEY M. (ed.). *Culture and the Direction of Human Evolution.* Detroit: Wayne State University Press, 1964. Pp. iii + 98.

HARRISON, GEORGE RUSSELL. *What Man May Be: The Human Side of Science.* New York: Morrow, 1956. Pp. 278.

HONIGMANN, JOHN. *Understanding Culture.* New York: Harper & Row, 1963. Pp. viii + 468.

HOWELLS, WILLIAM WHITE. *Mankind in the Making: The Story of Human Evolution.* Garden City, N.Y.: Doubleday, 1959. Pp. 382.

HUXLEY, JULIAN S. (ed.). *The Humanist Frame.* New York: Harper & Row, 1961. Pp. 432. An excellent symposium presenting the "humanist" conceptions of the nature of man and the universe, stressing Huxley's emphasis on "idea-systems."

LABARRE, WESTON. *The Human Animal.* Chicago: University of Chicago Press, 1955. Pp. xiv + 416.

LEE, DOROTHY. *Freedom and Culture.* Englewood Cliffs, N.J.: Prentice-Hall, Spectrum Books, 1959. Pp. vii + 179.

LINTON, RALPH. *The Tree of Culture.* New York: Knopf, 1955. Pp. xvix + 692. A very detailed, thorough summary of knowledge in the field of the anthropology of nonliterate man.

LIPSET, SEYMOUR MARTIN, and LEO LOWENTHAL. *Culture and Social Character: The Work of David Riesman Reviewed.* New York: Free Press of Glencoe, 1961. Pp. xiv + 466.

LYNN, KENNETH S. *The American Society.* New York: Braziller, 1963. Pp. viii + 245.

MEAD, MARGARET. *Cooperation and Competition Among Primitive People.* Enlarged Edition. Boston: Beacon Press, 1961. Pp. viii + 544.

MONTAGU, ASHLEY (ed.). *Culture and the Evolution of Man.* New York: Oxford University Press, 1962. Pp. xiii + 376.

————. *Man in Process.* New York: New American Library, 1961. Pp. xiii + 278. A good presentation of man's social evolutionary development.

————. *On Being Human.* New York: Henry Schuman, 1951. Pp. 122.

MULHERN, JAMES. *A History of Education: A Social Interpretation*, Second Edition, Chapters 1–2. New York: Ronald Press, 1959. Pp. vii + 754.

POTTER, DAVID M. *People of Plenty: Economic Abundance and the American Character*. Chicago: University of Chicago Press, 1955. Pp. xxvii + 219. An excellent analysis of the relationship of the "American character" to American economic abundance.

RICHARDS, O. W. *The Social Insects*. New York: Harper & Row, 1953. Pp. xiii + 219.

RIESMAN, DAVID. *Individualism Reconsidered and Other Essays*. New York: Free Press of Glencoe, 1954. Pp. 529.

——. *Lonely Crowd*. Garden City, N.Y.: Doubleday, 1956.

——. *Selected Essays from Individualism Reconsidered*. New York: Free Press of Glencoe, 1954. Pp. 529.

SHAPIRO, HARRY L. (ed.). *Man, Culture, and Society*. New York: Oxford University Press, 1960. Pp. vii + 380.

SPINDLER, GEORGE D. (ed.). *Education and Culture: Anthropological Approaches*. New York: Holt, Rinehart & Winston, 1963. Pp. 542.

TAX, SOL (ed.). *Anthropology Today*. Chicago: University of Chicago Press, 1962. Pp. viii + 481.

TEILHARD DE CHARDIN, PIERRE. *The Phenomenon of Man*. New York: Harper & Row, 1959. Pp. 318.

WAGNER, PHILLIP. *The Human Use of the Earth*. New York: Free Press of Glencoe, 1960. Pp. xv + 270.

WHITE, LYNN JR. (ed.). *Frontiers of Knowledge in the Study of Man*. New York: Harper & Row, 1956. Pp. xii + 330. An excellent symposium.

SELECTED FILMS

The Color of Man (Columbia University) 20 min
    Examines those conditions in the history of mankind which brought about differences in the color of man's skin. Shows the impression of modern science and transportation on these forces.

Earth and Its People Series (Louis de Rochement Assoc.) 20 min each
    Includes the titles: Malaya—*Nomans of the Jungle*; Norway—*Farmer-Fisherman*; Java—*Tropical Mountain Land*; Guatemala—*Cross section of Central America*; South Africa—*Riches of the Veldt*; and Argentina—*Horsemen of the Pampas*. Malaya films particularly recommended.

Mirror of America (Norwood Films) 36 min
    A reflection of the American way of life from 1914–1921, this movie portrays a cross-section view of people and progress. It is an historical documentary taken from the Ford Film Collection recently presented to the National Archives.

Monkey into Man (Library Films) 20 min
    Traces development through the baboon, gibbon, orangutan, chimpanzee, and gorilla, showing the family and social life of these animals and the variation in brain power among them. A comparison is made between the most intelligent of these apes and man.

Our Changing World (Ott and Methodist) 60 min
    The story of the development of the earth since the beginning of time.

The formation of the oceans and continents and the emergence of life are shown. Time-lapse photography is used to show the succession of higher forms of plant and animal life. Ends with the advent of man on earth.

Science and Superstition (Coronet Films) 10 min
Demonstrates technique for guiding elementary school children's thinking to scientific method. Shows means of helping children to conduct research and arrive at conclusions therefrom.

Social Change in a Democracy (United World) 29 min
Students in a social science class discuss the conditions that exist in a democracy and those that exist in a totalitarian state, and learn firsthand how a problem in their own community, arising from a social change, is solved by law and assembly rather than by violence.

Social Process (Encyclopedia Britannica Films) 20 min
Patterns of behavior common to all cultures. Develops concept of social process from the statement, "Man seeks values through institutions using resources."

Social Revolution (Encyclopedia Britannica Films) 18 min
Describes the process of social change, especially that instigated by technological developments. Illustrates the process with scenes of the Industrial Revolution in England, the French Revolution, emigration to the U.S., and the rise of totalitarianism in Germany and Russia.

Southern Highlands (Ford Motor Co.) 22 min
Provides a picture of folk people and affords insight into their responses to the processes of change.

The Story of Prehistoric Man (Coronet Films) 11 min
This description of the life, appearance, habitat, and achievements of prehistoric man is reconstructed from authentic evidence, prehistoric tools and weapons, cave paintings and stone carvings, and skeletal remains. The periods of the Old and New Stone Ages are indicated and the geographical areas in which prehistoric man lived are mapped.

Chapter 3. *The Historic Relationship of Schools to Their Societies*

THE FUNDAMENTAL THESIS underlying this chapter is: Schools tend to reflect the societies in which they are found. There is a similar proposition, which may seem to be contradictory to the first but actually is not: Schools tend to lag behind their societies, particularly in periods of rapid social change.

THE NATURE OF THE SCHOOL AS A SOCIAL INSTITUTION

All human institutions are a product of culture and as such must be called social institutions. The word "institution" itself implies that the school is social in nature. The school as an institution in most cases has been developed consciously by a people in order to carry out certain ideas deemed appropriate by them. Although the school as an institution sometimes has lost touch with its society and has tended to become a conservative force, it has always been established as an agency of society to carry out its purposes. Even where the schools have been institutions of a private nature, not controlled by any form of government, this has still been true.

In another sense, the school itself is a social institution. Persons attending it learn the methods of their society—merely by living in a cultural milieu that reflects the society in which the school is found. Many times the lessons learned from the social structure of the school (reflecting that of the society) may be more important in the development of the individual than the course content—sometimes academic and little related to life—that the students learn. This appears to have been just as true in earlier schools as in those of the immediate past. However, it was not until the modern period that the importance of nonformal learning was recognized by the people directing the schools and consciously given some status, in the form of extracurricular activities, student organizations, and others.

THE EARLY DEVELOPMENT OF THE SCHOOL AS A SEPARATE SOCIAL INSTITUTION

In Chapter 2 we have gone into some detail concerning the development of institutionalized education and some of the functions of the school among preliterate peoples. In the simple organization of the preliterate peoples, there were no well-defined institutions in the sense of their having a separate structure from that of the total community. The family probably emerged first as a separate institution, together with the other trappings of tribal organization, probably just an extended family at first. The various forms of governmental organization, such as the office of chieftain or an advisory body of elders, may have emerged next as social institutions. Soon the religious activities of the tribe became institutionalized with the development of a priestly caste with special training and activities.

In the more simply organized tribes, all of the adults were responsible for the education of the children. Formal education was limited to mystic rites of initiation into the tribe; these rites usually were held for certain age groups or puberty groups. The children learned by doing, by imitation of what the adult did. Later on certain persons, usually members of the priestly class, were given responsibility for the special training of children in the tradition and other formal instruction of the group.[1]

Until a written language and literature appear, it is not necessary to develop a distinctly separate institution for the purpose of educating the young. When this happens, it means that the group has reached the second level of development—the Oriental-type civilization. Those types of civilizations that first developed in the Fertile Crescent and in Egypt had quite a high level of culture; in most cases this culture was based upon amalgamation of existing cultures of various tribes. They also began to have a written language and literature. Similar changes were taking place in China. Only a few members of the culture at these early times could write or read. It became necessary, then, to train others to do this. Special schools were set up for those who were to be versed in reading and writing, who were to be the guardians of the culture. In most cases these persons were closely connected with the religious institutions. In some cases there were also scribes (those who could read and write) whose functions were not necessarily religious. Special books were written for the instruction of the young, usually containing admonitions, words

[1] See James Mulhern, *A History of Education*, Second Edition (New York: Ronald Press, 1959), Chapter 2, for more details of education among nonliterate peoples.

of wisdom, or important myths to be passed on to the next generation. Methods of instruction were devised for these schools. In many cases, however, the work of the schools became quite formal in nature, with the main attention directed to the language *as such* rather than to the material to be taught.

Prior to the period of the Greeks, and for that matter practically until modern times, the school did not differ greatly from other institutions with respect to its purposes or goals. Throughout most of the area of the Fertile Crescent, in Egypt, and in China, the school was tied in closely either to religious ceremonies or to government or both. Its primary difference in function was in teaching persons to read and to write the literatures and to understand and to interpret the sacred literature of the society or culture. Education was usually limited to a relatively small portion of the total population. It was provided primarily for people who would have to use it in their governmental or religious tasks. In that sense the school was vocational in nature. In all the thinking about schooling that took place prior to the time of the Greeks, there seems to have been little conception of education as being a broadening experience or as being intellectually stimulating for new ideas. Part of the reason, of course, lies in the fact that early cultures were repressive or restrictive in nature with respect to any kind of innovations. It is not until we come to the Greek culture that we find any idea of progress or of creativity. Since the school reflects the prevailing attitudes of the culture, it is not surprising that the schools of the pre-Greek period were as they were.[2]

In the next four sections, we shall discuss the school as an institution as it developed during each of four significant periods: the period of Greek influence, that of Roman influence, the Medieval period, and the period of the Revival of Learning.

In each case we will discuss briefly (1) the social and intellectual developments of the period; (2) the school as an institution; and (3) the goals of the school as they were established at that time.

THE GREEK SCHOOL AND ITS SOCIETY

The study of the Greeks and their civilization is an intriguing one because so many of the problems that they faced and the ideas with which they struggled were similar to our own.

It is difficult to understand why there developed on the Attic peninsula a different kind of civilization from that which developed in far Asia, the Middle East, or the Nile area. There had come into being on or near this peninsula, prior to the invasion by the various Greek tribes, two

[2] Details with respect to these early schools are too involved to be discussed in this book. The reader, however, is referred to an excellent discussion of Egyptian society and education in Chapter 3 of Mulhern, *A History of Education*, and of ancient Indian (Hindu) society and education in Chapter 4 of the same book.

fairly highly developed civilizations, the Mycenaean and the Cretan. Their level of art and culture was quite high. These peoples were then invaded by certain Aryan tribes from the north, who called themselves the Hellenes but whom we call the Greeks. They were much less civilized. However, in conquering the old civilizations they absorbed them. Although there was an early period somewhat resembling our medieval period when the civilization tended to decline, it did eventually recover and reach new heights.

Instead of becoming one large group dominating the entire peninsula, the Greeks tended to develop politically into small city-states that were more or less independent. This left a great deal of local initiative for them to develop and experiment. There were quite considerable differences existing among the various city-states, although a common language and a common alphabet and literature eventually developed. There was a contrast between the rigorous, autocratic type of city-state, such as Sparta, and the much more democratic ones, such as Athens. However, in both cases the power to rule was dispersed fairly widely among an oligarchy. In the case of Sparta the number of people who had freedom to make choices was probably, during most of the time, less than 5 per cent. The remainder of the populace were "free" men who were not citizens, plus a vast number of slaves. The same thing was true of Athens except that the number of free men was higher. Furthermore, the democratic rights held by the free men were much greater. Life was freer as a whole, and a great deal more individual initiative was allowed. Sparta was really a "garrison state." It was at Athens that the "liberal state" permitting a great deal of freedom of thinking was developed. Publicly the state was religious; however, there was no priestly class that dominated it. There was no dogma that could cause a stifling of man's intellect. Authorities are fairly well agreed that the Greek level of culture was achieved largely as a result of accident of social structure rather than because of any superior inherited characteristics of the Greeks, since they were closely related by blood to many other Aryans who did not accomplish so much so early.

The Greeks never were able to solve the problem of getting along with each other, and the peninsula was beset during the later period by a succession of civil wars, which tended to weaken them greatly. They were finally conquered by Alexander the Great. The Greek culture, however, was dispersed throughout the Mediterranean region and eventually absorbed by the Roman culture and civilization. It had great influence upon Roman life and also on Christianity. It also had influence upon the Saracen, or Islamic, culture. During one period of history the Greek influence was much greater upon the Saracen culture than it was upon Western civilization. A discussion of Greek developments would not be complete without considering at least three of the outstanding teachers and intellectual leaders of that country: Socrates, Plato, and Aristotle.

These men constituted a kind of "triumvirate" with the latter two each being a student of the older.

Socrates (469–399 B.C.) left no writings. Consequently it is difficult to determine exactly his ideas or his methods of teaching. Primarily he taught by a method that has become known as the Socratic method, a question-and-answer technique. When a pupil would come to him with a question to be answered, Socrates would retort with a question to the student. As the student began to answer that question and others to follow, he eventually discovered that he knew nothing. Up to this point, this is called the *ironic* or *destructive* stage. Then by a series of constructively worded questions, Socrates would build up the idea that he wished to place in the student's mind. This is called the *maieutic* stage (based on the Greek word for midwife)—giving birth to ideas. Socrates thus apparently thought that one could get at truth by skillful handling of ideas. However, his questions were always related to life. Among the Greeks he comes closest to the pragmatic or modern experimentalist method. But he was not a thorough-going pragmatist in the modern James-Dewey sense.

Plato (427–346 B.C.), although a student of Socrates, represents a withdrawal from the practical period. Plato moved his classes away from the marketplace to the Grove of Academius so that he would not be bothered by practical things. Hence comes our word "academic"—relating to things that are not necessarily practical. Plato developed a philosophical point of view that held that truth was decided ultimately by reason alone. Ideas existed quite apart from man's experience with things. As a matter of fact, to Plato the real world was a shadowy representation of the *ideal* world. The real end of education consequently must be to deal with those ideas. It must be abstract, intellectual. However, modern followers of Plato must, of course, remember that Plato's concepts about education were laid in the context of his time. Basic Greek education then allowed for the well-rounded development of the student, physically, mentally, and otherwise, through songs and literature and athletic activities. As shown by his suggestions for education contained in his *Republic*, he would continue this. Plato's emphasis upon the intellectual was, of course, the crowning part of the education he proposed for those people whom he believed capable of receiving it. However, for Plato this was not an exclusive form of education. Some of the modern followers of Plato attempt to define the education of the intellect as being the only kind that is worthy of the name of education. Plato's influence on the thinking of his time—and of the period to follow, when Greek culture was disseminated throughout the Mediterranean region—was immense. Through neo-Platonism, a mystical form of Platonic doctrine that spread throughout the area soon after Plato's time, he exercised a profound influence upon Christianity as it began to develop.

Aristotle (386–322 B.C.) was Plato's pupil. He agreed basically on most matters with Plato, but certainly he had more interest in the things of this world—in material things. In the first place, Aristotle was a great scientist.[3] He wrote prolifically about practically all matters that are now embodied in the various fields of knowledge. As a matter of fact, our organization of fields of knowledge still closely follows that of Aristotle. Aristotle was a collector and classifier of knowledge. Although he wrote many books on different phases of scientific knowledge, he did not understand the scientific method of experimentation as it has developed in recent years. Largely for this reason, his work contained errors. Aristotle's philosophy as such did not influence Western civilization until about the eleventh and twelfth centuries A.D., when his works, which had been lost, were recovered through Moslem scholars. Aristotle's philosophy, with its acceptance by St. Thomas Aquinas and by the Roman Catholic Church, became dominant in the universities of Europe and in European thought for almost four hundred years. It was not until the coming of the scientific method that it began to be seriously challenged.

Platonic and Aristotelian ideas still exert a strong influence in Western civilization. They provide largely the basis for the neohumanistic point of view discussed in Chapter 15 of this book.

The Greek ideal of education, particularly in Athens and in others of the freer Greek states, was to develop the well-rounded, thinking individual. In Sparta the aim was more to develop a hardy, militaristic type of individual. In both cases, education was quite thorough and much broader than the purely intellectual. One of the significant differences between Athens and Sparta lay in the attitude toward freedom and toward freedom of thinking. It is well to note here, as in other cases, that the Greek schools did put into action the Greek set of values and thus did reflect their society.

THE ROMAN SCHOOL AND ITS SOCIETY

In the early Roman period, as in the early development of other peoples, the school was not clearly separated from the society as a separate institution. Primarily it was the job of the family to carry on education. When Rome began to dominate the peninsula of Italy and the Roman state began to develop, schools as institutions began to separate from other institutions with respect to functions served. The early schools were private and seemed to be influenced little by either religious groups or the state. In the later Roman period, however, the state tended to exert much more influence. The Roman schools, just like schools in other countries, tended to reflect the nature of society whether or not they were run by

---

[3] The authors realize that Aristotle was not, strictly speaking, a scientist in the modern sense, since he did not know or use scientific experimentation to validate his hypotheses. Nevertheless his observations and classification of scientific data were a contribution, in spite of the few (but major) errors in his work.

the church, private nonreligious influences, or by the state. Roman schools in the early and middle period were divided into three levels: the *ludus*, or elementary school; the school of the *grammaticus*, or the intermediate schools; and the schools of the *rhetoric*, or the higher schools. The Roman schools were primarily organized to develop citizens and to stress the duty of the citizens to their state. The schools of the rhetoric, for example, were never as broad in their approach as were the Greek schools even though they were modeled after them. There was emphasis primarily on speaking and oratorical ability. However, this was certainly considerably broader than would be similar education at present. There was very little emphasis on the all-around development of the body, as there had been in Greek education. In the later Roman period, the schools tended to degenerate, laying emphasis upon grammatical structure and form rather than upon thinking and the spirit. The study of philosophy itself never became a central feature of the school. The Romans were largely men of action rather than philosophers, and they tended to play down this aspect of education, which had been so prominent in Greece.

Only a small fraction of the Romans were educated completely (as was true of all countries until modern times). During the period of the decline of the Roman Empire, education tended to languish and to come more under the control of the emperor.

In the medieval period, which is discussed next, education was closely associated with religion. Neither in Greece nor in Rome (in contrast to most of the other countries that were contemporary with Greek and Roman civilization), were the schools closely tied to religious ideas. Education was primarily a secular function. This does not mean that the schools were antireligious or that they ignored religious materials. They simply were not controlled by the religious authorities, and their central purpose was not the teaching of religious ideas. Furthermore, the schools did not use members of the priesthood in teaching functions. Clerics were almost exclusively used during the medieval period—even into the period of the revival of learning.

THE SCHOOL AND THE SOCIAL CLIMATE IN THE MEDIEVAL PERIOD

The medieval period of history is generally considered to be roughly from the fifth century to the fifteenth. This period has been erroneously called "the Dark Ages." Although there was a decline in learning and in the number of schools due to the social conditions of the time, they never disappeared. Furthermore, during part of this time there was an increase in the amount of learning and education due to various forces. The decline of learning was due in part to the breakdown of the Roman Empire, the invasion of the Germanic tribes, and the early opposition of Christianity to pagan learning. Since pagan learning was the only kind of learning there was, this meant that there was a tendency to look down upon schools and schooling of any kind other than religious. The first Christian schools, the catechumenal schools, were established before 500 A.D. and were connected with either a cathedral or a monastery. These schools and the later catechetical schools were established primarily for religious instruction. They often included instruction in ability to read along with that in theological doctrines. The best instruction in religion and theology was that developed for the clerics, which took place mostly in the monasteries. At the time of Charlemagne (742–814 A.D.) there was considerable revival of learning in the sense that Charlemagne issued several edicts to improve the education of the clergy and to establish other types of schools. However, this progress did not continue uninterrupted. The purpose of education was primarily that of instruction concerning Christian doctrines and preparing for the world to come—the "otherworldly" aim.

During this period of uncertain social conditions, many of the literary works of the Greeks and Romans were lost. Most of those that were preserved were from Plato. During the eleventh or twelfth centuries, Aristotle's works were found and revived through contact with the Moslems. In the eleventh and twelfth centuries, a group of scholars (called the scholastics) in the monasteries did a thorough reconciliation of Greek thinking (primarily that of Aristotle) with the Christian tradition. This philosophy, usually called scholasticism or Thomism (the latter term from St. Thomas Aquinas, 1225–1274), dominant in the Western world at least until the sixteenth century, was formally accepted by the Roman Catholic Church as its official philosophy in 1879 and has continued with some modifications to this day. Although no striking changes were brought about by the work of the scholastics, intellects were stimulated in preparation for the revival of learning that took place from the fifteenth to the eighteenth centuries. There was practically no interest in science during the medieval period, and most of the errors that Aristotle had made were incorporated in the ideas that were prevalent. The revival of interest in things scientific foreshadowed the greater interest in the period of the Reformation and the scientific revolution, the seventeenth and eighteenth centuries—to be discussed later. Although kings and other nonreligious authorities took an interest in education from time to time, and sponsored schools and universities, primary control of the schools was in the hands of the clerics, and their primary purpose was religious— that is, to prepare people to be better Christians, to strengthen their doctrines, and to get them ready for the world to come. Since both the the political state and the church were considered to be ordained by God and both were considered to be equally under His control, there was no such thing as the separation of church and state. Although there were disputes concerning the control of the Pope, by and large the political authorities were subservient to the religious authorities during the medieval period. Only a small percentage of persons were in schools, were educated, or were literate. The interest in mass education was to await the period of the Reformation and the Counter Reformation.

One of the major contributions of this period was the foundation of the university. Starting with the University of Salerno in the ninth century, many such institutions were founded throughout Europe in the medieval period. These became the repositories of learning and the centers for many new ideas. Though almost all of the scholars operated within the framework of the medieval outlook—the otherworldly, Christian outlook—they did maintain standards of learning as far as was possible during those times. The emphasis was upon the liberal arts and upon what was written in books rather than upon the development of new knowledge. The answer to a dispute was found by going to the authorities and attempting to reconcile the conflicting views. However, the freedom of the universities during this time laid an excellent background for the revival of learning and for the educational importance of the university in the early modern and contemporary scenes.

The School in the Period of the Revival of Learning
Fourteenth and Fifteenth Centuries

Starting with the work of Petrarch (1304–1374), the leaders of the period of the revival of learning were interested in changing the attention of the schools from otherworldly preoccupation to the joys of this world. This was primarily accomplished by a return to the use of the ancient Roman and Greek literary classics, all of which were much broader in outlook than the materials that had been used during the medieval period.

The political situation at this time helped to secularize education. There was a breakdown of feudalism, with the strengthening of the central monarchy in the case of France and England and a strengthening of the central power of the dukes and princes in the case of Italy, Germany, and possibly Spain. In many cases the hold of the church had been somewhat weakened. The growth and development of town schools for the rising middle class helped to bring about a school based more upon the ideas of this world.

Many of the outstanding educational leaders of this period wrote books on their ideas. Da Feltre (1378–1446), at Mantua, Italy, who taught in a school maintained by a duke, had ideas concerning education that were surprisingly modern. Although the course of study was quite classical in content, there was mild discipline in the school and it was aimed at the harmonious development of mind and body. This seems more like the Greek ideal than the philosophy of other schools of its time. The work of such other leaders as Rabelais, who was very critical of the schools and other social institutions of his time, stands out during this period.

It must be remembered that although the revival represented a new orientation, it was not in complete opposition to the general orientation of this theological-centered period. The leaders were not in rebellion against prevailing theological ideas. They were merely placing more emphasis upon the affairs of men (humans). Hence they came to be called "humanists," and the subjects they studied were called the "humanities." During the sixteenth and seventeenth centuries, religious leaders accepted humanistic ideas and the two were encompassed together under the name of "religious humanism."

In considering the pronouncements of earlier leaders on education, any ideas that they set forth must always be examined in the light of the times. The suggestions for milder discipline or for consideration of individual differences of the student must always be considered in the light of the fact that the main aim was to produce the classically trained leader and upper-class gentleman. These schools were purely for the upper class and for the leaders. In almost all cases the emphasis was upon classical learning and the use of the classical languages. Only a few of these people believed that education should be conducted in the vernacular. Emphasis was still heavy upon grammatical form and upon a literary type of education, as opposed to any attempt to utilize the first beginnings of science. The revival of learning saw the beginnings of interest in scientific knowledge, but this interest had little influence upon the education of the time.

The School in the Period of the Reformation and Scientific Revolution, Sixteenth to Eighteenth Centuries

During the sixteenth to the eighteenth centuries, the power of the church was both weakened and strengthened. Through the Reformation movement, the northern part of Europe mostly broke away from the control by the Church of Rome. On the other hand, the church was strengthened immensely by the Counter Reformation so far as the southern part of Europe was concerned. It also was the period of the scientific revolution, which began to affect education. The Reformation itself reflected a strengthening of the power of the secular rulers against the Pope as well as a religious reformation. At the end of this period, the national states were pretty well established. This laid the basis for a national system of schools.

The Protestant reformers were much interested in the education of the masses. While they did not have in mind the same kind of education for the masses as for the classes, at least they were interested in enabling them to read the Bible. This interest in the education of the masses did not, by and large, lead to any differences in school methods or curriculum. As a matter of fact, the Protestant schools under the influence of Luther and Calvin were probably more rigid and more repressive than had been the schools prior to that time. They largely stressed memorization and learning of the rules of grammar. Luther's own concept of liberal education reflected the classics in which he had been educated. The Protestant schools of this period were gloomy schools indeed. There was little emphasis upon the child as an individual or on developing an educational program suited to his level or on other such modern ideas.

A few developments during this period were the beginning of some things that were to come later. These were largely the results of the influence of modern science. It is generally felt that the work of Comenius (who is held by some to be the first modern educator) was influenced by the development of science. Comenius emphasized learning through sensory experience. He developed the idea of the textbook with pictures, so that the youngsters would understand the words that they were trying to learn. He was thus far in advance of his time, but he had very little influence because he was a Protestant bishop and in the minority as far as his section of Europe was concerned.

In Catholic Europe there was an improvement in education through the development of the Jesuit schools with quite high standards and through the work of the Jansenists and the Christian Brothers during this period. Each of these groups set up special teacher-training programs in order to better prepare teachers. LaSalle of the Christian Brothers developed a special institute, which was one of the first examples of an institution largely for the training of teachers in the elementary school.

The developments of this time did not greatly affect the relationship of religion to education. The Protestant reformers were even more interested in continuing education in religion than were the humanist educators of the previous period. Even when the schools were taken more and more under the control of the civil authorities, it was still done for the central purpose of preparing people for the world to come. Not until the middle of the nineteenth century was there an emphasis upon a secular type of educational program. Moreover, the Calvinistic and Lutheran emphasis upon the state being subordinate to religious authority led eventually to education becoming a function of the state. They held that the state had the right to decide which religion should hold sway and to require all citizens to conform. The church became established in the sense that it was protected and supported by the state. Even when the state did not have the actual ownership and control of the school, there was increasing government interest in education. Edicts of princes and kings quite often determined the content of the school curriculum. This was especially true of some of the work of universities in France and England during this period, where through edicts the king controlled the emphasis upon studies. One example is the move toward humanistic emphasis in the French schools as opposed to the earlier theological curriculum. In some cases, the king even took sides with respect to theological controversies.

One other point might be made with respect to the attitude of religious authorities toward the developing sciences. Both the Protestants and the Catholics were very much opposed to some of the findings of modern sci-

ence. For example, both the Lutheran Protestants and the Catholics de-
nounced the teachings of Copernicus in regard to the sun being the center
of the universe. It was almost a hundred years after the time of Copernicus
that his ideas became widely accepted. This delay was largely due to the
opposition of church leaders, who felt that the new ideas were opposed
to their theology. On the other hand, men like Descartes tried to reconcile
the new scientific view with the older theology; however, it was some time
before Descartes was accepted by religious authorities.

THE DEVELOPMENT OF NATIONAL SCHOOL SYSTEMS, NINETEENTH CENTURY

Prior to the nineteenth century, education in Europe was predominantly either religious in nature or private in character and available to a
very small segment of the population. There was a tendency for some
national (state) systems of education to be developed in Germany during
the Reformation period, as a part of the determination of the particular
religion of the subjects of each of the German states. The purpose of such
a national support of religion was primarily to give the young child proper
background to understand his religion, particularly in the Protestant faith.

With the French Revolution, the Napoleonic era in France, and the
development of Germany under the Fredericks, a new purpose of education evolved. This purpose was to use the school to develop the general
level of the people for the welfare of the state. The Prussian kings were
very much concerned about developing a minimum of education for
their subjects in order to develop their state. In this period there was no
thought of educating citizens to exercise the right of suffrage, since these
were despotic states, albeit benevolent. During democratic periods, there
was emphasis in the French schools upon educating persons for freedom
and the exercising of the rights of citizenship; during periods of despotism,
this influence disappeared, only to be revived again under the next democratic government. Throughout Europe the prevailing emphasis in schools
was on the indoctrination of the student with love for the emperor (or
king) and with the religious viewpoint that was prevalent in the particular
country. The German kings did espouse freedom of learning and teaching
in the German universities for the purposes of fostering research; however,
this was not carried into the *Gymnasien* and the elementary schools.

The general trend in the national school systems in France, Germany,
and other European countries was toward two school types: the elementary school for the masses, compulsory for those who could not afford
private tutors; and the secondary school for the classes, leading to the
cultural development of the student divorced from work, and perhaps
then to study at the university. Although there was much talk during
the Reformation period concerning compulsory education for all, this
ideal was not realized in Europe for some time. The first country in

Europe to establish a compulsory system of education was the German state of Prussia. One of the next was the democratic United States of America. Although the reasons in both cases were nationalistic, certainly the climate of political thought in the United States was quite different from that of Prussia, and certainly the citizenship (voting) reason was more prevalent in the United States. There is evidence that some of the leaders in education in this country were considerably influenced by what was taking place in education in Europe.

The nineteenth century was the period when the work of the educational reformers became quite well known, although certaintly the character of the work of the schools did not reflect to any great extent the teachings of such men as Herbart (1746–1827), Pestalozzi (1776–1841), and Froebel (1782–1852). The minimal influence of these men upon the typical school situation is an example of the lag of the school behind society in periods of rapid change. Very few of the teachers of Europe were well trained. Most saw learning as memorization, in spite of some of the emphasis of the theorists upon concrete, realistic education. It was only after people became concerned that there be changes in education, in line with the proposals of theorists, that there began to be set up special schools for the preparation of teachers—professional teacher education. When the people were fairly well satisfied with the kind of education that was being given, there was little agitation for professional teacher education. In some cases there was opposition to it for fear that the school system would change and become more modern—as witness recent developments in the United States.

The development of the European national systems of schools did not change the relationship of church and state that had existed previously. Whereas the schools of the previous period had been primarily dominated by the church for religious reasons, the schools of this period were still largely influenced by the prevailing religion of the time. This was true except at those times during the French Revolutionary period when anticlerical feeling caused the schools to become completely secular. Considerably later in the history of France, they were made secular again—around the turn of the twentieth century. Of course in America they did become secularized because America did disestablish the church and adopt a policy of separation of church and state. This is one of the marked contrasts between the development of the American education system and the systems of European countries.

THE INFLUENCE OF DEMOCRACY ON EDUCATION IN AMERICA BEFORE 1865

The European colonists who moved to this country brought with them their European institutions. This was as true of the schools as it was of other institutions. The European schools of the seventeenth century (the period of early colonization) were aristocratic and classical in background. These schools were hardly in keeping with life on the rugged coast of New England and other parts of the colonial area. Many of the schools that were established were narrowly sectarian. The breakdown of the sectarian character of the colonies, together with the growing feeling that education was not adapted to the life its colonists lived, led to the languishing of educational standards in the early part of the eighteenth century. There was some revival of interest in education by the middle of the eighteenth century. This was a part of the renewed interest caused by the age of enlightenment in Europe, the growth of science, and the stirring ideas concerning the freedom of man. Outside of the New England colonies very little was done to make education universal because most people had not yet thought of education as being other than a private matter.

The schools that were established in New England were public schools, in the sense that they were established by the state even though they were narrowly sectarian. This was not true of schools in Europe. As the schools changed from being sectarian, in the early part of the nineteenth century, they remained public schools. Thus in America the principle of governmentally owned and operated schools was established. Also in New England during the colonial period the idea of having a committee of the town selectmen to run each local school was established. This arose partly because of the difficulty of communication from one school to another and partly because of the desire of the parents of each school to have control. Local school committees eventually became boards of education.

The attempts to establish a better secondary school, to take the place of the European grammar school, which had been transplanted to America, also represented an effort to develop an institution to meet the needs of life on this continent. The academy temporarily was successful, but it was to be replaced by the high school around 1890. The academy was quite often sectarian, and it was generally privately run. It developed later into the college-preparatory type of school even though it was not originally so designed.

The influence of the democratic spirit in America after the Revolution eventually caused the school system to take on the four characteristics of being (1) *free*, (2) *public*, (3) *nonsectarian*, and (4) *universal* (compulsory). The framework of the first three of these was developed in the period preceding the Civil War[4]—although all aspects were not fully realized. The fourth was not realized until well after the Civil War and in many states not until the twentieth century. One aspect of the develop-

---

[4] At one time persons in the South objected to the use of the term "Civil War," preferring the "War Between the States." Since the Civil War Centennial the term, used officially by the joint committees, is more acceptable.

ment of universal education was the setting up of the American "ladder" system of education[5] as well as the compulsory aspects of the law.

We shall discuss the important trends during the period before the War under two headings: The Free Public School System; and the Secular (Nonsectarian) School System.

The Free Public School System

The public control of our school system and its free aspect are so common now that we take them for granted. It is hard for those of us of the twentieth century to realize the tremendous struggle that occurred in order to bring about a free school system.

We have noted how the custom of having the school run under public auspices developed in New England. However, public control was not nearly so prevalent in some of other states. In Pennsylvania, for example, many religious groups developed private schools. This differed from the situation of the theocratic states that set up the original *public* school system in New England—albeit a sectarian one. With the development of great heterogeneity of the population and with an increased demand for education, the question concerning the payment of tuition began to be raised. This became increasingly important with the extension of suffrage to all people. At first this meant that the persons of average wealth and wealthy people paid for their education by the use of the rate bill (being billed for their portion of the costs of education at the end of each term). In time, the question was forcefully raised as to whether or not a democracy could exist with universal suffrage unless all the people were literate. Thus it developed that the people who could not afford to pay for education—the paupers—would be able to get education free through public funds. In this way universal education was established, with those who could afford to pay doing so directly and with the fees of the rest being paid out of taxation. Of course there was always the difficulty of knowing where to draw the line as far as the pauper was concerned. Some people of very modest means resented the idea of the paupers getting free education. Furthermore, a great number of people who were not paupers and who should have educated their children were not doing so. A vigorous battle for free public education was begun. This became a hot political issue in many of the state legislatures. The idea of free education for all, paid out of public taxation, was considered by many to be socialistic or communistic. Furthermore, it was held to be a denial of man's right to individual initiative toward education. In the state of Pennsylvania, for example, a permissive free school law was passed; but then the next

[5] Under the so-called "ladder" system, a child may move without examination from one level of education to another and be transferred freely from one school system to another.

assembly elected by the people contained a majority opposed to the free public school. However, a speech by Thaddeus Stevens swayed the legislature and allowed the bill to stay. His speech ranks as one of the great pleas for free public education.[6]

Gradually the advocates of free public education did win in the various states. In some states it was made obligatory on the school districts to furnish free education. In other states it was made permissive for the local boards of education. Moreover, the states and the local communities within the states were very uneven with respect to providing free education even after it was legalized. It must also be remembered that free public education at first applied only to the elementary school. Free public education on a completely legal basis at the high school level came later.

The Secular (Nonsectarian) School System

We have seen that the early schools were largely sectarian. They were either public and sectarian as in the democratic states in New England or they were private and sectarian as in New York and Pennsylvania. Several factors had led to the breakdown of the sectarian schools long before the legal matter was debated. One factor was the great religious heterogeneity of the colonies. In order to encourage people to settle in the various colonies, the concept of freedom of religion had to be extended to include the freedom from being taught a sectarian doctrine other than one's own in the schools. This tended to cause sectarian differences to be played down as far as school instruction was concerned.

Another factor was, of course, the disestablishment of the church. Several colonies had disestablished the church before the Revolution. In the federal constitution, the church was disestablished under the First Amendment. All of the states eventually disestablished the church either by law or by constitutional amendment. When the new states set up constitutions, they all included sections preventing any kind of religious establishment, thus adopting officially the principle of the separation of church and state. Massachusetts was one of the last states to disestablish the church. However, Massachusetts had long had multiple establishment and in practice had fallen considerably away from "true establishment" before the passage of the law against any kind of establishment (1833). A third factor in eliminating sectarian instruction in the schools was the practical difficulty in deciding which sectarian doctrine was to be taught. Several board of education elections were fought in New England on the issue of whether trinitarian or unitarian doctrines should be taught, before the silliness of such a method of determination became apparent to most people. In many cases, by the time the states had decided on passing laws

---

[6] "Thaddeus Stevens' Speech Opposing Repeal of the Law of 1834," in Elwood P. Cubberley (ed.), *Readings in Public Education in the United States*, No. 121 (Boston: Houghton, 1934).

forbidding the teaching of sectarian doctrine in the schools, they no longer were teaching it in practice.

It must be remembered, in connection with the current discussions over the question of teaching of sectarian religious ideas in the schools, that these people were God-fearing. It was out of their experience in attempting to teach sectarian doctrines that they decided it was impossible in a publicly controlled school system. This became even more apparent when compulsory education laws were considered. In this instance, pupils would be compelled to go to school and to receive sectarian doctrine if it were taught there. This, of course, would be contrary to the First Amendment of the Constitution as it has been interpreted by the United States Supreme Court.

THE EXPANSION OF THE AMERICAN SCHOOL, 1865 TO 1929

Whereas the period preceding the Civil War represents the beginning of the expansion of the school, with many solid bases being laid, it was in the period following this war that a tremendous expansion of both elementary and high schools occurred.

Starting with Massachusetts in 1852, the states in turn passed compulsory attendance laws until there was complete acceptance in principle of compulsory education with the Mississippi law of 1918. While attendance laws were variously enforced by the different states and the range of years of required attendance varied considerably, the net effect was to establish the fourth of our principles of public education, namely, universal (compulsory) education. This meant that no longer did the parent have freedom to keep a child out of school or not as he wished. The child must attend school if he were physically and mentally capable of doing so. With the freeing of the slave and the coming of other non-Caucasians to the United States, the number of people of non-Caucasian races attending the public schools also increased.

After the turn of the century, some attention was paid to the raising of the standards of both training and certification of teachers. In around a hundred years we have gone from the early period for certification of teachers by lay examination (school boards) to certification by written professional examination and finally to state certification on the basis of credentials from accredited teacher-training institutions. There were also movements for the upgrading of elementary school standards, such as the demarcation of students into grades, the giving of objective examinations, and the setting up of standard courses of study.

The high school, which had its beginnings in the 1820's, expanded quite rapidly, and by 1870 it was seen to be the institution that would replace the old academy. Although ostensibly set up to take care of those who were not going to college, it soon developed a college-preparatory type of curriculum much like the academy it imitated and replaced.

The Kalamazoo decision, in 1874, legalized the use of common-school money in public high schools. The high school thus became an important part of the public school ladder system, filling in the gap between the common or elementary school and the state university. The Committee of Ten (reporting in 1893) by setting up the principle that one subject is good as another provided it is taught in the "right" way, reaffirmed the importance of the traditional subjects and in so doing tended to make the high school a preparatory institution, even though the committee recognized that the majority of students were not going on to college. It held, however, that the traditional college-preparatory subjects were good for training the mind, a mental-discipline argument. The Commission on Reorganization of Secondary Education, which published its report in 1918, developed a different concept as stated in the Seven Cardinal Principles. These are based on an analysis of the democratic culture. However, this did not influence the school curriculum very much—the high school in particular.

Starting with 1890, the high school doubled its enrollment each decade through 1930. The high school thus became a "people's college" in which programs of all kinds were set up in order to meet the varying needs of the increased number and range of students. This rapid expansion of the public schools, in a period when there were not adequately trained personnel, led to many types of consequences. The standards of education, particularly at the higher levels, were not always very well maintained. The salaries of the personnel always ran quite low. Teaching in too many cases was something that one did while one was waiting for a job that would bring in more income. This condition did not begin to be remedied until the 1920's, when increasing industrial expansion and the general prosperity of the country were such that the teachers were paid somewhat better. In the depression period of the early 1930's and in the period following World War II, this situation of low salaries recurred.

THE UNCERTAINTY OF A PERIOD OF RAPID SOCIAL CHANGE IN AMERICA, 1930 TO PRESENT

The general characteristics of the period from 1930 to date can be set forth roughly thus: First, the school was criticized during the 1929–1934 depression for at least two reasons: (1) Its poor standards were held to be one of the factors that caused the depression to occur. (2) It was maintained that it had not done a good job of teaching Americanism and therefore had caused people to become too radical in their ideas. Second, during World War II, the school was looked upon as one of the bulwarks in helping the defense effort. In the third stage, following general social unrest, the school was again looked at critically and blamed for some of the unrest and lack of stability in our society.[7]

The success of the U.S.S.R. in launching the first earth satellite, Sputnik I, launched a new criticism of American education. Our failure to be first in this field was blamed upon the schools. Newspaper, magazine, radio, and television appeals were made for strong science and mathematics programs. Open condemnation was voiced of the programs of fine arts and socialization as found in the present school curriculum.[8]

At the very time when the school was being criticized most for not fulfilling its function, it was being given the greatest tasks of its history. Throughout this period, however, there was a continued expansion of school enrollment, with the exception of a slight trough in the late 1930's and early 1940's due to the low birth rate of depression years. The great masses of people, wanting education and having great faith in its value, placed enormous burdens upon the school, both in gross numbers of children to be educated and in demands for increased services such as lunchrooms, health clinics, classes for the gifted and for the handicapped, and the like, and for broadened curriculums. Furthermore, the school was unable to compete salary-wise with other groups in the post-World War II period, as a result of inflation; and therefore it had difficulty getting adequate personnel. One of the ironies of the existence of criticism of the school was the fact that educational leaders were criticized for having the school take on the tasks that had been forced on it by social pressures, many times over the protests of educators who were, on the whole, very conservative.

One of the increasingly insistent criticisms of the school in the post-World War II period relates to the inability and alleged lack of interest in the public schools in teaching the moral and spiritual values. The private religious schools of today are, and the schools of the sixteenth and seventeenth century had been, strongly oriented in religious and theological ideas. Therefore, when the problems of the 1930's and of the postwar period arose, one of the arguments used was that the public schools were not grounding people thoroughly in moral and spiritual values. Whenever there is a period of social change, there has always been a period of reorientation of values and an increase in crime and other moral lapses. When this occurs, people seek some cause other than the difficulties of adjusting to a changing society. Noting that the schools did not specifically teach religious ideas, the critics hit upon this as being one possible reason. Actually the schools have not ceased teaching moral

[7] N.E.A. Research Division, "Ten Criticisms of Public Education," *Research Bulletin* 35 (December 1957), pp. 131–174. This research bulletin presents an interesting summary of the ten important and most repeated criticisms of the public schools in the early fifties. It also gives the information from research to support or contradict these criticisms.

[8] Current literature in the fifties and early sixties was replete with examples of these criticisms.

values just because they have ceased to teach religious doctrines. Early in the nineteenth century Horace Mann had advocated that they continue to stress moral teachings in his fight for the secularization of the school. But with greater emphasis on other things and the inability of the schools, under the legal restrictions, to teach sectarian ideas (which in the minds of many persons, including many teachers, were inextricably tied in with moral and spiritual values) there was a decline in the formal teaching of moral precepts. In newspaper and magazine articles during World War II and after, the problem began to be stated more clearly: Is it possible for the school to teach moral and spiritual values without using a sectarian theological base or without directly teaching religion? Many persons held that the school was already doing this and could continue to do it, although a greater stress could be placed upon the teaching of values. In 1952 the Educational Policies Commission published a book called *Moral and Spiritual Values in the Public Schools,*[9] in which they called on the schools to teach those moral and spiritual values that were common to our democratic society, regardless of differences in sectarian viewpoints. This point of view was accepted by many, and the schools have had a great revival of interest in attempting to teach moral and spiritual values as one of their aims. There have been three notable departures from this point of view:

1. Those who hold that the school cannot possibly teach moral and spiritual values without having a theological base. These people advocate a system of private religious schools, either financed by public funds or privately financed.
2. Others who advocate that denominational religious classes be established in the public schools and be given for credit.
3. Those who hold that the schools, while not teaching any one sectarian idea, can teach about religion. This is the point of view that has been sponsored rather fully by the Danforth Foundation and other influential groups.

The recent Supreme Court decisions forbidding the required use of prepared public prayers or the Lord's Prayer or any other religious exercises in the classrooms of the public schools seem to make rather clear that such denominational classes cannot be established in the public schools under the constitution as presently interpreted.[10]

There recently has developed a new way of solving the problem concerned with the conflict between the advocates of the teaching of religion in private schools and those of the continuation of the secular classes in

---

[9] N.E.A., Educational Policies Commission, *Moral and Spiritual Values in the Public Schools* (Washington, D.C.: National Education Association, 1951). See further discussion in Chapter 14.

[10] N.E.A., American Association of School Administrators, *Religion in the Public Schools.*

publicly financed classes. This is the "shared-time" concept. It is thought by its proponents to be constitutional. All that would be required would be arrangements providing for the easy shift of students during the day from public schools to private religious schools. In the case of secondary education, it would be necessary to provide for the transfer of credits from courses taken in part-time attendance in the public schools to the private schools or vice versa. Under this plan the child would take his religious classes and perhaps some other "theologically sensitive" courses such as social studies or literature in the church-related schools and take his courses in mathematics, science, and others (vocational, etc.) in the public school. He would then get his diploma eventually from one of the two schools by the transfer of credits.[11] Title II of the 1965 Federal Aid to Education bill grants money to promote schools (channeled through the public school in the area). This appears to be governmental (federal) approval of limited shared time concept.

The uncertainty over the role of the school did not come about entirely because of a social struggle or the rapid rise of the masses wanting an education. It was also the result of increasingly conflicting philosophies that were developing as a result of the rapid social and intellectual change that was coming about in America and in the world. (See Chapter 15.)

European Stirrings in Response to Democratic Ideas and Social Change

Until recent times the European countries maintained more or less the same type of school they had at the time of American colonization. Although common school education had been made available to the masses, and there had come to be compulsory education for four to six years in most countries, there was a great gulf between secondary and elementary education. Secondary education was held to be for the few. For example, in England a smaller percentage of persons went to the secondary school than were going to colleges in this country during the same period.

In the post-World War II period European schools experienced significant changes. Factors precipitating changes were the same forces that were affecting America, the attention the American educational system was receiving because of America's position of world leadership, and the contact with Americans in the armed services. The schools of the various countries of the world began to consider the possibility of lengthening the required period of the common school. In England, France, and Germany there was great effort to increase the compulsory attendance period and to provide higher schools to meet the differentiated needs of youngsters. Under the impetus of the Education Act of 1944, education in England

[11] N.E.A., *Religion in the Public Schools.*

is undergoing a great change. England is providing education of a broader sort in the English modern secondary school and in the comprehensive school (the latter enrolling secondary-age students with many different backgrounds and a variety of goals in one school). There has recently been a greater concern in England for the education of boys and girls beyond the age of fifteen to eighteen, an interest in providing more adult classes, and a very rapid increase in the amount of university-type education provided, somewhat the same as the increased interest in higher education that America started to have in the 1920's.[12]

In only one other country of the world was there any claim of providing the amount of advanced education for as great a number of persons as in America. That country was the U.S.S.R. By 1956 and 1957 information began reaching this country that Russia had developed an educational system, particularly of the technical type, that included ten years of school for the great majority of children. Also, the Russians were giving advanced training to a relatively high percentage of persons in the technical university or postsecondary schools. This education certainly was not as broad as that of other European countries, nor as broad as American education. It tended to be concentrated on the sciences, technical subjects, and the theory of communism. In 1958 Khrushchev initiated his reforms in which education was broadened and to some extent, vocational training ("polytechnical education") was tied in more directly to the other subjects taught. Many students of education think that the importance of the educational development that has been taking place in the Soviet Union recently cannot be minimized. With the development of eleven years of school for the great majority of children, the Russians probably now have, next to the United States, the greatest mass of their students in school at a high educational level. It seems probable that the economic and social status of the school teacher in Russia may be, relatively speaking, much higher than it is in the United States.[13]

CONTEMPORARY CONFLICT AS TO THE ROLE OF THE SCHOOL

The predominant theme underlying this chapter is that the school has developed as a separate institution in order to carry out the aims of its society—or at least the aims of the dominant portion of the society—for the education of the young. In the period of rapid social change that has come about recently, there has been confusion regarding the purposes of the school because there is confusion also with regard to predominating

[12] A good summary of this Act is found in John Francis Cramer and George Steffens Brown, *Contemporary Education: A Comparative Study of National Systems,* Second Edition (New York: Harcourt, Brace, and World, 1965), pp. 67–76. See also H. C. Dent, *The Education Act of 1944* (London: University of London Press, 1944).
[13] George Z. F. Bereday, and others (eds.). *The Changing Soviet School* (Boston: Houghton, 1960). Recent developments (1964–65) indicate further far-reaching changes in Soviet education. Education, of course, is in a state of flux in all countries.

ideas of our culture. The problem of the separation of the church and state and that of the relation between the secular and the sectarian have helped to becloud the issue. The tremendous diversity of opinions with respect to the base for our moral and spiritual values and other points of view in our culture, including those directly bearing on education, has also served to becloud the issue further. The recent advent of the Sputniks has highlighted the urgency of these questions. In Chapters 15 and 16 we will attempt to clarify some of those conflicting concepts. In this chapter we have merely attempted to indicate how these things came to develop, and to show the historic relationship of the school to its culture or its society.

SUMMARY

The school as a social institution has been developed consciously by a people to carry out the ideals of a culture or segment of a culture. Once established, the schools, like other institutions, tend to lag behind their cultures. Much of what one learns has been learned outside of the school.

In this chapter brief descriptions of the school at different stages in man's development have been made to illustrate the theses: the tendency for schools to reflect their societies, and their lag behind its development. The recent changes in the school in Europe and in America in response to unprecedented social change and the resultant conflict with respect to the role of the school are set forth.

SELECTED BIBLIOGRAPHY

BAYLES, ERNEST E. and BRUCE L. HOOD. *Growth of American Educational Thought and Practice.* New York: Harper & Row, 1966. Pp. x + 305.

BOYD, WILLIAM. *The History of Western Education,* Seventh Edition. New York: Barnes & Noble, 1965. PP. xii + 489.

BRUBACHER, JOHN S. *A History of the Problems of Education,* Second Edition. New York: McGraw-Hill, 1965. Pp. xiii + 688.

BUTTS, R. FREEMAN. *The American Tradition in Religion and Education.* Boston: Beacon Press, 1950. Pp. xiv + 230. The most authoritative source on the history of the separation of church and state in America, particularly as it relates to education.

————. *A Cultural History of Western Education,* Second Edition. New York: McGraw-Hill, 1955. Pp. xii + 645.

————, and LAWRENCE CREMIN. *A History of Education in American Culture.* New York: Holt, Rinehart & Winston, 1953. Pp. 628.

CRAMER, JOHN FRANCIS, and GEORGE STEPHENSON BROWNE. *Contemporary Education: A Comparative Study of National Systems,* Second Edition. New York: Harcourt, Brace & World, 1965. Pp. x + 598.

CREMIN, LAWRENCE A. *The Transformation of the School: Progressivism in American Education, 1876–1957.* New York: Knopf, 1961. Pp. xv + 387 + xxiv.

EDWARDS, NEWTON, and HERMAN G. RICHEY. *The School in the American Social Order,* Second Edition. New York: American Book, 1963. Pp. xiii + 694.

FROST, S. E., JR. *Historical and Philosophical Foundations of Western Education.* Columbus, Ohio: Merrill, 1966. Pp. 560.

GOOD, HARRY G. A *History of American Education,* Second Edition. New York: Macmillan, 1962. Pp. vii + 610.

———. A *History of Western Education,* Second Edition. New York: Macmillan, 1960. Pp. ix + 620.

HARTFORD, ELLIS FORD. *Education in These United States.* New York: Macmillan, 1964. Pp. xiv + 576.

MEAD, MARGARET. *The School in American Culture.* Cambridge, Mass.: Harvard University Press, 1951. Pp. 48.

MEYER, ADOLPHE E. *An Educational History of the Western World.* New York: McGraw-Hill, 1965. Pp. 516.

MULHERN, JAMES. A *History of Education,* Second Edition. New York: Ronald Press, 1954. Pp. vii + 754.

N.E.A. Educational Policies Commission. *Moral and Spiritual Values in the Public Schools.* Washington, D.C.: National Education Association, 1951. Pp. x + 100.

N.E.A. Research Division. "The State and Sectarian Education." *Research Bulletin,* **34** (December 1956).

———. "Ten Criticisms of Public Education." *Research Bulletin,* **35** (December 1957), pp. 131–174. An excellent summary of ten important and most repeated criticisms of the public schools in the fifties, together with information from research to support or to contradict them.

RIESMAN, DAVID. *Constraint and Variety in American Education.* Lincoln: University of Nebraska Press, 1956. Pp. 160.

SELECTED FILMS

The Children's Republic (AFF) 23 min
A new approach to education; operation of child-governed organization in France.

Clasping Hands (Grubbs) 20 min
How cooperation is taught in the French public schools.

Colonial Children (Ind.) 11 min
Re-enacts with authentic settings, costumes, and furnishings the home life and self-sufficiency of a family in colonial New England during the late seventeenth century. Describes how colonial children received their education by studying at home and portrays the duties and chores of each member of the family. Reveals the spirit of helpfulness between families and emphasizes the vital role of religion in the home.

Education in America: The Seventeenth and Eighteenth Centuries (Coronet Films) 16 min

Education in America: The Nineteenth Century (Coronet Films) 18 min

Education in America: Twentieth Century Developments (Coronet Films) 16 min

Horace Mann (Emerson Film Corp.) 19 min

Portrays important episodes in the life of Horace Mann, the "father of the common schools"; reviews his activities as teacher, lawyer, state senator, board of education member, and college president; emphasizes his work in pointing up the need for well-built schools, good textbooks, democratic methods of learning, schools for teachers, and universal education in the United States.

Near Home (International Film Bureau) 25 min

A class and teacher study the English community in which they live. The use of resources at hand, problem-solving procedures, and the role of the teacher are vividly portrayed. The report in the community at the culmination of the project is especially well done. Developed as a teacher-training film.

Outposts of American Education (Near-East Col.) 20 min

Story of life at American colleges in Near East; also historic spots, peoples, cities of Greece, Turkey, Syria, Lebanon, Iraq.

Schools of Mexico (Ind.) 10 min

Presents a comprehensive view of educational institutions from the ultra-modern Ministry of Education in Mexico City to remote one-room adobe schools far in the interior. Includes normal schools, vocational, and agricultural institutions, and kindergartens.

Soviet Education Today (University of Michigan) 72 min

A Soviet documentary with English sound and an American introductory statement.

Village School (BIS) 12 min

This documentary on education illustrates the philosophy underlying the British system of education.

Part II. *Social and Economic Trends in America*

In part II the writers present an over-all survey of the social and economic trends in the United States of America. Chapter 4 places in their historical setting the important social trends from the beginning of the American nation to the present time. Twelve current trends are summarized near the end of the chapter.

In Chapter 5 emphasis is placed upon economic problems. A detailed analysis is made of the development of American technology and of the American industrial system. An appraisal of alternatives in terms of economic choices facing the United States is also presented. Because economic and technological trends are basic to the general over-all development of the society and to the other problems being considered, the authors felt that they should be set forth in broad perspective early in the book.

Chapter 4. *An Overview of American Social Trends*

THE JOB TO BE UNDERTAKEN in this chapter may seem an almost impossible one in view of the fact that whole books have been written on one period of American history, even on one aspect of social change during one period. The attempt is made, however, to bring together in a clear picture the more significant American social trends and to show how they came to develop.

Many things confuse the picture. One is the disjointedness between the changes actually occurring and any widespread verbal or ideological realization of the change. In some cases, the most vigorous denial of the fact of change was being made at the very time of occurrence of the actual change and its acceptance for all practical purposes. The confusion among the various spokesmen for the people in respect to the meaning of a particular change has also been evident throughout our history. As an example, the new Darwinian science was accepted; but in some cases the implications were seen in terms of reactionary ideas tending toward ruthless exploitation and antihumanitarianism. As a further example, new philosophic viewpoints underlying new social action were rejected; but the action was advocated on the basis of selected phases of the most ancient of traditional philosophic ideas. Certainly any clarification of trends in American society must recognize the two threads: (1) the actual changes themselves—many times wavering, partial, and hazy; and (2) men's ideas, particularly those of vocal spokesmen in literature and the arts, concerning the proposed or actual changes and the necessity for or opposition to them. The second thread, like the first, presents a chaotic picture, with almost all combinations of the traditional and the new, agitations for change and defense of the old being often mixed in the same individual.[1]

---

[1] Cf. Merle Curti, *American Paradox: The Conflict Between Thought and Action* (New Brunswick, N.J.: Rutgers University Press, 1956).

79

PERIODS OF DEVELOPMENT OF AMERICAN SOCIAL TRENDS

We have divided the development into four periods similar to those used by Butts and Cremin in their book, A *History of Education in American Culture*.[2]

The first period, "The Colonial Period, 1600 to 1779," covers the era from the beginning of colonization up to the time of independence from Great Britain in 1779. Many changes were brought about during this period by the colonists who had come to America to find religious and political freedom, or to gain wealth, or both. They experimented with various governmental forms that were to eventuate in a federal type of republic. By the end of this period the separation of church and state was coming about, and a bill of rights was being established to bulwark democratic processes.

The second period, "The Formation and Expansion of the Nation, 1779 to 1865," covers the actual formation of the nation and the coalescing of its institutional forms and precedents, and encompasses a rapid geographic expansion. The influence of the frontier on the further democratization of social and governmental institutions was very marked during this period. The abolition of slavery and the enfranchisement of the Negro, which occurred at the end of this period, marked great progress in the strengthening and the extension of democratic institutions.

The third period, "Expanding America, 1865 to 1929," covers the time of the rapid industrial and further geographical expansion spurred by railroad development and by other forces of the industrial revolution. The effect of these forces was felt in ever growing impact on social institutions. The development of more rapid communications, the increase in population, the change from rural to urban backgrounds, the effect of all these changes on the family and in turn on society, the cumulative effects of scientific changes on fundamental thinking (philosophy)—all are important aspects of social trends during this period.

The fourth period, "Contemporary Changes, 1929 to the Present," primarily is concerned with changes in the role of government with respect to the economic system, with a great shift from the earlier laissez-faire conception toward a "welfare state," and with other trends arising from America's position of world leadership. This period is especially difficult to evaluate and describe because it is too close for complete objectivity.

Each period will be discussed with the following types of changes as subheadings:

Governmental and Political
Industrial and Commercial
Religious and Philosophical
Social Customs and Institutions

[2] R. Freeman Butts and Lawrence A. Cremin, A *History of Education in American Culture* (New York: Holt, 1953).

THE COLONIAL PERIOD, 1600 TO 1779

Governmental and Political

The governmental and political institutions established in America during the early colonial period were largely transplanted from England. In the main, those groups who came to seek freedom from political or religious oppression did not grant such freedom to all those who arrived later in their colonies.

In the case of the proprietary colonies such as New Amsterdam (later New York) and the Carolinas, a definite attempt was made to perpetuate a modified feudal system with a landed gentry. Many considerations, primarily economic but partially ideological, stemming from the ideas of French and British philosophers, prevented this feudalistic development.

New England at first was settled by people very desirous of self-government and freedom. The Puritan majority initially established a theocracy and restricted the suffrage to orthodox property owners. This group also set up an established church in which it was difficult to distinguish church officers from civil magistrates. However, by 1700 a reaction had set in. A rising secular feeling, a large number of dissident sects (such as the Quakers and Baptists), and the interests of even the former strict Puritans in the growing commerce in rum and slavery, led to a relaxation of strict Puritanism and to a widening of the gap between church and state.

The shortage of labor, the influence of the frontier, and the necessity for a common front against the Indians were all factors in the extension of self-government throughout all the colonies. This came about through representative councils and through the widening of the suffrage, which, however, was still far from universal at the end of this period. The actual practices in the colonies were quite often more benevolent than the rules promulgated from abroad for the governing of the colonies. The colonies were in competition for settlers and tended to vie with each other with respect of favorable conditions to attract newcomers.

By the time the homeland had begun to increase controls over foreign trade in such a way as to threaten many of the colonists commercially, the people had had such a taste of freedom and had absorbed sufficient ideas concerning liberty that they were ready to stand up for what they considered their rights. The experience of the colonists in developing self-governing institutions under British rule and the experiences of the revolutionary Committees of Correspondence stood them in good stead when they were confronted with post-Revolutionary problems of creating governments.

Industrial and Commercial

The economy of colonial America was predominantly agricultural, with lesser interests in trade, lumbering, fishing, and trapping. Although the country remained essentially a land of farmers until the Civil War, even in the eighteenth century trade and commerce began to prosper. With this prosperity a wealthy merchant class appeared, and the gulf widened between rich and poor. Economics invaded politics and religion when the merchant class gained power enough to resist the political control of the clergy and the landed gentry.

Climatic and geographic forces operated to fix a slave economy on the South, to stimulate attention on commerce in barren-soiled New England, and to make of the rich land of the middle colonies the granary of the nation.

Economic considerations were perhaps decisive in the final action of the colonies leading to independence. Century-old English mercantilism, climaxed by irritating taxes and new measures of trade control, drove men of commerce into questioning the work of the Empire. Their protests were translated into action by the propertyless classes, who felt that abandonment of the old order would somehow bring them a new economic dispensation. The political and social ideas of Locke and others (discussed briefly in the next section) had permeated all classes, to provide ideological undergirding for movements toward greater freedom. In America, economic problems led men to feel that independence from England was the only method of achieving this freedom.

Religious and Philosophical

Although divided into many sects on refinements of theology, colonial Americans with virtual unanimity were believers in Christian theism. This conception held the universe to be governed by one God Whose essence was infinite and spiritual. He was the All-good, All-wise, All-powerful Being who created the world for man and operated it according to His laws. Man was created with a soul and a material body. The immortal soul linked man to God, and the body was a part of the world that tempted man to corruption. The escape from worldly corruption was provided by God in the form of Christ, whom all men should follow. The Bible was the word of God, and the highest type of knowledge emanated from God through the Scriptures. Man was to use the knowledge set forth in the Bible to reveal the Heavenly Father.

Based upon this common body of belief, sectarian differences were somewhat in the form of minor superstructures built upon a vast, single foundation. The Calvinists (primarily the Puritans and later the Presbyterians) chose to emphasize predestination and election; the Anglicans, the sacraments and elaborate ritualism; the Roman Catholics, the sacraments, ritual, and a priestly intermediary; the Quakers, the inner life; the Lutherans, justification by faith and a priesthood of all believers. Of all religious groups in the colonies, the Calvinists and the Anglicans were the most numerous, and all "established" or "state" churches in the colonies were either Calvinist or Anglican. Of the two, the Calvinist church was, in the early period, the more authoritarian and its followers the more group conscious and aggressive.

The church in early New England was more than just that. It was a theocratic state, with the magistrates of the town and the leaders of the church being the same person or persons who worked in close cooperation, and with the suffrage being denied to members of dissident sects. Although some dissidents were tolerated, Quakers and others (such as Roger Williams) who advocated religious tolerance and complete separation were persecuted and driven out.

By 1700 the extreme form of theocratic state as set up by the colonists in New England began to crumble. The preoccupation of the people with commercial developments, the coming of many new sects with diverse ideas, and a slackening of interest by the Puritans (now Congregationalists) in matters theological, caused a separation of things civil from things religious; but the church still remained an established one. Later, other minor sects in New England were able to become established. This multiple church establishment continued in Massachusetts after the American Revolution and into the nineteenth century (until 1833), even after church and state had been completely separated in all other states.[3]

The ideas of Newton, Locke, Berkeley, Hume, and others, which were influential in starting the rational movement in Europe called the Enlightenment, reached America during the early decades of the eighteenth century and exerted strong influence after the middle of that century. The Enlightenment was a reaction against the absolutism of government, classical mercantile economics, and rigid theology. It was based on a growing faith in the common man, in science, and in human reason. In politics, it held that the rights of man were natural rights and were self-evident through the use of reason. In religion, there was a growth in deistic ideas,[4] which were held by many prominent leaders in the colonies including Franklin, Jefferson, and Thomas Paine. The political ideas were more acceptable to the masses than the religious ones. Thus John Locke may well be considered as a source of much of the political philosophy underlying the Revolution and the new American government.

In the theological field, Calvinist views (but with less emphasis on predestination) were strengthened in the eighteenth century by a series of religious revivals, called the Great Awakening. These revivals were probably a reaction to the secularism and religious indifference that had become prominent in America. Spreading from Pietist sources in Europe, these revivals were spearheaded in New England by Jonathan Edwards and soon swept over the colonies. Religious forces throughout the colonies were given a new life under such leaders as George Whitefield. The educational influence was particularly significant. Denominational colleges were brought into being to propagate the creeds and doctrines of their founders. Religious leadership and power gained tremendously.

The Enlightenment did affect religious ideas among many individuals

[3] Butts and Cremin, *A History of Education in American Culture*, p. 163.
[4] Deism—a belief in a personal god or creator who is unrevealed—opposes dogmatic orthodoxies based on revelation.

and among certain churches in several denominations. There was a questioning of church dogma, especially of the trinitarian conception of God, original sin, and eternal punishment. In 1785 King's Chapel in Boston, the first Episcopal church in New England, became the first Unitarian church in the Western Hemisphere.[5]

Social Customs and Institutions

Certainly not all immigrants to America during the colonial period had ideas favorable to social democracy. The views prevailing in Europe, which was witnessing the enormous upsurge of the middle classes, were transferred to America. The colonists were largely of this middle class, particularly of minorities whose political or religious rights had been oppressed. The upper class did not migrate. Neither did the peasants and the serfs of the lower class. The indentured servants and slaves of the colonies made up the lower class. The fact that the colonies were predominantly middle class did not mean that there were no class distinctions. There was a merchant and landed gentry who soon came to dress differently and to be addressed as "Mister" and "Mistress." There was also a lower middle class called "Goodman" and "Good woman." Members of an extremely lower class were often called only by their first or "Christian" names. These social distinctions persisted until well after the Revolution, although they never were as rigid as those in Europe, and broke down only where there were frontiers. Harvard had continued to classify its students by precise rank according to father's status until 1772.[6]

Class lines played an important part in separating loyalists from patriots at the time of the Revolution. The wealthy landowners of New England and New York were Tories and fled to Canada or England, while the merchants joined with the lower classes in the revolt. In the South, the planter landlords sided, by and large, with the patriot cause. The effect of the Revolution was to eliminate almost all of the upper middle class of the North, the gentry.

THE FORMATION AND EXPANSION OF THE NATION, 1779 TO 1865

Governmental and Political

The United States was gradually becoming a secular society in which religious institutions played an important but an increasingly subordinate role. Public attention was diverted to the growth of political democracy,

---

[5] Harvey Wish, *Society and Thought in Early America* (New York: McKay, 1950), pp. 207–208.

Unitarianism is a religious doctrine that does not accept the trinitarian ideas of orthodox Christianity and has quite different ideas concerning the nature of the divinity of Jesus.

[6] Edgar W. Knight, *Education in the United States* (New York: Ginn, 1951), p. 81.

the expanding role of the government, and the rise of nationalism. The achievement of independence inaugurated a struggle at home as to who was to rule. The earliest important conflict was that between the Jeffersonian ideas of democracy and the Federalist conception of rule by a wealthier class.

Jeffersonian doctrines, derived principally from the French humanitarian ideas of politics and economics, appealed to the frontier element, the small landowners, and the debtor class. The Federalists, adhering to the tradition of the English Whigs in opposing the wide extension of democracy, were supported by the wealthier merchants and the planter class. The struggle for rule was momentarily won by the wealthier class at the constitutional convention, but the Bill of Rights and the constitutions of the several states reflected the demand for democratic control and wider suffrage.

Voters who believed in a wider extension of democracy elected Jefferson to the presidency in 1800. This group conceived of political and economic freedom as meaning also political and economic democracy, and the Jeffersonian party controlled the national elections almost entirely during the earlier part of this historical period.

There was a trend toward increased federal control. A spirit of nationalism was also evidenced by the "War Hawks" in 1812. The first protective tariff was passed in 1816, and there were repeated increases in tariff rates until 1828. In this period political and economic ideas began to dominate the thoughts of men.

The majority of people in the western migration, particularly into Kentucky, Ohio, Indiana, and Illinois, tended to develop nationalist ideas, since they lost their identity with their original states as they intermingled in the new territory. They looked to the national government for the lands they purchased, and to the national government also for protection from the Indians.

The doctrine of states' rights developed by the South to defend itself and its agrarian economy against Northern capitalism, and the Northern assault on slavery, tempered the sense of nationalism. At the same time, the Democratic Party adopted the slogan of "manifest destiny," which demanded and defended expansion to the Pacific and to the Rio Grande. The Democratic Party, appealing to the common man and the Southern voter, dominated the national scene almost entirely during the later part of this era.

Differences of many kinds, economic, political, and cultural, led to the Civil War, in which an agrarian minority in the South sought to preserve a distinctive way of life based upon Negro slavery. The Southern move for independence was thwarted in the great Civil War, and the indivisibility of the Union was established. Both nationalism and capitalism became increasingly important forces in the developing country.

Industrial and Commercial

The years following the Revolution, and particularly the War of 1812, produced a change in the economic system. The frontier retained an agricultural economy. Along the seaboard there was a shift from an agrarian to a commercial society, which led to the development of capitalistic enterprises. Cities grew, and a demand for improved communication and transportation resulted in construction of canals, better roads, and other means of travel. The Cumberland Road was begun. Fulton's steamboat began operations in 1809, and the *Savannah* crossed the Atlantic in 1819. The Erie Canal was opened in 1825, and the Baltimore & Ohio Railroad inaugurated service in 1828, although the steam locomotive did not appear until 1829.

The most significant development of these years was, by all odds, the triumph of the economic doctrine of laissez-faire capitalism. Throughout the United States there was approval of Adam Smith's ideas of laissez-faire. This conception was based upon relatively few fundamental principles, which were probably more nearly achieved in the early American economy than at any other time in the world's history. These principles were private property, the profit motive, free competition, flexible prices, and little or no governmental interference with business. The idea was that the owners of the numerous small business enterprises would compete freely with one another to produce an exchange of the goods and services required by people to meet their daily needs. The profit motive would provide the driving force, and the open market would serve as an automatic device for regulation of prices and quality of goods and services. It would not be necessary to have any kind of governmental regulation except to prevent dishonesty or misrepresentation. Even though America had already partially violated the ideas of laissez-faire in passing a tariff law, the people still fully believed in them. The expanding American frontier helped to make laissez-faire principles successful at this time. The high tariff laws and the giving away of lands, however, were a direct violation of the pure principles of laissez-faire.

American economy entered an era of revolutionary industrial changes. The Industrial Revolution of eighteenth-century England had hit America in the early part of the nineteenth.

The spirit of individualism stimulated new inventions and the growth of manufacturing. The application of technology to industry got under way: in 1790 Slater developed power cotton machinery; in 1793 Whitney invented the cotton gin; in 1797 the first cast-iron plow was made; and in 1803 the grain cradle was produced. In 1802 the Du Pont Powder Company was organized. In 1814 the first complete factory in America was established in Waltham, Massachusetts. Manning's mowing machine appeared in 1831, the reaper in 1834, the telegraph in 1835, the screw propeller in 1836, the vulcanization of rubber in 1839, photography in

1839, iron rails in 1840, and the sewing machine in 1846. These laid the bases for industrial society and simultaneously extended the benefits of the machine to man.

Business continued to expand and to lay the groundwork for the era of "big business" late in the century. Western Union, the first trust, came into being in 1851. Pork-packing grew into a major industry in Cincinnati during the 1830's. The railroads became an important means of transportation. In 1850, when the federal government indirectly granted land to the Illinois Central Railroad, the government seemed committed to a policy of encouraging business activities. The National Bank Act of 1863 marked the long-deferred establishment of a sound national banking system. Sectional pressure and the ascendancy of the Democratic Party kept the tariff generally low until the Republican triumph in 1860 ushered in a period when a high tariff became a permanent characteristic of American economy.

Religious and Philosophical

The principal writers during the earlier part of this period were political philosophers, notably Jefferson, Franklin, and Paine. These men held a deistic conception of the world similar to that of the French humanitarians. Their championship of deistic ideas came about as a reaction to orthodox Calvinism; but, as Townsend has indicated, "deism is far too complicated a theory to be set down as a simple revolt against Calvinism."[7]

Muelder and Sears state that deism was dominant in the South.[8] Among intellectuals in New England, William Ellery Channing attacked the traditional Calvinistic views and proclaimed the Unitarian doctrine that "God is love, man is potentially noble, and religion is an excellent life."[9] Channing defined religion as "the adoration of goodness," and his doctrine of "sweetness and light" was set over against the Calvinist dogmas of retribution and election.[10]

In spite of these influences, the more orthodox forms of Christian theism were still the religious faiths of the majority of the people in the United States, but there were clear indications that the dominating influence of religion was on the wane. The traditional religious outlook was partially reinvigorated by a series of revivals called the Second Great Awakening, which spread among the pioneer settlements of the frontier

[7] Harvey Gates Townsend, *Philosophic Ideas in the United States* (New York: American Book, 1934), p. 66.

[8] Walter G. Muelder and Lawrence Sears, *The Development of American Philosophy* (Boston: Houghton, 1940), p. 65.

[9] Vernon L. Parrington, *Main Currents in American Thought*, Vol. 1: The Colonial Mind (New York: Harcourt, 1930), p. 332.

[10] *Ibid.*, p. 332.

and intermittently persisted past the Civil War.[11] Calvinism was still the prevailing doctrine among those who were religious at the opening of the Jacksonian era, but the time was opportune for a new liberalism. As Parrington has stated, "It [Calvinism] was deeply entrenched in the inertia of custom, but intellectually it was in really desperate straits."[12]

Organized religious groups were feeling the effects of democracy and the liberation of the common man. A doctrine of self-expression was abroad in the land, and from it new cults were springing to life. Merle Curti has termed this phenomenon "come-outism," and he lists Shakerism, Perfectionism, Millerism, and Mormonism as products of the new liberalism.[13]

Transcendentalism, growing out of but going beyond Unitarianism, was in a sense a part of the romantic protest against the rationalism of the previous century. Transcendentalists such as Emerson, Thoreau, and Melville believed in a daily rebirth of God in each individual's soul, and they taught that the "divinity in man should rule the world." They held that each man, by "virtue of being identical with nature," must enjoy "equal rights and privileges."[14]

Organized religion, although sanctioning many social inequalities, was not entirely blind to the conditions resulting from industrialism. Reformers, often denouncing religious bodies, appealed to the spirit of the teachings of Jesus. Northern churches "declared war" on slavery. This declaration split all the major denominations, except the Roman Catholic, into sectional camps. The Seneca Falls Congress of 1849 proclaimed a beginning of a worldwide campaign for women's rights, and various other groups advocated reform movements.

Ralph Henry Gabriel has advanced an interpretation that during this period there emerged a new democratic faith. It rested, he says, on the earlier belief in a law-governed universe, but it also accepted the transcendental faith in the worth of the individual. The emerging of these ideas implied a faith in the superiority of American democratic institutions.[15]

Harvey G. Townsend has summarized the philosophic views of this period in these words:

There was a dramatic issue . . . in America—heaven and earth had been sundered. The great question . . . was how they could be brought together again. The generation . . . had a firm grip on the earth. It was heaven which had

11 William Warren Sweet, *Religion in the Development of American Culture 1765–1840* (New York: Scribner's, 1952), pp. 146–153.

12 Vernon L. Parrington, *Main Currents in American Thought*, Vol II: The Romantic Revolution in America (New York: Harcourt, 1930), p. 323.

13 Merle Curti, *The Growth of American Thought* (New York: Harper, 1943), pp. 309–313.

14 Merle Curti, *op. cit.*, pp. 304–305.

15 Ralph Henry Gabriel, *The Course of American Democratic Thought* (New York: Ronald Press, 1940), pp. 37–38.

escaped that generation. The geographical expansion, the exploitation of nature, and the discovery of vast riches in an uninhabited continent awakened acquisitive desires. Men became drunk with the idea of their own importance. They had lost the humility of the Puritans, and . . . they had lost a sense of the sacred and the holy. As a substitute for theology, they half-consciously accepted the notion that the world was made for man and perhaps by him.[16]

Social Customs and Institutions

The class structure, which had broken down considerably by the time of the Revolution, was further weakened by the removal of the props of feudal stability—primogeniture, entail, and quitrents.[17] These were almost universally abolished by the various states by the turn of the century.[18] The reaction of the people against the establishment of the state church must be considered a part of this movement. Such establishments (that is, the official sponsorship of churches by government) came to be looked upon by Americans as a relic related to ancient feudalism. All establishment was gone by 1819, except in the state of Massachusetts (1833).

The property qualifications for voting almost universally became abolished during the first half of the nineteenth century. The Jacksonian attitude toward the eligibility for public office (rotation in office) represents the extreme of this influence toward democratization of politics and toward equalitarianism. It resulted in the spoils system. Even the Jeffersonian Democratic Republicans had been somewhat doubtful in the early decades of the nineteenth century as to the ability of the common man to carry on the actual business of government.

The democratization movement, while having a complicated set of multiple causes, was affected, more than by any other one factor, by the influence of the ever advancing frontier, where the worth of a man was measured by what he could do, not who he was. Turner, writing in 1920, was among the first to study the relationships of the social conditions of the frontier to governmental and social institutions. His theory that life on the frontier continually influenced American political thinking and institutions is now widely accepted.[19]

The fact that there was a movement toward greater democratization does not mean that there were no social classes. The range in wealth and in possession of worldly goods still remained, especially in the East. The

[16] Harvey Gates Townsend, *Philosophic Ideas in the United States* (New York: American Book, 1934), pp. 85–86.
[17] Primogeniture: Limitation of land inheritance to the eldest son, to prevent breakup of large estates.
Entail: Restriction on the sale of large landholdings such as the William Penn estate in Pennsylvania.
Quitrent: A hangover from feudal days; original proprietor maintains title and the farmer-owner pays a perpetual but small rent.
[18] Harvey Wish, *Society and Thought in Early America*, *op. cit.*, p. 203.
[19] Frederick Jackson Turner, *The Frontier in American History* (New York: Holt, 1920).

result of the development of industrial capitalism was an immediate rise of a very wealthy upper class and the appearance of a city proletariat. The latter were in some ways in a more pitiful condition than the peasant classes of the sixteenth and seventeenth centuries of Europe. The upper-class families, however, took care not to stand too aloof from the people. Distinctions in dress between the classes had practically disappeared by 1830. The labeling of persons of different classes by special names and courtesies tended also to fade out. The contempt that the upper classes in Europe had for work with the hands, which still persisted there, had almost disappeared during this period in America. All work was honorable. It was felt that everyone should work. Class lines were fluid, and it was relatively easy to move from one class to another.[20]

An Expanding America, 1865 to 1929

Governmental and Political

Every period of American history seems to offer a repetition of the simplicity-to-complexity theme. That course of development was certainly present in the period between Appomattox and the Great Depression. In these years the American population quadrupled; statehood was bestowed on the last bit of land between the two oceans; seven amendments were added to the Constitution; a world war was fought in defense of security; the American people shared in the building of an organization of states to preserve the peace of the world, although they themselves declined membership; and they sought to establish legislative control of colossal combinations of bankers, of industrialists, and of laborers. The government continued to aid bankers and industrialists, and it timidly ventured into a new field to extend a helping hand to farmers. Labor was little recognized until after 1932.

Even by 1929, the simple government at Washington had grown into a "wonderland of bureaucracy," with federal assistance of many kinds made available to businesses and to the public. Political habits, however, remained essentially unchanged. There were two major parties, and although third parties came into existence as the result of special issues, they were soon absorbed by the two major parties. Suffrage was extended to women. New devices of secret voting and of direct government (such as initiative referendum, and recall) were developed to aid in making a more honest and efficient government.

Chronologically, the United States passed successfully through the Reconstruction, the heyday of the cattlemen and the "robber barons," and the war against Spain to liberate the Cubans and the Filipinos, which made the country a world power. It then survived the "trust-busting" and

[20] Butts and Cremin, *A History of Education in American Culture, op. cit.,* pp. 146–147.

the "square deal" of Theodore Roosevelt, the "new freedom" of Woodrow
Wilson, World War I and the League of Nations, the "normalcy" and
scandals of Warren G. Harding, and the "jazz age" of Coolidge prosperity.
By 1928 it had come into the administration of Herbert Hoover.

Industrial and Commercial

Scientists and inventors again made a startling impact on the American
economy. Transportation became more rapid: in 1869 the first trans-
continental railroad was completed; in 1893 Clarence Duryea built one of
the first automobiles; in 1903 the Wright brothers left the ground in a
heavier-than-air machine; in 1911 the American continent was spanned by
air in four days; and in 1919 the Atlantic was flown by a multipassengered
plane. Communication, too, progressed: in 1866 the Atlantic cable was again
laid, this time permanently; in 1876 Bell gave the world the telephone; in
1901 Marconi added the wireless telegraph; and twenty years later commercial radio broadcasting opened new vistas of entertainment, education,
and sheer annoyance.

Strange new industries became both colossal and matter-of-course: meat-
packing, oil-refining, rubber, automobiles, radio, road-building, cosmetics,
commercial nitrates, sporting goods, and many others. Technological advances took the farmer to the city and the city to the farm. Electric lights
supplanted the "wonder light," the gas lamp, which in its turn had supplanted the "perfect light," the kerosene lamp.

Congress and the state legislatures repeatedly intervened to control the
influence and operations of economic combinations and enterprises. Beginning with the Interstate Commerce Act of 1887, Congress passed a
series of major laws to regulate the common carriers of the nation, taking
up the job where the Supreme Court forced the states to relinquish it.
Beginning with the Sherman Antitrust Act of 1890, Congress sought again
and again to bring industrial combinations to a sense of public responsibility; a stream of laws was aimed at the improvement of the nation's
banking system; various laws were enacted to adjust the rights and liabilities of organized labor; and pieces of legislation were directed at other
public problems—pure food acts, corrupt practices acts, workmen's compensation laws, old-age pension acts, mothers' and widows' pension acts,
educational aid acts, and many others.

The national economy of the years between 1865 and 1929 must be
described as one of heightening capitalism, defended and abetted by the
power of the government, and to an increasing extent restrained by well-
organized and articulate labor. Despite the failure of certain classes,
notably the farmers and the people in some areas, especially the rural
South, to earn a proper income, the country was almost wholeheartedly in
support of "rugged individualism." The doubts and compromises were to
come out of the Great Depression of the next period.

Religious and Philosophical

Possibly the most significant development in thought during the early part of this era was the appearance of Charles Darwin's theory of evolution. *The Origin of Species* was first published in 1859, but the real impact of its ideas came several years later. As recently as 1925, the fundamentalists, adhering to a literal interpretation of the Bible, attacked the Darwinian concept in the famous Scopes trial in Tennessee.

The philosophical position of idealism was subjected to scrutiny when Peirce, James, and Dewey combined science and the temper of American life to formulate the philosophy of pragmatism. Basic to this development was a philosophical-psychological conception of how people learned. Faculty psychology, based on rationalism, was attacked by the empirical methods of the experimental psychology of Thorndike.

The extension of organized knowledge raised the material horizons of life. The contributions of modern science were great during this period. The new scientific ideas of Albert Einstein, although announced during this period, were to affect science greatly during the following period, and their effect on thought cannot even yet be evaluated. Einstein's theory of relativity, first announced in 1905, changed the conception of gravity, of light, and of the fundamental nature of space and the universe, and this gave physics and the other sciences an entirely new perspective.[21]

The revolutionary philosophy of the class struggle, enunciated earlier by Karl Marx and Friedrich Engels in the *Communist Manifesto*, had few converts in America, although it gained impressive acceptance in Europe in this period and eventually provided the battle cry of a large portion of the world. In Russia, Marxian philosophy—which has been described by Arnold Toynbee[22] as a "reaction from and a criticism of the Western Capitalism"—was accepted by Lenin and his associates. In 1917 Lenin, Trotsky, and their followers successfully overthrew the Czar and attempted to establish a government based on Marxian principles. The importance of the 1917 Russian revolution must not be underestimated; for, as Toynbee has stated, Bolshevism is the "only semblance of an effective external challenge to our society [Western civilization] since the Osmanlis' [Turkish faction] second failure to take Vienna."[23]

Social Customs and Institutions

So far as social customs and institutions are concerned, there actually were two separate periods from 1865 to 1929. The change in customs was very slight from 1865 to somewhat past the turn of the century. A variety

---

[21] Lincoln Barnett, *The Universe and Doctor Einstein*, 2d rev. ed. (New York: Mentor, 1957).

[22] Arnold J. Toynbee, *A Study of History*, abridgment by R. C. Somervel (New York: Oxford University Press, 1947), p. 204.

[23] Arnold J. Toynbee *A Study of History*, p. 203. It is important to note that Toynbee wrote this analysis well before World War II; and, as a matter of conjecture, the Japanese militarists might have been considered at a later time as an "external challenge."

of causes led to a rapid change in customs after 1900, with a great acceleration after World War I and through the 1920's.

In 1865, with the exception of some of the quite wealthy people, the
living conditions of most Americans were very little improved over the
living conditions of the European lower and middle classes. By 1900 there
had been added, at least in the cities, many of the conveniences that now
are called "modern." Most middle-class homes had a bathtub and running
water. There were electric lights in most city homes, although some still
had gas light. The rural areas were still in the kerosene-lamp stage, which
had replaced the candle period some time after the Civil War. The rural
areas were to continue in the period of the gasoline lantern (and their
own private light plants for a few of the wealthy farmers) into the 1930's
before they received any extensive electrification.

At the beginning of this period the work week was quite long. Vacations
were scarcely heard of, except for the very wealthy. The expense of travel
(on the trains, or by the slower horse and buggy) and the amount of time
involved practically precluded the ordinary individual taking a vacation at
a spot away from his own city. Even drives from the city out to the country
were very rare. With the coming of the automobile, and particularly with
the mass production of a "Model T," this whole pattern was changed. Now
the average person was able to go quickly out into the country or to visit
relatives in some other town. Vacation spots for people of little means
sprang up at the seashore and in the mountains. This was only one aspect
of the changing social customs arising from ease of transportation. The
whole set of customs with respect to dating and chaperones was changed
by the automobile era. No longer was it possible to maintain the strict
chaperoning that had accompanied the courting period. The effects of the
automobile on the city and countryside were very obvious: people moving
to the suburbs, the improvement of highways, the filling stations, road
markers, and billboards. Frederick Lewis Allen, in his book *The Big
Change*, lists the following as being the effects of the automobile on society
during this period:[24]

1. "It developed the motorized suburb."
2. The automobile age "caused a wide-spread shift of business, and of
   economic and social importance, from the railroad town to the off-
   the-railroad town; from the farm that was four miles from the railroad
   station but had poor soil to the fertile farm that was twenty to fifty
   miles from rail."
3. "The automobile age brought a parking problem that was forever
   being solved and then unsolving itself again."
4. "The new dispensation brought sudden death.... The number of
   people slaughtered annually by cars in the United States climbed
   from a little less than 15,000 in 1922 to over 32,000 in 1930."

[24] Adapted from Frederick Lewis Allen, *The Big Change; America Transforms Itself,
1900–1950*, pp. 125–130. Copyright, 1952, Harper & Row. Adapted by permission of
the publishers.

5. "The automobile revolution ended the isolation of the farmer."
6. "The automobile broadened geographical horizons especially for people who hitherto had considered themselves too poor to travel." This also increased the mobility of our population, with people being able to move to other places for better land or better jobs much more easily than in the days of the covered wagon.
7. "The automobile revolution engendered personal pride." The American of relatively poor economic status who could afford a second-hand model T had a certain pride which was quite above that of any European enduring the humiliation that accompanied poverty in the European scene.

Let us now turn attention from such basic changes to some that on the surface may appear more superficial. In 1900, even in summertime, every woman would be wearing a dress that swept the street. She would have several layers of underclothes, including a chemise, drawers, corset, corset cover, and one or more petticoats. Men's clothing was very stiff and formal. The dressed-up man would have a high and stiff collar, and he would have to wear the waistcoat (or what we now call a vest) under his coat even in hot weather. It was never proper for a man to go hatless out of doors. In the early 1900's it was improper for a middle- or upper-class man even to be in shirt sleeves. The change in styles came about very gradually, with the most rapid changes occurring after World War I, with the shortening of the dresses to the knees and with the coming of sleeveless dresses with a low neck.

The so-called jazz age of the 1920's gave rise to many kinds of changes in conventions. Most of the Puritanical ideas of the early American period were done away with or minimized by the rapid changes that occurred during this period.[25]

Class differentials in wealth were great, particularly during the period around 1900. Many millionaires had been created by the rapid industrial expansion of the country, and their fortunes were maintained partially through the lack of income tax. It was quite the fashion to display wealth by building elaborate homes and by having elaborate entertainments. Frederick Lewis Allen tells of an affair held by the Guggenheims in which the cost of the meal per head was $250 (which would be nearly $1,000 a head at the present time).[26] Andrew Carnegie, the most wealthy man of the time, took in 23 million dollars in the year 1900 with no income taxes to pay! Later on, when attacks were being constantly made against the "monopolists and the wealthy," they tended to display their wealth considerably less. With the coming of the income tax and, later, with the increasingly progressive nature of this tax, the wealthy were much more

[25] Frederick Lewis Allen, *op. cit.*, pp. 9–10.
[26] Frederick Lewis Allen, *op. cit.*, pp. 37–39.

heavily taxed. There tended to be less of the "vulgar" display of wealth because of the public displeasure that it caused.[27]

Professional people around 1900 with a reasonably good income of two to three thousand dollars a year (which would be the equivalent of ten to fifteen thousand dollars now) lived much better than the corresponding class at present. One of the reasons for this, of course, was the fact that the average wage was quite low: four to five hundred dollars a year. It was easy for a man living on a professional income to hire other persons to work for him and to have at least one full-time servant. A professional income today will not support a full-time servant because domestic servants are getting incomes more nearly commensurate with those of professional people. On the other hand, the mass production of goods as of the present time, even though the cost of labor is much higher, enables many goods to be produced at relatively lower prices. The masses today can use articles that were not available except at a very high price to the wealthy few in the earlier period. Of course many of the conveniences of today—electric sweepers, refrigerators, and others—just were not available at all then; they had not yet been developed.

In looking at the situation as a whole, we should remember that, even though at the present time we still have a wide differential between the upper and lower classes, the filth and poverty of the cities, particularly around 1900, were much worse than at present. The accident rate among the workers was very high, and there was practically no workman's compensation. There was considerable child labor, with all of its attendant bad results on the health of the children. The average work week was about sixty hours, which left very little time for recreation. The average wage was quite low, $400 to $500 per year. Adjusting this wage to dollars of current purchasing power, the average wage still would be the equivalent today of only about $1,500 per year. This is less than half the real income of the wage today, slightly over $4,580 in 1965.[28]

Another interesting change came with respect to magazines. Magazines with mass circulation were almost unheard of before 1900. They were to come in the later part of this period, when persons had more time to read and when magazines could be mass-produced more cheaply.

CONTEMPORARY CHANGES, 1929 TO THE PRESENT

Governmental and Political

This period can be said to be marked by two major themes in domestic politics and two foreign relations; but it must be pointed out that in the twentieth-century world there can be no sharp distinction between the domestic and foreign problems of any nation.

[27] Frederick Lewis Allen, *op. cit.*, pp. 81–108.
[28] *Economic Report of the President*, January, 1966 (Washington, D.C.: Govt. Printing Office, 1966), p. 224. Labor force of over 78 million, counting armed forces but not unemployed; total wages and salaries around 357 million dollars.

Starting in 1929 with a serious breakdown in their economic and industrial system, Americans found that their first domestic problem was the organization of all their resources to end the Great Depression. Later it was necessary to bring about a *total* mobilization of the nation to prosecute to a successful termination the greatest war so far in history. The early period was dominated by the remarkable personality of Franklin D. Roosevelt, four times elected to the Presidency. His program for domestic rehabilitation, termed the "New Deal," called for a vast amount of legislation designed to lead to "relief, recovery, and reform." Much of this legislation was new in conception and liberal and progressive in nature, although roots can be found in controversies even prior to the days of the Populist agitation of the 1880's. The full impact of the New Deal on the eventual permanent trends in the philosophy of American government is as yet uncertain. The influence of the events of this earlier period on the Truman administration, and even on the Republican administration following, indicates that many of the New Deal changes seem to be here to stay, including the concept of responsibility of government in stabilizing and bolstering the economy.

Foreign relations were dominated by two major themes. The first of these was the effort to reconcile American security with the growing belief that the people of the United States ought to share in solving the problems of the world. For a number of years the United States had adhered to a policy of economic nationalism, as exemplified by the passage of the Smoot-Hawley Tariff of 1930 and by the insistence on payment of war debts even when the debtor nations of the world had defaulted. Even Roosevelt, in the early days of his administration, bolted the London Economic Conference (1933), preferring to solve America's problems at home and alone. The attitude of the United States influenced the breakdown of world economy. This hastened the rise of militarism in Japan and of nazism in Germany. This, in turn, helped to lay the groundwork for World War II. The apparent success of the isolationist foreign policies of the United States in increasing its own material prosperity was believed to be sufficient justification for refraining from closer economic collaboration with other nations. Effective neutrality legislation was sought at the same time that antiwar pacts were being framed and disarmament conferences were taking place. When isolationism eventually was abandoned, it was done in the name of national security.

Even before the end of World War II, the Roosevelt administration had turned to the second of the major foreign interests of the period, the preservation of the fruits of victory. The Atlantic Charter of 1941 was only the first of the persistent efforts of the Roosevelt administration to organize peace and understanding on the basis of morally defensible principles.

In the San Francisco conference of 1946, the United States was successful in its leadership in setting up the organization of the United Nations, which eventually settled in New York City. The United Nations is not a world government, but merely a body in which the opinions of the various nations can be sounded out and some action can be taken so long as it is supported by the nations concerned. During the early post-World War II period, many persons were advocating that a world government be set up. In the 1950's actions taken by Communist China and other nations of the world led to a worsensing of conditions and to a lack of faith in the co-operative method of the United Nations in solving problems. This led to a resurgence of nationalism in the United States and in some parts of Europe. This further led to a breaking apart of some of the cooperative efforts for the solution of international problems.

Although the United Nations was successful on many important but minor problems related to world peace, the major conflict between Russia and the United States deepened. This conflict, which became almost a cold war between the nations, flared into a "hot" war when North Korean forces invaded South Korea. The United States had withdrawn its troops but had pledged support to the maintenance of the integrity of both the North and South Korean republics. The United States then re-entered South Korea; and, with the support of the United Nations (Russia dissenting), fought an indecisive war that eventually ended in an armistice.

The Eisenhower administration pursued a foreign policy very similar to that of the Roosevelt and Truman administrations. On the economic front it also had plans to use the powers of government, if necessary, in order to prevent economic depression should one threaten. The major differences claimed by the new Republican administration were a cleaner and more honest government and a greater emphasis upon private enterprise. The opponents of the Republican administration claimed that in this respect the aims and achievements of the two parties were not different. In spite of much political heat and smoke with reference to the tendency for the Democratic Party to be favorable to a "drift toward socialism," it seems apparent that both the Kennedy and Johnson administrations in the sixties were center, middle-of-the-road, movements. This is particularly evident when they are contrasted with the tendencies of the democratic parties in European countries, which were much more blatantly socialistic in their policies and trends.

Industrial and Commercial

Two considerations in the area of industrial and commercial developments invite attention: the course or fortunes of the national economy, and the changing theory of that economy. The first can be quickly outlined. The Great Depression that began in 1929 reached its worst stage in 1932. Business casualties increased from 21,000 per year before the depression to nearly 32,000 in 1932. In 1933 almost 20 per cent of the nation's banks closed. In March, 1933 (with the monthly average of 1924–1925 at 100), the index of industrial production stood at 60, construction at 14, factory employment at 61, factory payrolls at 38, and wholesale prices (1926 at 100) at 60.[29]

A slow upward trend began in 1933, was reversed temporarily in 1937, and then after 1939 reached prosperity on the basis of orders from belligerents and from the defense-minded government. American entrance into the war in 1941 brought full employment, high wages, and—inevitably— inflation. The national debt increased from $16 billion in 1930 to a peak of $270 billion in 1945. After dropping for a while in the late 1940's and 1950's, it was to go above $260 billion in the mid-1960's.[30]

The theory of the national economy underwent changes. Although Herbert Hoover, in a sense, the precursor of the New Deal, it was President Roosevelt who threw tradition and precedent to the winds in a desperate effort to prevent complete economic collapse. The philosophy that emerged was both implicit and explicit: the government was no longer on the side lines, it was an active partner of every legitimate business interest and the guardian of the welfare of every individual. This thinking meant food and shelter to millions of Americans, because at one time a third of the population was on federal relief.

The war itself emphasized the economic thinking that the government could rightfully use its power to set aside the operation of the "natural law" of supply and demand as the determinant of prices. This economic theory was not new, for rationing and priorities had been used in World War I. Price controls on consumer's goods, however, were a different feature; and they were justified on the grounds that the national emergency was artifically curtailing supply and stimulating demand. Hence the "natural law" of the economist had no application.

There were many fears voiced to the effect that World War II would be followed very quickly by a depression. There was quite a controversy concerning whether the controls should be taken off or left on. Finally, due to political pressure, particularly from the members of the Republican Party but also from other influential persons, price controls were abruptly taken off and there was a rapid inflationary period following World War II, which led to prices considerably higher than in the prewar period. Considerable time was spent by industry in replenishing the inventories that had become low during the war period, and the inflationary trend tended to cause the public to buy things rapidly, thus preventing stock on the shelves from piling up. At about the time when there might have been a mild recession as a result of piling up of inventory in industry's warehouses, the Korean War broke out and there was a rush to buy materials for the war. Consequently a further inflationary trend caused prices to continue to rise and therefore to accentuate further buying. During most of this post-

[29] Louis M. Hacker, *American Problems of Today* (New York: Appleton, 1938), p. 178.

[30] *Economic Report of the President* (Washington, D.C.: Govt. Printing Office, 1966), p. 272.

war period, the national budget was out of balance; and this, of course, added to the inflationary trends. There was considerably more money spent by the federal government than was taken in. The change of administration made very little difference in this pattern of an unbalanced budget. There was some decrease in the amount of money spent on domestic matters by the Eisenhower administration as compared with the Truman administration; but the worsening international situation, including a stepped-up military budget and aid to friendly governments, caused the federal budget to be considerably out of balance. It is difficult, therefore, to determine what would have been the policies of the Republican administration in normal times as opposed to those of the Democratic administration. The postwar period was not "normal times." The question of whether or not there would ever be "normal times" was also in the minds of some persons because there was envisioned a long period of cold or moderately hot war between the United States and the Soviet Union. Although the Cold War between these two countries cooled off during the period of the sixties, the situation was complicated by the conflict 'between the Soviet Union and China within the Communist world and the growing disaffection of De Gaulle's France from other democratic countries in the early sixties.

Religious and Philosophical

By 1929 certain earlier religious views had been on the defensive for some time. Traditional social and ethical principles, including sex mores, were held by the conservatives to be allied to religion; and these were being violated. Religious interpretation of the Bible ranged from the literal and orthodox to more liberal positions. Complete atheism attracted only a small minority.

One trend appeared to be significant. Religious emphasis had been diverted from academic debates on divineness to the application of religious principles to problems of social welfare. Many ministers felt that theological problems were to be envisaged as they interacted with the industrialized world. One of these men, Reinhold Niebuhr, whose ministry brought him into personal contact with the industrial workers of Detroit, indicated that since he had "stopped worrying so much about intellectual problems" there was more of a thrill in preaching.[31] Niebuhr was largely concerned with the religious implications of economic, political, and social theory and practice. Although as a "neo-orthodox" he accepted an orthodox apostolic creed "as the whole genius of Christian faith" and advocated a Paulistic doctrine of "original sin," Niebuhr attempted to synthesize traditional religious thought with modern sociological thought.[32]

[31] Reinhold Niebuhr, *Leaves from the Notebook of a Tamed Cynic* (Chicago: Willet, 1929), p. 27.
[32] Reinhold Niebuhr, *Human Nature*, Vol. I: The Nature and Destiny of Man (New York: Scribner, 1941), pp. 260–265.

Secular thinking, too, showed the impact of the Great Depression. Men turned increasingly to science to solve the dilemma, and there was a range of opinion concerning how we get and interpret knowledge. Some men decried the emphasis on modern social and economic theories, reasserting the claims of the great tradition, which was based on the historical-philosophical outlooks of idealism, rationalism, and dualism. These reactions sometimes took the form of the new humanism as advanced by Stewart P. Sherman or Paul Shorey, of Catholicism as conceived by Jacques Maritain, or of intellectualism as proposed by Mark Van Doren or Abraham Flexner.

Other men, borrowing from Newtonian science and the positivism of Comte and Spencer, described the world as a machine that obeyed fixed natural laws in which supernatural and rationalistic interpretations had little place. These men believed in the scientific method, narrowly conceived. When the concepts of Newtonian mechanism were applied to explaining what caused man to function as he does, man was described as a complicated machine. The psychology of behaviorism stems from this view.

Reacting against intellectual rationalism and Newtonian mechanism was the point of view of experimentalism and experimental naturalism attributed to John Dewey and others. Drawing from all fields of knowledge, including the philosophic traditions of naturalism, empiricism, pragmatism, biology, anthropology, Gestalt psychology, and social psychology, this group attempted to devise a theory of life and education that they felt would assimilate many social and intellectual trends and would be appropriate for twentieth-century America. Experimentalism denied the traditional dualisms that separated man from nature, mind from body, individual from society, and knowledge from action. As Bode indicates, experimentalism held "that the world is all of one piece."[33] Human nature was not conceived as something fixed and eternal, but as a mode of reaction that had developed in a surrounding culture. Life was viewed as a continual interacting adjustment between an active individual and an active environment: in this adjusting process the environment influenced or changed the individual's behavior and, in turn, was changed by the individual's behavior.

In the sixties, two other philosophies tend to become emergent within the democratic culture: existentialism and logical positivism in the form of the analytical philosophy movement. Existentialism came to America out of the literary and logical movements among European philosophers that portrayed man as a tragic, grimly ludicrous figure in a world that lacked meaning. In this meaningless world, man has the awful task and the awful freedom to choose the nature of his being. He must face the problem of choice and the responsibility for the choice he makes. The philosophical analyst, on the other hand, tended to discount most of tradi-

---

[33] Boyd Henry Bode, *How We Learn* (Boston: Heath, 1950), p. 264.

tional philosophy as being meaningless and to reduce philosophy to the problem of clarification of the language philosophers use. This tended to rule out much of the earlier philosophy, including pragmatism, and to interpret most value statements as meaningless.

The churches and religious thinking were influenced greatly by the changes in scientific thinking and philosophical thinking. There was an increase of the liberal movement within the church and the further development of the "modernism" movement, which went much beyond the liberal thinking of the earlier period. The church as an institution prospered, however. The number of persons who were members of churches increased in all denominations—Jewish, Roman Catholic, and Protestant—to a level that probably included a higher percentage of the population than at any previous time in American history.[34] Within the Protestant denominations there was a strong ecumenical movement. This was an attempt for the Protestant churches, which had separated again and again into many denominations, to come back together because some of the reasons for which they had originally separated were now considered to be superficial. Several branches of the Methodist Church joined together, and many other minor denominations were united into larger groups. Most of the Protestant groups also worked together through the Federal Council of Churches, which later merged into the National Council of Churches. There was also a World Council of Churches, which took in most of the Christian churches of the world with the exception of the Roman Catholic Church. However, there are still a large number of denominations that are quite independent of each other administratively; and the big organizations like the National Council of Churches and the World Council of Churches are merely cooperative endeavors, rather than an actual union of the churches into one large group. With the administration of Pope John XXIII (1958–63), there was a renewed interest in liberalizing to some extent the practices of the Roman Catholic Church. With the calling of the Vatican II Ecumenical Council in 1962 and its continued sessions during the sixties, there were numerous changes made in the policies and practices of the Church which made for much better relations between it and the other branches of the Christian church and the other world religious. In 1964, for the first time a Catholic diocese joined the State Council of Churches, hitherto Protestant (New Mexico).

Social Customs and Institutions

The period from 1929 to the present represents an extension of the changes that had been taking place rapidly during the latter half of the previous period. In addition to the changes in the standard of living and the way in which goods were produced, there were changes in two other

[34] News item, Religious News Service, *Cincinnati Times-Star*, August 26, 1954. This item reported a church membership of 59.5 per cent or 94 million persons in 1953. This is certainly a higher percentage than in 1800.

major areas. One was a change in the character of the family, and the other was the further change from the rural to the urban type of population.

We shall discuss the changes in the family briefly, even though they are to be treated more fully in Chapter 7. In the first place, caused by and paralleling other social changes, there was a considerable reduction in the size of the family. This took place first in the cities, but there was also a reduction in the size of the rural family. Even the population increases that were to come in the post-World War II period were not due so much to a greater number of large families as the increased number of persons marrying and the increased number of families with one or two children that would have had none before.

The first noticeable characteristic about the family is, of course, the decrease in its stability—the increase in the number of divorces.[35] About one out of four marriages were ending in divorce in the post-World War II period. The character of the families that did hold together had been changing. Because divorce had become easier and more socially accepted, the husband and wife tended to stick together on the basis of mutual affection.

Not nearly so much of the life of the family is now centered around the home. In earlier days the family earned a living in the home, and almost all recreation and even many important aspects of education were centered there. The home has now changed to a point that, in some cases in which the mother works, it is little more than a place to get an occasional meal and to sleep. This last characteristic, of course, is an extreme example, because there were, in the period of the 1930's and early 1940's, numerous families that were completely stable. In spite of some predictions of a dire end to family life, most writers in the field have indicated that the family was in a transitional stage and that the kind of family that was to emerge might be also stable, although of a quite different character from the family of the 1850's.

The type of clothes worn, as well as other characteristics of living, have changed markedly during this period. The changes in the bathing suits worn at the beach are indicative of the changes occurring elsewhere. One-piece bathing suits for men and the two-piece for women became quite prominent during the 1930's. The wearing of shorts in the home by women (at least in the suburbs) and, to some extent, by men, was quite prevalent in the post-World War II period.

By 1955, some aspects of recreation were reversing the trend that had occurred in the early part of this period. Recreation, for a time, had been taken out of the home. The development of radio in the 1920's and early 1930's, and of television in the 1950's, tended to keep people at home, although it could hardly be called family recreation. There is some expression of opinion that television is killing the art of family conversation

---

[35] Cf. discussion of recent trends of divorce in Chapter 6.

and limiting other forms of family group recreation. Commercialized recreational facilities, such as mass sport events, bowling alleys, and commercial movies, tended to dominate the period of the late 1930's and early 1940's, and continued significant for adolescents who wished to get out of the home for their amusements during the period of the 1950's.

A tendency toward an increased amount of travel was apparent in the 1920's. The amount of travel was accelerated during the 1930's, was cut down during World War II because of gasoline rationing, and then again increased by leaps and bounds. After World War II almost everyone took some kind of vacation trip some time during every year. The tendency to travel in automobiles rather than by train was so great and the motel business so prevalent that it was possible to go almost anywhere in the United States and find a clean and reasonably priced place in which to sleep at night. All these factors caused a greater mobility of population, with the net movement being to the west and north. There were also tendencies to movement on a permanent basis from farm to city, and to states with climates such as Florida, that created minor eddies.

The increase in travel already in evidence before World War II was accentuated further by the enormous number of young men and some young women traveling because of the war situation, either in uniform or to defense plants. They found out about other parts of the world; and therefore they were interested in traveling all the more. Young men who, except for the war, would have grown up and stayed in their communities all their lives, were in Europe or the South Pacific, and they came back with a greatly broadened concept of the world in which they lived.

The tendency of Americans to move about also was accentuated after World War II. In the 1950's over 30 million persons moved in a single year. Ten million families went out of their counties, and 5 million of these moved out of their states. The population movement from the country to the city is, of course, one of long standing in American culture. It was greatly accelerated with the rapid industrialization of the country after 1900. The increasing productivity of the American farmers enabled an increasingly smaller percentage of them to provide the necessary food for a more adequate diet for an increasingly larger percentage of urban dwellers. A little over 11 per cent of the total employed labor force were farmers. Seventy-five years ago the labor force was divided about equally between farm and nonfarm.[36]

SUMMARY OF THE MAIN SOCIAL TRENDS

The purpose of this chapter has been to provide some understanding of the cultural setting in which the American educational system has arisen and in which it has striven to enhance those values in which its leaders

[36] *Economic Report of the President*, January, 1965, p. 280.

have believed. The American history reviewed here is filled with twists and turns of many kinds. Always there have been problems, each with its peculiar complexities and each doing something to induce a new perspective. Some awareness of these problems and of the conflicts they reflected and produced is necessary to an appraisal of the efforts of the school in its contributions to the society in which it exists and to any suggestions for future trends in education and in society.

Perhaps, in the brief review of the nation's social trends, enough has been seen to realize that at no time were Americans members of a static society. Always events were on the march; ever present was the fact of change, or as Faulkner once stated, "The only certain factor is continual change."[37]

In order to summarize the actual changes that are taking place in American society, we have in this section set forth a list of definite trends, together with some of their implications for our society and specifically for education. The authors acknowledge their heavy indebtedness to many sources.[38]

Trend I.   Development of Atomic Energy and Automation

The potentialities of the development of atomic energy and the rapid movement toward automation of the productive process have served to pose pressing problems for the American economic and industrial system.

One of the most pressing problems of the last few decades is that imposed by the increasing technology of the American economic and industrial system. There have developed in recent years new trends in this area of improved technology, and the potentialities that have now been opened for atomic power have served to make this problem even more acute. The rapid trend toward complete automation has been almost completed in some of the newer oil-refining plants. This trend has served to make quite evident that the newer productive processes are going to require even less labor of the unskilled and semiskilled types than did the earlier mass-production techniques based on the methods used in the production of the Model T by Henry Ford starting in the early 1900's.

A practically unlimited source of power will become available when the atomic power plant has been made successful and practical. This enormous increase of power arises from the fact that the fuel of the atomic power plant, the radioactive material, is not consumed in the same way as is coal, oil, or gas. In atomic furnaces new radioactive materials can be produced, which can be refined and used again in other atomic piles. The

[37] Harold Underwood Faulkner, *American Economic History*, Fifth Edition (New York: Harper, 1943), p. 641.

[38] An excellent list was prepared in 1935 by the (Yearbook) Commission of Education for New Social and Economic Relationships appointed by the Department of Superintendence of the NEA (now called the American Association of School Administrators).

use of atomic energy, therefore, gives almost unlimited productive potentialities in terms of the quantity of products that can be produced automatically. This dawning age of plenty challenges the ability of our present distribution facilities to take care of the results of the increased productivity of our industrial system. The economic and industrial problems related to this and to other problems arising out of our industrial system will be discussed more fully in Chapter 5.

This trend has come about so recently that it is difficult to explore all the implications for education that are present in our contemporary culture. On the one hand, in a culture in which the productive process has become largely automatic and in which there are tremendous potentialities of power, there will be increased amounts of leisure time and an increased accentuation of the trends toward unskilled and semiskilled jobs, or toward jobs that require a minimum of skill in operating machines that are fairly automatic. On the other hand, it will mean, of course, an increasing number of persons with highly technical skills to design the automatic machines and to design the productive systems under which they operate, and to prepare the blueprints for new machines in terms of new models and new products.

Trend II. Increased Leisure Time Made Possible by Technological Efficiency

The rapid development in the efficiency of American technology has made possible an increase in the amount of leisure time that has been released from the time previously required for the production of those goods and services necessary for the maintenance of a minimum standard of living.

This increased time for leisure pursuits has posed problems for the wise use of leisure as far as our society is concerned. In some cases, where leisure time has been used unwisely, it has been a contributing factor to increased delinquency and crime.

(1) There are some persons who would say that preparation for leisure-time activities is not basically the responsibility of the school, since it already has its own job to do and consequently should not be interested in expanding its program to include the development of resources within the pupils for the wise use of their leisure time. (2) Others, however, indicate that education should be concerned about all human possibilities and that the school therefore should teach the significance of our expanding technology. This point of view implies that the pupil could be helped to see the possibilities inherent in the increase in the extent of our material-centered living. It would also stress the need for the pupil to get ready to use his leisure time for the enrichment of life rather than to allow deterioration due to lack of wise use of such time. There is also a possibility that helping the person understand more fully his place in the quite often mechanical, routinized processes of the modern mass-production system will help him

appreciate his work more, so that he will not look upon it as purely routinized and therefore will be able to enjoy it more and also do a better job.

Trend III.   Social Lag of Institutions Behind Material Changes

Our modern society is characterized by a serious social lag, which is due to the failure of our institutions and our ideology to keep pace with the very rapid rate of material changes brought about by the expanding technology.

This lag, of course, is the occasion for many of the conflicts of our society and for many of the problems that exist. The problem of the lag of the school has been fully discussed in the appropriate sections of Chapter 2 and throughout Chapter 3. The problem of lag in regard to economic problems is documented throughout Chapter 5.

(1) One point of view would say that this lag should be of little or no direct concern to the school. The school is not concerned with current conflicts as such. The school's job is to pass on the basic values found in our cultural heritage and in this way help to avoid some of the difficulties that may arise due to conflict and change. (2) Other groups say that the school must help society change over to the new ideas and ideals and work hard for changes in institutional arrangements adapted to whatever is implicit in the rapid social change and in psychological understandings found in our society. If the school will help to do this, the changes can be brought about by democratic means. If, however, the school and other institutions in our society ignore the necessity for subsequent change in our ideology, values, and institutions, it may be that the very foundations of our society will be threatened because of the fact that the basic institutions are too much out of gear with it.

Trend IV.   Increased Necessity for Cooperative Action

The complexity of the modern industrial processes, the interdependence of different processes on each of its many parts, and the necessity for various specialists and other persons concerned with a process to work closely together result in an increased necessity for cooperative action in almost all of industrial as well as social enterprises.

This tendency toward the necessity for cooperation brought about by the complexity of our society, and, particularly, in the complex industrial process, has become evident in our modern society. The efficiency of the modern productive process depends upon a very careful working together in a cooperative manner of all the various aspects of that productive process. This necessity for careful coordination apparently is present whether the matter concerned is an industrial production line, a complex engineering job, or some type of social process taking place in nonprofit-making enterprises. Some research has shown that the failure of an individual to be successful on the job is due in more cases to his lack of ability to get along with other persons than it is to lack of skill.[39] Increasingly the type of skill needed for industrial jobs can be learned very readily by the average individual on the job itself. There is an increase in semiskilled and un-skilled jobs. Of course there are a certain number of jobs, such as engineer-ing and production design, that require a quite high level of skill.[40] Again, however, along with these skills is the necessity for knowing how to work cooperatively with others in the highly technical planning processes.

(1) Some persons would say that, in spite of this, the important thing to stress in our society is individualism. The individualist in our society will cooperate with others if it is profitable to him and if it is worthwhile for himself to do so. According to this point of view it would not be necessary to teach cooperation, because that would come about normally when the individual saw the necessity for it in terms of his own self-interest. Thus it would be the job of the school to teach each individual to be as highly skilled as possible with respect to the contributions that he might make to a productive or a social process. (2) Others would stress that the school should, in addition, help the individual see the importance of his job in the total productive process, indeed the place of his work in society as a whole. Also, they would stress the importance of teaching in the school the necessity for cooperation, including experiences in working with others within the school, so that the child will learn the know-how of group en-deavor and therefore be able to adjust better to the kinds of situations in which he will most certainly be placed when he leaves school. Except for a few very highly skilled jobs that require large numbers of specific skills to be learned in advance, the emphasis would be upon the all-round develop-ment of the individual, including the ability to work with others, rather than upon a very high level of specific skills. (3) Still another group feels that the necessity for cooperative action in modern society, plus the necessity for intelligent cooperative action of the entire group in the solu-tion of the problems we face, means that the school must play a much more positive role. It must play that role in developing new techniques for our society to use in helping to reorganize itself on a more collective basis for the common solution of our problems, including production and distri-bution problems in our economic system. The necessity for the school to take this particular role is brought about, they say, by the increasing complexity of the problems that we face, together with the increasing knowledge of the way in which our problems can be solved. The school is the institution best able to help society reorganize or reconstruct itself in such a way as to better enable itself to meet these problems.

[39] E.g., see T. L. Norton, *Public Education and Economic Trends* (Cambridge, Mass.: Harvard Graduate School of Education, 1939).

[40] E.g., see much studies as that of Charles A. Koepke, *A Job Analysis of Manu-facturing Plants in Minnesota*, cited by Newton Edwards and Herman G. Richey, *The School in the American Social Order*, Second Edition (Boston: Houghton, 1963), pp. 479–480.

Trend V.   Increased Necessity for Long-range Planning

Modern technology, other aspects of the industrial process, and other aspects of modern life have become so complex that they apparently have necessitated an increase in the amount of careful, long-range planning in order that there be the maximum efficient use of our productive processes so that there will be, in consequence, an ever-increasing improvement in our modern living.

Certainly a characteristic of modern times is the increasing amount of long-range planning by private industrial groups, nongovernmental social agencies, and governmental groups in general. There seems to be some opposition to this long-range planning when it is applied to governmental operations. It is difficult to see how, in a complex society such as we have now, there is any way in which we can avoid the necessity for making plans in advance so that complex devices and institutions can be geared and developed in line with those long-range plans.

(1) Some persons object because they evidently feel that the long-range planning of any group, private or governmental, tends to restrict the freedom of the individual to make choices. If you have long-range planning, there must of course be some way to bring about the cooperation of individuals in such long-range planning. Certainly, they say, the school has no place in this, as its service should be devoted to helping the individual to develop, rather than stressing procedures that may lead to the lessening of the importance of the individual and his decisions in our society. (2) On the other hand, there are those who notice that in spite of verbal opposition there is, in fact, increased planning on the part of private enterprises as well as on the part of nongovernmental and governmental social agencies. They hold that it should be the place of the school to teach persons about this necessity for planning so that they may be able to understand it and may learn to make their own individual plans within the framework of the larger plans of our society. Furthermore, it should be the job of the school to *teach* people how to work with others on a cooperative planning basis, so that whatever plans are made are the result of the widest possible participation of individuals and groups in our society.

Trend VI.   Increased Social Control and Increasing Remoteness of Social Control

The present machine age has tended to reduce the direct personal relationship both between the producer and the consumer on the one hand and between the worker and the manager on the other, and thus tends to increase our dependence upon new forms of social control (other than the former simple interpersonal relationships) in various aspects of our economy and of our society and has caused the source of the control to be increasingly remote from its individual beneficiaries.

The use of machine processes in production brings about an apparent necessity for the productive system to be quite complex and to involve a large number of persons doing different tasks. The growing complexity of the productive and marketing systems has caused us to lose the person-to-person contact between the consumer and the craftsman that existed prior to the development of the industrial age. At the same time, the complexity of the industrial process has also caused the close interpersonal relationship between the worker on one hand and the entrepreneur or manager of the plant on the other to be partially destroyed. The development of powerful labor unions, collective bargaining, and trade associations, and the larger ramification of governmental control in many aspects of life, all are indications of the growing amount of social control. This increased social control, of course, is resisted by certain elements of our population and accepted or promoted by other elements. At times, individuals have resisted social control when it was restrictive of them but have asked an extension of social control in areas favorable to their interests. This dichotomy of thought and action is quite common at present in the various groups of our society, and it includes, of course, persons in both labor and management groups. Sometimes persons may take one point of view in their consumer interests and another in regard to their producer or other interests.

Time was when the most important things that impinged upon local citizens were those under the control of the local government. Because of the complexity of society, many elements have been moved more and more to higher levels of government. The schools, for example, have had their administration and financing transferred more and more to the state level. Many other aspects of our society, involving as they do wide geographical areas, have become important on the federal level rather than on the local, county, or state level. This has been true not only in governmental aspects but also in business organizations, with their many ramifications of plants. It is true also with nongovernmental social groups such as the organized charities, where in many cases one large Community Chest campaign has replaced many smaller campaigns. This tends to make relationships very impersonal, with a lack of direct contact, for example, between the individual giver and the agency, or worthy enterprises within that agency, to which the person is making his contribution. It is difficult for the individual to see clearly that the giving of his money enables him to help out someone who is sick or some poor child, because all the machinery of a complex social organization is between him and the actual recipient.

There is a question as to what part the school may have to play in the recognition of this fact of increasing of social control: (1) On one hand, we might strengthen the individual as a consumer by teaching him how to make wise decisions in the purchase of his clothing, for example, so as to avoid the necessity for so much social control over such matters as the quality of materials and prices. (2) On the other hand, it certainly is true that we do have to have social control of some things because the matters of control are highly technical, such as the purity of our water supply, the competency of our doctors and teachers, and the soundness with which our buildings are constructed. This list of technical matters can be greatly extended. The complexities of checking on the satisfactoriness of matters of this type mean control and inspection of a very high level. One of the jobs of our schools would be to give an understanding of this, so that all would appreciate the necessity for social control.

The tendency on the part of society to operate more and more on a highly abstract level requires, of course, the ability of the person to read and understand things on an abstract basis rather than on the concrete basis of an earlier period. This means that a higher level of education of our populace must be maintained. One of the things that must be done is to establish communication as to purposes between the agencies and the people who must make the contributions or who must support them by means of their votes. This calls for a high level of literacy and of interest. Both of these latter undertakings can well be helped by the school as an institution in developing an educated and functionally literate populace that will be able to understand the complexities of the interrelationships of the remotely controlled social groups of which they are a part.

Trend VII.   Increased Need for Specialization

The extremely complex nature of industrial and social relationships has resulted in the increased need for expert knowledge and therefore in the need for specialists, particularly in the leadership roles in our society.

This leads to two implications for the school: (1) It must play an important part in developing the kind of individuals who will become the specialists and in maintaining a well-rounded background of those specialists aside from their field of specializations. (2) It must develop some way of teaching to all an understanding and respect for the contribution of the specialists but still maintain the ultimate control outside the oligarchy or minority of specialists. In the case of medical doctors, for example, to what extent must we leave the power to make certain decisions in their hands? To what extent should decisions relating to medicine that are social in nature be taken out of the hands of persons who may be somewhat biased in terms of their own self-interests? The same question arises with respect to our politicians or our civil servants in government. To what extent must we leave technical decisions in their hands? To what extent must broad policy be brought back and ratified on some kind of a basis, for example, to a board representing broader problems of school administration with a specialized school administrator, or to an analogous group in industry or in the various branches of government?

Trend VIII.   Increased Differentiation in Providing for Individuals

The growing recognition of the differences in individuals in our population is resulting in a differentiation of the provisions made available to people in a democracy and, therefore, in increased potentiality towards individual choice and creativity.

Our rapidly improving industrial system is capable of providing goods and services of great variety, so that individuals have a right to make a wide range of choices with respect to the kind of housing, clothing, and other consumer goods and rational needs they would like to have. Despite this technical capacity for diversity, there is increasing opinion among scholars which insists that the tendency in the United States is toward conformity. In Riesman's study of the other-directed man, he indicates that the tendency in modern industrialized society is toward conforming to the approval of the group as opposed to individualization of tastes and activities and interests. This problem cannot be completely resolved on an objective basis. However, it should be sufficient to indicate here that there was conformity in the tradition-directed individuals who lived in the middle of the nineteenth century. However, this conformity was to a much smaller group, both quantitatively and geographically. Consequently, people may have appeared to be more individualistic. Whatever conformity there is in the middle of the twentieth century, it is conformity to a larger social group that has been tied together through mass circulation magazines, radio, television, etc. This tends to make what conformity there is an even more uniform one throughout a larger geographical area and gives the appearance of greater conformity. The writers hold that whatever may be the final decision with respect to the *facts* of the extent of conformity, it is increasingly possible for persons in our affluent society to make choices that are quite creative and individual.

This potential for greater differentiation in the possible services provided the individual, of course, does have implications also as to the kinds of education that need to be provided. (1) An important implication here for the school is in terms of a differentiated program to meet the differentiated needs of the various individuals who go to the school. Equity of education does not necessarily mean the same education for all. (2) On the other hand, there is a general core of common knowledge that we should provide in the school, so that people who are facing the same general problems in our society will have the background for it. There are some differences of opinion on this particular problem. Some think that the school should be limited to the common needs of all. Others emphasize the differential needs and to some extent may even de-emphasize the common needs in preference to a greater stress on specific individual needs, particularly vocational.[41]

Trend IX.   Weakening of Traditional Controls over Human Conduct

The extreme diversity of our various cultural patterns, the very widespread dissemination of the knowledge arising from the scientific method,

---

[41] In 1965, for example, the Office of Economic Opportunity embarked upon a vast Youth Job Corps Training Program for out-of-school youth aged 16–21. This will be discussed more fully in Chapter 10.

*and the rise of the scientific attitude toward testing all hypotheses, together
with the generally changing and dynamic character of our industrial society
—all have tended to weaken the authoritarian and conventional controls
over human conduct.*

A breakdown of conventional controls over human conduct has almost
always been present in periods when society has been in rapid change or
has been rapidly deteriorating. At the present time, material changes are
occurring much more swiftly than at any other period in the history of
mankind, and they have been coupled with a more profound change in
some of the basic assumptions, ideologically speaking, underlying our
society. These material and ideological changes, together with the general
pattern of diverse culture in America—due to the many groups that make
up our country and to our policy of encouraging diversity—have caused
a partial relinquishing of the authoritarian controls that normally have
helped to regulate human conduct.

This breakdown in the controls that have been held over human conduct in the past has caused some to see weaknesses in our present educational system. (1) Some persons insist that the primary reason for the
breakdown of authoritarian control has been the fact that the educational
system has not stressed strongly enough the traditional values of our
culture. Others, of a more theological bent, have held that the reason lies
in the fact that our present public education, being nonsectarian, has not
been able to teach the theological foundations that help to strengthen
the many kinds of authoritarian moral controls. The net result has been a
considerable agitation for increased emphasis of the school on traditional
values, including, in some cases, emphasis on the religious values to the
extent to which they are compatible with the traditional separation of
church and state. (2) There are other groups who hold that the breakdown
in values is merely a characteristic of all changing societies and that the
remedy is not to be found in the schools but within society itself, in terms
of: increased family attention to such matters as the instruction of the
young; better work by the churches in attracting and maintaining the attendance of the young at church services; and other religious education
experiences. Some persons of this same general point of view would hold
that the lack of authoritarian values is not in itself bad, and that our value
systems will become more stable as society stabilizes itself after passing
through this period of rapid change. To this group, the present period is
not the forerunner of a time of serious deterioration of our society. (3)
Still another group would indicate that we should place a great deal more
stress upon the common values *inherent* in our culture, particularly those
related to its democratic aspects. The main job of the school from this
point of view should be that of helping boys and girls to clarify the values
that are inherent in our democratic culture and to see what their implications are for human action in our society.

Trend X.   Increased Strains and Tensions

The increased specialization of our society and other factors have caused the society to tend toward becoming compartmentalized into groups both vertically and horizontally, thus deepening the strains and tensions in American life.

There is an increased tendency for us to owe our main allegiance to the particular occupational or social group with which we are associated. Our political and economic ideologies tend to correspond more closely with those of the industrial group or social class in which we operate than with that of any other element of our population. There is a tendency, there-fore, for action to be taken more often on the basis of this narrower class interest than on the basis of what may be good for society as a whole. It is, of course, true that there is greater mobility of persons from genera-tion to generation (or even within one lifetime) between the various classes in America than there would be in most European or other countries at the present time. The person who is making his way from one class to another tends very quickly to assimilate the points of view of the new group in which he is found. This mobility, therefore, tends to preserve the class structure. These fractionated points of view increase the problems that America is facing; but some inherent tendencies toward stability help to minimize these class differences in points of view. One characteristic of American society that helps to give stability is the identification of most persons with the middle class. There are very few persons who wish to classify themselves at the extremes. This is in marked contrast to many of the other countries of the world, where most people are at the extremes and think of themselves as being either wealthy or poor. (1) The school, since it is a nonsectarian, non-class-interest institution in our society, probably has played a very important part in reducing class consciousness without consciously attempting to do so.[42] Most of our people attend public school, which helps them better to understand persons different from themselves. (2) Some persons feel that the school might play a more definite part in helping to reduce class tension by helping to explain the various points of view of the different classes (groups) in our society so that they will be better understood. The school might further help the pupil to see in broader perspective the problems of the entire society rather than that of the specific group to which his parents may happen to belong. (3) There are others, of course, who feel that the school should ignore these tension problems. They feel that focusing attention on prob-lems will tend to accentuate them rather than to alleviate them. The school, according to this latter point of view, should emphasize the com-mon culture of our society. This would help to mitigate the differential nature of our society, which tends to cause groups to come in conflict with each other.

[42] However, see the discussion of social class structure in Chapter 9.

Trend XI.   Population Explosion

*Because of improved medical care and a better understanding of disease,
resulting in decreased infant mortality and in a sharp increase in longevity,
the United States and the world are confronted with the possibility of
enormous increases in population of each of the different countries and of
the world as a whole. This possibility raises problems as to the availability
of food, living space, and the proper distribution of natural resources
among the countries in face of uneven population distribution.*

It is perhaps a strange anomaly that the two most serious problems the
world is facing are so opposite in nature. The awful threat of the nuclear
bomb, whether of the A or H variety, is the possibility of wiping out all
human life or all life on this planet. On the other hand, if we do not have
a serious atomic war or some type of disease that will decimate our population, we face the possibility, perhaps even as serious, of a world in which
we will be so crowded that life will not be very pleasant. The details in
regard to our population will be discussed more fully in Chapter 11. However, at this point it should be noted that this increase in population is not
only a matter of the total numbers, and that it is uneven in the various
parts of the world, but also that it does create changes in the nature of the
population, particularly in the numbers of people of an older age, above
65, in each of the populations. This creates economic problems concerning the support of these people after their working period has been finished. This is also a psychological problem as well as economic in terms of
their own psychological well-being. Further, it raises questions as to the
distribution of the world resources because in some cases, as in the underdeveloped countries, the population is rising much more rapidly than the
resources can be developed. In some cases, the resources are not there
within the geographical area to support the population. Furthermore,
eventually the question will be raised as to whether we can find room to
house the people and provide any kind of living that is worthwhile. Housing already has encroached upon some of the agricultural land that could
be used for the production of food. Although this is not an immediate
problem in the next twenty-five years in the United States, it will and can
soon become so. It is, however, an immediate problem in India and China.

The population of the United States is increasing at approximately the
average rate of the increase in the world in general. The population in
large countries such as China, India, and in the South American countries
is increasing very rapidly. The rapid increase, of course raises the possibility
that countries with less highly industrialized development and with values
and a way of life not acceptable to Western civilization are increasing so
much as to dominate eventually the rest of the world. Consequently, their
population increase is not only a problem to India, to China, and to the
South American countries, but it is also a worldwide problem—that of
maintaining an appropriate balance in the world between the different

levels of culture while allowing underdeveloped countries sufficient time to develop a higher level of civilization as they take over a greater position of dominance in the world.

Some of the implications for the school, of course, might include: (1) giving the boys and girls some understanding of the population problem and the unevenness of the population; (2) helping them to understand the possibility of regulating the size of the family to make it reasonable to be able to meet its education and other needs in terms of the family resources. The latter, of course, raises the question of birth control and birth control techniques. At the moment, because of the controversial nature of the methods of birth control to be used—not birth control itself—the school is not in a position to provide information concerning the necessity for the use of birth control nor, of course, the methods to be used. The understanding of the economics and the problems that are entailed by the terrific expansion of the population in the world certainly ought to be presented to the students in our schools at some time during their educational program.

Trend XII.   America in Position of World Leadership

Increased transportation, more rapid communication and America's industrial and military power have thrust her into a position of world leadership.

Even though change is the most evident feature of history, and even though history never exactly repeats itself, many unsolved problems persist from generation to generation. The aftermath of World War II revealed several persistent, unsolved problems. Although the power of Italian fascism, German National Socialism, and Japanese militarism was destroyed by the war, the problem of aggressive totalitarianism was not removed. With the peace there came to the forefront a totalitarian Soviet Union, which became one power of a two-powered world. Totalitarianism is certainly not a new development created in 1945. In its present form it has been threatening democracy since 1920, and its roots may be traced far back into history. Neither is it likely to be a unique characteristic of the few years after World War II, for it is quite probable that future generations will struggle with this same problem.

Many writers point out that World War II created a different attitude on the part of the American people in that it caused more Americans to think in worldwide terms; that more Americans are conscious that an open society with a free flow of information and goods should be maintained; and that more Americans feel that the United States should collaborate with the British Commonwealth, Western Europe, and Latin America. Yet it should be noted that these ideas are not basically new and that the underlying fundamentals of international relations have undergone no radical change.

Perhaps of all the trends listed, this is the one that might be questioned most in the light of the events occurring in the mid-sixties. Western Europe had emerged as stronger in its industrial and military power, and the Soviet Union had developed a great military force and had become a technical and industrial power. Numerous other nations as well had become stronger, and seemingly were challenging the leadership of America. Questions were, therefore, being raised concerning America's relative strength and also her ability as a world leader. It might well be that in the decade to come, the concept of one nation taking upon itself the responsibility for the entire world will cease to be. At the moment, however, the United States, by virtue of its industrial and military power, is the leader of the world. It is the only single nation that possesses financial, economic, and military power to exercise this leadership. This fact has not made America popular in the world, either among her friends or those who consider America to be their enemy. All this, of course, leads to some confusion in appraising the implications of America's position of world leadership. This will be discussed somewhat in the next paragraph and also more at length in Chapter 13.

There are differences of opinion as to what some of the above implications mean for the school. (1) There is a particularly vociferous minority opposed to all efforts of the United States that jeopardize even slightly its sovereignty, even by participating in such organizations as the United Nations. This group is particularly fearful of such organizations as UNESCO (see Chapter 13). It opposes all efforts of the school to teach international-mindedness and to give information concerning UNESCO if this means, as they think it does, jeopardization of the patriotic love for America and a consequent weakening of nationalism as far as American citizens are concerned. (2) The majority of educators apparently are in favor of teaching for better understanding of the other peoples of the world in which we can work together more cooperatively. (3) There is a small minority who feel that the school ought to teach more positively ways in which we could strengthen international cooperation, including the possibilities of world government. The history of the world has been, of course, the progression of government from the level of the family to the tribe to the small nation, then to the present large nations that are predominant in the modern world. The next step, say these persons, is a government at the world level; and the schools ought to do their job of preparing people for this final and logical step, which would lead to world order and peace.

PERSISTENT VALUES IN AMERICAN CULTURE

In spite of the changes indicated by the twelve preceding trends, there are other ways in which the United States remains primarily the same, and these lie in the ideas that Americans hold dear. In many ways ideas are the heart of a nation's power; and most certainly Americans cherish the conception of liberty and man's place in society—a heritage derived from the Magna Carta and John Locke among other sources. Although there are varying interpretations among our 190 million odd people, generally Americans still believe in such ideas as respect for truth, rule of law, sanctity of human life, open-minded critical inquiry, and freedom of the individual and of the mind. Many of these ideas are as old as America itself; most have remained basically the same throughout all of American history, although means advocated or used to achieve them may have changed radically.[43]

Americans in the postwar period appear to be in general agreement that our nation and the world have reached a turning point or crossroads. They seem to feel that the decisions and events of the next few years will fix the course of history for a long time to come. It may be that the atomic and hydrogen bombs, the prospect of space exploration, and the clash between the United States and Russia are the major conditioning factors of the period; but some writers have taken care to point out that there are problems of other kinds: economic rehabilitation and a more equitable distribution of income, overpopulation, the exhaustion of natural resources, general lawlessness, mass education, racial discrimination, and the utilization of the blessings of medical science. Unfortunately, technical advances have outstripped advances in the social sciences. America knows how to produce; but it has not solved the distribution problem *at home*. In spite of its obvious domestic failures, as evidenced by the masses of the poverty stricken and swelling welfare rolls, America aspires to world leadership through helping the underdeveloped nations of the world to solve their problems both of production and of distribution. Social inventions are badly needed, if Western culture as we know it is to survive.

The solution of the problem of the control of nuclear energy and others related to it must involve not only science, economics, and politics, but also philosophy, religion, and ethics. There are some grounds for hope that a solution may be reached, for the religious and philosophical problems of today are increasingly concerned with the place of the individual in society and the relation of society to the individual. To improve the material standards of living of the people of today is a mission commanding the same kind of moral fervor as formerly went into the task of winning their souls. There are some indications that mutual respect, cooperation, and understanding are increasing. A large number of organizations seeking racial and religious understanding have appeared in the last few years, and in 1946 the World Council of Churches had an auspicious beginning.

The question of freedom is at the center of the political and social

[43] Further discussion of the agreements and disagreements concerning the nature of American democracy appears in Chapter 14.

problems. It has been estimated that nearly three out of every ten Americans are not sure that everyone should have the five freedoms advocated in America, and one authority has found that 17 per cent of Americans would deprive others of certain rights.[44] This is a forceful reminder that freedom has to be fought for in every generation. If America is to survive, Americans must face the issue squarely. There are two choices. She may try to achieve (through Marshall Plan, Peace Corps, etc.) a reality of all freedoms in an understanding, interrelated world. She may elect self-preservation through military dominance, as indicated in Korea and in Viet Nam.

An interrelated world appeared to be a possibility at the close of World War II; but events since that time seem to indicate that instead there is a divided, two-power world. Both powers, the United States and Russia, advance claims of being truly "democratic," although the Americans tend to measure democracy in political terms and the Russians to measure it in terms of economics.[45] The United States, and for that matter all Western countries, according to Toynbee, have recently become aware of the challenge of the economic democracy implied in communism, since there is "an irresistible encroachment of planning in the once-unregimented economics of the democratic countries."[46] On the other hand, the Russians have put up a case for political democracy; they conceive the working class and peasants as the majority of the nation, and therefore they argue that the "proletarian democracy" expresses the "will" of the great masses of people more clearly than does the "bourgeois democracy" of the United States.[47]

There is little doubt that Russian Communistic ideas have had a tremendous influence in Eastern and Central Europe, an influence that John Gunther believes to be the "permanent transforming force" of a contemporary revolution that "can no more be ignored than that of the industrial revolution of a century ago."[48] The extent of direct Communistic influence within the United States, in spite of Toynbee's insight, is more problematical. The question, however, in which Americans are intensely interested is whether the great powers will engage in a struggle that might destroy Western civilization or whether they can peacefully coexist.

The challenge of the Soviet/Sino philosophy to the educational ideas of the United States is significant. If the educational system of this country is to meet the challenge successfully, it must inspire a continual struggle for freedom, for a living democracy, for a better distribution of worldly goods, and for the extension of democratic privileges to all the people.

[44] Elmo Roper, "How the Public Feels About Some Freedoms in America," *Pittsburgh Post-Gazette*, May 19, 1948, p. 10.
[45] Edmund J. King (ed), *Communist Education* (Indianapolis, Ind.: Bobbs-Merrill, 1963), pp. 18–27.
[46] Toynbee, *A Study of History, op. cit.*, p. 400.
[47] King, *op. cit.*, p. 5.
[48] John Gunther, *Behind the Curtain* (New York: Harper, 1949), p. 335.

These are the goals. The procedures and techniques are yet to be developed.

SELECTED BIBLIOGRAPHY

ALLEN, FREDERICK LEWIS. *The Big Change: America Transforms Itself, 1900–1950.* New York: Harper & Row, 1952. Pp. xi + 308. A very interesting and penetrating (although popularly written) review of the effect of technological and social change on the average American's thinking since 1900.

ARENDT, HANNAH. *On Revolution.* New York: Viking Press, 1963. Pp. 343.

BELL, DANIEL (ed.). *The Radical Right: The American Right, Expanded and Updated.* Garden City, N. Y.: Doubleday, 1963. Pp. xiii + 394.

BRICKMAN, WILLIAM W., and STANLEY LEHRER (eds.). *Automation Education, and Human Values.* New York: School and Society Books, 1966. Pp. 419.

BRUCKBERGER, RAYMOND LEOPOLD. *Image of America.* New York: Viking Press, 1959. Pp. x + 277.

Center for the Study of Democratic Institution. *A Conversation: The American Character.* Santa Barbara, Calif.: The Fund for the Republic, 1962. Pp. 48.

COGLEY, JOHN, *et al. The American Character: A Conversation.* Santa Barbara, Calif.: Center for the Study of Democratic Institutions, 1962. Pp. 47.

COMMAGER, HENRY STELLE (ed.). *The American Mind: An Interpretation of American Thought and Character Since the 1800's.* New Haven: Yale University Press, 1950. Pp. 476.

CURTI, MERLE. *American Paradox: The Conflict Between Thought and Action.* New Brunswick, N.J.: Rutgers University Press, 1956. Pp. 116.

EDWARDS, NEWTON, and HERMAN G. RICHEY. *The School in the American Social Order,* Second Edition. Boston: Houghton Mifflin, 1963. Pp. xi + 694. Some excellent material on the topic, particularly on the economic and industrial aspects.

FOSTER, GEORGE M. *Traditional Cultures and the Impact of Technological Change.* New York: Harper & Row, 1962. Pp. xiii + 292.

FRIEDENBERG, EDGAR Z. *Coming of Age in America: Growth and Acquiescence.* New York: Random House, 1965. Pp. xii + 300.

GRODZIN, MORTON, and EUGENE RABINOWITCH (eds.). *The Atomic Age: Scientists in National and World Affairs.* New York: Basic Books, 1963. Pp. xiii + 616.

HENRY, JULES. *Culture Against Man.* New York: Random House, 1963. Pp. xiv + 495. A critical examination of contemporary American culture.

LERNER, MAX. *America as a Civilization: Life and Thought in the United States.* New York: Simon & Schuster, 1957. Pp. xiii + 1036. An extremely well-written and thorough analysis of American civilization presented from a liberal point of view but on the whole factual and objective.

MARTINDALE, DON. *American Social Structure: Historical Antecedents and Contemporary Analysis.* New York: Appleton-Century-Crofts, 1960. Pp. xiv + 521.

MILLS, C. WRIGHT. *The Power Elite*. New York: Oxford University Press, 1956. Pp. 423.

N.E.A., AMERICAN ASSOCIATION OF SCHOOL ADMINISTRATION. *Social Change and Education* (Thirteenth Yearbook). Washington, D.C.: National Education Association, 1953. Pp. 384.

NEF, JOHN. *Civilization, Industrial Society, and Love*. New York: The Center and the Fund for the Republic, 1961. Pp. 13.

POTTER, DAVID M. *People of Plenty: Economic Abundance and the American Character*. Chicago: University of Chicago Press, 1955. Pp. xxvii + 219. An excellent analysis of the relationship of the "American character" to American economic abundance.

RIESMAN, DAVID, and others. *The Lonely Crowd: A Study of the Changing American Character*. New Haven: Yale University Press, 1950. Pp. xvii + 386. A thorough detailed study of a hypothesis about the different types of Americans and the changes in the past few years.

ROSENBERG, BERNARD, and DAVID MANNING WHITE (eds.). *Mass Culture: The Popular Arts in America*. New York: Free Press of Glencoe, 1957. Pp. x + 560. An excellent symposium on the culture of the American masses; covers many areas and points of view.

SCHLESINGER, ARTHUR M., JR., and MORTON WHITE (eds.). *Paths of American Thought*. Boston: Houghton Mifflin, 1963. Pp. viii + 614.

SPILLER, ROBERT E., and ERIE DARRABEE (eds.). *American Perspectives: The National Self-Image in the Twentieth Century*. Cambridge, Mass.: Harvard University Press, 1961. Pp. vii + 216.

SWEET, WILLIAM. *Religion in the Development of American Culture, 1765–1840*. New York: Scribner, 1952. Pp. xiv + 358.

TOQUEVILLE, ALEXIS DE. *Democracy in America*. New York: New American Library, 1956. Pp. 317.

TURNER, FREDERICK JACKSON. *The Frontier in American History*. New York: Holt, Rinehart & Winston, 1920. Pp. 375.

TOWNSEND, HARVEY GATES. *Philosophic Ideas in the United States*. New York: American Book, 1934. Pp. v + 293.

WATSON, G. (ed.). *No Room at the Bottom: Automation and the Reluctant Learner*. Washington, D.C.: National Education Association, 1963. Pp. ix + 112.

WATTENBERG, BEN J. *This U.S.A.* Garden City, N.Y.: Doubleday, 1965. Pp. 520. "An Unexpected Family Portrait of 194, 067, 296 (March 31, 1965) Americans Drawn from the Census."

WHITE, M. C. *Social Thought in America*. New York: Viking Press, 1949. Pp. viii + 260. Very good historical development of liberal thought in United States up to 1930. Covers principles of Beard, Holmes, Veblen, and Dewey.

SELECTED FILMS

The Age of Specialization (McGraw-Hill) 13 min
> In a country store in 1900, a farmer, shoemaker, store owner and country doctor speculate about changes the new century will bring in their occupations. The contrast between the work done by the four men in 1900

and that done today is vividly drawn through technological changes in production, communication, and transportation.

American Farmer (Ford Motor Co.) 28 min

An intimate and beautifully photographed story of a modern farmer and the changes wrought in his life by mechanization and scientific farming.

The American Road (Ford Motor Co.) 25 min

An excellent film of the changes in American culture brought about by changing technology, particularly changes in transportation.

Automation—Part I (McGraw-Hill) 34 min

The film points out the effect of automation on the work of various people. It compares the fabrication of a specific item by new method and by method standard five years earlier. It explores the many problems connected with the revolutionary development of automation.

Automation—Part II (McGraw-Hill) 25 min

The film illustrates automation in this country in the field of communication. In addition the film depicts the problems created and their effect upon human relationships involving leisure time, unemployment and re-training.

Automation—Part III (McGraw-Hill) 25 min

Views of the payroll division of a large corporation show how paper work is being taken over by machines and lead to predictions of new industries resulting from the trend. The film shows that what is taking place is really an intellectual revolution, challenging teachers as well as workers.

Cities: Why They Grow (Coronet Films) 10 min

A study of our increasing urban population. By departing from the usual statistics and the sociological problems that are a result of the cities' growth, we learn that by observing what the workers of the city do we can find out why the city grew.

Expanding World Relationships (U.S. State Dept.) 11 min

Contrasts the slow transportation and communication of Thomas Jefferson's day with the machine age, in which technological advances have lightened men's work and brought all the countries of the world into close contact and interdependence on raw materials and manufactured goods; emphasizes the necessity for worldwide cooperation.

Four Teachers (Nat'l Film Board of Canada) 60 min

Filmed in Japan, Poland, Puerto Rico, and Canada, *Four Teachers* presents many illuminating comparisons of the world of the classroom, of student-teacher relationships, of the status of the teacher in the community, of the importance placed on education in these four countries.

H-Bomb over U.S. (Public Affairs Films) 10 min

A clear and direct scientific estimate of the impact of a 10 megaton H-Bomb warhead on Los Angeles (as an example of a large U.S. city). The film presents no program of solutions; it does provide a clear, lively and vital basis for discussion of civilian and military defense programs and the physical and moral aspects of nuclear war.

How Do American Schools Compare with Yours? (NET) 29 min

A forum with representatives comparing their school with American. Includes Australia, Guatemala, Norway, and Turkey.

The Individual in the Modern World (Association) 28 min

A provocative discussion of the crucial problems a rapidly-changing industrial civilization has created in the 20th century.

Man in the Twentieth Century (CS-573) 18 min

Discusses the fact that Man's material progress is now at a higher peak than ever before, but that his daily routine is often one of dissatisfaction. Although he wants peace, his world is split into two conflicting philosophies—communism and democracy. Emphasizes the fact that through public education and the United Nations, man is looking toward peace.

Man Who Changed the World (TFC) 11 min

Story of James Hargreaves, English spinner, whose invention of the spinning jenny in 1767 laid the foundation for the machine age. How the conflict between man and machine came about.

Passion for Life (Brandon) (full-length feature)

A dramatic French film with English subtitles describing how a schoolmaster vitalized learning in a village. His activities are atypical and represent a protest against the traditional French school. However, the film depicts some activities, such as the oral examination system, which are common in French schools.

Satellites, Schools, and Survival (N.E.A.) 28 min

A pictorial history of education in the U.S. during the last half century. Points up the challenge of present problems. Shows close relationship of the American system of education to survival as free nation. Interviews supplemented by dramatized section on our school since 1900 and a present-day class at work.

The Second Hundred Years (Crane Co.) 27 min

Traces an exciting hundred years of progress in America, with a glimpse of the future, in the colorful record of a pioneering company's growth to supply our modern comforts.

Section 16 (N.E.A.) 14 min

Traces the history of public education in America from the Dame Schools of early New England through the colonial schools of Pennsylvania, the one-room schools of the Middle West, the mission schools of the Far West, the accomplishments of Horace Mann and other leaders in education, up to the public schools of today. Narrated by Raymond Massey.

Schools of Mexico (Ind.) 10 min

Presents a comprehensive view of educational institutions, from the ultra-modern Ministry of Ed. in Mexico City to remote one-room adobe schools far in the interior. Includes normal schools, vocational and agricultural institutions, and kindergartens.

Social Revolution (EBF) 17 min

Traces the social changes during the past two hundred years.

Techniques for Tomorrow (Ford Motor Co.) 25 min

A description of one of the new automatic factories—an engine plant near Cleveland—and what it means for industry.

Village School (BIS) 12 min

This documentary on education illustrates the philosophy underlying the British system of education.

Chapter 5. *The Development of the American Economy: Problems and Alternatives*

IN THE PRECEDING CHAPTER, the over-all social trends in the United States were traced, with some mention of the developing American technology and of the American economy in general. In this chapter the development of the American economy will be described in greater detail.

In order to understand what is happening in the American economy, including the expansion of productivity, and the increasing complexities of distribution in an urban, industrialized society, it is necessary that we trace the history of the economy from the time of the American Revolution. In general, this history starts with what has been called "laissez-faire" economics, the principles of which were more nearly realized in the early American frontier period than any other time in American history, as was pointed out in the preceding chapter. Well before the Civil War, it had in practice broken down in a number of aspects. Governmental aid to home industries through tariff and the expansion of American industry through the rise of various large companies and the consequent monopolies were all part of this picture, to be more fully discussed later. The Industrial Revolution, which took place in Europe in the 1790's and which hit America in the early 1800's, was one factor underlying the increase in productivity in the United States. However, as will be pointed out in more detail later in this chapter, America has been hit by a series of industrial revolutions, each of a different nature.

OVER-ALL TRENDS IN THE AMERICAN ECONOMY

Several over-all trends can be identified and will be given more attention later.

1. The first of these trends is the development of the laissez-faire economy and its subsequent breakdown due to forces most of which

123

originated within the economy itself. Other forces were changes in the nature of the emerging technology and in the structure of industrial enterprises.

2. The most outstanding of all these trends is, perhaps, the enormous expansion in productivity, in agriculture, in industry, in transportation, and in communication; most of this increase is a direct result of modern technological change. This is America's continual revolution.

3. Another outstanding change that took place during this period was the rise of the capitalistic system of control of the economy, as opposed to the small-shop and handicraft system of the earlier period. It is likely that Adam Smith had in mind the very small enterprises with which he was familiar in his day (1750–1780) rather than the large finance-controlled capitalistic enterprises that began to emerge after the Civil War and are quite typical of our industrial system in the latter half of the twentieth century. The development of the corporate system and the control of industry by corporations (rather than by single entrepreneurs or by partnerships) were only two of the factors that enabled large companies to develop. These large corporations could devote themselves completely to the dictates of profit and "good business," irrespective of any kind of moral purposes to maintain some responsibility for the general welfare of their employees. This attitude was scarcely noticeable (even to a small extent) in the period immediately following the Civil War. The development of "big" business, as opposed to the prevalence of small business, is seen by most students as a necessary characteristic of the development of American technology.

4. From 1870 to some time following the early 1920's, nearly the entire economy of America shifted from one of scarcity to one of plenty. From the 1920's on, our main problem in peacetime had become: How can we distribute the products of our factories and farms in such a way as not to cause the goods to pile up on our shelves? The problem was to work out some system of distribution—some relationship between wages, availability of products, prices, and the maximum efficiency of the production system—that would enable the economy to keep operating without being flooded with unsold goods as it was during the period of 1929–1937 depression. There is practically no question but that the prevailing problems of our economy today arise out of conditions of plenty, rather than out of those of scarcity that had been characteristic of almost all economic systems of the world up to modern times.

5. Finally, then, the over-all trends in American economy reveal a shift from the laissez-faire capitalism of the early period toward a mixture of both corporation and state capitalism with some cooperatives, some state socialism, and some small private enterprise.

After a comparison of American productivity to that of other nations in the next section, the development and current extent of each of the preceding trends will be discussed. The way in which the productive processes are geared with the economy and the way in which the money economy operates in our system will also be described later in this chapter. In the latter part of this chapter we will take up in more detail the problems faced by the economy and will explore the possible alternatives to be used in attempting to solve them.

AMERICAN PRODUCTIVITY COMPARED TO THAT OF OTHER NATIONS

The full significance of the trends in the American economy can be understood only as economic development in the United States is compared with that of the rest of the world. The people of the United States have lived better than those of other countries. This is true in the twentieth century even if we compare our periods of depression to the best times in other countries. The United States has approximately one fifteenth of the world's population and about the same proportion of the world's land area and natural resources, yet the United States:

1. Produces about half the world's manufactured goods.
2. Has more than half the world's telephone, telegraph, and radio networks, more than a third of the railroads.
3. Has more than three-quarters of the world's automobiles.
4. Has almost half of the world's radios and consumes more than half of the world's coffee and rubber, over half of the steel, one half of the coal, and nearly two-thirds of the crude oil.[1]

The comparison of this American productivity with that of other countries can perhaps best be shown by such concrete illustrations as those in Table 1. This shows a comparison of cost in dollars and of work time for certain commodities in the year 1964 in the United States and in the Soviet Union. It is true that some of the well-industrialized democracies can more nearly equal the United States in this respect.

It is also instructive to see the annual Gross National Product (GNP) per person (defined later in this chapter) in the leading countries of the world, expressing all GNP's in American dollars. Figure 1 illustrates this.

The increase in American productivity that has brought about its world leadership has been accompanied by an ever-decreasing work week. In the early part of the nineteenth century, the handworker usually had to work from twelve to sixteen hours a day to make a living. Now the five-day, forty-hour week is quite common.

[1] Adapted from "The Miracle of America" (pamphlet), p. 12 (New York: The Advertising Council, Inc., n.d.). Used by permission.

TABLE 1

COMPARATIVE COST IN U.S. $ AND MINUTES OF WORK REQUIRED TO
PRODUCE SELECTED ITEMS IN THE U.S.A. AND THE SOVIET UNION

	Cost in U.S. $		Work Time in Minutes	
Item	*N.Y.*	*Moscow*	*N.Y.*	*Moscow*
Loaf Bread	$ .27	$ .13	8 min.	16 min.
Macaroni, lb.	.22	.23	5.5 min.	24 min.
Rice, lb.	.23	.48	6 min.	54 min.
Beefsteak, 2 lb.	1.75	1.76	46 min.	190 min.
Pork, 2 lbs.	1.35	2.10	35 min.	225 min.
Chicken, 2 lbs.	.88	2.93	23 min.	315 min.
Sugar, 2 lbs.	.25	1.00	6.6 min.	107 min.
Milk, qt.	.28	.66	7 min.	72 min.
Coffee, lb.	.95	2.50	26 min.	267 min.
Vodka, qt.	4.29	6.75	112 min.	729 min.
Taxi	1.00	3.30	26 min.	356 min.
Subway	.15	.06	3.9 min.	6.5 min.
Movies	2.00	.50	52 min.	54 min.
Haircut, men	1.75	.55	46 min.	59 min.
Newspaper	.10	.02	2.6 min.	2.2 min.

Source: Estimates from Radio Liberty quoted in Sylvia Porter, "Your Money's Worth,"
Cincinnati *Post and Times-Star,* November 11, 1964. Used by permission.

Laissez-faire Economics and Its Breakdown

A set of principles and practices that can best be termed "laissez-faire" economics was accepted by the American people quite early in the development of the American economy. Adam Smith had published his book, *Wealth of Nations,* in 1776, just at the time when the American colonists found it necessary to formulate for themselves an economic theory under which to operate. The American people had a fear of government regulation based on their colonial experience, and like John Locke they held a rather negative conception of the place of the state.

The Nature of Laissez-faire Economics

The theory of Adam Smith, which came to be known as "laissez faire," was based upon a few fundamental ideas or basic assumptions. The economic system would be characterized by very small businesses or productive enterprises, such as small firms, factories, and shops. These would compete with each other to produce and exchange the necessary goods and services. The competition of the numerous, independent, small producers on an open market would operate automatically to regulate prices. This market mechanism would serve, without the necessity for any positive governmental policy to coordinate it, to self-regulate all of the activities that made up the economic life of the people in the best possible fashion. Not only was the government to interfere as little as possible except in

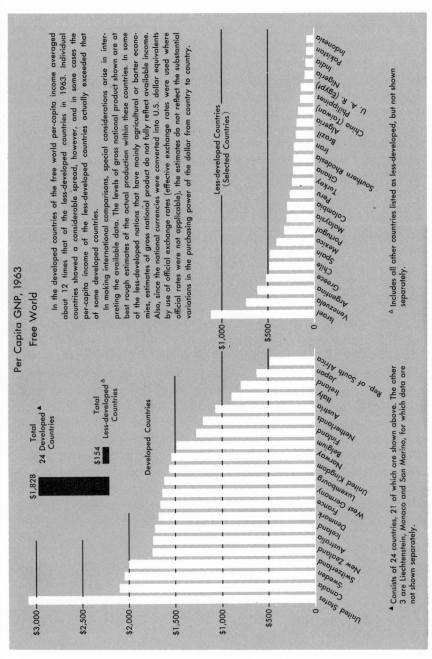

Figure 1. Gross National Product per Capita (1962) in Selected Countries.
Used by permission National Industrial Conference © 1964.

cases of downright fraud, but any important interference by the government would theoretically serve to destroy or upset the balance that would be automatically brought about in the free play of competition on the market.

As noted above, in laissez-faire economics a great number of small, independent producers of various kinds and the absence of any kind of restraint of trade, either governmental or otherwise, were presumed. It was assumed that, if each of these small independent producers operated in a way that was best for his own immediate self-interest, the entire system would operate for the best interest of the economy as a whole. If there was a producer who was charging too high prices, he could not sell his product on the market. He would then be forced to bring his prices down. If there was a producer who was putting out inferior products, he also would not be able to sell on the market at the same price and would therefore be forced to reduce his price or not be able to sell his product. In any case, he would be driven out of the market unless there was a demand for a cheap, inferior product. To summarize, the characteristics of the economic system were private property; the profit motive; free competition; flexible prices; and little or no government interference with business.[2]

Although the conditions that were present on the new American continent shortly after the Revolution fulfilled very nearly the assumptions of Adam Smith's theory, it is doubtful if his conditions ever were fulfilled perfectly anywhere at any time. It would be extremely difficult for a free market, in the modern stage of transportation and communication, to prevent one successful business from becoming large and monopolizing the market or dominating it in such a way as to be able to control prices so that they were not freely set by the market. One of the interesting points about the history of American thought has been the persistence of the American people, and in many cases also of their intellectual spokesmen, in talking about the perpetuation of the laissez-faire type of economy long after it had been drastically modified. What we were *doing* in the gradual abandonment of laissez-faire practices, and what we were still *saying* about the central ideas of our economy, were quite often different.

Breakdown of Laissez-faire Before the Civil War

The government of the young American nation broke away from its neutral position in economic affairs quite early, as evidenced by the establishment of high tariffs for the protection of "infant" industries, bounties to the railroads, patent rights, and, later on, the giving away of the free land as homesteads in the West.

Conditions in early nineteenth-century America were very favorable for

[2] Newton Edwards and Herman G. Richey, *The School in the American Social Order*, Second Edition (Boston: Houghton, 1963), p. 465.

the expansion of an economic system. We had a virgin continent of excellent resources. We started our government at a time when the Industrial Revolution was getting under way, so that, in addition to the possibilities for the exploitation of our abundant natural resources, there was an opportunity to build our industries in accordance with the technological advances of the time. Our country was experiencing a rapid growth of population, including, of course, that which came about through the influx of immigrants throughout this period.

The laissez-faire system partially broke down, then, when government began to participate as more than an interested, neutral spectator. The participation usually was in favor of business enterprise. However, laissez-faire also broke down partially in the agitation for laws controlling conditions of work. For example, the establishment of the textile mills in New England, which should have brought a greater prosperity to the people, seemed to lead to the crowding of workers into cities, with relatively low wages, a long work week, and deplorably low living conditions. Conditions became so bad that many humanitarians of the 1830's and 1840's were agitating for various kinds of reform laws, such as the reduction of the work week and child-labor prohibitions.

Corporate Monopoly Practices As a Threat to Laissez-faire

There was, therefore, some breakdown of laissez-faire before the Civil War. But this breakdown was greatly increased in the period immediately following the war. The advent of the corporation as a prominent form of ownership of industrial enterprise, and the extension of legal and constitutional protection to the corporation as a person under Supreme Court decisions, led to a tremendous expansion in the size and power of the corporations in the postwar period.

It was estimated that, in 1904, there were 26 trusts that controlled about 80 per cent of the production in their respective fields. Of these 26 trusts, 8 controlled 90 per cent or more of the output of their respective products. Among these trusts were those that specialized in tin cans, cigarettes, agricultural machinery, oil, and shoe machinery. These corporations were the object of a vigorous "trust-busting" campaign during the administration of Theodore Roosevelt. This crusade actually did not break up very many trusts. As a matter of fact, no satisfactory answer to the problem of large business has as yet been worked out.[3]

In 1946 an investigation made by a special governmental committee (included in the report *Economic Concentration and World War II*) showed that the 200 largest nonfinancial corporations, leaving out such firms as those in banking, owned 33.3 per cent of the total assets of all

[3] Clifford L. James, *Economics: Basic Problems and Analysis* (New York: Prentice-Hall, 1951), p. 111.

the nonfinancial corporations in 1909, 43 per cent of them in 1929, and 55 per cent in 1933.[4]

In addition to the concentration of assets into a relatively few corporations, there was an increasing tendency for only a minority of the stockowners to be in actual control, since the rest of them usually were apathetic or disorganized. A study made in 1933 showed that the Rockefeller family was controlling Standard Oil of New Jersey with holdings of 20 per cent of the outstanding stock. Similarly, the Du Pont interests controlled General Motors with holdings amounting to only 32.6 per cent of the outstanding stock.[5]

The fact that a great number of people in the United States did own some stock does not alter the fact that the stock was concentrated in the hands of a few. For example, in an investigation made in 1937, it was found that 8 million persons in the United States received all of the dividend payments reported by all corporations for that year. However, the Temporary National Economic Commission, which made this report, found that more than half of the total dividend payments received by individuals went to persons numbering fewer than 75,000, less than 1 per cent of the total number of stockholders in the nation.[6]

Most authorities hesitate to indicate the effect of World War II and the postwar period on economic concentration, some indicating that there has been a lessening of concentration and some indicating an increase. However, a government document cited earlier, *Economic Concentration and World War II*, indicated that from June, 1940, through September, 1944, of the $175 billion in contracts that were awarded to 18,539 corporations by the federal government, two thirds of the total amount went to the top 100 corporations and about 30 per cent to 10 corporations alone. It is true that these large corporations did some subcontracting to smaller firms, but even then three-fourths of the subcontracts were awarded to other large firms (firms with over 500 workers). These same top 100 corporations were responsible for the construction of 51 per cent of privately financed war production facilities and for the operation of 75 per cent of the value of government-owned facilities.[7]

Some of the corporations, such as the Aluminum Corporation of America, lost part of their leadership in the field due to the effect of the heavy demand on the output of some of the smaller companies. It is also true that the effect of the income tax probably led to some reduction in

[4] U.S. Special Committee Report, *Economic Concentration and World War II*, Senate Document No. 206, 79th Congress, Second Sess., pp. 6, 352 (Washington, D.C.: Govt. Printing Office, 1946).

[5] Adolph A. Berle and Gardiner C. Means, *The Modern Corporation and Private Property* (New York: Macmillan, 1933), pp. 102–103.

[6] U.S. Temporary National Economic Committee, Monograph No. 29, *The Distribution of Ownership in 200 Largest Non-financial Corporations*, p. 13 (Washington, D.C.: Govt. Printing Office, 1940).

[7] U.S. Special Committee Report, *op. cit.*, pp. 29–33, 47.

the amount of total relative wealth held by individuals, and thus at least a reduction in the concentration of industry into the hands of a few corporations and of the control of a particular industry in the hands of a few individuals, if it did not stop it completely.

In the above discussion there is no attempt to point out that either size or concentration is bad or good. As a matter of fact, there is a difference of opinion among students of the problem, some indicating that the large corporation was an inevitable result of the trends taking place in American industry. It is true that in some respects the large corporations, by using mass methods, were able to produce goods much more cheaply than could many inefficient, small corporations. However, there was considerable evidence of price leadership and of agreements concerning price in some cases where there was still quality competition among firms, such as among the typewriter companies. A study of the changes in prices that had come about in the period from 1926 through 1938, under the effects of the depression, indicated that there was a considerable difference in the amount of drop as a result of that depression. In a government report prepared by Gardiner C. Means, it was found that in the "administered-price" group (that is, cases in which there was an almost complete control of the prices of a given commodity[8]) prices fell from 1927 to 1935 by about 10 per cent. In the case of the "market-price" group, where prices were set largely on the basis of what the product could bring in the market, there was a fall of more than 50 per cent during the period from 1927 to 1932. By 1935 prices had come back to within 25 per cent of what they had been in 1927.[9]

TECHNOLOGICAL CHANGE: AMERICA'S PERMANENT REVOLUTION

In an earlier section it was pointed out that American productivity had been made possible through tremendous changes in technology. "Technology" refers to the methods used in the productive process. It relates to the production of both goods and services. Technological change may increase both the quantity and quality of both goods and services. In the following sections it is planned to spell out a little more fully the extent of the technological change that has taken place in America.

The Extent of America's Technological Change

The following point is clear in any discussion of technology. The output per man-hour has increased over a long period of years. This has been

---

[8] This discussion does not mean to imply that all cases of administered prices are due to corporation decisions or collusion. Policies of labor unions or even government regulations may contribute to it.

[9] U.S. National Resources Planning Commission, *The Structure of the American Economy*, Part I: *Basic Characteristics*, pp. 145–147. A report prepared by the Industrial Section under the direction of Gardiner C. Means (Washington, D.C.: Govt. Printing Office, 1939).

especially noticeable since 1929. The ability of this country to take care of civilian needs quite satisfactorily while maintaining supplies for an army of some 11 million men and giving aid to its allies during World War II indicates that this technological efficiency had improved. We do not have as accurate figures on the amount of recent technological change as we did before the war. With the advent since World War II of automation (to be discussed more fully in the next section), there apparently has been another enormous increase in the technology. A rise of 35 per cent in production in American industry from 1947 to 1955 illustrates vividly the technological change that was taking place at that time.[10]

The increase in the pre-World War II period was striking. In 1936 Mordecai Ezekiel reported that the annual output per worker in agriculture had increased 140 per cent between 1870 and 1930.[11] This would mean that agriculture in 1930 was producing almost two and one-half times as much per worker as it had produced in 1870. These figures, of course, represent changes taking place before the day of the more complete mechanization of agriculture. Comparable figures today would probably reveal an increase since 1930 equal to that from 1870 to 1930.

A study made by the Temporary National Economic Committee indicates that in four big segments of our economy the percentage increase in output per man-hour between 1909 and 1930 was as follows: manufacturing, 163.5; steam railroads, 81.7 (1914 to 1939); bituminous coal mining, 102.7; anthracite mining, 111.1.[12] These figures indicate, for example, that manufacturing had more than doubled—in fact nearly tripled.[13] Some of the reasons for the amount of this technological change will be discussed in the next section. Suffice it to say at this time that there is some evidence that technological change could have been more rapid in some cases had it not been held back by the pressure of monopoly and other interests that benefited by producing products that would not last as long as those products that could have been produced by inventions available at the time.[14]

What are some of the factors underlying the rapid technological changes? Whatever the dynamics back of the changes that did come about, they can be explained in terms of industrial "revolutions." Many history books speak of the Industrial Revolution as an event taking place

[10] Adapted from U.S. Bureau of Labor Statistics.

[11] Mordecai Ezekiel, "Population and Unemployment," *Annals of the American Academy of Political and Social Science,* **189** (November, 1936), pp. 238–239.

[12] U.S. Temporary National Economic Committee, *Technology in Our Economy,* adapted from table, p. 90. Investigations of Concentration of Economic Power, Monograph 22, 66th Congress, 3rd Session Senate Committee (Washington, D.C.: Govt. Printing Office, 1941).

[13] *Ibid.,* pp. 95–96.

[14] See U.S., National Resources Committee, *Technological Trends in National Policy* (Washington, D.C.: Govt. Printing Office). See especially Section IV, pp. 39–66.

at a specific time. In England the date used usually is the late eighteenth century, in America the early nineteenth. Actually what happened is of much longer duration and much more complex. Barnes speaks of these changes in terms of "four" industrial revolutions. The conception as he developed it may give us insight into what has been happening in this respect in America.[15]

The first industrial revolution was the period of the development of new textile machinery in Europe (especially in England) from about 1750 on; of Eli Whitney's cotton gin, appearing in America in 1793; of the steam engine, which provided the power necessary to operate machinery to produce steel, to build better roads and canals, and later, to operate railroads and steamships.

The second industrial revolution took place in America from about the time of the Civil War to perhaps the second decade of the twentieth century. The machinery used became larger. During this period there emerged the vulcanization of rubber and the rubber industry; the petroleum industry and the application of its discoveries to the internal combustion engine; the development of better methods of communication such as the telegraph, telephone, and wireless telegraphy (early radio) of the late 1890's; and the production of high-speed printing presses that increased cheap production of books and magazines for mass reading.

The third industrial revolution could be considered to be the "power age" or the "electric age." One of the characteristics of this age has been the development of the mass-production line brought about partially through the standardization (and therefore interchangeability) of parts.[16] Most of the technological change of the period from 1913 to 1940 can be ascribed to the improvement of production-line techniques, the improvement of the use of power—especially the use of electricity in running very complex machines—and the setting up of automatic machines that require only a minimum of control by the worker. Improvements of radio and the development of better high-speed newspaper processes also occurred during this time.

The fourth industrial revolution could be considered that occasioned by the use of automation and "atomic energy." It is just now beginning to show promise.

Successful atomic power plants eventually will produce power in quantities that were unheard of in the days of the production of electricity from either steam or water power. This will enable some hitherto uneconomic processes to be undertaken, such as the converting of sea water to fresh

[15] Harry Elmer Barnes and Oreen M. Ruedi, *The American Way of Life: An Introduction to the Study of Contemporary Society*, ed. (Englewood Cliffs, N.J.: Prentice-Hall, 1950), pp. 18–24.
[16] Although parts had been standardized by Eli Whitney in his gun factory, the use of the conveyor belt and the highly specialized production line was first put into operation on a large scale by Henry Ford in 1913.

water, the pumping of water from one area to another for irrigation, and the complete automatization of factories run by an abundant supply of power.

Automation itself, of course, is perhaps as important a revolution as any other. It means that the productive process will be made almost completely automatic. From the raw material to the finished product, automatic machines will feed the productive stream in a continuous process with little supervision. This has occurred now in the case of some of the chemical industries where the flow process is possible. It is rapidly becoming widespread in the production of certain items, such as auto engines and TV chassis. At such time as it can be applied to the productive process from raw material to finished product, it will mean another enormous increase in the output per man-hour. Many fewer but more highly skilled persons will be necessary to design, install, maintain, and operate the machines, as compared to the number manufacturing the same product previous to automation. Of course the men released from one process could very well be absorbed in another, as cheaper products could release purchasing power for new products.

Similar changes are taking place in the field of agriculture. With the agricultural methods now available, it is quite likely that one-fifth of our agricultural population with completely efficient methods could produce as much food and other agricultural products as are now being produced.

"U.S.A.: The Permanent Revolution"

Other persons surveying the nature of the technological changes taking place in America have not felt it necessary to analyze the industrial revolution in separate phases, but have spoken of it as a "permanent revolution," industrial and otherwise.[17] This means to these writers that America has always been in a dynamic situation where something was continually happening to change the technology, and the changing technology was influencing other social changes. Consequently, we have never been in a completely static situation. "Revolutionary" changes have been occurring at all times. This has been so continuous that it is incorrect to speak of an "industrial revolution" or a "first industrial revolution." We are undergoing a permanent (or continuous) revolution in many aspects of American life at any given time.

We have traced the development and the decline of laissez-faire as a central set of principles underlying the American economy, and we have considered the nature of technological change and its accompanying industrial revolution. We shall now consider two other important trends in the American economy before making an analysis of the productive process. In the first of these we shall analyze the changing nature of the or-

---

[17] *Fortune* editors in collaboration with Russell W. Davenport, *U.S.A.: The Permanent Revolution* (Englewood Cliffs, N.J.: Prentice-Hall, 1951).

ganization and control of enterprise itself. Then we shall indicate the changes in the relative amounts of different kinds of enterprises present in the structure of our industrial economy.

THE RISE OF BIG BUSINESS AND THE SHIFT TO "MIXED" CAPITALISM

In this section we shall trace the development of the way in which enterprises were owned and operated, as an indication of some of the changes that were occurring. The nature of the ownership and the size of the corporation in particular are central to the discussion. The shift from the economy of scarcity to one of plenty will be detailed. Then the tremendous shift of economic structure to a mixture of corporation and state capitalism, cooperatives, state socialism, and some small private enterprise will be traced.

The Rise of Capitalism, Corporations, "Big" Business

In the earlier period of the application of the laissez-faire philosophy of Adam Smith, most industrial enterprises were conducted as relatively small businesses, quite often owned by one entrepreneur. In many cases they were small shops or small factories employing only a few men. Sometimes the structure of ownership was complicated by a system of partnerships. As technology improved and the nature of the industrial process became more complicated, it was found that the method of establishing corporations provided for more efficient expansion and operation of industrial enterprises. The earlier ownerships or partnerships were not adequate for the size of organization made necessary by the type of economy emerging under the pressure of technological change. The Adam Smith theory could have applied as well to a system of goods exchange without any capital or money economy at all. Of course, the use of money does simplify the problem of exchange. The accumulation of large amounts of money for the purpose of purchasing capital goods or means of production, however, constitutes a contribution that modern money methods have made to a better and more effective organization of our productive process. For this reason we speak of our system as a "capitalistic" system. It is the concentration of the ownership of capital goods, because of the concentration of wealth in the hands of a few persons or a group of people joined in a corporation, that makes the word "capital" significant as applied to our economy.

The corporation, with its board of directors and president operating under a charter granted in most cases by one of the states, was to pursue policies that were fairly flexible and was thus to expand readily to meet the demand for its product. The Supreme Court decisions of the late nineteenth and early twentieth centuries declaring the corporation to be a person in the sight of the law and therefore subject to the protection of the Fourteenth Amendment added to the effectiveness with which the corporation was able to operate in our economy.[18] The rise of capitalism and the discovery that corporations were the most effective way of handling modern mass-production methods led to the rise of big business. This phenomenon has been discussed earlier under the heading of monopoly. However, even in those industries where competition still existed, such as in automobiles, the size of the company seemed to be important in maintaining efficiency of operation. The mergers of many smaller automobile corporations in the 1950's serves to highlight this.

The reasons for the importance of the factor of size in success have been analyzed. In general, it is because large companies have greater operating efficiency than do small ones. David Weintraub indicates that the use of large-scale equipment results in greater efficiency. He says: "The obvious implication of the trend toward larger capacity equipment is that during the recovery period after 1933—as idle plants were being put into operation and as old obsolete machinery was being replaced—considerably smaller capital outlays and less construction of equipment were required than in the middle twenties to secure the same or even an increased volume of output."[19] The ability of some large corporations to control distribution outlets, again for efficiency and economy, illustrates another advantage.

In addition, the Temporary National Economic Commission in their publication *Technology in Our Economy* found that in general the larger enterprises were able to employ a larger amount of electrical energy per man-hour. This same publication shows that these larger enterprises also could afford to employ larger research staffs.[20] This enabled the larger enterprises to refine old products, to create new ones, and to improve the productive process. It was pointed out also by this same publication that the larger companies could more easily control patents, which made for greater economic concentration as well as efficiency. The larger enterprises were also able to provide more readily the huge advertising campaigns requisite to mass merchandising of present products and the introduction of new ones. Crum[21] summarizes the results of his study by saying: "The larger the corporation, the higher is the rate of return on the average; and this relation holds with surprising constancy, in each of the six years 1931–36."

[18] For example, see Hillman M. Bishop and Samuel Handel, *Basic Issues of American Democracy* (New York: Appleton, 1949), pp. 136–141. This contains excerpts of the Supreme Court decision in the case of *Lechner* v. *New York* (1905).

[19] David Weintraub, "Effects of Current and Prospective Technological Developments upon Capital Formation" (pamphlet), pp. 5–6 (Philadelphia: Works Progress Administration, National Research Project, 1939).

[20] U.S. Temporary National Economic Committee, *op. cit.*

[21] William L. Crum, *Corporate Size and Earning Power* (Cambridge: Harvard University Press, 1939), p. 32.

The Shift from an Economy of "Scarcity" to One of "Plenty"

The history of mankind up until recent times (and of the major part of the world even at present) has been one of a continual striving for food and the other necessities of life in an environment in which there was not enough to go around. The population and the desires and needs of the people have increased, by and large, more rapidly than has their ability to produce food and other necessities. A factor in this "scarcity" of course has been the increasingly higher standard of living based upon an increasingly higher level of aspiration of mankind from the days of the cave man.

It has only been in the last few years, however, that at any point on the earth's surface a people was able to produce goods in such great quantities as to raise a serious problem of how to distribute those goods more equitably. The technological changes described are now coming about at such a rapid pace in America as to make this problem more acute.

In one of the most comprehensive surveys of American economic directions of recent years, financed by the Twentieth Century Fund, Dewhurst,[22] predicted that the trend in America would continue to be to have much more goods per person than ever before. The growth in the national product is rising at a more rapid rate than the growth in the labor force. The average income per family even when translated back into the constant dollars is such that the amount of equivalent dollars to be spent for household income each year is growing more rapidly than the price of the product. Although this rosy picture of the American economic system is blurred somewhat by the stubbornly high rate of unemployment and the threat of a higher rate through the increased automation, it is likely that the rate of productivity will continue to rise and therefore the work week will continue to drop. The effects of automation on the amount of technological unemployment, on the possibility of an accelerated shift from skills no longer usable, and on greater demands for highly trained persons to the detriment of those that are unskilled and to some extent untrainable are not known. One thing at least is certain—that, barring unforeseen economic or other type of disaster, the productivity of a highly industrialized nation has the capability of reaching to "astronomical" heights.

THE SHIFT FROM LAISSEZ-FAIRE CAPITALISM TOWARD A MIXED CAPITALISM. The third major trend is away from simple laissez-faire capitalism toward a mixture of many forms of structure for various enterprises.

We have noted that the predominant pattern of small enterprises of various kinds, operated largely by individual entrepreneurs, continued throughout the Revolutionary period, not only with respect to the farms but also with respect to most of the small shops and industry. The exception in the case of farms was in the New Amsterdam-Hudson Valley, where there were some large tracts owned by the Dutch patroons, where

---

[22] J. Frederick Dewhurst, *America's Needs and Resources: A New Survey* (New York: Twentieth Century Fund, 1955).

other persons worked for the owner. There were also some large plantations in the South, the growth of which was accelerated with the increase in slavery.

In the period from the American Revolution to the Civil War, there was increase in the amount of enterprise controlled by those with money as opposed to that owned by the worker himself and run by him with a few assistants or apprentices. The period preceding the Revolutionary War could scarcely be called one of laissez-faire capitalism, since it was dominated by laissez-faire enterprises in which the worker had very little financial commitment other than his shop. In the succeeding period between the two wars, the change was in the direction of what can more nearly be called laissez-faire capitalism, since control through money was more predominant. In the period following the Civil War there was a rapid trend toward control by means of the corporation. The tendency for our production system to be dominated by one or a few corporations led to corporation capitalism and away from the strictly laissez-faire type.

In addition to this trend toward corporation capitalism, there was also a trend toward to what Barnes has called a "state capitalism." This term is used here in the sense of the controls by state, national, or other branches of government over the policies and practices of private enterprise. Historically, this starts with the latter part of the nineteenth century when controls were established over the railroads as a result of the Populist revolt that occurred in the Midwest, largely over the inequity of railroad rates. These controls soon spread to cover many of the other so-called "public utilities." These are businesses that are privately owned but are monopolistic by their very nature, because competition has no practical way of manifesting itself. Examples are electricity, gas facilities, and the telephone. In addition to the controls that were established over rates and other such matters in the public-utility field, there was, of course, the later establishment of workman's compensation laws and other laws dealing with minimum wages and conditions of work, applying to all industries. These amounted to control over the policies of all private enterprise. Then in the 1930's there was a movement toward unemployment insurance and other laws dealing with minimum wages and conditions of work, again applying to all industries. These and other social security measures represent a further move toward state capitalism and added control over the policies and actions of private enterprises. These latter controls have been placed over institutions that are still "free" to set their own prices.

Cooperatives developed during this period. Producers banded together to form their own brokerage houses for the purchase of supplies and equipment and for the distribution of their products. The profits formerly absorbed by entrepreneur distributers or "middlemen" thus reverted to the producer-consumer cooperative owners. Examples of such corporations are the Farm Bureau enterprises and the cooperative elevators. The federal government has entered into the spirit of eliminating the middleman's profit through such activities as the Rural Electrification Administrations.

There has also been a movement toward what might be called "state socialism." This is the actual ownership and operation of various kinds of enterprises by the national, state, or local governments. It dates to the nineteenth century as far as many enterprises are concerned—for example, municipal ownership of the water system, the taking over of the firefighting enterprises, the collection of garbage by the city, and in some cases the operation of a municipal light plant or a transit system. It is also represented in some respects in the development of public power, particularly in the Northwest. In this case the power is usually distributed to anyone at its actual cost, including local private power-distributing companies and to other businesses.

The public mail system and the public school system are still earlier examples of state socialism. A distinction can be made between state socialism and communistic enterprises at this point. As the terms are being used here, they are defined in a more technical sense than that in which the term "Russian communism" is typically used. In this stricter sense, a "socialistic" enterprise is one where the state or governmental subdivision operates the enterprise but sells the services at cost to the people. Examples of this would be water supply, a municipal light plant, or a public transit system. A communistic enterprise, technically defined, is one in which some branch of the government owns and operates the enterprise and supplies the services without cost to those who need it. Examples of this would be garbage collection, the public school system, and fire-fighting services.

It can be recognized readily that there has been a decided trend, and there still is a continuing trend, in the direction of socialistic or communistic operation in an increasing proportion of our enterprises. As a matter of fact, many of the services described in the preceding paragraphs are fully acceptable to most people. Terminology, of course, remains a very real problem. The strongest supporters of public postal and educational systems might present vigorous opposition if these systems were labeled "socialistic" or "communistic." It would seem that, in the light of the history, the question to be raised in the case of a proposed change is not whether the new direction is technically classified as socialistic, communistic, or toward private enterprise, but whether it is the most efficient and effective way of conducting the particular piece of business with due reference to its over-all effect upon the economy.

In spite of all these trends toward larger and larger corporations, and in spite of the fact that a very large percentage of our manufacturing is in the hands of a very few firms in each industry, there are still large segments of our economy in the hands of small private enterprises. This was largely true in the 1950's in the fields of farming and retail business. In the case of farming, the amount of capital outlay necessary for efficient agricultural production had become so great as to lead to a sizeable trend toward larger farms and absentee ownership. But there are still a large number of small individually owned farms. There are still a great number of small individually owned retail stores and establishments. This residue of smaller proprietors has been gradually reduced by the increasing trend toward larger farms and toward chain stores in almost all areas of retailing from groceries and auto accessories to big department stores. One of the outstanding aspects of this shift is the increasing domination of the whole industrial enterprise by the large corporation. Whether in newspapers, or in radio or television or movies, or in manufacturing, the advantages of the large corporation are becoming increasingly evident.

In the next section we shall analyze the nature of the productive and distributive processes in the present American economy before we consider, in the following chapter, some of the problems posed by all these changes in the American economy.

An Analysis of the Productive and Distributive Processes

In this section there is presented an analysis of the productive and distributive processes as they have developed and seem to operate at present in a modern industrial society such as that of the United States. The writers have attempted to do this by making the process as simplified as possible. It is their belief that even the most complex of processes can be understood by a layman. Although understanding a process sufficiently well to hold a general opinion is not the same as knowing it technically, in our democratic society such an understanding seems to be of paramount importance. As long as the person preparing the simplification does it honestly, with every attempt to convey the correct interpretation, it would seem to be a desirable service. There *is* danger, of course, of misunderstanding due to oversimplification. There are always many exceptions that cannot be put into a greatly simplified picture.

In order to explain the effects of technological change on a productive system, we have imagined a system in which there is at the start a balance between production and consumption. By means of a series of charts (Figures 2 through 6), we have attempted to show the situation existing in such an industry. This generalization could be generalized to the whole productive process and will be so at times in this section in order to illustrate the effects upon the productive system if all industries were affected similarly or made the same decision with respect to technological changes.

Before the charts are discussed consecutively, some of the assumptions underlying the charts should be stated. In the first place, this is a static picture of the productive enterprise as seen at different times permitting only certain kinds of changes and certain kinds of response to those changes. It is assumed, of course, that no other changes occur during the period of discussion. For example, there can be no change in the value of the dollar, no change in the amount of credit available, no change in the balance of trade, no change in the size of the federal budget surplus or deficit, no increase or decrease in the total public and private debt. These conditions are, of course, never realized because an economic system is a constantly changing, kaleidoscopic complex, interrelated system. The problems involved in the economic system can perhaps be understood if the system is considered simply. It is this possibility of the simplification for nontechnical presentation of the very complex relationships existing within many aspects of the modern social and natural world that makes it at all possible for every person to have some understanding of matters concerning which he must make decisions as a citizen. The authors do consider this feasible and present this illustration for the topic of economics.

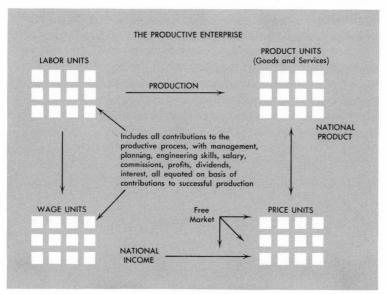

Figure 2. A Balanced Productive and Distributive System—No Changes.

It will be noted that in Figure 2 the productive process has been analyzed into four separate divisions. These are illustrated by means of formations of squares in the chart. One of these is called *labor units*. The utilization of these units (man-hours per week) in the productive process leads to the production of the product unit (goods and services), which on the national level can be called *national product*. The labor units, on the other hand, give rise to *wage units*. The total wage units are held to include all contributions to the productive process, including management, planning, and engineering skills, each being equated on the basis of its contributions to successful production. All wage units together can be termed *national income* when all of the country's productive enterprises are included. This income from production or national income then goes into the free market to purchase the product units. The *price units* in a free market situation would be established by supply and demand conditions.

It should be pointed out that, for purposes of simplification, we have arbitrarily set up units so that we have in each case exactly twelve to start with. In the case of the labor units, they would represent such things as hours of labor per week, with management and other skills converted to the equivalent of other labor. The wage units would represent so many dollars per hour or per week. A size of unit has been chosen in each case such as to enable us to start out with exactly twelve units at the beginning of a balanced productive and distributive system. Similarly, we have chosen a unit for goods and services that enables the productive process to be listed as twelve such units during a given period, which could arbitrarily be a week, a month, or a year, depending on the size of the unit chosen. Similarly, for the price unit, a number of dollars has been chosen that would enable the price paid for the product to be on the basis of one price unit for each product unit at the beginning of the balanced productive and distributive system—twelve price units in all.

Now if there is no technological change and if the factory is putting out a number of product units sufficient to meet the normal demands of the society, as illustrated in Figure 2, we will have a balanced productive and distributive system, with the national income and national product (if considered on the national level) balanced, with no inflationary or deflationary trends, and with no piling up of goods in the warehouses.

Now let us look at Figure 3. One of the outstanding characteristics of our productive system has been the great increase in productivity. We have assumed in this chart that in a given period of time there has been a 33⅓ per cent increase in productivity. We have assumed that other things have remained constant in the charts that are to follow and have so indicated. The 33⅓ per cent increase in productivity is not out of line with the figures quoted in the section on technological change earlier in this chapter.

Let us note, therefore, what effects this increased productivity will have on the balance of production and distribution if there are no other changes. The first will be a 33⅓ per cent increase in the number of products (product units). This has been indicated on the chart by means of adding four crosshatched squares, indicating that one-third more product units are now available for the market. If the same prices are maintained and if the situation is generalized over the entire economy, there will be an oversupply if there is no other change in the total national income. Other factors that might affect the balance, such as increased credit from borrowing or the introduction of money from outside the nation, have been ruled out. The increased production would then mean that there would be an oversupply of goods and of services. The services would go unpurchased, and the goods would tend to pile up in the warehouse.[23]

Going back to Figure 3, the situation would then call for decisions by management and by others concerned (such as government). Let us suppose that the decision is made by management, as shown in Figure 4, to

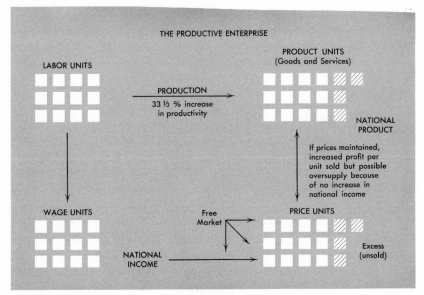

Figure 3. Increase in Productivity—No Other Changes.

reduce the amount of labor units, since the same amount of labor can produce more goods and since the goods have not been purchased. Then we can reduce the number of labor units and produce as many goods; but of course, since there is no change in wages, we can produce goods much more cheaply and therefore make a better profit. If we reduce the number of labor units without increasing the wages, then the number of wage units will also be reduced. We indicate this on the chart by blacking out three of the twelve labor units and three of the twelve wage units, indicating

[23] It will be noticed that we have indicated that the profit per unit sold will be increased. Actually, since we have included profit in the wage units, this would not directly produce a decrease either in the wage units or in the national income. If the persons receiving the profits would expend the same balance in capital goods and consumer goods as would those receiving wages, theoretically this would make no difference in the productive economy. Consequently, the additional profits from the sale of sixteen product units as against twelve would then be spent in the market. This, generalized to the national level, would bring about a balance in the economic system. However, in a period of static or declining production, there is no incentive for a person to spend excess money gained by profits for capital goods or for new productive enterprises. Usually, therefore, the money gained through profits is withheld from the productive system, leading to a further slowing down of the process. This is more clearly shown in the flow chart in the next section.

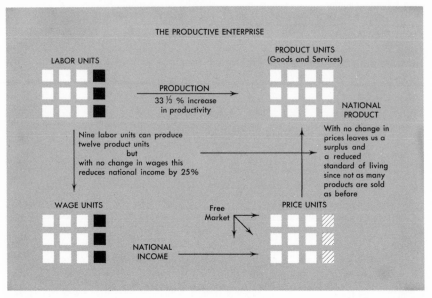

Figure 4. Increased Productivity—Reduction of Labor to Avoid Oversupply.

that there are now just nine labor units and nine wage units. However, there still are twelve product units. But this, generalized on the entire national scene, means that there is less national income to take into the market to purchase the product units. With less national income and with no change in price, there will still be a surplus of products (indicated by crosshatched squares), which cannot be purchased unless persons borrow money or go into debt, a condition that has been ruled out for the purpose of our present discussion. Consequently we again have an oversupply of goods and services that cannot be purchased. However, in this case, since no more products are being produced, this will bring about a reduced standard of living, for not as many products can be sold as before. The result, then, of laying off men without reducing prices while still producing the same number of units as before, would be to reduce the standard of living. One way of reducing the labor units, instead of laying off men, would be to reduce the length of the work week by an amount (one-fourth) that would still produce as many units.[24]

Now let us suppose that we attempt to solve our problem by a reduction of the labor units without a reduction of the wage units. Since nine labor units can produce as much as twelve, we could reduce the work week

[24] Some of our readers may perhaps be a little puzzled and disturbed by the fact that the reduction in labor and wage units amounts to one-fourth whereas productivity went up one-third. Actually it is mathematically the same. The reduction in one-fourth of labor units will enable the nine persons with a 33½ per cent increase in productivity to produce as much as twelve labor units did before.

without a reduction in the amount of wages paid or the men employed. This can be done by raising the hourly or weekly wage by 33⅓ per cent. This plan is shown in Figure 5. Now it will be noted that we have reduced the number of labor units from twelve to nine but that the wage units stay the same; and so, generalized to the national level, the national income

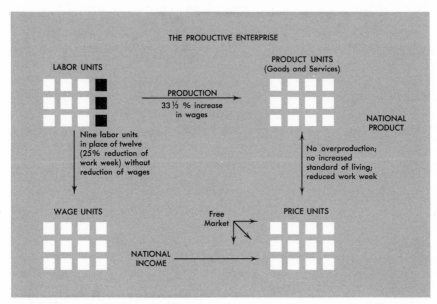

Figure 5. Increased Productivity—Reduction of Work Week with No Reduction in Wages.

would stay the same. We are producing the same amount of units, so we have the same national product. The wage units (national income) then going out into the free market with the same price units enable the purchase of all the products produced. The net result of all this, generalized to the national level, means that we do not have overproduction, we are able to reduce the total amount of hours that we work, but we have no increase in our standard of living. We have merely reduced the amount of work that is necessary to maintain the stame standard of living.

Now let us solve this problem in still another way. Suppose that we maintain the same amount of labor units, which would give us the same amount of wage units (with no change in the wages). We can thereby produce sixteen product units in place of the previous twelve (Figure 6). However, we can reduce the prices by 25 per cent, which means that, generalized to the national level, the same amount of income can absorb the 33⅓ per cent increase in product units. The twelve price units will purchase sixteen product units. The net result of this is that we have been able to absorb the increased production into our economic system in such a way that we have an increased standard of living without any change in

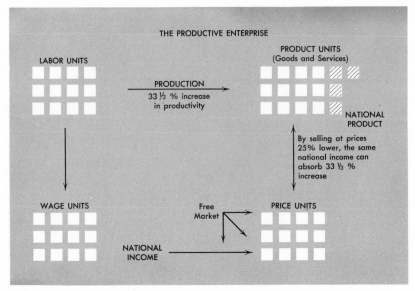

Figure 6. Increased Productivity—Reduction of Prices.

amount of work week but with a reduction in prices. This tends to lead to a deflation and an increase in the value of money measured in products.

Suppose, as is shown in Figure 7, we decide to pass along the increase in productivity to labor in the form of increased wages, so that they will be able to purchase the increased national product. We have therefore in-

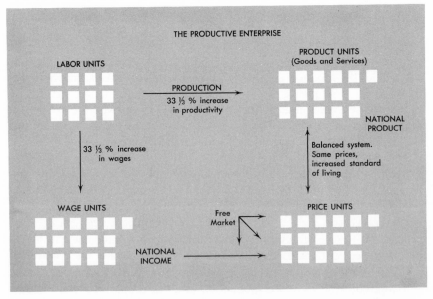

Figure 7. Increased Productivity—Increased wages: No Change in Prices.

creased the number of wage units by four, a 33⅓ per cent increase. This would thereby increase national income by 33⅓ per cent. The product units of course have increased by 33⅓ per cent (four on our chart). We thereby have again a balanced system. With the same prices we now have sixteen price units to correspond to the sixteen wage units that can produce the sixteen product units. We have a balanced system, with the same price per product but with an increased standard of living. This is a result of an increase in wages to correspond with the increase in productivity.

No attempt has been made in this explanation to indicate which of these methods should be used or whether it should be a combination of these.[25] The attempt was to show the effects of various decisions on industry itself, and, by inference, on our national economy if such decisions were universally made. It can be readily seen, and it will be more fully shown in the next chapter, that decisions of this kind have an important effect on depressions, on inflationary trends, and on other similar economic matters.

This presentation has been a static analysis of the productive process. In the next section, since our economic system is not really static, we are going to illustrate the dynamic process of the flow of money through our economy.

The Nature of the Flow of Money Through the Economy

In this section we will portray the economic system as a circulatory system in which the flow of income to the economy is illustrated. The presentation, of course, again has been greatly simplified. The actual economic system is an extremely complex one, in which each of us with our income and purchasing power would be represented by little capillaries or pipes and in which other elements could be represented by many larger arteries, veins, and so forth.

Figure 8 represents a clarification of this simplified process by a relatively simple sketch.[26]

Before describing and defining the circulatory system in detail, the reader's attention is called to the fact that the Gross National product, a representation of the nation's productive power, is a major driving force of the economy. At the other end the Disposable Personal Income, which goes into the market for personal consumptive expenditures, represents

[25] Alternatives are presented in the latter part of this chapter.

[26] The statistical discrepancies in Figure 8 can be reconciled as follows: Some are due to rounding. Some are due to the statistical inadequacy of the data sources. For example, the National Income amount necessitates the adding of government subsidies and subtracting business transfer payments. The Personal Income amount necessitates the adding of Business Transfer Payments and Inventory Valuation Adjustments. If the figure were three-dimensional, these extra flow pipes could be pictured. The discrepancy between Gross Savings and Gross Investment represents government surplus, a type of savings. The amount of net foreign investment must be added to incoming flow to give Gross National Product.

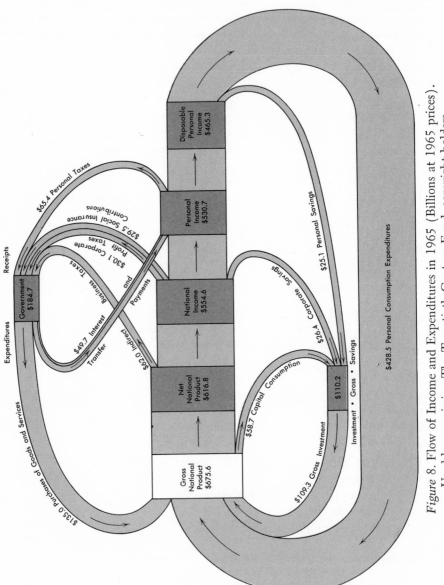

Figure 8. Flow of Income and Expenditures in 1965 (Billions at 1965 prices). Used by permission The Twentieth Century Fund, copyright holders.

also a major driving force of government expenditures and private capital investment.

One of the results of the recent study of economics has been the sharpening of the definition of certain terms used in that field and the development of reliable statistics on them. In Figure 8 we have used the latest statistics taken from the *Economic Report of the President*. We shall define some of the terms found in this figure as an illustration of the precise definition of certain indicators that can be carefully measured to indicate how our economy is progressing.

Gross National Product (G.N.P.) represents the total national output of goods and services at market prices. G.N.P. measures the product attributable to the factors of production—labor and property—supplied by the residents of the continental United States. *National Income* is the aggregate of earnings by labor and property from the current production of goods and services by the nation's economy. It is the sum represented by the compensation of employees, proprietors' income, rental income, net interest, and corporate profits; thus it measures a total factor cost of the goods and services produced by the economy. Earnings are inclusive of taxes on those earnings. *Personal Income* is the current income received by individuals, by unincorporated businesses, and by nonprofit institutions (including pension trusts and welfare funds from all sources). *Disposable Personal Income* is equal to personal income less taxes on individuals.

Now let us look at the chart itself and follow through the analysis there given. The indication that is of greatest interest to economic statisticians is the Gross National Product. This was $675.6 billion for 1965. This figure less the capital consumption (that is, material spent by industry for building of new plants and purchasing of tools of production) becomes the *Net National Product*. The Net National Product less indirect business taxes becomes the National Income. The National Income less corporate savings and corporate profits and social insurance contributions plus interest payments and other government transferable payments becomes the Personal Income, the total amount received by individuals in our economy. The Personal Income less personal taxes gives us the Disposable Personal Income—the amount that individuals have to spend in any given year. This was $465.3 billion in 1965. Some of this may go into personal savings and then back, of course, into various types of investment, as indicated in Figure 8. The various taxes collected by the different governmental units are also spent in the purchase of goods and services, which keeps the blood stream of our economic system going and adds, of course, to the Gross National Product. The capital investment is a very important part of the economic system; it is investment of capital goods that facilitates machinery and processes for increased productivity. For example, if there were *no* money set aside in the productive process for the purchase of capital goods (those goods used to set up and develop the productive process itself), our productive system would become obsolete and eventually would disintegrate through normal wear-and-tear.

So long as this system maintains a fairly constant and balanced circulation, we have a relatively healthy circulation of money. If for some reason the consumers feel that they must purchase goods very rapidly, even borrowing money to do so (as, for example, in an inflationary period), then there tends to be an increase in the total amount of income, since the rate of acceleration affects the amount of income. The Total National Income is equal to the total of wages, salaries, rent, interest, and profit. If people spend their money rapidly so that it passes through many hands and therefore is counted several times in a given period, in effect we have more money in our economy, even though the actual amount of printed dollars may be the same. Other things that may affect the system are the pumping in of credit by governmental and private borrowing. The pumping out of credit by paying off debts also affects the system by reducing the amount in circulation. A "favorable" balance of foreign trade and the taking of products off the consumer market, as in the case of military products blown up or stored for future action, also affect the amount of income in circulation. In both cases, the wages are available for the purchasers of consumer goods, but the goods are not available.

It is interesting to note that, as far as the flow of income is concerned, it makes no difference whether the wages and other income are secured through private enterprise or through governmental enterprise. For example, money paid to teachers for their services looks just the same to the economist as money paid to the doctor for his services on a private basis or as money used to buy products through private enterprise. Money paid for products bought from a publicly owned utility such as a water plant affects the economic system in exactly the same way as money paid for gas or electricity bought from a private electric company. Perhaps the amount of money set aside for capital improvement and the amount going into the division called profit may differ slightly in these respects, but as long as the money goes into the economic system, it affects the system in much the same way.

We will discuss later, at greater length, the problem of private versus public enterprise with respect to a working economy. Suffice it to say at this point that the incentive for production is held by the proponents of the private-enterprise system to be stronger in that system than it would be in the government-owned situation such as is found in extreme forms of socialism.

The nature and the development of the American economy has now been set forth. The remainder of this chapter will present some of the problems faced by the American economy and possible alternatives in the solution of these problems. In presenting facts indicating the problems of the American economy, the authors do not mean to be condemnatory concerning the nature of the economic system. It is an attempt to describe what has happened. Possible alternative actions designed to solve the problems presented are discussed fully in the latter part of this chapter.

Concentration of Economic Power

Some of the trends with reference to the concentration of economic power will now be traced.

Many big corporations have a large number of stockholders. In theory, this might make it seem that the ownership of a particular corporation is actually quite widely dispersed. In fact, many of the holdings are very small ones. Most of the money value of the holdings in a given corporation is concentrated in the hands of relatively few persons. In a study of 208 common stock issues reported by Purdy, Lindahl, and Carter, it was found that in one half of the cases only 1.5 per cent of the total of individual shareholders was needed to reach a majority (over 50 per cent) of the shares of common stock outstanding. In three quarters of the issues, 2.5 per cent or less we needed to reach a majority; and only in a few cases did it take over 5 per cent to make up a majority of the issue.[27]

Because of the wide scattering of the various small shareholdings, quite often a minority of stockholders is able to control the company. Often a sizable portion of the stock may be owned by another company in closely related business, such as the telephone and telegraph industries, and in some cases by oil companies.

The control of proxies (signed delegations of voting rights) by the management, usually in conjunction with an already existing minority control, helps to prevent the overthrow of this minority control of stock. In many cases, the management itself controls the votes of the larger minority stockholders and thus can determine who the directors are to be.

Except in cases of stock manipulation (where the minority may manipulate a given company in order to cause a change in the value of the stock to its own betterment, even though it would not necessarily be an advantage to the company itself), such concentration is not always necessarily bad for the company or for the industry as a whole. It does, however, pose certain potential dangers if the interests of the minority in control are not consistent with the interests of the industry and with those of the country at large. The right to work in gainful employment is coming to be considered as one of man's basic rights. If the time should come when practically all the opportunities for employment were controlled by a few companies, which in turn were controlled by a minority, it would place in the hands of these persons more power than has ever existed in the hands of an oligarchy before in the history of mankind. However, we shall show in

[27] Harry L. Purdy, Martin Lindahl, and William H. Carter, *Corporate Concentration and Public Policy* (Englewood Cliffs, N.J.: Prentice-Hall, 1950), p. 71.

a later section that as far as the American scene is concerned, this is not as serious a threat to our freedom, at the moment at least, as it might appear to be to those who may wish to use the information for rabble-rousing.

Inequality of Wealth and Income

The second problem faced in American society is the inequality of wealth and income. When we talk about the low income of certain Americans, we must think of it within the American context. There is not as great a disparity between the income of the masses and that of the wealthy as that found within some of the undeveloped countries of the world. The income of the "underprivileged" class of America is well above the average income of the masses in some other countries, but this makes their deprivation none the less painful. They desire material comforts on the American standard.

There have been numerous studies made of the disparity of income. One of the most recent is that made by Michael Harrington, whose book *The Other America* was very influential in the development of the program of economic opportunity (the "antipoverty" program) in the mid-1960's. He indicated that there existed in America at that time approximately 50 million Americans, nearly a third of the population, living below the borderline of what could be considered a decent income within the American economy.[28] This at a time when American affluence was climbing and the middle class was able to have more than one automobile, better homes, even swimming pools and boats. The problem of depressed areas, both urban and rural, will be discussed in Chapter 10. At the moment, the problem of discrepancies in income between the upper and lower level is merely noted.

Monopoly and Administered Prices

It has already been seen, in the analysis earlier in this chapter, that the setting of prices has an important effect upon the economic process. Among the problems inherent in monopoly (or duopoly or oligopoly)[29] is the effect of such concentration of economic power in producing rigidity of price structure. This phenomenon is called by economists *administered prices*. It occurs in situations where prices are controlled, either by government (as in the case of utilities or during a war) or by a company (or group of companies) that sets prices at will.

It is possible that a monopoly, through the use of administered prices,

[28] Michael Harrington, *The Other America: Poverty in the United States* (Baltimore, Md.: Penguin, 1963), Chapter I.

[29] *Monopoly*—control of a production of a product by one company; *duopoly*—control of production of a product by two companies; *oligopoly*—control of the production of a product by a few companies working in concert.

can increase its income (based on profits) by maintaining prices at the expense of the amount of production. This may be especially bad during a period of depression in the business cycle because it further accentuates the trends already present.

It should be noted, however, that there are other factors that tend to mitigate the possible disadvantages in monopoly control. One of these is the fear of punitive measures by government, such as antitrust suits. Another is the fact that there really are no such things as absolute monopolies. Even though a company may control the manufacture and sale of a given product, when the price becomes greater than the market can bear, the consumer tends to find substitutes or to delay purchases. This means that there will be some tendency toward self-regulation in any economy in which there is not an absolute control over the products that can be purchased by the consumer. The theory of this, known as *countervailing power*, will be more fully discussed later. It has been found that various powerful interests in our society tend partially to counteract one another, thus mitigating the possible force of monopoly or the concentration of economic power in the hands of a few.

Business Cycles

If the business activity in the United States over a period of years is measured on almost any scale, it tends to show peaks and valleys. This represents our business cycles.

This rapid variation in business activity leads to considerable waste in the production system. At times of low level, production capacity is not used efficiently, and there is heavy unemployment with resultant social disabilities and misery. The periods of boom may seriously affect other persons in the population because boom periods usually are accompanied by inflation, which means that persons on a fixed income may suffer from the lack of buying power. At this point we are not attempting to indicate the possible solution to the problem but merely to indicate that it is an important one. It is particularly interesting that the extremes of the business cycle seem to have been greater in the highly industrialized and advanced technology of America than they have been in some of the other countries of the world. It remains to be seen whether some of the remedies that have been worked out by government since the 1929 depression will be of any help in reducing the ups and downs of the business cycle or their effects.

Technological Unemployment

The paramount problem of the displacement of workers due to rapid technological development has been present for some time in our economy. Even though the total number of workers needed in the economy may remain the same or even be increased under an improved technology, there is the problem of the worker being displaced from one job and unable quickly to make the transfer to a new position.

With the advent of automation the situation may become quite acute, with very few men actually producing what a great number of men had produced before. This could lead to the production of an enormous quantity of goods per person, but it raises the question as to whether or not we shall be able to employ as many persons as before.

Peter Drucker has the following to say on automation:[30]

If automation were a simple matter of technology or replacement of human labor by machines, its social impact would be large-scale displacement of workers. There may actually be no workers on the production floor of tomorrow's "push-button factory." There are practically none in a power-generation station or oil refinery. But at the same time incredibly large numbers of men will be required behind the scenes in new, highly skilled jobs as machine builders, machine installers, repair men, controllers of machinery and its performance, and "programmers" to prepare information and feed it into the machines. In addition, large numbers of highly educated men will be needed in new jobs as designers of machinery, draftsmen, system-engineers, mathematicians, or logicians. Finally, large numbers will be needed for new managerial jobs requiring high ability to think, to analyze, to make decisions, and to assume risks, and this increase both in the numbers of managers and in the demands made on them may well be the largest of all the social impacts of automation.

The workers needed per unit produced may be less under automation. If the results of technology are reflected in lower prices, the workers per unit cost may be the same (in an economy with stable money). The productive capacity not used in one process must be routed into another to use the man power and to absorb the purchasing power, both of which should be released by the new technology of automation if workers are released and prices lowered.

Since automation and technological unemployment do not affect the service industries in the same way that they do the production industries, we might expect that there would be a leveling off of persons employed in production even with increasing activity, productivity, and increase of those employed in services. This apparently is true. In 1920 there were about 14 million persons employed in the services-producing industries and 26 million in goods-producing industries. In 1952 there were approximately 27 million employed in each. By 1954 the number of persons employed in the service-producing industries had exceeded the number in the goods-producing industries, roughly 28 million and 26 million respectively.[31]

[30] Peter Drucker, "The Promise of Automation: America's Next Twenty Years, Part II," *Harper's Magazine* (April 1955), p. 44.
[31] United States Department of Labor, Bureau of Labor Statistics, *Occupational Outlook Handbook*, 1957, p. 25, chart 8.

The National Budget, Inflation, and Taxation

One of the outstanding phenomena among recent social trends has been the tremendous amount of money involved in governmental expenditures. The total money spent for all governmental purchases from 1929 to 1964 increased from $8.5 billion to 128.7 billion. Furthermore, in 1929 only $1.3 billion was spent by the federal government; whereas in 1964, $97.6 billion was spent by the federal government.[32] Of course a large part of the increase in the interim period was due, first to an attempt to stop the depression, and secondly to the efforts to achieve national security through the waging of World War II, the maintenance of military forces in Europe, Korea, and Southwest Asia, and preparation for other military eventualities. Regardless of the reasons, the size of the governmental budget has had an important effect upon the national economy. Much of the material required for war purposes was either stored in inventories or blown up in combat. Consequently, goods were not made available to be purchased on the market. Since the production of these goods required payment for raw materials and for labor, large amounts of money tended to be spent and thus set loose in the economic system. This excess of purchasing power over production made it necessary to establish controls on prices in order to slow the inflation of the value of money, and also to ration certain goods in short supply so that they would be equitably distributed among the people. This problem of controlling the value of money—or, putting it another way, the price of goods—then becomes an important one.

It is now thought that peacetime tendencies toward inflation and deflation can be controlled partially by the power of the Federal Reserve Board to control credit. A large part of the money available in the American economic system arises through the credit that can be given by a local commerical bank as loans. The bank needs to maintain only a certain proportion of its deposits in reserve. The rest can be loaned out again. Furthermore, the local commercial bank can, by going to a Federal Reserve bank with the loan paper (notes, mortgages, etc.), get additional credit, which permits it again to lend money on security loans. This pyramiding of credit can go on and on unless the cycle is topped by such regulations as those restricting the amount of the discount rate required by the Federal Reserve Bank.

Problems Involved in the Growth of Unionism, the Expansion of Government, and the Pressure of Organized Agriculture

The early developments in the growth of larger power blocs go far back into the history of this country. Unionism is not a recent phenomenon; however, it has become a major industrial feature only in the last thirty or

---

[32] *Economic Report of the President,* January 1965 (Washington, D.C.: Govt. Printing Office, 1965), p. 159.

forty years. Section 7a of the National Recovery Act gave legal status to collective bargaining by labor and thus tended to give labor more power than it ever had before. This was in response to the increasing power held by industry, caused by the increasing concentration of power into the hands of fewer and larger corporations. The individual workingman was not able to bargain effectively with such massive antagonists as the large corporations.

Because of the magnitude of problems of all kinds that we face, including the necessity for alleviation of suffering caused by depressions, there has been a rapid expansion of governmental services. This expansion is not entirely a recent phenomenon, for there has been a growth in the services demanded of the federal government over a long period of time. Many of these expanded services grew out of legitimate need for the aid that only the government could furnish, such as agricultural research, direct advice in helping farmers grow more crops, weather information, and other such services. It is difficult, when one starts to analyze any one of these services, to see how it can be eliminated; but the over-all result is that a sizable portion of the national income is given over to goods and services furnished by the federal government and by other governmental subdivisions.

In the growing concentration of industrial enterprises, labor, and government into larger and larger groups, agriculture was apparently losing out in the 1920's. In the 1930's the farmers combined politically with other proponents of the New Deal to secure various kinds of legislation to give it more power. By means of guaranteed parity payments, payments for land conservation, and other similar bounties, farmers were able to achieve what they considered to be their just share in the economy. Although they were still not well organized as a group, their voice was felt politically. By the early sixties this voice had lessened considerably due to the rural-urban population shift.

Agriculture is still in the economic picture along with big labor, big business, and big government. The prospect of these giants facing each other presents a quite different picture than Adam Smith envisioned many years ago. It poses a problem of the place of the individual in the picture. Individuals are only small elements within large groups battling for power or for their "just" share of the national product. Then what place is there for individuality? The basic question is: How can we maintain and protect the individual personality in a massive power conflict, such as has developed rapidly after the 1930's?

The Place of Private Property in the Modern Democratic State

The concept of the right of private property seems to have developed quite early among some of the nonliterate peoples. We have seen, in the example in Chapter 2, how private property as an institution developed among the Tanala as a result of a change in technological process. Private property has always played an important part among the institutions the various civilizations have evolved as part of their total network of institutional arrangements. With the development of democratic theories, including those of the social and political philosophers preliminary to the development of democratic institutions, the idea of private property as being one of the basic rights became very prevalent. John Locke speaks of the rights of "life, liberty, and property." In the Declaration of Independence, this was changed (perhaps deliberately) to read "life, liberty, and the pursuit of happiness." At the time of the writing of the Declaration of Independence, men of property were only a small minority among the influential leaders. By the time of the Constitution, the propertied interests were much stronger. Numerous laws were passed quite early in the history of our country to limit the absolute right of property; for example, primogeniture (or the inheritance of all land by the eldest son) had been abrogated by laws passed early in the nineteenth century in almost all the states.

Basic growth of various forms of social legislation some time after the Civil War, such as the regulation of railroad rates, the regulation of other utility rates, the regulation of working conditions, have all been considered to be a "chipping away" at the rights possessed by owners of industrial property. The battles over these laws were usually fought on the idea of the relative value of "property rights" versus "human rights." The development of extremely heavy inheritance taxes and of the steeply progressive income tax has been a further chipping away at the "property rights" idea in the American economy.

The right to property is not commonly considered to be an absolute right in America at present; for example, a person who owns a lot is restricted by zoning laws as to the kind of house or industry that he can build on it. The lot may be taken away from him under due process with compensation in order to build a schoolhouse, a road, or some other public construction. If he builds an industry on the property, he is restricted in many ways as to its working conditions, such as safety, hours of work, minimum wages, and so on. In general, then, the rights of private property of almost all kinds have been restricted by numerous laws supposedly in the public interest. When property rights have conflicted with human rights, human rights have increasingly won out.

Despite the above, the right of private property in terms of the right to the ownership of instruments of production, to the distribution of product, or to the dispensing of services, is held by the American people to be a fundamental one—within limits. In this respect the general tenor of opinion within America is different from that of the countries of the world that have tended to go toward socialistic (national) ownership of the instruments of production, or from the situation in Soviet Russia, where ownership of private property is mostly restricted to consumer goods.

Atomic Energy for Military and Industrial Use

One of the causes, and also a concomitant result, of our technological process has been the great increase in the amount of energy available for man's use. In the far past almost all of the energy used was man power. Later animal power was added, then wind and water power. In the recent past the tendency has been toward the fuel sources of power. These included first wood, then coal, then, of course, oil and gas. All such sources are potentially a form of energy derived from the sun. This is true even of water power, which is tied to the sun by the evaporation process and the subsequent falling of rain and the flow of the streams down to sea level. Gas and oil represent a storing up of potential energy through plant photosynthesis by action of the sun's rays. Power from such fuels is achieved entirely through the releasing of the energy latent in them by means of oxidation, and the consequent release of the stored energy (changed in form so that, after use, the energy is lost or dissipated). Atomic energy, however, embodies an entirely new principle. There is a destruction, in part, of the mass fuel material in return for release of enormous quantities of energy.

The development of atomic energy has been very rapid. The stimulus of competition, at first from the Nazis and later from the Russians, brought about the subsidization of research by all those governments that had the resources to put into the technological development of atomic power. The result was an extremely rapid growth of know-how in this field.

Although some scientific work had been done before 1939, serious efforts toward the development of the atomic bomb were not made until about that time. On December 2, 1942, the first chain reaction based upon the fission process (breaking down of the molecules into simpler parts) was successful at the University of Chicago. On July 16, 1945, the first atomic bomb was exploded at Alamogordo, New Mexico.[33]

The release of the bombs over Hiroshima and Nagasaki served in a destructive fashion to dramatize for the world, the opening of the atomic age. From the very beginning it was felt that the fission process could be controlled for power purposes as far as the atomic energy reactions were concerned. On July 18, 1955, the General Electric Company announced the start of production of energy in an atomic energy plant that furnished electricity for power and light in West Milton, New York. This was just about ten years after the first bomb was exploded.

The hydrogen bomb employs a different process, namely, the fusion of lighter substances, such as deuterium (heavy hydrogen) or lithium. It was at first thought to be usable only in destructive explosives such as bombs or shells, and therefore to have no industrial applications. Little success has as yet been achieved in efforts to develop the fusion process in such a way as

[33] Samuel Glasstone (ed.), *Source Book on Atomic Energy* (Princeton, N.J.: Van Nostrand, 1950), pp. 202–203.

to make it controllable and therefore available for atomic power purposes. The abundance of fuel for the fusion process opens completely new vistas of energy capabilities.

Even in the use of "conventional" atomic energy, namely, the fission process, there are unusual possibilities for fuel because of the possibility of breeding. Let us now explain this process. U-235, the fissionable isotope, is a very scarce form of uranium. It makes up about 0.72 per cent of refined uranium. (The remainder is U-238.) The process of refinement is extremely complicated, and it takes a great amount of energy to get the relatively pure (99 per cent) U-235 used in an atomic pile.[34] In a process known as *breeding*, quantities of U-238 placed in the atomic pile while the U-235 is undergoing reaction can be converted by the action of extra neutrons into plutonium, which can then be purified and used in other atomic piles just as U-235 is. The amount of fuel recovered from such an atomic pile is more than the amount of fuel used up in the reaction. Therefore there is no diminishing of the amount of fuel. Of course there is a potential limit in the amount of U-238 available in the world. The possible use of the fusion processes (indicated above), coupled with the possible utilization of further information concerning the nature of the atom to lead to the use of other elements in fission or fusion, add to the probable *potential* amount of energy available.

Stuart Chase, writing in the *Saturday Review* for January 22, 1955, states that at the estimated rate of energy consumption for the year 2000, there will be sufficient atomic energy, based on uranium supplies *alone*, available for seventeen hundred years. The best estimate now is that the coal, oil, and gas supplies (if used alone) would last about eighty years at the rate at which we will be probably consuming energy in the year 2000.

The possibility of the utilization of this great amount of energy for increasing the productive capacities of the world challenges the imagination. Processes that have been economically impossible, such as the purification of sea water, the pumping of water over great distances to irrigate deserts, the synthesis of many products from raw materials, may all become possible. The amount of energy that can be used to run automatic factories with very complex machinery almost completely without human guidance also staggers the imagination.

The dark cloud that hangs over all is the use of atomic power for destructive purposes. Indications are that two nations fighting an atomic war could very well destroy all human life on the globe, if not all animal and plant life, if they so chose. Whether this fact will lead to increased tension and war, or whether the enormity of the power available in atomic energy will cause the groups to compromise on some "live and let live" basis, remains to be seen.

[34] It has been asserted that sufficient amounts exist in sea water to make it the equivalent as a fuel to an equal amount of petroleum.

Man's Problems Ahead in the Economic Area

Before we examine the alternatives for the solution of problems that man faces, it may be well to summarize the main problems in the economic area. This list is not intended to be exhaustive.

1. How can we make adjustments in our production and distribution system to allow for extremely rapid changes in technology, including the effects of automation and atomic energy on production?
2. How can we prevent the extremes of the economic cycle with its attendant boom periods and its inflationary trends, which are harmful to the worker on a static income, and the bust periods (depressions), which are hard on the workers who become unemployed?
3. How can we avoid an undue concentration of economic power, which may endanger our individual liberties, without destroying the efficiency that grows from the advantages of large businesses?
4. How can we avoid the extremes of wealth and poverty, with the usual deterioration of character and personality at both of the extremes?
5. How can we avoid the rigidity of our economic system caused by the control of certain industries by monopolies or by a few companies that cooperate in maintaining a fixed price structure?
6. How can we operate the federal budget in periods of heavy military or social needs when large sums need to be expended, without causing undue hardship due to inflation or to excessive taxes on certain groups?
7. How can we avoid the problems arising out of the large organized forces in our economy, such as monopolies, manufacturers' groups, labor groups, agriculture, and strong governmental pressure and regulation?
8. How can we provide for protection against the unexpected emergencies, such as unemployment, accidents, and sickness, and for retirement after old age, without stifling the independence and initiative of the individuals involved?
9. How do we establish the just distribution of income and product to labor, management, owners, and government?

ALTERNATIVES FACED BY THE AMERICAN ECONOMY

In view of these problems, what are the possible alternatives faced by the American economy? Such possible alternatives might be discussed in several ways. They might be classified under the possibility of return to the traditional business system, the possibility of complete government ownership (socialism), the possibility of some combination of the two, or the possibility of movement toward more cooperatives. The writers have chosen to make the analysis a little more detailed to indicate a wide range of logical possibilities, though some of these alternatives are very unlikely to be chosen, and it is equally unlikely that any one of these will be selected exclusive of the others.

For the alternatives chosen by the writers for purposes of discussion, the reader is referred to Figure 9, labeled, "Alternatives Faced by the American Economy." These alternatives have been taken from two sources: the one is William Van Til, *Economic Roads to Democracy*,[35] a book sponsored

Van Til	Traditional Business System	Restoring Competition	Leadership by Business	Two-Front Economy / Mixed Economies	Governmentally Planned	
Edwards and Richey	Negative Laissez-faire	Positive Laissez-faire	Administered Economy — by Business	Administered Economy — by Government		Socialistic Economy
Other terms; alternative proposals	Laissez-faire Individualism	Free market enforced by government action / "Trust-Busting"	Enlightened Self-Interest / Committee on Economic Development ←	Compensatory System / Keynesian Economics / Cooperatives →	State Capitalism	Democratic Collectivism / State Socialism

Figure 9. Alternatives Faced by the American Economy.

by the Consumer Education Study of the National Association of Secondary School Principals; the other is Newton Edwards and Herman G. Richey, *The School in the American Social Order*.[36] We shall start with the ones at the left, discussing and comparing the names given by each to these possible alternatives. Inasmuch as the classifications are somewhat different, there are six alternatives even though each source actually lists just five.

Return to Negative Laissez-faire

The first alternative is called by Van Til *the traditional business system*.[37] It is called *negative laissez-faire* by Edwards and Richey.[38] This is the traditional system, as elaborated by Adam Smith,[39] in which the government *would keep its hands completely off* business enterprise, leaving it to the operation of economic laws for any self-correcting influence. The

35 William Van Til, *Economic Roads to Democracy* (New York: McGraw-Hill, 1947), *passim*.

36 Newton Edwards and Herman G. Richey, *The School in the American Social Order*, (Boston: Houghton, 1963).

37 Van Til, *op. cit.*

38 Edwards and Richey, *op. cit.*, Chapter 14.

39 Adam Smith, *The Wealth of Nations*. A classic published in many editions. See, for example, the Modern Library edition (1937).

government would conduct the punishment of persons who violate the law in such matters as honesty, but would exercise absolutely no positive action toward the working of the economic system. This is sometimes also referred to as the system of *laissez-faire individualism*. This system is based on the assumption that if each one works for his own immediate self-interest, the interest of society will be furthered through the automatic operation of the self-adjusting characteristics of the system.

Positive Laissez-faire

The next alternative, *positive laissez-faire*, is what Van Til speaks of as *restored competition*. In this case it is recognized that we have, in fact, moved a considerable way from the original laissez-faire idea. It would be the job of the government to exercise a positive influence to restore the original conditions. This was the purpose of what has been called the "trust-busting" program of the government. In this proposal there is set forth the anomalous idea of the government actually using its power in order to restore the laissez-faire system, which itself means "let alone." The idea is that if we can break down the power of large monopolies and restore competition, whatever is wrong with our economic system will be taken care of. The problem has been that trust-busting has not been able to accomplish much toward the restoration of laissez-faire. Much faster than the government has been able to operate in the very complicated lawsuits that have been brought, industry has been combining and forming larger corporations, and more and more segments of our economy have come under either monopoly, duopoly, or oligopoly. It is difficult to say that there has been much positive action with respect to this particular alternative, even though it has been pursued as a government policy ever since the days of Theodore Roosevelt and by each of the administrations since—Republican and Democrat alike.

The first two alternative views were predominant before 1929 and are still widely held in the United States today. The remaining alternatives are those that arose into prominence after the depression of 1929.

Administered Economy—Business Leadership

The next alternative has been called by Van Til *leadership by business*, and by Edwards and Richey the *administered economy*, of which they list two kinds: one being administered by business (discussed here) and the other being administered by government (to be discussed in a later section). The idea involved is that we have to recognize the fact that we live in an extremely complicated economic world that requires much coordinated planning and action. Someone (or some group) has to take the responsibility for this coordination and planning. The proponents of business leadership ask who better could do this than the businessmen who are in positions where they can know what should be done? Instead of each businessman working for himself, businessmen would work together to develop those policies that would be best for our economy. The enlightened self-interest of businessmen, in seeing more than just their noses and in looking ahead to the things that are happening and would happen in our economy in the future as a result of their plans, would enable them to make the kind of plans that would bring about a better economic system. There is self-interest operating here, but supposedly an enlightened self-interest rather than the extremely narrow form of self-interest that operated under the traditional laissez-faire system. A group of industrialists who call themselves the Committee for Economic Development was organized during World War II, to pursue, more or less, proposals and actions based on this point of view. They have been at least partially in opposition to the National Association of Manufacturers and the United States Chamber of Commerce, which, by and large (at least publicly), operate according to one of the two points of view already set forth, usually that of the traditional business system. The Committee for Economic Development, which includes some of our leading businessmen, has called upon business to take an interest in the welfare of the entire country and to pursue policies in regard to wages and other industrial practices that will lead to a better economic system.[40]

An example of action (although somewhat ill-fated) based on this point of view was the NRA, the National Recovery Act. This was sponsored by government, although it basically was leadership through business. Early in Franklin D. Roosevelt's administration, the idea was developed that if the various industries could get together and agree upon fair codes of trade practices, then the government would enforce those codes. The representatives of an individual industry, such as, let us say, textiles, were first to agree on such things as the payment of minimum wages and the setting up of certain similar working conditions, and the government would then enforce the desires of the industry so that one business would not undercut another. The idea back of this was that if we could raise the amount of money being paid out to labor so that people had more mass purchasing power, then we would be able to get the economic machine going again. But if one business raised wages and another did not, then the one that did would be unable to compete. So the plan was that they would all get together and agree upon minimum wages, working conditions, hours, and other things, and perhaps even prices, and then the government would put the agreement into operation as an administrative law. Once this law was in force, all businesses, even the minority that had not gone along with the majority, would have to operate in accordance with it. Several hundred of these codes were set into operation. The

[40] The Committee for Economic Development, "Neither Right nor Left but Responsible" (pamphlet) (New York: Committee for Economic Development, n.p., n.d.).

Supreme Court of the United States declared the NRA unconstitutional in 1935, in the famous "sick chicken" case, as it was called (*United States vs. Schecter Brothers*); consequently this particular plan went out. But it appears that the Committee for Economic Development is not in favor of precisely this way of operating, because they tend to operate on the basis of voluntary cooperation among businessmen rather than to use enforcement by government as was done in the period of the NRA.

Dual Economy—Keynesian Economics

An alternative that became very prevalent throughout various parts of the world, including the United States in the late 1930's, has been called by Van Til the *two-front economy*. It is also sometimes called the *compensatory system*, and at times *Keynesian economics*, after Lord Keynes, a famous British economist who espoused the idea. Many of the policies brought about under the New Deal were based upon this theory, in spite of some of the criticisms that have been launched against Keynesian economics.

One of the characteristics of our capitalistic economic system, in spite of its many good points, is that it tends to lead into business cycles, or inflations and depressions. If the products of the factories are not bought, the deeper will be the depression, the more factories will be closed, and the fewer people will be getting money. We have not yet been able to eliminate depression, but we can use the power of government to prevent depressions from being so acute. When the industrial system starts to go into a depression, dropping off in employment and production, then the government borrows money and pumps it into the credit stream. Such means as public works are used to set people to work. Without such government aid, we sink deeper and deeper until we get so low we can't go any further.

Under the plan of older Keynesian economics, the government expands credit so that the cycle is prevented from going down as low as it might. On the other hand, as business begins to recover and starts up to new boom heights, the Keynesian theory then indicates that taxation must be heavy in order to prevent an inflationary boom. In other words, we take the purchasing power away from the people during the boom days and pay back the national debt so that we will be able, in the next depression period, to pour that money back into the economic system. What this system does at best is not to stop business cycles but to prevent them from going to extremes, a condition which has tended to become greater in recent years. The Keynesian economics was expressed in the early sixties in the tax-cut method of placing more money in the hands of consumers. It was also used not only to prevent depressions but to maintain a steady rate of economic growth.

Administered Economy—Through Governmental Planning

Administered economy through governmental planning goes well beyond either economy administered by business or the two-front economy described in the immediately preceding section. In the two-front economy the government interferes very little with what is happening in private enterprise. Under a governmentally planned economy, the government does over-all planning in terms of allocation of raw materials, minimum working conditions, and perhaps price controls, such as we have had in periods of inflation or periods of war (as for example, World War II). Although there had been no well-defined program of administered economy by government consciously pursued in times other than war, the whole trend during the last fifty to seventy years had been toward more and more of what can be called state capitalism—or toward the policies of business being dictated by administrative law rather than being left to business itself. In general, except in wartime this has not included any attempt at restricting the amount of certain products produced, the controlling of prices, or consumer rationing, although quotas for certain farm crops have been set annually. During wartime such measures have been necessary in order to steer the economy into a productive program geared to meet military objectives. Most of the advocates of governmental planning think that we should bring together some kind of planning board (such as the National Resources Planning Board set up in the early 1940's) and determine just how the resources of the country should be used for the welfare of the people. Then various kinds of regulations, encouragement incentives, and other policies would be set forth by the government to see to it that the effort of our industrial system was employed in those areas where it would do the most good for our economy.

Socialistic Economy—Largely Governmentally Owned

A socialistic economy is an alternative not cherished by a large number of Americans. It is perhaps difficult for Americans to realize that, outside of America, ideas of this kind are widely held even in countries that are not Communistic. Major political parties in France, Italy, and England hold modified ideas leaning toward a socialistic solution some of the problems that their economies face. It is therefore, worthwhile for those of us in America to study this particular alternative, even though it is not likely to be accepted as a complete answer to our economic problems, at least in the near future.

The government geographically closest to the United States that approximates a socialistic approach is that headed by the Co-operative Commonwealth Federation of Canada, which has been in control in the province of Saskatchewan (but not of Canada as a whole) over a period of years. It is interesting to note that one of the things that this Canadian party has done within the province is to make available life insurance that can be bought at cost through provincial auspices. Another interesting item is that when you buy your automobile license you also must buy your liability insurance—at a slight additional cost. Other than that, this particular party has made no major changes in the economy, although it does advocate some.

Distinction should be made here between democratic socialism and socialism of the type sponsored under dictatorships such as Russian communism. Most of the Socialist parties in noncommunistic countries are democratic; that is, they believe that the policies they want to bring about should be established through discussion and majority vote. This, of course, is in opposition to the attitudes of those Marxian Communists who think that it is necessary that there be a revolution in order to bring it about. Many of the Socialists do base their philosophy on Marxian economics, as do the Russian Communists, but break with Marx with respect to the use of violence.

There is considerable difference among Socialists, both in the United States and other parts of the world, as to the extent to which they would socialize the economy. Almost all of them agree that the noncompetitive types of enterprise, such as public utilities, should be publicly owned, either through the central government or through some local branch of government (state, county, or city). Most of them also agree that the major instruments of production, such as the manufacturing industries, should eventually be governmentally owned. When it comes to agriculture there is a marked disagreement among the different types of socialistic parties, with very few, among the democratic Socialists at least, actually advocating nationalization or collectivization of farms on some kind of a public basis. Many of the democratic Socialists (outside of Communistic Russia) believe in the private ownership of personal property, such as clothing, cars, and, in most cases, housing. At least private housing is one of the alternatives of most of the democratic Socialist proposals. It is difficult to make an evaluation of this highly emotionalized, controversial issue within the present world scene without being, or appearing to be somewhat biased. However, most Americans—and this includes most American economists—feel that the Socialist "doctrinaire" theorists have oversimplified the problem. Although it might simplify the steps toward solution to have industry owned by a government rather than by private enterprise, it does not necessarily solve the problems per se, as the British Labour Party discovered following World War I. Many of the basic economic problems of our society are still present even if we hand the ownership and management of an enterprise over to a representative of the government, or (theoretically) the people. We would still have a conflict of interest between management (which in the case of socialization is directly representative of the government) and the actual workers in industry. In other words, there can be strikes in government-owned enterprises, as Britain discovered. We would still have the problems of deciding what shall be the distribution of the proceeds from the productive process as between management on one hand and labor on the other and of the amount that shall be set aside for capital improvements. Most American economists, although some of them may favor increased socialization, do not believe that socialization per se is an automatic solution to many of the problems that we are facing. As Adams puts it:

And yet it is not so much the economic systems as the social and political systems of the two parts of the world that are divergent. The similarity of the economic forces working upon all contemporary systems [is apparent and] it may be pointed out here that industrialism, mass production, ever closer integration of industrial operations, and even an increasing measure of economic control and planning are characteristic of both systems. The Russians, to be sure, have so far freed themselves of the scourge of the business cycle, but they have exposed themselves to the inflexibilities of planning, which may produce its own maladjustments. The responsibility of Russian business management to the state has certain similarities to the responsibility of the American corporate director to the stockholders: both serve as agents. Even the financial conditions under which enterprise operates in the two systems are not as dissimilar as might at first appear.[41]

Cooperatives—Private "Nonprofit" Enterprise

The history of the cooperatives actually goes back much farther than that of some of the other alternatives found here. As a matter of fact, the cooperative is not an independent alternative, but parallels, in a sense, several of the possible alternatives found on the chart. Cooperatives were organized only for a specific purpose, and their proponents did not make any claim that their particular method was one that would solve all problems. However, there are some outstanding enthusiasts who feel that if we could organize a large portion of our economy in the cooperative fashion —cooperatives of producers, perhaps cooperatives of distributors, cooperatives of consumers, retail stores organized without the profit motive but only from the motive of service ("production for use")—we would solve some of the problems that arise out of "exorbitant profits and concentration of too much wealth in the hands of a few people." Furthermore, they believe that this could be done on a basis that would avoid the alleged inefficiency of government-operated enterprises.

Other Possible Economic Analyses

In addition to the various alternatives listed above, there are other possible economic analyses. Other possible solutions may come out of these analyses. In addition to the use of nonprofit cooperatives discussed above, there is also the idea of profit-sharing. In this proposal, firms would be

---

[41] From George P. Adams, Jr., *Competitive Economic Systems* (New York: Thomas Y. Crowell Company, 1955), p. 362.

privately owned but would share the profits (or profits over a certain amount) with their workers, and in some cases also with the consumers. This is held to avoid the frequent conflict of interest between the workers and the management found under nonprofit-sharing systems. This has been called vigorously to the attention of the American people in the campaign by Walter Reuther of the United Automobile Workers in 1958. We cannot go into the details of this and of other analyses, but brief résumés will be presented of a few alternatives that we feel are particularly pertinent or promising.

(1) SCANDINAVIA—THE MIDDLE WAY.   In the Scandinavian countries, Sweden, Norway, and Denmark, we find mixed economics that have gone farther away from laissez-faire, perhaps, than in any other of the countries of Western civilization. In Sweden, for example, the enterprise is divided as follows: private enterprise, one-third; governmentally owned enterprises, one-third; and cooperatives, one-third. It is interesting and intriguing to note that during the period of the depression, when such countries as the United States were suffering seriously, Sweden maintained a fairly even keel even though her exports were down because of the condition of world trade. Apparently by having a mixed economy (although perhaps there were other factors involved), she was able to avoid the excesses of the business cycle that affected the other countries of the world.[42]

(2) DRUCKER'S "NEW SOCIETY."   Peter Drucker, in *The New Society*,[43] has made an analysis of the present American industrial system and points out that we are not headed toward either more socialism or communism or back toward laissez-faire capitalism. He makes an analysis of the industrial process particularly from the point of view of the production process itself in the individual enterprise, even when within the large corporation. This analysis is largely based upon the human relations existing within the enterprise. He points out that whether the eventual ownership of the enterprise is governmental or private or corporational, the same types of problems are faced in the relationship between management responsible for the overall functioning of the productive process and the laborer carrying on some atomistic part of the process.

The laboring man, powerless as an individual in bargaining with management as to his share of the proceeds of the productive process, has joined with others in organizing himself into a union. The union has been formed primarily for the purpose of trying to get for its members as large a share as possible of the returns from the productive process. In this narrow, limited view into which the union has been forced by the circumstances of its existence, the larger welfare of the productive enterprise, the worker, and the consumer sometimes has been lost to sight. In some

[42] See, e.g., William L. Shirer, *The Challenge of Scandinavia* (Boston: Little, Brown, 1955), pp. 5–7.
[43] Peter L. Drucker, *The New Society* (New York: Harper, 1950).

cases the union leadership has manipulated the members to serve its own selfish interests. In these cases it is imperative that the union itself must be democratized in the opportunity for "feed-back" from the rank and file to the union management.

Certain technical matters in regard to the productive process must be placed in the hands of management. The narrow self-interest of the individual workers may be destructive of the productive process. Management must be in the position of making production decisions. Each enterprise must make a profit, whether operating as the only enterprise of a private company, or as a government enterprise, or as one of the many atomistic enterprises of one large corporation.

Mr. Drucker thinks that his so-called *new society,* or *industrial society,* is "beyond" capitalism and socialism.[44] He apparently feels that his proposal would be less advantageous in an industrial system of the kind favored by democratic socialism than it would be in one in which the legal ownership was still vested in private or corporate management hands. Management must be allowed to run the productive process on an efficient "business" basis, receiving whatever powers are necessary in order to make decisions consistent with the most efficient production.

(3) GALBRAITH's THEORY OF "COUNTERVAILING POWER." Another interesting analysis of the American capitalistic system is that of John K. Galbraith.[45] Galbraith has been concerned about analyzing the dynamics of the whole system, as opposed to Drucker's analysis of each enterprise within the system. Galbraith, however, agrees with Drucker that American capitalism has moved far away from laissez-faire capitalism as it was earlier conceived. He thinks that it has been gradually supplanted by a *differing* system until now its success can be explained entirely in terms of a *differing theory.* This is the theory that he calls *countervailing power.* This explains the success of our economic system because of somewhat automatic regulation by the opposing giants, the many big corporations, big labor, and big government. This replaces the automatic self-regulation of the old laissez-faire system.

As industry got larger and larger and control of the various productive processes became concentrated more and more in the hands of monopolies or oligopolies, an attempt was made to restore the competitive system by the means of "trust-busting." Galbraith indicates that this proves unsatisfactory because the large size of the industries is necessitated by the type of technology we have.

Monopolies, however, might well have tended to lead to inefficiency of the productive process and a static condition that would have been bad in terms of general industrial progress had it not been for the developing of

44 *Ibid.,* p. 351.
45 John K. Galbraith, *American Capitalism: Concept of Countervailing Power* (Boston: Houghton, 1952).

countervailing power against monopolies. One of the bulwarks of this power is the force of the labor unions. With the help of the government through the National Industrial Relations Act, as well as through earlier laws passed to assist labor in its fight against management, the unions were able to obtain concessions in regard to their share of the returns of the productive process, as well as in other matters such as working conditions. Also, agriculture, a group that found it very difficult to organize itself to maintain its fair share of the productive process, was aided (after political pressure upon the government) through various forms of governmental action such as price-support methods.

According to Galbraith, these are not the only countervailing powers. Corporations are consumers of the products of other corporations. An example of this kind is supplied by General Motors and United States Steel. In other cases, corporations such as the Atlantic and Pacific Tea Company or Sears, Roebuck are marketing organizations and are able to match or even master the manufacturers in price and quality tussles. In between, all around, and keeping an eagle eye over the procedure, is the force of the government, which has become over a period of years and still is becoming an ever stronger factor in the whole productive process through laws of various kinds to prevent any one element in the economy from overstepping itself. This whole process has led to a system of checks and balances, which Galbraith gives as the reason why the American capitalistic system has been able to go to great heights of productive efficiency and capacity.

(4) PEOPLE'S CAPITALISM.   Another possible interpretation of ways in which our economic system might move is toward what is called People's Capitalism. Kelso and Adler, in their book *The Capitalist Manifesto*[46] indicate that the best direction in which the economic system could move would be toward more and more mass stock ownership. This has happened to some extent, of course, for there is widespread ownership of the stocks in some of our large companies. There is, however, still high concentration of the deciding power of the companies in the hands of a relatively few persons. Kelso and Adler suggest that laws be set up to prevent too great a concentration in the hands of a few people and through provisions to encourage the widespread purchase of stocks. Provisions could be made for people to buy stock in smaller quantities without the expense of purchase through a broker because this makes it somewhat prohibitive for small investors at present. Stocks, for example, might be sold "over the counter" at banks or even stores. This proposal is based on making an economic system like profit-sharing companies in which the general public, workers, and others, would feel an important vested interest in the capitalistic system as do the present owners and managers.

[46] Louis O. Kelso and Mortimer J. Adler, *The Capitalist Manifesto* (New York: Random House, 1958), Chapter IX–XIII.

AMERICANS WILL PROBABLY SEEK A PRAGMATIC SOLUTION

In spite of the fact that all shades of opinion are present in the American social scene, the vast majority of Americans are probably very close to the middle of the road as far as range of opinion on the world scene is concerned. There are few Americans who are at the extremes of communism or other forms of dictatorial socialism, only a relatively few who are in favor of a thorough democratic socialism, and only a very few at the opposite extreme who would expound some form of neofascism or closely related view. Some of our extreme reactionaries are very close to a fascistic point of view, even though not openly avowing such. This latter group, in spite of the publicity sometimes given to them, makes up a relatively small portion of our population.

Trueblood indicates a balanced appraisal of these familiar views as follows:[47]

There are obvious dangers in what is called a welfare state, the chief of these being that people who are secure often become supine and relatively unproductive, but we must run some slight risk in this direction if we are to keep the tenderness toward persons which the good life requires. There may be some argument about what ought to be done for the lazy man, but there cannot be any serious argument about what ought to be done for his children. They, in any case, are innocent of his sins, and ought not to suffer hardship because of the shiftlessness of their parent. The free society will avoid coddling the lazy, but it will seek at the same time to take fear of absolute destitution out of every heart. The good life advances when the people in a society are free from the haunting fears and anxieties of catastrophic changes in their lives. The encouragement of group insurance and the widening of social security are, therefore, not at variance with the idea of free society, but essential to it, if the freedom to live is one of the primary freedoms. The task is to give full scope to this freedom without, at the same time, losing the freedom of enterprise and initiative. But this, as in the other situations already reviewed, comes best by deliberate moral development rather than by legal restraint. Neither this nor any other system is foolproof. It is part of the idea of a free society that it never, at any point, releases the individual from the necessity of moral effort.

In spite of the vehemence with which Americans fight their political battles and in spite of the fact that they quite often seem to be irresistibly committed to one of a set of alternatives, the probability is that Americans in the future will continue to solve their problems in the same way as they have in the past. This is by the method of a pragmatic solution, one by one, of the problems that they face. Americans apparently hesitate to theorize and thus solve a whole set of problems together. Once having achieved an immediate solution, they can rationalize it in terms of their

[47] From Elton Trueblood, *Declaration of Freedom*, p. 68. Copyright, 1955, Harper & Row. Used by permission.

present theory or as an exception to their theory, without developing a new theory to encompass the complete solution. It is quite likely that Americans will choose to improvise or to select for isolated instances from the many alternatives listed above in the solution of their economic problems. This means that at times the solution will be delayed beyond the point at which it should be put into effect. However, there is apparently a growing feeling that economic problems can be solved by man because they *are* "man-made." Consequently the public will not be very patient unless some sort of solution is attempted. The use of better measuring devices to determine the direction our economic system is going on the one hand, and to determine the efficacy of economic remedies on the other, will help to determine the direction of economic remedies and their success as they are tried.

RESPONSIBILITY OF SCHOOLS TO EDUCATE PUPILS TO UNDERSTAND CONSEQUENCES OF ECONOMIC TRENDS

Economic problems are basic to our lives. The growth of technical economic knowledge recently has been so rapid that very few of the American people understand such problems. It can be stated more strongly: the American people are economically illiterate. Conceptions about economics are held that are manifestly and demonstrably false. Many of the decisions that are made in economic matters must be formed through public opinion and public action. The people need to be better educated as to how the economic system works, what its problems are, and the possible alternatives for their solution.

Before we take up other implications in the study of economics, it is interesting to note that economists have recently become interested in studying education from an economics point of view. A good case in point is the study by Schultz.[48] This study of education has been interested in determining what the costs of education are if the loss of earning power while going to school are included. This is not topically considered in the total when the amount of money spent on education is announced. Further, the economists are interested in knowing what is the return on investment in terms of "human capital." In searching for the sources of improved productivity in Gross National Product, one of the things which has to be considered is capital. The normal definition of this term refers, of course, to the plant, equipment, and methods of productivity used. However, the economists have discovered another factor called "human capital," a part of the capital stock. Part of this human capital is related directly to education. Some of it is indirectly related to education to the extent to which the culture has been improved by education. The economists

[48] Theodore W. Schultz, *The Economic Value of Education* (New York: Columbia University Press, 1963).

make an estimate concerning the rate of return on the investment in terms of improved national product as well as in earnings that accrue to the individual concerned. As of 1939 Schultz reports that for four years of high school the return on the investment was 14.3 per cent per year. College education had a return of approximately 11 per cent as based on 1958 data. In the meantime, the 1958 data had indicated a reduced return on high school education of 10 per cent. The 1958 data also support a 35 per cent return per year on elementary education based on the return on the total cost over the life span of one's earnings.[49] The import of these data seems to indicate that education gives the highest return on an investment both from the standpoint of the investment by government and of the investment by the individual in loss of time and in money for his education.

Returning now to the discussion of the study of economics in the schools: the authors hold that there should be a greater emphasis on economics in the school's curriculum. This does not necessarily mean on courses in economics. Economic ideas can be taught quite early in the elementary grades and in courses other than economics. Some of this is done now, but much more could and should be done. The fundamental concepts of economics can be made interesting and clear even to average persons in our population. Of course some of the more complex ideas of economics are for the specialist. What the average man needs to understand is the basic outline of economics. We have attempted to present such an outline of the fundamentals of our economic system in these two chapters.

Implications for education of the future growth of automation and of the possible ramifications of atomic energy, however, go much beyond the mere understanding of the economic system that now exists. The following quotation from Stuart Chase in the *N.E.A. Journal* serves to indicate the problem ahead of us:[50]

Robert Bendiner in the *Reporter* has posed the $64 long range question: "Are we capable of developing a culture that does not depend upon work to give meaning to our lives?" This is a question that education must face. It will call for changes in the curriculum, to train the new types of industrial workers needed—mathematicians, scientists, designers, skilled electronics operators, and those extraordinary virtuosos who cut the tapes. Even more important, practically everyone will need training to live with a degree of leisure unknown in any human culture—even under the breadfruit trees of the South Seas.

Homo sapiens is not a loafing organism. Without something to engage his mind and muscles, he rapidly degenerates. Studies of workers retired at 65 *with no outside interests* show many cases of nervous breakdown. In some

[49] Schultz, *op. cit.*, pp. 62–63.
[50] From *N.E.A. Journal*, October, 1955, p. 393. Copyright, 1955, the National Education Association. Reprinted by permission of Stuart Chase and the National Education Association.

companies, the poor chaps are permitted to go back to the shop and watch somebody else do what they used to do.

Automation, after its introductory period, may well mean more leisure than the human organism was designed by nature to tolerate. How to transform this leisure into fruitful activity, and so escape biological disaster, will be the particular job of the teaching profession.

Other implications for the school flow from an understanding of the nature of the free enterprise system through which America has been able to make great progress because of freedom, in the sense of the right to make suggestions and to carry them out. The authors would like to encourage some of the activities the schools have carried on in the past, while asking them to accentuate and extend them in the future. We quote herewith again from an earlier writing of the senior author that stresses this point:[51]

It can be readily seen that the trend in the schools toward the stimulation of self-expression and creativity on the one hand and the more recent movement toward helping boys and girls and youth to work together in groups are both elements which assist the schools in teaching for values which are dominant in our "free enterprise" society. The emphasis upon creativity in our schools contrasts sharply with the Russian communist system, which does not permit free expression or creation by artists, musicians, or writers.

The schools have done and are doing a great number of things in the areas of creativity, group planning, and group work. Certainly we can do more, and it becomes necessary from time to time to clarify our thinking and to explore new possibilities of improvement in this area. Conflicts concerning the fine points of the meaning of "free enterprise" in special instances are not likely to have meaning in the early levels of school, since those elements which are significant at these maturity levels are generally not matters which are in conflict in our society.

The school, of course, must assist the child in clarifying those elements which are not in conflict. Moreover, it should be pointed out that criticism which teachers and others as citizens in our society may at any time make of certain interpretations of "free enterprise" should not be regarded as a criticism of free enterprise itself. While teachers should avoid airing in the classroom their own private opinions about this and all other matters, the teacher should be free, where such issues are pertinent according to the maturity of the child, to discuss all sides of such questions without fear of reprisal, since such freedom itself is a part of our free enterprise system.

In summary, the writer envisions "free enterprise" in a broad sense as being one of the fundamental values of our democratic culture, a value which the school should emphasize. While the school should not as such take sides on points in which aspects of the concept are under dispute, the school should actively and openly help boys and girls to understand the concept and con-

[51] Ralph L. Pounds, "Teaching for "Free Enterprise," *Progressive Education*, July 1956, pp. 119–120. Copyright, 1956, John Dewey Society. Used by permission.

flicting ideas concerning it at their level of maturity. Such aspects as stimulating and developing creativity, independent and critical thinking, and the ability to work with others and to submerge one's self in constructive contribution to group activity (without sacrificing individual creativity) are certainly among the more important contributions that the schools can make. The concept is to be thought of as applying as well to non-profit-making enterprises such as government, charity, and education. If America can maintain a kind of creative individuality in a world that, because of its conflicts and its interdependence, requires a high degree of coordination on one hand and of skilled specialization on the other, America's future is safe, because she will have thereby guaranteed the free flow of ideas and innovations so necessary to the growth of a society and to its adaptability to changing world conditions.

SUMMARY

In this chapter the development of one of the outstanding economic systems of the world has been described. The American industrial enterprise compared to that of other nations ranks quite high both in total quantity and in quality, and in the productivity per worker as well.

The first of the over-all trends in the development of the American economy has been the rise of the laissez-faire economy and its subsequent breakdown due to forces that originated within the economy itself and rose out of the emerging technology and the structure of the industrial enterprises. Outstanding also among the trends has been the expansion of the productivity in all fields. The American capitalistic system has changed —from the small shop and handicraft system of the earlier period, to the finance-controlled capitalistic enterprises, and on to the large corporations characteristic of the "big business" of the modern period. Economy has shifted from one of scarcity to one of plenty, probably sometime in the 1920's. The over-all trend in the type of enterprises has been the basic shift from the laissez-faire capitalism toward a "mixed" capitalism consisting of both corporation and state capitalism, along with some cooperatives, some state socialism, and some small private enterprises.

The effect of the improved technology on a productive enterprise has been illustrated by charts, with the effect shown of the change in certain factors, wages, work-week, prices (other factors being held constant), upon productivity and the relationship of such within the individual enterprise to the total national enterprise. A description of the American economy in terms of the flow of goods and money has also been presented. The problems of the American economy have been listed: possible concentration of economic power; inequality of wealth and income; monopoly and administered prices; business cycles; technological unemployment; the unbalanced national budget, inflation, and taxation; the growth of big units, labor government, business; and the changed notions concerning private property. Six alternatives for the American economic system have been set forth: negative laissez-faire, positive laissez-faire; administered economy by business; administered economy by government; two kinds of governmentally planned economy—i.e., "state capitalism"—"two-front" economy or "Keynesian economics"; and socialistic economy.

Other possible alternatives were discussed but it was pointed out that the Americans would probably seek a pragmatic solution to each of their economic problems as they face them rather than develop some type of clear-cut doctrinaire, theoretical base upon which to work out logically solutions for all problems faced.

SELECTED BIBLIOGRAPHY

American Assembly, John Dunlop (ed.). *Automation and Technological Change.* Englewood Cliffs, N.J.: Prentice-Hall, 1962. Pp. vi + 184.

"American Capitalism: An Introduction for Young Citizens." Study on Economic Education, CASE Economic Literacy Series, No. 1 (Pamphlet). Washington, D.C.: Council for Advancement of Secondary Education, 1958. Pp. xi + 116.

American Round Table Digest Report. *People's Capitalism.* Series, sponsored by Yale University and the Advertising Council. New York: Advertising Council, 1957. A series of discussions by experts purporting to explore numerous aspects of the effects, benefits, and problems of American capitalism. Part II, for example, is entitled "An Inquiry into Cultural Trends under the American System of Widely Shared Benefits."

BAZELON, DAVID T. *The Paper Economy.* New York: Random House, 1963. Pp. 467.

BRICKMAN, WILLIAM W., and STANLEY LEHRER (eds.). *Automation, Education and Human Values.* New York: School and Society Books, 1966. Pp. 419.

BERLE, ADOLF A. *The American Economic Republic.* New York: Harcourt, Brace, & World, 1963. Pp. xv + 247.

Center for the Study of Democratic Institutions. *A Conversation: Labor Looks at Labor.* Santa Barbara, Calif.: The Fund for the Republic, 1963. Pp. 32.

Committee for Economic Development, Research and Policy Committee. *Economic Growth in the United States: Its Past and Future.* New York: Committee for Economic Development, 1958. Pp. 63.

Committee for Economic Development. *Union Powers and Union Functions: Toward a Better Balance.* New York: The Committee, 1964. Pp. 42. A statement of national policy by The Research Committee of the Committee for Economic Development.

COTTRELL, WILLIAM FRED. *Energy and Society: The Relation Between Energy, Social Change, and Economic Development.* New York: McGraw-Hill, 1955. Pp. xix + 330.

CRUM, WILLIAM L. *Corporate Size and Earning Power.* Cambridge, Mass.: Harvard University Press, 1939. Pp. 418.

CUBBEDGE, ROBERT E. *Who Needs People?* Washington, D.C.: Robert B. Luce, 1963. Pp. ix + 114. Deals with automation.

DARCY, ROBERT L. "Economic Education for Teachers: Preservice Program,"

Bulletin of the National Association of Secondary School Pupils, 49 (November 1965), pp. 74–85.

DEWHURST, J. FREDERICK, and Associates. *Amercia's Needs and Resources: A New Survey.* New York: Twentieth Century Fund, 1955. Pp. xxix + 267.

DILLARD, DUDLEY. *The Economics of John Maynard Keynes.* Englewood Cliffs, N.J.: Prentice-Hall, 1953. Pp. xv + 364.

DRUCKER, PETER F. *The New Society: The Anatomy of the Industrial Order.* New York: Harper & Row, 1950. Pp. xv + 356. Believes that a "new society" is emerging in the American democratic culture that is neither capitalistic nor communistic.

DUNLAP, JOHN (ed.). *Automation and Technological Change.* Sponsored by the American Assembly. Englewood Cliffs, N.J.: Prentice-Hall, 1962. Pp. vi + 184.

EBENSTEIN, WILLIAM. *Today's Isms: Communism, Fascism, Capitalism, Socialism,* Second Edition. Englewood Cliffs, N.J. Prentice-Hall, 1958. Pp. 256.

The Economic Almanac, 1953–54. New York: Crowell, 1953. Pp. 442.

Economic Education Experiences of Enterprising Teachers. A Report developed from the 1962 entries in the Kazanjian Foundation Awards Program for the Teaching of Economics, 1963. Pp. x + 93.

Economic Education in the Schools. Summary of the report of the National Task Force on Economic Education (September 1961). Pp. 14.

Economic Policies and Practices. Paper No. 5. Unemployment Programs in Sweden. Washington, D.C.: Government Printing Office, Joint Economic Committee, 1964. Pp. 8–9.

Editors of *Fortune. America in the Sixties: The Economy and the Society.* New York: Harper & Row, 1960. Pp. xvi + 266.

Educating for Economic Competence. A report prepared by the Association for Supervision and Curriculum Development of NEA, Washington, D.C., 1960. Pp. 78.

Educational Policies Commission. *Manpower and Education.* Washington, D.C.: National Education Association of the United States, 1956. Pp. 128.

FERRY, W. H. "Caught on the Horn of Plenty." New York: Center for the Study of Democratic Institutions, 1962. Pp. 8.

———. "The Triple Revolution." The Ad Hoc Committee on the Triple Revolution, Santa Barbara, California, 1964. *Advertising Age Magazine* (March 22, 1964). Reprint.

FOSTER, GEORGE M. *Traditional Cultures and the Impact of Technological Change.* New York: Harper & Row, 1962. Pp. xiii + 292.

GALBRAITH, JOHN K. *American Capitalism: The Concept of Countervailing Power.* Boston: Houghton Mifflin, 1952. Pp. xi + 216.

———. *Economic Development in Perspective.* Cambridge, Mass., Harvard University Press, 1962. Pp. 76.

GIDEONSE, HARRY D. "Economic Growth and Educational Development" (Reprinted from *College and University* (Summer, 1963). Brooklyn College. Pp. 421–433.

GINSBERG, ELI (ed.). *Technology and Social Change.* Columbia University. Seminar on Technology and Social Change. New York: Columbia University Press, 1964. Pp. vii + 158.

———, and HYMAN BERMAN (eds.). *The American Worker in the Twentieth Century: A History Through Autobiographies.* New York: Free Press of Glencoe, 1963. Pp. xii + 368.

GRAHAM, BENJAMIN. *The Flexible Work-Year: An Answer to Unemployment.* Santa Barbara, Calif.: Center for the Study of Democratic Institutions, 1964. Pp. 12.

GROVES, HAROLD M. *Education and Economic Growth.* Washington, D.C.: The Committee on Educational Finance, NEA, 1961. Pp. 58.

HALSEY, A. H., and others (eds.). *Education, Economy and Society: A Reader in the Sociology of Education.* New York: Free Press of Glencoe, 1961. Pp. ix + 625.

HARRINGTON, MICHAEL. *The Other America: Poverty in the United States.* New York: Macmillan, 1962. Pp. 191.

HEILBRONER, ROBERT L. *The Great Ascent: The Struggle for Economic Development in Our Time.* New York: Harper & Row, 1963. Pp. 189.

HEILBRONER, ROBERT L. *The Making of Economic Society.* Englewood Cliffs, N.J.: Prentice-Hall, 1962. Pp. xiii + 241.

HOLSTEIN, RALPH, GERARD PIEL, and ROBERT THEOBALD. *Jobs, Machines, and People.* Santa Barbara, Calif.: Center for the Study of Democratic Institutions, 1964. Pp. 23.

JACOBSON, HOWARD, and JOSEPH S. ROUCEK (eds.) *Automation and Society.* New York: Philosophical Library, 1959. Pp. 553.

KELSO, LOUIS O., and MORTIMER J. ADLER. *The Capitalist Manifesto.* New York: Random House, 1958. Pp. xviii + 265. Argues for a "capitalist revolution," which in essence would consist of the limitation of capitalist holdings to an individual family and the paying out of all earnings in dividends. All corporate income taxes would be abolished. The corporation would go to the market for additional capital needed for expansion.

KEYSERLING, LEON H. *Agriculture and the Public Interest Toward a New Farm Program.* Washington, D.C.: Conference on Economic Progress, 1965. Pp. 8 + 123.

LARRABEE, ERIC, and ROLF MEYERSON. *Mass Leisure.* New York: Free Press of Glencoe, 1958. Pp. x + 429.

LEVY, LESTER S. and ROY J. SAMPSON. *American Economic Development: Growth of the U.S. in the Western World.* Boston: Allyn & Bacon, 1962. Pp. 623.

LYNCH, DAVID. *The Concentration of Economic Power.* New York: Columbia University Press, 1946. Pp. x + 423.

McKEE, C. W., and H. G. MOULTON. *A Survey of Economic Education.* Washington, D.C.: Brookings Institution, 1951. Pp. viii + 63.

MARKHAM, J. W. (ed.). *The American Economy.* New York: Braziller, 1963. Pp. 74.

MASSWELL, MARK S. *Competition and Monopoly: Legal and Economic Issues.* Washington, D.C.: Brookings Institution, 1951. Pp. viii + 63.

MICHAEL, DONALD N. "Cybernation: The Silent Conquest." A report to the Center for the Study of Democratic Institutions. Santa Barbara, Calif.: The Center, 1962. Pp. 46.

MOORE, WILBERT E. *Economy and Society.* Garden City, N.Y.: Doubleday, 1955. Pp. ix + 48 (Pamphlet). An excellent brief discussion.

MORGAN, JAMES N., and others. *Income and Welfare in the United States.* New York: McGraw-Hill, 1964. Pp. x + 531.

MYRDAL, GUNNAR. *An International Economy: Problems and Prospects.* New York: Harper & Row, 1956. Pp. xi + 381.

————. *Challenge to Affluence.* New York: Pantheon, 1963. Pp. viii + 172.

NEA, *Automation and the Challenge to Education.* Washington, D.C.: The Association, 1962. Pp. 200.

NORTON, JOHN K. *Changing Demands on Education and Their Fiscal Implications.* Washington, D.C.: National Committee for Support of the Public Schools, 1963. Pp. 4 + 109.

Organisation for Economic Co-operation and Development. *Higher Education and the Demand for Scientific Manpower in the United States.* Paris: The Organisation, 1963. Pp. 101.

PACKARD, VANCE. *The Wastemakers.* New York: David McKay, 1960. Pp. x + 340.

PHILIPSON, MORRIS (ed.). *Automation: Implications for the Future.* New York: Vintage Books, 1962. Pp. 456.

PIEL, GERARD. *Consumers of Abundance.* New York: The Center and the Fund for the Republic, 1961. Pp. 10.

POMFRET, JOHN D. *New Opportunities for Depressed Areas.* Public Affairs Pamphlet No. 351 (October 1963). New York: Public Affairs Pamphlets, 1963.

PURDY, HARRY L., MARTIN LINDAHL, and WILLIAM A. CARTER. *Corporate Concentration and Public Policy.* Englewood Cliffs, N.J.: Prentice-Hall, 1950. Pp. xv + 725.

RIESMAN, DAVID. *Abundance for What? and Other Essays.* Garden City, N.Y.: Doubleday, 1964. Pp. xiv + 610.

ROBINSON, MARSHALL A., and others. *An Introduction to Economic Reasoning.* Washington, D.C.: Brookings Institution, 1956. Pp. x + 335.

ROGERS, VIRGIL M. "What Teachers Should Know About Automation" *NEA Journal,* **52**, No. 7 (October 1963), 50–52, 69.

ROSTOW, W. W. *The Stages of Economic Growth: A Non-Communistic Manifesto.* Cambridge, Mass.: University Press, 1960. Pp. xi + 179. A comparative study of national development based on a theory of economic growth.

SAMUELSON, PAUL A. *Economics: An Introductory Analysis,* Sixth Edition. New York: McGraw-Hill, 1964. Pp. xx + 810.

SCHEIBER, HENRY N. *United States Economic History: Selected Readings.* New York: Knopf, 1964. Pp. xi + 583.

SHIRER, WILLIAM L. *The Challenge of Scandinavia: Norway, Sweden, Denmark and Finland in Our Time.* Boston: Little, Brown, 1955. Pp. 437.

"Shorter Hours: Tool to Combat Unemployment," *The American Federationist* (n.p.) (American Federation of Labor and Congress of Industrial Organizations). Pp. 53.

SHULTZ, THEODORE W. *The Economic Value of Education.* New York: Columbia University Press, 1963. Pp. xii + 92.

SIEVERS, ALLEN M. *Revolution, Evolution, and the Economic Order.* Englewood Cliffs, N.J.: Prentice-Hall, 1964. Pp. vii + 173.

SKINNER, B. F. *Walden Two.* New York: Macmillan, 1951. Pp. 266. An utopia, employing modern terms, including view of psychology. Written as a novel.

SMITH, ADAM. *The Wealth of Nations*. New York: Modern Library, 1937. A classic.

THOMSON, GEORGE. *The Foreseeable Future*. Cambridge (Eng.): University Press, 1955. Pp. vii + 166. An excellent nontechnical discussion of the technical problems and possibilities of future advances in world technology.

United States, Special Committee Report. *Economic Concentration and World War II*. Senate Document No. 206. 79th Congress, 2nd session. Washington, D.C.: Government Printing Office, 1940. Pp. vi + 48.

United States, Temporary National Economic Committee. *Competition and Monopoly in American Industry*. Investigation of Concentration of Economic Power, Monograph 21, 76th Congress, 3rd Session, Senate Committee Print. Washington, D.C.: Government Printing Office, 1941. Pp. xii + 344.

————. *The Distribution of Ownership in the 200 Largest Non-Financial Corporations*. Investigations of Concentration of Economic Power, Monograph 29, 76th Congress, 3rd Session, Senate Committee Print. Washington, D.C.: Government Printing Office, 1940. Pp. xviii + 1558.

VAIZEY, JOHN. *The Economics of Education*. London: Faber and Faber, 1962. Pp. 165.

VAN TIL, WILLIAM. *Economic Roads for American Democracy*. New York: McGraw-Hill, 1947. Pp. ix + 252.

WIRTZ, WILLARD W. (Chairman). *The Challenge of Jobless Youth*. Washington, D.C.: Government Printing Office, 0–681922, 1963. Pp. iv + 20.

WOYTINSKY, W. S., and Associates. Employment and Wages in the United States. New York: Twentieth Century Fund, 1954. Pp. xxxii + 777. A careful study made by the Twentieth Century Fund (a nonpartisan philanthropic foundation) of this difficult problem.

SELECTED FILMS

A Is for Atom (GE) 15 min
An animated cartoon on basic atomic information.

The Age of Specialization (McGraw-Hill) 13 min
From the country store of 1900 to the complex specialization of today.

Allocating Our Resources (Carousel) 30 min
America has rejected the mechanism of total planning; however, because of our desire for fair distribution of goods or for reasons of efficiency, we have put some restrictions on a totally free market. The film illustrates some of the areas where the government has limited the free market as the sole criterion of economic allocation.

American Farmer (Ford Motor Co.) 28 min
An intimate and beautifully photographed story of a modern farmer and the changes wrought in his life by mechanization and scientific farming.

American Harvest (Jam Handy Organization) 29 min
Surveys American production, highlighting the latest developments in the mechanization of agriculture, the integration of agriculture with creative

chemistry, and the newest, largest and most efficient operations in agriculture, industry, transportation and distribution.

Atomic Energy (Encyclopaedia Britannica Films) 10 min

Animated drawings on concepts fundamental to understanding the nature of atomic energy and its releases.

Atomic Power (McGraw-Hill) 28 min

A basic film on atomic power and on the bomb. Produced by the March of Time.

Beginnings and Growth of Industrial America (Coronet Films) 11 min

Discussing economic and social change in the period between the Revolutionary and Civil Wars, the film shows the development of American manufacturing from a system of home crafts to an industrialized factory system. Factors that contributed to industrial growth—inventions, investments, and labor—are explained. The film includes many actual, reconstructed, historical scenes, such as Hopewell Village and Slater's Mill.

Cage (McGraw-Hill) 29 min

Portrays High Martin, a capable business executive, caught on the treadmill of a competitive society. Suggests that each man has to find his own way out of the cage that modern living imposes on everyone.

Capitalism (Coronet Films) 11 min

In this film students see some important aspects of the capitalistic system—private property, profit, competition, freedom of contract, and free enterprise. A high school radio forum provides an opportunity to listen to the conflicting opinions of several people, each of whom tries to tell what our system means to him.

The Case of Competition (Carousel) 30 min

The film points out that competition begets lower prices, provides a greater variety of products and is generally favorable to all consumers. The film examines how government and business might view four subjects outside the area of competition—monopoly, labor, profits, and subsidies—and illustrates a "self-fulfilling prophecy."

Communism (UWF) 32 min

Documentary film on communism and its history, contrast between communism and the American system, and a warning to avoid labeling as communists all who disagree with the majority.

Competition and Big Business (Encyclopaedia Britannica Films) 22 min

Assists in clarifying the meaning of competition by analyzing the role of big business in terms of its bearing on entry into the market, technological progress, and the problem of monopoly in a society where public interest and social responsibility is crucial.

The Cooperative and the Community (Social Science Films) 12 min

Shows high school students in a current problems class defining the difference between a private corporation and a cooperative. Defines and gives examples of three general types of cooperatives and then describes in some detail various marketing cooperatives.

Crossroads for America (Cincinnati Chamber of Commerce) 30 min

What America is, what it has to offer, and what it could become. The film exposes and explodes communism from a practical point of view.

Enough for All (Massey-Harris) 40 min

A review of agricultural science and its application to modern farming. Basic scientific developments and techniques in the field of agriculture demonstrate the ever increasing ability of agriculture to meet the food requirements of a growing population.

Farmers Working Together (United World) 19 min
Describes the operations, organization, and general activities of farmer cooperatives through the United States.

A Free Economy: Theory and Practice (Encyclopaedia Britannica Films) 30 min
The film outlines the essential ingredients of the classical, or laissez-faire, model of a free economy, and shows how this has become a myth in the United States.

Goals and Growth (Carousel) 30 min
In the film it is explained how we must achieve continued or accelerated growth in the GNP, and the importance of the question of choice, especially in the context of economic freedom, is revealed.

How We Live in America (The American Economic Foundation) 30 min each
A series of nine films on economics. Factually well done. Strongly favorable to the American competitive system.

Introduction to Foreign Trade (Coronet Films) 10 min
First establishes the importance of foreign trade to our economy and then presents a general picture of the mechanics of international commerce. The role of monetary standards and control, national policies in reference to those controls, distribution of raw materials and markets are shown. Then, in an actual exchange of goods, the detailed domestic and foreign operations involved in the sale, shipment, and payment are portrayed.

Knowledge and Skills (Association) 21 min
Alex Drier reports on today's growing need for workers with skilled and technological knowledge and shows how vocational training courses are preparing both young and old for future jobs.

A Look at Communism (NEP) 13 min
Basic philosophy, tactics, and strategy. A look at dialectical materialism, economic determinism, and atheism.

A Look at Socialism (NEP) 13 min
A thorough study of the philosophy and record of socialism in practice. Uses dramatization, actual scenes in England, and other material.

Man Who Changed the World (TFC) 11 min
Story of James Hargreaves, English spinner, whose invention of the spinning jenny in 1767 laid the foundation for the machine age. How the conflict between man and machines came about.

The Meaning of the Industrial Revolution (Coronet Films) 11 min
Tells of the beginning and the meaning of the Industrial Revolution.

Productivity: Key to Plenty (EBF) 20 min
Greater use of machine power has given America top place in productivity with resultant high standards of living, says this film. Research by Twentieth Century Fund.

The Rise of Organized Labor (McGraw-Hill) 18 min.
Explains the economic reasons that forced workers to join unions. Il-

lustrates the past and present problems and responsibilities of unions in our economic system.

Seed for Tomorrow (Brandon) 20 min

Surveys the problems of the small farmer and discusses how the cooperative effort of the National Farmers Union can help the farmer to stay on the land.

Sweden (McGraw-Hill) 22 min

Narrated by Walter Cronkite, this film explains the cradle-to-the-grave security as experienced by the Swedish people, and answers such questions as "Is it worth it?" "What are its drawbacks?" Swedish leaders in several fields are interviewed on the central issue of whether the nation's welfare state legislation is related to its chronically high rates of anti-social behavior.

The Story of Creative Capital (U.S. Chamber of Commerce) 16 min

A clever animated film of the evolution of business and capital investment in this country. It shows where capital comes from and what it does.

Traveling the Middle Way in Sweden (Harmon) 90 min

Divided into three two-reel units, each of which may be obtained separately. A pictorial record of Sweden's progress through a coordination of public ownership and consumer and agricultural cooperatives. Unit I, Land of Sweden; Unit II, Consumer Cooperatives; Unit III, Agricultural Cooperatives.

Trip to Cooperative Europe (Co-op League) 20 min

A first-hand report on "co-ops" in seven of Europe's most cooperatively developed countries. Covers cooperative development from the original Toad Lane Store in Rochdale to the modern co-op factories in Sweden. Describes how the cooperatives of England, Scotland, France, Holland, Denmark, Finland, and Sweden are working to strengthen their nations' economies, badly shattered by the war.

Trouble in Paradise (Association) 12 min

An animated film that shows what inflation is, how to recognize it, and how to solve it. It shows further how it reduces purchasing power and threatens the foundations of free enterprise.

Two Views on Socialism (Coronet Films) 15 min

Arguments for and against the socialistic proposals.

Valley of Tennessee (U.S. Government.) 30 min

Change in agricultural methods made possible by TVA.

Valley Town (New York University) 27 min

The story of how machines made a boom town with factories running at top speed, stores crowded with shoppers, money flowing freely and of how more machines broke it. Considers the problem of capable men thrown out of jobs because of high-speed machinery. Gives an idea of what this does to the spirit of the man and of the effect on the family. Finally offers as one solution the constant training of adults to keep them abreast of new developments for new and better jobs.

Waves of Green (Ford Motor Co.) 43 min

This is the dramatic pictorial story of the amazing development of American agriculture due to the combined efforts and skills of science and industry, the land grant colleges, and, on the local level, the county agent.

What We Have (American Economic Foundation) 15 min

An active, dynamic presentation of the meaning of free enterprise system —from the standpoint of production, consumption, and investment. Basic economic freedoms are pointed out.

Where People Count (Midland) 25 min

Story of two families and the importance of various kinds of cooperatives to them; how coops begin and grow; democratic participation and owner-ship.

Why Play Leapfrog? (Harding College)10 min

Shows how increases in wages result in increased prices. Points out that wage raises based on increased productivity increase purchasing power, but that wage raises without corresponding increases in productivity force prices higher, so that the two can, and frequently do, "play leapfrog."

Years of Progress (Chrysler Corp.) 32 min

An informative picture whose primary objective is to acquaint students with the unique and outstanding facilities for research and engineering that exist for the purpose of creating new and improved products in the interest of broader services to public needs.

The '29 Boom and 30's Depression (Atlantis Productions) 14 min

Recreating this period in American history, the film examines the pros-perity and boom of the 1920's with special attention to factors which later led to the depression.

Part III. *Problems Facing the Individual in Modern American Society*

I<small>N PART III</small>, the authors have selected typical problems in modern American society and have gone into some detail in an analysis of them. In many cases implications are drawn for the school, in the broad context of the point of view set up in the first two parts. The types of problems discussed in this part and the choice of individual problems for discussion within each type are not intended to be exhaustive; but it is hoped they will be typical and will give the student a well-balanced overview with respect to the important trends in the present American society, the nature of persistent current problems, and some of the implications for the school of these problems and trends.

Chapter 6. *Problems of Family Life*

It is FITTING that our study of problems facing the individual in modern American society should consider problems of the family. A recent volume devoted to an analysis of modern social problems states:[1]

All contemporary cultures make some provisions for marriage and family life. History fails to record a time when the family did not constitute a significant social group.

It is not surprising that a specialized text on the family should echo:[2]

In all known peoples—contemporary, historical, prehistorical—human societies have regulated the relations between the sexes through some type of marriage. Thus, marriage is an ancient, venerable, and universal institution.

The importance that students of the family attach to this institution as a determinant of the entire warp and woof of our present social fabric may be gleaned from the following statement:[3]

This broad overlap of generations is what makes the family, under our present type of social organization, the most basic of all social groupings. It is the institution recognized by society as being chiefly responsible for biological survival and social well-being, for it provides a socially approved method both

---

[1] Morris G. Caldwell and Laurence Foster, *Analysis of Social Problems* (Harrisburg: Stackpole, 1954), p. 375.

[2] Henry A. Bowman, *Marriage for Moderns*, Fifth Edition (New York: McGraw-Hill, 1965), p. 1.

[3] By permission from *Marriage and the Family* (p. 1), by Ray E. Baber, Copyright, 1953. McGraw-Hill Book Company, Inc.

187

of bearing and rearing children. The family provides almost the total social environment of the child for the first five years in its life and a very considerable portion of its environment for many years thereafter. It is the matrix of human personality. To this small primary group the state entrusts the initial care and training of its future citizens in the most formative period of their lives. This makes home and family the center of our total culture pattern.

Despite the consensus among modern authorities with respect to the vital importance of the family, it is only in the past four decades that serious and systematic study of the family has been undertaken. In reviewing this research, Baber says, "All these efforts together have thus far been able to make only a slight impression on the work needing to be done."[4] Any serious consideration of family life courses for inclusion in the curriculum has been of even more recent origin. The first impetus came from the youth on college campuses who wanted to know "how to meet desirable members of the opposite sex, how to attract them, how to choose a mate wisely, how best to practice sex relations and birth control, how to spend their money intelligently, and how to bring up children."[5] The noncredit, guest-lecture, loosely organized "courses" originally designed to meet this need gradually are giving way to systematic courses in family and marriage, usually in the sociology department. Baber reports 632 colleges and universities offering such courses in 1948–1949. Bowman takes an optimistic view of the quality of these courses, even though he recognizes their shortcomings in the lack of specialized preparation of the instructors, with attendant problems of inadequate materials and facilities designed for adapting the courses to the needs of prospective teachers.[6]

The high schools are beginning to see the need for family-life education, only to realize that adequate teachers are scarce. A report of one of the most comprehensive surveys of potential sources of teachers in this field in the high schools, with guidelines for their training was published by the American Social Hygiene Association.[7]

Underlying this chapter, then, are three basic assumptions: (1) The family remains one of the most important institutions in modern culture. (2) Research on the family is limited, but enough materials of recent origin are available for a scholarly presentation. (3) Family life education in the high school is in such an exploratory stage that any propositions presented by our authors must be considered as tentative suggestions only.

[4] Ray E. Baber, *ibid*, p. 647.
[5] Willard Waller and Reuben Hill, *The Family: A Dynamic Interpretation* (New York: Dryden, 1951), p. x.
[6] Henry A. Bowman, "Marriage Education in the Colleges," *Journal of Social Hygiene*, 1949, p. 11.
[7] American Social Hygiene Association, *Education for Personal and Family Living: A Working Guide for Colleges* (New York: American Social Hygiene Association, 1955).

Proceeding upon these assumptions, this chapter will develop (1) the sociological significance of the family; (2) trends in the changing nature of the family; (3) reasons for the trends and present status in the changing nature, characteristics, and functions of the family; (4) problems facing the modern American family; and (5) tentative solutions to these problems, with stress upon family life education from the cradle to the grave.

SOCIOLOGICAL SIGNIFICANCE OF THE FAMILY

The Family Remains One of the Major Institutions of Society

Several institutions have a pervasive influence upon most individuals from the cradle to the grave. The church, the state, and the family are prime among these. It is a commonly accepted tenet of the science of social psychology that those institutions that have primary contact with an individual make the most significant and lasting impressions upon both his personality and his behavior. The family, by definition, is a primary group. Burgess, Locke, and Thomas define the family in terms of the following four characteristics:[8]

1. The family is composed of persons united by the ties of marriage, blood, or adoption.
2. The members of a family typically live together under one roof and constitute a single household.
3. The family is a unity of interacting and intercommunicating persons enacting the social roles of husband and wife, mother and father, son and daughter, brother and sister.
4. The family maintains a common culture, derived mainly from the general culture, but in a complex society possessing some distinctive features for each family.

A shorter and more workable definition is that used by MacIver: "The family is a group defined by a sex relationship sufficiently precise and enduring to provide for the procreation and upbringing of children."[9] Although the family usually is a primary group, bound by strong emotional ties, some families more nearly typify the impersonality of relations of the secondary group; in either case, the family influences personality development and behavior during the entire life span of most individuals. Brown states, "The extent to which the individual shows warmth and congeniality or is cold and reserved in relation with others is largely the product of the

---

[8] Ernest W. Burgess, Harvey J. Locke, and Mary Margaret Thomas, *The Family: From Institution to Companionship*, Third Edition (New York: American Book, 1963), p. 2.

[9] Robert M. MacIver, *Society: A Textbook of Sociology* (New York: Holt, 1937), p. 196.

family pattern."[10] The family, then, builds the basic personality structure of our citizens. Certainly this is of major importance in any society.

The Family Is in Transition Because It Is Adapting to Conditions of Modern Life

The many changes that have occurred in the nature, characteristics, and functions of the family have led some writers to view its future with gloomy forebodings. Sorokin sees the family passing from a stage of instability to complete disintegration.[11] He sees divorce and separations becoming so common that marriage will become *passé*, and children will be separated earlier and earlier from their parents. Anshen states: "The present collapse of marriage and the family is a perverted triumph of a profaned passion which in truth now largely consists in a reversion to abduction and rape."[12] Zimmerman is pessimistic about the survival of the family, seeing a parallel to the breakdown of Greek and Roman family life.[13] Russell hopes for the continuation of the family, because the affection of parents for their children makes the family a far better place for the development of personality than are institutions for children.[14] His hope for the continuation of the family seems inconsistent with his continued championship of those factors in modern life to which the authors cited above attribute the disintegration of the family: increased sex experimentation of young persons before marriage, "trial" marriage without benefit of legal ceremony, and freedom to commit adultery after marriage.

Many sociologists hold a much more optimistic view of the future of the family. Table 8, presented later in this chapter, statistically documents their position. Elmer reminds us that there is a vast difference between reorganization and disintegration.[15] As Linton so aptly put it, "The ancient trinity of father, mother, and child has survived more vicissitudes than any other human relationship."[16] The authors are inclined to agree with the statement of Burgess that the apparent disintegration of the modern family is only an expression of the symptoms of transition of a major social institution in changing its form from one adapted to a stable culture to one adapted to a rapidly changing culture.[17] Such an interpretation is in harmony with the entire tempo of modern American life and

---

[10] Francis J. Brown, *Sociology of Childhood* (Englewood Cliffs, N.J.: Prentice-Hall, 1939), p. 111.

[11] Pitirim A. Sorokin, *Social and Cultural Dynamics*, (New York: American Book, 1944), Vol. IV, p. 776.

[12] Ruth Anshen (ed.), *The Family: Its Functions and Destiny* (New York: Harper, 1959), p. 512.

[13] Carle C. Zimmerman, *Family and Civilization* (New York: Harper, 1947), p. 798.

[14] Bertrand Russell, *Marriage and Morals* (New York: Liveright, 1929), p. 308.

[15] McC. Elmer, *The Sociology of the Family* (Boston: Ginn, 1945), p. 223.

[16] Ralph Linton, in Ruth Anshen, *op. cit.*, Chapter 2.

[17] Ernest W. Burgess, "The Family in a Changing Society," *American Journal of Sociology*, **53** (May 1948), pp. 417–422.

education, where adaptability is becoming more essential to success in most fields than is stability. Adaptability as a major personality characteristic of the members of the family well may become the most important single factor in the success of marriage and family life.

It may be significant to note the differential marriage status between suburban males and other males as reported in the United States Census of Population, 1960. In suburban areas 73.9 per cent of males were reported as married, whereas only 67.4 per cent of males in central cities and rural areas were reported as married. The metropolitan suburbs are characterized by a middle-class culture more typical of traditional American ideals than the more rapidly changing urban and rural areas. It may be that the status of the males living in the more fluid areas may be indicative of the shape of things to come. This would be true, of course, only if American culture were to move farther and farther away from the middle-class values cherished by the suburban dweller. Currently available evidence seems to point to the contrary. Statistical gradient is presented in Table 8. The "Great Society" movement stresses involvement of the lower-class citizen in the development of solutions to his problems. Prized solution, at the time of this writing, seems to be the fitting of the lower-class inhabitant of the core-cities and of impoverished rural areas with the job skills and the social attitudes that will enable him to move to the preferred suburban areas. These vast governmental programs reinforce the indoctrination of the schools toward prizing of middle-class values, with the attendant higher marital status. Table 8 emphasizes the steadily increasing percentage of married males in the total population, 1890–1962, with a sharp upward gradient in the 1940's. Current statistics indicate that the family is, indeed, here to stay.

In the past hundred years we have shifted *from* a rural, handicraft society based on primary-group production with a versatility of skills shared by the family group as an independent social entity *to* a highly specialized, interdependent, urban, industrial, secondary-group society.

We have experienced a complete cycle of the "three R's." In the past, the sole formal education of the family member was limited to basic instruction in reading, writing, and ciphering. These skills were all that were needed to conduct the business and social affairs of the independent family group in a simple rural culture. Now the family and the school have to teach children to meet the basic problems of modern living in a highly complex, interdependent modern world. This necessitates delegation (by the family) to the schools and to other agencies of an ever-increasing portion of the educative function of the family, and a tremendous expansion in the curriculum of the school and in the scope of other governmental activities. Paradoxically, this only further emphasizes the importance of the "three R's" as tools to unlock the content of the added curricular offerings. In modern America, we are doing a better job of teaching the "three R's" to more people than at any time in any culture in the world.

Governmental programs are reinforcing the schools in placing stress upon literacy and computational skills through Operation Headstart, the Manpower Development Training Act of 1962, Job Corps, and similar programs. These programs tend to be operated with personnel recruited from the teaching profession. Concurrently with the stress upon literacy and computational skills, conscious effort is being made to implant middle-class values in the participants in these programs. A group of professors employed as consultants to Federal Electric Corporation in the operation of the Job Corps Center at Kilmer, New Jersey, withdrew from their consultative role in protest against what they termed the "middle class colonialism" of the policies of the Office of Economic Opportunity. This new partnership of government with school and family in the education and training of lower-class children and youth portends an ever-increasing acceptance of middle-class values by the American populace. This assumes, of course, that the governmental programs will be more successful in dealing with these lower-class youth than were the traditional schools. It seems reasonable, however, to assume that the increased time and energy expended by the government will at least increase the effect of the schools in stressing such characteristics as honesty, punctuality, and chastity. In the face of the rising tide of juvenile delinquency, adult crime, and unemployment rate, the significance of these contributions toward strengthening the moral and social fabric of America cannot be overestimated.

A fact of modern life in America is the shift from home to the school and to other governmental agencies of the responsibility for furnishing education in many areas that once were considered the exclusive prerogative of the family, but that now have become areas in which the family has neither the technical competence nor the desire to guide the education of the child. Prime among these areas are experiences in social relationships and in direct participation in decision-making.

These shifts in the tasks of the schools have been accompanied by a shift in the nature of the school. Many authorities feel that the school no longer can dare be oriented toward the past, focused upon simple transmission of the cultural heritage. The modern school must be oriented toward the present and the future, using history as a tool to solve present problems and to design a better future.[18] Thus many "conservative" families are delegating the education of their children to "progressive" schools, thereby creating conflicts in the basic philosophies of the several family members. The children and youth of the underprivileged segments of the American population increasingly are becoming involved in other governmental programs of education and training. These programs foster even greater gaps between children and parents. Consider the situation, for example, of the Job Corps graduate who has been intentionally mal-

[18] Othanel B. Smith, William O. Stanley, and J. Harlan Shores, *Fundamentals of Curriculum Development* (Yonkers-on-Hudson: World Book, 1950), p. 123.

adjusted to return to slum environment. He is uncomfortable in the home of his parents. He no longer thinks, acts, or believes as they do. He now has the job skills to enable him to purchase a home in the suburbs—and the social attitudes to enable him to live comfortably there. But he has discarded the social attitudes that formerly served him in the slums. If he returns to his "home," conflict is inevitable. He has no choice but to make a new life for himself apart from his family and his former friends.

The magnitude of the changes, mentioned above, in the social matrix gives new perspective to the disorientation of the modern family. People are confused by the rapidity and complexity of change in modern life and are uncertain as to procedures and values even in such traditional areas as the family. Much reorganization must occur in the form of the family—but one can state with certainty that the family will survive.

TRENDS IN THE CHANGING NATURE OF THE FAMILY

Changes in the characteristics of the family are presented in Table 2. A cross-sectional view of the trends in family life may be gained by looking

TABLE 2
CHANGING CHARACTERISTICS OF THE FAMILY

FORMERLY	Now
Large Many children, with little personal attention given to each by the overworked mother. Average household size in 1790: 5.9.	*Small* Few children (1 or 2). They strive to be economically and socially independent of the family unit. 1940–1965: fluctuated around 3.7.
Consanguineal Several generations under the same roof. Oldest man was the head of the family.	*Conjugal* Husband, wife, and children. No parents or other relative. Accelerated in the 1940's—more new houses than new marriages.
Rural Nine of ten families rooted to the soil. 1800: only five cities over 10,000. 1790: New York only city of 50,000.	*Urban* More than half of the population living in cities. 1940: cities over 1,000,000. 1950: urban areas over 50,000.
Agrarian (Producer) An economic unit. Self-sufficient.	*Industrial* (Consumer) Neither an economic unit nor self-sufficient. Income from outside home. No present or future security.
Authoritarian Mate selection by parents. Little or no courtship. Marriage for economic necessity; a partnership. Many children who received little attention, but had high economic value.	*Democratic* Weakened authority of parents over children. Mate selection by individual, based on romance. Husband and wife equal. Decisions reached in family council.

TABLE 2 *Continued*

Formerly	Now
Patricentric Father head of household. Child followed father's vocation. Obedience to father first duty of child.	*Many Types* *Emancipated.* An urban phenomenon. Young parents. No plans for children until education is completed and/or business is established. Living in the present. Rebels against convention. *Patriarchial.* Father head of household by common consent, but family operates democratically. Typical of rural families (30 per cent of total U.S. population) and workingmen's residential areas. *Equalitarian.* Based on equality of husband and wife. Many working wives. Apartment houses. Many decisions reached in family council. *Matricentric.* Mother head of household. Father commutes to work.
Institutional High degree of solidarity. Activities entered into jointly and cooperatively. Respect for secular and religious education. Permanence of marriage. Unplanned parenthood. Sense of duty. Economic necessity.	*Companionship* Low degree of solidarity. Individualism prevails, except in the rural areas. Little group participation in common activities. Education left to experts. Divorce. Planned parenthood. Happiness the goal.

Note: Majority patterns are given, with the exception of "modern types" of families. The modern rural family tends to develop a majority pattern, but modern city families defy attempts at a single classification. All majority types in the charts on characteristics and functions, of course, exclude the many deviations from same in an attempt at clarity in presentation of trends.

Source: Adapted from Ernest W. Burgess, Harvey J. Locke, and Mary Margaret Thomas, *The Family: From Institution to Companionship* (New York: American Book Company, 1963), pp. 63–72.

next at the changing functions of the family. These are presented in Table 3. The underlying causes of these trends, and the problems they create, are presented in the two sections that immediately follow this section.

TABLE 3
CHANGING FUNCTIONS OF THE FAMILY

Formerly	Now
Reproductive Fostered by: Taboos on extramarital sex experiences. Sense of duty of women. High economic value of offspring.	*Reproductive* Hampered by: Breakdown of sex mores. Marital unhappiness. Birth control knowledges. Great economic liability of offspring. Despite the above, the birth rate has risen rapidly from the early 1940's to the present. The reduction in the size of the household from 1940 to 1950 reflects an increase in housing units available and money available for rent.

TABLE 3 Continued

FORMERLY	Now
Emotional Little attention to emotional adjustments. Marriage for economic necessity and partnership. Despite the above, a high degree of emotional solidarity through functioning of the family as a unit, with the labor of all necessary for its maintenance.	*Emotional* Warmth and affection lavished on the young. Greater emotional attachment for the individual. Despite the above, emotional stresses due to: Extreme individualism of modern life. Care and training of young increasingly shifted outside the home. Consumer families. Commercial recreation.
Accultural Folkways and mores transmit the cultural heritage—democracy, etc. Political beliefs, customs of dress, table manners, social manners and the like shared by entire family.	*Accultural* Home atmosphere still a potent force in shaping the attitudes of the young. Despite modern individualism, high correlations exist between parents and offspring in cultural behavior.
Economic Self-sufficient. Made own clothes, food, etc.	*Economic* Needs depend on outside income. Most goods purchased. More women work outside home. Packaged foods or restaurant meals. Electric appliances do housework.
Educational Secular and moral training mostly received in home.	*Educational* School and church taking over both secular and religious training. Advanced education outside the home increasingly an economic necessity.
Protective Head of house kept firearms. Legal business as unit.	*Protective* Government taking over. Police department. Fire department. Social security, etc. Life and health insurance policies.
Religious An established part of family life.	*Religious* Decrease in worship and prayers. Increased reliance on scientific explanation of natural phenomena. Decrease in supernatural beliefs and in church attendance.
Recreational Long hours of work. No place to go. Remained home. Play often frowned upon.	*Recreational* More leisure. Higher standards of living. More money and recreation. Growth of public facilities.

Source: Adapted from Ernest W. Burgess, Harvey J. Locke, and Mary Margaret Thomas, *The Family: From Institution to Companionship* (New York: American Book Company, 1963), pp. 63–72.

RATIONALE OF CHANGE IN THE AMERICAN FAMILY

Industrialization, urbanization, the rising tide of individualism, and increasing governmental participation both in job training and in provisions for care of the aged are beyond the control of the family. These great national forces, however, have had immediate and profound effect upon the nature of the American family. Other forces in our culture have contributed in a somewhat lesser degree toward accelerating changes in the characteristics and functions of the family; among these are national crises such as wars and depressions, and cross-cultural marriages fostered by the increased mobility of our population. Most of these contributory forces, however, are natural outgrowths of the larger national forces earlier noted.

Industrialization

Chapter 5 traces the development of the American economy. Now let us see what these economic, industrial, and technological trends have meant for the American family.

First, the shift from family handicraft to factory production has forced the family to shift from a producer unit to a consumer unit. The emotional impact of this shift has been tremendous. Man needs to be needed. Children, and in some instances wives or husbands, have become economic liabilities. The producer in the family is the wage earner, who works outside the home for money with which he provides the material needs of all members of the family. The work of other members is less needed for the promotion of the material welfare of the family. The nonproducing members of the modern family lack the emotional security of the members of the older producer-unit family. The additional warmth and affection lavished on children and spouses by the modern wage earner can only partially compensate for the emotional security formerly provided through the simple fact of being needed.

Industrialization takes the father from the home for the major portion of the day, at least for five days per week. His commuting time plus work time plus meal time total almost the entire waking hours of the child. Some writers suggest that this factor alone is developing a majority pattern of matricentric families, for the mother has the predominant contact with the children. Both boys and girls learn to turn to the adult woman in the household for guidance. What more natural development after marriage than for the boy-child grown-up to continue to turn to the adult woman in the house for guidance in family affairs?

Not all women in an industrial culture are content with the role of wife and mother. Tables 4 and 5 reveal significant trends in the number of women who are emulating the producer-male in the household. They are securing gainful employment outside the home, not just as a temporary measure but as a permanent feature of their way of life. Over one third

TABLE 4
MARITAL STATUS OF WOMEN
IN THE CIVILIAN LABOR FORCE: 1940 TO 1964

[Persons 14 years old and over, except per cent. Beginning 1960, includes Alaska and Hawaii. Includes institutional population. Figures for 1940 based on complete census revised for comparability with intercensal series. Data for 1944–1964 based on Current Population Survey: see Technical Note, p. 215. Beginning 1953, figures not strictly comparable with previous years as a result of introduction into estimating procedure of 1950 Census data through 1961, and of 1960 Census data beginning March 1962.]

Month and Year	Female Labor Force (1,000)					Per Cent Distribution of Female Labor Force			Female Labor Force as Per Cent of Female Population, 14 and Over				
			Married		Widowed or Divorced			Widowed or Divorced			Married		Widowed or Divorced
	Total	Single	Total	Husband Present		Single	Married		Total	Single	Total	Husband Present	
March 1940	13,840	6,710	5,040	4,200*	2,090	48.5	36.4	15.1	27.4	48.1	16.7	14.7	32.0
April 1944	18,449	7,542	8,433	6,226	2,474	40.9	45.7	13.4	35.0	58.6	25.6	21.7	35.7
April 1947	16,323	6,181	7,545	6,676	2,507	37.9	46.2	15.9	29.8	51.2	21.4	20.0	34.6
March 1950	17,795	5,621	9,273	8,550	2,991	31.6	52.1	16.3	31.4	50.5	24.8	23.8	36.0
April 1953	19,304	5,223	10,908	9,763	3,174	27.1	56.5	16.4	32.8	48.5	27.7	26.3	36.3
April 1954	19,726	5,412	11,209	9,923	3,105	27.4	56.8	15.7	33.1	49.0	28.1	26.6	36.0
April 1955	20,154	5,087	11,839	10,423	3,227	25.2	58.7	16.0	33.5	46.4	29.4	27.7	36.0
March 1956	20,842	5,167	12,278	11,126	3,397	24.8	58.9	16.3	34.2	46.4	30.2	29.0	36.9
March 1957	21,524	5,378	12,696	11,529	3,450	25.0	59.0	16.0	34.8	46.8	30.8	29.6	37.6
March 1958	22,000	5,365	13,032	11,826	3,604	24.4	59.2	16.4	35.0	45.4	31.4	30.2	37.9
March 1959	22,376	5,162	13,586	12,205	3,628	23.1	60.7	16.2	35.2	43.4	32.3	30.9	38.0
March 1960	22,516	5,401	13,485	12,253	3,629	24.0	59.9	16.1	34.8	44.1	31.7	30.5	37.1
March 1961	24,199	5,663	14,612	13,266	3,924	23.4	60.4	16.2	36.8	44.4	34.0	32.7	39.0
March 1962	23,978	5,481	14,770	13,485	3,727	22.9	61.6	15.5	35.7	41.7	33.7	32.7	36.6
March 1963	24,675	5,614	15,362	14,061	3,699	22.8	62.3	15.0	36.1	41.0	34.6	33.7	35.8
March 1964	25,399	5,781	15,790	14,461	3,828	22.8	62.2	15.1	36.5	40.9	35.3	34.4	36.1

* As of April.

Source: 1940–1958, Dept. of Commerce, Bureau of the Census; Current Population Reports, Series P-50. Beginning 1959, Dept. of Labor, Bureau of Labor Statistics; Special Labor Force Report, Nos. 2, 13, 20, 26, 40, and 50. Reprinted from Statistical Abstract of the United States, 1965 (Washington: Government Printing Office, 1965), p. 226.

TABLE 5
CIVILIAN FEMALE POPULATION—TOTAL AND LABOR FORCE, BY MARITAL STATUS AND AGE: 1964

[In thousands of persons 14 years old and over, except per cent. As of March. Includes Alaska and Hawaii. Includes institutional population.]

MARITAL STATUS AND AGE	POPULATION	LABOR FORCE		MARITAL STATUS AND AGE	POPULATION	LABOR FORCE	
		NUMBER	PER CENT OF POPULATION			NUMBER	PER CENT OF POPULATION
Total	69,503	25,399	36.5	*Married, husband present*	42,045	14,461	34.4
14 to 19 years	9,609	2,326	24.2	14 to 19 years	782	243	31.1
20 to 24 years	6,446	3,176	49.3	20 to 24 years	3,947	1,445	36.6
25 to 34 years	11,271	4,199	37.3	25 to 34 years	9,452	2,891	30.6
35 to 44 years	12,549	5,585	44.5	35 to 44 years	10,379	4,093	39.4
45 to 64 years	19,697	9,114	46.3	45 to 64 years	14,001	5,525	39.5
65 years and over	9,931	999	10.1	65 years and over	3,484	264	7.6
Median age (years)	40.9	40.7	(X)	Median age (years)	41.6	41.7	(X)
Single	14,132	5,781	40.9	*Other marital status*	13,326	5,157	38.7
14 to 19 years	8,639	2,029	23.5	14 to 19 years	188	54	28.7
20 to 24 years	2,002	1,481	74.0	20 to 24 years	497	250	50.3
25 to 34 years	786	685	87.2	25 to 34 years	1,033	623	60.3
35 to 44 years	571	474	83.0	35 to 44 years	1,599	1,018	63.7
45 to 64 years	1,348	961	71.3	45 to 64 years	4,348	2,628	60.4
65 years and over	786	151	19.2	65 years and over	5,661	584	10.3
Median age (years)	18.4	22.9	(X)	Median age (years)	61.2	50.6	(X)

X Not applicable.
Source: Dept. of Labor, Bureau of Labor Statistics; *Special Labor Force Report*, No. 50. Reprinted from *Statistical Abstract of the United States, 1965* (Washington: Government Printing Office, 1965), p. 226.

of the married female population of the United States is employed through age 64. This suggests that many women have chosen to continue working until they reach retirement age and can draw old-age insurance benefits under the Social Security Act, thus assuring themselves of a measure of independence in later years. It seems reasonable to predict that this trend will accelerate with the advent of the significant increases in taxes and benefits under the Social Security Act commencing on January 1, 1966. The economic independence attained by these women, coupled with their equalitarian relations with fellow workers, has contributed heavily to the development of the equalitarian family.

Even more revealing information is gleaned from an analysis of the percentages of single and married women in the labor force. Nearly two thirds of all women 14 years of age and over are married and living with their husbands. Of these women 34.4 per cent are in the labor force. They make up more than half (57 per cent) of the woman labor force.

Several factors combine to set the stage for an unprecedented high in juvenile delinquency.[19] The growing child has no household tasks to occupy his time. Both mother and father may be working outside the home, so the child receives a minimum of family guidance in the utilization of his tremendous amount of leisure time. When immature minds are forced to rely upon their own ingenuity for utilization of leisure time, unwise choices may be expected. The resultant experiences and associations set the stage for further delinquent acts.

Not all aspects of industrialization have been harmful for the family. Modern technology has increased productivity, with corresponding shortening of the work week. Gas and electric appliances, coupled with packaged foods, have cut the amount of time necessary for essential housekeeping chores. "Thirty years ago, the average housewife had to spend five to six hours of her day in the kitchen preparing meals. Today she spends less than half that time. That reduction is primarily due to her use of foods which are partially or fully prepared for her—foods that have built-in services. For example, bread, cake mixes, canned fruits and vegetables, canned soups, frozen foods of all kinds, baby foods, packaged dairy products, precut and prepared meats, prepared desserts including ice cream."[20]

Shortening of the industrial work week and of time required for housework theoretically makes possible more time for the family to spend as a unit. Manufacturers are completely remodeling the kitchen, to make it a feasible spot for conversational family gatherings. The rising tide of individualism, urbanization, modern transportation, and expanding commer-

---

[19] See Chapter 8 for treatment of delinquency as a factor in modern life.
[20] William B. Murphy (President, Campbell Company), "Revolution in the Kitchen: New Foods—Better Meals, Less Work," *U.S. News and World Report*, February 15, 1957, p. 56.

cial amusements is retarding this return to family unity—except for television, which is at least bringing some families again into physical proximity, albeit without intercommunication. The trend seems to be the dispersion of the family to separate leisure-time activities.

Urbanization

Urbanization has further weakened the emotional security of the family. The rural family knew its neighbors and shared with them close ties of friendship, developing a community culture that further strengthened the security of the component families. The impersonal, secondary-group society of the modern city isolates the family among strangers. This lack of family-to-family contact accentuates the dispersion of family members fostered by industrialization. Father tends to make his circle of friends among his business associates. Mother tends to associate with an entirely different group of families in her ladies' social clubs. The children may encompass still a third group of families by forming their friendships with their classmates at school. The minimal overlap of common acquaintances makes "family" gatherings for leisure-time activities a rarity; when they do occur, they are confined to the conjugal family rather than to two or more families sharing a common experience.

A further weakening of family stability due to urbanization is the effect of the gathering of the forces of evil that occurs in any area in which population is concentrated. Social parasites have existed in all ages. The vendor of illicit entertainment must seek population centers to find a market. Not only youth but also parents may become involved in drunkenness, drug addiction, prostitution, theft, and other illegal and/or immoral activities, simply because the sources are readily available. Deviant social behavior by any family member causes family disorganization.

Urbanization and modern transportation have combined to foster a "transition from a sacred to a secular society."[21] The family no longer shares Bible reading. In many families the rush of modern living does not leave time for a simple prayer before meals. The church and the Sunday school have taken over the religious education of youth. The more than 250,000 ministers of the approximately 250 denominations in the United States do not say the same things about family life.[22] Not only moral precepts but family concepts have suffered through lack of integration between home and church in the moral instruction of youth.

Urbanization has had some salutary effects upon the family. The diversity of cultural activities in any metropolitan area offers great opportunity for the broadening of worthy interests and activities for all members of the family—opera, theater, symphony, zoo, conservatory, library, ath-

[21] Clifford Kirkpatrick, *The Family: As Process and Institution* (New York: Ronald Press, 1963), p. 129.
[22] Clifford Kirkpatrick, *ibid.*, p. 142.

letics, and the like. Both industrialization and urbanization have contributed to improved family health; in the past century the life span of the average individual has increased from 45 years to 67 years. The cities have more than their proportional share of doctors and hospitals. Drugstores, life-squads, and the like are immediately available. Despite Dewhurst's analysis that more than one fifth of the population are ill-fed,[23] more than one fourth are ill-clothed,[24] and nearly one third are ill-housed[25] (by modern standards), we are the healthiest, most prosperous, and longest-lived nation in history.

The term "urbanization" has been used to refer to the complex of technological and social aspects of life in the metropolis and in the large city. Suburbs have characteristics different from those of central cities; these characteristics are developed in detail in Chapter 11. Often these characteristics, when stated statistically, fall between those for central cities and rural areas. For example, Table 6 shows that in 1960 this was

TABLE 6
FAMILY SIZE, SEX RATIO, AND PER CENT 18 YEARS OLD AND YOUNGER
FOR CENTRAL CITIES, SUBURBS, AND RURAL AREAS, 1960

Characteristics	Central Cities	Suburbs	Rural Areas
Size of private family	3.50	3.66	3.85
Sex ratio	90.9	92.2	104.3
Per cent 18 years of age and younger	32.3	37.2	39.0

Source: U.S. Bureau of the Census, *U.S. Census of the Population, 1960.* Volume 1, Characteristics of the Population. Part 1, U.S. Summary (Washington, D.C.: U.S. Government Printing Office, 1964), pp. 148–157.

true for the average size of the family, the sex ratio (the number of men per 100 women), and the per cent of the population 18 years and younger.

Individualism

Although American origins of the philosophy of individualism were largely economic, commencing with the religious individualism of the early settlers, accentuated by the familial individualism of the producer-family, and reaching its economic heights in Carnegie's "Gospel of Wealth,"[26] individualism has become an established part of the *total* American way of life. Let us see how this emphasis upon individualism has affected the modern family.

[23] J. Frederick Dewhurst and Associates, *America's Needs and Resources: A New Survey* (New York: Twentieth Century Fund, 1955), p. 158.
[24] Dewhurst and Associates, *ibid.,* p. 194.
[25] Dewhurst and Associates, *ibid.,* pp. 202 and 204.
[26] Ralph Henry Gabriel, *The Course of American Democratic Thought* (New York: Ronald Press, 1940), p. 158.

Choosing a career and choosing a mate surely are two of the most important decisions in the life of a man. Historically, the family heavily influenced, if not actually dictated, both choices. The extreme emphasis upon individualism in modern America has developed a cultural expectation that the youth of the nation shall make these choices for themselves, with a minimum of parental guidance.

That the choice of youth should be on a basis that stresses individual happiness is to be expected. In discussing reasons for marriage, Baber states:[27]

Why do people marry? The answers, if one went into detail, would be numerous, including sheer romance, desire for wealth or position, assurance of care in old age, a steady source of sex satisfaction, escape from unpleasant home conditions, love of children, perpetuation of family name, the expectation of society, fear of ridicule if one does not marry, salary promotion or preference, spite against another, and a host of other reasons. But all these are minor compared with the dominant urge for continuous and intimate companionship with a loved person.

Individualism probably is the major underlying factor in changing attitudes toward divorce. Kirkpatrick states:[28]

There is also a pattern of individualism. The tendency is to think in terms of "what I want," of personal advantage, of good business. An individual who has just fired a secretary for inefficiency may take a dim view of his wife's inadequacy as a household manager. While the home is the last refuge of collectivism in the sense that most property is communally owned, there is a growing tendency to think in terms of personal possessions and personal gains. If it is good business to break an economic relationship, why should it not seem desirable to break up a family when personal satisfactions are not completely fulfilled? There is an impact then of individualism, engendered by the economic system, which strikes powerfully at the traditional pattern of family life.

National Crises

Depressions and wars are the major national crises affecting family life.

Economic depressions cause tremendous strain on the modern family. The sole source of material necessities and pleasures is the wage earner's pay check. Even temporary unemployment severely dislocates the family budget. Continued unemployment, such as occurs in periods of national economic depressions, forces a complete reorganization of family finance. Burgess, Locke, and Thomas report a study of the reactions to the depres-

[27] By permission from *Marriage and the Family* (p. 162), by Ray E. Baber. Copyright, 1953. McGraw-Hill Book Company, Inc.

[28] Clifford Kirkpatrick, *The Family as Process and Institution* (New York: Ronald Press, 1963), p. 130.

sion of the 1930's.[29] They conclude that integrated, well-organized families meet and solve depression problems with rational behavior and little emotional disturbance, emerging from the experience with greater family solidarity. Disorganized families tend to become further disorganized in the face of crisis, and may even disintegrate through separation or divorce. Thus it appears that national depressions are not one of the major determinants of family structure, excepting as they intensify inherent family tendencies toward stability or instability.

Although depressions do not seem to have a significant effect upon the nature of the family, they have a definite effect upon marriage and divorce rates, both of which decline sharply in times of depression.[30]

Wars appear to have more varied effects upon the family. The entire supply of available marriage mates is disrupted by such factors as men of military (and marriageable) age being concentrated in training camps or going overseas, defense industry towns becoming clogged with women workers, and seaports being flooded with transient hordes of pleasure-seeking males in uniform. Hasty marriages often are contracted between persons of badly mismatched backgrounds under the psychological tensions of a nation at war. A considerable portion of wartime marriages culminate in early divorce.[31] Of much more statistical importance is the drop in marriage rate during the war years, with a corresponding increase in the immediate postwar years. In the United States, for example, the marriage rate per 1,000 population fell from 12.2 in 1939 to 10.5 in 1944 and rose 16.2 in 1946.[32] Parenthetically, one should not assume from the partial data above that the long-term marriage rate is on the increase; quite the reverse is true.[33]

After a careful analysis of the effects of World War I, World War II, and the Korean conflict upon American family life, Burgess, Locke, and Thomas conclude that wars, like depressions, are not major determinants of trends in family life:[34]

To the degree that war weakens institutions buttressing and supporting the family, it disturbs family relationships and is an indirect factor in family disorganization.

Family instability in American society is essentially a phenomenon of the transition from the institutional to the companionship type of family. The effect of a crisis like war is both to accelerate the transition and to introduce temporary disrupting conditions.

[29] Burgess, Locke, and Thomas, *op. cit.*, pp. 435–436.
[30] Philip M. Hauser, "Population and Vital Phenomena," *American Journal of Sociology*, **18** (1942), p. 311.
[31] Burgess, Locke, and Thomas, *op. cit.*, pp. 484–485.
[32] Metropolitan Life Insurance Company, "Recent International Marriage Trends," *Statistical Bulletin* (New York: Metropolitan Life Insurance Company, 1952), p. 2.
[33] See Table 7 for details.
[34] Burgess, Locke, and Thomas, *op. cit.*, p. 486.

Certain factors favorable to family unity emerge in wartime. First, the actual danger to family members in war may draw them more closely together. When a member of a family enters the army, with the actual or potential dangers involved, petty difficulties may be submerged and the family may become more united than before. Second, some men in the services, feeling that they are mere cogs in a huge machine, desire the intimate and personal appreciation of a sweetheart, a wife, or parents, and may be drawn more closely to their families than formerly. Third, to most men a war is a disagreeable job, to be finished as soon as possible in order that they may return to civilian life, settle down, and enjoy home life, made all the more attractive by contrast with the army camp.

When one examines the divorce rates during World War II and the immediate postwar years, it is well to guard one's thinking against the common-sense fallacy of assuming that a given reversal of a trend, due to temporary wartime conditions, is indicative of a permanent change. Divorce rates per 1,000 inhabitants jumped from 2.9 in 1944 to 3.5 in 1945 and 4.3 in 1946.[35] They declined almost as rapidly in the immediate postwar years, dropping to 3.4 in 1947 and 2.8 in 1948. From 1951 through 1962 they have stabilized at about 2.2, which is about what the long-time trend in rising divorce rate would have projected; thus the dramatic fluctuation caused by the war apparently has not significantly affected the long-time trend in a slowly rising divorce rate. This is in sharp contrast to the pessimistic predictions of some authors that by 1965 there would be one divorce for every two marriages. The apparent stabilization at about one divorce to every four marriages from 1947 through 1962 suggests that this ratio may not significantly be exceeded in the coming years. If this proves to be true, then the transitional period from the institutional to the companionship type of family may be nearing its completion.

Analysis of marriage rates does not present such a clear picture. The expected drop in the rate occurred during the depression years, but it failed to materialize immediately in World War II; in fact, the first full year of American participation saw the highest marriage rate ever recorded in American history. One must remember, however, that marriage rates rise during periods of prosperity; one can only surmise that the forces of wartime prosperity following the Great Depression more than counterbalanced the effects of war. The typical pattern of depressed war rate followed by a dramatic postwar rise (as noted above in the divorce rate) held true for 1943–1946. A disturbing facet of recent years is that marriage rates for 1952–1962 (rate per 1000 females aged 15 to 44) continue to be the lowest recorded since the depression year of 1935. A detailed listing of the data appears in Table 7. A marked upswing of the rate is expected,

[35] For marriage and divorce rates, see Table 7.

however, between 1965 and 1970, when large numbers of young people from the "baby boom" of the middle 1940's reach marriageable age.

There has been great debate among demographers about the significance of the currently rising birth rate. Suffice it to say here that the trend of slowly rising birth rate from 1935 to 1962 apparently has not been seriously affected by the customary wartime depression of birth rate in 1944 and 1945, or the expected sharp rise in the immediate postwar years of 1946 and 1947. It is too early to make a prediction as to what effect the apparent stabilizing of the marriage rate from 1949 to 1962 will have on the birth rate. For a full discussion of birth rate, with detailed data in tabular form, see Chapter 11.

PROBLEMS FACING AMERICAN FAMILIES

Let us consider in roughly chronological order the family problems faced by the individual from birth to death.

Child Socialization

We have noted earlier the repeated reference by several writers to the importance of the first few years of life in shaping the basic personality of the child, and to the importance of the family not only in this but also in transmitting the cultural heritage. Now let us examine problems facing the child in these areas.

First, in this scientific age, parents are not quite sure they are equal to a task of this magnitude. For guidance in this area, parents eagerly read the publications of Gesell, Spock, Hymes, and other modern authorities. The philosophy of earlier treatises, such as Watson's *Psychological Care of Infants*,[36] was diametrically opposed to the central thesis of modern child-care techniques. The apparent confusion among the "experts" increases the insecurity of the parent. Insecurities and inconsistencies in parental guidance of children seriously hamper adequate personality development in these young citizens of our democracy.

Fortunately, modern authorities have available much research in the field of personality on which to base their advice. Modern techniques include an abundance of warmth and affection, especially for the very young child, to assure early emotional security and to free the infant for concentration on normal developmental tasks. They stress parental understanding of the strong egoism of the very young; the importance of the language of behavior; the need for being an attentive audience when the child feels that he has something important to express; the need for setting limits on the child's behavior, teaching him the bounds of behavior beyond which family and society say he cannot go; and the critical importance of

---

[36] John B. Watson, *Psychological Care of Infants* (New York: Norton, 1928).

TABLE 7
MARRIAGE AND MARRIAGE RATES, DIVORCES AND DIVORCE RATES, UNITED STATES

	MARRIAGES			DIVORCE*		
	TOTAL PER YEAR (THOUSANDS)	RATE PER 1000 INHABITANTS	RATE PER 1000 FEMALES 15–44	TOTAL PER YEAR (THOUSANDS)	RATE PER 1000 INHABITANTS	RATE PER 100 MARRIAGE
1887–1891	555	9.0	39.3†	31	0.5	6
1892–1896	609	8.9	38.7†	39	0.6	6
1897–1901	683	9.1	39.3†	52	0.7	8
1902–1906	829	10.1	42.8	67	0.8	8
1907–1911	919	10.2	42.9	81	0.9	9
1912–1916	1027	10.4	44.0	101	1.0	10
1920	1274	12.0	50.9	171	1.6	13
1925	1188	10.3	43.6	175	1.5	15
1930	1127	9.2	38.4	196	1.6	17
1935	1327	10.4	43.3	218	1.7	16
1940	1596	12.1	49.7	264	2.0	17
1941	1696	12.7	52.3	293	2.2	17
1942	1772	13.2	54.2	321	2.4	18
1943	1577	11.7	47.9	359	2.6	23
1944	1452	10.9	43.9	400	2.9	28
1945	1613	12.2	48.5	485	3.5	30
1946	2291	16.4	68.4	610	4.3	27

1947	1992	13.9	59.2	483	3.4	24
1948	1811	12.4	53.5	408	2.8	23
1949	1580	10.6	46.4	397	2.7	25
1950	1667	11.1	48.7	385	2.6	23
1951	1595	10.4	46.4	381	2.5	24
1952	1539	9.9	44.7	392	2.5	25
1953	1546	9.8	44.7	390	2.5	25
1954	1490	9.2	43.0	379	2.4	25
1955	1531	9.3	44.0	377	2.3	25
1956	1569	9.4	45.4	382	2.3	24
1957	1518	8.9	43.2	381	2.2	25
1958	1451	8.4	40.9	368	2.1	25
1959	1494	8.5	41.8	395	2.2	26
1960	1527	8.5	42.2	393	2.2	26
1961‡	1547	8.5	42.3	n.a.**	2.2	n.a.**
1962‡	1580	8.5	42.5	n.a.**	2.2	n.a.**

Note: Based on estimated population figures as of July 1. For 1940 to 1950, population-based figures for marriage represent population, excluding armed forces overseas. Those for divorce represent total population including armed forces overseas for 1941 to 1946; for 1947 to 1962, excluding armed forces overseas.
* Includes reported annulments.
† Not strictly comparable to later data.
‡ Preliminary.
** Not available.
Sources: Samuel A. Stouffer and Lyle M. Spencer, "Recent Increases in Marriage and Divorce," *American Journal of Sociology*, (January 1939); Department of Health, Education, and Welfare; Bureau of the Census; The Conference Board. Reprinted by permission from *The Economic Almanac, 1964* (New York: The National Industrial Conference, Board, Inc., 1964), p. 13.

TABLE 8
MARITAL STATUS OF THE POPULATION 14 YEARS OF AGE AND OVER, 1890–1962

| | MALE | | | | FEMALE | | | |
| | TOTAL (THOUSANDS) | PER CENT DISTRIBUTION | | | TOTAL (THOUSANDS) | PER CENT DISTRIBUTION | | |
YEAR		SINGLE	MARRIED	WIDOWED OR DIVORCED		SINGLE	MARRIED	WIDOWED OR DIVORCED
1890	21,501	43.6	52.1	4.0	20,298	34.1	54.8	11.0
1900	26,414	42.0	52.8	4.8	25,024	33.3	55.2	11.3
1910	33,362	40.4	54.2	4.9	30,959	31.8	57.1	10.9
1920	37,954	36.9	57.6	5.3	36,190	29.4	58.9	11.6
1930	45,088	35.8	58.4	5.6	44,013	28.4	59.5	12.1
1940	50,554	34.8	59.7	5.5	50,549	27.6	59.5	12.9
1950	54,762	26.2	68.0	5.9	56,970	19.6	66.1	14.4
1960	60,273	25.3	69.3	5.3	64,607	19.0	65.9	15.1
1961	61,238	25.9	68.8	5.3	65,847	19.4	65.3	15.3
1962	62,129	25.3	69.2	5.5	67,166	19.6	65.3	15.2

Note: Beginning 1960 data include Alaska and Hawaii. Totals for 1890–1940 include persons not reporting marital status (5% of total at maximum).

Differences between the number of married men and the number of married women are due partly to the absence of husbands or wives from the country at the time of the enumeration. Examples are women whose husbands were in the Armed Forces overseas and immigrants whose husbands or wives were still abroad.

Data relate to total population for 1890–1940 and to civilian population thereafter. The latter includes members of the Armed Forces living off post or with their families on post, but excludes all other members of the Armed Forces.

Source: Bureau of the Census. Reprinted by permission from The Economic Almanac, 1964 (New York: The National Industrial Conference Board, Inc., 1964), p. 13.

assisting the child to evaluate himself, to decide which plans and goals are realistic for him.

All of these modern techniques of child care are designed to build personalities who are creative and adaptable, who respect and show a genuine concern for others, who expect that same consideration from others, and who can make choices independently. These are personality traits that are essential to survival in a rapidly changing world. These techniques are understandably different from those designed to build personalities to live in the stable community of a hundred years ago, where security was gained through extended-kinship families and where choices were made for youth by the family.

Modern parents are confused by the conflicting ideas on child-rearing of their own grandparents (who were reared in a stable culture), the ideas of Watson and others of the coldly "scientific" school of child-rearing that influenced their own parents, and the advice of the modern authorities. Development of a sound philosophy of child socialization is a very real problem for parents of today's child. If society is to progress, sound child-rearing practices *must* be followed. Personality defects acquired in infancy will handicap the child and his society for all of his life. If the parents remain confused, the child can find no sound foundation on which to build a healthy personality.

Second, complicating the confusion about proper child-rearing techniques may be the ambivalent attitudes of parents toward their children. "The child may be an economic burden to the parents, may conflict with parental ambitions or desire for freedom from responsibility; as a consequence, parents may develop the ambivalence of love and hate toward the child."[37] The reverse, of course, may be true; the imposition of necessary restraints upon the child may create temporary hatred toward the parent. But so long as love remains the dominant emotion, this ambivalence is no real problem. "No matter which way parents express their feelings, they assert strong hates and equally strong loves toward their children as a normal part of parent-child relations."[38] It is when the hate feelings lead to frequent rejection of the child that personality damage results.

A third problem in parent-child relations is the conflicting values between some homes and outside agencies such as church and school. The child is caught in a conflict of loyalties. He must disobey either the teaching of parents or the teachings of church or of school. If he disobeys the parent, family conflict probably will result; at the very least, family solidarity will be weakened. The conflict in values between lower-class homes and the school affects a significant portion of the population.

[37] Morris G. Caldwell and Laurence Foster, *Analysis of Social Problems* (Harrisburg: Stackpole, 1954), p. 397.

[38] John Levy and Ruth Monroe, *The Happy Family* (New York: Knopf, 1948), pp. 270–271.

Fourth, the indiv̈idualism of the equalitarian, companionship marriage centers many of the family activities about adult interests. This is particularly true of suburban apartment dwellers. The child may have real difficulty in discerning himself as "an important person" when so few of the activities of the total family are centered about his interests. Failure to develop adequate concepts of self may result.

Fifth, the conflicts of adolescence are a major problem area for most families, with the growing adolescent's need for independence from adult supervision, the conflict in values between the adolescent group and their parents, and the lessened control of parents over adolescent sex behavior.[39]

Finally, the high percentage of commuting husbands, working wives, and broken homes deprives the child of guidance by one or both of the parents for most of the time. Basic personality traits of these children are formed by persons other than the parents, who have intimate contacts with them in the formative years: nurses, baby-sitters, stepparents, personnel of child-care institutions, and the like. Many of these children form very real feelings of inferiority and other negative personality traits because they feel they are not important enough to be loved and cared for by their parents.

Careers and Family Roles

At first blush, this seems to be a feminine problem: Shall the young woman get married, or shall she embark upon a career? The modern woman, assisted by the equalitarian concept of husband helping the working wife with the housework and by the host of mechanical and other devices for reducing household drudgery, seems to be choosing both. Nearly two thirds of all women 14 years of age and over are married and living with their husbands; 34.4 per cent of these women were in the labor force in 1964, up 6.4 per cent from 1952.

This trend toward combined careers and families has created many problems for female youth. Shall the young woman marry early and settle for a low-paying job? Shall she defer marriage until after the college training necessary for a real career? "Even at the high school level there is the problem of emphasis on grade-getting in preparation for a job as compared with boy-getting in preparation for courtship, marriage, and motherhood."[40] Shall she have children? If so, how can she best manage simultaneously the roles of wife, mother, and career woman?

The young man must answer the same questions faced by the young woman as to the immediacy of marriage. Further, he must learn to compartmentalize his life into a career segment and a family segment. When work is brought home from the office night after night, no opportunities are provided for real family life.

---

[39] The problems of adolescents are more fully treated in Chapter 7, under "Attaining Puberty."

[40] Clifford Kirkpatrick, *The Family as Process and Institution* (New York: Ronald Press, 1963), pp. 255–256.

Sex Behavior

Urbanization, the growth of scientific knowledge of birth control, and the lengthening period of formal education have accentuated the problems of modern youth in defining and conforming to changing sex mores. This does not necessarily mean that the problem of living within the sex mores is peculiar to recent generations. In the past sixty years, the median age of first marriages for men declined from 26.1 to 20.4.[41] Thus we see that the period from the attainment of puberty to marriage has decreased in modern times for the average American; but this fact does not make the period any less traumatic. "Kinsey reports that males attain their strongest sex drives in their late teens, which is still several years before most of them marry."[42]

Complicating the problem for modern youth is the supercharged atmosphere of sex stimulation that seems to pervade present-day culture. Sex is glorified in newspapers, magazines, and books; on billboards, radio, and television; in the cinema. As a populace, we seem to be saturating ourselves with the physical aspects of sex. Since sex taboos largely have been based on the doctrines of ancient theologians, this verbal flaunting of the taboos may be expected in a society that is in transition from a sacred to a secular base. That the flaunting is inconsistent, at least with parents, is revealed by their insistence upon rigid adherence to their own interpretation of acceptable sex mores by their children, even though they themselves have violated them. In fact, they may be violating their own verbalizations of the mores by what Waller defines as "party behavior"[43] at the very time they are insisting on chastity in their offspring!

The "dating" complex that has grown up in the United States since World War I, combined with the automobile, has thrown young people upon their own moral resources in the area of sex behavior. They must decide for themselves the nature and the frequency of the physical intimacies permitted the opposite sex. Boys tend to be the aggressors in this area, both through earlier sex drive and through cultural expectation. The young lady must decide where to draw the line in the progression that leads from holding hands through kissing and fondling to coitus.

Despite the writings of Edward Carpenter, Ellen Key, Havelock Ellis, Bertrand Russell, Aldous Huxley, William Reich, and others, who preach varying degrees of sex freedom, the thoughtful writer has little difficulty in marshaling an array of arguments against premarital sex experience. Baber summarized these arguments as follows:[44]

[41] Ray E. Baber, *Marriage and the Family* (New York: McGraw-Hill, 1953), p. 585.
[42] Ray S. Baber, *ibid.*, p. 585.
[43] Willard Waller and Reuben Hill, *The Family: A Dynamic Interpretation* (New York: Dryden, 1951), pp. 584–587.
[44] By permission from *Marriage and the Family* (pp. 596–599), by Ray E. Baber. Copyright, 1953, McGraw-Hill Book Company, Inc.

1. Premarital coitus will not prove whether the couple will be well mated and will make a successful sex adjustment in marriage. . . . Even if both reached full physical satisfaction, it would be no indication that they would be suitable marriage partners, for love is far more than a "sexual outlet."

2. Premarital sex experience, instead of being a helpful introduction to the sex life in marriage, may actually be one of the poorest possible introductions, especially for the girl. The act usually occurs after she has long resisted the idea and is finally persuaded against her better judgment. In such circumstances it is entered into not with anticipation and freedom, but with misgivings that magnify her normal inhibitions to such an extent that she gets no pleasure from the act.

3. Young folks of real character have great difficulty with their consciences when they indulge in sex behavior which they know runs squarely against all their home training, their moral and religious teaching, and the established tenets of society. Their sense of guilt makes them unhappy, especially when they think of the faith their parents have in them.

4. The possibility of pregnancy is a constant source of worry.

5. Frequently, when a young couple are in love and have engaged in sex relations before marriage, suspicions arise in the minds of each as to whether the other has had similar intimacies with others.

6. Furthermore, it frequently happens that a young couple who are engaged and begin sex relations do not marry after all. They feel differently, and conduct which they had justified in their own minds becomes just an illicit relationship.

7. The difficulty sometimes carries over into marriage, when either bride or groom has had previous sex relations and is afraid to tell the other . . . there is a tendency to try to wipe the slate clean by telling all, but it doesn't always work out as wished, for past indiscretions, even when consciously repudiated, still persist as lurking anxiety.

8. Premarital sex relations sometimes lead to varying degrees of personality disorganization, especially in girls who have been reared with a high regard for moral and religious standards.

To the psychological costs of irregular sex expression must be added the social costs. Exact statistics, of course, are unavailable; but it was estimated in 1953 that there are 150,000 illegitimate births and 350,000 abortions annually in the United States.[45] The 1963 estimates are nearly double the above figures, as noted below in Table 9.

The Children's Bureau estimates that one half of the illegitimate mothers are eighteen or younger.[46] This would mean that about one half of these girls, or from 60,000 to 70,000, were enrolled in high school at the time of conception. Surely this is a challenge for educators![47] Many of these unwed

[45] Ray E. Baber, *ibid.*, pp. 909 and 916.

[46] Maud Morlock and Hilary Campbell, *"Maternity Homes for Unmarried Mothers,"* Children's Bureau Publication 309, p. 13.

[47] This is a challenge to families, first. A family put a daughter into one of the strictest girls' schools, that they might feel she was safe. She had an abortion within the year. This is similar to families who can't control their sons and hope that the military school or the army can teach them values that should have been learned at home.

TABLE 9
ILLEGITIMATE LIVE BIRTHS (IN THOUSANDS),
BY AGE AND COLOR OF MOTHER, 1940–1963

Age and Color	1940	1945	1950	1955	1960	1961	1962	1963
Total	89.5	117.4	141.6	183.3	224.3	240.2	245.1	259.4
Rate*	7.1	10.1	14.1	19.3	21.8	22.6	21.5	22.5
By age of mother:								
Under 15 years	2.1	2.5	3.2	3.9	4.6	5.2	5.1	5.4
15 to 19 years	40.5	49.2	56.0	68.9	87.1	93.3	94.4	101.8
20 to 24 years	27.2	39.3	43.1	55.7	68.0	74.0	77.3	82.6
25 to 29 years	10.5	14.1	20.9	28.0	32.1	33.7	34.0	35.4
30 to 34 years	5.2	7.1	10.8	16.1	18.9	19.8	19.8	19.8
35 to 39 years	3.0	4.0	6.0	8.3	10.6	11.1	11.1	10.9
40 and over	1.0	1.2	1.7	2.4	3.0	3.2	3.2	3.5
By color of mother:								
White	40.3	56.4	53.5	64.2	82.5	91.1	93.5†	102.2†
Nonwhite	49.2	60.9	88.1	119.2	141.8	149.1	147.5†	150.7†

Note: Beginning 1960, includes Alaska and Hawaii. Includes estimates for States in which legitimacy data were not reported. No estimates included for misstatements on birth records or failures to register births. Beginning 1960, based on 50 per cent sample of live births in the reporting States.

* Rate per 1,000 unmarried (never married, widowed, and divorced) women aged 15 to 44 years enumerated as of April 1 for 1940 and 1950 and estimated as of July 1 for all other years.

† Excludes data for residents of New Jersey since this State did not require reporting of color.

Source: Dept. of Health, Education, and Welfare, Public Health Service; annual report, *Vital Statistics of the United States.*

Source: *Statistical Abstract of the United States* (Washington: Government Printing Office, 1965), p. 51.

mothers receive adequate care in reputable nursing homes and place their children for adoption through legal channels. Some of them retain their children, despite social disapproval amounting almost to ostracism. Some fall victim to the adoption racket operation in "black market babies." In any case, most of them are forced to leave home and family for a "secret" lying-in and delivery period at the very time they most need sympathetic family guidance. The personality disorganization of these girls must be added to the social costs of bearing and rearing children in socially disapproved ways.

It has been estimated that perhaps 90 per cent of all abortions are performed on married women, especially wives in the 25- to 35-age group who already have several children.[48] Except when legally authorized to save the life of the mother, abortion commonly is held to be the taking of life. Society pays the bill when human energies, and even human life, is wasted in these illegitimate and abortive results of irregular sex expression. Of these costs, the economic one seems minor compared with the moral decay

[48] Ray E. Baber, *op. cit.*, p. 616.

of society and the accompanying personality disorganization of its members. Upon the moral standards of youth rests the solution of this problem.

Mate Selection and Courtship

For so long as the romantic ideal exists, mate selection cannot be a coldly scientific process in a culture in which youth is free to choose his or her own mate—and probably it should not be. Much of the tenderness that makes of marriage a satisfying relationship in this era of individualism probably is based on physical attraction, and this sudden, mutual attraction is the basis of the romantic ideal.

One of the blocks to rational mate selection is that our cultural definition of "romance" encourages youth to idealize the loved one. In the first mad infatuation, love is blind to any and all faults of the object of affection. "If one is to use his head in mate selection, he must do it early. The only time in the process that the intellect is capable of functioning successfully is before, not after, one has fallen in love, for that rather rare pasttime known as cerebration frequently varies inversely as the intensity of emotion."[49] Parental or peer comments on the "ideal one" can lead only to conflict with the persons making the derogatory remarks.

A second block is the impetuousness of youth. Long engagements are not the mode of modern life. Often the infatuated couple rush to the altar or the justice of the peace, only to discover after the honeymoon is over that their mate is not at all the person whom they thought they were marrying.

Fortunately, society has evolved several procedures that make mate selection a trifle less hazardous.[50] To begin with, children and youth make many contacts with members of the opposite sex in "dating" situations at an early age. Many of these relations appear to resemble sibling relations rather than approaches to mate selection. Secondly, the phenomenon of "going steady" (as puberty comes to pass and the "sibling" relations cease) provides first-hand experience with the complete cycle of infatuation-disillusionment-separation on a premarital basis. The caution provided by these experiences may make youth a bit more careful in the selection of the next recipient of his affections.[51] Finally, the courtship period itself normally allows for one to meet the parents and friends of the loved one. Obvious cultural dissimilarities may at least prolong the engagement. The additional time thus purchased not only allows for gradual dissipation of the intensity of emotion, with the return of a more rational viewpoint,

---

[49] Ray E. Baber, *op. cit.*, p. 136.

[50] For excellent treatments of the courtship period, see part two of E. E. Le-Masters, *Modern Courtship and Marriage* (New York: Macmillan, 1957). Also Chapters 4–9 of Henry A. Bowman, *Marriage for Moderns* (New York: McGraw-Hill, 1965).

[51] There is no research evidence to document this conjecture.

but also provides much more material as a basis for rational consideration. Folsom indicates something of the variety of these materials:[52]

Prospective partners need especially to know each other's attitudes regarding the number and timing of children, their management and discipline, the role of the wife as homemaker or worker outside the home, and regarding housing, accumulation of possessions, money, travel, extramarital friendships, the role of sex in life, the duty of the family toward the community and its institutions. Each needs to know what the other is likely to do under emotional strain. Will he resort to drink, illness, quest of excitement, or will he retreat into a world of fancy? When hurt, will she "freeze up" for a long while toward the person who hurt her, or will she develop a rage which can be easily softened into love and reconciliation? She needs to know what he is apt to drop out of his life when he becomes busy and preoccupied; what pleasures he will most likely retain under these circumstances. She needs to know what is his pattern of work. Is it normal for him to become preoccupied for long periods with his work, puctuated by intense "sprees" which she may share with him by proper timing of her activities; or does he thrive best on a little work, a little play, a little love, each day with regularity? He needs to know whether she likes to save money cumulatively, or to save merely so as to keep always a little ahead of the game, or is comfortable to be always a little in debt. Each needs to know whether the other really wants to be told everything, or whether he would rather remain ignorant of possible unpleasant facts which do not affect him in practice.

Other factors also are operating to influence marital choices along lines favorable to marital success. Families tend to live in neighborhoods composed of others of like cultural backgrounds. Bossard found that of the applicants for 5,000 consecutive marriage licenses issued in Philadelphia, nearly one quarter lived within two blocks of each and more than one half lived within twenty blocks of each other.[53] Cumulating this effect toward likeness, families who visit other families farther removed in residence tend to visit families of like backgrounds. This broadens the field of contact with possible life mates for children of both of the families, still within the framework of families of like acculturation. A further accentuation in this pattern of influencing the field of candidates from whom one might select a mate is parental attitudes of encouraging children to associate only with the "right" playmates. Normally, the "right" playmates means "our kind of people."

The importance of length of engagement and of similarity of cultural backgrounds stressed above is further documented in Table 10, "Basic Background Factors in Marital Success," compiled by Waller and Hill after

[52] J. K. Folsom (ed.), *Plan for Marriage* (New York: Harper & Row, 1937), pp. 96–97. Reprinted by permission of the publishers.

[53] James H. Bossard, "Residential Propinquity as a Factor in Marriage Selection," *American Journal of Sociology*, September 1932, pp. 219–224.

TABLE 10

BASIC BACKGROUND FACTORS IN MARITAL SUCCESS

	FAVORABLE	UNFAVORABLE	UNRELATED
Personality Characteristics	Permissive and considerate attitudes (both). Cooperative attitudes (both). Compatibility of temperament. Combinations where neither is neurotic. Combinations where both are intellectually superior.	Lacks self-confidence (husband). Man daydreams and woman does not. Man feels inferior and woman does not. Woman makes friends easily and man does not. Self-sufficiency in facing troubles alone (both). Proneness to argue points (wife). Unhappy temperament (both). Variability in moods (both). Feelings easily hurt (both).	Extraversion-intraversion. Friendliness or offishness.
Cultural and Family Backgrounds	Similarity of cultural backgrounds. Similarity of educational level. Father of high occupational level (both). Firm but not harsh home training (both). Happiness of parents' marriage (both). Happiness of childhood (both). Conservative home backgrounds.	Dissimilarity in cultural and family backgrounds. Wife's cultural background higher than husband's. Residence in the city during childhood.	Number of siblings. Birth order in family. Differences in educational achievements of parents. Modernist or fundamentalist religious beliefs. Economic circumstances at marriage.

Sociability Factors	Frequency of attendance at church and Sunday school. Number of friends (both sexes). Residence in single-family dwellings. Social conservatism.	Unconventionality with respect to religion, sexual ethics, drinking. Religious inactivity.	Number of persons with whom one has "kept company."
Response Patterns	Love based on companionship. Length of acquaintance before marriage. Similarity between parent of opposite sex and affianced (both). Strong attachment to father (both).	Romantic infatuation as basis of love. Disapproval of marriage by parents (especially husband's). Conflict with father (both).	Amount of "petting" before marriage. Fear of pregnancy.
Sex Factors	Sex information received from parents first (both). Frank and encouraging attitudes of parents toward child's curiosity about sex (important for husband). Similarity in sex desires. Orgasm capacity in wife. Amount of pleasure wife experienced at first intercourse.	Premarital intercourse by either or both (low but negative relationship to subsequent marital adjustment). Fear of sex (wife). Prudishness and excessive modesty (wife). Husband-wife differences in strength of sex drive.	Sex techniques used. Frequency and duration of intercourse. Degree of pain experienced by wife at first intercourse. Methods of contraception used.

Source: Reprinted from *The Family: A Dynamic Interpretation* (p. 352), by Willard Waller, Revised by Reuben Hill, by permission of The Dryden Press, Inc. Copyright 1951 by The Dryden Press.

an examination of the research studies bearing on factors related to marital success. The other factors noted in the table may be beyond the control of the individual by the time that he has reached the age of mate selection. For the approximately one half of the population who do not marry within their residential area, knowledge of the importance of these factors is surely critical to propitious mate selection.

Certainly mate selection designed to produce happy marriages is one of the major problems facing youth today, not only for the sake of the individuals doing the selecting but for the future of the marriages of their children. Close examination of Table 10, in all five major areas, stresses the importance of happily married parents in the development of characteristics that are favorable for happy marriage of the children. Stability in marriage, in an individualistic age, depends on the continued happiness of both partners. The happiness of tomorrow's marriages will be largely determined by the wisdom employed in selecting today's mates. The future stability of the family will be determined by the happiness of the marriages of today.

Married-pair Living

The newly married couple faces a host of new problems. The major task is that of submerging one's individuality in the building of a new unity between the married pair.[54] The personality of the newly formed family, with its offspring, will be a harmonious, integrating one or an inharmonious, disintegrating one largely to the degree to which the individual marriage partners willingly and cheerfully can subordinate individual desires to group welfare. In this age of individualism, this is indeed a difficult task.

The young couple are faced immediately with choices in furniture, life insurance programs, health, recreation, religious and social organizations, political affiliation, sex adjustment, and a host of lesser problems. Most of these, of course, are tied to that difficult problem, the family budget. Two people simply cannot maintain the same standard of living on a man's salary as he maintained when he was supporting only himself. The wife may choose to work; if so, this affects the couple's plans for children. If the choice is for an immediate family, soon three or four people may be living on the single salary. In such case, the wife in the moderate-income bracket must assume the roles of mother, housekeeper, cook, seamstress, and keeper of the family budget if the couple are to make ends meet financially. The impact of these personal and financial problems on immature youth (approximately 70 per cent of all youth aged 20 to 24 already are married)[55] is revealed in divorce statistics. Many simply cannot cope with problems, and call it quits early in the game. Most divorces occur in

---

[54] J. L. Hirning and Alma L. Hirning, *Marriage Adjustment* (New York: American Book, 1956), Chapter 14, "Unification of Two Personalities," pp. 257–278.

[55] Morris G. Caldwell and Laurence Foster, *Analysis of Social Problems* (Harrisburg: Stackpole, 1948), p. 388.

the first five years of marriage, and two thirds of all divorces are granted within the first ten years of married life.[56]

Parenthood

A major problem facing the newly married couple is the conscious choice of parenthood. Birth control knowledges are as readily available as the family physician, except in Massachusetts and Connecticut, where medical prescription of contraceptives is illegal. Even couples living within the moral framework of religions that ban the use of contraceptives are tending toward the modern mode of planned parenthood, through abstinence from sexual intercourse during the fertile period of the female.

There are two major facets of the birth-control aspects of planned parenthood. One involves the decision as to whether to have children at all. The cost of bearing and rearing children obviously must result in other adjustments to most family budgets. If the wife worked previously to childbirth, the loss of her income coincides in time with an increase in family expenses if they are to support a child; they may mean fewer party clothes (and fewer parties!) and less frequent trips to the golf links, the hairdresser, the theater, the symphony, and the like. Couples who enjoyed travel during summer vacations may find that they no longer can afford it. The restaurant meal that used to be a regular routine now becomes a rare luxury.

The above, of course, is all relative to the family income. It has been estimated that it costs a family with an annual income of $2,500 nearly $8,000 in cash, or a family with an income between $5,000 and $10,000 over $16,000, to rear a child to the age of 18.[57] To the cash outlay must be added the personal services attendant upon rearing a child. This total cost is more than some families are willing to bear.

The second aspect of birth control, once the decision to bear children has been reached, is in regulating the number and spacing of the children. The economic and personal-service costs of rearing children definitely affect the total number of children in the family. (As noted in an earlier section, when birth-control techniques are faulty, abortions may be induced in the effort to control family size, particularly in the group of married women aged 25 to 35 who already have several children.) Health of the baby is a major factor affecting spacing of children. "The National Committee for Planned Parenthood claims that when births are one year apart, the loss of babies is nearly 50 per cent higher than when the births are two years apart."[58] The adverse effects of too closely spaced

---

[56] Howard Becker and Reuben Hill, *Family, Marriage, and Parenthood* (Boston: Heath, 1955), p. 685.

[57] Louis I. Dublin, "The Cost of Raising a Child in Higher Income Families," *Statistical Bulletin*, Metropolitan Life Insurance Company (January 1944).

[58] Ray E. Baber, *op. cit.*, p. 546.

babies upon the health of some mothers is another reason for the wide-spread practice of birth control for the spacing of children.

Once the baby has been born, the process of child socialization proceeds. These parent-child relations have been discussed previously under "Child Socialization." It is not amiss, however, to review a major point (discipline) on which so many parents and teachers are confused; it is the crux of the socialization process, on which depends the success of the child in developing self-direction and self-control. As Brown puts it:[59]

A complicating factor in the American home is the lack of standardization regarding maturity. Among primitive peoples, the initiation ceremony marked the transition from child to adult. In our times, a person must be 21 years of age to vote in all but one state; he is allowed to work at ages varying from 14 to 18 depending on the state laws; the age at which young people can marry is a matter of state lines, varying from 21 for both, without parental consent. The variation in the attitude of parents toward the maturity of their children shows similar contrasts, from those who believe that home discipline should be retained until marriage—and sometimes afterward as well—to those who assume that young children should be given much the same sense of responsibility as adults.

The Empty Nest

Married pairs are often startled to discover that their "babies" have grown up. The departure of the last child from the home for college or for marriage signals the start of a period of major readjustments for both parents. The father faces a less serious problem than his wife, for he has devoted a relatively larger portion of his interests and energies to his occupation, with correspondingly less involvement in the process of child-rearing; further, his occupation offers him not only an outlet for the energies that formerly were expended in the family situation, but also the opportunity to escape the place so full of memories of the recently departed children. The mother is in a less favorable position. Her child-bearing and child-rearing span is comparatively short.[60] She reaches the stage of the empty nest in physical and mental condition appropriate for many more years of useful service, only to realize that her life's function apparently is complete. The empty house symbolizes the emptiness of the years ahead. Her emotional adjustment may be a difficult one.

Parents who have kept alive interests other than parental duties can cope more successfully with this crisis. Particularly is this true if the companionship roles of husband and wife have been satisfactorily fulfilled through the years of parenthood. The married pair who can "do what they always wanted to but hadn't the time because of the children" re-

[59] Francis J. Brown, *Educational Sociology* (Englewood Cliffs, N.J.: Prentice-Hall, 1954), p. 240.

[60] Paul C. Glick, "The Family Cycle," *American Sociological Review*, 12 (April 1947), pp. 167–168.

ceive assistance in adjustment not only from the revived interests but also from the mutual reinforcement of the sympathetic mate. This type of married-pair adjustment builds a much more stable foundation for the childless years ahead than the individual adjustments through mutually exclusive interests such as father's vocation and mother's social clubs.

The Aged

The extended-kinship family of rural America considered the care of the aged a family matter. The shifts from rural to urban residence, from agriculture to industry, and from extended-kinship family to conjugal family, have combined with an increased longevity of population to create an increasing number of old people who are unemployed, impoverished, and cannot depend upon their family for support. For a discussion of this problem, see Chapter 11.

The economic support of the aged is still a legal responsibility of the family in many states. Further, the folkways of the extended-kinship family linger in the memories of the people. A major factor is that children who love their parents cannot see them suffer economic deprivation without making some effort to relieve their suffering. In discussing the problem of economic dependency of the aged, Kirkpatrick says:[61]

The familial group in the past has taken heavy responsibility for support of the aged. Now the OAA program creates confusion in regard to the roles of the familial group and the state. The laws of some 35 states still bear witness to the social expectation that consanguineal and affinal relationships imply responsibility for aged family members who are in need.

In some 14 of these states OAA benefits are withheld on the assumption that relatives should bear their share. Contributions from relatives determined by complicated schedules must be deducted from the old age assistance benefits. The aged may even be encouraged to sue their own relatives to obtain these contributions, thus jeopardizing familial good will and discouraging voluntary contributions. Since the relatives of the aged are often poor, they may take aged relatives into their own homes unwillingly with a possibility of familial disharmony. Confusion as to the responsibility of family and state is further indicated by the laws in about half the state which seek to recover OAA payments from the estate of a deceased beneficiary. The total effect of efforts by the state to coerce support of the aged by family members is probably a weakening of voluntary cooperation.

The burden of economic support of aged family members often is unfairly distributed among the children. Married children readily shift the burden to the single sibling, especially if this sibling still resides with the aged parent. Even when the burden is shared, the yoke may be heavy. The life insurance programs, pensions, social security programs, and the like men-

[61] Clifford Kirkpatrick, *The Family as Process and Institution* (New York: Ronald Press, 1963), p. 549.

tioned in Chapter 11 may relieve this burden in many cases. The sharp rises in social security taxes and benefits, commencing in January 1966, together with the concurrent legislation on Medicare, may portend a future in which the aged will retain economic independence, even to the extent of provision of home care for the physically feeble and/or incapacitated. Governmental programs seem to be moving rapidly in this direction, financing them from payroll deductions in the productive years of the worker. Realization is not yet here.

Aside from the loss of economic independence, two major problems face the aged parent. One is loss of status. This varies by class level. "In the lower class the context is one of a relatively unified mutual-aid economy in which old folks manage their statuses in a larger kinfolk entity. In the upper class, old people normally retain status and honorific positions, including power, to the end. In the middle classes old people retain status only if they are economically competent and worthy. A middle-class person loses social respectability when he no longer can hold his own economically."[62] The aged who have lost status face a major adjustment problem. To have advice to their own children rejected as being old-fashioned or impractical is bitter medicine for the person who has guided these same children through the years of their mental immaturity. An even greater gap exists between the aged and the grandchildren, who sometimes have difficulty even in communicating.

The second major problem is one of social isolation. The conjugal family has no place for grandparents or for aged aunts and uncles. Even when physical residence is enforced, social communication is at a minimum. Ways of thinking, behaving, and even of speaking have changed so rapidly in American culture that there is little real basis for social interaction among three generations. Old age is becoming increasingly a lonely time for most persons.

Family Disorganization

Not all families enact a continuous drama, with a resident cast, from the cradle to the grave. The actors change in far too many casts. Too many actors are "muffing their lines." Family disorganization occurs when there is serious and prolonged conflict or when the family unit is broken. Either of these situations suggests an unhappy family. The members of the family carry their unhappiness with them to work and to play, infecting society with their tensions. Society pays for the unhappy family, for the changing casts, and the inept actors.

Divorce, legal separation, or desertion normally come only after serious and prolonged family conflict. The obvious remedy for these causes of broken homes is to discover and to eliminate the causes of unhappy

---

[62] Willard Waller and Reuben Hill, *The Family: A Dynamic Interpretation* (New York: Dryden, 1951).

marriages. The legal causes of divorce, listed in the order of the number of states recognizing their validity, are as follows: adultery, cruelty, desertion, insanity, pregnancy at marriage, bigamy, separation, indignities, drug addiction, violence, and fraudulent contract.[63] These may or may not be the real reasons for divorce. New York State, for example, recognizes only adultery as a ground for divorce; collusion of the marriage pair in manufacturing false evidence is common. The real causes of the family discord preceding desertion, separation, or divorce are more elusive. Basically, all conflict results from blocking of goal-seeking behavior.[64] Whenever the gratification of the wishes of one marriage partner means frustrating the desires of the other, there is conflict. These bases of marital unhappiness are as broad as life itself—so the "obvious" remedy cited above must elude the social scientist.

If a positive approach were taken—that is, concentrating on the building of *happy* marriages—then more rapid progress might be made toward reducing the number of unhappy homes. We have indicated earlier that the building of healthy personalities in children, with stress upon adaptability and upon consideration for others, is the best possible preparation for happy marriage. The importance of this second trait (consideration for others) is noted by Cohn in the negative sense by referring to disruptive marriage behavior as "an orgy of the ego ... an indulgence of the gratification of the immediate desires of man or wife without regard to family, children, or state ... individualism gone mad."[65]

The common causes for broken homes are death, separation, and divorce. Hunt indicates that about 10 per cent of all broken homes are headed by divorced persons, approximately twice as many by those legally separated, and nearly three-fourths by individuals who have been widowed.[66]

When children are involved, the problems of broken homes are magnified. Truxal and Merrill emphasize that it is the unhappy marriage that poisons the world of the child. Whether the marriage be broken psychologically by bitter and continuous conflict, or legally by divorce, or by separation or death, the child loses an emotional security that he may never recover.[67]

Remarriage of the surviving spouse (or of the separated or divorced spouse retaining custody of the children) may provide economic security for the children, and eventual emotional security, but not until many difficult adjustments have been made. New roles need to be defined not only

[63] *Information Please Almanac* (New York: Macmillan, 1965), p. 304.
[64] See Chapter 7.
[65] David L. Cohn, "Are Americans Polygamous?" *Atlantic*, 180 (August 1957), pp. 30–33.
[66] Elgin F. Hunt, *Social Science* (New York: Macmillan, 1955), p. 186.
[67] Andrew G. Truxal and Francis E. Merrill, *Marriage and the Family in American Culture* (Englewood Cliffs, N.J.: Prentice-Hall, 1953), pp. 545–546.

between the newly married couple but also between at least one spouse and one or more children. When both partners bring children to the marriage, a whole host of new relationships and roles need to be defined. Unfortunately, there is no script to follow; each member must "ad lib" his way, defining his own role in the new group.

Some emotional support is given to the family broken by death through the bereavement rituals designed by society. Friends and neighbors gather, saying only complimentary things about the deceased, and offering material assistance during the adjustment period. The divorced person has no such ritual to support him. The tendency is to condemn the defects of one or both spouses, and possibly to ostracize those involved.[68] The family separated by desertion often has no public notice taken of their plight until the initial shock of the separation has been dissipated; by that time the "deserter" frequently has returned home. The family separated by a legal step short of divorce suffers much the same discrimination as the divorced person.

Statistics reveal little of the human suffering involved in broken homes. Death may mean the passing of the one human being with whom genuine affection and respect was shared—or it may mean release from a drunken, sadistic monster. Divorce normally is the result, not the cause, of family suffering; but, especially with children, it may cause much new or further suffering. Statistics can reveal only the number of broken homes. Various estimates follow. "In 1960 there were 7.9 million widows and 2.2 million widowers in the United States. This refers to current marital status and not those who have ever been widowed. The larger number of widows than widowers is due to two factors: (1) Women have a longer life expectancy than men; in 1961, white men and women at age 20 could expect to live to age 69.4 and 76.2 respectively. And (2) a greater per cent of widowers remarry. Widowed men are more inclined to find it easier to remarry than widowed women. Of all men and women who had the marital status of widowed in 1960, 70.8 per cent of the men and 57.4 per cent of the women were 65 years or older."[69] Part of the difference is the result of the greater incidence of remarried younger widowers. "It would appear that a figure of 100,000 deserters per year is conservative. This would be roughly one desertion to every four divorces—1950."[70] If one adds the divorce and desertion totals and compares them with the marriage totals, one can well understand the concern of many for the future stability of the family. In recent years this ratio has been approximately one desertion and four divorces for every sixteen marriages; in short, nearly one-third as many homes annually are being broken by desertion and divorce as are being created by marriage. Fortunately, not all broken homes involve children.

[68] Ernest W. Burgess, Harvey J. Locke, and Margaret Thomas. *The Family: From Institution to Companionship* (New York: American Book Company, 1963), p. 460.
[69] Burgess, Locke, and Thomas, *ibid.*, p. 593.
[70] Ray E. Baber, *op. cit.*, p. 494.

Childless couples are twice as prone to divorce as couples with children; further, as the size of the family increases, the likelihood of divorce decreases.[71] It will be remembered from the statistics quoted on homes broken by death that the great majority of these involved marriage partners over 45; obviously, fewer young children are present in homes with parents over 45.

In summary, family disorganization occurs when there is serious or prolonged family conflict or when the family unit is broken. The bases of marital unhappiness are as broad as life itself; but extreme individualism is the greatest contributor. The greatest hope for reducing the number of unhappy marriages destined for dissolution by desertion or divorce seems to be in premarital and marital counseling designed to create happier marriages, thus providing a better environment for the development of healthy personalities in the offspring. The basic personality traits needed are adaptability and consideration for others. Death is the greatest contributor to broken homes. Divorce and desertion affect over 300,000 minor children each year.[72]

PROPOSALS TO IMPROVE FAMILY STABILITY

In a culture exhibiting as much free choice by the individual as is apparent in modern America, education of the individual is the surest approach to the solution of social problems. However, in any urbanized, industrialized culture, the government increasingly restricts freedom of the individual in order to protect the welfare of the group. Social legislation is necessary, therefore, to assist the individual in the solution of problems that are partially or completely under governmental regulation. In Chapters 9 and 10 considerable space is devoted to necessary social legislation designed to improve the physical and social welfare of the individual in terms of health, housing, vocational opportunity, and economic welfare. All of that legislation is applicable to the individual as a family member.

Legislation

Special social legislation is needed in the field of family stability. Our present medley of divorce laws is a national disgrace. "The confusion produced by the difference among state laws is well known; a man may be a respectable married man in New Jersey and a bigamist in New York State."[73] Even the Supreme Court has reversed its position on migratory divorce on three separate occasions within a seven-year period.[74] The moral of the story seems clear: persons had better stay married—or else marry, divorce, remarry, and live the rest of their lives, all within the same state.

[71] Ray E. Baber, *ibid.*, pp. 502–503.
[72] Willard Waller and Reuben Hill, *op. cit.*, p. 542.
[73] Willard Waller and Reuben Hill, *op. cit.*, p. 502.
[74] Ray E. Baber, *op. cit.*, pp. 477–478.

The alternatives may be charges of bigamy and illegitimacy, and confusions regarding inheritance of property.

Another aspect of divorce law that needs clarification is alimony. State differences are large; the range in percentage of divorce cases involving alimony, from state to state, is approximately from 10 per cent to 50 per cent.[75] The range in size of award may be as great as from $1.00 per month to a New York award of $90,000 a year.[76] Certainly there is social justification for alimony. The middle-aged wife who has neither training nor experience in earning a living cannot be expected to culminate twenty years of keeping house and rearing children with a penniless start on a new life. Neither can the sick or aged be cast upon the charity of society. On the other hand, alimony "careerists" have abused the alimony provisions of the law. Many women stoutly refuse alimony, maintaining that they are well qualified to support themselves; others insist upon support in a style far better than the former husband's income can maintain. Despite the provision of the federal Constitution that individuals cannot be imprisoned for debt, nonpayment of alimony is an offense punishable by imprisonment. The thesis is that the defaulter is not being jailed for debt but for contempt of court in refusing to pay. The penalty maintains in some states even though the wife is using the alimony to support both herself and a new husband. Alimony may be claimed by the wife even though she be the "guilty party" in the divorce. Certainly, the changed political, social, and economic status of women in the modern world entitles men to a re-examination of the alimony statutes.

The greatest single change that needs to be made, however, is in the concept of the "guilt" of one party to the marriage as a condition to divorce. "The legal theory is that a divorce is granted to the injured party because of some violation by the other of the marriage *mores* or customs which govern the married state. .... A couple cannot agree to get a divorce. If any evidence of such collusion comes out in a trial for divorce, the judge is in duty bound to throw the case out of court."[77] Such a state of affairs makes criminals out of every couple who jointly decide that their interests and those of society would be served best by a dissolution of their marriage. Much more important, from the viewpoint of the stability of marriage, their legal lines of communication are severely restricted from the time of their decision to separate. For prosecution of the case, the law insists that they must be antagonists rather than two adults cooperatively trying to solve a problem. Basic to this assumption is the theory that if the guilt of one be proved, then divorce is the just punishment for the offender. Divorce is not so impartial; both parties suffer from it. Further, society pays a large part of the cost in terms of the unhappiness of both parties, loss of time and energy in court procedures, the turning back into the

[75] Ray E. Baber, *ibid.*, p. 480.
[76] Ray E. Baber, *ibid.*, pp. 481–482.
[77] Willard Waller and Reuben Hill, *op. cit.*

marriage market of poor matrimonial risks, and the emotional and economic problems of the dependent children who may be involved in the divorce action.[78] The emphasis needs to be shifted legally to a consideration by the court as to whether the divorce action is in the best interests of the parties involved and of society. The American Bar Association has advanced a proposal based on a counseling relationship between the court and the marriage partners. Claims of success in reintegrating marriages on the verge of divorce have gone as high as the 90 per cent advanced by the Department of Domestic Relations in Cleveland.[79] Evidence of the willingness of couples to try again if someone will encourage them to do so is gleaned even from the cold statistics of the divorce courts: Marion County, Indiana, reports that about 45 per cent of the divorce suits filed there never even come to trial.[80] Certainly we need to change the function of our divorce courts from one of "trying guilt" to one of "trying to help."

Social agencies have been working recently on agreements concerning qualifications for the marriage counselor. If such specially trained persons were available, they might well prevent most divorce cases from ever coming to trial. Waller and Hill comment on the promise of this field as follows:[81]

No activity is at present more chaotic and none is riper with promise than the salvaging of families through skilled counseling. A husband and wife are worried about their heated tiffs; a parent feels that friction at home is producing anxiety in a child; a doctor has a patient whose home difficulties are delaying his recovery; a lawyer finds that his client needs his marriage strengthened, not dissolved; an employer has a good workman who is falling down on the job because of personal problems; a minister desires advice regarding care for a member of a family in his church; an engaged pair wonder whether they are ready to marry, they have so many doubts and mixed feelings—these are problems for the marriage-and-family-counseling agency which yesterday would have been solved over the backyard fence or with the help of an older relative. Or worse, they are problems that might have been postponed indefinitely, never to be solved.

It is hoped that the day will come when every divorce court judge will insist upon counseling by a member of his staff before agreeing to hear a divorce case.

[78] It is estimated that a total of three children under eighteen are involved in every five divorce actions.

[79] David G. Wittels, "Perjury Unlimited," *The Saturday Evening Post*, February 18, 1950, p. 138.

[80] *Indianapolis News*, December 2, 1953, p. 34.

[81] Reprinted from *The Family: A Dynamic Interpretation*, by Willard Waller, Revised by Reuben Hill, by permission of The Dryden Press, Inc. Copyright 1951 by The Dryden Press.

Education

The period in which family life education is most desperately needed is young adulthood. Readiness for learning is at an optimum. The need for learning is evidenced by the high divorce rate in the early years of marriage; and most newlyweds are young adults. The student body of these adult education classes, however, should not be limited to young adults. The need is for enrollment by engaged couples, other single young adults, the newly married, married people with unresolved problems, *ministers, doctors*, and *teachers*. As we noted earlier, the minister, doctor, and teacher often are called upon in the role of marriage counselor. All too often, they possess neither the knowledge of family life nor the techniques of counseling requisite to adequate fulfillment of the role.

The content of such adult education classes in family living should include at least the following: study of and practice in democratic principles of family living; development of a set of moral and ethical principles on which to base family decisions; human dynamics, with special stress upon the courtship and marital roles of the adult couple; sex relations in marriage, personal hygiene, birth control, and planned parenthood; the human development of the child through adolescence; home management, including family finance; consumer education; the wise utilization of leisure time; planning for the periods of the empty nest and of old age; and techniques of counseling.

Another social invention that contributes much to family life is the nursery school. Of recent origin, it has not yet been fully accepted. The assistance given parents in child socialization in good nursery school centers surely will yield handsome dividends in better adjusted, more adaptable individuals better equipped to meet all life problems, including those related to the family. Operation Headstart should extend those benefits to more families.

Pending further assistance from the nursery school and from adult education, the elementary, secondary, and university schools must accelerate their own programs in family-life education.[82] The content is basically the same as that noted for adult education, with high school and college counselors rendering personal, vocational, and marital counseling. The teacher competencies and methodologies are basically the same as those to be outlined in Chapter 9. Areas that currently are weak are the assimilation of high ideals and the development of skills in critical thinking.[83] The historic separation of church and state, with proscription against doctrinal instruction, has led many good teachers to evade their responsibility to help youth develop a set of moral and ethical principles that will guide life decisions. This is part of the cultural tradition the school is charged to

---

[82] For an excellent treatise on the role of the schools in the family life education, see Joseph K. Folsom, *Youth, Family and Education* (Washington, D.C.: American Council on Education, 1941).

[83] Problem-solving as a technique is discussed in Chapters 8 and 14.

transmit.[84] This omission on the part of many good teachers may well be a heavily contributing factor in the secularization of our society. This weakening of the moral fabric of our people adds considerably to the emotional insecurity of our times, which further distorts the judgment of all. Man needs the security of something greater than himself to which he can cling in times of trouble. Too many families are trying to find the answers to their problems in the physical world alone. Religious expression has been a basic need of man from time immemorial. Teachers probably exceed Constitutional limitations in their emphasis upon Christian holidays —yet they fail to guide children in the development of those daily moral and ethical principles that all of us so badly need for guidance in coping with life's problems. The family cannot survive so long as man and woman find their only strength in each other.[85]

SUMMARY

The family always has constituted a significant social group; but sociological research on family life is of recent origin. Some sociologists interpret this research to indicate that the family is disintegrating. The authors concur with the contrasting interpretation that disorganization is only a symptom of the adaptation of the family to a rapidly changing culture. Urbanization, industrialization, and increasing governmental participation are changing the size, functions, characteristics, and stability of the family. There is evidence of a shift in family structure from an institution to a companionship, based upon equalitarian roles of family members and with stability dependent upon continued happiness of its members.

The major problems facing the American family are child socialization, dating, choosing a career, developing physically and morally satisfactory sex behavior, selecting a mate, courting, defining family roles, parenthood, and adjusting to the stages of the empty nest and of old age. Family disorganization may occur at any of these stages. Basic personality traits of adaptability and consideration for others are the greatest integrating forces in building harmonious, effective families.

Social legislation is sorely needed to improve present divorce procedures. Education, however, offers the greatest hope for successful transition of the family to a new form adapted to present society; it is increased stability of the family, not improved methods of dissolution, that is needed. Basic to this education must be concern for wholesome personality development of children, for it is upon the personalities of today's children that the future of the family depends. Educators need to recognize that modern

[84] Educational Policies Commission, *Moral and Spiritual Values in the Public Schools* (Washington, D.C.: National Education Association, 1951), pp. 6–7.

[85] The legal separation of church and state in America need not mean the abandonment of moral and ethical principles in the schools. The American moral code has as strong roots in our secular history as it has in doctrinal teachings.

youth is faced with a bewildering variety of decisions; sound moral and ethical principles on which to base those decisions must be integrated into total personality development. Upon the moral and ethical integrity of modern youth rests the future of America.

Selected Bibliography

Bell, Robert R. *A Bibliography of American Family Problem Areas*. Philadelphia: Temple University, 1964. Focuses on problem areas in the family in American society; not intended as a comprehensive bibliography of works on the over-all study of the family. Organized in eighteen categories of commonly recognized family problem areas. Cross indexed at the end of each subject-matter category. Especially helpful in locating pertinent articles in periodicals; articles listed from 186 different Journals.

Barrich, Dorothy. *How to Live With Your Teen-agers*. New York: McGraw-Hill, 1963. Pp. xiii + 261. A guide for parents.

————, and Hyman Miller. *Sex in Marriage: New Understandings*. New York: Harper & Row, 1962. Pp. 277.

Bowman, Henry. *Marriage for Moderns*, Fifth Edition. New York: McGraw-Hill, 1965. Pp. xx + 709. This college text emphasizes the importance of attitudes in marriage. Comprehensive presentation of most aspects of premarriage and marriage relations and conduct. Films available that are correlated with the text.

Burgess, Ernest W., Harvey J. Locke, and Mary Margaret Thomas. *The Family: From Institution to Companionship*. New York: American Book, 1963. Pp. 582. Analysis of historic forces that are changing the family from institution to companionship. Stresses role of family in shaping personality. Claims family is successfully adapting to social change.

————, and Paul Wallin with Gladys Denny Schultz. *Courtship, Engagement, and Marriage*. Philadelphia: Lippincott, 1954. Pp. 444. A popular version of the Burgess-Wallin study of one thousand engaged couples covering dating in the modern age, the engaged couple, what makes marriage sound.

Cavan, Ruth Shonie. *Marriage and Family in Modern World: A Book of Readings*. New York: Crowell, 1960. Pp. 607.

Despert, Louise. *Children and Divorce*. Garden City, N.Y.: Doubleday, 1953. Pp. 382. Describes the effect of marriage failure on the child before and after divorce. Suggests ways of safeguarding the child and explores such questions as, "When children experience divorce are they bound to experience failure in their own marriages?" Presents a child's eye view of failing marriage.

Duvall, Evelyn Millis, and the Class in Methods and Materials in Teaching Family Relations, Syracuse University, Summer 1949. *Family Life Materials*. Syracuse: Syracuse University Press, 1949. Pp. 52. Text and reference books; annotated lists of pamphlets; annotated lists of professional periodicals; annotated lists of films and film strips; glossary of frequently used terms.

————, and Hill, Reuben. *Being Married*. New York: Association Press, 1960. Pp. 440. Gathers previously published materials from periodicals, journals, and monographs. Designed for young people—the engaged and the just-married.

ELLIS, ALBERT, and ROBERT A. HARPER. *Creative Marriage*. New York: Lyle Stuart, 1961. Pp. 288. Popularly written. Psychiatrically oriented.

FARBER, BERNARD. *Family: Organization and Interaction*. San Francisco: Chandler Publishing Company, 1964. Pp. 536. Organized in three sections: General aspects of family life, contemporary family structure and membership, and interaction between family members.

FOLSOM, JOSEPH K. *Youth, Family, and Education*. Washington, D.C.: American Council on Education, 1941. Pp. xv + 299. Report on the development of family-life education, from nursery school through adult education. Still an excellent source of practical ideas for the teacher.

GRUENBER, SIDONIE, and HILDA CRECH. *The Many Lives of Modern Woman*. Garden City, N.Y.: Doubleday, 1952. Pp. 255. A mother-daughter team emphasizes marriage as a partnership in which the modern educated woman creates her own design for significance as she seeks her role as an individual as well as wife and mother.

KIRKPATRICK, CLIFFORD. *The Family as Process and Institution*. New York: Ronald Press, 1955. Pp. 651. This book elaborates the dilemmas of families in our inconsistent culture and portrays the family process as successive dramas over the life cycle of familial experience. Reflects a lifetime of research and teaching courses on the family.

LEMASTERS, E. E. *Modern Courtship and Marriage*. New York: Macmillan, 1957. Pp. xii + 619. Emphasises upon "subcultures" of the adolescent, the male, the rural dweller, class levels, and other groups. Excellent section on the American courtship system. Crisp, effective, readable.

Look (January 11, 1966), "The American Woman." Special 50-page feature. Interesting cross-sectional overview of problems facing the modern American woman.

MCIVER, ROBERT. *Challenge of the Passing Years*. New York: Simon & Schuster, 1962. Pp. xxiv + 133.

MUDD, EMILY. *Success in Family Living*. New York: Association Press, 1965. Pp. 254.

———. *The Practice of Marriage Counseling*. New York: Association Press, 1951. Pp. 366. Discusses the process of marriage counseling. Includes a list of institutions and center providing reliable help on problems arising in marriage.

REISS, IRA L. *Premarital Sexual Standards in America*. New York: Free Press of Glencoe, 1960. Pp. 286. A sociological investigation of the relative social and cultural integration of American sexual standards.

SUSSMAN, MARVIN B. (ed.). *Sourcebook in Marriage and the Family*. Boston: Houghton Mifflin, 1955. Pp. 431. A selection of essays and research articles that are sometimes hard to place on reserve for college students. Supplements most texts nicely.

VAN EVERA, JEAN. *How to Be Happy While Single*. Philadelphia: Lippincott, 1949. Pp. 181. A guide for the young woman who by choice or necessity may remain single through adulthood.

WALLER, WILLARD, and REUBEN HILL. *The Family: A Dynamic Interpretation*. Revised 1951 by Reuben Hill. New York: Dryden Press, 1951. Pp. xviii + 637. Mature and meaningful study on the college level.

ZIMMERMAN, CARLE and LUCIUS F. CERVANTES. *Successful American Families.*
New York: Pageant Press, 1960. Pp. 226.

SELECTED FILMS

Age of Turmoil (McGraw-Hill) 20 min
  The picture goes from one adolescent type to another, focusing on be-
  havior that mirrors the emotional turmoil of the persons involved.
Children's Emotions (McGraw-Hill) 20 min
  Shows sources of common emotions. Discusses normal fear, anger, and
  jealousy, and points dangers of emotions.
Choosing for Happiness (McGraw-Hill) 14 min
  Portrays through dramatized situations the reactions of a girl to various
  boyfriends and her rejection of all of them—and they of her; and sug-
  gests that the girl should re-evaluate herself and her demands on others.
  Follow-up filmstrip: 38 frames.
Early Social Behavior (ERPE Classroom Films) 10 min
  Illustrates the social significance of the home through scenes reflecting
  parent-child relationships. Analyzes the social behavior of ten children,
  eight weeks to seven years old. Stresses individual differences and sibling
  relations.
Families First (New York State Department of Commerce) 17 min
  By a series of everyday episodes in the lives of two contrasting families,
  this film demonstrates the causes of tensions, frustrations, and antisocial
  attitudes as well as the results of affection, achievement, and harmonious
  personality adjustment.
Family Circles (McGraw-Hill) 31 min
  Shows how the role of the family has changed in our society, placing
  emphasis on the relation of home and school. The importance of recogniz-
  ing the child's emotional needs is shown in four parents' attitudes in
  their homes.
How Much Affection? (McGraw-Hill) 20 min
  Dramatized presentation of situations and questions concerning the extent
  of physical affection between a couple who are going steady.
Human Growth (E. C. Brown Trust) 20 min
  Demonstrates for parents how sex education can be handled smoothly.
  Provides the classroom teacher with a suitable instructional aid for presenting the biological facts of sex.
In Time of Trouble (McGraw-Hill) 14 min
  Portrays the family minister counseling a young married couple and help-
  ing them understand the reasons for their disagreements and ways in
  which satisfactory adjustments can be made. *Follow-up filmstrip: 36
  frames.*
Is This Love? (McGraw-Hill) 14 min
  Contrasts the romances of two college girls, one impulsive and eager to
  get married, the other wishing to go more slowly through the stages of
  dating, courtship, going steady, and engagement. Concludes with open-
  end questions directed to the audience.
It Takes All Kinds (McGraw-Hill) 20 min

Portrays a series of young couples reacting to tense situations; relates their reactions to their possibilities for marriage success or failure; and emphasizes the point that marriage partners should be carefully chosen.

Jealousy (McGraw-Hill) 16 min

Portrayal of a young wife, jealous of her husband, and her gradual realization that her behavior is an expression of her dissatisfaction with her role as a homemaker. *Follow-up filmstrip: 38 frames.*

Life with Grandpa (March of Time) 17 min

Portrays problems confronting older people in our society: disease, economic insecurity, emotional difficulties. Suggests several solutions.

Marriage Is a Partnership (Coronet Films) 16 min

Shows some of the realities of early marriage adjustment; considers specific problems of in-laws, finances, housing, job adjustment; exemplifies arguments, responsibilities, decision-making, loyalties.

Marriage Today (McGraw-Hill) 22 min

Dynamic treatment of goals and ideals of married love. Three couples are depicted: one idealizing marriage, one working toward building a secure future, and one in the process of adjusting interests and day-to-day living.

Meeting Emotional Needs in Childhood (New York University) 33 min

Shows children's need for security for emotional development.

Meeting the Needs of Adolescents (McGraw-Hill) 19 min

Attempts to indicate some of the things parents can do to prepare their children for the future.

Preface to a Life (United World Films) 29 min

Parental influence in a child's developing personality, illustrated by episodes showing the effects of an overly solicitous mother and an overly demanding father contrasting with the healthy childhood resulting when both parents accept their child as an individual.

Social Development (McGraw-Hill) 15 min

Factual description of the developmental changes in children's social behavior. Most of film centers on the preschool years.

The Steps of Age (International Film Bureau) 25 min

Portrays the confusion, fears, and far-from-easy struggle to understand herself that Mrs. Potter, age 62, faces as she embarks on the last quarter of her life. The picture suggests that people need to begin early in life to handle well the situations that come with increasing age.

This Charming Couple (McGraw-Hill) 19 min

Shows how the marriage of a couple who refused to evaluate each other's good and bad points realistically ended in divorce.

When Should I Marry? (McGraw-Hill) 19 min

A minister advises a young couple, eager to marry, by describing the experiences of two other couples who married at an early age.

Who's Boss? (McGraw-Hill) 16 min

Portrays a young married couple, both of whom are individualists, their differences, and their decision to adjust their differences through co-operation. *Follow-up filmstrip: 36 frames.*

Who's Right? (McGraw-Hill) 18 min

Dramatization of a quarrel between husband and wife, caused by her seeing his forcefulness as "bossism" and by his labeling her good taste as extravagance. *Follow-up filmstrip: 36 frames.*

Chapter 7. *Problems of Mental Health in an Era of Rapid Social Change*

WE ARE LIVING in an anxious age. A multitude of personal and social pressures are impinging on individuals and on groups, creating personal tensions and cultural stresses that threaten to destroy us. The statistical significance of this problem was reported in 1950 by the Public Affairs Committee in the following terms:[1]

The problem presented by nervous and mental diseases is an enormous one —the most serious medical problem facing our nation. Out of every twenty living persons, one will spend part of his life in a mental hospital. Recent studies indicate that one out of every ten persons in the United States is emotionally or mentally maladjusted and needs treatment for some personality disorder. More than half the patients who visit their family doctor for some physical ailment are really suffering from some type of emotional disorder. Nervous and mental disease take a larger toll than do cancer, infantile paralysis, and tuberculosis combined.

Not all nervous and mental diseases are caused by the pressures of modern social living. Serious personality disturbances usually have multiple and deep-seated origins. There is no single cause of mental illness. Nevertheless, isolation of single causes and single catalytic events is an essential step in the diagnosis and treatment of the illness. Such diagnosis and treatment, of course, is the prerogative of the trained person such as the clinical psychologist, physician, or psychiatrist. The purpose of this chapter is to introduce laymen and professional educators to the general area of mental hygiene as a vantage point from which to assay the role of the teacher in promoting sound mental health in the children under his charge.

[1] George Thorman, *Toward Mental Health* (Public Affairs Pamphlet No. 120), pp. 22–23 (New York: Public Affairs Committee, Inc., 1950).

234

CONFUSIONS IN TERMINOLOGY IN THE FIELD OF MENTAL HEALTH

Both popular and professional literature in the field of mental hygiene tend to use terminology loosely. Note the apparent interchangeability in the quotation cited above of such terms as "nervous and mental diseases," "persons . . . emotionally or mentally maladjusted," "personality disorder," and "emotional disorder."[2]

Need

This indeterminateness in terminology extends to the foundational field of psychology, from which is drawn much of the rationale of mental hygiene. The inclusiveness of the term *need* is noted:[3]

A *need* exists as a state of tension in a person which serves to direct his behavior toward certain goals. In Chapter IX this goal-directed behavior was attributed to *motives*, or *goal set*. Here the word "need" is chosen to emphasize its primary importance to the person. It is used as an inclusive term to embrace drives, impulses, goal sets, urges, motives, cravings, desires, wants, and wishes. The choice of a term is arbitrary, of course, because in our present state of knowledge it is impossible to disentangle the aspects which these concepts have in common and the differences between them. A need, then, exists as a state of tension which leads a person toward activities which will relieve the tension.

Here the term "need" embraces "drives, impulses, goal sets, urges, motives, cravings, desires, wants, and wishes."[4] It exists "as a state of tension."[5] This tension "leads a person toward activities which will relieve the tension."[6] The sections that immediately follow will define "Needs" as delineated by the psychologists. In a later section of this chapter will be presented a briefer and more generalized listing by the sociologist Thomas.

NEED: THE NEED THEORY APPROACH. Carl Rogers contends that the organism has one basic tendency and striving—to actualize, maintain, and enhance the experiencing organism.[7]

Rather than many needs and motives, it seems entirely possible that all organic and psychological needs may be described as partial aspects of this one fundamental need. It is difficult to find satisfactory words for this proposition. The particular phrasing is from Snygg and Combs. The words used are

---

[2] George Thorman, *ibid.*, pp. 22–23.

[3] Arthur I. Gates, Arthur T. Jersild, T. R. McConnell, and Robert Challman, *Educational Psychology* (New York: Macmillan, 1950), pp. 617–618.

[4] Gates *et al.*, *ibid.*, p. 617.

[5] Gates *et al.*, *ibid.*, pp. 617–618.

[6] Gates *et al.*, *ibid.*, p. 618.

[7] Reprinted by permission from Carl A. Rogers, "Client Centered Therapy," in William S. Sahakian (ed.), *Psychology of Personality: Readings in Theory* (Chicago: Rand McNally, 1965), pp. 477–478.

an attempt to describe the observed directional force in organic life—a force which has been regarded as basic by many scientists, but which has not been too well described in testable or operational terms.

We are talking about the tendency of the organism to maintain itself—to assimilate food; to behave defensively in the face of threat, to achieve the goal of self-maintenance even when the usual pathway to that goal is blocked. We are speaking of the tendency of the organism to move in the direction of maturation, as maturation is defined for each species. This involves self-actualization, though it should be understood that this too is a directional term. The organism does not develop to the full its capacity for suffering pain, nor does the human individual develop or actualize his capacity for terror, or, on the physiological level, his capacity for vomiting. The organism actualizes itself in the direction of greater differentiation of organs and of function. It moves in the direction of limited growth, expansion through extending itself by means of its tools, and expansion through reproduction. It moves in the direction of greater independence or self-responsibility. Its movement, as Angyal has pointed out, is in the direction of an increasing self-government, self-regulation, and autonomy, and away from heteronomous control, or control by external forces. This is true whether we are speaking of entirely unconscious organic processes, such as the regulation of body heat, or such uniquely human and intellectual functions as the choice of life goals. Finally, the self-actualization of the organism appears to be in the direction of socialization, broadly defined.

Need: Self-actualization.   A need to actualize the self, as the individual perceives himself to be, is an important concept. The term is not original to Rogers, but may be seen in the writings of other "needs" theorists such as Maslow[8] and Roe.[9] If one would think of needs as having some priority order within each individual, the need to actualize the self may in any given situation supplant or take precedence over some higher order need. Perhaps an example would clarify this. Assume that a particular article of clothing, pegged trousers, was the "fad" in a given peer culture. The student's parents have refused to purchase these pegged trousers for their son. However, he receives a lunch allowance of 50¢ per day. If the need to dress like his fellow students is of sufficient strength, the boy may pass up his noon meal in order to save enough money to purchase the pegged trousers. This would be an indication of self-actualization where the need to be like one's peers temporarily would supplant the need for bodily nourishment. This is a common occurrence in the everyday existence of most of us. It can take more extreme forms.

Need: Self-Maintenance.   The need to maintain one's self encompasses what has been referred to as self-preservation. The need for physical survival is broadly accepted for all forms of life. It does, however, go be-

[8] A. H. Maslow. *Motivation and Personality* (New York: Harper, 1954). Pp. xvi + 411.

[9] Anne Roe, "Early Determinants of Vocational Choice," *Journal of Counseling Psychology*, Vol. 4 (1957), pp. 212–217.

yond this restricted limitation. It also encompasses the maintenance of the psychological self. An individual needs to maintain his psychological self as well as his physiological self. This expanded use of the term self-preservation permits an explanation of behavior such as martyrdom, suicide, and other forms of apparent physical self-destruction. When one voluntarily chooses to relinquish his physical life, he could not be thought of as being concerned with physical self-preservation or maintenance. However, if we consider each individual to have a psychological existence as well as physical, then such behavior becomes more plausible. The individual may see himself psychologically (in terms of his self-concept) as one who would give up his physical existence for a religious belief. In the case of martyrdom, he has decided that it would be better for him to give up his physical existence rather than change his view of himself as a person. A soldier in Viet Nam may have a concept of himself as a person who would lay down his life for his friends. If a live hand grenade were thrown in his vicinity he would fall on the hand grenade to save his friends' lives even though it meant his own destruction. This would illustrate the need on the part of the soldier to maintain his psychological self. The physical world of the suicide is so threatening or intolerable for him that he destroys his body rather than alter his self-concept.

Need: Self-enhancement. Self-enhancement and growth occur in each individual under favorable environmental conditions. This self-enhancement and growth is not always easy. Rogers contends that it would be perhaps more correct to say that the organism moves through struggle and pain toward enhancement and growth. The whole process may be symbolized and illustrated by the child's learning to walk. The first steps often involve struggle, and usually pain. Often it is true that the immediate reward involved in taking a few steps is in no way commensurate with the pain of falls and bumps. The child may, because of the pain, revert to crawling for a time. Yet, in the overwhelming majority of individuals, the forward direction of growth is more powerful than the satisfactions of remaining infantile. The child will actualize himself, in spite of the painful experiences in so doing. In the same way, he will become independent, responsible, self-governing, socialized, in spite of the pain that is often involved in these steps. Even where he does not, because of a variety of circumstances, exhibit growth of these more complex sorts, one may still rely on the fact that the tendency is present. Given the opportunity for clear-cut choice between forward-moving and regressive behavior, the tendency will operate.[10]

This definition of need, in its broadest sense, presupposes that man in his basic nature is similar to all forms of organic life. That is to say, man has the potential for growth. Placed in a favorable environment, man's growth both psychologically and physiologically would be maximized.

[10] Carl A. Rogers, *op. cit.*, pp. 478–479.

Providing man with a favorable climate for maximum growth and development is critical to the whole picture of mental health. We need to identify those elements of our society that contribute to or retard maximum growth and development.

NEED: SELF-PRESERVATION. Maslow[11] has listed needs according to their priority or power in relationship to each other. This and the following paragraphs constitute a slight modification of Maslow's list. At the top of Maslow's listing of needs is the need for self-maintenance, or self-preservation, which has been adequately treated in prior discussion.

NEED: SELF-REPRODUCTION. Maslow's second priority of need is the tendency or need of man to reproduce his species, which seems to be passed genetically from one generation to the next. If this need is not of sufficient intensity, in a given species, that species disappears. We can see here the relationship between self-actualization and self-reproduction. Even though the self-reproduction need is present in man, some people, for a variety of reasons, do not reproduce their kind. When preservation of the psychological self is more dominant, as in previously cited cases of suicide, martyrdom, etc. (assuming they had not reproduced prior to death), or where, for reasons meaningful to the individual, celibacy is practiced, (priests, old maids, and bachelors), self-reproduction does not occur. If people in these categories existed in a large majority, the species would disappear.

NEED: SECURITY. Security may be defined as the preservation of the inviolability of the self and freedom from fear and excessive anxiety. This occurs when the individual interacts with his environment in such a way that he has a confident feeling about his needs being satisfied in the present and some reasonable assurance that they will continue to be satisfied in the future. The degree to which this feeling is nonexistent is related to his level of anxiety. The knowledge that the universe may be destroyed by a thermo-nuclear war threatens his need for self-preservation and reproduction. This concept will be developed in more detail in other parts of this chapter. Its application will be noticeable as we continue a more detailed description of needs.

NEED: SELF-RESPECT. The need for self-respect is quite closely tied to the interaction of the child prior to age six with the significant people in his world. Each person needs to view himself as being worthy of love, respect, and dignity. It is an attitude one develops towards one's self and is learned. Although socioeconomic status may affect the atmosphere in which the child may obtain gratification of his need, it appears to operate regardless of one's status in life. A hypercritical parent who is constantly saying "No, no—bad boy!" to curtail the behavior patterns of her child, may indeed teach him to view himself as a person who is bad and cannot trust himself to do the right thing. He may conclude that when he is behaving

[11] A. H. Maslow, *op. cit.*, pp. 80–98.

as he thinks he should, his mother sees it as being bad. Frequent repetition of this kind of child-parent interaction may leave him with a concept of himself as a bad boy.

A parent who encourages and permits her child to do things that he can master and tells him how well he has done, creates in him a feeling of self-respect and accomplishment. He begins to view himself as a person who can succeed, as a person who is wholesome and worthy of love and respect, a person who can accomplish goals. The stabilizing effect of a strong sense of personal adequacy can hardly be overestimated. The parents exert prime influence in determining how the individual comes to view himself as a person. They can produce an inferior, insecure child or one who considers himself to be a person of worth.

NEED: ACCEPTANCE BY OTHERS. The individual needs to feel that he is accepted by the significant people in his environment. Nonacceptance by others sets up the basic cleavage of man from himself. Let us examine how this could occur. It is fairly well established that man needs love and affection. This has been also called mothering. Love is indeed a many-splendored thing. Harlow found that love, mothering, or as he calls it "contact comfort" was the most significant variable in his study.[12] If we generalize his findings, we discover that the age-old argument of breast versus bottle feeding is not an important factor in child development. Regardless of the method used, it is the amount of contact comfort in a warm intimate relationship that is crucial. It even surpasses the need for nourishment, Harlow found. The primates preferred the warm soft mother surrogate to the wire mother surrogate regardless of which one gave the milk. Those primates forced to live with a wire mother become overly anxious. The study of marasmus in children who received little, none, or inconsistent mothering indicated that they literally withered up and died. They were unable to make use of food even when it was fed intravenously. They soon died of malnutrition. While the medical doctors were looking for some virus, it was discovered that they only lacked response and mothering.

The parents usually are the ones to give this response to the child. He needs love, affection, or contact comfort more than food. Unfortunately, some parents give or withhold affection from their child as a condition of his behavior. When the child does not behave the way the parents think he should, they convey their dislike. The child feels rejected. He sees himself as a person not worthy of being loved when he acts a certain way. Because of his overwhelming need for acceptance, he generally does what the parents feel he should do, and in this way he takes on parental values. What they view as right and wrong and good and bad, he does also, even though these values are not confirmed by his experience. He adopts,

[12] Harry F. Harlow and Robert R. Zimmerman, "Affectional Responses in the Infant Monkey," in Paul H. Mussen, John Conger, and Jerome Kagen, *Readings in Child Development and Personality* (New York: Harper 1965), pp. 112–139.

as Rogers has postulated, a set of values rather than learns a process by which he may value. He has not the opportunity to learn for himself. We start with the conclusion and try to make it compatible with our experience. This need to be loved and accepted by others causes the person to become alienated from himself.

As with other forms of treatment by parents, acceptance of the child as he is and for what he may become is a matter of degree rather than of kind. In cases of extreme deprivation of the fulfillment of this need, persons may develop, in later years, a neurotic need to be liked by others. This is evident in much adolescent behavior when he will do most anything, even commit antisocial acts, in order to be accepted by his peer group. The threat of loss of love and acceptance for those who have not had this need gratified sufficiently can produce extreme anxiety and panic.

We find no discrepancy in the literature or research indicating that individuals are indeed unique and different. Still, many people have difficulty accepting individuals as being different. Many parents, teachers, and others attempt to remake them in terms of their values and perceptions of what they should be. *"Wie man wird, was man ist . . .* how one becomes what one is,"[13] is still a paramount question that demands the attention of parents and of educators. This need can be met in the parent-child relationship, heterosexual love and attachments, close friendships, and in the general sociability of the human being under favorable conditions.

NEED: RECOGNITION, SELF-EXPRESSION, AND ACCOMPLISHMENT. The individual has a need to use his talents or abilities for gratification purposes or role accomplishments in areas dictated by his interests. As one would imagine, this need should and can be gratified in early years in the home. Effective school settings also may become a facilitator for self-expression and recognition. The teacher is in a key position to accord acclaim as he structures the classroom situation and evaluates the child's progress. In the foregoing paragraph, the terms *interest* and *ability* were not used loosely. It is the responsibility of the teacher to set goals for the individual with some considerable assurance that these are attainable in terms of the child's abilities. It is a difficult task to accomplish this under our present school structure.

There are those educators and administrators who feel that the educative principle and the competitive principle are compatible bedfellows. Barker has found that children who experienced continual success set their aspirations at a realistic level, that is, at a level where success frequently was achieved.[14] Children with a history of chronic failure, on the other

---

[13] Martin Heidegger, "Being and Time," in Rollo May, Ernest Angel, and Henri F. Ellenberger (eds.), *Existence: A New Dimension in Psychiatry and Psychology.* (New York: Basic Books, 1958), p. 31.

[14] Roger G. Barker, "Success and Failure in the Classroom," in Haimowitz and Haimowitz, *Human Development: Selected Readings* (New York: Thomas Y. Crowell, 1960), pp. 543–547.

hand, set their aspirations with little regard for the achievements. To make self-expression, achievement, and recognition within the realm of need gratification he suggests the following:[15]

(a) Broaden the basis for evaluating pupils;
(b) reduce to a minimum the prominence of the relative standing of the pupils;
(c) allow maximum freedom to pupils to set their own goals and to alter them as their success and failure experiences require; that is, make success possible at all levels of achievement;
(d) reduce the dominance of the teacher.

Other areas for the fulfillment of this need are in the occupations we choose. In the complexity of our modern society the individual may have a difficult time finding employment compatible with his interests and abilities. With the exception of the professions, the major bulk of our employment opportunities are repetitious assembly line tasks.

It is postulated here that the recent increase in leisure-time activities is an attempt on the part of the individual to gratify these needs when his principal occupation fails to do so. Increased participation in such areas as in camping and traveling as well as do-it-yourself kits and hobbies might be considered further evidence in support of this contention.

NEED: ESTHETIC EXPRESSIONS. The existence of artistic forms of expression such as music, art, drama, may be viewed as expressions of the gratification of this need.

NEED: AS THE PRIME MOTIVATOR OF BEHAVIOR. Rogers has stated (WSS) that "Behavior is basically the goal-directed attempt of the organism to satisfy its needs as experienced, in the field as perceived."[16] He stressed that man's reaction or behavior is not to what reality is, but to his perception of what is real. A man in the desert will struggle just as hard to reach a "lake" that he perceives in a mirage as he would to reach a real waterhole. Or man may strive for money as a source of security even though in fact this may not satisfy his needs. Man's perception of his world is, for him, his reality. Rogers departs quite remarkably from Freud and the psychoanalysts when he states that man behaves to meet present needs, that behavior is not caused by something that happened in the past. What happened in the past may alter the way that we perceive our present situation. However, we behave to satisfy present-felt needs and to reduce present-felt tensions.

The reason that Maslow arranged his needs in a hierarchy was that he contended the individual must attend first to the basic needs before he can satisfy higher order but less powerful needs. Anne Roe, in much the

15 Roger G. Barker, *ibid.*, p. 543.
16 Carl A. Rogers, *op. cit.*, p. 479.

same vein, contends that a higher order but less powerful need that is not gratified over a long period of time will wither and die.[17] This is not true, however, with the more basic needs. She contends that when basic needs are not gratified, they become the prime motivator of our behavior. Thus, an individual from an economically deprived area of this country may have very little need for esthetic expression. He is primarily concerned with the more basic needs of self-preservation. We may postulate, from the foregoing, that the need for self-preservation in terms of food and shelter and protection from the elements may dominate his behavior pattern.

Need satisfaction as a determinant for behavior has wide applications for our society in general and for the school and home in particular. While recognizing that behavior is infinitely complex, people who deal with children and youth could, nonetheless, use need satisfaction in an attempt to understand behavior. Beginning with the most basic need, and going upward on the hierarchy, one might ascertain at what level the individual is operating in terms of need satisfaction. An attempt might be made to begin at that point.

Tension

Tension is another major concept about which there is confusion. Gates, Jersild, McConnell, and Challman seem to use it as meaning a complex emotional and physical state resulting from unfulfilled needs.[18] Hilgard defines it as a contraction of the muscles of the body.[19] Although some authorities support Hilgard in the more narrow definition, the authors of this text will use it in the broad sense—a state of emotional excitement and muscular contraction that drives man to action.

Emotion

Emotion is another nebulous term. Prescott says, "Emotions . . . are defined usually as inherited pattern reactions involving extensive visceral behavior and intense feelings."[20] Here the definition of emotions includes the "extensive visceral behavior," or contraction of the smooth muscles of the intestinal tract, which we have been describing as muscular tension. Emotions, then, like tension, involve both muscular contraction and feelings. Common emotions are fear, anger, and joy.

Emotions in man are differentiated from emotions in infrahumans primarily by man's ability partially to control and to conceal his emotions through the use of reason. This emotional control is accompanied by muscular tension. It is the muscular tension that leaves one fatigued after a day in which one has done little physical labor but that has sorely tried

---

[17] Anne Roe, *op. cit.*, pp. 212–217.
[18] Arthur I. Gates *et al.*, *op. cit.*, pp. 617–618.
[19] Ernest Hilgard, *Introduction to Psychology* (New York: Harcourt, 1953), p. 612.
[20] Daniel A. Prescott, *Emotion and the Educative Process* (Washington, D.C.: American Council on Education, 1938), p. 17.

one's emotional control. Teachers are particularly prone to this type of fatigue. Respect for the personality of children puts a heavy strain upon emotional control in the face of the many conflict situations that occur in every teaching day. The teacher is the adult in the learning situation, and must meet ignorance and innocence alike with tolerance and restraint.

Mental Health

A working definition of mental health may be "that dynamic state of adjustment or maladjustment resulting from man's eternal quest for emotional equilibrium." Man never attains perfect equilibrium—or, at least, he attains it only for very brief periods. As soon as emotional balance is achieved, some new force impinges upon the individual and again throws him off-balance. The resulting attempt to adjust to this new force usually either falls short of reachieving balance or goes just a bit too far in the other direction. A common example is the incitement of anger in a normally considerate individual. Actions taken in anger frequently are overcompensated by a lavishing of affection on the recipient of the angered action, in an attempt to "make up."

With certain exceptions, any state of emotional adjustment that approaches equilibrium for extended periods of time is indicative of sound mental health. An obvious exception is the depressive, who is so completely withdrawn from society as to be immune to emotional stimulation. The ideal of a democratic society is that state of mental health that enables one to live harmoniously within his culture, to assimilate its values, and to maintain and improve the culture.

Mental Hygiene

Mental hygiene is a study of the causes of poor mental health and of the techniques for improving and maintaining mental health.

Adjustment and Maladjustment

The term *adjustment* may be used to refer to one's attempt to regain emotional balance, in response to emotional stimulation from his environment. Ineffective responses are referred to as maladjustments. These may be either failures to regain composure or recapturing temporary balance by the use of techniques (such as daydreaming or destructive acts) that will only further upset one's emotional balance. Levy reminds us that destructive acts may secure temporary release from tension; but that such acts are followed by self-punishment, restitution, or verbal defense of the action.[21] The presence of self-punishing, restoring, and defensive activities is evidence of the temporary nature of the emotional balance achieved through the performance of destructive acts.

[21] David M. Levy, "Experiments in Sibling Rivalry," in Barker, Kounin, and Wright (eds.), *Child Behavior and Development* (New York: McGraw-Hill, 1943), p. 407.

Mechanisms

We shall refer in a later section to adjustment mechanisms indicative of poor mental health. These emotional, or indirect, reactions to conflict situations are typically unconscious and designed to ameliorate immediate distress. The destructive acts cited above are illustrative of such ineffective mechanisms. Not only is the relief they afford of a temporary nature, but also they may accentuate the original cause of frustration and may lead to serious mental illness.

It is the destructive effects on mental health of these mechanisms that lead to the common misconceptions that all mental illness is progressive in nature and that all mental illness exists on a continuum from mild maladjustment to legal insanity. Continued ineffectual emotional reactions to conflict situations may lead to serious neurosis, or psychosis; but not all serious mental illness develops in this way.

Personality

The term *personality* generally refers to the organization of a person's habits, attitudes, and traits. It is the individual version of "human nature." As we have demonstrated in the opening chapters, we learn our "humanness" from the culture; it is, therefore, obvious that we learn to be the kind of person we become. One's basic attitudes toward self, things, ideas, and other persons are shaped by his environment. Much of this learning is emotionally toned and takes place at an unconscious level.

Mental Illness

Mental illness refers to that state of being that seriously impairs one's ability to live harmoniously within his culture. It is evidenced by behavior noticeably different from the norm. Obviously, the "normal" person in one culture may be the "mentally ill" person in another. Mead's study of primitive people is discussed in Chapter 2.[22] Certainly the individual reared in the Arapesh culture would be maladjusted in a Kwakiutl community. Biesanz and Biesanz[23] interpret this maladjustment in terms of a conflict between the basal personality pattern of the individual and the demands of the society in which he finds himself. This conflict is both caused and evidenced by behavior patterns that differ from the prevailing pattern of the culture. Disarmonious states of being may be caused by the conflicts described above, or they may be the results of physical impairment of the individual. In either case, the resultant state of disharmony with the culture represents some degree of mental illness. The terms that are employed to refer to these states of disharmony are neither limited nor

[22] Margaret Mead, *Cooperation and Competition Among Primitive People* (Boston: Beacon, 1961).
[23] John Biesanz and Mavis Biesanz, *Modern Society* (Englewood Cliffs, N.J.: Prentice-Hall, 1964), pp. 177–202.

precise. The varying degrees of disharmony may be referred to as "mental illness," "mental sickness," "nervous disease," "emotional disturbance," "emotional maladjustment," "emotional deviation," "personality conflict," "personality disturbance," "personality maladjustment," "deviant behavior," "psychoneurosis," "psychopathic personality," "psychosis," and others.

Some of the states mentioned above represent only mild deviation from cultural norms; others may be so serious as to be labeled legal insanity. There are no precise boundaries on the continuum—if, indeed, such a continuum from mild deviation to legal insanity exists at all. It is more probable that many disharmonious states are merely normal reactions to frustrating situations and are temporary in nature. It is states of persisting disharmony, however, with which we are concerned in a definition of mental illness. These are not easy to isolate. Bloch says:[24]

> The pathological individual possesses the traits of the normal individual, but in distorted and extreme form. There is no clear-cut dichotomy between normal and abnormal states of mind. Rather, the two states seem to blend into each other. Pathological mental states are recognized as matters of degree; they exist in the extent to which an individual's adjustment-capacities are seriously impaired.

We now turn to a child psychiatrist for definitions of three of the more common terms referring to pathological emotional functioning.

Psychoneurosis

"When unresolved emotional conflicts . . . absorb the person's energies and thus interfere with his intellectual and physical efficiency without greatly altering the basic personality, we look upon the person as psychoneurotic."[25]

Psychopathic personality

"When powerful antisocial feelings habitually or frequently overpower the emotional control of the individual . . . even though the person can reason logically and distinguish between what is generally accepted to be right and wrong, we are inclined to consider the person to have a psychopathic personality."[26]

Psychosis

"When powerful feelings completely overwhelm the individual, causing sweeping changes in the personality and obscuring the individual's ability

---

[24] Herbert A. Bloch, *Disorganization, Personal and Social* (New York: Knopf, 1952), p. 535.
[25] Hale T. Shirley, *Psychiatry for the Pediatrician* (New York: The Commonwealth Fund, 1948), p. 235.
[26] Hale T. Shirley, *ibid.*, p. 235.

to distinguish between reality and fantasy and between accepted standards of right and wrong, we consider the person to be psychotic."[27]

It is recognized, then, that one encounters difficulties in communication when writing in the field of mental hygiene. With these limitations of terminology in mind, we shall discuss briefly several causes of poor mental health, some adjustments to these causal situations, severe mental disturbances requiring special care, problem-solving as a technique for achieving sound mental health, and the implications of mental hygiene for the school.

THE RELATIONSHIP OF PHYSICAL AND MENTAL HEALTH

Mental hygiene is the study of the causes of poor mental health and of the techniques for improving and maintaining mental health. The study of causes is complicated by the fact that mental illness is not distinct from bodily disease. "Probably every case of physical disease has some effect on mental health, and vice versa. An outstanding example of this may be the asthmatic attack due to allergy, with fear superimposed and often becoming dominant. Hence the treatment often becomes psychiatric in nature, even though a physical cause initiated the attack. Some psychiatrists look upon asthma as purely psychological in origin; others accept an allergic explanation, plus psychological overlay."[28] Further examples of the relationship between physical and mental health are found daily in doctors' offices, where patients exhibit very real symptoms of physical pain, although there is no apparent organic basis for pain. Common examples are psychosomatic backache and nausea.

Prolonged emotional conflicts may even produce real changes in bodily tissue, changes that we call physical disease. Ulcers of the stomach, certain types of heart disease, and other comparable physical ailments may be so induced. Such physical illnesses, when caused by emotional disturbances, are called psychogenic, meaning that they are psychological in origin. Fink records successful psychotherapy in a case involving "alternating diarrhea and constipation, abdominal colic, mucus and sometimes blood in the stools."[29] Since these cases are psychological in origin, successful treatment depends upon removal or amelioration of the psychological cause of the physical condition.

Just as emotional disturbances may cause physical disease, so also may physical deviations cause mental illness. Any or all of the physiological "causes" of mental illness in the paragraphs to follow may form only a small portion of the total picture—but the picture certainly would be

[27] Hale T. Shirley, *ibid.*, p. 236.
[28] Oliver E. Byrd, *"Causes of Mental Illness"* (unpublished paper, Stanford University, 1950).
[29] David Harold Fink, *Release From Nervous Tension* (New York: Simon & Schuster, 1963), pp. 33–34.

incomplete without them. This isolation of physiological phenomena is not to be interpreted as an indication of dualistic thinking on the part of the authors. We believe in the organismic nature of man—that any physiological or psychological phenomenon manifested by an individual affects both the mind and the body of that individual. Nevertheless, some phenomena are related most closely to injuries, disease, or malfunctions of the bodily structure, and these may be classified for clarity of discussion as primarily physiological in nature. Other phenomena are related primarily to emotional reactions to symbolic stimuli or to other persons, or to external situations in general, and these may be classified as primarily psychological. This section comprises an attempt to list some of the major physiological phenomena affecting mental health, in an endeavor further to emphasize the organismic nature of man—that forces affecting the physical aspects of man also affect the mental aspects.

Infections

Infections are a more widespread source of mental illness than it was previously thought. Worry over chronic illness—even such as excessive susceptibility to the common cold—may so upset a person that petty irritations become magnified, tensions mount, and emotional unbalance results. A less obvious result of infections is the damage to the neural system caused by impurities deposited by the infections in the blood stream.[30]

Nutritional Deficiencies

Nutritional deficiencies have much the same twofold effect. In addition, they may result in physical impairment of one's ability to meet the demands of his everyday world, thus causing frustrations due to inability to perform tasks that the nutritionally adequate person could accomplish with ease.

Accidents

Accidents, especially traffic injuries, imply all of the hazards listed above. These are accentuated by the incidence of sharp blows to the head, resulting in direct and immediate injury to the brain. Brain injury may cause disabilities such as lack of muscular control, loss of speech, or loss of ability to think coherently.

Anemia

Anemia, if severe, may result in insufficient supply of oxygen to the brain. The resultant damage to the brain may be more serious than that occasioned by a sharp blow to the head.

---

[30] J. Victor Greenebaum and Louis A. Lurie, "Encephalitis as a Causative Factor in Behavior Disorders of Children," in Oliver E. Byrd (ed.), *Health Instruction Yearbook*, 1948, (Stanford: Stanford University Press, 1948), p. 66.

Deterioration of Brain Tissue

Thorpe[31] lists deterioration of brain tisue such as that accompanying senility or in hardening of the arteries, and growth of foreign tissues in the brain (whether benign or cancerous), as among the most frequently recognized causes of organic psychosis.

Food Allergies

Food allergies may cause severe disturbance to otherwise well-adjusted persons if the allergy is such that it results in inflammation of the brain with resultant damage to its tissue.[32] The social effects of food and other allergies are similar to those discussed in the next two items.

Glandular Deficiencies and Imbalances

Glandular malfunction may be a direct cause of mental illness, such as glandular imbalance related to depression; or it may be social in its effect. A glandular imbalance leading to obesity, for example, could cause serious damage to the personality. This may be true even though the particular personality being damaged never has been rejected or ridiculed. The simple knowledge that one is very different from one's fellows may prevent development of adequate concepts of self. This knowledge may lead one to imagine that one is being rejected and ridiculed. Feelings are facts, so far as emotional balance is concerned.

Physical Defects

Physical defects, such as facial disfigurement, may have social effects similar to those resulting from glandular deficiences. A second major result of limitations on one's ability imposed by physical defects is the frustrations that accompany inability to participate effectively in the activities enjoyed by one's age-mates. A heart condition or an allergy to dust may prevent a boy from playing baseball. This enforced separation from his age-mates not only may cause immediate frustration but also may lead to the isolation of the boy from the group in other activities. Man is a gregarious creature. He does not thrive on isolation.

Alcoholism

Alcoholism is one of the leading causes for commitment to mental institutions. The relationship of causation here is not entirely clear. It is generally agreed, however, that alcoholism is the result of personality disturbance rather than the cause. Bloch synthesizes the research in an interesting refutation of the well-intentioned but misguided propaganda of

[31] Louis P. Thorpe, *The Psychology of Mental Health* (New York: Ronald Press, 1960), p. 203.
[32] T. Wood Clarke, "The Relation of Allergy to Character Problems in Children," in Oliver E. Byrd, (ed.), *Health Instruction Yearbook, 1950* (Stanford: Stanford University Press, 1950), pp. 70–71.

prohibition zealots.[33] That alcohol in itself may be a contributing factor to personality disorganization, however, on a solely physical basis, may reasonably be assumed from the disclosures of the Yale University Laboratory of Applied Physiology. Nutritional deficiency was shown to be one aspect of alcoholic neglect, caused not so much by the specific action of alcohol upon the body as by the upsetting of ordinary vitamin balance through the excessive intake of alcohol.[34] We have discussed earlier the effects of such nutritional deficiency.

Drugs

Drugs are another source of possible mental disorder. Many drug addicts lead useful and productive lives, relatively unaffected by their habit.[35] It is the withdrawal of drugs that causes the addict intense physical and mental anguish. "The resulting physical shock to the organism may be severe in many cases, even after the cure has been attained."[36] It must be admitted that the physical damage of the withdrawal shock probably is of less importance in personal demoralization than the association with the criminal procurers of drugs or the effects of methods necessary to obtain money to buy the expensive drugs. In any discussion of physical causes of mental illness, however, drug addiction surely deserves at least passing mention.

THE RELATIONSHIP OF EMOTIONAL NEEDS TO MENTAL HEALTH

The importance of the emotional component in the development of personality and the emotional nature of mental illness are recognized by all. The physical components of mental illness have not been so commonly known. We have spent considerable time developing the inseparability of physical and mental health and the physical nature of several causes of mental illness.

Before we examine emotional causes of mental illness, it may be well to pause to restate two major concepts: First, abnormal behavior is a matter of degree, not of kind. The neurotic individual may use the same mechanisms as the normal person, but he uses them excessively and unrealistically. Secondly, the mental diseases customarily are classified into two major groups—the organic and the functional. In organic mental disease, it is contended that physical factors are present that can be shown to be the most important causes, or perhaps the only causes, of the deviant behavior. In functional mental illness no such organic defects can be found.

Some authorities claim there is no such thing as an organic cause for mental illness. They build their case by contending that if organic dis-

[33] Herbert A. Bloch, *op. cit.*, pp. 443–449.
[34] Herbert A. Bloch, *op. cit.*, p. 446.
[35] Herbert A. Bloch, *op. cit.*, p. 459.
[36] Herbert A. Bloch, *op. cit.*, p. 461.

orders cause or produce a mental disorder, in a direct relationship, then this would be the end result in all cases of a similar kind. In alcoholism, for example, excessive intake may affect the brain, liver, kidneys, and other parts of the body. What the individual does as a result or reaction to this organic insult may produce mental illness. Then again, it may not. The fact that many alcoholics are not psychotic or even seriously maladjusted is a matter of record. A majority of alcoholics continue to perform their everyday assigned tasks quite effectively. The manner in which an individual reacts, that is to say, his functional reaction to the organic insult, impairment, or deterioration is what causes mental illness. It is not proposed here to throw out the concept of organically based mental illness and maladjustment but rather to postulate that direct cause and effect relationship has not been clearly demonstrated.

Despite the recent dialogue on the topic, most textbooks still dichotomize mental illness as organic and functional. Under such a classification, deviant behaviors due to physical causes may be considered as organic disorders. Emotionally induced deviant behavior, however, is functional illness. It is these functional mental illnesses with which we shall be concerned in the remainder of this chapter.

The major causes of functional mental illness are psychological in nature. Although many single causes enter into any serious case of mental illness, the damaging effect of most of them may be traced to the denial of man's basic emotional needs. Many listings of these needs have been published by many eminent authorities: psychiatrists, psychologists, sociologists, anthropologists, educators, and others. For purposes of discussion here, the organization suggested by the sociologist Thomas is used.[37] He reduces basic emotional needs to four major areas: response, recognition, new experience, and security.[38]

Response

Thomas uses the term response to refer to that warm, intimate relationship found between individuals in primary groups. The cuddling, the fondling, and the terms of endearment employed by a loving parent are evidence of a responsive feeling. The billing and cooing of young lovers is another good example of responsive behavior. The degree of responsive feeling is not measured by the innate worth of its recipient; it is determined by the depth of emotional attachment felt by the bestower of affection. Margaret Ribble refers to the evidence of this feeling as "mothering" and stresses the importance of adequate mothering in the development of personality.[39] While there is not unanimous agreement among authorities

[37] W. I. Thomas, *The Unadjusted Girl* (Boston: Little, Brown, 1923), p. 4.

[38] For contrast with more extended listing of emotional needs by modern psychologist, see "Needs" section under *Confusions in Terminology* as presented earlier in this chapter.

[39] Margaret A. Ribble, *The Rights of Infants, Early Psychological Needs, and Their Satisfaction* (New York: Columbia University Press, 1943), p. 9.

in child development, Ribble's position is indicative of the trend in the literature away from the austerity of the child-rearing practices recommended by some pediatricians in the 1920's. Experts in child development now are emphasizing the importance of the giving of an abundance of love to very young children in order to foster the development of an inner sense of adequacy and security. Although the innate worth of any individual may not determine the number or intensity of responsive behaviors received by that individual, it becomes readily apparent that the number and intensity of responsive feelings received by the individual will determine his own feelings as to his innate worth. Mental health is primarily a matter of emotional balance, only secondarily a matter of intellectual perception.[40] The stabilizing effect of a strong sense of personal adequacy can hardly be overestimated. This sense of personal adequacy is best developed through an abundance of responsive behaviors showered upon the infant. It is best maintained by the continuing evidence of responsive feelings throughout the life of the individual.

The effectiveness of responsive behavior in the development and maintenance of wholesome personalities is directly related to the degree of response that the recipient feels toward the giver. Persons who hold the following roles in the successive primary groups clustered about any individual bear a civic responsibility for the evidencing of responsive feeling toward that individual: parents, siblings, teachers, "best friends," lovers, mates, and children. Those persons in our culture who seem to need the most encouragement to display affectionate behavior are fathers and teachers. Some fathers seem to feel that it is "unmanly" to display affection toward their children—especially toward their sons. Some teachers seem to feel that it will ruin their "discipline" if they display affection toward their students.

Response is a basic emotional need of modern American man. Failure to meet this basal need often results in disturbed personalities, already off-balance and susceptible to severe mental illness upon the receipt of serious emotional shock.

Recognition

A second emotional need is for recognition. By this, Thomas refers to the more impersonal acclaim accorded by members of secondary groups. The teacher will fill a role either in one of the primary groups surrounding the child or in one of the secondary groups, dependent partly upon the age of the child and partly upon the personality of the teacher. The teacher is in a key position to accord acclaim, as he not only evaluates all of the child's schoolwork but also structures the classroom situation so as to ac-

---

[40] Even our perceptions are colored by our feelings. Emotional blocks may make it impossible for any given individual to perceive the "truth" about colorful political personalities, much less about himself.

cord or deny the individual child the acclaim of his peers.The teacher does not always recognize his own importance in controlling to a significant degree the amounts both of response and of recognition received by the school-age child. The three R's are paramount, "to fit the child to get along in the world." If teachers would only realize that jobs are lost not nearly so often because of ineffectiveness in the three R's or in technical skills as they are for ineffectiveness in human relations! Basic to good human relations is sound mental health. Basic to sound mental health is the meeting of one's basic emotional needs. Specifically, awarding of recognition bolsters one's sense of personal adequacy through the feeling of worthiness of self that comes with the acknowledgment by others of a job well done.

Unlike response, recognition is directly related to the "worth" of the individual. Particularly is this so in our competitive American culture. The more outstanding are one's accomplishments, the greater is the amount of recognition accorded. But recognition need not be limited in our classrooms only to the "best" products. Primary-grade teachers seem to be particularly skillful in eliciting group recognition even of the "poorest" products. A primary child will glow with pride over group acclaim of the first completed project—even though the rest of the group had mastered that phase of their work months earlier! For older children, differentiated tasks need to be devised. Each child can do something acceptably well; teachers of older children need to discover these limited abilities and to assign these particular tasks only to the child who can do nothing else well. They need to follow up with warm personal recognition and with guidance of group recognition of the completed task, even though it be such a menial task as carrying in the realia for a class culminating activity.

New Experience

The term *new experience* we should like to define as both different and independent experiences. To state that one needs only "new" experiences is trite. Personality is learned. All learning is based upon experience. With no new experiences, one not only ceases to develop as a person, one also reaches a plateau in other areas of learning.

This drive for different and independent experiences is evidenced at a very early age. One who knows intimately a two-year-old child knows precisely why some psychologists refer to this as the "wastebasket age." His eager, inquisitive fingers are everywhere. He delights in emptying the wastebasket just to see what is in it. The three-year-old may cross that forbidden traffic artery just to see what is in the next block. The ten-year-old may plan with his gang for Huckleberry Finn adventures—a trip on a raft down the Mississippi—not only to enjoy the rigors of camp life and to explore the unknown, but also to demonstrate that he can exist for considerable periods of time in unusual circumstances independent of the protection of his family. Teachers must meet this need if they are to safeguard the mental health of their children. Classroom situations need to be varied, to provide children not only with different group approaches but also with independent experiences.

This need for different and independent experiences persists throughout life. Adults may enjoy much of their adventure vicariously, through books and films and television programs; but they do satisfy their need, or suffer emotionally from the deprivation. The wealthy thrill-slayer and the celebrity drug addict are good examples of the extremes to which mentally diseased individuals will go in seeking new and different experiences.

Security

The final basic emotional need listed by Thomas—security—may be defined as the preservation of inviolability of self and the freedom from anxieties and fears. Certainly the experiencing of adequate amounts of response and recognition will contribute greatly to emotional security. One can never receive too much love.

One can, however, receive only love and protection—without a corresponding balance of new experience—and become emotionally insecure despite massive doses of affection and acclaim. Child developmentalists refer to this phenomenon as overprotection. Mother loves her child so much that she cannot bear to see him climb on a chair—he might fall and hurt himself. She cannot bear to see him play with other children— he might catch a contagious disease. She is anxious about his walking alone to school—he might get hit by an automobile. She is fearful about his working with tools with Father or engaging in team sports with his classmates—he might get hurt. So she protects him from all of these possible ills by preventing him from having the experiences that might produce them. She loves him too much? Not so—she loves him unwisely! It may be that she loves him not enough, that she loves herself so much that she cannot bear the pain of seeing him endure the ordinary ills of boyhood. The personality damage to the growing child is many sided: development is retarded due to limitation of new experience; fears of specific situations are effectively taught through mother's obvious fear of them; and a general feeling-tone of anxiety is learned through constant association with a fearful mother (or teacher!).

Related to this need for independence of experience as a means for attaining emotional security is the concept of inviolability of self. The child who always had to be tucked into bed and kissed good night may suddenly slam the bedroom door in our faces as she approaches adolescence. She needs to establish herself as an independent person. She wants no encroachment on her private domain. An example from earlier life is the inquisitive toddler who wanders the length of the train aisle, peering solemnly at each new passenger as he approaches his chair; but as soon as one of the passengers attempts to pick her up—or even to talk to her—

she beats a hasty retreat to the security of her mother's skirts. To reach into adulthood for examples, how many executives will allow their secretaries access to every drawer in their desk? Or allow their sons free access to all of their items of clothing? Each of us needs some things or places to call his very own. Just so, some dreams are shared with no one—not even wives, mothers, or sweethearts. Some innermost recesses of our hearts must remain inviolate, or we have nothing left to call our very own. This inviolability of self is essential to emotional security.

The attainment of security, however, involves more than just the psychological experiences of inviolability of self and adequate amounts of response, recognition, and new experience. It involves also protection of the physical welfare of the young. When baby is cold and wet and hungry, he is insecure. When mother changes and feeds him, holding him gently in the warmth of her arms, he is learning that the world is a good place in which to live; he is building emotional security. Provision of the physical things that make this a good world in which to live is essential to the emotional security of the human organism. These are such things as food, shelter, clothing, and recreation. Not all of us have as much as others; but all must have at least minimal amounts if we are to create and maintain an emotionally secure populace. Basic to the attainment of physical security in our society are skills in problem-solving, both for personal attainment of this world's goods and for the solution of social problems that threaten the security of all mankind.

In summation, prolonged denial of any of the basic emotional needs will tend to cause mental illness.[41] The method of denial, however, is not always obvious. These needs are psychological and are elusive of description. They are even more elusive of recognition in the commonplace workaday world. The authors, therefore, will attempt, in the next three sections, to survey some of the broad social areas in which man's basic emotional needs are being met or are being denied. Social relations with groups and individuals in this interdependent world will be surveyed, with attention to limitations of the physical, economic, and social environments. Personal adjustment to new ways of living will be considered—being born, starting to school, making sex adjustments, choosing an occupation, selecting a mate, entering military service, and attaining retirement. Finally, some attempt will be made to indicate some of the cultural limitations placed on the process of realistic goal-setting by the individual; special attention will be paid to unrealistic levels of aspiration, incompatible goals, restriction of alternatives (especially in the field of recreation), and religion—both as a source of strength and as a source of weakness.

[41] The needs listed by the sociologist Thomas have been discussed here. The needs listed by the psychologists Rogers, Roe, and Maslow were discussed earlier in the chapter. Regardless of the terms in which man's basic emotional needs are defined, both sociologists and psychologists agree that denial of these needs has destructive impact upon personality and behavior.

SOME SOCIAL CAUSES OF POOR MENTAL HEALTH

Fear Occasioned by an Interdependent World

Anxiety is contagious. Research has shown that anxiety should be considered a communicable disease and that the chief method of spread is through sound (voice, loud noises, etc.).[42] Children especially are apt to absorb the tensions of parents or other adults. Is it any wonder that we are living in an anxious age! Modern methods of communication have brought the furious sounds and sights of global conflict into the living room of nearly every American child. Television screens report the battles of the "Crusade in Europe," the sobbing of Vietnamese orphans as they wander aimlessly through the rubble of their cities, and the battle tactics of the armed forces as they maintain a state of readiness for our protection in the event of a third world war. Films of race riots in our own cities come into our homes through televised news report. Television, radio, and newspapers are an essential link in the chain that is slowly binding the entire globe into one world. The prospect of one-world unity seems to frighten many people even more than the specter of the continuous armed conflict that seems to be the concomitant of a divided world. These fears are being communicated as specific fears from one adult to another—and as a generalized feeling of anxiety from adults to their children.

Limitations of Physical Environment

In our complex, interdependent modern world the sources of fears and anxieties are found in all of man's relations with man and with the physical world in which he finds himself. For example, the relationship between the rice fields of China and the mental health of the children of Middletown, U.S.A., is not obvious; but it is very real. The unrest in the Far East today is in part a reflection of the inability of the land to support such a large population in an agricultural economy. When man's physical existence is threatened by starvation, tensions mount and drive him to action. Evidence of such behavior was the surge of the Chinese army over the Yalu River. Televised scenes of weeping Korean orphans directly disturbed American children, for the orphans depicted were similar to them in age. More sweeping in effect, though less obvious, is the transmission of anxiety from adults to children when adults become disturbed by this evidence of the inadequacy of the rice fields of China. The confusions as to causes and goals of the Viet Nam conflict, coupled with the heavy casualty rates in the escalated stages of the war, accelerated and extended the anxieties both of adults and of children. These anxieties may be blamed on a Communist plan for world conquest—or they may be attributed

[42] Jurgen Ruesch and A. Rodney Prestwood, "Anxiety," in Oliver E. Byrd (ed.), *Health Instruction Yearbook, 1950,* (Stanford: Stanford University Press, 1950), p. 72.

directly to the physical deprivations suffered by the Vietnamese as a result of their environment.

Limitations of the Economic System

Let us come closer to home for another example of the contagiousness of anxiety, leaving limitations of the physical environment in the Far East for a brief sketching of one limitation of the American economic system. We turn to opportunities for vertical mobility in American society. True, the term "limitation" is used here in a relative sense. One of the great strengths of American democracy has been its tradition that "any boy can become President." Recent evidence of the operation of that tradition is the rise of a relatively unsuccessful haberdasher to the Presidency of the United States. Despite that recent dramatic evidence, the trend has been toward a diminishing of opportunity. As business corporations have become larger and more complex, the junior executive posts have come more and more to be filled by sons of the senior executives. Harvard, for example, draws its student body largely from the homes of the well-to-do. It places its graduates in positions of eminence—at least partly due to the social connections made by students during their years at Harvard.

College enrollments are growing because of an increasing population of youth of college age; but only slightly over half of the young electorate of the country have completed even a high school education. Median years of school completed, by states, range from 8.7 in South Carolina to 12.2 in Utah.[43] Education is one of the major ladders of vertical mobility in Modern America. For so long as nearly half of the nation's children are being denied a high school education, the opportunities for that half to become President are being materially decreased.

The denial of the education ladder for vertical mobility to a large segment of the population has destructive effects far beyond the anxieties it creates in the minds of young people facing the problem of vocational placement with inadequate preparation. It limits further contact with middle-class culture in a society that is based on middle-class values, thus making individual problems of life adjustment more difficult in all areas; stated negatively, it fosters juvenile delinquency and adult crime. Basically, it is a denial of vocational and intellectual security to those who come from homes already faced with physical insecurity.

Limitations of the Class-caste System

A third major source of tensions in America society is the limitation imposed by our class-caste system. The authors hold no brief for a classless society. In all cultures, at all times, man has rewarded his leaders with power, prestige, and money. Admitting the necessity for such unequal

[43] *U.S. Census of Population, 1960,* Volume 1, Chapter 6 (Washington, D.C.: Department of Commerce, Bureau of Census).

(but equitable) division of this world's goods and services, the fact remains that those on the lowest rung of the economic ladder must have enough goods and services for adequate existence if they are to remain physically and mentally healthy. Our caste system, however, discriminates on a basis other than leadership (or other productive) ability. Color of skin has denied first-class citizenship to some ten million Americans. The clash between the ideals of equality and brotherhood embodied in the Judaeo-Christian tradition and the reality of class privilege causes many anxieties and insecurities.

Our class-caste system, then, has limited opportunities for the achievement of security on the basis of economic class, color, and religion. These limitations will be developed in Chapter 9. All of us are aware of the tensions created by these denials of man's needs. Social legislation may increase these tensions for brief periods in restricted areas—but the proud record of America is a gradual lessening of these tensions through reductions in discriminatory practices. We note these tensions here only as another source of the many anxieties of our times. Any anxiety is contagious; it affects not only one's own class, race, or creed, but all of America.

Making Adjustments to New Ways of Living

Being born is probably one of the greatest shocks suffered by any human being. Baby is faced with the task of doing many things for himself that Mother had been doing for him, such as breathing, eating, eliminating, and adjusting to changes in the temperature and humidity of the air about him. He had not even supported his own weight—mother had suspended him in a bag of liquid. The postnatal period, or first ten days of life, is one of great adjustment to a new way of living.

Other periods in one's life that necessitate great readjustment to new modes of living are starting to school, attaining puberty, leaving school to earn one's living, beginning married life, entering the armed forces, and retiring. To these may be added the major readjustments faced by selected portions of the populace as they move from rural to urban areas, from one state or region to another with sharply different ways of living, or from one country to another.

Any period necessitating major readjustments to life's problems endangers mental health. It is in these periods of stress that personality damage may be done to the mentally healthy person, and that severe mental illness may develop in the previously mildly unbalanced individual. Evidence from the battle zones of World War II indicate the significance of these periods of stress for the mental health of our most physically and mentally fit young men:[44]

---

[44] Robert J. Carpenter, "Early Recognition and Treatment of Neuropsychiatric Conditions in the Combat Zone," in Oliver E. Byrd (ed.), *Health Instruction Yearbook, 1944* (Stanford: Stanford University Press, 1944), pp. 88–89.

Ordinarily neuropsychiatric disorders are thought to occur only in weaklings or in individuals with personality defects. This is not true. Information at hand indicates that a significant proportion of the neuropsychiatric casualties are occurring in individuals who give no history suggesting predisposition. Under the extremes of stress and fatigue of modern combat the most stable individual may reach his breaking point. Thus the presence of neuropsychiatric disorder must be looked for in normal as well as predisposed individuals.

Even those well-adjusting individuals with emotional security and a high level of problem-solving ability, who cope successfully with the less traumatic problems of life, may find adjustment to new modes of living extremely difficult.

THE PRESCHOOL PERIOD. The preschool period of rapid growth in all aspects of development—motor, intellectual, school, and emotional—encompasses the most critical years of personality formation. "The basic personality traits and reaction patterns are acquired in this period (early childhood) and are, for the most part, merely strengthened in the succeeding years. . . . In the home the young child encounters the initial experiences which determine whether he will develop a sense of personal security and of being loved and accepted; in the home the child meets the situations which determine the extent of his sense of adequacy and of personal worth."[45] But this does not mean, as some of the earlier psychologists had contended, that personality patterns are rigidly set by the age of 6. Sherman lists "critical periods in the growth of personality" through the "crystallization period—variously estimated as occurring between the ages of 35 and 45."[46]

It seems obvious that there is greater danger of basal personality damage at the very youngest ages. It seems somewhat less obvious that the cumulative effect of a life of emotional instability would make the older person more susceptible to severe mental illness. This is not to imply that mental illness is a prerogative of old age. At least 150,000 children are seen in psychiatric clinics each year.[47] Schizophrenia, the leading cause of first admissions to mental hospitals in 1950, was most commonly found in youth.[48] As we develop briefly each of the periods creating stress on emotional stability, two factors should be kept in mind. First, although emotional security and problem-solving ability will enable most individuals to experience transitional periods successfully, they are a potential source of danger to the mental health of every individual. Secondly, "personality maladjustments" and "functional mental illness" are probably varying

[45] Barney Katz and George F. J. Lehner, *Mental Hygiene in Modern Living* (New York: Ronald Press, 1953), p. 75.
[46] Mandel Sherman, *Mental Hygiene and Education* (New York: David McKay, 1945), pp. 58–60.
[47] Katherine Glover, *Mental Health—Everybody's Business* (Public Affairs Pamphlet No. 196), p. 23. (New York: Public Affairs Committee, Inc., 1953).
[48] Katherine Glover, *ibid.*, p. 23.

intensities of the same psychological phenomenon and are found at all ages.

STARTING TO SCHOOL. Certainly the young child is expected to make major readjustments as he enters school life. The small size of the modern American family provides the average child with relatively few individuals with whom he must share the affection of his parents. In this strange new world called the school, he must share with thirty or forty other equally self-centered children the attentions of the teacher. By and large, his needs had taken priority at home. As a very young child, he consumed his meal under the complete and undivided supervision of his mother before his parents sat down to dinner. During the immediately preschool years, he had moved to the family dinner table at their regular dinner hour—but his needs still were the center of attention. Smaller portions were arranged for him. Special provisions were made to prevent his spilling food. Little games were played to make certain foods more attractive. If his father commuted to work, the family dinner hour may have been the major period of the day in which he and his father had time to visit (in his terms, to play) with each other. Now he must learn to participate in kindergarten lunch periods where he is only one of a large group, receiving only one thirtieth of the attention of the sole adult present. Food is very important to the young child. The relative impersonality of the school lunch program may present a very real problem to him.

His freedom of movement is curtailed, and even the ways in which he receives directions are changed. In the home he had free access to the cookie jar and to the toilet facilities. He played when, where, and with what he pleased, with the exception of fragile bric-a-brac. Now he must adjust to routines, to taking turns, and to sharing. He must learn to take directions from written symbols on a chalkboard or chart, as a member of a group, rather than receiving the individual oral instructions, to which he has been accustomed. He must learn that for the authority of only two parents there has been substituted the authority of many individuals, some of whom have only infrequent contact with him—bus-driver, teacher, principal, nurse, dentist, custodian, traffic policeman, and safety patrol boy. Little children need much affection and close physical contact with adults at this period if they are to make a satisfactory adjustment. True, basal personality patterns are taking shape; but they have not completely jelled. They are subject to great modification now and to lesser modification in later life. A normal, healthy, outgoing child may be transformed by a harsh first-grade teacher into a shy, withdrawn child or into a hostile, aggressive one.

ATTAINING PUBERTY. The attainment of puberty is another great milestone in personality development. Freud makes more of the sex drive than most modern psychologists; but most of us are forced to agree with him that the prolonged period of (legal) infancy in modern man has created a host of problems that adolescents in earlier cultures did not face. Biologically, most children are mature before they enter senior high school. If they have aspirations for professional life, they must remain dependent upon parents for at least seven more years of schooling—three of high school and four of college. If they have vocational aspirations higher than that of semiskilled labor or the lower echelons of the distributive trades, they must postpone marriage for at least the three years requisite for the completion of high school. Further complicating the picture are compulsory-education and child-labor laws that limit the amounts and kinds of employment available to them until the normal age of completion of high school.

Youth is biologically ready for procreation, then, several years before our society will sanction marriage—and premarital intercourse violates both the social and the religious mores of our culture. The biological organism is driving youth to the satisfaction of its needs. Society says that sexual desires cannot be satisfied. Many youths, of course, defy convention and satisfy the biological urge; but they only intensify their emotional conflicts through guilt feelings and lowered moral standards as youths, and through excessive worry about the sexual behavior of their own children when they become parents of teen-agers.

Some other problems of adolescents are their anxieties about "growing up" earlier or later than the group; making a transition from the unisexual gang age to the bisexual social life of adolescence with its conventions such as dating and its new skills such as dancing; developing and refining a personal set of values and a coherent philosophy of life; and the growing need for freedom from adult supervision. This latter task faces them just as surely if they go on to college as it does if they drop out of high school to take a job.

LEAVING SCHOOL TO EARN ONE'S LIVING. Whether the youth leaves school at the end of the sixth grade or at the completion of the doctorate, many of his problems will be the same—establishing a life independent of his family,[49] becoming established in a vocation or a profession, assuming full legal and moral responsibilities for his actions, selecting a mate, establishing and supporting a family, making choices of social and political allegiances, and assuming responsibility for adult citizenship. It seems as though at both the beginning and the end of one's school life a whole host of critical decisions are forced upon one as a result of entering a new way of life. Many youths drift along the path of least resistance with apparent serenity—only to regret bitterly those casual decisions as they assess their accomplishments and survey the future from the reality of middle age. The time of leaving school is a critical age in terms of personal mental hygiene, even though the emotional conflict may be delayed for many years.

One of the choices of youth most dramatically affected by an era of

[49] Youths who attended colleges outside their home community have made many of these adjustments; but even for them graduation symbolizes final severance of many major family ties, especially financial ones.

rapid social and technological change is the choice of a vocation. The choice of a semiskilled vocation, with its high job obsolescence, gives little real security to the employee. Technological unemployment—the elimination of jobs through the invention of labor-saving machines—may wipe out the family source of income just as the new baby is arriving. Complicating this picture is the fact that the percentage of semiskilled jobs is increasing. These semiskilled jobs are the ones most susceptible to technological unemployment. The recent trend of entire factories toward automation may eventually wipe out all but a handful of these jobs in production work.

A second change in the composition of the labor force that will affect youth's choice of vocation is the decline of the extractive occupations—farming, mining, and forestry. This is coupled with a sharp increase in the distributive and service trades—retail sales, repair, and maintenance. It is becoming increasingly difficult for a youth to drift into the occupation of his father. Many youths are having to select from a host of new jobs created by the rapid changes in our technology and our whole social order.

BEGINNING MARRIED LIFE. No matter how cooperative and understanding one may be, learning to share one's life with another person is accomplished only to the accompaniment of conflict situations. To begin with, one may learn that the person one married is not at all the person one thought he was marrying. The fastidiously perfect beauty queen may be a sloppy housekeeper. The handsome "prom trotter" may refuse to leave his fireside. Further, few individuals realize just how carefully they have preserved their inviolability of self until they discover that their mate expects to share all of their most intimate secrets, their feelings, and their thoughts. Petty incidents become magnified out of all proportion to their significance—they serve as focal points for venting pent-up hostilities. Sharpening the pencils with a razor blade may provoke a scene—when the real source of irritation was the wife's curiosity about an office deal that had not gone well.

Sharing also means giving up. Bowling may have to be discontinued. Favorite television programs may have to be forgotten. One is no longer free even to choose one's own friends—they must be acceptable also to the mate. The weekly trip to the hairdresser may not be within the family budget, even though it was a pleasant necessity when the girl was working. If the wife continues working, Business and Professional Women's Club meetings may have to be skipped to iron hubby's shirts or to clean the house. In the 1960's the courts of these United States were granting one divorce for every four marriages. In 1945 an all-time high was reached of one divorce for every 3.3 marriages.[50] Need more be said about the emotional impact of marriage, if nearly one fourth of our modern marriages are ending in complete failure and dissolution? And what of the emotional conflict in those unhappy marriages that never reach the divorce courts?

[50] *The Economic Almanac, 1958* (New York: The National Industrial Conference Board, Inc., 1958), p. 16.

What can we predict for the future of the mental health of our nation, as measured by the stability of marriage as an institution? Children are involved in nearly half of all divorce cases. It is true that often a child can be happier and feel more secure when living with one parent with a minimum of confusion and conflict than when living with both parents amid a storm of criticisms and accusations; but "the child's basic difficulty in the disappearance of one or more parents arises from the fact that his parent could care so little for him as to desert him."[51] His basic security is threatened by the disruption of the marriage of his parents. If we are concerned that the marriages of the future become more stable, society must assume responsibility for more and better marriage counseling in an attempt to improve the happiness of current marriages. "Education for successful marriage begins in infancy. Upon the success of today's families depends the success of those established a generation hence."[52]

FULFILLING MILITARY SERVICE. Many young men will state bitterly that military service was the most "snafu" period in their entire lives. Statistics will at least partially support their statements. "For every soldier hospitalized in World War II for wounds due to bombs and shellfire, there was one (or more) hospitalized for an emotional difficulty. The great majority of emotional crack-ups occurred during the first three months of training."[53] When one considers the sources of man's emotional security—family, friends, job, locality—this high incidence of personality disturbance in the early months of training is readily understandable. The civilian-soldier is suddenly torn away from all his emotional anchors. He usually has little choice in his new life as to his associates, the type of job to which he will be assigned, or even his freedom of movement. Regimentation and restraint are thrust upon individuals trained from birth to exist in a free society. To attempt to escape from this disagreeable situation is to be stigmatized as a traitor. The civilian-soldier has no choice but adjustment—or discharge as an emotional deviate. Despite the 1964 and 1965 "draft card burnings" and "Viet Nam Protest Demonstrations," the stigma attached to the draft-dodger persists. The "bleed-in" staged by students at Indiana University still symbolizes the spirit of patriotism characteristic of the great majority of American youth.

If the civilian makes a satisfactory adjustment and becomes a "good soldier," then new emotional stresses are placed upon him. The fatigue, sleeplessness, irregular diet, physical danger, noise, and confusion of battle may break even the best-integrating individual. It is no wonder that reports from all theaters of operation indicated that neuropsychiatric disorders caused more hospital admissions than did all battle casualties.[54]

[51] J. S. Plant, *The Envelope: A Study of the Impact of the World upon the Child* (New York: Commonwealth Fund, 1950), p. 22.
[52] John Biesanz and Mavis Biesanz, *op. cit.*, p. 247.
[53] Barney Katz and George F. J. Lehner, *op. cit.*, p. 426.
[54] Barney Katz and George F. J. Lehner, p. 426.

ENTERING RETIREMENT. We realize what a great source of emotional security we find in our jobs when we see the aimless wandering and early demises of men and women forced into retirement by compulsory age limitations on service. Many of these unfortunates only complicate their own problems by voluntarily severing ties with many other sources of security; they leave children, friends, and places with which they have been associated all their lives to move to the "retirement colonies" of Florida and California. They are "starting a new life" almost in the sense of the army draftee: new climate, new house, new associates, new occupation, and, usually, a restricted financial income. About all they retain of their old life is their mate, their personal and household possessions, and their freedom of movement. Of those who remain in their old homes, the former wage-earners face major readjustments to an entirely new way of life.

MOVING FROM RURAL TO URBAN AREAS OR FROM ONE REGION TO ANOTHER REGION WITH SHARPLY DIFFERING FOLKWAYS. The impersonality, loneliness, bustle, and confusion of a large city have a seriously disintegrating effect upon the personalities of many persons born and reared in rural communities. Old sources of security have been left behind. Ways of doing things are strange and different. Apartment dwellers do not "neighbor" like the folks back home. Clothing is worn differently. Speech patterns are strange. All of these differences and many more make the newcomer visible as an "outsider" and tend to keep him that way. New friends are few and far between. Just sheer loneliness can overwhelm one!

MOVING FROM ONE COUNTRY TO ANOTHER. The immigrant faces all of the above problems; but they are intensified because of the greater degree of differences in ways of doing, thinking, and believing. To these barriers to social integration may be added the extra visibility of a foreign accent or of a foreign tongue being spoken in the home, a difference in skin color, and even a "foreign" name. The difficulty of finding emotional security in a strange culture is probably the greatest single reason for the formation of "foreign colonies" in large cities. This segregation may afford immediate relief from tension; but it only intensifies the long-range problem, as it slows the process of the cultural integration that is essential to the eventual acceptance in the culture that in turn is prerequisite to the finding of emotional security in the new culture.

Cultural Limitations on Realistic Goal-setting

Goals must be set in the major areas of living in order to give direction and meaning to life. Frustrations result from inability to set goals, or from inability to achieve unrealistic goals, or from inability to achieve incompatible goals simultaneously. These frustrations are caused by the absence of realistic goals. Conversely stated, the achievement of realistic major life goals foster sound mental health. By "realistic goals" we mean attainable goals that contribute to the integration of the individual and to the maintenance and improvement of the culture. The major limitation upon the setting of realistic goals by the average individual is the tendency of parents to encourage youngsters to set life goals without due consideration of the children's innate abilities; upper-class parents tend to encourage aspirations beyond the child's ability; lower-class parents sometimes discourage capable children from pursuing professional goals.

The four broad areas of life in which one should concentrate his mental health efforts are work, love, recreation, and a personal philosophy.[55] We shall speak, in a later section, of scientific problem-solving as a technique for setting realistic goals in these major areas of life. Unfortunately, many individuals set their major life goals not on the basis of rational problem-solving but on the basis of emotional attitudes. These attitudes have been conditioned by the child-rearing practices of parents and by other forces in the cultural matrix. The extent of such emotional goal-setting is not amenable to scientific measurement; but informed opinion is reflected in the statement attributed to the Dean of the School of Education in a major American university: "We feel our way through life on the basis of our emotions. We think only as a last resort, for thinking is painful."

UNREALISTIC EXPECTATIONS OF PARENTS. A significant source of culturally imposed frustrations is the tendency of upper-class parents to encourage their children to set an unrealistically high level of aspiration. This level is related to the child's concept of self, and it will determine the types of goals that he sets for himself. The mean intelligence of children of professional parents will correlate about 0.50 with the mean intelligence of their parents, regressing toward the mean intelligence of the total population.[56] Many professional parents, however, wish their children to be as good as, or better than, themselves. They anxiously watch for the first baby step, the first word, and other measuring sticks of development, eagerly comparing such developmental status with that of the children of their friends and relatives. The child constantly is reminded of superior progress. He is encouraged to think of himself as a very superior fellow indeed! Sport ambitions, vocational choices, and other goals will be based on the expectation of superior accomplishment. What does this do to the personality of the individual of near-average ability when he constantly fails to achieve superior accomplishment? He may make a choice early in life, for example, to become a physician. His orientation for years has been toward that goal. Now he makes such a poor record in premedical training that he is denied admission to medical school. A major readjustment to a new choice of a life work must be made. Both the making of the new choice and the period of adjustment to it will be very trying experiences. A more realistic setting

---

[55] Oliver E. Byrd, *"Mental Health for the Normal Person"* (unpublished paper, Stanford University, 1950).

[56] Anne Anastasi, *Differential Psychology* (New York: Macmillan, 1964), pp. 275–279.

of the original goal by the child was prevented by the unrealistic expectations of the parents.

The discouragement by lower-class parents of professional ambitions in their children may contribute to self-recrimination in later life, with the attendant anxieties and frustrations; but the major tragedy here seems to be the waste of human resources in menial jobs.

AMBIVALENT CULTURAL VALUES OF INDIVIDUALS. Another major source of externally imposed frustrations lies in the ambivalent patterns of our culture. We offer the child inconsistent guidance in the making of important choices. How shall the child decide to feel about people of another color if brotherly love is taught in the home and racial segregation is practiced in the schools, or vice versa? Or if the most important agencies for education in his life—home, school, and church—all preach brotherly love but practice discrimination? How shall the child decide to feel about honesty if he is scolded for stealing an apple and made to return it, only to hear his dad brag about a "sharp deal" in which he made a big profit at the expense of a gullible customer or business associate?

AMBIVALENT CULTURAL VALUES OF GROUPS. A major source of internally imposed frustrations is the effort of the individual to work simultaneously toward incompatible goals (or apparently incompatible goals). Such dilemmas may be personal, as in the case of the girl who can't decide between two prospective mates or between a mate and a career. On the other hand, it may be largely a social dilemma, even though the selection of the alternative may be almost wholly within the individual. We have mentioned earlier the moral conflict within the child who experiences inconsistent racial attitudes at home and at school. The child has little choice about maintaining membership in the home and the school. He does have autonomy, however, in pledging allegiance to various subgroups within the school and the community. For example, a child may accept or reject membership in a school sorority, a Y.W.C.A. youth group, or a Sunday school class. Simultaneous membership in all three of these groups may involve behavior that violates the customs of one or more groups; friendship may be expected in the Y.W.C.A. group toward a girl who was excluded by the sorority. Such friendship may horrify the sorority sisters, who just can't understand such behavior from "one with such a good background— associating with trash just isn't done!" "In these cases, the individual is not reacting contrary to his past experience, as might at first appear. This would be psychologically impossible. His (her) behavior is the result of psychological membership in various conflicting groups."[57] Simultaneous membership in many conflicting groups may be maintained to the ultimate improvement of the individual. Awareness of their differences may provide for more realistic evaluation of all the groups and for more sound moral choices. In some cases, however, as in the case of open conflict between a

[57] Anne Anastasi, *ibid.*, p. 628.

labor union and a political party, the individual may be forced to choose affiliation with one group at the expense of surrendering friendships in and cherished ideas of the other group. Such surrender, of course, gives very real pain and may cause serious personality damage. An illustration of such damage is the adoption of dogmatic attitudes in defense of the organization chosen. The gradual growth in the rigidity of personality that may result from such painful choices not only may impair one's problem-solving skills but also may leave one less prepared to bend rather than to break under other emotional impacts.

IMPOVERISHED CULTURAL ENVIROMENT.   Some goals may be recognized as poor ones, but may be structured by limitations of the physical environment. The young adult may "choose" movies, bars, and "lover's lanes" as preferred entertainment solely because they offer the only recreational facilities available in the community. The frustrations that come from such forced choices are keeping many good young teachers out of some rural communities. They are draining the potential leadership in many other areas of life from some areas of the hinterland, as young people gravitate to metropolitan areas that offer sports, the fine arts, and intellectual stimulation. The effects on mental health of the "bar-lover's lane" routine were discussed earlier under the headings of *alcoholism* in this chapter and *sex behavior* in Chapter 6.

RELIGION.   Religion may be a source of strength or of weakness. Man can comprehend the finite; he can only contemplate the infinite. When scientific explanations of life's problems and mysteries have proved inadequate, when tensions seem unbearable, peace may be attained through faith in the ultimate wisdom of a Supreme Being in so arranging events. Religious faith can be a great source of emotional security.

Religion as a source of weakness has both social and personal ramifications. On the social side, there have been religious wars and discrimination against religious sects throughout recorded history. On the personal side, religious teaching is often the source of the greatest emotional disturbance —the dichotomy of perfection taught and imperfection practiced on all sides.

Another personal aspect of religion as a source of emotional disturbance is concerned with the basic reorientation of the thinking patterns of modern Western man. For the Western world the day of "one faith, one King, one country" has gone forever. For the unreasoned acceptance of the authority of church and state we have substituted the application of Newtonian science to most areas of life. Religious freedom is one expression of this reorientation in thinking. A man no longer must belong to the Universal Church or be damned to eternal fire (and secular persecution); he has the right to make his individual peace with God, either alone or within the religious sect of his choice. But as man probes the eternal mysteries of life in search of religious faith, he cannot escape his problem-solving frame of reference. He wants to understand, to explain, the meaning of life and the nature of God.

To call things supernatural is no explanation of them according to the modern scientist, for to explain is simply to point out the natural connection between phenomena. The new general attitude has become so instinctive and so much a part of our world-view that most of us never think of interpreting extraordinary any more than ordinary occurrences in other than a naturalistic way. Fairies, witches, ghosts, angels and demons, once freely assumed to account for all sorts of phenomena, have simply dropped out of the mind of the average modern man and no longer play a part in his experience. Not that their existence has been disproved, but that they have become superfluous.[58]

Man needs the security that has been supplied by religious faith. The Communists have used this need and have avoided the conflict between modern naturalistic thinking and the unreasoned acceptance of a religious dogma by making of communism a secular religion—one that demands a fanatical adherence to its dictates.

He alone has the true faith. The party line alone is truth. To it he owes blind obedience. It is his God on Sinai delivering the law. Any deviation from the dictates of the party line must be confessed as a sin. To a Communist, the state is the all-powerful, all-embracing Numen (Universal God). The party leaders are high priests and exercise the enormous social control of a priest-hood.[59]

Probably more important than the "faith" noted above (since it applies only to the party members) is the fact that the Soviets have put everybody to work and have attached high praise to its performance. Some, probably many, though not party folk, enjoy better mental health because they feel they are engaged in a common enterprise. Further strengthening their mental health is the climate of political opinion in Russia; the common man has few choices to make; hence, he has few anxieties concerning the "right" decisions. One can only speculate as to the effect of purges and reversals of the party line on the mental health of the common man in modern Russia.

Western man has reached no easy solution. He is committed to the freedoms implied in the individual, scientific search for truth. He is bound by the thinking patterns of that search as he tries to establish an individual faith. He cannot accept on a supernatural basis the spiritual values enshrined in the Hebraic-Christian tradition.[60] There seems to be an unconscious realization that the moral and spiritual values that he needs to

[58] Arthur C. McGiffert, *The Rise of Modern Religious Ideas* (New York: Macmillan, 1951), p. 36.
[59] John Biesanz and Mavis Biesanz, *op. cit.*, p. 27.
[60] Many individuals, of course, do accept spiritual values on a supernatural basis. The adherence of devout Catholics to church dogma is a case in point.

give direction and meaning to his life must arise from the experiences of modern culture—but the church teaches that the source of these values is Divine Revelation, as recorded in the Bible. The intensity and significance of the conflict caused by the attempt to apply naturalistic thinking to mystical phenomena cannot readily be measured. Some writers take a more pessimistic view of the dualism of reason and faith in the modern world than do your authors; but the presence of the problem cannot be denied. The position of one writer is that "we shall continue to develop intellectually and emotionally maladjusted people so long as the total educational influences of our culture perpetuate this split between the head and the heart—between modern man's tested methods of achieving knowledge and control and his ideal objects of aspiration, allegiance, and devotion."[61]

ADJUSTMENT MECHANISMS INDICATIVE OF POOR MENTAL HEALTH

The problem situations sampled in the preceding sections have implied a need for action by the individual. The well-integrating individual will react both emotionally and rationally to problem situations. It is only when emotional reactions become habituated as the major "solutions" to problems that poor mental health is indicated. In this section we shall list some of the better known emotional reactions that are typical of most people. Individuals with good mental health use them sparingly and accompany or follow them with rational attacks upon their problems. Persons with poor mental health use them excessively and often employ them as their only response to problem situations.

Anger

We refer here to emotional outbursts of *anger*. When this anger is directed against people, it is referred to as *aggression*. When anger is vented against things, it is referred to as *destruction*. When anger is repressed, or when it is a constant, deep-seated feeling-tone indicative of many unresolved frustrations, we refer to it as *hostility*. By whatever name —anger, aggression, destruction, hostility—this emotional reaction and its accompanying behavior form ineffective techniques for the solution of problems and are accelerants of mental illness. Levy emphasizes the fact that aggression is not a constructive form of tension release by noting that it is invariably followed by compulsive self-punishment, restoration (restitution), rationalization, or all three.[62] These compulsive behaviors are indicative of the heightened, rather than lowered, level of tensions that follows aggressive behavior. The aggressive behavior to which we are referring is not rational aggression in socially approved ways, but sheer outbursts of anger resulting in antisocial behavior.

[61] John L. Childs, *Education and Morals* (New York: Appleton, 1950), pp. 124–125.
[62] David M. Levy, *op. cit.*, pp. 397–410.

Withdrawal

Withdrawal from the conflict situation is a common response at the unconscious level. Tensions may be relieved through withdrawal techniques; but such withdrawal indicates either abandonment of the goal or a postponement of goal-seeking activity. In either case the relief is only symptomatic; the immediate tensions are relieved, but the source of anxiety is unchanged. At best, withdrawal maintains a *status quo* of unresolved frustrations and a potential source of intense and prolonged anxiety.

Some of the common withdrawal techniques will be sketched very briefly. Physical withdrawal from the conflict area may be a perfectly rational action, if there is real physical danger present and/or if there is no goal to be attained by remaining. It is the habituation of this response to frustrations that builds anxieties; unresolved frustrations mount in number, tensions multiply, and more severe withdrawal techniques are demanded. In psychological withdrawal, the person lives in an inner world into which no conflict can intrude. Emotional equilibrium is maintained through emotional apathy. This is incipient schizophrenia, a psychosis perennially holding top rank in first admissions to mental hospitals. Regression to less mature levels of behavior is another withdrawal defense against tensions. The sick or younger person is not expected to be able to cope with adult problems. Occasional use of the regression technique does little harm. A good cry may relieve tensions and leave one more relaxed, which may aid in problem-solving if one soon retackles the problem. Continued infantile behavior, however, neither solves perplexing problems nor builds confidence for meeting new ones. Psychosomatic illness is one form of withdrawal behavior. The inefficient bank clerk or bookkeeper may develop sick stomach, backache, sleepiness, or other physical symptoms of distress as the time for the bank examiners approaches; if he is ill enough, he can stay away from work while his books are being examined. Postponement of decision and compulsive use of alcohol or narcotics are withdrawal techniques that have been discussed earlier. The use of fantasy is another withdrawal technique that has consequences all the way from beneficial effects on mental health to development of psychosis. Daydreams are common in childhood. The vicarious achievement of daring deeds through fairy tales, comic books, movies, radio, television, and adult fiction may serve a very real emotional need for recognition for most of us. It is when the individual resorts to fantasy in the compulsive fashion of the alcoholic, to escape reality, that we recognize the symptoms of serious mental illness.

Rationalization

Rationalization is an easy way out of difficult situations, because it involves merely inventing plausible statements as to the desirability of the *status quo*. This may mean attributing altruistic motives to selfish behavior, claiming insightful behavior upon the fortuitous resolution of an unwise decision, feigning indifference or dislike of a group by which one has been rejected, and the like. If the original goal was unrealistic, rationalization probably promotes better mental health. The danger is that rationalization involves fantasy. Such distortions of fact may make future goals even more unrealistic.

Repression

Repression of our real reasons for behavior, while verbalizing rationalizations until we actually are unaware of our real motives, may lead to marked mental illness. The real motives usually are so socially unacceptable as to cause shame and humiliation if we admit them, even to ourselves. An example is that of the young man who has homosexual tendencies. He is so ashamed of them that he disavows all interest in sex, on the basis of moral precepts, until he himself actually has forgotten why he became so sexually moral. Such behavior involves tremendous tension, to the point of severe physical fatigue.[63]

Projection

Projection of our original motives on another is a mechanism that has its amusing as well as its tragic aspects. A respectable businessman was standing at a bus stop, innocently reading his newspaper. A frustrated spinster was standing beside him. As the bus arrived and he moved to board it, he accidentally brushed against her. She had him arrested for indecent advances! The woman had so wanted to be touched, though not admitting it to herself, that she actually thought that he had run his hand caressingly over parts of her body.

Sublimation

Sublimation refers to the channeling of the energy generated by a primitive urge into culturally or ethically high patterns of behavior. According to some psychoanalytical theories of genius, some of the finest art and music is attributed to sublimation of the sexual drive into esthetic experiences. For some persons, in some situations, sublimation is the only possible positive adjustment.

Identification

Identification is one of the more important of the adjustment mechanisms. The importance of the adult model in shaping behavior patterns of children and youth can hardly be overemphasized. If a child likes an adult and is liked in return, the behavior and personality patterns of the child may show a striking similarity to those of the adult model. This can be one of the major forces contributing to sound mental health when the

[63] Barney Katz and George F. J. Lehner, *op. cit.*, p. 50.

child selects wholesome models. It can be a most disrupting influence when the models are socially or emotionally deviant, or when two or more models adopted by the same child hold conflicting values and/or exhibit conflicting behaviors.[64]

SEVERE MENTAL DISTURBANCES REQUIRING SPECIAL CARE

The diagnosis and cure of advanced cases of mental illness require long and complex treatment by highly specialized personnel. The inexpert meddling of the lay person can only make more difficult of attainment the eventual rehabilitation of the mentally ill. It is probable that the meddling of well-intentioned but poorly prepared classroom teachers and inexpert psychiatrists has accentuated the problems of some individuals who were suffering from curable mental illness. Many of the functional psychoses probably are only accelerated neuroses. "The conviction is becoming widespread among psychiatrists, psychologists, and sociologists that the same kind of personal, social, and environmental factors are operative in preparing the ground for and in precipitating the functional psychoses as in the case of the neuroses."[65]

This section is designed to emphasize the fact that emotional deviates differ in behavior from normal individuals only in the intensity of the frustrations experienced and the frequency and appropriateness of the techniques employed to reduce their tensions. As Katz and Lehner put it:[66]

Maladjusted people differ from those who are well adjusted principally in degree. They use the same defense mechanisms as adjusted individuals, but they use them more rigidly and in ways which are less desirable socially. The difference can be stated as follows: Whereas the adjusted individual uses mechanisms sparingly and appropriately, the moderately maladjusted person uses them frequently and inappropriately, and the psychoneurotic or psychotic individual depends on these mechanisms constantly and frequently uses them in ways which antagonize, repel, and in general, alienate him from other people.

The very terms "adjusted" and "integrated" indicate the relativity of mental illness, if we remember that we are referring to emotional balance. One is never really "adjusted" or "integrated" except for fleeting moments of time. We are constantly "adjusting" to new influences, and we are constantly "integrating" new experiences into our total personality. To be technically correct, one would speak of "well-adjusting" people when

[64] Lee J. Cronbach, *Educational Psychology* Revised Edition (New York: Harcourt, 1964), pp. 424–434.

[65] N. Cameron, "The Functional Neuroses," in J. McVicker Hunt (ed.), *Personality and the Behavior Disorders* (New York: Ronald Press, 1944), Vol. II, p. 869.

[66] Barney Katz and George F. J. Lehner, *Mental Hygiene in Modern Living* (New York: Ronald Press, 1953).

referring to those of sound mental health. The emotional deviate simply has more difficulty in adjusting. He exhibits the same behaviors and uses the same techniques for adjustment as anyone else; he simply does not use them so effectively, and consequently remains further off-balance than the normal individual. All of us will recognize some of our own behaviors in descriptions of deviant behavior; that does not mean that we are neurotic or psychotic (although, in fact, we may be!); it means simply that we are recognizing "human behavior."

For a presentation of the major neurotic and psychotic syndromes in language understandable to the lay person, the reader is referred to Carroll.[67] The hysterias, psychasthenias, neurasthenias, schizophrenias, paranoia, and manic-depression are outlined in accordance with classification developed by the American Psychiatric Association. These states are beyond the scope of this text, requiring the attention of highly trained specialists.

PROBLEM-SOLVING AS A TECHNIQUE FOR MAINTAINING SOUND MENTAL HEALTH

Certainly the problem-solving process is not a technique to be suggested to psychotic individuals as a method by which they may regain mental health. Individuals in advanced stages of psychoneurosis may no longer be able to attack life's problems rationally. But the normal and mildly maladjusted person who learns to apply the problem-solving technique to life situations may expect to enjoy sound mental health. This is not necessarily true in every case—battle fatigue can occur in the best-integrating individual—but a scientific approach to life's problems offers the greatest hope for sound mental health.

This is neither the time nor the place for a detailed discussion of the problem-solving technique. Dewey,[68] Thorndike,[69] and others have presented in great detail both the technique and ways of learning it. If the reader is unfamiliar with the application of scientific method to life situations, the authors recommend intensive readings in the field.

The basic problem of mental hygiene lies in the blocking of the individual in his attempts to satisfy his needs. Success in the fulfillment of needs results in feelings of satisfaction and the release of tension. Failure to satisfy needs sets the stage either for the adjustment mechanisms discussed in a previous section or for a constructive learning situation, the successful conclusion of which will contribute to sound mental health.

The well-adjusting individual, in the face of failure, will marshal his

---

[67] Herbert A. Carroll, *Mental Hygiene: The Dynamics of Adjustment* (Englewood Cliffs, N.J.: Prentice-Hall, 1964), pp. 239–291.

[68] John Dewey, *How We Think* (Boston: Heath, 1933), pp. 106–115.

[69] Robert L. Thorndike, "How Children Learn the Principles and Techniques of Problem-Solving," *Learning and Instruction: Forty-ninth Yearbook of the N.S.S.E.*, *Part I*, pp. 192–216 (Chicago: University of Chicago Press, 1950).

knowledges and skills to cope with his frustrations in a rational fashion. Mary Elizabeth Keister has this to say:[70]

Mental hygienists have employed the concept of failure in two ways. They have used it in connection with a situation which is ultimately impossible for the individual to overcome because of his own incapacity; under such circumstances it is important for him to realize this fact and adjust himself to the idea of impossibility. In a second sense, they have thought of failure as a step in the process of solving a problem, as involved in the individual's working his way out of a difficulty.

The first adjustment noted above is obviously the more difficult one because it involves emotional as well as intellectual acceptance of failure. The second procedure treats failure as a temporary state in the application of provisional tries for the solution of the problem and eventual success. We shall consider first, the rational adjustment of the individual to limitations of self; and secondly, some of the common rational attacks on surmountable sources of failure.

Understanding and Acceptance of Self

We have indicated in an earlier section some of the child-rearing practices that contribute to unrealistic conceptions of self. In a prior section we took a brief look at physical disabilities. It may seem relatively simple to the objective observer to assess the physical and mental capabilities of an individual in terms of the goals that he realistically may set for himself. It is, in actuality, an extremely difficult task for any individual to assess his own capabilities objectively. The task is even more difficult when the individual is inferior in any aspect, as objective appraisal violates his sense of personal adequacy. The rational person, however, is forced to conclusions of limitations of self when faced with insurmountable difficulties. Then comes the most difficult task of all, a realistic acceptance of these limitations as a basis for setting new and attainable goals.

Aggression

The problem-solving approach involves an aggressive attack upon the cause of failure. This may be either at the physical or at the verbal level. The boy who was too poor to afford a college education, but whose football prowess and high grades in high school earned him the opportunity to achieve a degree through a football scholarship, exemplifies the virtue of both types of aggression. Physical aggressiveness on the football field and verbal aggressiveness in the classroom demonstrate respectively his ability to score touchdowns and his understanding of the concepts presented in

[70] Mary Elizabeth Keister, "The Behavior of Young Children in Failure," in Barker, Kounin, and Wright (eds.), *Child Behavior and Development* (New York: McGraw-Hill, 1943), p. 429.

texts and lectures. Both aggressive behaviors are essential if he is to achieve his goal of a college education. Despite the negative connotations attached to the word "aggression" in our modern world, our football hero's behavior is a positive expression of a virtue highly prized in that same world—a drive to assert self, to excel. The successful aggression on barriers to goals, in socially approved ways, is the reaction to frustration most conducive to sound mental health. Such aggression is a rational attack upon the very source of the anxiety.

Circumvention

The barrier to the goal may be circumvented by following a circuitous path to the original goal. A stenographer may have her heart set upon the prestige and the salary that accompany the position of private secretary to the boss. The barrier, in this case, may be a very efficient secretary to a junior executive. The seniority practices of the firm may make it quite clear that the secretary to the junior executive has first claim to the position as secretary to the boss when such position becomes vacant. A circuitous route to the original goal may be followed through moving to another firm where seniority practices are not followed.

Substitution

If prestige and money are the crucial goals of the stenographer cited above, the position of wife of the boss may make a quite satisfactory substitute for the position of secretary to the boss.

We assumed above that the only barrier to attainment of the stenographer's goal was the seniority practices of the business firm. Now let us assume that the roles are reversed: that our subject is the secretary to the junior executive and holds seniority, and that the stenographer is promoted over her head because of our subject's demonstrated inability to handle the high-level routine demanded of the secretary to the boss. The problem now becomes one of understanding and acceptance of limitations of self. This task will be considerably eased if the original goal is not simply abandoned but substituted for. Such an acceptable substitution might be to become the best possible secretary to a junior executive. Such a goal is well within the realm of attainment, because ability already has been demonstrated to be a "good" secretary to a junior executive. Just that bit of extra effort, just that bit of extra training, or just a bit of adroit bringing of one's merits to the attention of the junior executive, may bring forth the assurance that he has the "best possible secretary." Attainment of this realizable goal will bring the feelings of success, of adequacy, and of achievement that contribute to personal mental health.

Not all substitution, of course, is appropriate. Particularly poor substitutions, from the viewpoint of mental hygiene, seem to be the substitutions of academic goals for social ones. The withdrawal from attempts to improve social skills will result in a progressively crippled social life. Cronbach notes, "Not only artists like Van Gogh and Beethoven, but also scientists like Cavendish are celebrated for their moodiness, eccentricity, and temperamental outbursts as well as for their work. These men achieved, but they appear to have been far from happy."[71]

Choice Between Goals

Conflicting goals present very real barriers, each to the other. A choice, of course, has to be made at the intellectual level of reality. A girl has to verbalize an intellectual choice between mates if she is to participate in a wedding ceremony. A man has to verbalize an intellectual choice of professions at an early age if either of them involves a prolonged period of highly specialized training.

If such choice is unwillingly made with a "now let's wait and see if this is the right decision" attitude, the period of anxiety that accompanies decision-making either is prolonged until the final psychological choice (emotional commitment to the intellectual choice) is made when the decision is proved the correct one, or the anxiety is intensified when the choice is proved to have been a poor one. A problem-solving and mental-hygienically sound approach to such decisions involves making one deliberate and final choice—a choice as scientifically sound as is possible at the time of decision—and a willingness to accept the consequences of a wrong decision. Later twinges of regret are not repressed, but are faced with a "counting of the blessings" that flowed from the decision reached. This procedure terminates at the time of the choice-making, the period of anxiety that always accompanies choice-making. Freedom from this anxiety assists the individual in making this a "good" choice and in maintaining the emotional equilibrium necessary for successful coping with all the new choices that occur in everyone's lifetime.

IMPLICATIONS OF MENTAL HYGIENE FOR THE SCHOOL

The recurring emphases in this chapter have been upon the importance of emotional security and of problem-solving skills in the attainment of sound personal mental health. The prevalence of mental disturbances has been indicated, the relationships between physical and mental health and between emotional needs and mental health have been explored, various causes of poor mental health have been sampled, and defense mechanisms indicative of poor mental health have been briefly summarized.[72] But in all of these discussions, the stress has been upon the significance of emotional security and of rational problem-solving.

These techniques are not designed primarily to rehabilitate damaged personalities nor even to prevent mental illness. Emotional security and

[71] Lee J. Cronbach, *Educational Psychology* (New York: Harcourt, 1954), p. 532.
[72] Severe mental disturbances, of course, are beyond the scope of the classroom teacher's responsibilities.

skills in problem-solving are designed to promote and maintain sound mental health. Rivlin summarizes the responsibility of teachers for provision of classroom conditions conducive to sound mental health in the following terms.[73]

The teachers and the parents have the responsibility for seeing that the child achieves so sound a degree of emotional stability that he can take in stride the frustrations and disappointments that may be disastrous to others. More important still, they may help him function so effectively that he will have fewer frustrations and disappointments.

The classroom teacher, the supervisor, and the administrator are referred to the above-cited reference as one of the best syntheses of current professional opinion on the most effective methods of providing such classroom environment. The bibliography for this chapter lists texts, pamphlets, and films bearing on this topic. From this wealth of professional literature, the authors will select what they consider the three most important ideas in the provision of a classroom environment conducive to sound mental health.

First the teacher must have such basic personality patterns that she can be both permissive and firm. She must love children and be willing to make allowances for their behavior when they are tired or hungry or sick. Most important, she must be patient when children are frustrated and are striking out at her in an attempt to relieve their tensions. But she must also be firm and clear in setting the boundaries for behavior. Children need to know what is expected of them if they are to build behavior patterns that will conform to societal expectations. Further, the mental-health-oriented teachers must assist in breaking what Kubie refers to as the "conspiracy of silence." Children and youth must be free to analyze their experiences and feelings. Only through full and free exploration may children and youth receive moral education based on personal decision-making. The authors agree that it is "more important that a child be taught to be "moral"—that he become capable of moral choice, and, hence, become fully "human"—than that he be "right" in the sense of conforming to the established dictates of society."[74] The permissiveness of the teacher, and the involvement of the student in the decision-making process, perhaps is best stated by Kubie:[75]

[73] Harry N. Rivlin, "The Role of Mental Health in Education," in Nelson B. Henry (ed.), *Mental Health in Modern Education: The Fifty-fourth Yearbook of the National Society for the Study of Education*, Part II, p. 10 (Chicago: The University of Chicago Press, 1955).

[74] William F. O'Neill, "Existentialism and Education for Moral Choice," *Phi Delta Kappan*, 1964, XLVI–2, p. 49.

[75] Lawrence S. Kubie in Richard Jones, *An Application of Psychoanalysis to Education* (Springfield, Ill.: Charles C. Thomas, 1960), pp. vii–viii. Reprinted by permission.

This does not, however, force us to the impossible conclusion that every teacher must be an analytically trained psychotherapist or that every school child must be psychoanalyzed. It brings us rather to conclude that all education should be conducted in an atmosphere in which the universal and recurrent emotional disturbances and repressive tendencies of childhood can be resolved as soon as they arise, and before they become chronic. The child's fifth freedom is the right to know what he feels; but this does not carry with it any right to act out his feelings blindly. This will require a new mores for our schools, one which will enable young people from early years to understand and feel and put into words all the hidden things which go on inside of them thus ending the conspiracy of silence with which the development of the child is now distorted both at home and at school. If the conspiracy of silence is to be replaced by the fifth freedom, children must be encouraged and helped to attend to their forbidden thoughts, and to put them into words, i.e., to talk out loud about love and hate and jealousy and fear, about curiosity over the body, its products and its apertures; about what goes in and what comes out; about what happens inside and what happens outside; about their dim and confused feelings about sex itself; about the strained and stressful relationships within families, which are transplanted into schools. All of these are things about which school must help children to become articulate in the schoolroom.

Second, she must possess the professional skills that are necessary for understanding the needs of children. Permissiveness and firmness are sound foundations on which to build a classroom environment that will provide emotional security for children—but each child has both normative and unique needs. The teacher must discover the needs of each child if she is to assist him in building realistic plans for the satisfaction of those needs. Only if his needs are satisfied can he be emotionally secure.

Third, the teacher must possess a high level of problem-solving ability and must develop a host of techniques for assisting children in learning the attitudes and skills necessary for effective problem-solving. The students *must* be intimately involved in the decision-making process. The process seems to be best learned through application. The teacher, then, will need to assist students in discovering, clarifying, and attacking major problems of significance to them. He will need to guide them in evaluating the success of their endeavors, in formulating new plans of attack when faced with failure, and in maintaining an attitude of continuing appraisal of successful endeavors.

Summary

We are living in an anxious age. The tensions of the Cold War, the insecurity of an industrial economy, the insecurities of the class-caste system, and the unique problems of urban living have fostered a national disease of anxiety—one which is as contagious as measles. Diagnosis and treatment of the mental illnesses stemming from this generalized anxiety—and other sources—are not so far advanced as the diagnosis and treatment of physical illnesses.

This chapter only touches upon the varied causes of mental illness, and the relationships among them. Broad overview of the complexity of the problem is attempted, in an effort to sensitize the beginning teacher to the magnitude of the problems other than academic content that affect both the academic and the social learnings of her pupils. Stress is placed upon structuring classroom situations in which children are free to learn —situations providing an abundance of response, recognition, security, and new experience for the pupils.

Milestones of personality development are sketched, with suggestions to teachers for ways in which school experiences can foster, or hamper, development of the wholesome personalities essential to effective citizenship in a democracy. Conscious effort has been made to write in lay language, in the hope that this chapter will serve as the springboard for many parent-teacher conferences, and as a stimulus for parents to digest the entire text as a means of strengthening the parent-teacher relationship.

Stress is placed upon the problem-solving technique as a means toward sound mental health. The psychology of the decision-making process still is imperfectly understood; but a wealth of literature is available concerning the formal processes of attacking a problem. Implications for mental health of the various reactions to problem situations are developed.

Final section of the chapter, "Implications of Mental Hygiene for the School," summarizes the pedagogical principles developed in the context of the presentation of the problems of mental health.

Selected Bibliography

Allport, Gordon W. *Becoming: Basic Considerations for a Psychology of Personality.* New Haven: Yale University Press, 1955. Pp. ix + 106. A quite readable presentation for the beginner of the concepts presented in the more technical psychiatric treatises.

Baruch, Dorothy Walter. *New Ways in Discipline.* New York: McGraw-Hill, 1949. Pp. xiv + 200. A penetrating analysis of the principles of child discipline which includes alternative patterns for parental leadership in dealing with preschool and school age children.

Bettelheim, Bruno. *Truants from Life: The Rehabilitation of Emotionally Disturbed Children.* New York: MacMillan, 1964. Pp. xii + 511. Through four detailed case studies, the author illustrates the nature and scope of the work carried on at the Sonia Shankman Orthogenic school of the University of Chicago.

Bloch, Herbert A. *Disorganization, Personal and Social.* New York: Knopf, 1952. Pp. xvi + 386.

Byrd, Oliver E. (ed.). *Health Instruction Yearbooks, 1944–1954.* Stanford: University Press, 1944–1954. A series of yearbooks dedicated to health instruction. One chapter in each yearbook on mental hygiene. Summaries of the significant current research.

CARROLL, HERBERT A. *Mental Hygiene: The Dynamics of Adjustment,* Fourth Edition. Englewood Cliffs, N.J.: Prentice-Hall, 1964. Pp. vii + 408. Technical explanations in terms understandable by the layman.

CROW, LESTER D., and ALICE V. CROW (eds.). *Mental Hygiene for Teachers.* New York: Macmillan, 1963. Pp. xii + 580. A guide for teachers to the needs and problems of learners, with the emphasis on human relations in the classroom.

FARBER, SEYMOUR M. (ed.). *Man and Civilization: Control of the Mind.* San Francisco: McGraw-Hill, 1961. Pp. xvi + 340. Record of a symposium held at the University of California San Francisco Medical Center, January 28–30, 1961. Psychological, physiological, and philosophic approaches to the control of human behavior.

FRANK, LAWRENCE K. *The Fundamental Needs of the Child.* New York: National Committee for Mental Hygiene, Inc. Pp. 29 (Pamphlet). Sociological interpretation of the psychological needs of the preschool and primary age child. A challenging equation of the needs of the child to the needs of society.

GROSSACK, MARTIN M. (ed.). *Mental Health and Segregation.* New York: Springer, 1964.

HAIMOWITZ, MORRIS, and NATALIE HAIMOWITZ. *Human Development: Selected Readings.* New York: Crowell, 1960. Pp. xvi + 799. Book of selected readings of eighty prominent people in the field of human growth and development from prenatal through the adolescent years.

HEATON, MARGARET M. *Feelings Are Facts:* New York: National Conference of Christians and Jews, 1962. Pp. 60 (Pamphlet). Suggestions for helping children to analyze their feelings and to make wholesome adjustments to them.

JOSEPHSON, ERIC, and MARY JOSEPHSON (eds.). *Man Alone: Alienation in Modern Society.* New York: Dell, 1962. Pp. 592.

KATZ, BARNEY, and GEORGE F. J. LEHNER. *Mental Hygiene in Modern Living.* New York: Ronald Press, 1953. Pp. 546. Simple, clear, comprehensive coverage of the mental hygiene aspects of all areas of modern living.

LAYCOCK, S. R. *Mental Hygiene in the School.* Toronto: Copp Clark Teachers Handbook Series, 1960. Pp. 117. A handbook for the classroom teacher.

MENNINGER, KARL, and others. *The Vital Balance: The Life Process in Mental Health and Illness.* New York: Viking Press, 1963. Pp. 530. Synthesis by a recognized scholar in the field of the changes that have taken place in scholarly positions regarding mental health in the past fifty years .

MUSSEN, PAUL H., JOHN CONGER, and JEROME KAGEN. *Readings in Child Development and Personality.* New York: Harper & Row, 1965. Pp. ix + 480. Selection of thirty-one readings by prominent authors in the fields of child development and personality from infancy through adolescence.

N.E.A., Association for Supervision and Curriculum Development. *Growing Up in an Anxious Age: 1952 Yearbook, A.S.C.D.* Washington, D.C.: National Education Association, 1952. Pp. xvi + 263. An analysis of the cultural sources of anxieties in children. Clearly written. Suggestions for school practice.

———. *Learning and Mental Health in the School: 1966 Yearbook*, A.S.C.D. Washington, D.C.: National Education Association, 1966. Pp. viii + 174. Synthesizes current theories of learning and of mental health. Designed for the sophisticated scholar of curriculum. Too technically written to be useful to the average teacher.

NEMIAH, JOHN C. *Foundations of Pyschopathology*. New York: Oxford University Press, 1961. Pp. xx + 338. Of special interest for this chapter is the position of this recognized scholar in clarifying the relation between physical and mental health in the very opening pages of his text.

REDL, F. *Children Who Hate*. New York: Free Press of Glencoe, 1965. Pp. 286. Utilizes case studies to tell what these aggressive children are like, how it feels to live with them, and how people can survive with such children.

———, and WILLIAM W. WATTENBERG. *Mental Hygiene in Teaching*. New York: Harcourt, Brace & World, 1959. Pp. xiv + 562.

———, and DAVID WINEMAN. *Controls from Within: Techniques for the Treatment of the Aggressive Child*. New York: Macmillan, 1965. Pp. 332.

SAHAKIAN, WILLIAM S. (ed.). *Psychology of Personality: Readings in Theory*. Chicago: Rand McNally, 1963. Pp. xviii + 504. Brings together generous selections from the writings of twenty-one prominent psychologists. Use of primary sources exclusively brings the students into direct contact with the significant theories of personality.

SCHOECK, HELMUT, and JAMES W. WIGGINS (eds.). *Psychiatry and Responsibility*. Princeton, N.J.: Van Nostrand, 1962. Pp. 288.

SHIRLEY, HALE F. *Pediatric Psychiatry*. Cambridge, Mass.: Harvard University Press, 1963. Pp. xiii + 796. Highly recommended for reading by parents and by teachers of young children. Language of the text is readily comprehensible to professional teachers and to most parents.

SELECTED FILMS

Emotional Health (McGraw-Hill) 21 min
> Shows interviews of a college student with a physician and then with a psychiatrist, who uncovers his fears and helps him to become emotionally adjusted; uses occasional flashbacks to the boy's childhood.

Feeling Left Out (Coronet Films) 13 min
> Attempts to stimulate understanding for the socially isolated and offers suggestions to meet the problems involved in dealing with them.

Feeling of Depression (McGraw-Hill) 30 min
> Presents the case history of a businessman who suddenly suffers feelings of great despondency. An examination of his earlier life reveals the reasons for his plight and suggests help.

Feeling of Hostility (Natl. Film Board of Canada) 27 min
> Case history of Clare, showing how feelings of insecurity in childhood produced a lonely person underneath the outward appearances of success. Calls attention to various compensatory devices expressive of feelings of hostility.

Feeling of Rejection (Natl. Film Board of Canada) 21 min
> Presents the case of Margaret, who as a young adult had not yet learned

to make decisions independently. When she goes to a psychiatrist to learn the reasons for her headaches and tired feeling, she reveals that when a child she was afraid of losing the love of her parents and friends and, as a result, learned to acquiesce to all their demands. When she realizes the cause of her trouble, she begins to assert herself and becomes well adjusted.

Meeting the Emotional Needs in Childhood: The Groundwork of Democracy (Dept. of Child Study, Vassar College) 32 min

Opens with a scene of students graduating from college, then shows and analyzes behavior in various childhood situations related to needs and experiences that shape adult behavior. Causes are shown, along with suggestions as to how problems might be met by those working with children.

Nation's Mental Health (McGraw-Hill) 18 min

A March of Time film; a survey of the mental health problem for community and other adult groups and for beginning students in psychology and education.

Overdependency (Natl. Film Board of Canada) 32 min

Deals with understanding the causes of overdependence, with the discussion presented through flashbacks to childhood experiences.

Preface to Life (United World Films) 30 min

The story of a boy and two dreams, one that of his father who expects great things and pushes him too fast, the other of his mother who wants him to remain a baby. Attempts thereby to show how attitudes of adults are reflected in incidents of the child's experience, and that both stimulation and pressures are involved.

Problem of Pupil Adjustment (McGraw-Hill) 2 reels. 39 min

First reel: "The Drop-out"

In an employment office Steve Martin, on the day he should be graduating from high school, sits reminiscing about things gone awry at school and his succession of mediocre jobs held after his "drop-out." Shows Steve's eagerness as a freshman, then the withering effect of repetitious drills over textbook material that seemed pointless. Truancy comes easily and, finally, becomes his escape.

Second reel: "The Stay-in"

Explains how one high school has reduced its "drop-outs" to less than 5 per cent of its total student population: stresses learning in terms of student interests and shows how even "required" subjects are made vital by enlightened teaching methods.

Self-Conscious Guy (Coronet Films) 10 min

Feelings of self-consciousness keep a high school boy from doing classwork well or making friends easily. He discovers that many of his classmates suffer from similar feelings. Works to become better adjusted by thinking about others, developing skills, taking part in activities, and finally by developing a perspective on his own relationship to the social situations in which he moves and lives.

Shyness (McGraw-Hill) 23 min

Shyness in children, its causes, and how, through a greater understanding by parents and teachers, this problem may be dealt with. From the lonely existence of a typically shy adult, the film turns to a study of three children: Anna, shy but wistfully wanting association with others; Jimmy, whose excessive timidity is really a symptom of profound emotional disturbance; Robert, aloof but happily independent. Studying their conditions, a psychiatrist from the child guidance clinic reveals the confidence-destroying demands of parents that predisposed the children to shyness. Together—teacher, psychiatrist, and parents—bring about a change in the children's attitudes.

Understand Your Emotions (Coronet Films) 13 min

A general understanding of emotions, what they are, what they do, where they come from, and how they are changed. Shows that emotions have main effects on the body, both on voluntary behavior and on involuntary behavior, and that people have different emotional responses to the same stimulus pattern.

What's On Your Mind? (National Film Board of Canada) 11 min

This documentary film explains modern psychiatry and clinical psychology. The film opens with a definition of psychiatry and shows in close-up a case of schizophrenia.

You Are Not Alone (Association) 32 min

An emotional health documentary that dramatically tells the story of a businessman who suffers a disappointment that creates great emotional anxiety. Emphasizes self-understanding and emotional adjustment.

Chapter 8. *Problems of Crime and Delinquency*

IN THE EARLY STAGES of man's development almost all of the problems he faced as a community member were those that resulted from disasters in his physical world or from his contacts with neighboring tribes. Today many of our important social problems come from stresses and strains within the society. As community members we still face some disasters that are due to forces beyond our control. Floods, fires, earthquakes, hurricanes, volcanic eruptions, tidal waves, and—yes—the possibility of bombings may challenge the resources of a community. Problems of traffic conditions, problems of eliminating slums—these and similar other municipal problems must be faced squarely by individuals in their own communities, if we are to have—from the grass roots—a strong nation and a good world. Overshadowing these physical and external problems, however, are major problems of human relations developing *within* the society. One such major set of problems relates to the area of adult crime and juvenile delinquency. This chapter will concentrate on the implications of crime and delinquency for the local community.

EXTENT OF CRIME IN THE UNITED STATES

The cost of crime in the United States, ranging from minor felonies to actions of highly organized gangs and syndicated gambling, was estimated by J. Edgar Hoover to be $27 billion in 1964.[1] These estimates include the cost of damages done by criminals as well as the expenses of apprehending, convicting, and confining them. By far the largest number of crimes are those against property. Next in frequency are those related to sex.

[1] Letter to authors, January 6, 1965.

283

Many murders are the result of gang warfare, although some are caused by temporary anger or are the work of psychopaths. The annual homicide figure for the United States is usually between 8,000 and 9,000 a year.[2] Actually, however, the numerical importance of homicide as a part of the crime picture in the United States can be greatly exaggerated. For example, the suicide rate probably is almost twice as great for a given year. Furthermore, the accidental deaths probably run about 100,000 annually. The above comparisons do not mean to indicate that we should not take whatever measures may be necessary to reduce the homicide rate—or, for that matter, the suicide and accident rates as well.

A part of the picture of trends in crime is the increase in the amount of white-collar crime. Such matters as embezzlement, confidence games, and stock-market manipulation, as well as other marginal practices (such as reported dishonesty on the part of watch repairmen and garagemen) have shown a considerable increase in American society in recent years. Such trends, together with the prevalence of crimes against property (robbery, theft, and gangster racketeering) indicate the extreme emphasis upon the economic motive lying behind most crimes.

A careful study by Sutherland[3] has revealed the extent and nature of white-collar crimes:

White-collar criminality in business is expressed most frequently in the form of misrepresentation in financial statements of corporations, manipulation in the stock exchange, commercial bribery of public officials directly or indirectly in order to secure favorable contracts and legislation, misrepresentation in advertising and salesmanship, embezzlement and misapplication of funds, short weights and measures and misgrading of commodities, tax frauds, misapplication of funds in receiverships and bankruptcies. These are what Al Capone called "the legitimate rackets." These and many others are found in abundance in the business world.

In the medical profession, which is here used as an example because it is probably less criminalistic than some other professions, are found illegal sale of alcohol and narcotics, abortion, illegal services to underworld criminals, fraudulent reports and testimony in accident cases, extreme cases of unnecessary treatment, fake specialists, restriction of competition, and fee-splitting. Fee-splitting is a violation of a specific law in many states and a violation of the conditions of admission to the practice of medicine in all. The physician who participates in fee-splitting tends to send his patients to the surgeon who will give him the largest fee rather than to the surgeon who will do the best

---

[2] J. Edgar Hoover, *Crime in the U.S.*, Uniform Crime Reports (Washington, D.C.: U.S. Govt. Printing Office, 1963), pp. ix + 170.

[3] From Edwin H. Sutherland, "White-Collar Criminality," *American Sociological Review*, Vol. 5, No. 1, February 1940, 1–5, 7–8, 11–12. Copyright, 1940, The American Sociological Society. Reprinted by permission of the Society and of Mrs. Myrtle C. Sutherland.

See also fuller statement in Edwin H. Sutherland, *White-Collar Crime*, New York: Dryden, 1949.

work. It has been reported that two-thirds of the surgeons in New York City split fees, and that more than one-half of the physicians in a central western city who answered a questionnaire on this point favored fee-splitting.

These varied types of white-collar crimes in business and the professions consist principally of violation of delegated or implied trust, and many of them can be reduced to two categories: misrepresentation of asset values and duplicity in the manipulation of power. The first is approximately the same as fraud or swindling; the second is similar to the double-cross. The latter is illustrated by the corporation director who, acting on inside information, purchases land which the corporation will need and sells it at a fantastic profit to his corporation. The principle of this duplicity is that the offender holds two antagonistic positions, one of which is a position of trust, which is violated, generally by misapplication of funds, in the interest of the other position. . . .

The financial loss from white-collar crime, great as it is, is less important than the damage to social relations. White-collar crimes violate trust and therefore create distrust, which lowers social morale and produces social disorganization on a large scale. Other crimes produce relatively little effect on social institutions or social organization.

ORGANIZED CRIME

One of the characteristics of modern crime trends is the increasing tendency for crime to become highly organized. The beginning of this trend can be found in the prohibition era of the 1920's when gangs organized for the distribution of bootleg liquor. However, the trend has continued through the 1930's, the 1940's, the 1950's, and into the 1960's. It is probably now centered mostly around gambling activities; however, the tendency toward organized crime can also be seen in narcotics, trade, prostitution, labor racketeering (protection), "Murder Incorporated," and so on.

The effects of organized crime upon the public are many. Stock manipulation and other marginal business practices eventually increase the cost of a product to the public. Racketeering control of such industries as trucking and construction also increases the cost to the public. Emphasis upon gambling activities diverts a lot of money to nonproductive enterprises. The total energies persons devote to these activities could very well be devoted to constructive enterprises that would add to the total amount of goods produced and services in our country. The demoralizing influence of the close tie-in of gang leaders to local municipal governments and the sometimes "respectability" of the very wealthy gangsters have a bad effect upon the youth and others of our society.

Narcotics Problem

One of the problems that has become especially acute, particularly among adolescents, is that of narcotics. The basic and most important narcotic is that derived from the poppy—opium and its various derivatives.

It is usually used in the form of heroin. The use of marijuana, a drug that does not have as powerful an effect on the user but is much more difficult to stamp out, is also now very prevalent in the United States.

The use of narcotics, except for medical purposes, is completely illegal. Any traffic in these drugs is a crime. There is great variation in the extent to which the narcotics laws are enforced in various parts of the country. Furthermore, there is great variation in the penalties provided by the laws of the various states and cities. The use of narcotics results in a serious habit, which requires that the addict be given very special treatment. Aside from the harmful effects produced directly by the drug, there is the demoralization of the person in terms of his efforts to obtain it. Since drugs are very expensive (as well as illegal) and the habit requires increasing amounts, the addict is willing to go to any length to obtain money to buy the drug, or will engage in criminal acts, sometimes induced by the seller of the drug, in order to obtain it. By legal definition, of course, all addicts are criminals. Therefore it is easy to be driven into other types of criminal acts once one has become a drug addict.

Gambling

Gambling has existed from time immemorial and exists in various forms to the present day—from the "harmless" little private bet and the private poker party to carefully organized syndicated gambling. In some states a certain amount of control has been obtained by legalizing gambling, as in pari-mutuel betting at races.

In spite of the fact that the gambling addict is always in hopes that he will be able to make a strike, mathematical study of gambling devices indicates that there is, in the long run, no chance for the gambler. Even if the gambling machines were on the "up and up," the odds are so set as to play entirely into the hands of the gambling operators. Many of the gambling devices are not on a fair basis. Just enough winnings are made available to the customers to keep up their interest.

Because gambling does involve so many persons and so much money, it has become closely allied with corrupt politics. Many persons, thinking there is no harm in some gambling, wink at the violation of the laws in those states prohibiting it. This plays into the hands of the gambling racketeer. Many persons who need money badly for the necessities of life spend it on the various types of gambling, including the "numbers racket." The numbers or "policy" racket is based on a sale of chances on the payoff of some number based on the total number of stock or bond sales or of some other public figure that has at least a semblance of being unfixed. However, in many cases such numbers can be fixed. Even though the numbers racket involves relatively small sums of money from each individual each day, the annual take is very large, and it comes mainly from people who can least afford to lose it.

CRIME AND POLITICS

By far the worst problem related to organized crime is that of the possible corruption of the local municipal government. It is unlikely that organized crime can operate successfully on any large scale without the connivance of the local police force. By conniving with the ward politicians and other local political bosses, some of whom may even be racketeers themselves, persons engaged in organized crime are able to get protection from arrest. Whenever arrests and convictions do occur, they are usually of some small person who is not important in the total picture. Through access to great amounts of money, the organized criminals are able to hire brilliant lawyers who use legal devices in such a way as to make them almost immune from successful prosecution even if arrested. It is all too well known that such gangsters as Al Capone were finally convicted only for income tax evasions, not for the more serious crimes of which they were guilty.

This possibility of a fundamental breakdown of law enforcement at the local level places the crime problem squarely in the hands of the people of the various communities. By electing the right people to office and by taking an interest in their government, particularly by supporting non-corruptible officials, the citizens of a community can minimize the crime in their community. However, many citizens either are indifferent or else are interested in being able themselves at times to have access to one or more of the illegitimate enterprises. Every person who seeks to have his traffic ticket "fixed" is technically on the same basis as those who buy protection from the police to carry on illegal enterprises. Those participating in illegal gambling, even for a spasmodic special occasion, are also contributing to the corruption of their city government.

Legal Prohibition Versus Legalized Control

One of the big controversies arising out of the relationship between crime and politics relates to difference of opinion over the respective merits of prohibition versus legalized control. As a first case in point, let us look at the prohibition of the manufacture and sale of alcoholic beverages. This legal step, opposed by a large minority of United States citizens, led to the racketeering gangs of the 1920's who managed to finance themselves through the sale of alcoholic beverages to many otherwise law-abiding citizens. The passing of the repeal of prohibition managed to eliminate this source of revenue. However, the gangs have continued, largely ensconced now in the fields of gambling, narcotics, and other illegal activities.

The proponents of legality think that if such marginal pursuits as gambling could be controlled so as to reduce the gambling take and a campaign of education concerning the harm of gambling could be conducted, we could eliminate the gamblers' influence and their payoff protection, on the one hand, and reduce the amount of gambling in the community on the other. There is very little sentiment for the legalization of the use of narcotics. In this case most persons think that this traffic, which actually involves few people, can be eliminated through more careful and uniform law enforcement. This would have to be accompanied by increased access to institutions for the treatment of addicts. There are even some who argue for legalized prostitution, which is still so prevalent in Europe and was almost universal during the Middle Ages and later.

The difficult problem of the better enforcement of prohibition laws as against a careful system of legalized control in these areas of gangster activities is one that requires careful study. On that level, it is a social problem. On the level of helping the individual to solve his problems related to it, it becomes an educational problem.

Development of Corruption-free Municipal Government

One of the most important problems related to the crime situation is corruption in the local government. This has come about for a wide variety of reasons. One is the indifference of the average urban dweller to his city government. Another is the attempt to fight city election battles on the basis of some national political affiliation. If a city is predominantly of one party or the other, the municipal government tends to stay in power regardless of the efficiency or honesty of the administration. Over a period of years, this tends to lead to corrupt government. From time to time, in the large cities, various reform groups have attempted to bring about good government by electing good officials. In most cases such efforts are sporadic and the city soon resumes its traditional practices. Efforts have been made in some of the cities (mostly medium-sized and small ones so far) to set up a politics-free government on the city manager or commission plan. There have been other efforts to make city elections nonpartisan so that they would not be related to national or state politics.

Juvenile Delinquency

Although in the legal sense the primary distinction between delinquency and crime relates to the age of the persons involved, the concept of delinquency also implies a completely different attitude on the part of society. This differing attitude toward acts committed by younger persons goes back far in the history of mankind. Among the Romans and Greeks younger persons were not held to be responsible for crimes that they had committed. This same point of view prevailed in the Napoleonic Code. In the English jurisprudence, however, there was little differentiation among children, youths, and adults until relatively modern times. The Chancery Courts of England were sometimes used for special legal processes including cases involving children. Not until 1899 was there one special court in the United States for juveniles. In that year the first juvenile court was set up in Illinois.

The Nature of Juvenile Delinquency

A delinquent is someone below a given age, as defined in the law of the specific state, who commits an illegal act for which society must take some kind of action. This age is usually set at sixteen, seventeen, or eighteen. In practice, delinquency is generally held to involve something more than a one-time minor infraction of the law. In the first place, the concept includes repeated violations, and in the second place, it denotes violations by someone who deviates consistently from expected normal behavior. It does not include, therefore, the common misbehaviors of persons who are normally cooperative toward society. The use of the term "delinquent" ranges from its application to someone who has persistently violated the law but has not been detected, to someone who has been taken into the juvenile court and actually adjudged to be a delinquent and been assigned to be given special treatment.

It is likely that, for most purposes, a sociological and psychological definition is more helpful than a strictly legal one. Furthermore, it is probably better not to define the term too strictly but to leave it somewhat amorphous. In general, then, the writers are using the term *delinquency* in the following sense in this chapter and other parts of this book: *Chronic and persistent failure (of young persons) to conform to the expectations of the society as a whole.* This would mean that some persons are delinquent even though they are not being treated in a juvenile court. It would also mean that in some cases persons might be legal delinquents who are not so in terms of this definition. An example of the latter case would be that of a child who ran afoul of his family where the family itself was somewhat antisocial. In this case the child's behavior would conform to that of society as a whole but not conform to that of the family, and the child, consequently, might be falsely remanded by the family to the court.

The writers are of the opinion (and believe that most students of the basic social sciences are of the same opinion) that just as normal personality is the product of culture, so is deviant personality. Both crime and delinquency are caused. It is so important that pliable, plastic youth be handled on a psychological and sociological basis, rather than on a legalistic one, that it is essential for the society to set up special procedures. The use of the juvenile court to handle these cases—a procedure that is now almost universal in the United States and is spreading to other parts of the world—is one illustration of this point of view. Before going into the details of these procedures, let us see exactly what is the nature of the problem.

Trends in Delinquency

Most of the statistics quoted in the field of delinquency are not completely accurate. This is true for a number of reasons. There are differences in the definition of delinquency in the several states, both in terms of the general types of behavior called delinquent and in respect to age range. Delinquency figures include only court cases and not those handled by other agencies. Good agency handling of delinquency cases may preclude the need for court. The discrepancy in figures varies from state to state and from time to time.

Most authorities are agreed that, in the post-World War II period, there has been a sizeable increase in the delinquency rate in the United States. The figures may vary in different parts of the country. They may vary in a given year from two to three youths per hundred up to about six or seven youths per hundred who are actually picked up by police, some of whom are studied by the juvenile court (or its equivalent) in any one of the several states or jurisdictions. The Children's Bureau of the United States Department of Health, Education and Welfare reports that, excluding traffic cases, approximately 555,000 different youths were brought before juvenile courts in 1962.[4] A much greater number (1.1 million, again excluding simple traffic cases), dealt with directly by the police but did not go to juvenile courts are included. There was an increase of over 100 per cent in the number appearing before the courts between 1950 and 1962.[5] According to this figure, the number of juvenile delinquents is rising faster than is the increase in the population as a whole.

Studies of trends over a period of years have indicated that delinquency rates, as well as crime rates, periodically rise and fall. Delinquency rates, as opposed to crime rates, tend to rise during periods of prosperity and full employment. They also tend to rise during war periods. Both of these conditions were present during World War II. They were also present during the period of heavily increasing delinquency from 1950 to 1955, with the continued draft for the Korean "affair" and the general unrest with respect to national security, and with a high level of prosperity in the United States. It may well be, also, that periods when the public is very much interested in delinquency may cause the rate to appear to rise even farther, merely because the enforcement agencies are more zealous in the apprehension and prosecution of cases.

Differentiated Rates by Socioeconomic Backgrounds and by Other Factors

Almost all available studies indicate that the delinquency rate is much higher in industrial areas (where the families are of a lower social-economic status and are in overcrowded and/or poor housing) than it is in the better residential areas. Among the important factors behind this difference are the lack of recreational facilities in the former areas and the poor

---

[4] Richard Perlman, Chief, Juvenile Delinquency Statistics Section, Children's Bureau, "Statistical Aspects of Antisocial Behavior of the Minor in the United States," (Washington, D.C.: U.S. Department of Health, Education and Welfare, 1963), p. 8. (Processed.)

[5] Richard Perlman, *ibid.*, pp. 3, 11.

facilities in the home, as well as the standards of conduct that are more likely to be learned by the young person and to bring him into conflict with the law.

Part of the difference in delinquency rates in the two types of areas must be attributed to the fact that a child who is apprehended in a lower socioeconomic area is more likely to be brought before the juvenile court and thus to become a "statistic." In the better areas the case is likely to be settled without being taken into court, and thus it does not go on the record. In some cases, in the more wealthy residential areas, the influence of prominent persons who are acquainted with the parents of the delinquent prevents anything at all from being done. However, most sociologists agree that there is a "real" differential of rates, which is not totally accounted for by this difficulty with the statistics.

In the recent postwar period there has been a greater increase in delinquency in the low-delinquency areas (that is, the areas with the higher socioeconomic status) than there has been in the formerly high-delinquency areas. There has been a significant increase in both types of areas.

Youth Gangs

An important aspect of the problem of juvenile delinquency is the youth gang. The youth gang meets a very definite need that the youth apparently has for adventure, a feeling of belongingness, and a desire to lose one's self in some type of "cause." Although not all gangs are necessarily delinquent or criminal, a large portion of those in urban areas do tend to be so. They tend to become schools for delinquency and crime. In some cases the law is broken through episodes arising from competition with some other gang. In other cases the group has joined together in order to have a thrill, "borrow" automobiles, or actually commit thefts or sex crimes.

This problem is especially difficult to solve since the work of the juvenile court and other agencies tends to be nullified by the strong forces of the gang, which do fulfill a real social and psychological need of the youth. The problem is one of redirecting the activities of the gang toward constructive social efforts. This can be done through increased recreational facilities, competitive athletics, and other worthwhile youth projects. However, the problem of getting the gangs interested in these things is not an easy one.

Delinquency and Social Factors

Persons working with the problems of delinquency, and other concerned citizens, are always attempting to find a cause for it. Authorities are fairly generally agreed that there is no one cause nor one "pat" solution. This problem, like so many social problems, is multicausal. Sometimes factors that might normally appear relatively insignificant and that, in other circumstances, would not lead to delinquency may cause a particular child to become delinquent. Reasons such as comic books, poor housing (in and of itself), oppressive teachers, and broken homes, which have been given as causes for juvenile delinquency, probably are *not* the basic causes. But they may be factors that trigger delinquent behavior if other conditions are also unfavorable.

An analysis of the reasons for the *increase* of delinquency at the present time probably would reveal some of the following general social conditions: First, there should be listed the general insecurity of the world at the present time, due to war and threat of war, coupled with some vague feelings about economic insecurity and the possibility of depression; second, closely related to this general insecurity is the emphasis of our society upon measuring success by material criteria. This places enormous pressure upon the individual—the youth as well as the adult—to display those material things that have become the symbols of success. He is sometimes thoroughly tempted to use short cuts to get them, such as stealing an automobile or other objects that are evidence of material prosperity. This results in increases in crimes against property. Another factor is the very great mobility of the people, with the problems of adjustment that are entailed. Persons who live in relatively settled neighborhoods tend to develop sets of values and ideals that are not threatened as long as they stay in the slower-changing community. Moving into a new group tends to challenge these values and may cause the individuals to do things that they would not otherwise do. The sedate businessman who goes on a "toot" when he is in a strange town is an example of this at the adult level. This example can be duplicated many times, especially by children, in the relatively anonymous environment of the large city. Still another factor, of course, is the changing mores of our times. These changes lead to confusion of choices. The conflict between the mores of youth and the mores of adults leads to confusion, and this, in turn, can cause persons to assert that there are no moral standards. Consequently many youth and young adults are not motivated by a clear set of values or of moral standards. Still another factor is the difficulty of finding facilities for the wholesome use of leisure time, particularly in the urban situation. In spite of the fact that many cities have done excellent work in trying to develop leisure-time activities, there probably still are not completely adequate facilities in any of the cities of the United States. Another factor that probably affects delinquency is the attitude in our society toward lack of emphasis upon the individual as such and on his responsibility for his own actions. This attitude has recently become increasingly prevalent. It results from the increasing complexity of society, the increasing emphasis upon group activity, and the increasing lack of recognition of individual achievement. Institutions such as the home, the school, and the church can do much to combat all of these trends and to counteract to some extent the harm that these attitudes may do to youths and adults of all ages.

THE JUVENILE COURT

The *juvenile court* is the name applied to the specialized institution now used by all forty-eight states, the federal government, and the various territories for handling the delinquency cases of special groups of persons who are below a given age. The definition of the type of cases to be handled by this court apparently varies with the political jurisdiction. In many states it is defined to include all cases "below a certain age." In other states it may be the cases of persons between certain ages, such as between twelve and seventeen inclusive, as in Ohio. In the case of Ohio, there is a *children's registry* for children twelve years of age and under.

The philosophy of the juvenile courts is that the cases of immature, plastic children should be handled differently from those of hardened criminals. In a sense, the juvenile case is not a criminal one at all. The child is neither "charged" nor "tried." He is carefully studied and some recommendation is made. This may sometimes entail sentencing for a period of time in a reform school. A very careful study is made of the problem by psychologists, sociologists, and others before any recommendation is made to the judge. There are no lawyers. The action of the juvenile court, or the referee, is taken on the basis of the sociological and psychological factors rather than on the nature of the crime per se.

One of the important methods used by the juvenile court, as well as by other criminal courts for minor offenses by younger adults, is to pass sentence but to withhold it pending a probation period. The delinquent is assigned to a trained probation officer to whom he must report periodically. This probation officer works with him on any problems he may have, and, when the probational period ends, he is free from any sentence that the delinquency might have entailed. The work of the probation officer has been relatively successful. Its success depends upon a great many factors. The child or young criminal going back into the same environment sometimes has considerable difficulty. If he has served a certain amount of time in a reform school prior to the probational period, this hangs over his head. Sometimes the probation officers are not as well trained and as skilled in handling their cases as they should be. A major block to effective probation work is the extremely large case load of the probation officer.

The opinion of most criminologists and experts on juvenile delinquency is that the philosophy of the juvenile court, by and large, is the one under which we must solve our delinquency problems. What improvements are needed are in the quantity and quality of the facilities available for the study of the child and of the places to send him for rehabilitation when necessary. In many cases juvenile courts are handicapped by inadequate funds for staff and facilities. At present the facilities for detention and rehabilitation are *very* poor. Many of the so-called reform schools are "schools for crime." They are poorly staffed and poorly equipped, with very few facilities for the actual study of juveniles or for remedial work to be done. Some of the farms that have been set up with relatively small groups on large areas of land under fairly wholesome conditions have done a reasonably good job in respect to rehabilitation.

In spite of the fact that the philosophy under which the juvenile courts operate, and the general methods that are used are appropriate in the light of what is known about the nature of juvenile delinquency, there is much to be said about the way in which the philosophy is carried out. Some of the criticisms of "mollycoddling" launched against juvenile courts are, in reality, results of poor methods of administration, lack of appropriate number of personnel, or lack of trained personnel. Criticisms have been launched (which seem, in some cases, to be substantiated) that youthful delinquents brought in by the police sometimes are released and returned home before the police can return to the precinct. Although the extent to which this occurs may be exaggerated, in many cases the investigation is probably quite perfunctory. It is difficult to see how a juvenile investigation can be carried out without bringing in the parents and without putting some responsibility on them for whatever rehabilitation program may be worked out. In some cases the parents are not of the type to participate in such cooperative planning. However, this does not negate the need for a thorough investigation to include conferences with parents and others, such as ministers or youth-group leaders, who have some knowledge concerning the juvenile and who could help in his rehabilitation. School people should be of great assistance in this area. Unfortunately, some juvenile courts tend to ignore school personnel or even to reject assistance proffered by the school. Much of the criticism of the juvenile court probably can be laid to a lack of effective administration or a defect in the carrying out of its ideals rather than in the philosophy of the court itself. Possibly one of the new areas to be explored is that of increased involvement of the parent in responsibility for the delinquent act and in the rehabilitation and educational program.

EDUCATIONAL IMPLICATIONS

The facts concerning crime and the problems originating from crime do, of course, have implications for the school. Our citizens should be aware of the extent and importance of crime as a problem in our society. They should also be aware of the danger of such problems as narcotics and gambling. Positive emphasis in the curriculum should be on values that would tend to counteract any tendencies toward criminal action on the part of the person. Most of the implications for rehabilitation of the persons who tend toward criminality are the same as the implications for treating delinquency. The educational implications for the treatment of the delinquent are of two sorts. One is to take care of those who have become so badly delinquent that they require a special treatment, either in the form of clinics or in the form of some kind of school for rehabilitation. The other is the case of the various agencies trying to work with children in the pre-delinquent stage.

Child Guidance Clinics

It is necessary that each school system or community have full facilities for the study of individual children who have become serious problems either in school or in other institutions and who are either potential delinquents or have already become delinquents. These child guidance clinics are quite extensive. Each child must be dealt with individually. Opportunities must be given, at times, for the child to take residence for more complete study. In many cases an investigation of the family and other environmental conditions must be made. Such clinics are an essential part of the total handling of many problems of behavior or delinquency.

Schools for the Socially Maladjusted

There are schools for cases that are not so bad as to need to be completely separated from society and sent to the so-called reform school, but that may need to be taken out of their home environments for a period of time. These schools are usually resident schools—often in a rural area outside of town—where there can be a farm program and usually also some special type of educational program directed toward the rehabilitation of the children.

Classes must be small, teachers must be specially trained, and facilities for individualized work must be made available. Facilities for further psychological and psychiatric study of the children must be available. The length of time the child stays at the school should be determined by careful study and restudy of the individual and of his home. Some of these schools have been very successful in rehabilitating some cases involving badly maladjusted delinquents.

General Implications for Schools and School Programs

School programs have an important part to play, particularly in the prevention of delinquency. In the first place, an important matter is the attitude of the teacher toward his pupils and particularly toward those who are serious behavior problems in school and, therefore, potential delinquents. Whatever the treatment that may be given to behavior problems in a school, there must be a real warmth of understanding and every effort must be made to give genuine meaning to the school program. A teacher who works in a neighborhood where the backgrounds of the children are quite different from the background of the teacher himself must learn to understand these unfamiliar cultures if he is to work effectively with them. Even when cultural differences do not exist, to some extent the teachers (the adults of one generation) tend not to understand the boys and girls of another generation because of the present rapidity of change. This disparity in points of view is bad enough in a community where the teacher comes from the same general socioeconomic status. The problems are complicated with the socioeconomic statuses, attitudes, and mores are markedly different. Probably the most important *one* thing the school can do is to take a *genuine personal interest* in each child.

In addition to the teachers' attitudes and understanding, there needs to be a heavy emphasis in the curriculum upon those matters that will help the coming generation to work toward the solution of social problems so that fewer situations conducive to the development of behavior and delinquency problems will exist. This means, among other things, an emphasis on developing skills in helping people to get along with each other—good human relations, good intergroup relations (see Chapter 9). It also means heavy emphasis upon the ideals and practices of good family living, so that the graduates of our schools who are normal boys and girls will go out equipped (among other things) with the attitudes and desires to develop a good family living (see Chapter 6).

Mental-Health Program of the School

Efforts should be made to develop a good mental-health atmosphere in all schools. Antagonism between groups of pupils in a school, or antagonism between teachers or groups of teachers, or between teacher and principal does not result in a situation where wholesome personalities can readily be developed. Some of the suggestions that have been covered in the chapter on mental health (Chapter 7) are applicable here in a program for developing a good mental-health atmosphere.

SUMMARY

Crime in the United States has become a very important social and political problem, both in terms of the amount of money and in the effect the criminal and his crimes has on the rest of society. Prominent in the increase in crime is the increase in the amount of "white collar" crime. Much crime is related to the problem of control or prohibition of certain things such as the use of alcohol, the use of narcotics, gambling, and prostitution.

In the United States by and large the juvenile delinquent is treated differently from the adult criminal. The special court, the juvenile court, at present has an adequate point of view but an inadequate staff to do the job assigned to it. Juvenile delinquency has increased markedly, particularly in the spread into the previously low delinquency areas, of those of the middle- and upper-classes. Educational implications point toward greater services for the help of children who are socially maladjusted and hence potential delinquents—through special schools and classes as well as specialized personnel. Important implications for school programs based upon good mental health principles can also be formulated.

SELECTED BIBLIOGRAPHY

BARUCH, DOROTHY. *New Ways in Discipline.* New York: McGraw-Hill, 1949. Pp. xiv + 280.

CHANDLER, B. J., LINDLEY, J. STILES, and JOHN I. KITSUSE (eds.). *Education in Urban Society.* New York: Dodd, Mead, 1962. Pp. viii + 279.

EVANIER, DAVID, and STANLEY SIVERZWEIG (eds.). *Nonconformers.* New York: Ballantine, 1961. Pp. viii + 184.

FYREL, T. R. *Troublemakers: Rebellious Youth in an Affluent Society.* New York: Schocken Books, 1962. Pp. 347.

GLUECK, SHELDON, and ELEANOR GLUECK. *Delinquents in the Making: Paths to Prevention.* New York: Harper & Row, 1952. Pp. viii + 214.

GOODMAN, PAUL. *Growing Up Absurd.* New York: Random House, 1960. Pp. xvi + 296.

KVARACEUS, WILLIAM C. *Juvenile Delinquency.* Washington, D.C.: Department of Classroom Teachers, American Educational Research Association, of the National Education Association, 1958. Pp. 32.

———, and WALTER B. MILLER. *Delinquent Behavior: Culture and the Individual.* Washington, D.C.: National Education Association, 1959. Pp. 147.

———, and WILLIAM E. ULRICH. *Delinquent Behavior: Principles and Practices.* Washington, D.C.: National Education Association, 1959. Pp. 350.

MOORE, BERNICE MILBURN. *Juvenile Delinquency: Research, Theory and Comment.* Washington, D.C.: Association for Supervision and Curriculum Development, 1958. Pp. vii + 68.

OJEMANN, RALPH H. *Personality Adjustment of Individual Children.* Washington, D.C.: Department of Classroom Teachers, American Educational Research Association, of the National Education Association, 1954. Pp. 37.

PASSOW, A. HARRY (ed.). *Education in Depressed Areas.* New York: Teachers College, Columbia University, 1963. Pp. xiv + 369.

PERLMAN, I. RICHARD, Chief, Juvenile Delinquency Board, Children's Bureau, "Statistical Aspects of Anti-Social Behavior of the Minor in the United States." Washington, D.C.: The Bureau, 1963. (Processed.)

SCHREIBER, DANIEL (ed.). *Guidance and the School Dropout.* Washington, D.C.: National Educational Association, 1964. Pp. 267.

———. *The School Dropout.* Washington, D.C.: National Education Association, 1964. Pp. 214.

SHEVIAKOV, GEORGE V., and FRITZ REDL. *Discipline for Today's Children and Youth.* Washington, D.C.: National Education Association, Association for Supervision and Curriculum Development, 1956. Pp. 64.

SILBERMAN, CHARLES E. "Give Slum Children a Chance." *Harper's Magazine,* Vol. 228, No. 1368 (May 1964), 37–42.

SUTHERLAND, EDWIN H. *White Collar Crime.* New York: Dryden Press, 1949. Pp. x + 272.

SYKES, GRESHAM. *Crime and Society.* New York: Random House, 1956. Pp 125.

TYLER, GUS. *Organized Crime in America: A Book of Readings.* Ann Arbor, Michigan: University of Michigan Press, 1962. Pp. xvi + 421.

U.S. Department of Health, Education and Welfare, Welfare Administration. Children's Bureau. "Children's Bureau Statistical Series," *Juvenile Court Statistics.* A series.

SELECTED FILMS

America on the Edge of Abundance (Indiana University) 55 min

Am I Guilty? (Normand Haule) 15 min
Cases are taken from the files of the Los Angeles Police Department and are presented mainly as an aid to combat the problem of juvenile delinquency. Especially useful if round table discussion follows each short feature. Provides excellent educational material.

Better Use of Leisure Time (Coronet Films) 10 min
There are many leisure-time activities that are both interesting and educational open to young people. This film serves as a helpful guide in developing a constructive attitude about leisure time, showing how time can be used best through a self-planned program of leisure and activities. Compare the amount of leisure time now with that of fifty and one hundred years ago.

Chance at the Beginning (Anti-Defamation League) 29 min
Discusses an experimental program for the culturally disadvantaged three- and four-year-olds, carried out by Dr. Martin Deutsch.

A Chance to Learn (N.E.A.) 30 min
Shows how the Elementary and Secondary Education Act of 1965 will open up educational opportunities to underprivileged children.

Children in Trouble (N.Y. State Youth Com.) 11 min
Discusses the causes of juvenile delinquency, what happens to the juvenile delinquent, and the role of the home, the church, the school, the police, and community clubs in preventing and controlling juvenile delinquency.

Children of the City (BIS) 31 min
Frank discussion of juvenile delinquency problems illustrating practice of Scottish courts under recent act of Parliament. Story of three boys accused of petty thievery—how overcrowding and shortage of recreating facilities breed delinquency—how education, social, and civic authorities unite in treating delinquents.

Children's Village (McGraw-Hill) 19 min
Produced at the Children's Village, Dobbs Ferry, N.Y. This film shows the work of this well-known institution in the rehabilitation of delinquent boys. Founded in 1951, the village is today a community of more than fifty buildings and four hundred boys. It is both a school and a pre-adult society in which each boy learns and works. It has its own businesses, shops, and banks, elects its own mayor, judge and town clerks, and its citizens pay taxes to run their own community projects. We are shown a new boy, Richard, who is accepted by the community, and how he reacts to his new environment.

Children Without (Anti-Defamation League) 30 min
> Shows a Detroit Public school where teachers and counselors establish the warm relationships such children need, and provide positive learning experiences for them.

Dropout (Atlantis Productions) 27 min
> Studies the case of a school dropout. Explores the reasons for his action and the results.

Marked for Failure (NET) 59 min
> Educational problems of deprived children in Harlem, New York.

Portrait of a Disadvantaged Child (NET) 59 min

Portrait of the Inner City (NET) 58 min

Portrait of the Inner City School: A Place to Learn (NET) 59 min

Superfluous People (Atlantis Productions) 54 min
> This film argues that welfare aid is a material and moral problem. It looks at people in trouble. It presents the thoughts of social workers, clergymen, authors, educators, and city planners.

Chapter 9. *Problems of Intergroup Relations*

Successful societies probably always will be stratified. Without leadership, and without power vested in the hands of the leaders, there is anarchy. A central thesis of this book is that democracy is the best method yet devised for the selection of those leaders and for the prevention of the abuse of power by the leaders. Recognizing this, we realize further that American democracy has not yet reached its full fruition; we have many problems. A parallel thesis is that American educators bear a responsibility for recognizing current American problems and for providing leadership in the search for solutions. It is the responsibility of American educators to recognize the diverse groups in American culture, to become aware of the problems created by conflicts of interest among these groups, to ameliorate the suffering caused by conflicts (especially as it affects the personality development of their school children), *and to develop adult citizens who can meet these conflicts with mutual respect, reason, cooperation, and high morale.*

Adequate treatment of intergroup problems would require a series of volumes. This chapter will briefly sample, in sequence: (1) the basic problems of intergroup relations in America; (2) reasons for the origin and persistence of these problems; (3) proposed action toward their resolution; (4) the role of the school in treating them; and (5) the school integration crisis of the 1960's.

Broad Areas of Intergroup Problems

Most of the intergroup problems in America today fall into the areas of social class, race, religion, national origin, and regional differences. Each of these broad areas will be discussed. The school integration crisis will

300

be treated in a concluding section, as the authors feel that the traumatic nature of resistance to school integration in the early 1960's was not only a question of racial prejudice, but it was also a matter of social class differences among those being integrated.

Class Differences

In spite of the fact that America is generally considered to be a classless society, social stratification is a major source of intergroup problems in this country today. One reason for the popular impression that America is relatively free of class differences probably lies in the high degree of vertical mobility in American culture; that is, one can move readily from one class to another. The popular phrase "Any boy can become President" epitomizes America's pride in her relative freedom from the rigid class barriers that inhibit vertical mobility in many cultures. The extremity of the phrase also emphasizes the popular belief that vertical mobility is more easily accomplished than is actually the case. Despite relative mobility, great masses of the American populace suffer discrimination based on social stratification. This is particularly true of the lower-class Negro.

Class barriers in many societies are so rigid as to approach a caste system, wherein one is born into a certain caste and can never escape it, no matter how great his individual abilities. The Negro has been relegated to such a caste status in America. Within the Negro caste one finds class differences quite similar to those described in succeeding sections of this chapter as an integral part of the total American culture.

Social research has indicated that class differences in America make important differences in the behaviors of individuals in at least four areas of human experience: sexual behavior, values and motivation, cultural practices such as child-rearing, and political and economic ideologies. These differences often serve as bases for the rationalization and reinforcement of prejudices.

Because of the importance of class differences affecting the entire populace of the nation, we shall develop in some detail (1) the Communist theory of class structure and struggle; (2) the development of class structure in America; (3) the method of analysis of contemporary social structure in America; and (4) the nature of contemporary American social structure.

(1) THE COMMUNIST THEORY OF CLASS STRUCTURE AND STRUGGLE. There are two main ideologies in conflict in the world today: democracy and Marxian totalitarianism. Struggle between the social classes is basic to the Marxian theory. It is, therefore, pertinent at this point to examine the Marxian theory of class struggle and structure in relation to what has happened in America. According to the Marxist theorists, the class struggle in modern time was to result in all existing classes being reduced to two major social classes—the proletariat (or working class) and the bour-

302   *The School in American Society*

geoisie.[1] Marx postulated that the rich would become richer and the poor would become poorer. He based his generalization on certain trends that were present during the period in which he wrote—in nineteenth-century industrialized Europe. Events of recent years, particularly in the United States, have tended to demonstrate that in this respect the Marxian analysis is faulty. It is true that the wealthy have accumulated more wealth, but so have the poor. Amelioration of the living conditions of the lower-middle and lower classes since 1900 has been tremendous. Even though there is wide economic difference between the upper and lower classes, the gulf between them has not become wider. Furthermore, many persons in the lower classes have risen in class level through occupational or professional advancement. This means that there has been a very heavy increase in the size of the middle class. Although there is a large group of wealthy persons in American society, neither the number of those persons nor the amount of wealth above the middle-class level has increased proportionately in recent years. It is likely that the program of economic legislation starting with the antitrust laws and continuing with the regulation of utilities, the income tax, the social legislation and executive orders and agencies of the Franklin D. Roosevelt administration, and probably the increased strength of labor unions, all have served to prevent Marx's predictions from coming true. Rather than all classes being reduced to two sharply defined groups, at least six groups have been identified in contemporary American class structure, with lines of demarcation emerging as being very hazy.

(2) THE DEVELOPMENT OF CLASS STRUCTURE IN AMERICA. The colonists brought to this country many of the class distinctions that had existed in Europe. Since for the most part the upper class did not migrate, the colonists were mostly middle- and lower-class persons. Certain class distinctions existed well into the period of the development of the American republic itself.[2] Some class lines tended to become obliterated by the time of the Revolution. The Revolution accelerated this trend by eliminating a portion of the wealthy landowning class and thus reducing the extent of class differences. In addition, the whole climate of political opinion affected by the Age of Enlightenment in Europe was toward greater emphasis upon equality and brotherhood, which tended to blur class lines.

On the American frontier a man was worthwhile for what he could do and not for his class status. The frontier tendency toward blurring of class lines had great influence on what was occurring in the more settled East. This does not mean that there were no classes. There was considerable range in wealth and in the possession of worldly goods. There were no

[1] Louis Untermeyer, *Makers of the Modern World* (New York: Simon and Schuster, 1955), pp. 26–33.
[2] These class distinctions are discussed in some detail under "Social Customs and Institutions" in Chapter 4.

sharp lines between the classes, however, except perhaps those between the wealthy mill owners and the laboring groups.

Especially in the larger cities, social class distinctions tended to become somewhat more fixed in the period following the Civil War. In most of the large cities a society consisting of the "best families" developed; frequently there was a special book to list them. Of lesser status was a group of wealthy persons who tended to associate together, and who had both wealth and tradition. Then there was the great mass of people, who quite often tended to associate on the basis of craftsmanship or mercantile ties. Next in status came the unskilled laborers and the lower classes.

The expansion of the economy during the latter half of the nineteenth century promoted the amassing of wealth, with accompanying vertical mobility; but cultural practices among the classes necessitated major reorientation of habits of speech, dress, and social courtesies on the part of those aspiring to raise their class standing. The climate of opinion that followed the administration of "Teddy" Roosevelt was such that there was a reaction against the extremely wealthy, and the open display of wealth typical of the early 1900's tended to decline. The income tax, following 1913, has tended to remove the great surplus of wealth even from the very rich. Present social structure maintains wealth as one of the indices of social position, but family tradition still is an essential ingredient of entree into the upper-upper class.

(3) Methods of Analysis of Contemporary Social Structure in America. Research in class structure has tended to be based upon empirical findings, although sometimes hypotheses are set up, to be verified later by experimentation or by field study. The Lynds felt in *Middletown* that there was a twofold social class system: one of the business class and one of the working class. In a later study, *Middletown in Transition*, they divided the working class into two groups.[3] Another study by Centers divided the United States into a fourfold class system, including upper, middle, working, and lower classes.[4]

By far the most thorough and far-reaching study of American class structure has been done in a series by W. Lloyd Warner and his associates. Basing their work entirely upon an empirical analysis of thoroughly detailed data in specific towns in which they worked, these investigators have postulated a class system as follows: upper-upper, lower-upper, upper-middle, lower-middle, upper-lower, lower-lower. The major techniques employed in arriving at the above classification system and assigning persons to it involved the development and application of two indices: an index of status characteristics consisting of such criteria as occupation and place of residence; and an index of participation in social activities such as to

[3] Robert S. Lynd and Helen M. Lynd, *Middletown in Transition* (New York: Harcourt, 1937).

[4] Richard Centers, *The Psychology of Social Classes* (Princeton, N.J.: Princeton University Press, 1949).

reveal the social class rating of persons in the community by other members of the community.[5]

Although the Warner studies have been subjected to some criticism, they are by far the most far-reaching and penetrating of all available studies. They seem to indicate definitely that there are social classes and that people are aware of them. Class consciousness is illustrated in such areas as selectivity of social invitations and differential codes of conduct toward selected groups.

(4) THE NATURE OF CONTEMPORARY SOCIAL STRUCTURE. A careful study of the research done by Warner and by other researchers indicates that social class structure is a fact in America and must be taken into account in any analysis of the American scene. We have indicated earlier that even within the Negro caste there can be identified a class structure, which is similar to that found in the Warner studies.

As a result of the empirical study of Yankee City, an heterogeneous industrial city in New England, Warner and his associates found it to be divided into classes as postulated. The class structure of Yankee City is shown in Figure 10.

Race, social reputation, religion, national origins, and wealth—all enter into the composite picture that comprises the class structure of Yankee City. Old American stock, Swedes, Russians, and Negroes have class preference in that order. The basis for prestige is social reputation. The upper-upper, old-family, native-born formulate standards and ideals, which serve as models of social conduct for the lower-lower, who lack job security and are unskilled and poorly housed. The norm is a middle-class society. The upper class is predominantly Episcopal in religious faith; the lower class is predominantly Catholic, Jewish, or unchurched.

To be born into one of the classes does make it difficult to move into another. In spite of the difficulty, there is a great deal of vertical mobility in the American scene. It probably is becoming increasingly difficult for one to move from the lower-middle class or the lower class to the position of executive in the industrial world. But by means of higher education— albeit with a struggle because of economic handicaps—a person can move from the lower class into a profession such as teaching, law, or medicine, and thus break out of class bonds.

The breaking of lower-class bonds through higher education is popularly thought to be becoming more difficult; the ever-increasing costs of Bachelor's degree is cited. Statistics on college enrollments do not support this position; an ever-increasing proportion of college-age youth are enrolled in college. True, many modern youth are enrolled in terminal courses in

[5] There is a whole series of books in the study, but see especially W. Lloyd Warner and Paul Lunt, *The Social Life of a Modern Community*, Yankee City Series, Volume I. (New Haven: Yale University Press, 1941). Newest paperback edition of this data appears as W. Lloyd Warner and others, *Yankee City* (New Haven: Yale University Press, 1963).

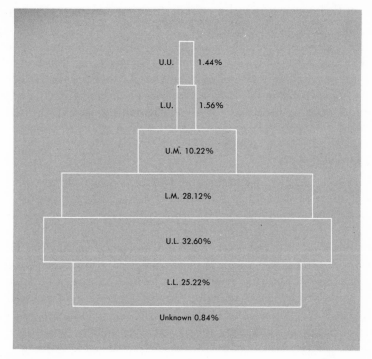

Figure 10. The Class Hierarchy of Yankee City (From W. Lloyd Warner, *et al.*, *Yankee City*. New Haven: Yale University Press, 1963, p. 43. Used by permission).

two-year colleges, or in similar courses at major universities; but the fact remains that more and more of modern youth are receiving at least some college education. The campus associations not only prepare them for technical vocations with relatively higher salary and status, but also significantly modify their value patterns and cultural behaviors.

If one has assimilated the middle-class mores emphasized in our public schools, breaking lower-class bonds relieves misery. If an individual becomes an urban professional person, however, while maintaining lower-class standards of dress, language, and personal habits, he may become an unhappy isolate. He belongs professionally with one group and socially with another; he receives only an uneasy tolerance from each group and no real acceptance from either, with an attendant reduction in his personal emotional security. Fortunately, many such professional men marry middle-class wives who re-educate them; but such marriages may have turbulent beginnings, or even may culminate in divorce, because of these class-value conflicts. If both members of a marriage of urban professional people maintain lower-class mores, unhappiness almost certainly will result. In the small rural community, however, the professional members may achieve greater social and emotional security by conforming to the lower-class mores of the community.

There can be an overemphasis on the class structure of America because it is less restrictive here than in many other places on the face of the earth. However, to ignore the existence of the lines, even though they may be somewhat blurred, is to ignore one of the important facts about American culture. Especially in the larger cities, class distinctions are important in modern America.

Racial Differences

The anthropologists maintain that two facts alone are important for any definition of race. They state that a race is a large group of people (1) possessing in common certain distinctive *physical characteristics* that are (2) *determined by heredity*. Such a "pure" race has not been located in the modern world. The most commonly accepted scientific classification of the modern races of mankind is the Negroid, or "black," the Mongoloid, or "yellow-brown," and the Caucasian, or "white."[6] Laymen often confuse "race" with natural characteristics, confusing genetic and political concepts; Hitler capitalized on this fallacy. Further confusions relate to linguistic, religious, or cultural differences; for example, Judaism is a religion and Hebrew is a language—there is no Jewish "race."

Racial differences pose some of the most traumatic problems in intergroup relations facing the American populace today. The Negro suffers most from racial discrimination. The American Negro has been relegated to second-class citizenship solely on the basis of skin color. This historic fact has made very real differences in the behavior of both whites and blacks. The resentment over deprivation of their birthright has made large numbers of the American Negroes militant in their fight for first-class citizenship. Highly articulate Negroes with great organizational abilities have capitalized on this militancy. The clarion call of the freedom sermon is effectively expressed in Martin Luther King's letter from a Birmingham jail:[7]

. . . I am in Birmingham because injustice is here. Just as the prophets of the eighth century B.C. left their villages and carried their 'thus saith the Lord' far beyond the boundaries of their home towns, and just as the Apostle Paul left his village of Tarsus and carried the gospel of Jesus Christ to the far corners of the Greco-Roman world, so am I compelled to carry the gospel of freedom beyond my own home town. Like Paul, I must constantly respond to the Macedonian call for aid.

[6] Stewart Henderson Britt, *Social Psychology of Modern Life* (New York: Rinehart, 1941), p. 427.

[7] Martin Luther King, Jr., *Why We Can't Wait* (New York: New American Library, 1964), p. 77.

Unfortunately, even the most capable of the Negro leaders cannot control the lunatic fringe of their followers—witness the bloody and apparently senseless riots in Harlem, Philadelphia, etc., in the summer of 1964.

"Moderate" Negro leaders such as King were being pushed aside by late 1964; and many responsible Negro leaders had considered King to be "radical" in early 1963. Negro militancy mushroomed in 1963 and 1964. 1965 saw the responsible leaders further losing control, while spontaneous street riots broke out with no apparent leadership or organization. The extended riots in Watts, California, in the summer of 1965, finally communicated to the leaders of the power structure of America that the Negro was committed to a genuine grass-roots rebellion. Clear need had been demonstrated for prompt and positive programs to strike at the roots of the conditions of poverty which generated a "Watts." Had the leaders seen the need in time? Popular support must be generated for such sweeping programs if they are to be successfully implemented. Congress saw the need—and embraced *in toto* the legislative programs proposed by President Johnson for the War on Poverty. Only time will tell if these programs will be accepted by the great mass of the American people. A realistic appraisal of the situation appeared in the August, 1965, issue of *Change,* publication of the Center for the Study of Democratic Institutions.[8]

Members of the Center, like most Americans, have been discussing the meaning of the Los Angeles riots and speculating about what should now be done. There is general agreement that repressive or punitive measures make no sense. "It depends on what you're aiming at," one staff member commented. "Some people want to strike back because of the discomfort and guilty feelings that the riots have caused in them. So they ask for more police, and want the entire community penalized. This course will merely insure bigger and more costly commotion in the future. The right thing to aim at is a program that will do away with the conditions—personal, economic, and social—that brought on the uprising in the first place. The effort should be to show that an intelligent city can learn from its mistakes by turning the devastated area into a model community."

Extremist groups, both black and white, further contributed to the turmoil of the times. Groups such as the Klu Klux Klan, the White Citizens Council, National Association for the Advancement of White People, and certain activities of the John Birch Society deliberately inflamed the white man. They sought to intensify racial prejudice where it existed, and to create racial prejudice where there was none. The Black Muslims were perhaps the best known of the hate groups on the Negro side of the ledger in the 1960's—but there were many such organized groups of

[8] "Can We Learn from the Riots?" *Change,* Vol. I, No. 6 (August 1965), p. 1 (Santa Barbara: Fund for the Republic, Inc.)

Negroes dedicated to fostering of racial prejudice. Unscrupulous leaders, both black and white, used these extremist groups for personal ends. Among the many and varied causes of the Watts and other riots of the 1960's surely must be counted the hate-fostering activities of these extremist groups.

Segments of the Negro population have become outwardly subservient to the white man. The confusions in the American culture as to the value to be placed upon aggressiveness make it easy for the white man to rationalize his prejudices; no matter whether the Negro fights for his birthrights or accepts the *status quo*, the white man rejects the Negro's behavior as containing either too little or too much aggressiveness. The Negro who maintains a judicious balance in his behavior is not credited with such wisdom, for selected portions of his behavior are misrepresented by the whites as examples of both extremes. The deep prejudice felt by many whites, combined with his high visibility and large numbers (approximately one of every ten Americans), have made the American Negro the center of the greatest intergroup conflict in America today. The contemporary Negro rebellion intensifies this conflict on all levels. Some authorities on human relations, as well as some scholars in the field of social psychology, are conjecturing as to whether the greatest potential source of conflict lies in this very segment of the Negro populace. The subservient Negro is labeled as an "Uncle Tom" and rejected by his own people. These are angry men. To the resentment engendered by his very subserviency is added the pain of total social isolation. Normal outlets for relief of tension are denied them. The role of subserviency demands a calm demeanor. In the face of a genuine Negro rebellion, how long can the "Uncle Toms" contain their righteous wrath? When and how will it be vented? These are among the most intelligent, best-adjusting Negroes. If the power structure does not take intelligent action before this group joins the Negro Revolution, the power structure may find itself out of power. This may be in the best interests of the future of America—but it will come only after long and violent struggle.

Evidence of discrimination against the Negro exists in nearly every area of American life: housing, recreation, church membership, economic opportunity, and education. Negroes have a larger incidence of disease and a shorter life span than whites, largely due to deficiencies in health facilities, education, housing, and economic opportunity. Negroes have suffered a greater ratio of delinquency and crime than have the whites, largely because the discriminatory practices of the whites have forced Negroes to live in conditions that breed vice; for example, the big city slums are largely owned by absentee landlords who perpetuate slum conditions for personal profit. Furthermore, if the Negro tries to escape slum conditions by moving out of them, he finds that houses in desirable locations are not readily available to him. If he does succeed in locating in a desirable area, "For Sale" signs are likely to sprout on his neighbors' lawns.

Finally, the whole complex of lower-class Negro culture violates the middle-class mores of the white-Anglo-Protestant majority group in America. Honesty, cleanliness, and thrift are noticeably deficient in large segments of lower-class American Negro culture. The white man accepts none of the blame for this, any more than he accepts the blame for similar deficiencies in lower-class white culture. Rather than examine his own discriminatory practices, which have forced a large proportion of the Negro population into a lower-class way of life, he shrugs his shoulders in superior fashion and says, "Negroes are born that way." These are the attitudes which must be overcome if the War on Poverty is to be accepted—and be successful! Mr. Van Henderson, Associate Director for Program Services of Atterbury Job Corps Center, comments:[9]

In a social situation such as the Watts riots, we cannot assume that there is any one given cause, but many causes. The unorganized and leaderless lower classes of the Negro society can be considered dangerous. They must have education and leadership. President Johnson's War on Poverty programs are not a luxury but a necessity. The whole of American society depends upon all Americans operating as a unified force to combat the racial, economic, social, and morale problems of the Negro. Our whole system is threatened. We must unite as Americans, not as Negroes and Whites, to preserve the greatest way of life yet extant.

Orientals are held in minority status in most places where they are found in America, but usually they are not subject to the type of discrimination suffered by Negroes. The Oriental problem is a minor one in the total American culture because of the small number of Orientals presently in this country and because of our restrictive immigration policy. But the human misery suffered by any individual Oriental is none the less severe: the Nisei (Japanese-American) camps of World War II offered a dramatic example of the cruelty of the white-Anglo-Protestant group to a minority group.

The American Indian is the one ethnic group that can escape caste status if it so desires. Because of their low visibility, many Indians can leave the reservation and start a new life if they so choose; this is more true for some tribes, of course, than others. Substandard education, housing, health facilities, and economic opportunity characterize the several Indian cultures in America today; all of these factors make especially difficult the breaking of lower-class bonds, even though caste status is escaped.

Whereas severe cultural conflicts currently exist in some sections of the country between Indian groups and the white-Anglo-Protestant majority group, the relatively small numbers of the American Indian and his low visibility make the Indian problem a relatively minor one on a national

[9] The comments by Mr. Henderson do not necessarily reflect official Job Corps policy or opinions; they are the private views of one Job Corps executive.

scale. This does not lessen for the individual Indian the human misery caused by deprivation and discrimination suffered by those who choose to remain with their relatives and friends in the Indian areas.

Religious Differences

Religious discrimination is on a long-term decline in America. Anti-Semitism is our largest religious problem. Entire sections of our large cities have become Jewish in population—at least partly because the Jewish family that moves into a Christian neighborhood does not receive full social acceptance by the neighbors. This social distance is emphasized in our public schools, in which Christian holidays are joyously celebrated— but in which the Jewish child who remains at home to celebrate a Jewish holiday often is counted as an "unexcused absence" on the school rolls and is given "make-up" assignments. This works a special hardship on the Jewish child because his whole culture prizes education and places a premium on good relations with the teacher.

Discrimination against Jews in the better hotels is declining—but "Sorry, no rooms available" still is a common response in selected establishments. Some housing areas still have restrictive covenants in the deeds against sale to Jews and Negroes. These restrictive deeds have been declared illegal; but "gentlemen's agreements" are an effective technique in the continuing of discriminatory practices.

Anti-Catholicism has taken an upsurge in recent years. The constitutional separation of church and state in the schools may be at least partly responsible. Separately maintained schools may lead to lack of understanding between groups with different backgrounds (Roman Catholic versus Protestant, Jew, and those with no religious affiliation): although two recent studies, separated by half a continent, found no empirical evidence to support this assumption.[10, 11] The rock of contention on which federal aid to the schools has foundered in the past several sessions of Congress has been the method of distribution within the states as related to children in private and parochial schools versus children in public schools. In the aftermath of the Supreme Court decision of May 17, 1954, holding racial segregation unconstitutional, the racial problem has overshadowed the religious one; but the religious issue alone effectively blocked further federal aid to schools. The crux of the problem is that some states furnish free transportation, textbooks, health services, and the like to all children of the state; some states furnish money for the support of education only to *public school* children. N.E.A.-sponsored bills have proposed that any new federal aid funds be distributed in the same fashion as other state funds. Some Protestants as well as some Catholics have attacked this

[10] Joseph H. Fichter, S.J., *Parochial School* (Notre Dame, University of Notre Dame Press, 1958).

[11] Peter H. and Alice S. Rossi, "Some Effects of Parochial School Education in America," *Daedalus*. Cambridge, American Academy of Arts and Sciences, Vol. 90, No. 2 (Spring, 1961), pp. 300–328.

provision. A high point of the controversy was reached in the widely publicized debate between Eleanor Roosevelt and Francis Cardinal Spellman
in 1954; then debate subsided until the early days of the Kennedy administration. The emphasis on federal aid to education shifted from "general"
aid to highly specific programs for provision of science equipment, language laboratories, government loans and grants to college students, etc.
The Catholic universities profited from these federal funds. Much furore
has been created in educational and in religious circles over this use of
federal funds to further Catholic higher education, thereby further contributing to the consolidation of anti-Catholic prejudices.

Religious discrimination against Catholics has been most pronounced
in the area of job opportunities. To write "Catholic" in the space provided
for religious preference on some job application forms was, in the 1920's,
tantamount to automatic loss of chance to secure the job; on others, religious preference was the deciding factor in choosing between equivalent
candidates. Civil rights legislation designed to assist the Negro has proved
of significant value to the Catholic job-hunter. Many states now have civil
rights laws, enforced by separate civil rights commissions, making illegal
the identification of a job candidate by race, color, or creed. These laws
were codified at the national level by the *Civil Rights Act of 1964*. Both
labor and management are experiencing major difficulty with this Act. If
one cannot discriminate on the basis of sex, then does a *man*, also, lose
his job after the birth of his first child? Or a second illegitimate child?
These are common management policies affecting women. Test cases are
in the courts at the time of this writing. The language of the Act appears
clear. Management policies affecting only women appear doomed.

There has been much discussion as to the effect of separate parochial
school systems in maintaining religious discrimination against Catholics.
At the very least, separate school systems limit contact between the Catholic and Protestant children. This deliberate segregation of children of the
two faiths could mean limiting the growth of understandings between the
groups, limiting the friendship ties that play a large part in securing some
jobs, and even the conscious building of antagonistic feelings through the
demonstration of differences fostered by the maintenance of separate
school systems. In the light of recent studies that find no evidence to support these assumptions, it seems more likely that anti-Catholic sentiments
have continuing reinforcement from the feeling among many Protestants
that the vigorous recent growth in the parochial school system of the
Roman Catholic Church has been accompanied by growing Catholic resistance to school taxes for public schools. The "federal aid to education"
controversy has reached the local level.

As in the case of anti-Semitism, parental fears of intermarriage probably
play a significant part in the building of anti-Catholic and anti-Protestant
prejudice in children. Research evidence indicates the instability of mixed-
faith marriages, thereby reinforcing the fears of parents. Whatever the
reasons, there seems to be some increase in anti-Catholicism in recent

years.[12] This is not to intimate that individual Catholics cannot overcome the generalized feeling of anti-Catholicism—witness the popularity of President John Fitzgerald Kennedy.

National Differences

National differences, fortunately, are mainly of historic interest in America; the treatment of Spanish Americans is the exception to the trend. During the past generation there has been little immigration. Our high population mobility has helped to disperse the second generation from the "foreign Colonies" in our large cities. With differences mini-mized through removal of the foreign accent and through dispersion of residence throughout the total population, second-generation immigrants have only minor problems of acculturation. Some discrimination based on national origins still persists, but severe problems are limited to a few recently immigrating groups.

This has not always been true in America. The waves of Irish in the 1850's, the Germans in the 1880's, and the southeastern Europeans in the twentieth century have suffered, each in their turn, from discriminatory practices of the established residents. In times of prosperity the immigrant was welcomed as source of cheap labor—but was held at a social distance as an inferior being. He did not talk, dress, think, or even eat like the older Americans. He had different ideas on how to rear his children. His diet seemed peculiar. In short, he was different. Because he was different, he must be inferior. Because he was inferior, he was not acceptable to "100 per cent" Americans. He could secure housing only in slum areas; since the areas where he lived had a high incidence of crime and violence, he was blamed for "crime waves." In times of economic depression, dis-criminatory practices grew much more severe. He was blamed for the de-pression. He was vilified by movements such as the Know Nothing Party of the mid-nineteenth century, the Ku Klux Klan of the 1920's, and the National Council for American Education of the post World War II period. He was subject to all the physical misery of the lowest class in times of depression, plus the psychological torture of the social outcast.

Spanish Americans currently are subject to many of the historic dis-criminatory practices noted above. Puerto Rican immigrants, particularly in the New York City area, are suffering heavy discrimination. The un-skilled laborer with limited or no command of the English language re-ceives only the lowest-paying positions, and lives in the least desirable quarters. Acculturation is to the norm of his neighbors—the lower-class American Negro. Severe problems related to itinerant Mexican laboring groups occur in the Southwest and Far West. Negro-Mexican and Negro-Puerto Rican marriages produce offspring that are subject to the minority-status problems of both groups.

---

[12] For an excellent study of the many problems merely touched on in this section, the student is referred to Will Herberg, *Protestant—Catholic—Jew: An Essay in American Religious Sociology* (New York: Doubleday, 1956).

Regional Differences

As we have indicated in Chapter 11, there are great currents of population movement in America. Some of these relocations of large segments of the population cause severe problems of intergroup relations. The southern white mountaineer who moves to the industrial cities of the North enters an entirely new culture, where he may experience discrimination from the established residents. The southern Negro who moves from the cotton fields to the northern cities must adjust to new ways of living; his problems of adjustment may be accentuated by discrimination based both on color and on regional differences. The pensioner who retires to the West Coast may be resented by families with school-age children as a potential threat to the passage of school tax levies, and by the general populace as a potential drain on the entire taxable wealth of the state through eligibility for state pensions. The problems of each group are different and are specific to the characteristics and needs of the groups involved—but the general pattern of discrimination through fear of the newcomer is employed against most of them.

So it goes for the victims of discrimination, whether the prejudice be based on differences in social class, race, religion, national origin, or region. Each minority group is different from another, but all suffer discrimination—for, as Hirsh so aptly put it, " . . . the victims of prejudice have little to do with the cause of it. They are likely to be people whom a tragic combination of circumstances has rendered both accessible and vulnerable and therefore eminently suited for victimization by those casting around for someone on whom to unleash the full force of their fears."[13]

RATIONALE OF INTERGROUP PROBLEMS

There must be some reason or reasons for Americans who profess to believe in democracy to violate those beliefs through maltreatment of fellow Americans. This dilemma is compounded when one reflects that most Americans profess to adhere to the values of the Judaeo-Christian tradition, and that discrimination and persecution violate all the precepts embedded in these faiths. Teachers need to summarize the salient facts of the psychology of groups in an attempt to clarify these reasons.

We have tended to treat the diverse groups in America on a majority-minority basis. The majority have power on their side, so we have not concerned ourselves with their problems. This does not mean that they have no problems, *for the deterioration of the moral fiber of the majority group through discriminatory practices that violate their democratic and Judeo-Christian values is a major reason for the psychic unrest of our times.* Allport estimates that "group prejudice is an active force in the lives of perhaps four-fifths of our fellow-citizens."[14] In the following brief pres-

13 Selma G. Hirsh, *The Fears Men Live By* (New York: Harper, 1955), p. 104.
14 Gordon W. Allport, *The Bigot in Our Midst* (New York: American Jewish Committee, 1957), p. 2.

entation of the social psychology of discrimination, perhaps the implications for deterioration of the moral fiber of the majority group will become more clear. The major purpose of this section, however, is to enable educators better to understand the psychology of prejudice as a first step in formulating plans to combat it.

Minority Status

Minority status is not a quantitative affair but a qualitative one. The basis for minority status is lack of power and prestige. The evidence of minority status is discrimination. The attitudinal configuration that leads to discrimination is prejudice; namely an attitude of prejudging individuals on the basis of their race, social class, religion, national origin, region, or some other characteristic.

Origins of Prejudice

How does prejudice come to be? Basically it stems from a feeling that one culture, class, race, religion, or other group is superior to another. Then how do we get that way? Why do we feel superior? In the past decade much new knowledge has become available on the dynamics of prejudice. A monumental series has been completed under the sponsorship of the American Jewish Committee.[15] In a popular interpretation of this series, founded in great part on *The Authoritarian Personality*, Hirsh states that "the central thesis of this book is that people are prejudiced because they are afraid. They use their prejudices to conceal their fears."[16]

Men suffer from fears largely because they fail to develop as children the basic emotional security necessary for the integrating personality. Disturbed personalities may reach for emotional security through feelings of superiority. If an individual feels that his group is superior to another group, he enjoys the personal security of his own worth as compared to that of individuals of the "out-group," and also the group security gained by power of group action. Hitler capitalized on this phenomenon of group psychology by propagating the myth of Aryan superiority.

Another major origin of prejudice is the sociological fact that majority influence establishes the patterns of behavior for any society, and that minorities are "judged" by their degree of conformity to the established cultural norms. The white-Anglo-Protestant figure is dominant in contemporary America. Middle-class values are the cultural norm. Any other color, national origin, religion, or class value will be prejudged by the majority group in terms of its degree of conformity to the majority pattern. Your authors will maintain, in a later section on the integration crisis, that this was a major source of the resistance to school integration. Your authors feel that white parents did not picket the public schools of

---

[15] Max Horkheimer and Samuel H. Flowerman (ed.), Studies in Prejudice Series. *The Authoritarian Personality; Dynamics of Prejudice; Anti-Semitism and Emotional Disorder; Rehearsal for Destruction;* and *Prophets of Deceit* (New York: Harper, 1949–1950).

[16] Selma G. Hirsh, *op. cit.*, p. xi.

New York City because their children were attending school with Negroes and Puerto Ricans, but because their children were in classes with children whose cultural background did not allow them to progress academically at the same speed as children with middle-class backgrounds. In short, they felt that their children were being sacrificed on the altar of integration. This is a common source of great tensions in our culture. Those persons now accepted as middle class strive to maintain their place, while others exert great effort to attain these coveted values.[17]

Another good example of judging by degree of conformity to the established cultural norms is discrimination based on national origins.

The newly arrived immigrant was the subject of much discrimination. He had left his old culture but had not yet assimilated the new. He clung to old ways of doing things because he knew no other ways. He might not even have had a working knowledge of English. Second-generation immigrants were reared in the new culture and assimilated as many of its patterns as were not in violent conflict with parental patterns. The third generation had virtually escaped discrimination based on national origins, for the new ways of living were firmly entrenched—but social class discrimination may persist because of the relegation of his grandfathers to the lower class. Individuals may escape class bonds. The middle-class values taught in the public schools are their greatest aid in escape.

Finally, the psychological climate of the times may intensify mild prejudice into overt discrimination by the majority group.[18] This may be only verbal, as exemplified by name-calling. More often it develops into denial of job opportunities, with the attendant deprivations in health, nutrition, housing, and clothing. Some of the crises in men's affairs that accentuate prejudice are wars, depressions, floods, drought, and other national calamities. In such times the psychological insecurity of the majority group leads them to seek a scapegoat. Minority groups are convenient victims on which to vent their frustrations. It has been reported, for example, that the incidence of Negro lynchings in the South is highly correlated with the price of cotton.

The psychological climate of the times also may intensify existing prejudices through actions of the minority group. The mass sit-ins, freedom marches, forced school integration, etc., of the 1960's undoubtedly forced many whites to re-examine their color prejudices. Surely many persons subject only to mild, generalized feelings of prejudice became victims of intensified, specific prejudices when their children were bussed from the white, suburban school to the predominantly Negro school in a slum neighborhood.

Perpetuation of Prejudice

An oversimplification of the basic reasons for the persistence of prejudice and discrimination in a democratic Judeo-Christian nation would be the

[17] Margaret Rasmussen (ed.), *Implications of Basic Human Values for Education* (Washington: Association for Childhood Education International, 1964), p. 38.
[18] Gordon W. Allport, *op. cit.*, p. 3.

statement that prejudice persists because of (1) ignorance and (2) insecurity. Both are broad terms. Some space will be devoted to delineating the ways in which ignorance and insecurity perpetuate prejudice.

By *ignorance* we mean lack of understanding, both of one's own self and of other people. A man does not always possess full knowledge even of the values by which he guides his own life. He may pledge $1,000 to his church for the support of African missions and secure the $1,000 by charging exorbitant rentals to Negro inhabitants of his slum tenements. He may be convinced that he gave to the mission fund because of Christian compassion for fellow human beings. Could it be that he really pledged because his church group expected it of one in his financial position? And that he fulfilled that expectation in order to maintain his social status? If so, then ignorance of one's own motivations, with the attendant failure to live by a consistent set of values, is one major reason for the perpetuation of prejudice. Certainly the first step toward success in intergroup relations is to "know thyself."

Ignorance of the conditions in which one's fellow man lives certainly is a contributing factor toward the perpetuation of minority status. Full knowledge of minority cultures and full understandings of *why* different groups behave differently would provide a sound basis for rational solutions to intergroup problems. These knowledges must be implemented by emotional conditioning designed for acceptance and appreciation of others.[19] Absence of accurate data about minority group fosters stereotyping, tabloid thinking, racism, and chauvinism. This is not meant to imply that the supplying of knowledge alone will yield significant returns in improved intergroup relations; experience with informational programs has indicated their limitations, as will be shown later. Effective use of informational techniques involves utilizing knowledge as a first step in emotional acceptance of likenesses. Understanding without identification is of limited effectiveness; what is needed is empathy, not sympathy.

Insecurity is a second major block to the Brotherhood of Man. Basically, all insecurity is psychological; but for purposes of discussion, two broad areas contributing to insecurity will be discussed separately: denial of man's emotional needs, and denial of man's physical needs.

One means of finding emotional security is through association with people like one's self in order to convince one's self of one's own worth. This leads to the formation of "in-groups." The in-group then comprises a pressure group to foster its own welfare. Discrimination against other groups thus enhances not only the political, social, and economic welfare of the group but also bolsters the psychological security of its members through a feeling of superiority to other groups. When things go wrong, the minority group becomes a scapegoat, thus allowing the majority group to escape guilt feelings (feelings of inferiority) for allowing its affairs to deteriorate. The challenge to the White-Anglo-Protestant "in-group" dur-

---

[19] Hilda Taba (ed.), *Elementary Curriculum in Intergroup Relations* (Washington: American Council on Education, 1950), p. 25.

ing the integration crisis of the early 1960's led to frustrations among Caucasians so evident that a national candidate for office attempted to capitalize on the "white back-lash." It is a tribute to the white man's conscience that, despite his obvious feelings of insecurity in the face of the apparent power of the Negroid minority group, no significant block of votes seems to have been delivered to the candidate—with the possible exception of the eleven states of the old Confederacy.

Tabloid thinking plays a significant part in perpetuating prejudice. Man thinks only as a last resort, for thinking is painful; what is more natural than the acceptance of stereotyped concepts as a basis for justifying the venting of his angers and frustrations on a minority group? Why complicate matters by thinking of individuals when we can rationalize our discrimination against an individual by claiming that his entire group is characterized by negative traits? The verbalizing of these stereotyped concepts leads still others of our own group into tabloid thinking; thus is started a new cycle of bigotry, spreading from the newly affected individual.

Allport notes: "Besides venting our fury upon scapegoats for their alleged vices, we go still further and blame them specifically for our *own* sins and shortcomings. The term psychologists give this mental twist is projection."[20] Projecting our faults upon others allows us to escape our feelings of personal guilt, thus bolstering our emotional security.

Economic insecurity leads to at least retrenching of man's physical needs for food, clothing, shelter, and recreation, if not to actual deprivation. Economic insecurity tightens the bonds of the majority group and intensifies its discriminatory practices to protect its own welfare, at the same time that it intensifies scapegoating to relieve guilt feelings and to reassert its own status. Previously mild prejudices may grow into bigotry under the pressures of physical insecurity. Some recognition of the importance of this aspect of the situation seems to have been evident in the federal "War on Poverty" commencing with the *Economic Opportunity Act of 1964* and continued through a series of legislative and executive actions designed to relieve economic insecurity.

Nonrational Nature of Prejudice

The above discussion of the social psychology of discrimination presupposes a basic knowledge of the psychology of learning on the part of the reader. Let us briefly summarize, at this point, the psychology of the learning of attitudes as it affects the above discussion.

Discrimination is overt action. Prejudice is the attitudinal configuration that motivates the act of discrimination. Like most attitudes, *prejudice is learned nonrationally*. Davis[21] says that attitudes are learned (1) by integration of numerous specific responses of a similar type; thus, a series of unpleasant emotional experiences with a certain group of people will lead

---

[20] Gordon W. Allport, *op. cit.*, p. 4.
[21] Jerome Davis, "Study of 163 Outstanding Communist Leaders," *Proceedings*, American Sociological Society, **24** (1930), pp. 42–45.

one to generalize, "All such people are unpleasant," without any rational investigation of the total group; (2) through a single traumatic experience; (3) through general approach or withdrawal tendencies; and (4) through imitation of the attitudes of others in order to secure their affection.

The nonrational nature of prejudice has implications for educators, both in the original learning of these attitudes and in the relearning process that supplants negative attitudes with positive ones. Nonrational, emotional experiences are the ones that implant prejudice. The educator needs to utilize this knowledge. The approach to intergroup problems dare not be a coldly scientific one or it is doomed to failure. Attitudes are not formed in rational fashion. Rational approaches need to be strongly reinforced through presentation in highly emotional situations. The teacher needs to be an "actor," with a sound working knowledge of all of the dramatic techniques available to the intergroup educator. This is true both for the original implantation of attitudes and for the supplanting of negative attitudes. Psychiatrists utilize psychodrama for the securing of maximum emotional involvement of the individual in psychiatric treatment of negative attitudes. The educator does not have the technical competence for the use of psychodrama; but sociodrama and other techniques that secure a relatively high degree of emotional involvement are available to him. The above notation by Davis about the adoption of the attitudes of others in order to gain their favor certainly operates daily in classroom and playground situations, through the adoption by children of the attitudes that teacher displays toward members of minority groups. Teachers need to demonstrate clearly their own warm, friendly feelings toward minority-group members, and must utilize emotional techniques with individuals and with groups, if they are to be successful in the supplanting of negative attitudes and in the implanting of positive ones.

The above is not meant to imply that educators are not currently using emotional techniques. The daily pledge to the flag, the giving of thanks before the mid-morning lunch, class discussions of emotionally charged problems, the satisfying experience of successful committee work with members of other groups, the warm smile and hug of the primary teacher for the newcomer in her room, and the use of dramatic films are but a few examples of the many ways in which educators are recognizing the interdependence of intellectual and emotional learnings.

Toward the Resolution of Intergroup Problems

The short-term solution to intergroup problems in America seems to be legal action to protect the rights of minorities and to improve the economic and social status of underprivileged groups. The long-term solution seems to be education. Both legal action and educative forces must be brought to bear on those areas where the effects of discrimination are most severely felt: employment, housing, recreation, and education. Industry must bear a major share of the responsibility for ending discriminatory practices in employment. Labor must open the doors to apprenticeships in the skilled trades. Surely the public schools bear a major responsibility, but full discussion of the role of the school will be deferred until the final sections of this chapter. Federal legal action—including federal legislation, Presidential investigations, executive orders and enforcement agencies, and Supreme Court decisions—and agencies of education other than the schools will be discussed below.

Legal Action

Social legislation needs both to protect the legal rights of the populace and to improve the economic and social welfare of all citizens. We shall discuss briefly American social legislation and other steps of a legal nature currently affecting minority groups, with some consideration of the speed with which such steps should proceed.

(1) LEGAL STEPS TO PROTECT THE RIGHTS OF MINORITIES. Laws do not, of course, eliminate prejudice. However, a state may be neutral with respect to the acts of the citizen affecting the rights of minorities, or it may be positive in taking measures to prevent acts of discrimination against those minorities. Some states, such as Nazi Germany or the Union of South Africa, have taken active steps to deny or restrict rights and privileges to certain minorities. The trend in recent years in the United States has been toward positive efforts on the part of the government to protect the rights of minorities, as opposed to a somewhat neutral policy followed in earlier years.

Most of these legal measures have been taken since 1941, under the pressure of World War II and of post-World War II events. President Franklin D. Roosevelt in 1941 and 1943 issued executive orders prohibiting discrimination on government contracts and requiring a clause in such contracts that would prevent discrimination against any employee or applicant because of race, creed, color, or national origin. He set up the Federal Fair Employment Practice Committee to police these executive orders. After World War II, President Truman attempted to make the FEPC a permanent agency, but the proposal was turned down by Congress. President Truman soon afterward issued an executive order declaring nondiscrimination to be government policy and requiring the same policy of all government contractors. President Eisenhower, in 1953, confirmed the policy of nondiscrimination and in 1955 set up a President's Committee on Government Employment Policy to supervise the nondiscrimination program in federal employment. The President's Committee on Government Contracts set up by Eisenhower in 1953 continues the work of President Truman's early committee in this area. By 1956 at least fifteen states had FEPC laws. However, some of these laws were in the nature of general education, persuasion, and consultation. Many of the latter were not very effective even in this area. In addition, thirty-six towns and cities (many of these in states not having FEPC laws) had set up their own fair-employment groups by 1956. Presidents Kennedy and Johnson capitalized

on the climate of the early 1960's to secure formalization of nondiscrimina-
tory (and, in many instances, compensatory) employment practices among
the large corporations through the President's Committee on Equal Employment Opportunity's "Plans for Progress" programs.

In 1945 President Truman set up a committee on civil rights[22] which
investigated the condition of civil rights for minorities and made a report
in 1947. A considerable change has been made in the segregation rules of
the armed forces. Starting in 1946 changes were brought about so that by
1954 almost all of the segregation practices of the armed forces had been
eliminated. In 1946 the Navy opened all of its jobs to Negroes and slowly
began to mix the races. In 1948 the Air Force did the same. Although the
Army made some earlier attempts to integrate, it was not until the period
of the Korean War that integration actually was achieved and given a
first test in battle. By June, 1954, all Negroes were serving in nonsegre-
gated units.[23] By contrast, Civil Service regulations prohibiting discriminatory practices continued to be ignored through the 1950's.[24] It was not
until the late President Kennedy made it clear to the heads of all government agencies that he expected them to increase the number of Negroes
in government jobs, especially in jobs at the middle and upper levels of
responsibility, that integration became truly effective in the Civil Service
structure.[25] The most sweeping civil rights law since Reconstruction days
was signed into law by President Johnson on July 2, 1964. The thirteen
titles of the *Civil Rights Act of 1964* encompass voting rights, places of
public accommodation, public facilities, public education, commission on
civil rights, federally assisted programs, equal employment opportunity,
registration and voting statistics, intervention and procedure, community
relations service, and miscellaneous provisions.

Prior to the enactment of the *Civil Rights Act of 1964*, Supreme Court
decisions with respect to the enforcement of civil rights provisions and
with respect to declaring unconstitutional certain laws and practices had
been more important than new laws. Starting with the Gaines decision
concerning the right of Negroes to higher education and continuing to the
school segregation decision of 1954, the Court has strongly affirmed a
nonsegregation policy in the schools; this is consistent with the many
decisions with respect to civil rights on railroads and other similar matters.
The 1954 school segregation decision is a complete reversal of the Plessy
vs. Ferguson decision in 1896, which confirmed a law requiring racial segregation. This latter has been called the "separate but equal" decision. Im-

[22] *To Secure These Rights: The Report of the President's Committee on Civil
Rights* (Washington, D.C.: Govt. Printing Office, 1947).
[23] Cf. George Eaton Simpson and J. Milton Yinger, *Racial and Cultural Minorities:
An Analysis of Prejudice and Discrimination* (New York: Harper, 1953), pp. 451–
455. Also Elgin F. Hunt, *Social Science: An Introduction to the Study of Society*
(New York: Macmillan, 1955), p. 259.
[24] Mahlon T. Puryear, Associate Director of the National Urban League, in an
unpublished speech at the 1963 National Conference of the Urban League.
[25] Charles E. Silberman, *Crisis in Black and White* (New York: Random House,
1964), p. 241.

plementation of the Supreme Court decision of May 17, 1954, is another matter. Ten years after the decision, only one Negro child in 100 was attending school with white pupils in the eleven states of the Deep South.[26]

While northern school systems generally have rendered prompt compliance with the Supreme Court edict against *de jure* segregation, the major battles of school segregation of the early 1960's have been waged in the North. There has been an influx into central cities of Negro families. This has produced, because of neighborhood residential patterns, *de facto* school segregation in many of the big cities.

Among other developments has been the increase in the setting up of public and private intergroup agencies to assist in the protection of the legal rights of minorities and to work for the improvement of their status.[27] While most public agencies are less than twenty years old, the leading private agencies have contributed more than fifty years of service to date. There are a total of 61 private agencies. There are 48 state private agencies. There are 30 cities that have municipal (public) intergroup relations agencies with paid staffs, and in addition there are 266 local private agencies with paid staffs. This does not include certain special groups that work on special problems, such as those of immigrants. A trend is evident in the increase of both public and private agencies in this field.

(2) LEGAL MEASURES DESIGNED TO IMPROVE ECONOMIC AND SOCIAL STATUS OF UNDERPRIVILEGED GROUPS. Many of the social changes that have been inaugurated by the federal and state governments from the depression years to the present have been of special value to underprivileged minorities. Although these measures were designed to relieve distress from a number of causes, they have been especially helpful to the minorities that have been economically underprivileged. Federal laws dealing with minimum wages, unemployment benefits, housing, school lunches, aid to dependent children, relief, old-age insurance, medical aid, and other kinds of social security have been of great help to the underprivileged segments of our society. Although there are many problems here that have not as yet been completely alleviated (Dewhurst estimates that in 1950 one fifth of the population was ill fed, one fourth ill clothed, and one third ill housed[28]), certainly the net result of these laws has been to reduce the amount of serious suffering in the lower, underprivileged classes and thus to reduce the extremes of poverty in the United States. The March on Washington on August 28, 1963, the high point of good feelings between activists in the civil rights movement and white people sympa-

[26] "A Decade of Desegregation," *Education U.S.A.*, May 14, 1964 (Washington, D.C.: National School Public Relations Association, N.E.A.).

[27] The authors are especially indebted to Miss Janet Smith of the Cincinnati Mayor's Friendly Relations Committee, who made available to them the results of a recent study by the National Association of Intergroup Relation Officials (NAIRO) and gave them access to an advance copy of a directory of intergroup relations agencies having paid staffs.

[28] J. Frederick Dewhurst and Associates, *America's Needs and Resources: A New Summary* (New York: Twentieth Century Fund, 1955), pp. 158, 194, 224.

thetic to the cause,[29] seems to have triggered a series of legislative acts designed to alleviate poverty: the Anti-poverty Act, Appalachian Relief, etc. At the time of this writing, it is too early to assess the effectiveness of this legislation. Director Sargent Shriver says, "We are developing yard sticks to measure our achievements."

(3) THE TIMING OF DEMOCRATIC LEGAL ACTION.   Legislation that does more than to codify the mores precipitates conflict. A good example of this is the southern reaction to racial integration in the public schools. Many southern cities and states have laws that codify the mores of the southern whites on this issue. The Supreme Court has held these local laws unconstitutional. Where even the supreme law of the land, the Constitution, conflicts with local mores, violence erupts.

Legislators need to be aware of this basic sociological fact when drafting laws. Legislation that departs too radically from the established mores may cause more human misery than it alleviates. In the case of racial integration in the schools, Gunnar Myrdal points out that the white man's conscience is probably the greatest force operating toward eventual acceptance by the South of the Supreme Court's reinterpretation of the Constitution.[30] In one sense, this is codification of national mores before they had been fully assimilated by one section of the country. This was bound to lead to sectional conflict. One wonders, as one observes the caste status of the Negro in the North, if these mores had fully solidified in any section of the country.

Writing twenty years later, Silberman agrees with Myrdal that codification in advance of the mores causes conflict, but questions Myrdal's interpretation of the white man's motivation.[31]

Gunnar Mydal concluded that "the American Negro problem is a problem in the heart of the American," and titled his monumental study of the Negro *An American Dilemma*. Myrdal was wrong. The tragedy of race relations in the United States is that there is no "American Dilemma." White Americans are not torn and tortured by conflict between their devotion to the American creed and their actual behavior. They are upset by the current state of race relations, to be sure. But what troubles them is not that justice is being denied but that their peace is being shattered and their business interrupted.

Social legislation, of course, must go beyond the mores; otherwise there would be no need for such legislation. There is a fine line of demarcation, however, between social legislation that will be reluctantly accepted and social legislation that will precipitate bitter and prolonged conflict designed to further factionalize the nation. This psychological evaluation in terms

---

[29] William Lee Miller, "Civil Rights in the North," *Current*, October 1964, Number 52 (New York: Current, Inc.).

[30] Gunnar Myrdal, *An American Dilemma* (New York: Harper, 1944).

[31] Charles E. Silberman, *Crisis in Black and White* (New York: Random House, 1964), p. 10.

of predicted acceptance or rejection should be a critical factor in the consideration of even the most-needed social legislation. Democracy has demonstrated its ability to achieve *peaceful* change, at a moderate pace, through cooperative action.

Industrial Recruitment and Employment Practices

Concurrent with legal action by the government and partly as a result of it, industrial recruitment and employment practices significantly have altered the complexion of racial discrimination in employment in recent years. This has been a key area of progress. Of what use are integrated restaurants, if the average Negro cannot afford the price of a meal? Acquisition and retention of something more than menial jobs is the only solid fulcrum on which the Negro can lever his way upward.

(1) MANAGEMENT PRACTICES. Writing in the immediate wake of the "long, hot summer" of 1963, Reverend Martin Luther King, Jr., was caustic in his comments concerning management practices.[32]

The summer of 1963 was a revolution because it changed the face of America. Freedom was contagious. Its fever boiled in nearly one thousand cities, and by the time it had passed its peak, many thousands of lunch counters, hotels, parks and other places of public accommodation had become integrated.

Slowly and unevenly, job opportunities opened up for Negroes, though these were still more impressive in their promise than in their immediate numbers. In the larger northern cities, a more significant change in employment patterns took shape. Many firms found themselves under fire, not because they employed Negroes, but because they did not. Accustomed to ignoring the question, they were forced by its sudden overwhelming presence into a hasty search for absolving tokens. A well-trained Negro found himself sought out by industry for the first time. Many Negroes were understandably cynical as the door to opportunity was flung open to them as if they were but recent arrivals on the planet. Nevertheless, though the motives were mixed, the Negro could celebrate the slow retreat of discrimination on yet another front.

No less caustic were the critics of the new hiring policies. The public image of the large corporations undoubtedly suffered from the bitter satire of such writers as Art Buchwald.[33]

Ever since the Negroes have been protesting job discrimination and threatening to boycott any company that doesn't hire Negroes, the major corporations have been searching desperately to have at least one Negro on the payroll in something more than a menial position. For the first time the college-

[32] Martin Luther King, Jr., *Why We Can't Wait* (New York: New American Library, 1964), p. 117.
[33] Art Buchwald, "How it Goes with New Hiring Policy," *Cincinnati Enquirer*, September 13, 1963. Reprinted with permission from the *New York Herald Tribune*.

educated Negro is being wooed by large companies who need him desperately to avoid a national boycott. . . .

The search is going on very quietly and no one is willing to talk about it, but the competition is getting so fierce that we wouldn't be surprised if it went something like this. . . .

Two vice presidents of the Mackerel Soda Co. are sent to interview Thomas Jefferson Jones, who holds a B.A. and an M.A. and a Doctor of Philosophy degree from MIT. Before Birmingham, Mr. Jones was working as stock-room clerk in a large New York department store. But now everything has changed.

"Mr. Jones," the first vice president says, "we'd like you to join our company in an executive position."

"If I understand you correctly," Mr. Jones says, "you'd like me to be your executive Negro."

"No, no—that's not it at all," the second vice president says, "We've been searching for some time for somebody with your qualifications to head up our Interdepartmental Bottling and Sales Liaison."

"What is that exactly?"

"It's a new job which would require you to consult and report and make suggestions on managerial procedures that could improve consumer interest on a company level."

"I see," Mr. Jones says. "But you'd want me to sit near the door."

"As a matter of fact, we would, but that has nothing to do with job. . . .

It would appear, to an impartial observer, that writings such as those quoted above from King and Buchwald underrate the intelligence of top management officials in the larger corporations. The "spontaneous" search for the well-qualified Negro graduate by the larger corporations commenced no later than 1960. Management was preparing for the holocaust which seemed bound to come—and which the Southern Baptist Leadership Conference and allied organizations delivered in the summer of 1963. By the time the President's Committee in Equal Opportunity presented industry with a code, hiring policies already had been revised. Industry signed the code, claiming that it only codified their existing practices. It does seem significant, however, that industrial recruitment of Negroes on college campuses experienced a sharp increase in the 1963–64 school year.[34] Further evidence of the acceleration of pace in employment of Negroes appears in a report on the President's Committee on Equal Employment Opportunity on the "Plans for Progress" program, "Employment of non-whites in management categories rose by 43.4 per cent and by 37.4 per cent in professional and administrative jobs . . . in technical jobs, 31.6 per cent.[35] Paradoxically, this seemed only to increase the pressure on industry from Negro organizations. The National Urban League has taken the leadership, supported by other Negro organizations and by informal groupings

[34] "Industry Rushes for Negro Grads," *Business Week*, No. 1908 (April 25, 1964), pp. 78–82.

[35] "Negros Push for Employment Opportunities," *Dun's Review and Modern Industry*, Vol. 83, No. 6, (June, 1964), pp. 59–60.

of Negro ministers, in demanding "compensatory" employment practices. Management of most of the larger companies appears, at the time of this writing, to be honestly endeavoring to practice *equal* employment opportunity for all Americans, regardless of race, color, or creed. They are "compensating" for the difficulties experienced in locating well-qualified Negro applicants by intensifying recruitment activities designed to locate and attract Negro applicants.

This is not the type of "compensatory activity" acceptable to Negro leaders. Mr. Whitney Young, Jr., Executive Director of the National Urban League, has been the most vocal spokesman for the position that the Negro is "owed" compensation in all areas of life—employment, housing, recreation, education, etc.—for three centuries of maltreatment in exactly the same sense that the G.I. was compensated for *four years* of "lost" time during World War II.[36] Silberman[37] discussed the Urban League in 1964 as follows:

The Urban League is proposing that when a Negro and a white have equal qualifications for a job, the former should be given the preference. Militant Negro organizations are demanding considerably more; they are insisting, in effect, that business firms hire Negroes not because they are qualified but because they are Negroes. And they are developing a good deal of muscle to back up their demands for preferential hiring. The most widely used technique is the boycott, or "selective patronage campaign," as Negroes prefer to call it. "Don't buy where you can't work" campaigns were frequent during the 1930's, but they were sporadic and only occasionally effective. The contemporary use of the weapon began in the early sixties in Philadelphia. The campaign was organized and directed by a group of Negro ministers (some 400 ministers co-operated) with no formal organization. The ministers' technique is to approach one company at a time, usually a manufacturer or distributor of consumer products for which a number of competing brands are available—a baker, a dairy, an oil company, a supermarket chain. If the company refuses to negotiate with the ministers, it is given an ultimatum to hire a specified number of Negroes in specified job classifications before a given date; if the demands are ignored, a boycott ensues. With four hundred ministers using their pulpits to announce the boycott, a substantial portion of the Negro population takes part. Some firms—Pepsi-Cola and Esso, for example—have come to terms without a boycott. Others held out—but generally not for long; Gulf Oil capitulated in twelve days, Sun Oil in three months. All told, the ministers have won concessions from twenty-four firms so far. The technique has spread to Boston, New York, Atlanta, Detroit, and other cities, and is bound to be widely imitated. As Rev. Ralph Abernathy, Rev. Martin Luther King's chief lieutenant, says, "Not every Negro is able to go to jail, but every Negro can stop buying a particular brand of bread or milk or gasoline."

[36] Whitney M. Young, Jr., "Domestic Marshall Plan," *New York Times Magazine,* October 6, 1963.

[37] Charles Silberman, *Crisis in Black and White* (New York: Random House, 1964), pp. 238–239.

326 The School in American Society

While activities such as the Philadelphia boycotts attract wide press coverage, the major portion of management activities in selective recruitment and employment practices continue to be confined to the Negro community. Management is on the horns of a dilemma. If they do not provide at least equal—and the line between "equal" and "compensatory" seems very hazy in these middle 1960's—employment opportunity, the Negroes will most certainly boycott their product. If they provide and publicize compensatory employment opportunity, the whites may very possibly boycott their products—and the whites still provide nearly 90 per cent of their domestic market. Industry is frantically searching for appropriate corporate practices as a requisite to their survival.

(2) LABOR PRACTICES. Labor is not so vulnerable as management. Of what use is a boycott of a particular union as a technique for gaining admission into the union? To the discerning Negro, the situation is critical. Of the 18½ million union members, the 1½ million Negro card holders are concentrated in the poorest-paying jobs.[38] For the most part, the craft unions historically have excluded Negroes.

The only feasible solution to the problem of admission of Negroes to trades unions providing apprenticeships for skilled labor seems to be government intervention. The government may be moving in this direction. Adequate laws presently are on the books, if the government chooses to enforce them. At the time of this writing, such enforcement activities are not readily apparent. The President's Committee on Equal Employment Opportunity seems to be busily engaged in pressuring management to employ Negroes at all corporate levels. They do not seem to be quite so busy in pressuring labor unions to admit Negroes to apprenticeship programs that will qualify them for the very jobs for which management is supposed to employ them.

Public reaction to riots such as have hit Rochester, New York, Philadelphia, and Los Angeles may expedite governmental action. The employer contends that he cannot employ Negro skilled labor if Negro skilled labor is not available.[39] If riots tend to become a generalized response of the Negro to this position taken by the employer, some reform within the labor unions must result. Tear gas and riot clubs will not provide a permanent solution—nor should they; the Constitution guarantees every citizen equal treatment under the law. Discriminatory practices in union membership do not represent equal treatment. Job Corps may be the means for getting "one foot in the door." Labor appears, in the early stages of Job Corps, to be receptive to the concept that Job Corps graduates will be admitted to all AFL-CIO unions at the apprentice level. If this becomes reality, the Negro is well on his way to full union membership.

[38] Whitney M. Young, Jr., "Discrimination in Labor Unions," *Vital Speeches of the Day*, (New York: City News Publishing Company), p. 535.
[39] "Why Race Riots Strike 'Nice' Northern City," *Business Week*, No. 1822 (August 1, 1964), p. 24.

(3) NATIONAL URBAN LEAGUE. The Urban League is often mentioned by company executives as being the most professional of the Negro groups. It specializes in working on Negroes' employment and housing problems, while agencies such as NAACP, CORE, and SNVCC concentrate on education and voting. Urban League activities are not only nonviolent in nature—they lead to positive "action" programs. Active cooperation among the Urban League, industry, and philanthropic Foundations has resulted in large cash grants to institute and/or further retraining programs for Negroes.[40] There seems to be no question of the need for such retraining programs. [41, 42] The Negro suffers from cultural deprivation that handicaps him in the beginning reading programs of the elementary grades of school, in acceptance of vocational guidance in secondary school, and in development of positive attitudes in college courses and in job-seeking. There is a critical shortage of well-qualified Negro labor in all but the unskilled categories. The Urban League had taken beginning steps in the retraining program by 1964, and had completed a highly successful year in placing already trained Negroes in appropriate positions through the National Skills Bank.

The basic proposals of the National Urban League[43] in 1963 were (1) A Basic Skills Program for the "Hard Core" Unemployed Negro. The League was dissatisfied with existing federal retraining programs, claiming that the majority of Negroes enrolled in government-financed retraining programs were being trained for menial occupations—practical nursing, shirt pressing, cooking, and service station operation. Negroes were conspicuous by their absence in most of the programs in electronics, machine trades, welding, drafting, and other skilled areas. (2) Demonstration Projects to Increase Opportunities in Apprenticeships. Suggested activities were improving the backward and preparation of Negro youth through general and vocational education (the Deutsch research and demonstration project in ten New York public schools and five day-care centers is an excellent example of a successful demonstration project in general education); changing the attitudes of Negro youth *and of their parents* concerning Negro aptitude and opportunity in the skilled trades; changing the attitudes of the unions; and changing the attitudes of management. (3) An Experimental Recruiting and Placement Program for Negro College Students. The main thesis was that the Negro colleges were providing inadequate guidance and inadequate placement service. It was the respon-

---

[40] "Negro Push for Employment Opportunities," *Dun's Review and Modern Industry*, Vol. 83, No. 6 (June 1964), pp. 59–60.

[41] Stephen Habbe, "Hiring Negro Workers," *The Conference Board Record*, Vol. 1, No. 6 (June 1964), pp. 16–19.

[42] Stephen Habbe, "Recruiting Negro College Graduates," *The Conference Board Record*, Vol. 1, No. 8 (August 1964), pp. 7–9.

[43] Mahlon T. Puryear, "Problems and Trends in Job Development and Employment," (unpublished speech before the 1963 National Conference of the Urban League at the Statler-Hilton Hotel in Los Angeles, July 29, 1963).

328 The School in American Society

sibility of government and industry to provide these services for the students enrolled in Negro colleges. Industry recruitment programs were proposed for Negro students in Negro and in integrated colleges. (4) A National Skills Bank. This proposal was to establish in one central place the names, qualifications, and availability of any persons who wished to be considered for employment in a variety of work situations. The National Skills Bank was to be financed by the federal government, but was to be managed exclusively by the National Urban League.

Securing commitments from governmental leaders for legislative programs designed to achieve most of their objectives, but failing to secure governmental support for the National Skills Bank, the Urban League turned to the great Foundations for financial support. Supported by funds from the Rockefeller foundation, the National Skills Bank was established and widely publicized. A survey is done by each of the local Urban Leagues across the country to determine availability of jobs for Negroes, and companies' interest in cooperation in such a program. By late 1964, chapters of the National Skills Bank had been established in 65 cities. The National Urban League trains the personnel of its local chapters in how to contact Negroes in their communities, to understand their job skills, and to stimulate their desire for improvement. Once job candidates are identified, they are called in for personal interviews. The interviewers are often personnel specialists who themselves work for local companies. Through this process, a pool of available Negro talent is built up job level by job level. If applicants are not available in an area to match an employer's particular request, the National Urban League headquarters, where a master file is maintained, is contacted. The employer's request is matched with an applicant closest to the company and a meeting is arranged. The Skills Bank differs from private employment agencies in several respects: it operates nationally, and no fee is involved; its primary aim is to help more Negroes to gain entry to job levels where few or none are now employed.

Education

Education is a continuous process from the cradle to the grave. The following discussion will be oriented to this broader definition of education, with the role of the formal school deferred to a later section.

(1) APPLICATION OF CONSISTENT VALUES TO THE SOLUTIONS OF LIFE'S PROBLEMS. Democracy, Judaism, and Christianity should be more than a political philosophy and religious faiths. Many persons hold that the application of the Judaeo-Christian tradition in the American social scene should clearly indicate a way of life based on the values common to both democracy and the Judaeo-Christian tradition. There should be little conflict between Christians and Jews in arriving at a common set of values.[44]

---

[44] Those values common to all Americans are more fully developed in Chapter 14, with clear implications of their effects on the moral and ethical principles of both theists and nontheists.

Briefly stated, the American value system includes mutual respect, cooperation, rational thinking, and faith in the future.

Man needs constantly to be re-educated in the consistent application of these values. Conceptual grasp of a set of values is meaningless unless the values are *applied* to all areas of life. Parents, teachers, and peers, all bear a civic responsibility to assist in this educational process through precept and example.

Mutual respect involves both understanding one's fellow man and treating him as a brother. Confucianism goes beyond even the Sermon on the Mount in this respect; it expects one to do unto others as *they would have one do unto them*. This demands full understanding of one's fellow man, in order that one may know what he would have done unto him. No one can fully know all of the diverse groups in America; but consistent operation on a principle of mutual respect would eliminate the fears of the unknown and the pseudo-feelings of superiority that are at the roots of all prejudice. Further, it would lead one to search for *causes* when a group behaved in an apparently unexplainable way, rather than to treat them as stereotypes and scapegoats.

Cooperation involves the full efforts of *all* groups in the solution of common problems; it cannot consist of the majority group reaching a decision and handing it down to the minority group. Again, the very handing down of cultural decisions, such as proper dress, diet, and common courtesies, implies that the majority group is superior in that it knows the only "right" ways. Cooperative action on such problems often discloses the fact that there are many "right" ways. Sometimes the minority way of behaving proves to be the preferred way, as witness the gradual adoption by the socially élite of the loose, comfortable summer wear of the men of the lower classes. Formerly, a "gentleman" never appeared in public without his coat; such vulgarity was reserved for the masses at their popular resorts such as Coney Island. Now short-sleeved sport shirts are acceptable to all classes for casual wear.

Rational thinking strikes at one of the roots of prejudice: ignorance. Rational thinking demands factual data on which to base hypotheses. If the overwhelming weight of scientific data on the equality of races were accepted by all men, than racism would diminish. As indicated earlier, the difficulty lies in securing emotional acceptance; surrender of one's prejudices threatens personal security through closing of the escape valve for the venting of frustrations. Other problems of intergroup relations are not so readily susceptible to solution by rational thinking, even if men could be induced to think rationally in prejudicial areas; for example, no system of government to eliminate class differences has yet been devised. Rational thinking can minimize the adverse effects of social stratification, however, by providing a four-point program designed to (1) develop each person to his maximum potential; (2) provide equitable opportunities to all—political, economic, social, and educational; (3) help individuals to establish realistic life goals; and (4) help individuals to be happy in the position in life that they must fill.

Faith in the future is the very antithesis of psychological insecurity. It is emotional in nature and correspondingly difficult to define in operational terms. Basically, if one has faith in his fellow man and in the use of cooperation and reason for the solution of common problems, then faith in himself and in the future should result. Maintaining faith in the future becomes increasingly difficult in an age of atomic missiles and sputniks. First steps, for educators, lie in building the confidence of students in their classmates and in their teachers through cooperative classroom mastery of demonstrably important and difficult learnings.

(2) EFFECTIVE AND NONEFFECTIVE TECHNIQUES IN THE CHANGING OF ATTITUDES. We have stated earlier that prejudice is perpetuated through ignorance and insecurity. Prejudices based on insecurity are extremely resistant to modification, and there is some evidence that all prejudices are so based.[45] These prejudices may be of the group, or they may be personal in genesis. Examples of the two types are the scapegoating of one group by another to relieve group frustrations, and the expression of psychoneurotic symptoms of authoritarian personalities. Prejudice based on group insecurity may be made more susceptible to change by removing the source of group frustration. Prejudice based on rigidity of personality requires a reorientation of basic personality structure before pressures for attitudinal change can be effective.

Programs of information, per se, have not been effective in the reduction of prejudice. Americans pride themselves on their rational approach to life; they fail to recognize their own prejudices, believing them to be reasoned conclusions. Programs of factual information may modify attitudes based solely on ignorance. Unfortunately, one's attitudes affect one's interpretation of such data. Even highly factual research data may be perverted to reinforce established prejudices. This does not indicate an abandonment of the rational approach; it means simply that informational programs should be used not in isolation but as supplements to other approaches. "Although facts can always be forgotten or distorted, in the long run, accurate information is a most important ally in the effort to improve human relations."[46]

Effective techniques in intergroup relations, including even the manner of presentation of factual material, address themselves to an emotional response. The exchange of information must be emotionally conditioned for the modification of attitudes. The psychology of learning that structured the formation of attitudes is equally sound in their modification. Briefly stated, effective techniques in changing of attitudes include the following: (1) rewarding for desired behavior, which reflects the expression of desired attitudes; (2) punishing for deviant behavior; (3) associating

---

[45] Selma G. Hirsh, *op. cit.*, p. xi.
[46] Selma G. Hirsh, *op. cit.*, p. 124.

the new idea with positively charged symbols,[47] (4) associating the old attitude (prejudice) with negatively charged symbols; (5) entertaining (people are more receptive when in a pleasant mood); and (6) securing emotional involvement. Sociodrama is illustrative of the effective techniques of developing empathy as a preface to the presentation of information. Deliberate modification of attitudes involves action by persons or groups desirous of the attitude modification. Some of these groups will be discussed below.

(3) FORMAL WORKSHOPS IN INTERGROUP EDUCATION. The National Conference of Christians and Jews, the Anti-Defamation League, and the American Jewish Committee have fostered the development of workshops in intergroup education both as summer sessions at leading universities and as in-service programs in public school systems. Both educators and laymen are attending these workshops, studying the dynamics of intergroup problems and developing skills in techniques of combating them. The National Urban League goes beyond the informational techniques employed by the above organizations. Workshops are held, it is true; but the emphasis of this organization is on persuading the federal government and/or the philanthropic foundations to translate their conclusions into action programs.

(4) INFORMAL STUDY GROUPS. Many parent-teacher associations have informal study groups discussing intergroup problems. Women's clubs, both professional and social, are taking an increased interest in this area. Unfortunately, some social women's clubs have been the traditional bulwarks of the forces perpetuating discrimination, representing the women whose husbands' income frees them for club work and whose consciousness of ancestry reinforces their feelings of superiority. If the upper-class woman recently has come from a lower class, she has vested interest to protect; if she was born to the upper class, she is heir to all the prejudices illustrated in "Yankee City." One encouraging facet of social women's club work is the overt action that often follows their study of the area. They may adopt some civic project for the underprivileged. This first-hand contact with children and adults of minority groups can be of value in building understandings of these minorities; it is hoped that such contact will develop empathy rather than sympathy. The situation is not so structured, for it starts with an emphasis on difference in economic status rather than building bridges of understanding through sharing of likenesses.

Civic clubs such as Kiwanis, Rotary, Lions, and others long have been noted both for their programs of education of their members and for civic projects for the underprivileged. The American Legion, Veterans of Foreign Wars, and American Veterans Committee sometimes undertake like

[47] Note the authors' continuous equating of positive intergroup attitudes with values found both in democracy and in the Judaeo-Christian tradition.

projects. The men's civic clubs are prey to the same weaknesses as the women's social clubs. Too often a condescending sympathy blocks real understanding. The veterans' organizations are especially subject to chauvinism. Despite these weaknesses, both men's and women's clubs are making some progress in education in intergroup relations.

(5) LITERATURE IN INTERGROUP EDUCATION. If the proper literature finds its way into the hands of the groups listed above, progress is accelerated. Fortunately, there is a wealth of excellent material available. The National Conference of Christians and Jews has a number of sound pamphlets on a variety of topics in intergroup education. These are concise, clearly written, authoritative capsules designed for lay consumption. The Public Affairs Committee, the Anti-Defamation League, and the American Jewish Committee (sometimes publishing as Community Relations Service) have similar series. The United States Chamber of Commerce has some pamphlets bearing on the same topics that will bear critical reading. The National Association for the Advancement of Colored People publishes a limited amount of materials. All of the above organizations furnish materials at nominal cost. The National Education Association has publications in this area by a number of its commissions, such as the Educational Policies Commission and the Defense Commission. The American Council on Education has a scholarly research project in this field in process. A number of its reports are available in bound form. These should provide expert professional assistance to educators and serve as stimulating reading for the informed layman.

For the reader's convenience, these sources are listed below:

The National Conference of Christians and Jews, 43 West 57th St., New York 19, N.Y.
Public Affairs Committee, 22 East 38th St., New York, 16, N.Y.
Anti-Defamation League, 515 Madison Ave., New York 22, N.Y.
The American Jewish Committee, 386 Fourth Ave., New York 16, N.Y.
The Chamber of Commerce of the United States, 1616 H. St., N.W., Washington 6, D.C.
National Association for the Advancement of Colored People, 20 West 40th St., New York 18, N.Y.
Educational Policies Commission of the N.E.A., 1201 16th St., N.W., Washington 6, D.C.
Defense Commission of the N.E.A., 1201 16th St., N.W., Washington 6, D.C.
The American Council on Education, 744 Jackson Place, Washington, D.C.

(6) OTHER AGENCIES OF COMMUNICATION. Motion pictures, radio, and television have greatly accelerated the homogenization of America. Any factor that reduces differences among people retards discrimination by reducing the visibility of the minority group. In addition to this, docu-

mentary motion pictures such as *Gentleman's Agreement* provide sound education in intergroup relations. Fortunately, production policy in most film, radio, television, and periodical and other publishing companies currently seems to be favorable to the promotion of better intergroup relations, in terms of the treatment of the stories they present. Members of minority groups are presented as human beings with problems, and in such a way as to merit respect. Respect is what is needed, not sympathy. Sympathy connotes a feeling toward people who are less fortunate than (inferior to) ourselves. The agencies of public communication are to be commended on their traditional voluntary production policies. Governmental pressures of the Kennedy administration, the fear of Negro boycotts of their products, and, eventually, the *Civil Rights Act of 1964,* led to a far greater break-through in the early 1960's. Negro performers began appearing in major roles on nearly every major radio and television show. Constant exposure to presentation of Negroes in serious dramatic roles, rather than the exclusively song/dance/comedian routines of previous years, surely must have had some influence on the attitudes of the viewers.

Cultural Pluralism Versus the Melting Pot

Cultural monism was the traditional ideal of the American "melting pot." Immigrants were supposed to fuse the best of their diverse cultures into a common pattern. This cultural assimilation has not taken the ideal pattern that it was supposed to. Vices have been assimilated as readily as virtues.

Cole has proposed "cultural democracy" as an ideal.[48] This would follow the pattern of American political democracy, preserving the good things in all cultures but building common strands of behavior to unify the nation. This would give prestige to all cultures, religions, and other groups, recognizing their variances and efficiencies as part of democracy. The basic weakness here is the same as in cultural monism: Who shall decide what the common strands will be?

Cultural pluralism is advanced by some authorities as the most feasible approach. This means, in effect, admitting that the practical working of the melting pot is superior to the ideal that was posited for it. We recognize that there is not one "American" but many "Americans"; that there are many regional and subregional ways of life in America, rather than a common pattern, but with common strands of beliefs and behaviors unifying all groups into a national entity. These authorities would say that this cultural pluralism is good; that continued differences per se are not the problem, but that the discriminatory practices of the majority group are the problem. They cite as proof of the theorem that impartial foreign social analysts such as Gunnar Myrdal identify a common "American character" among the various groups that make up America. They main-

[48] Stewart G. Cole, I. James Quillen, and Mildred J. Wiese, *Charting Intercultural Education* (Stanford: Stanford University Press, 1946), p. 58.

tain that this proves that common strands of behavior will develop in time, in a pluralistic culture.

The cultural pluralists have the weight of history in their favor. Any culture that failed to develop and maintain strong common strands of behavior in all its peoples has disintegrated. America has been growing stronger. We have cited earlier the effect of public agencies of communication in building these common strands. Probably the effect of the editorial policies of our newspapers in shaping political opinion was insufficiently developed at that time. Here is cultural pluralism at work. Some papers are Democratic, some are Republican, but most are alert to the threat of foreign wars and see the need for foreign commitments for hemispheric protection. Midwestern papers are complacent in their isolationism, but all support the government in time of war, no matter how many foreign commitments become necessary.

The problem facing the American schools, of course, is not so much whether cultural pluralism, cultural democracy, or cultural monism is the better ideal. Cultural pluralism exists. The educator's problem is to develop citizens who optimistically utilize respect, reason, and cooperation in dealing with differences.

THE ROLE OF THE SCHOOL

Formal education must be concerned with more than intellectual perception if the school is to make any contribution to improved intergroup relations. We have indicated earlier the ineffectiveness of programs of information alone in the development and modification of the attitudes that guide our behavior. The schools must be concerned with understandings, yes—and with tools for gaining understanding, the three R's, and with high ideals and problem-solving abilities; but the crux of intergroup problems is human *emotions*.

This calls for a basic reorientation in the preservice preparation and the in-service training of the teaching profession. We shall summarize briefly the broad areas in which current practice needs to be re-examined: teacher purposes, teacher competencies, the scope and sequence of the public school curriculum in intergroup education, and the methodology of intergroup education.

Teacher Purposes

The task facing the teacher who is concerned with intergroup relations is that of developing in his students the understandings, ideals, and competencies necessary for effective, harmonious living as democratic citizens of a community, state, and nation in an interdependent world. This is no simple task of the presentation of the three R's. It demands of the graduates of our schools high levels of proficiency in the three R's, in understandings of our world and of the people in it, in techniques of working with people, in skills and attitudes of critical thinking, and in the development of high ideals. It means, further, that these competencies are to be expected of *all* children and youth, not just of the upper 10 per cent or 25 per cent or 50 per cent of the students—and certainly not just the white, middle-class student to whom the public schools traditionally have been oriented. Some students will become more proficient than others, but the goal of the human relations-minded teacher is effective citizenship for all of his graduates.

The effective teacher guides his pupils throughout their years of common education through an ever-expanding orbit of social understandings and skills—roughly from competencies in living as a member of one's own family to competencies in living as a member of the human race. The stress needs to be on constructive human relations, plus all other understandings, skills, and values contributing to the improvement of human relations. This means that the successive teachers who work with the child should set up a series of progressive goals, with the child working on successive developmental tasks as he gains the mental maturity and social skills requisite to their successful completion. These goals, in succession, are (1) clarification of concepts of self; (2) development of feelings of empathy (understanding of people cannot be accomplished unless the child can emotionally identify himself with them); (3) growth in skills in interpersonal relations, (4) growth in skills in group relations; and (5) growth in skills in intergroup relations. These tasks will need to be paralleled with continuous growth in (1) skills in forming value judgments; and (2) skills in critical thinking. Students will work concurrently on several developmental tasks, but success in the tasks farther in social distance from the child must be built upon at least partial mastery of preceding tasks. For a discussion of the importance of building first skills first, with stress upon clarification of concepts of self and development of empathy, see *Elementary Curriculum in Intergroup Relations.*[49]

Teacher Competencies

No teacher can hope to accomplish the above goals fully. Any capable teacher, however, can make substantial progress towards them. Certain personality characteristics, certain fields of knowledge, and certain special abilities will contribute toward increased teacher efficiency. Basic to teacher success is a real concern for people, demonstrable in such ways that children will readily recognize it. This is often referred to as a warm, outgoing personality. The teacher needs to include in his training a broad general education, with stress on the social heritage and on the social problems of his age. He needs specialized training in psychology and anthropology—the study of man, groups, and institutions. He needs, of course, specialized training in the basic theory and practice of teaching. Special abilities need to be developed in the human relations-minded teacher. He needs to see the school as a society. He needs to recognize the

[49] Hilda Taba (ed.), *Elementary Curriculum in Intergroup Relations* (Washington, D.C.: American Council on Education, 1950).

significant evidence of children's needs as revealed in their work and play. He must free himself of his personal background for an objective evaluation of children's needs; this is particularly true in reference to his own middle-class values. He must at all times recognize the interdependence of physical, mental, social, and emotional learnings.

Scope and Sequence of Intergroup Education

The scope of an elementary school curriculum in intergroup education is the sum of the skills, knowledges, and attitudes necessary for accomplishment of the developmental tasks mentioned above. Skills are necessary for working with people. Understanding of self is prerequisite to all other tasks. Knowledges about others are important mostly for their part in guiding the development of constructive attitudes; rather than just learning *about* people, intergroup education must foster emotional identification *with* and sensitivity *to* a variety of people, their feelings and attitudes.[50] Attitudes are the most important end product, for they structure our behavior in these prejudicial areas.

The sequence has been indicated in an earlier section as successive goals of the teacher. The traditional content of the school subjects can serve as a base for the emphasis indicated here, for the stress is not on content but on the provision of cooperative action in a problem-solving attack on all content. A school organized on a basic life functions curriculum, rather than on the traditional subjects, may be more amenable to the human relations emphasis—but, again, content is not the important part of the program. The end result is not the acquiring of a body of knowledge, but the learning and habituating of a way of approaching problems: with mutual respect, reason, cooperation, and high morale. In discussing a standard elementary school unit on transportation, Taba indicates the ways in which traditional content can be adapted to fit the purposes of intergroup education: "The study of communication (in the adapted unit) emphasized blocks instead of means of communication, because the aim of the unit was to develop insights into why people misunderstood each other; and a study of child's needs indicated their main difficulty was in not being understood."[51]

The secondary curriculum in intergroup education should continue the emphasis of the elementary school. Methodologically, the major block to an integrated curriculum in intergroup relations in the secondary school is the compartmentalization of course work, with the attendant impersonality in relations between teacher and student and the limitations in focusing the content of several traditional areas upon a central problem in human relations. Compounding the problem is the stress placed by many secondary teachers on the acquisition of bodies of knowledge in the

---

[50] Hilda Taba, *ibid.*, p. 25.
[51] Hilda Taba, *ibid.*, p. 207.

separate disciplines, almost to the exclusion of attention to the development of skills and attitudes in human relations.

The leadership in constructive human relations education shifts from the classroom teacher of the self-contained elementary school to the guidance department of the departmentalized secondary school. Conferences on individual and group problems, and the election of course patterns, are in the province of the guidance counselors. These counselors can do only part of the job. They can assist students in exploring their own potential, through testing, conferences, and patterns of exploratory courses. They can see that course patterns selected by students not only explore the potential of the student but also sample broadly the opportunities offered by the world. They can develop in individual and in group conferences, and through supervision of student cocurricular activities, the inseparability of individual and group welfare. They can urge the curriculum development department to offer to senior high school students those organized bodies of specialized knowledge in personal mental hygiene, family relations, and problems of democracy. But these tasks are administrative in nature. The real learnings still occur under the guidance of the classroom teachers who conduct the courses and who sponsor the cocurricular activities. Secondary classroom teachers must become human relations-minded if high school students are to receive guidance in the application of classroom concepts to the problems of life. The cocurricular program offers an excellent laboratory for the application of social understandings developed in the classroom. Values will become implanted and skills will be developed when these understandings are applied to areas of life *that are important to students.*

Methodology of Intergroup Education

An application of the knowledges of mental hygiene to classroom discipline is fundamental to the human relations approach. A dictator can maintain order and can instill intellectual concepts more rapidly than can a democratic leader. A dictator can indoctrinate with an authoritarian philosophy through use of highly emotional propaganda techniques. These authoritarian values are the antithesis of those valued in a democracy. Only in a permissive atmosphere, based on a sound knowledge of personality development, can attitudes and skills of democratic action be developed. Careful attention must be paid to the social climate of the group and to the personality adjustments of individuals.

Provisions for an extensive and varied base of three types of learning experiences are essential. First, situations involving strong emotional reactions must be structured. Second, discussion and analysis of those situations must explore those reactions, their causes, and ways of constructive adjustment to them. Finally, tasks requiring the ability to use inductive and deductive reasoning should include both these emotional situations and scientific ones, such as the gathering of research data to document discussion. We understand imperfectly how to build in others the skills of problem-solving.[52] The best solution seems to be the provision of much practice in the use of the technique, in order to develop a "mind set" for its use when one is faced with a problem.

Fostering understandings of people means more than the presentation of facts about them; it means an emotional identification with them. Producers of films for the elementary social studies program recognize this fact in focusing the content of the film on the children of other lands rather than on the adults. Primary teachers are adept in finding common strands that permit children to make a connection between what they know and understand and the strange and unfamiliar. John H. Elliott refers to this as "building bridges."[53] It means starting the study of other groups with an emphasis on likenesses, postponing the study of differences until the bridges of understanding are built. Finally, teaching should be organized in such a way to support the relationship among ideas, facts, and insights that are most difficult to see and to understand. Logical organization provides many clues to children in their attempts to solve problems related to understandings of people.

Building adequate concepts of self, developing empathy, and building skills in interpersonal relations are integral to the discussion in the above three paragraphs. Specifically, they mean freedom to practice interpersonal relations in the classroom and on the playground without the domination of the teacher. They mean class discussion of the successful and unsuccessful techniques evolving from the group, with stress upon understanding that all behavior is caused and that our behavior affects the other fellow. Sociological techniques such as panels, forums, sociodrama, and sociograms may serve to assist the teacher in better understanding her group and in helping them to understand themselves better.[54]

Building skills in intergroup activities can be accomplished at the secondary school level, if the school is so oriented. These skills build on all that has preceded; further, the cocurricular program of the high school provides an excellent laboratory. The Stanford Workshop on Intercultural Education[55] makes a number of suggestions applicable to intercultural education that are equally applicable to intergroup situations. They stress capitalization upon traumatic incidents precipitating group conflicts to assist youth in probing for the *causes* of those conflicts—not the episode that precipitated the conflict, but the underlying causes. They stress the values of the unit approach to teaching. They emphasize discussions of parent-child conflicts, housing deficiencies, athletic contests, and other cocurricular

---

[52] See Summary, Chapter 11 for a brief presentation of the difficulties faced by educators in developing skills of critical thinking in their students.

[53] John H. Elliott, *Building Bridges* (New York: Astoria Press, 1950).

[54] For a discussion of these techniques, see Hilda Taba and others, *Diagnosing Human Relations Needs* (Washington, D.C.: American Council on Education, 1951).

[55] Stewart G. Cole, I. James Quillen, and Mildred J. Wiese, *Charting Intercultural Education* (Stanford: Stanford University Press, 1946), pp. 36–41.

topics. Student participation is stressed, via the preparation of panels, programs, newspapers, plays, fiestas, and the like. This active participation by students not only fosters the understandings necessary for effective intergroup action but also provides practice in the skills necessary for the solution of intergroup problems.

THE SCHOOL INTEGRATION CRISIS OF THE 1960's

The great cities public school teacher of the 1960's has no choice as to whether or not there shall be a curriculum in intergroup education in his classroom. The curriculum, after all, is the sum of the experiences shared by the teacher and his pupils. A significant portion of that sum total, for at least the 1960's, promises to be that of dealing with the hostilities of his Negro pupils and of their parents (and, in specific cities, the hostilities of pupils and parents of Puerto Rican and Mexican extraction, whose fortunes tend to be tied to those of the Negro). Silberman analyzed the cultural matrix of the immediate future as it affected the business community. Your authors see no reason to believe that the implications for the school community differ from that of the business community. Partial quotation of the Silberman analysis follows:[56]

It would be fatuous to pretend that any set of policies adopted by business and government can bring racial peace within the next few years. For one thing, Negroes' impatience, bitterness, and anger are likely to increase the closer they come to full equality. This is not a quirk of Negro character but a characteristic of all disadvantaged groups; the closer they are to their goals, the harder it is to understand or justify the disparities that remain. Indeed, it is a commonplace of history that revolutions (and the Negro protest movement resembles a revolution in many ways) stem from hope, not despair; from progress, not stalemate. And the nearer to triumph the revolutionaries get, the tougher they usually become.

To justify the faith that teachers are professional people, rather than mere craftsmen, it seems essential that the teaching complex—teachers, supervisors, administrators, lay Board members, state departments of education, college professors of teacher education, college administrators, and the U.S. Office of Education—face up to the challenge. If the welfare of the child is the concern of the professional educator, then the teacher must "deal with hostilities" in the ways suggested in the preceding section on *methodology of intergroup education*. As the classroom teacher applies the best of current knowledge to developing vital experiences in intergroup education within his classroom, it is the responsibility of the rest of the teaching complex to develop new and better ways of fostering constructive

[56] Charles E. Silberman, "The Businessman and the Negro," *Fortune*, September 1963, p. 193.

intergroup living and to disseminate this new knowledge and methodology to the teacher. One good example of a highly successful project in inter-group research is the program developed in the Banner District of St. Louis. Dr. Sam Shepard, Banner District Superintendent, is in constant demand to speak to professional and lay groups in other cities to explain the workings of his plan and to suggest ways in which it might be applied to other cities. We have too few Sam Shepards! The teaching profession must invest prodigious quantities of time and energy (and money) in action research in intergroup education if the profession is to meet the challenge of the times.

The public and private schools of America traditionally have been as notoriously niggardly in the allocation of funds for research as American industry has been successful in the generous investment of significant por-tions of its budget in research activities. The massive involvement of in-dustry in the War on Poverty promises to yield significant dividends to American education. The education and training programs financed by the federal government under the *Economic Opportunity Act of 1964* and other legislation[57] appear to be developing new approaches to old educational problems. The United States government maintains a pro-prietary right in all of these developments. Those materials and methods that prove successful could be made available to the educational establish-ment at minimal charge through the Office of Economic Opportunity, and/or the United States Government Printing Office.

There are, in fact, many action research projects involved in these government-sponsored programs of education and training. Men's urban Job Corps Centers will be used as an illustrative program.[58] Many high Job Corps officials are disclaiming the research function as it applies to the operation of Job Corps Centers. This is understandable. Any new or-ganization undergoes an early period of ferment in the development of policies and procedures. Job Corps was created in late 1964; Policy Guide was not developed until mid-1966. The newer governmental programs encom-pass the fifty states, and other U.S. possessions and protectorates. They involve state and local governmental agencies, as well as private contractors drawn from industry, foundations, universities, local school boards, and other organizations such as Community Centers, Young Women's Chris-tian Association, etc. During the early days of Job Corps, the organizations operating the centers were under the loose and often contradictory con-trols of personnel from Job Corps Headquarters in Washington. There appeared to be little coordination of the efforts of the various departments in Headquarters; in fact, there appears to be little continuity of individuals assigned to responsible positions in the various departments. The research

[57] For a comprehensive listing of the programs under the Office of Economic Op-portunity and the other governmental agencies, see William A. Haddad, "Mr. Shriver and the Savage Politics of Poverty," *Harpers Magazine*, December 1965, pp. 46–47.

[58] The following material pertaining to Job Corps do not necessarily reflect official Job Corps policy or opinions; they are the private views of the authors.

function of the education and training programs in Job Corps Centers was a major source of many divergent opinions.

The action research activities of the urban Job Corps Centers both illustrate the divergence of opinion as to whether research is a function of a government-sponsored program of education and training and indicate the potential fruitfulness of this source of materials and methods for future application to the educational establishment. Within the diversity of opinions concerning research, the most commonly stated positions seem to be: (1) Governmental funds for the operation of Job Corps Centers shall not be utilized for research, but for the operation of the programs.[59] (2) The uniqueness of the student population of Job Corps demands innovative approaches to the education and training functions. Both positions concurrently were stated by many individuals, both in Job Corps Headquarters and within the various training centers, with little or no apparent recognition of the incongruency of these positions. Washington supervisors constantly stress "trying new ideas." As these new ideas are developed, implemented, and evaluated, action research results. The scope of this research is indicated by the fact that each of the large, urban centers developed its own, unique program!

The potential for development of materials and methods for application within the educational establishment, with particular reference to under-privileged children and youth, may be gleaned from a brief examination of the philosophic foundations on which one Job Corps program was based. In January, 1966, Director James R. Bryner presented the program of the Atterbury Job Corps Center. Synopsis follows. For detailed description of the program, see Chapter 10, "Problems of the Depressed Areas."

The Job Corps program at Atterbury is three fold. Obvious goals are the traditional ones: the teaching of job skills, and the provision of general education courses designed to lead the Corpsman toward attainment of a high school diploma. Not so obvious, but the tremendously exciting and more important goal, is the enculturation of educationally and culturally impoverished youth into the commonly accepted mores of American society.

If Dr. Bryner's goals are achieved at Atterbury, and similar goals in other Job Corps Centers, then one of the greatest contributions of Job Corps well may be to present to the public and private schools of this country new ways of educating culturally and educationally disadvantaged youth; contributions based on action research!

(1) DE FACTO SEGREGATION. The major school issue of the 1960's is what the Negro organizations have chosen to call *de facto segregation*, as differentiated from the *de jure segregation* declared unconstitutional by the Supreme Court in 1954. Court battles, demonstrations, freedom

---

[59] While Center contractors were prohibited from spending contract funds for research activities, special grants were available for research projects designed by Headquarters personnel. Contractors sometimes received these special grants for on-Center research activities as approved by Headquarters.

marches, sit-ins, etc., continue in the Deep South, where only one Negro child in 100 has been integrated in the ten years since the Supreme Court decision; but the major focus of Negro effort seems to have been shifted to the North. Responsibility for the integration of the schools of the Deep South seems to have been abrogated by the major Negro organizations—possibly under the assumption that the Attorney General of the United States has no choice but to proceed with legal action in compliance with the Supreme Court decision of 1954 and the *Civil Rights Act of 1964*—whereas their energies have been concentrated on securing from the Supreme Court a decision on *de facto segregation.*

De facto segregation has been defined as racial segregation in the public schools brought about by residential patterns. The core areas of the great cities have tended to become almost exclusively Negro in composition. By contrast, the surburban areas (both within and outside the city limits of the parent city) have tended to become almost exclusively white. The only truly integrated schools in the great cities in recent years have been those schools whose sites chanced to fall on or about the dividing line between the Negro residential areas and the white residential area—and many of them became predominantly Negro through redrawing of district lines to exclude the white areas (in all justice to school administration, this was a natural result of the heavier Negro inhabitation of what were formerly white residences; former white single-family residences usually became Negro multiple-family dwellings, with proportionately larger pupil enrollments. Either the school building had to be enlarged or district lines redrawn). James Farmer, executive director of the Congress of Racial Equality, said, "What we're getting in city after city in the North now is a black core at the center of the city and a white noose around it.[60] The schools in the black core are the subject of the *de facto segregation* battles.

The Supreme Court had not considered a case involving *de facto segregation* as of December, 1965. In 1963 the Supreme Court refused to review the case in Gary, Indiana, in which the plaintiffs had contended that inferior education was provided in the predominantly Negro schools. Fresh attack by the NAACP attorneys unsuccessfully was instituted against the Cincinnati Public Schools, on completely different grounds from those on which the Gary case was lost by the NAACP in the lower courts. The legal briefs for the Cincinnati case paralleled as closely as possible the reasoning used by the Supreme Court in the 1954 decision, as follows: "To separate them . . . [Negro children] . . . from others of a similar age and qualifications solely because of their race generates a feeling of inferiority as to their status in the community . . . which may affect their hearts and minds in a way unlikely ever to be undone."[61]

The dimensions of the problem perhaps may be indicated by the fact

[60] United Press International, "Negroes Will Dominate Cities if Trend Continues . . . Farmer," *Cincinnati Enquirer,* November 16, 1964.

[61] From a report *"Background Paper on the Integration Problem.* Made by The Cincinnati School Foundation, March 1964. Used by permission.

that the pupil enrollments in the great cities currently are approximately 50 per cent Negro and/or Puerto Rican in composition, and promise to approach 70 per cent by 1970. *De facto segregation* already has been declared unconstitutional by some lower courts. If it is so held by the Supreme Court, it is difficult to conceive how the neighborhood elementary school can persist in the great cities.

(2) SCHOOL ADJUSTMENTS TO THE CLIMATE OF THE TIMES. Cities, great and small, faced with charges of *de jure* and/or *de facto segregation*, are developing a variety of ways to resolve their problems. To date, none of them have been eminently successful. The Cincinnati School Foundation summarized the current techniques in March, 1964, as follows:[62]

A. *Appointment of Study or Advisory Commissions*

Public school systems have established commissions to study the problem and prepare recommendations for solution. In most cases the commissions have been composed of lay citizens, usually with professional staff participation. School systems which have reported the establishment of such commissions include Berkeley, Champaign, Chicago, Denver, Detroit, Englewood, Los Angeles, Minneapolis, New Rochelle, New York, Norwalk, Pasadena, Philadelphia, Plainfield, San Francisco, Stamford, Wichita, Boston.

B. *Statement of Policy by the School Board*

A number of school systems have adopted policy statements on de facto school segregation and/or equal educational opportunities for minority groups. Most cities have not issued such policy statements. On the state level, California, New Jersey, and New York have recognized that residential segregation results in segregated schools and that solutions to the educational aspects of this problem should be sought by the cities in those states. Cities which have issued policy statements include Detroit, Morristown (N.J.), New York, Norwalk, Pasadena, Wichita.

C. *Specific Plans to Promote Integration*

1. *"Princeton Plan"*

Two formerly separate neighborhood schools with populations of different races are reorganized so that all children in grades 1–3 attend one school and all children in grades 4–6 attend the other school. This plan was initiated in Princeton, N.J., 15 years ago.

2. *"Open Enrollment"*

"Sending" and "receiving" schools are established to alter the racial proportions that exist in both schools. Free bus transportation is generally needed to operate this plan. The term is also applied to "free-transfer" systems where parents may request the transfer of children to another school if there is space available.

3. *Pupil Dispersal*

In small communities a school with predominantly Negro pupils is closed and the students distributed among the other schools that are predominantly white.

4. *Rezoning*

[62] The Cincinnati School Foundation, *op. cit.*, pp. 9–10.

School attendance zones are changed to promote a deliberate mixing of children from different ethnic backgrounds. This method is most applicable for contiguous areas having different racial compositions.

5. *Feeder Patterns*

The combinations of elementary schools which feed pupils to secondary schools are altered to minimize the concentration of one racial group in a particular junior high school.

6. *Selection of Sites for New Schools*

Criteria are established for planning of new schools that take into account the racial makeup of the areas, and school sites are selected to promote an attendance district that has a balance of races.

D. *Concomitant Steps Proposed to Improve Educational Opportunities*

1. *Compensatory Education*

A greatly increased instructional program is instituted for children who come from "culturally disadvantaged" homes. Provisions include smaller class size, double periods in English, tutoring of individuals or small groups, assistance of psychologists and social workers. Major emphasis is placed on improving the achievement levels of students.

2. *Pre-School Programs for Children*

Efforts are concentrated on children from low socio-economic backgrounds, starting at the ages of 3 and 4 years in order to raise the level of communication and understanding before the children enter kindergarten.

3. *Use of Appropriate Textbooks*

Pictures and text of books, for lower grades particularly, show Negro children as well as white children; subject material includes situations that are familiar to the life of minority groups. Histories of the Negroes and their role in American history have been introduced in two school systems.

4. *Training for Human Relations*

The institution of training programs for teachers, counselors and administrators to work with children in integrated classrooms, and to work with parents and groups in the community.

To the "Specific Plans to Promote Integration" listed by the Cincinnati School Foundation should be added the very newest proposal.

EDUCATIONAL PARKS.   The educational park is the boldest and most imaginative proposal yet offered for coping with the segregated urban community and its school problems. The park is, in essence, a scheme for concentrating all the schools of a section of the city, or in some cases of the whole city, upon a single large campus.

"The plan applies to urban districts the principle, long accepted in rural areas, that when good schools cannot be provided close to a child's home, he should be transported to a site where an adequate program is possible. . . . Some advocates of the park plan would concentrate a whole school system in one large campus; some favor separate elementary and secondary centers; and others prefer several comprehensive parks strategically located about the periphery of the city."[63]

The bitter fruit of the above suggestions for integration of northern school systems has not yet fully been tasted by the northern negro school teacher. The same cannot be said of his southern colleague. The National Education Association reported in December, 1965, that hundreds of Negro school teachers had been fired or demoted in the wake of school desegregation in 17 southern and border states.[64] The NEA report stated that at least 452 southern Negro educators were dismissed or downgraded in 1965 alone, and that 1900 new graduates of predominantly Negro teachers colleges had not found work in the classroom. Industry is searching diligently for qualified Negro graduates. It is a sorry commentary on the educational establishment when the qualified Negro graduate is rejected by the schools. Who is leading whom?

SUMMARY

Intergroup problems are emotional in nature. The major areas of conflict are race, class, religion, and national and regional origins. Prejudice is the common denominator of intergroup problems. It has its roots in ignorance and insecurity. Because of the nonrational origins of prejudice, it is resistant to change based solely on reasoned understandings. Prejudice is most efficiently supplanted by constructive attitudes through the use of propaganda techniques. These techniques supply the emotional involvement necessary to assimilation of reasoned understandings.

The short-term solution to intergroup problems is legal action. The long-term goal is education, through all of the agencies of education, including family, peers, local and national voluntary organizations, philanthropic foundations, federal and state agencies, industrial management, organized labor, and public agencies of public communication. A major responsibility for intergroup education should be borne by the school. Most teachers have had little training in human relations. Success of the school in combating prejudice depends on the degree to which teachers can infuse human relations material and techniques into the total curriculum. This does not mean the addition of new bodies of knowledge for rote memorization but an application of democratic Judaeo-Christian values and problem-solving skills to problems of human relations as they arise in the regular curriculum.

The forces of history have thrown the spotlight on the public schools of the great cities as they attempt to resolve their integration problems. Solutions do not seem readily apparent. The 1960's promise to be times

[63] John H. Fischer, "Desegregating City Schools," *The PTA Magazine*, Vol. 59, No. 4 (December 1964), pp. 12–13.
[64] "Hundreds of Negro School Teachers Fired," *The Indianapolis Star*, December 23, 1965 (Washington, D.C.: United Press International).

of great turmoil as the schools search for practical application of democratic values to the schools' treatment of minority groups.

The thesis of this chapter, then, is that intergroup education is the capstone of a progressive curriculum in human relations. This curriculum is progressive in nature, with skills at each level based on those that preceded; but it is also concurrent in nature, in that basic attitudes of mutual respect, reason, cooperation, and optimism are essential at all levels. The progressive nature of a human relations curriculum demands the application of these attitudes to an ever-expanding number of people at increasingly greater social and geographic distances from the individual. It is the *application* of the attitudes, then, that is progressive. The same democratic Judaeo-Christian attitudes that are essential for happy family living are equally essential for effective citizenship in an interdependent world.

Selected Bibliography

Allport, Gordon W. *The "ABC's" of Scapegoating.* New York: Anti-Defamation League, 1948. Pp. 56 (Pamphlet). One of the most valuable brief summaries of the psychological mechanisms underlying prejudice and discrimination.

Baldwin, James. *Nobody Knows My Name.* New York: Dell, 1961. Pp. 190. A series of essays revealing the inner turmoil of a Negro expatriate during a ten year stay in Europe and through his return to America during the early days of the school integration crisis. Winner of awards and grants for his novels, *Go Tell It on the Mountain, Giovanni's Room, Notes Of a Native Son, Another Country,* and *The Fire Next Time.*

Baltzell, E. Digby. *The Protestant Establishment.* New York: Random House, 1964. Pp. xviii + 430. Traces the white-Anglo-Protestant power structure from a ruling class dominating our institutional life and setting our cultural norms to its deterioration into a stubborn caste more concerned with protection of its privileges than with encouragement of the widest possible participation by talented citizens in the management of our country.

Becker, Howard S. *Outsiders: Studies in Sociology of Deviance.* New York: Free Press of Glencoe, 1963. Pp. x + 179.

Chambers, Lucille A. (ed.). *America's Tenth Man.* New York: Twayne, 1958. Pp. 351. This volume has been compiled in an effort to present a composite portrait of the American Negro today.

Clark, Kenneth B. *Dark Ghetto: Dilemma of Social Power.* New York: Anti-Defamation League, 1965. A sociological and psychological study of the Negro ghetto; an attempt to understand the combined problems of the confined Negro and the problems of the slum.

———, (ed.) *The Negro Protest: James Baldwin, Malcolm X, Martin Luther King.* Boston: Beacon Press, 1963. Pp. 56.

Corwin, Ronald G. *A Sociology of Education.* New York: Appleton-Century-Crofts, 1965. Pp. x + 454. Emerging patterns of class, status, and power in the public schools.

Countryman, Vern (ed.). *Discrimination and the Law.* New York: Anti-

Defamation League, 1965. This book is an in-depth analysis of constitutional law as it applies to race discrimination. It deals with the sources of federal power under the Fourteenth Amendment in four basic areas—employment, education, public accommodation, and housing.

DUBERMAN, MARTIN B. *In White America*. Boston, Mass.: Houghton Mifflin, 1964. Pp. x + 112. A documentary play.

EICHLER, EDWARD P. *Race and Housing*. Santa Barbara: Fund for Republic, 1963. Pp. 23 (Pamphlet).

ELLIOTT, JOHN H. *Building Bridges*. New York: Astoria Press, 1950. Pp. 64 (Pamphlet). Stresses need for building mutual respect among all men as a means toward achieving international peace. Presents in capsule form the basic facts about religious and racial groups. Synthesizes personal guide lines toward elimination of prejudices through bridges of understanding.

ESSIEN-UDOM, E. U. *Black Nationalism*. New York: Dell, 1962. Pp. 448. The Black Muslim movement, its goals, strength, and meaning; the nature and extent of its appeal to the lower-class urban Negro.

HABENS, MURRAY C. *The Challenges to Democracy*. New York: Anti-Defamation League, 1965. Shows how our political unity has been threatened throughout our history—the Civil War, racial and religious bigotry, the Ku Klux Klan, Huey Long, Father Coughlin, McCarthyism—and discusses present-day dangers to American unity such as those connected with the acceptance government. The broad conclusions of this study are that our national unity is continuously in jeopardy, but that our democracy and nationalism are deeply rooted and possessed of considerable potential for survival. This book promises to become a classic on extremism in American life.

HERBERG, WILL. *Protestant-Catholic-Jew*. Garden City, N.Y.: Doubleday, 1956. Pp. 320.

HIRSH, SELMA G. *The Fears Men Live By*. New York: Harper & Row, 1955. Pp. xx + 164. Lay interpretation of the monumental series in the dynamics of prejudice prepared by Max Herkheimer and Samuel H. Flowerman (eds.) for the American Jewish Committee, published by Harper & Row. Based largely on *The Authoritarian Personality*. Effectively presents the thesis that the origin of prejudice is fear.

HODGES, HAROLD M. *Social Stratification*. Cambridge, Mass.: Schenkman, 1964. Pp. 307.

HOLTON, GERALD, and others (eds.). "Ethnic Groups in American Life." *Daedalus* (Spring, 1961), Vol. 90, No. 2. Middletown: Wesleyan University Press, 1961. Pp. 220–399. Quarterly issue of *Daedalus*, devoted to a series of essays and reports of research studies concerning ethnic groups.

JOHNSON, LYNDON B., ROBERT C. WEAVER, and others. *The Negro as an American*. Santa Barbara: Fund for Republic, 1963. Pp. 19 (Pamphlet).

KING, MARTIN LUTHER, JR. *Why We Can't Wait*. New York: New American Library, 1964. Pp. 159. Starting with *Stride Toward Freedom* in 1958 and continuing through *Why We Can't Wait* in 1964, Martin Luther King, Jr. has been the most widely recognized voice of the Negro leadership. Dr. King lays the facts on the line. He is bitterly critical of federal delay, and of southern law officials. He recognizes the danger of leaderless, violent rebellion if prompt and positive steps are not taken.

KVORACEUS, WILLIAM C., and others. *Negro Self Concept: Implications for Schools and Citizenship*. New York: McGraw-Hill, 1965. Pp. 144

LANDES, RUTH. *Culture in American Education*. New York: Wiley, 1965. Pp. vi + 330. Anthropological approaches to minority and dominant groups in the schools.

LOMAX, LOUIS, E. *The Negro Revolt*. New York: New American Library, 1963. Pp. 288. Explains the history behind the Freedom Riders, Sit-Ins, Prayer Marches . . . the development and meaning of the racial protest of the 1960's in America.

MYRDAL, GUNNAR. *An American Dilemma: The Negro Problem and Modern Democracy*, Revised Edition. New York: Harper & Row, 1944. Pp. iv + 1483. This monumental study in two volumes by a Swedish sociologist is the most comprehensive and profound analysis of the Negro in American life. The chapter on value formation is particularly significant and challenging.

NEWTON, JIM (ed.). *Negro Contributions in America*. Hamilton: Fort Hamilton Press, 1964. Pp. 28 (Pamphlet). Cross-indexed compilation of famous Negro leaders and events from the beginning of the Republic.

PASSOW, A. HARRY (ed.). *Education in Depressed Areas*. New York: Columbia University Press, 1963. Pp. 359. A compilation of many city schools' projects dealing with the underprivileged child and his problems and progress in school.

RASMUSSEN, MARGARET (ed.). *Implications of Basic Human Values for Education*. Washington, D.C.: Association for Childhood Education International, 1964. Pp. 64 (Pamphlet). Collection of statements by behavioral scientists, with application to basic human values and the educative process.

SILBERMAN, CHARLES E. *Crisis in Black and White*. New York: Random House, 1964. Pp. xii + 370. The boldest and most profound attempt to understand the Negro crisis in America, not only in relation to its history, but with respect to its possible solution. Stresses the need for America to restore to the Negro the dignity, initiative, and the ambition of which his countrymen traditionally have deprived him. Covers all aspects of American life. Chapter IX, "The Negro and the School," should be required reading for all teachers.

TABA, HILDA. *Leadership Training in Intergroup Education*. Washington, D.C.: American Council on Education, 1953. Pp. xii + 337. Dated, but remains among the best available series.

———, ELIZABETH HALL BRADY, JOHN T. ROBINSON, and WILLIAM E. VICKERY. *Diagnosing Human Relations Needs*. Washington, D.C.: American Council on Education, 1951. Pp. v + 154. Describes several devices for diagnosing the concerns and feelings children have about their relationships with others. Examples are given of the teacher's use of diaries, parent interviews, sociometric procedures, and other techniques.

———, and others. *Curriculum in Intergroup Relations: Secondary School*. Washington, D.C.: American Council on Education, 1949. Pp. vii + 168. Presents examples of ways in which the secondary school curriculum may be pointed to the development of better human relations. Excellent suggestions for ways of determining the real interests and concerns of adolescents. A good chapter on methods of teaching.

————, and others. *Elementary Curriculum in Intergroup Relations.* Washington, D.C.: American Council on Education, 1950. Pp. xiii + 246. Concrete illustrations of ways to discover the human relationship needs of children and select curricular experiences to meet these needs. Particularly good on the development of concepts regarding family and community life. Teacher will find helpful the explanation of the uses of sociograms and of role-playing. The final chapters appraise three types of curriculum planning in various school systems.

WRIGHT, RICHARD. *Native Son.* New York: New American Library, 1961. Pp. 399.

SELECTED FILMS

A Morning for Jimmy (Anti-Defamation League) 28 min
Negro boy encounters racial discrimination while seeking part-time job. A wise teacher takes Jimmy to visit Negroes successfully employed in their chosen fields. He begins to believe that with proper education and training he, too, can succeed.

All the Way Home (Brandon Films) 30 min
Examines the confused reaction of a community when a Negro family stops in front of a "For Sale" sign. Even before "anything happens," fear and hysteria encouraged by irresponsible elements threaten the long-resident couple whose house is for sale and shake the relationships built up in the community throughout the years. The film objectively explores the contagion of unreason and guilt, which are barriers to the solution of the integration problem.

Americans All (McGraw-Hill) 16 min
Film on minority groups. Product of March of Time. Material on the Springfield plan.

As Our Boyhood Is (American Film Center) 17 min
Shows the development of Negro education; emphasizes that a development was slow and difficult, from the schoolhouse with broken windows and the teachers only a few steps ahead of the pupils to the modern school that spreads its influence beyond the confines of its four walls through training in home economics, machine shopwork, and handcrafts.

Born Equal (Library Films) 10 min
Interprets the UN Declaration of Human Rights with special emphasis on rights for children.

Boundary Lines (Int. Film Foundation) 10 min
Describes by animated drawings the imaginary lines that divide us as people from each other. The lines that boys draw on pavements in youth are developed in the adult into boundaries based on differences in color, origins, wealth and poverty, fear, and confusion.

Brotherhood of Man (Consumers Co-op Assn.) 10 min, Color.
Animated cartoon in which the central figure finds a group of strangers in his back yard. His fear abates when he learns that people are pretty much alike, regardless of race or religion, and that people must learn to live together in order to survive.

The Burden of Truth (Anti-Defamation League) 67 min

A Negro family moves into a white suburban community and a mob gathers in protest. Through flashbacks, we discover the problems and prejudices that a Negro faces in growing up.

Cast the First Stone (Anti-Defamation League) 42 min

Interviews on location with Negroes in Los Angeles and Chicago, Jews in Detroit, Puerto Ricans in New York, Mexicans, Japanese, and Chinese in the Midwest, on their firsthand experience and outlook for the future.

Confronted (Indiana University Films) 1 hr

How or what does the northern white feel when he is confronted by the demanding Negro?

Crisis in Levittown, Pa. (Brandon Films) 30 min

When the first Negro family moved into this community, on-the-spot reactions were captured by the film crew of the complex forces and reactions that were released. Insight into a community in turmoil over an integration crisis.

Dallas at the Crossroads (Anti-Defamation League) 8 min

Describes desegregation in the city of Dallas, is an appeal for law and order during the process of desegregation in the public schools.

Democracy (EBF) 11 min

Presents the nature and meaning of democracy by analyzing four major concepts on which there is substantial agreement; points out how true democracy depends equally upon shared respect and shared power.

Earth and Its People Series (Louis de Rochemont Assn.) 20 min ea.

Includes the titles: Malaya—*Nomads of the Jungle*; Norway—*Farmer-Fisherman*; Java—*Tropical Mountain Land*; Guatemala—*Cross Section of Central America*; South Africa—*Riches of the Veldt*; and Argentina—*Horsemen of the Pampas*. Malaya film is particularly recommended.

Epitaph for Jim Crow (Anti-Defamation League) 30 min

Series of illustrated film-lectures focuses on the history and current situation of the American Negro. The historical, political, sociological, and psychological forces that shape patterns of prejudice and discrimination.

High Wall (McGraw-Hill) 32 min

Fear, frustration, and narrow bigoted thinking develop the hate chain—ways of building confident adult personalities. This film represents an excellent, new approach to the re-education of the prejudiced.

House I Live In (Young America) 10 min

Frank Sinatra appeals for intergroup understanding. An Academy Award winner.

I Wonder Why (Anti-Defamation League) 5 min

Film will appeal to children and adults. Delivers a powerful message against racial prejudice.

Incident on Wilson Street (Anti-Defamation League) 15 min

Film dramatically reveals how skilled and sympathetic teachers bring enrichment into the lives of educationally disadvantaged children.

It Happened in Springfield (NCCJJ) 21 min

How the Springfield Plan in Springfield, Mass., built an intergroup bridge.

No Hiding Place (Anti-Defamation League) 50 min

Leading performers are starred in the TV drama which dramatically traces the events in a neighborhood into which a Negro family has just moved. Panic and tension cause the collapse of an entire community.

Of Human Rights (UN Films) 20 min

An incident involving economic and racial prejudice among children is used to dramatize the importance of bringing to the attention of the peoples of the world their rights as human beings as set forth in the Universal Declaration of Human Rights, proclaimed by the UN General Assembly in December, 1948.

One-Tenth of Our Nation (International Film Bureau) 26 min

Education of Negro children in rural South, from one-room shacks and trade schools to universities.

Other Face of Dixie (Anti-Defamation League) 53 min

Progress report on Negro-White relations, as a vivid demonstration of integration achievement contrasting the old distrust with the new cooperative spirit among students in Clinton, Little Rock, Norfolk, and Atlanta.

Picture in Your Mind (International Film Foundation) 16 min

Through the use of symbols presents the earliest roots of prejudice and the reasons why any group, tribe, or nation thinks its way of life is superior to the other man's way of living. A forceful plea is made to every individual to re-examine his own mind to see whether his mental picture of the other man is distorted.

Segregation in Schools (McGraw-Hill) 28 min

A "See-it-now" report by Edward R. Murrow. Interviews with Negro and White leaders in Gastonia, North Carolina, and Natchitoche, Louisiana, in the wake of the Supreme Court ruling of May 17, 1954, against segregation in the public schools.

Social Class in America (McGraw-Hill) 15 min

Follows the lives of three young men representing the lower, middle, and upper classes. Points out that an individual may change his social status under certain conditions. Introduces such terms as vertical mobility and horizontal mobility.

Story of Dr. Carver (TFC) 10 min

Biography of Dr. George Washington Carver, born in slavery, university educated, whose agricultural experiments notably advanced science.

That All May Learn (UN Films) 19 min

Portrays UNESCO's part in correcting the evil of illiteracy as typified by a story of the exploitation of a Mexican farmer and his family. The farmer unwittingly signs away his rights to his land, but he and his neighbors are helped by his son who has left to get an education.

To Find A House (McGraw-Hill) 28 min

Depicts the rebuffs encountered by two middle-class Negro families as they unsuccessfully seek adequate housing in a northern city. Presents the variety of excuses used by landlords. Dramatizes the heartaches caused by denial of first-class citizenship to the American Negro.

Walk in My Shoes (Anti-Defamation League) 42 min

A documentary explores the innermost feelings of the Negro as he reacts to prejudice and discrimination in America.

Chapter 10. *Problems of the Depressed Areas*[1]

In considering "depressed areas" it may be asked, what conditions constitute such a defined area? Why do these areas come into existence? What are the factors relating to economic deterioration? And what of the human suffering that is endured in these areas?

DEPRESSED AREAS

A depressed area is one that has failed to keep economic pace with the growth of the nation. It actually has moved backward while the rest of the nation has moved forward.[2] Although no single remedy or short-term program offers itself as a solution, the United States government has moved ahead in the concern for these areas with far-reaching programs that provide varying measures and degrees of intensive aid.

This chapter will consider the far-reaching implications of the distressed areas and the human disability they engender. The constellation of factors are multiple in the human orientation: geographical, social, cultural, economical, and educational.

In an era of economic prosperity with vast scientific and technological innovations, there are geographical areas of substantial and persistent unemployment and underemployment in the United States. In the Public Works and Economic Development Act of 1965, Public Law 89–136, the following criteria, among others, determine that a particular region has lagged behind the whole nation in economic development:[3]

[1] The senior author acknowledges his indebtedness to Mrs. Rebecca Pittenger, one of his graduate students, who prepared the original draft of this chapter.
[2] C.E.D., "Distressed Areas in a Growing Economy" (New York: The Committee for Economic Development, 1961), pp. 24, 25.
[3] Title V, Sec. 501.

1. The rate of unemployment is substantially above the national rate;
2. The median level of family income is significantly below the national median;
3. The level of housing, health, and education facilities is substantially below the national level;
4. The economy of the area traditionally has been dominated by only one or two industries, which are in a state of long-term decline;
5. The rate of outmigration of labor or capital or both is substantial;
6. The area is adversely affected by changing industrial technology;
7. The area is adversely affected by changes in national defense facilities or production; and
8. Indices of regional production indicate a growth rate substantially below the national average.

The economic structure of depressed areas is typified by the following. Large numbers of people are jobless who are ill equipped to find gainful employment. Employment opportunities within the area are minimal because of lack of diversification in most of these areas.

Urban

Lack of diversification is more severe in urban areas that are too small to be able to support the kind of diversification that would allow a self-adjusting process by means of shifting a variable labor force from one firm to another as economic opportunities change. Employment has often been dependent on a major industry. When it has declined, other local industries, if existent, have not been able to take up the slack. New industry has not moved in. The unemployed then cease to play a productive role in their community. The social climate of the larger communities in which depressed areas are found tends to be one of "They don't *want* to work!" These attitudes only perpetuate the ghettos of the unemployed.

This condition has been illustrated very clearly in areas dependent on coal mining in West Virginia, eastern Kentucky, Pennsylvania and Illinois. Where anthracite and bituminous coal have lost out to gas or oil, or where technological improvements in the mines have increased productivity and thereby reduced the employment needs, the backbone of the economy is greatly altered with resultant unemployment. In industries other than coal mining, causative factors have been at work to produce negative economic changes. Textile industries, through their manufacture of synthetic products, have cut into the market for wool, cotton, and silk. Manufacturing of railway equipment and railway repair has succumbed to the decline of their passenger traffic, and the rise of truck transportation. The decline in defense-oriented jobs, competitive forces within the automobile industry, competition from abroad, automation, and change due to locational advantages—all have contributed to urban areas in depression. The human hardships involved in unemployment and the economic waste of human potential cause problems that are complex and numerous.[4] The demography of depressed areas accentuate their depression. The more able, the more highly skilled, leave the community. Property values deteriorate. New dwellers tend to be jobless, or minimally employed, attracted by the lower rents and by the psychological salve of association with similarly deprived persons.

It can be asked, why do distressed areas persist and get worse? The social and physical deterioration that take place are by-products of economic distress, usually not the primary fault of the workers involved. A spirit of individual and community defeatism grows when lack of productivity renders people dependent, directly or indirectly, on public assistance. This, in turn, leads to disunity, disorganization, and even apathy.

Internal migration has always been a part of American life. However, to move from a known to an unknown area in the face of adversity does require money, experience, and spirit, all difficult in the face of defeat and failure. While many have left, those who have not moved out of the depressed areas may be lacking in these requirements. They may lack knowledge of opportunities, or they may not possess skills for different jobs. Their familiarity with the home community, deep emotional ties with families and friends, or property investment may prevent their search for new opportunities. The factor that contributes most to continued depression is, however, the failure of new industry to move into the surplus labor area. Unfortunately, too often a single distressed region is lacking in appropriate occupational skills and in locational advantages such as utilities, school systems, adequate local government, and has poor local leadership, and, as well, often an eroded tax base and heavy welfare burdens.

Large urban areas, containing diversification of industry, massive public utilities, schools, government, and many kinds of facilities and expert services, are far more able to adjust to economic changes. Detroit, however, has been an example of a large metropolitan center with a concentration of employment in one or two major industries serving national markets. Until recently, the decline in unemployment in these industries was not counterbalanced by other industries benefiting from the above factors. In recent months, this and other regions are attacking their problems through far-reaching economic development and urban renewal projects. In 1960, 25 per cent of the total U.S. population lived in the ten largest metropolitan areas. It is understandable, therefore, that the major depressed areas, in terms of people affected, continue to be in urban locations.

Rural

As the dynamic growth of technology has continued into a permanent industrial revolution, radical changes have taken place in agriculture, business, industry, government, and labor throughout the United States and the world. The trend has been toward larger and larger enterprises. With mechanized farming methods, the agrarian system has changed from

[4] C.E.D., *op. cit.*, pp. 24, 25.

small units to "big" agricultural units, larger farms with less population needed to produce and harvest products.

Before the days of industry and mechanized farming, the small rural community was largely isolated from other communities. Difficulties in transportation and communication led not only to geographical, social, and intellectual isolation, but also to well-established and provincial patterns of behaviors and attitudes. Strict adherence to those established ways was learned at an early age, and divergencies were frowned upon. The mode of life was simple and continuing. The small farm unit allowed at least a marginal subsistence level and offered a life complete. However, this mode of life is for the most part becoming impossible.

In the long run, the small farmers have not been able to profit from technology, and have not been able to keep their way of living or to retain their land; the same end result has occurred where farmers have tilled marginal land, regardless of size of farm. Small land units, or unfertile areas, cannot support the cost of labor to till them, nor the capital necessary to invest in machinery. With increasing competition for agricultural commodities, governmental policies on acreage restriction for more efficient production, there are rural areas which, lacking diversification in other enterprises, also lack an adequate economic base. These factors have led to the social deterioration of rural society, depopulation, and a growing inadequacy of the old ways. Knowledge of opportunities and new ways have led either to leasing the land and becoming part-time labor in a nearby urban center or to migrating completely out of the rural area.

Those who have migrated from the rural to the urban centers have found all too often that this has not only failed to relieve their plight, but has led them to a situation in which they are unable to establish a satisfactory new life. These migrants are composed largely of Appalachian Mountain farmers, sharecroppers, tenant farmers (both Negro and White), landless Puerto Ricans, Mexicans, and reservation Indians who are generally poor and uneducated, with little chance for advancement. In this movement away from the land to the city, these people have found themselves to be victims of a system they do not understand and over which they have no control. Their predicament is further compounded by racial and class prejudice, and few or no marketable skills.

The urban center, large or small, has become the focal point of industry and organized community living. It has become the place for concentration of large numbers of wage earners. Discrepancies develop when technology outruns the wage earners' skills, and when changed circumstances require social adjustments. The city is the place in which problems are met and institutional practices must be refashioned toward ultimate better human social adjustments and more widely available economic opportunity. The migration of rural people to the city has a historical background with old patterns and problems that are being seen today in new perspectives. The following section is a brief view of the city as it has grown and developed in human history.

The City in Human Culture[5]

The Polis

Predating even the most primitive village, nonliterate man's social and religious impulses, his need for protection, together with his practical needs, drew him to family and tribal groupings. Though nomadic and concerned with physical survival, the human need for expression and the search for meaning and understanding of life and death led to communal rites and meeting places.

Cooperative life grew with burial practices and communal rites, hunting activities, and feasts. Evidences exist of division of labor displayed in tools and weapon making, and in highly developed art techniques.

The later domestication of animals and the practice of food production gave rise to the eventual establishment of more permanent settlements. With this humble beginning came the first expression of human institutions: the family and tribe, the religious shrine, and the protective fortress, all giving form to the primordial city.

The villages grew in number and size. As the invention of writing, engineering, and improved agricultural methods developed, old and new ways of living were brought into interaction, leading to the expanding of human energies and to the differentiation of occupational activities. The beginnings of organized law concerning justice, morality, and government gave rise to further structure in the lives of those whose village life was becoming more that of the city. For, as the village took root, trade came by way of merchant caravans that settled at the edges or outside the walled fortress. Here business was conducted; in case of danger, refuge could be sought inside the village. The influence of trade brought new life, growth, and complexity to the now emerging city. As ancient kingships were established, the city grew into the ultimate fusion of fortress, temple, and marketplace, and was the center of intellectual, artistic, economic, and political progress.

The cities, through the process just described, arose first in the areas of early Oriental civilizations; the Nile, Tigris, Euphrates, Yellow, and Indus Rivers. The development of a high level of civilization at this period of history is simultaneous with the rise of the city. In the Greek *polis* is found one of the most successful harmonization of the city with its surrounding territory—the city-state. In Rome the city-state expanded into an empire and the city-states, as such, passed out of history until the rise of the great trading cities of the late Medieval Period.

The Medieval City

In medieval Europe, the oldest cities were those that survived from Roman times. New cities grew out of population growths around castle

[5] Cf. Lewis Mumford, *The City in History* (New York: Harcourt, 1961).

strongholds, monasteries, or cathedrals. In the early Middle Ages the growth of the cities was relatively slow. Open spaces were plentiful for recreation and for rural occupations such as gardening and keeping animals. In this respect, the use of land can be likened to the small country town of the United States where such practices still exist in a limited sense today. In the later Middle Ages, population within these walls increased and became crowded. Land values rose, houses with upper overhanging stories were built to conserve land space, and the streets were dark, narrow, crooked, and unpaved. Life was crude and offered few refinements. Filth abounded as all refuse and garbage were thrown into the streets, to be removed only by rain or by the dogs and pigs which roamed at large. The frequently contaminated spring and well water supply served as fertile breeding grounds for disease. Certainly it can be said that the medieval city was beset by sanitation inadequacies. This problem continued to exist in the universal evolution of cities, with some making better provisions than others. Although today's modern cities do make contributions toward creating alleys of filth, toward making running sewers of the rivers, and toward contaminating the air into a disease-breeding element, Western civilization has made of the city a relatively sanitary environment—even within the depressed areas.

During the crusades in the late Middle Ages, profitable trade and commerce with the Near East grew rapidly. As this expansion took place, the cities grew in size, number, and importance. New markets developed and many people turned to manufacturing products like those of the Eastern cities. This resulted in the movement of much of the rural population to the cities to engage in commercial and industrial enterprises. A basic institution took the form of merchant and craft guilds, which were, in some respects—though superficially—the forerunners of present-day labor unions. These functioned to preserve the local market for their own members, to create a noncompetitive and stable economic system, and to maintain standards of goods, in addition to furnishing social services. The guilds served to raise the status of work and that of the wage earner, enabling him to become a free citizen; thus began the decline of a servile culture.

Although cities have emerged in different times and places and in different ways, it is significant that their growth has resulted primarily from a concentration of population, human energy, and social interaction, and the production of goods and services. The growth of industry with its differentiated occupations drawing a labor force from the land to the city is not a new phenomenon in human history.

The Modern Metropolis

The modern concept of the city is no longer one based on a fortress or religious shrine as in ancient and medieval times, but rather one based on the value of goods and services it facilitates. Changes in the internal patterns of cities have been occurring for centuries. With the extension of agriculture providing a varied food supply, and with advancements in medical science and sanitation, the nineteenth- and twentieth-century world has experienced a vast increase in population. The commercial and industrial revolutions have accommodated this population by furnishing increased trade and more work opportunities in factories, all of which has made it possible for resourceful areas to support many people. The geographical concept of the metropolis includes the central city and its surrounding area, boroughs, villages, towns, and townships. These are the suburbs, and the whole is referred to as the greater metropolitan area.

Sociologically, cities are large and permanent population aggregates, composed of heterogenous individuals, who are involved in diversified and specialized occupational roles. Cities are self-maintaining and are in the constant process of creating order in the face of disturbing life forces. Heterogeneity and mass, while tending to break down class lines and to cause increasing integration of persons, paradoxically also lead to a complicated and segregated class structure, which at times undermines social solidarity through class, ethnic, and racial conflicts. Race relations within an urban culture are today presenting a challenge no longer limited to just the local metropolitan scene, but extending to the state and national scenes as well, even affecting the foreign image and policy commitments. Glaring contrasts of close physical contact and distant social relations, mobility, security, and instability, slums, grey-areas, and affluent areas, are also marks of the enlarged city. The individual, who is largely anonymous, finds his effectiveness in organized groups, or institutions, and in group actions that tend to serve the mass. It is from the metropolis that massive communication media emanate, such as newspapers, magazines and book publishing, radio, television, and it is within this large city that dynamic financial and managerial moves are made.

Megalopolis

From the metropolis it is but a short step to "Megalopolis" which, in the words of Wolf Von Eckardt, is "a huge string of central cities, suburbs, and satellite areas that stretch along the eastern seaboard of the United States from north of Boston to south of Washington and is the largest, wealthiest, and most productive region on earth."[6]

This conglomeration includes arable land in spite of the spread of suburbs and growth of cities. It does, however, make less sharp the line of division, and alters the balance between city and country. The quantity, expansion, and overgrowth of the megalopolis create one vast complex of industry, commerce, financial power, and high population density.

It draws hope through its concentration of skills, learning, talents, job opportunities, schools, affluence, and institutions. It draws despair in its unemployed and low-income people, its blighted areas, its need for more

---

[6] Wolf Von Eckardt, *The Challenge of Megalopolis: Based on the Original Study of Jean Gottman.* Twentieth Century Fund Report (New York: Macmillan, 1964), p. 5.

schools, its lack of adequate housing, its increasing tax burden, and its maladjusted—those who have not become "urbanized."

Urbanization involves the adjustment of a whole range of behaviors, attitudes, and relationships to the conditions imposed by urban life. Successful adjustment is a high degree of organization allowing personal freedom of social activity, economic self-sufficiency, and a productive role in the urban milieu. Lack of urbanization, or lack of adjustment, results in a condition characterized by personal disorganization, poor mental health, crime, corruption, and allied forms of social disorder.

Significantly, the suburban areas have experienced great growth in recent years. These represent the affluent society. Population actually is declining within the core cities, with their blighted areas. In the urban matrix, the population of the depressed areas live within sight of the industries from which the suburban commuters draw their livelihood. It is lack of job skills that keep the urban resident in depressed area status.

EFFECTS OF URBANIZATION

Specialization

Whereas in Europe the growth of cities has dominated, preceding the growth of national states, in America until recently, rural life and growth has been dominant, with the growth of national power preceding that of cities. An urbanized society is rapidly emerging in the United States. The effects of this urbanization, although identified with abundance, security, and democratic freedoms, are also identified with negative social consequences, particularly in the core of cities.

Specialization has developed as the nature of industry, and society has become more complex. Those who have become trained and knowledgeable within the limits of particular occupation or service offer their limited roles to the whole of business or community enterprise.

Effective knowledge is professionalized and expert. In the complex metropolitan community, functions are performed better by those who possess knowledge and skills in specialized areas of influence. Persons find their roles occupationally and in social groups, and tend to function especially within these confines, thereby achieving their own special areas of living. The positive values of specialization notwithstanding, inherent dangers lie in overspecialization. It can foster passivity and even resistance, and a lack of interpersonal and intergroup communication. The possibility of oversimplification due to specialization negates a comprehensive view of the vast and complex nature of the total society. The loss of interaction between specialized parts, and the problem of recognizing the worth of the individual in relation to the whole of society has created human relations problems requiring more and more attention and research from the behavioral sciences. Specialization demands skilled labor. The unskilled, whether from lack of ability or from lack of training, drift toward the depressed areas of the core city. Deprivation breeds violence. The large cities *must* retrain the workers of the depressed areas, or face continuous riots of the magnitude of the Watts riots of 1965.

Fragmentation

When society began to demand specialization, fragmentation began. Life at one time could be viewed more as a whole, with a view of a certain product of labor from its inception to its completion. The labor and its product were enmeshed in the whole tone of the family and the community. More and more persons play different roles that become compartmentalized. People go to work, to church, to social, recreational, and cultural events that are all more or less unrelated. Observance of and participation in the life of the city by the individual does not take place as a total activity, but more as one fragmented into certain selected parts. With the relentless increase in specialization, a different framework has been created that disrupts the continuity of the "whole." Now only a small part, a single operation, in a whole complex of parts and operations, can be the fruits of a worker's labor. This change has brought about a subsequent fragmentation of relationships and created echelons of authority that are impersonal in human interaction. Today the importance of understanding human behavior, and the approach that work is getting done through people, has increased the need to understand the psychological needs in the large rank and file of wage earners.

Anonymity

Anonymity is the lack of adequate personal identification with the society in which one lives. With the impersonality fostered by *fragmentation,* associations are altered. On the urban scene the more intimate person-to-group relationship is replaced largely by a group-to-group relationship. Humans cannot tolerate a loss of individual identity, a sense of not belonging. According to some authorities, this in part explains the strength of labor unions. The union tends to give the worker a sense of belonging and it cares for its welfare. Men tend more to express themselves and gain identity through groups rather than individually.

Man measures himself in the structure of his values, beliefs, and work. He forms a sense of who and what he is. This is his ego-identity, which involves self-concept, self-attitude, motivation, and aspiration. Simple personal relationships of a more rural past were a relatively easy adjustment for people. In the complex, mechanized urban society, these simple relationships are much more difficult to achieve at much more than a superficial and transitory level. People need a personal identity in the role they play in society, and this role is difficult to select. It is getting to be more difficult to function adequately, and to achieve self-expression and to create a sense of belonging. If the individual sees society moving on irrespective of his existence, he feels his impotence and his feeling of anonymity is intolerable. He may rationalize his victimization, his shortcomings, his lack of striving, his humiliation—and his predicament becomes his crutch. Apathy or aggressive and hostile behavior may be turned into weapons of sabotage against the anonymity he suffers.

Anomie

Anomie implies a social state of degradation in which the individual is so dissociated from any productive role in society that the common rules of conduct fail to influence his behavior. There is no longer any sense of values or goal direction. The symptomatology of anomie incorporates a state of alienation, progressing further to antisocial forms of behavior, and leading finally to a loss of reality-sensitivity. The sequelae is a drifting and senseless existence, devoid of cultural impact, and lacking even rebellion in the form of hostile aggression. The finality of this anomic state is, upon reflection, identifiable only in the context of severe mental illness in which behavior no longer relates to reality, rationally or irrationally—a complete state of dehumanization or total withdrawal.

Anomie is decreasing in the depressed areas. Rebellions are based on hope of success as a result of the rebellious activities. The residents of the depressed areas are correctly concluding that the Civil Rights legislation of the mid-1960's was a direct result of the Civil Rights violence of the early 1960's. Success builds hope.

The Problems of the City

The violence can be predicted to accelerate, until concrete improvements are visible in the lives of the dwellers in depressed areas.

Urban problems have been articulated to some extent in the foregoing development of the city. It has a rapid, intense pace, complicated by the forces of technology. Its culture has seen great physical and social changes. Crowding people into limited space results in increased demands, such as public utilities, traffic regulations and movement, police protection, parks and other recreation centers, civic centers, schools, libraries, public transportation, fire protection, health and welfare measures, and housing. Communities in their organization to meet these needs find both opportunities in physical improvements and growing social problems.

Urban Renewal

Urban renewal remains a controversial issue, and many such projects have met with something less than long-range success. It is, however, generally agreed that the welfare of people is contingent on the prevention of slums and blight; that the preservation of natural beauty and the provision of decent homes and living environment are among the factors relevant to a healthy democratic society.

The problems of urban environment are enmeshed in critical issues of human welfare. Renewal projects precipitate the need to study housing, building codes, zoning and land use laws, traffic problems, and the disruption of private business and public enterprise. Such projects have been in effect, to one degree or another, since the Federal Housing Act of 1949. Very simply, the term *urban renewal* implies the rebuilding of a city through government subsidy and private enterprise. The procedure includes studies of the conditions mentioned above and of the needs of the local community, with a proposed clearance of specific areas and plans for reuse. Development standards must be clarified in these plans and the whole submitted to the federal government. The cost of land, raising buildings, and resale of this land to private enterprise represent a large loss which, upon the condition of federal approval, is made up by the federal government and city subsidy.

With the more economically sufficient class of people leaving the city for the suburbs, thereby reducing taxable income, and with the basis of urban taxation in its property and improvements, many cities have found their dwindling basis of taxation in need of reconstruction. One remedy to aid in obtaining higher revenue is to impose income taxes on residents of suburban areas who still earn their living in the city. Detroit was successful in levying this tax, and even managed to cut its city property tax while in the midst of extensive renewal projects.

Diversity of values, class, and social groups—a pluralistic society—has always been thought to characterize the urban environment. The population trend is for the discriminated-against lower-class minority groups and elderly people to remain in the central city, with the middle and upper classes moving out to the fringes and suburbs. Thus the social distance between classes and ethnic groups becomes more intense, and slums become singular areas for the poor, with all of their attending ills.

Housing

As urban renewal projects disrupt the small business merchants, so too do they involve the clearance of slums and subsequent removal of slum dwellers. Inadequate housing is a quantitative and qualitative problem of the city. Many residential areas located in the inner core are characterized by substandard dwellings. They are in a state of physical deterioration, housing too many people who are socially and economically impoverished. These areas whose high population density demands greater facilities, are often lacking in parks, playgrounds, and appropriate educational opportunities.

In providing better public housing that will rent to low-income people, the Public Housing Authority pays a figure in lieu of taxes to the city and county, thus making it possible to provide good housing for those who qualify. Rehabilitation of old housing has been pursued to some extent by nonprofit groups. Housing codes are effective in forcing the owner of property to improve it if there is adequate inspection service, and if the courts enforce housing regulations. Effective zoning is another aspect of residential planning, be it new housing developments or the rehabilitation of older areas, and the prevention of the encroachment of undesirable kinds of business and industry. It offers restrictions on the use of property and can prevent the deterioration of previously stable neighborhoods.

It is being more and more recognized that, in addition to a physical plan for renewal, a social plan is vital not only to serve people, but also to involve and educate people to the responsibilities of their care of property and their use of services. For neighborhood rejuvenation to succeed, the residents must, with intelligent leadership, participate in improvement of the neighborhood and must be instilled with civic pride. Civic organizations work in close alliance with the federal government. They try to achieve this citizen participation and to prove that the city is trying to improve itself, which is now a requirement in order to be granted government subsidy. The Community Action Programs of President Johnson's "Great Society" movement are logical outgrowths of the urban-redevelopment program. The emphasis in CAP is not upon housing, but upon job-training and employment service.

Traffic

Mass production has resulted in the use of the automobile, truck, and bus for the mass transportation of goods and people. These means of transportation have, in turn, resulted not only in urban congestion of traffic in the core of the city, but also in congestion on the routes into the city. Efforts thus far to render more efficient movement of traffic has resulted in the development of complex expressways leading into the city. Due to the rapid growth, particularly of American cities, and the lack of planning, city streets are too narrow to be able to handle the heavy influx of traffic. Efforts to widen them and enforce complicated traffic regulations have alleviated the problem in a minimal and temporary way.

The problem of traffic is further compounded by the need for parking space, with areas above and below ground being utilized for this purpose. The expressways, garages, and other parking areas consume land space, thereby reducing the space available for other purposes, such as parks, recreation areas, cultural centers, and residences.

A number of procedures to remedy traffic ills have been proposed, and some have been incorporated into renewal projects. Perimeter parking facilities at strategic points enroute to the central city, with fast electrically driven public transportation to complete the journey, have been projected. Special underground routes have been suggested for inner city traffic, especially facilitating the delivery of goods. Another device for commuters would be an underground tube through which passenger vehicles would travel at speeds in excess of 100 miles an hour. Within the core area, moving sidewalks and small electrically driven vehicles would be for pedestrian movement. The ideal is to enhance the core area for use by people, and to offer flexibility of design in city planning.[7]

Crime and Delinquency

The preceding chapter dealt with crime and delinquency in its several forms. It will suffice here to remind the reader that they represent some of the most serious of city problems. As the population migrates to the cities, there is more poverty, and as there is more poverty, so there is more antisocial behavior. Crime is the manifestation of the social ills of a community. The circumstances of city life such as poverty in the midst of material abundance, anonymity, the crowds of people, the need to conform to prevailing urban social mores, the lack of adjustment to these mores, and the one-time family activities moving from the home out into the community—all evoke the problem of crime and delinquency.

The Culturally Disadvantaged

There is a growing concern stemming from the contrast of economic well-being for so many in the American society, and of the condition of economic poverty and social alienation for others. The technology that has created great material advantages, better working conditions, and high levels of aspiration both educationally and vocationally, has passed by growing numbers of this society. These are not only failing to advance, but seem to be insulated against advancements, forming a culture of the poor. The term "culturally disadvantaged" is relative and is one of several that have been used to identify a segment of society that is being recognized today as nonproductive economically. In addition, this part of society creates welfare burdens and social hazards, with a set of values, habits, attitudes, and behaviors that are different from those of the large middle class of America. Whereas these "different" elements of a more provincial culture may have been acceptable at another time and in another place, when moved to the urban scene, they no longer serve their bearers well. Nor do they serve the larger society in the urban milieu. Recognizing that these people do have a culture, that they are not "without" or "deprived" of a culture, it seems that they are a truly disadvantaged culture.

The middle-class influences demand some measure of conformity in matters of education, success-striving, moral behavior, social adjustment, economic self-sufficiency, and belief and participation in the democratic way of living. It is possible that the very existence of a democratic form of government and way of life are contingent on a productive and educated citizenry.

Two cultures, though they may actually have a fundamental sharing of

[7] See Victor Gruen, *The Heart of Our Cities: The Urban Crises: Diagnosis and Cure* (New York: Simon and Schuster, 1964).

a basic democratic faith, cannot exist side by side without one assuming a position of leadership, or prominence, over the other. To a degree, the minor culture will have to be assimilated into the larger culture if a healthy society is to be maintained. This does not negate the right of subcultures to exist. That they do is healthy and good—offering, as they do, diversity of habits, talents, ideas, incomes, and institutions. However, when a subculture becomes insulated against the standards and norms that perpetuate the healthy survival of its offspring, and when it becomes enslaved in a downward spiraling cycle of poverty, then the whole of society is jeopardized. The culturally disadvantaged are those in American society who lack the resources—economically, educationally, and socially—to maintain norms acceptable in the middle-class culture, and who cannot contribute to their own well-being nor to that of society at large.

These people are mostly of southern origin, both Negro and white, and have been forced by economic necessity to leave their small farms, or their positions as farm workers, itinerant or tenant, to seek employment in the cities. Between 1950 and 1961 over 1½ million farmers and over 1 million farm laborers left the farm. Millions of farm laborers and small farm owners became either migratory or crowded into the cities, looking for work.[8]

Many of the migrants are products of depressed areas into which failure and defeat have invaded due to automation. These people move to the only area open to them in a large and confusing city, the slum. They bring with them few if any employable skills, their children, and their problems. The other minority groups, the Puerto Ricans, Mexicans, and Indians also comprise a part of the population of the slum. They too have the disadvantage of the lack of skills, and furthermore face even more prejudice than the white population because of language barriers and skin color.

While the case of the Negro is unique, it is unnecessary to go further into his plight, his history, and his enslavement to prejudice and discrimination (see pp. 307–328, Chapter 9). All that is said of the other disadvantaged groups may also be said of the Negro, only with considerably more emphasis, for he is discriminated against because of color.

Although the culturally disadvantaged cannot be stereotyped according to race, social class, nationality, or occupation, certain characteristics are held in common often enough to provide a fairly clear picture:[9]

1. A position in the lower-income and class level.
2. A low aspirational and educational level with little upward mobility.

[8] Grace Graham, *The Public Schools in the American Community* (New York: Harper, 1963), pp. 259–260.
[9] Martin Deutsch, "The Disadvantaged Child and the Learning Process," Harry A. Passow (ed.), *Education in Depressed Areas* (New York: Bureau of Publications, Teachers College, Columbia University, 1963).
See also Robert D. Havighurst, "Who are the Socially Disadvantaged," *The Education Digest*, Vol. 30, No. 3 (November 1964).

3. Victims of economic, class, and racial discrimination.

4. In a rural location in a depressed condition, or in a city location with a predominantly rural background and subsequent lack of adjustment to the urban environment.

5. Few, if any, marketable skills, with marginal or no employment.

6. Frequent regression to anti-social behavior.

THE CULTURALLY DISADVANTAGED CHILD AND THE SCHOOL

From the family enmeshed in the defeating circumstances of poverty, emerges the child. The disadvantaged child's environment and social relationships have not prepared him to grow and mature adequately.

What are the children like? What are their circumstances of poverty which so ill-prepare them for healthy growth. To provide answers to these questions it is best to look at the different aspects of these children's environments: the home, attitudes, and social activity.

The home:
1.   Is disorganized.
2.   Provides inadequate space for play and study.
3.   Is often characterized by maternal domination, with a poor male model.
4.   Has inequality in eating and sleeping habits.

Attitudes:
1.   Are fatalistic toward health.
2.   Are accepting of illness.
3.   Involve low aspiration.
4.   Indicate a poor self-concept, a feeling of worthlessness and rejection.
5.   Are distrustful of those in the larger society.

Social activity in which:
1.   Play is confined to narrow sidewalks.
2.   The child is kept close to him by parents.
3.   The child is not exposed to a variety of experiences.

The child from these circumstances is intellectually lacking on all fronts.[10]

The school represents a foreign culture. It has values of cleanliness and health. It offers a great variety of objects to be handled and identified— things to be seen and heard. It requires verbal expression and response. Long-range goals predominate over short-range goals. Emotional stability is a prerequisite. School learning requires regular attendance. Aggressive behavior is frowned upon. The educational process needs the parents' vital interest and involvement to motivate and develop the child. For the

---

[10] See Harry A. Passow (ed.), *Education in Depressed Areas* (New York: Bureau of Publications, Teachers College; Columbia University Press, 1963).

middle-class child these are normal enough requirements. Why can't the disadvantaged child achieve in this orientation? These are discussed under the following headings:[11]

Cleanliness and health are not the order in the home of poverty. Cleanliness holds a very secondary rating. The mechanical contrivances for cleaning taken for granted in a better home frequently do not exist. The rather fundamental knowledge of how to keep clean is often a missing factor.

Of considerably more importance is the factor of health, which affects the will to work and learn. The child has not only not learned good health habits, he has learned a carelessness regarding health. His has been a poor diet resulting in low energy, upset stomach, poor teeth and respiratory problems. The family, usually large and living in small, inadequate or dilapidated quarters, is disorganized and irregular concerning eating and sleeping habits, to say nothing of the lack of adequate beds, tables, and chairs to handle their needs. The attitude toward poor health is a fatalistic attitude—one of accepting poor health with apathy and fatigue.

Sensory development is inadequate. The disadvantaged child's ingenuity of hands and mind has not been challenged. He does not have a variety of toys with which to play, handle, and identify. He does not have picture books nor stories told and read to him. His home is sparsely furnished, bereft of decor and stimulating objects. Noise surrounds him, but much of it is meaningless. Intellectual stimulation does not exist and readiness to learn does not grow in the disadvantaged child. Rather, it seems that he learns not to learn, not to see, not to hear, and not to be attentive. His is a restricted range of experiences and his concept formations are limited. This ill-equips the child for the structure and demands of school activity.

Language development in the impoverished home is usually of a restricted nature. It is used to convey essential, concrete, and immediate information for immediate consequences. The use of short, grammatically simple, and often unfinished sentences with little variety suffices. This meager language use is compounded usually by colloquialized expression. Concurrent with the minimal use of language is the inability to interpret and express impressions and reactions. With these restrictions the child is preset for poor language and cognitive development unless the school can offer compensatory measures.

Long-range vs. short-term goals lie at the heart of middle-class values. The disadvantaged simply do not think this way. Life's basic needs are acute, and the effort expended to meet them is all-consuming. In addition, the attainability of future rewards is not realistic; the hurdles met are too great. The feelings of insecurity and failure repudiate the promise of some distant security and success, and make continued effort hopeless. Only

[11] See also Martin Deutsch, *op. cit.*, p. 163 ff. for similar list.

when basic needs are met, and successful experiences in the early school years are achieved, will long-range goals be meaningful to the child.

Emotional stability is a part of being acceptable and secure. The impoverished child has his parents' feelings of worthlessness passed on to him, and school may offer more feelings of rejection and failure.

At home the child is subject to harsh and quick punishment for behavior that displeases, but seldom rewarded for behavior that is pleasing. The parents are more adept at communicating *what they feel about themselves*—disgust, disapproval, and rejection. It is hard to show love when bitterness, discouragement, ill health, and anxieties dominate. Frequently, the home structure lacks a father, or the father, if present, is unemployed and presents a poor model to the child. There is no doubt that the implication here is to help the child achieve and gain a good self-concept, and to provide parental education and guidance.

Good behavior in the school means nonaggression. Compliance with rules, good sportsmanship, and rewards for success are indelibly inscribed in the middle-class concepts of good school behavior. As the deprived child progresses through school, he is often more and more of a behavior problem.

The rules of behavior are from another culture, and he has learned no respect for them. In his environment, fighting amounts to a way of life. Differences and arguments are not settled through logical reasoning. More often the child has not only witnessed the most gross of physical exchange between his peers, parents, and neighbors, but he has been a recipient of harsh punishment, many times undeserved. He has not been taught self-control. He has been taught quite the opposite and can be very volatile, with the result that subsequent school punishment for his aggression is of belated importance. His is a life of survival, and he is ready to defend what seems to him to be the slightest infraction of his tenuous position. His weapons are few, and he uses what he has. What may be a good adjustment in his home environment, however, is a poor adjustment in the school.

Parental attitudes are basically in favor of education. However, the attitude is ambivalent. The parent confusedly sees the need for education, but is opposed to the authority of the school. He himself has had only limited exposure to or success in school, and has no knowledge of what is required for readiness to learn and good study habits. The importance of regular attendance is not understood. The parent is embarrassed by his lack of education, and is aware of his poor showing in the company of middle-class school personnel, and is actually fearful. The school is an outsider who takes the child away from the home to better him in ways not fully comprehended by the parent. The school appears to point an accusing finger at the culturally limited parent, and this bears the threat of humiliation and raises barriers.

EFFECTS OF THE CHARACTERISTICS COMMON TO DISADVANTAGED CHILDREN ON THEIR SCHOOL LIFE

Children

As the child enters school he may not evidence many or all of these disadvantages. However, the bridge between the slum culture and middle-class school culture is a large one, and problems increase with time. Frustrations and failures begin and accumulate until by the sixth grade the student is alienated and negative to the degree that the prognosis for success is a doubtful one.

Older Youth

Adolescence is a period when there is a search for a new identity, a quest for new experience, when peer group relations and conformity are increasingly important, and future goals become more defined. All societies must have a set of universals—a set of values to which all persons must either adhere or face some ostracization. The child comes into conflict in the transition period between childhood and adulthood in his search for new self-identity. This is largely a case of maturing.

In contemporary American society, the teens have developed a real culture that is considerably isolated from the adult culture. These youth have trouble relating to authority and seeing the adult as helpful. Youth are also searching for identity in the world of skills and occupations. If there is a lack of proper identity development and adult relations, anti-social, delinquent, or outright psychotic behavior may result. The problem of youth then is threefold: (1) the search for new self-identity, (2) the adjustment to the adult world, and (3) the search for occupational identity.

For approximately one third of the youth who begin secondary education this critical period is one in which the student has little motivation and little aspiration for further education.[12] He fails to see the relevancy of his education to his living habits, and he has no clear vocational goals. The disadvantaged youth is rebellious and resentful of authority and school domination, which, for him, represent punishments and no rewards.

By ages 14–16, the way to be "in" is to be hostile to the dominant society, with conformity to the culture in which his rearing took place. Still, this presents an enigma. This youth knows that the completion of secondary education is essential to acquire work that will enable him to survive economically. But this awareness often does not generate the necessary will to overcome what are now internalized features of the poverty environment. He tends to push aside the grim reality of his future for immediate gratification. To the middle-class person, this is an irrational

[12] Erik H. Erikson, *Youth: Change and Challenge* (New York: Basic Books, 1961, 1963), p. 120.

response. To the psychologist, this is the only rational response to his situation. From school truancy and dropping out, of course, come the threatening behavior called juvenile delinqency, adult crime, and the spontaneous riots of depressed areas.

This youth is one out of every four under 20 years of age who today are the unemployed.[13] He has been ill equipped since his early schools to take advantage of the educational opportunities available. Passow states that the unemployment rate of youth between the ages of 14 and 21 is twice that of the labor force as a whole and is even greater among youth from minority groups.[14]

What is being said here is a natural conclusion to the preceding evaluation of the early school years of the disadvantaged child. The efforts of social and educational impoverishment are cumulative and culminate in the wasteful situation of school dropouts and unemployed youth. This concern is today being recognized as a problem of national dimensions in the United States. The school is recognizing that the deprivation endured by a child of the disadvantaged culture not only impinges on his academic achievement, but renders him incapable of ultimate social and economic adjustment, *within the framework of existing school programs*, both public and private. A new kind of education is needed.

PROGRAMS FOR THE ALLEVIATION OF THE EFFECTS OF POVERTY AND CULTURAL IMPOVERISHMENT

The culturally disadvantaged student does not make normal progress in school learning. This realization has affected all aspects of education, spurring educators and the public to view the immediacy of the problem and to define the task of reshaping curriculum and methods to attain full development for each individual. The need is for helping those who are impoverished to achieve personal dignity and freedom, thereby enabling them to identify with the larger society and to respond profitably to social and economic change. This calls for a system of education that can overcome deficiencies in the learning development of the child.

Enrichment and Compensatory Education

Special projects for schools with "problem" children evolve around a number of factors, and begin with the child at a preschool age. Considerations of adequate food, medical care, and clothing are fundamental concerns. Programs to aid the perceptual and cognitive ability of the child by helping him to experience the world around him, involve the structured nursery and kindergarten experience. In some areas these have existed as preschool academies, and in current federal programs are called "head start." Through these, which may involve the child as young as 3 years,

13 Erik H. Erikson, *op. cit.*
14 Harry A. Passow, *op. cit.*

language is extended, and new insights and discoveries are made. The child learns to see the adult as a source of help and information. He becomes motivated and ready to learn. Communication and involvement with parents is essential at this early stage. They are informed of these early programs, are encouraged to observe the classes and, when possible, even to assist in their operation.

For those whose deprivation has culminated in a lack of learning, the progress may be early retardation, frustration, and failure within the first three grades of school. Compensations must be created to halt further failure that can only become more pronounced as the child proceeds through the upper grades. In these critical early years, careful evaluation of the social and intellectual characteristics of each child should be made, with adjustive teaching methods and the freedom to try new approaches geared to help each child. Enrichment and compensatory programs may include a longer school day with special instruction for small groups, summer programs, and tutorial programs. Exposure to the performing arts through concerts and plays, field trips to parks, museums, recreation areas, and places of business and industry are more and more being incorporated into programs to alleviate the effects of impoverishment.

The importance of a positive relationship between the school and parents, thereby forming a conjunctive home-school effort, cannot be over-emphasized. The school reflects the community in terms of boys and girls, who in turn reflect their home environment and structure. As a community agent, the school can use neighborhood resources as a "community school." This concept involves a wide range of academic, vocational, recreational, and social pursuits that involve not only children, but also adults. Special classes operate on Saturdays and evenings through the week for children to acquire skills beyond those given during regular school hours. Adult education, recreation, health services, remedial education, social activities, and civic participation add special strengths to the school and community, and strengthen minority groups.

Study and work must have transfer value out of school. As the child progresses through secondary education, this statement claims more and more significance. Deprived students need special help in tutoring or small group instruction, with emphasis on basic skills and vocational education. In a work-study plan, learning takes place through a relationship that holds concrete value, providing some income and motivation to complete what is so essential—the secondary school. The study-work program requires school leadership and counseling, and the cooperation of community agencies, business, and industry. From this can evolve an organized peer society in which adolescent youth may find positive identity and support from others in the group, as well as helpful adult leadership.

Not of least importance in school programs for the disadvantaged is the need to recognize the changes necessary in the school staff and their qualifications—more counselors for both students and parents at all levels, social workers, and leadership that can intelligently reach out into the community from the school. Teachers who are equipped to grasp the problems of the disadvantaged children, and who are resourceful in coping with these problems, need to possess certain characteristics both in personality and in training. The following are basic essentials:[15]

1. Knowledge and understanding of the disadvantaged culture, including specific ethnic differences.
2. Knowledge of the various forms of prejudice and discrimination and ways of counteracting them.
3. Exposure to an orientation program, and specific training with regard to the problems and relevant issues of depressed areas.
4. An understanding of learning problems, with an emphasis on the students' fear of failure in the classroom.
5. The ability to objectively evaluate students' strengths and weaknesses.
6. Consistency in firmness and fairness of treatment, be it in disciplinary matters or structure of work.
7. An authoritative, straightforward, and direct approach, with the emphasis on physical presentation as opposed to a highly verbal presentation.
8. The ability to accept and respect children as they are.
9. The ability to establish good rapport and to motivate through interest, enthusiasm, and patience.
10. Conviction that these children can and will learn.

School programs such as those just described are geared toward a better tomorrow for children—by raising their aspirational, educational, and vocational levels, by providing better cultural and recreational horizons, and by intensive guidance to help students want to achieve in the midst of opportunity.

ANTI-POVERTY PROGRAMS

The 88th and 89th Congresses of the United States enacted laws to strengthen the social and economic potential of people through education, training, work opportunity, and through designs for a better living environment. This antipoverty legislation was overwhelming in its many aspects and perspectives, with extraordinary attempts to upgrade services in such broad fields as education, health and welfare, transportation facilities, employment, voting rights, farming, aid to distressed areas and conservation. The legislation symbolizes the growing outlook that the United States

---

[15] See similar list Harry A. Passow (ed.), *Education in Depressed Areas* (New York: Bureau of Publications, Teachers College, Columbia University Press, 1963). See also Frank Riessman, *The Culturally Deprived Child* (New York: Harper, 1962).

is a national community with problems that have grown to national dimensions.[16]

Why is the country so concerned about its depressed areas and disadvantaged population? The economy is one of plenty and keeps moving upward. This is a society of affluence, and the relative downward mobility of a growing segment of society stands out in contrast to this affluence and upward mobility. Too, a careful look at the present, and a further look into the future foretells of even greater problems if man doesn't develop a fuller human potential.

In historical perspective, education has been the function of the state and local community, with much controversy over the issue of federal aid. The state assumed this task, with the result that America became the first stronghold of universal education, this concept becoming an integral part of democracy. As the cost of education has increased, the federal government has responded with caution and reserve. Thus, in the past, aid has come through the Morrill Act of 1862, a device for setting up land grant colleges to promote agricultural and mechanical arts education. During each succeeding war, further aid was enacted, designed largely to support vocational high school training, and after World War II, the famous GI Bill of Rights enabled veterans to gain higher education.[17] With the advance into space by the Russians in 1957, Congress enacted the National Defense Education Act, which supported science, mathematics, and long-range instruction in the public schools, by the granting of further provision for loans to college students.

With the declaration that poverty must be eliminated, the legislation of 1964–1965 is of a vast nature and has long-range implications for fighting poverty on many fronts. It has provided federal initiative, but with allowance for local autonomy and latitude. Although most local communities had entered a war on poverty before 1964 and had supported their efforts by local foundations, the federal legislation made further funds available to existing or new agencies upon request, and subject to approval on the basis of utilization of the requested funds. These agencies have been organized as component parts of a whole antipoverty program, coordinated by a local community action commission. It is through this coordinating body that plans are màde, funds are requested, and federal approval is obtained, to implement the program.

The Economic Opportunity Act of 1964 provides a work-training program giving part-time work to boys and girls in their local communities on projects picked by local government or organizations thereby enabling them to stay in or return to school. Large training centers, the Job Corps, provide vocational training and educational skills, with an allowance and certain expenses paid for those 16 to 21 years of age who are out of school and out of work. Work-study programs to help needy college students,

16 *Time Magazine*, April 30, 1965, pp. 40, 45.
17 *Time Magazine*, *ibid.*

community action projects such as tutoring, training, recreation centers, grants for adult education, work experience programs for needy unemployed, loans for poor farm families, projects involving mental health, migrant workers, and neighborhood improvement groups, are areas of local effort. Organizations such as better housing leagues and American Committee to Improve Our Neighborhood (ACTION) are well-known examples of local organizations created to foster projects. Volunteers in Service to America (VISTA) is a federally operated domestic peace corps that serves in local areas with no pay.

The potential for development of materials and methods for application within the educational establishment with particular reference to under-privileged children and youth, may be gleaned from a brief examination of the philosophic foundations on which one Job Corps program is based. In January, 1966, James R. Bryner presented the program of the Atterbury Job Corps Center as follows:[18]

The Job Corps program at Atterbury is twofold. An obvious primary goal is to teach job skills. Not so obvious, but equally important, is the enculturation of youth into the commonly accepted mores of American society.

The job skill portion of the program is accomplished through provision of shops and instructions oriented toward specific families of job skills: food service, building trades, appliance repair, heating and ventilating, refrigeration, and automotives. Equal time is given to general education. Academic materials are programmed on an individual basis to fit the unique need of each Corpsman, in reading, computation, and science; the range of instruction is from beginning reading through twelfth grade competencies. During the final phase of shop instruction, full time is devoted to shop work. Final phase stresses advanced shop skills demanding technical skills in interpretation of manufacturers' manuals. Corpsmen who have not accomplished sixth grade levels in reading and arithmetic will not be allowed to proceed to the final phase of shop instruction.

Industrial research clearly demonstrates that jobs are lost not because of lack of technical skills, but because of lack of social skills in getting along with fellow workers and with supervisors. Atterbury Job Corps Center has no intention of accepting hostile, illiterate youth and of graduating hostile, illiterate mechanics. The total staff works constantly to maladjust these youth for return to the environment from which they came. The prevailing (middle class) American mores of thrift, honesty, cleanliness, courtesy, promptness, and pride in fine workmanship are stressed in all areas of Corpsman life. The goal is to graduate mechanics who have the technical skills to secure good jobs—and the social skills to hold them and to live comfortably in neighborhoods characterized by good housing and by responsible citizenship.

[18] The following materials pertaining to Job Corps do not necessarily reflect official Job Corps policy or opinions; they are the private views of the authors.

The population from which Job Corps youth are drawn is characterized by a rebellion against authority. Most of these youth are made of good stuff, but simply have known nothing but failure in the regimented class-rooms and heavily policed streets of the slums. They associate their failures with authority figures. They can be led; they cannot be driven.

Some Corpsmen have such extreme resistance to authority that they simply cannot adjust to institutional life: set hours for rising, meals, classes, and going to bed. These are the AWOLs, and the involuntary separations. They cannot tolerate controls, so they run away or they get thrown out.

Most Corpsmen simply come from disadvantaged backgrounds. As they experience success in individualized programs of academic instruction and of shop training, and as they earn rewards for conformance to social rules, they gradually discard their resistance to authority figures—for this new set of authority figures (Job Corps Staff) is associated with success! These Corpsmen are hungry for success experiences. They request *more* and *more stringent* rules so that "those of us who came here to learn something are not bothered by the guys who don't want to learn." This shift in atti-tudes and behaviors by individual Corpsmen generally is accompanied by significantly more rapid learning both in classrooms and in shops. Further, the social growth accelerates. These learnings go hand in hand. Both components of the program seem to be essential to success in either.

The research in education and in school work stresses the importance of development of concept of one's self as a worthy person as a prime prerequisite to successful living. This concept is built through success experiences. One is loved by family. One is accepted by peers. One is rewarded by authority figures in school, church, and civic institutions.

Job Corps youth have not had this love, acceptance, and reward. Job Corps staff is developing new materials and methods to meet these needs. Job Corps staff is providing these youth with their first physical and emo-tional security. It is providing youth with appropriate learning tasks, both in job skills and in social living. These youth are reading, computing, and working at skill levels that are suited to their ability and experience, in a relatively permissive atmosphere. They are being led, one small step at a time, toward acceptance of the prevailing modes of social behavior. As Corpsmen experience success, and develop worthy self-concepts, they start that long climb toward becoming responsible, self-directing, self-supporting citizens.

The successful American is an independent individual. He prizes his freedom of choice—in selection of friends, vocation, housing, and so on. Paradoxically, this "freedom of choice" leads him to value the same kinds of friends, vocations, housing, and so on, as are valued by those whom he respects. Job Corps staff predominantly is drawn from middle-class culture. Job Corps staff is dedicated toward earning the respect of the Corpsmen, as a prime motivator of Corpsmen toward accepting the prevailing values of American Life.

Many new instructional materials are being developed. Progress in the development of effective new methods is slower. The goal, in these early stages, is to apply the best of known techniques. By and large, Job Corps youth have not been exposed to acceptable techniques in education or in social living—or they wouldn't be in Job Corps. For the first time, they are being valued as human beings. They are respected as persons. True, they are expected to conform to a minimum of obvious roles of behavior; but these rules allow for a wide range in behavior. This range narrows as Corpsmen become enculturated to new ways of living. As Job Corps staff continues to work with Corpsmen, promising techniques are being experimentally implemented, both in formal instructional programs of general education and shop training and in the more informal programs of enrollee living. It is yet too early to appraise the effectiveness of these methods. Of this much we are sure. Job Corps youth are responding favorably to individualized materials presented through the best of the currently known techniques.

If Dr. Bryner's goals are achieved at Atterbury, and similar goals are achieved in other Job Corps Centers, then one of the greatest contributions of Job Corps well may be to present to the public and private schools of this country new ways of educating the lower-class citizen, contributions based on action research!

The Elementary and Secondary Education Act of 1956 offers aid to public, private, and parochial schools in low-income areas. Funds are allocated to school districts according to the number of pupils age 5–17 years within their boundaries whose families have an annual income of less than $2,000. Educational centers are supplemented to provide for remedial instruction, to finance instructional materials, and to expand federally supported educational research.[19] One illustration of a locally inspired, supported, and planned program conceived before this federal legislation is that operated by the Mutt Foundation in Flint, Michigan, since 1935. Based on the concept that the problems of society are the problems of the public school, their program has involved families and homes in the schools' attendance areas, and has attracted national and international attention. Briefly, this plan involves extra learning time after school hours and on Saturdays, adult educational, social, civic, and recreational activities, special classes for children with learning programs, and cooperative efforts and involvement of local businesses and clubs.[20]

The Public Works and Economic Development Act of 1965 provides assistance in improvements for public works and services, better employment opportunities, construction and rehabilitation within a redevelop-

---

[19] Hearings on Opportunity Act of 1964, Part I (Washington, D.C.: Govt. Printing Office, 1964), pp. 3–17.

[20] Peter L. Clancy, "The Urban Process," *The Community School and Its Administration*, Vol. 3 (February 1965), No. 6, 1–6.

ment area, and aid to Appalachia. It actually extends and revises the Area Redevelopment Act of 1961.[21]

The Housing and Urban Development Act of 1965 offers financial assistance to make private housing available to lower-income families who are elderly, handicapped, displaced, victims of natural disaster, or otherwise qualifying occupants of substandard housing.[22]

The Higher Education Act of 1965 in essence established funds to upgrade the quality of teaching by grants to colleges and universities. These grants extend services and resources within an institution, finance cost of cooperative exchanges of faculty, students, and facilities between institutions, student scholarships and loans, and advanced teacher preparation programs[23] (details and latest information about any or all of this legislation may be obtained by a request to the congressman of your district, or to one of your two senators).

LONG-RANGE IMPLICATIONS FOR PROGRAMS

A healthy society provides effective roles for its members. It has physical, economical, educational, governmental, and social aspects from which its members cannot be divorced. Civic pride and community conscience must be energized into involvement in setting goals for programs, and in determining values that prescribe the direction toward these goals.

Family planning services, which have existed in the past, must be made more effective for the future. Education in the material, physical, and psychological aspects of child rearing—so important to the development of physically and mentally healthy youngsters who later make up the adult social fabric—must be made more available to parents. Premarital education and marriage counseling must be made more available—the difficulty here is that it is often hard to find, educate, and counsel those who need it most. Communication is difficult on matters relating to family planning and other matters basic to the establishment of sound marriages.

The programs and the legislation just discussed have for the most part been constructed as a marshaling of resources to deal with complex and emergency situations. However, the immediate challenges must evolve into long-range measures that will effectively continue to prevent society from allowing inadequate roles for its members. The concern for human welfare cannot be indifferent to questions of poverty and its ills, education, social class and race, urban planning, rural environment, and physical and mental health. Basically, people must be educated to the problems that confront them and their society. The basis of this education must be laid early and proceed through the maturing of the individual as he develops

[21] Public Law 89–136, 89th Congress, S 1048, August 26, 1965.
[22] Public Law 89–117, 89th Congress, H.R. 7884, August 10, 1965.
[23] 89th Congress, 1st Session. Senate. Calendar No. 656. Report No. 673. September 1, 1965.

into a functioning member of the family (see also Chapter 7), social, civic, and governmental groups. This education must be a positive approach and must develop a sensitivity to just and preventative treatment measures. Consideration should be given to the different kinds of impoverishment: intellectual, biological, cultural, educational, and emotional. A whole complex of factors is associated with poverty.

Community services of whatever nature must be a collaboration of lay people, professional educators, social scientists, and social planners. Underlying all endeavors, there must be a human orientation, the planning for people.

SUMMARY

In this chapter the problems of the depressed areas—those areas that have not kept pace with the economic growth of the rest of the country—and the problems of the culturally disadvantaged child have been considered. The urbanization of our society with its attendant problems has been fully discussed. The nature of the rural depressed areas has also been described.

The effects of urbanization and the attendant specialization of the society, its fragmentation into groups in which it is difficult to "live life as a whole," and the increase in the amount of anonymity (lack of identification), with the consequent increase in the number of persons who are in a complete state of degradation—i.e., "anomie"—were clarified. Also were discussed the problems of urban renewal, the problem of urban housing, and the city traffic and highway problems as these affect the life of the people.

The problems of the culturally disadvantaged and the characteristics of the culturally disadvantaged children and youth in terms of their difficulties of adjusting to American social institutions, largely based on a middle-class set of values, were presented. Suggestions were made as to actions that might be taken to assist personnel working with disadvantaged children as these come into the schools or as they are helped by other social agencies.

Some of the programs developed as a part of the antipoverty movement, both by private and governmental groups, were discussed as these have come into play in recent years.

SELECTED BIBLIOGRAPHY

ABRAMS, CHARLES. *Man's Struggle for Shelter in an Urbanizing World*. Cambridge, Mass.: M.I.T. Press, 1964. Pp. xi + 307.

BAGDIKIAN, BEN H. *In the Midst of Plenty: The Poor in America*. Boston: Beacon Press, 1964. Pp. 207.

BEREITGER, CARL, and SIEGFRIED ENGLEMANN. *Teaching Disadvantaged Children in the Preschool*. Englewood Cliffs, N.J.: Prentice-Hall, 1966.

BETTELHEIM, BRUNO. *Truants from Life: The Rehabilitation of Emotionally Disturbed Children.* New York: Macmillan, 1964. Pp. xii + 511.
Through four detailed case studies, the author illustrates the nature and scope of the work carried on at the Sonia Shankman Orthogenic School of the University of Chicago.

BLOOM, BENJAMIN S., and others (eds.). *Compensatory Education for Cultural Deprivation.* New York: Holt, Rinehart & Winston, 1965. Pp. 192.

BROOKS, LYMAN B. "The Norfolk College Experiment in Training the Hard Core Unemployed." *Phi Delta Kappan,* **41** (November 1964), No. 3, 111–6.

BRYN, SEVERYN T. *Communities in Action: Patterns and Process.* New Haven, Conn.: College University Press, 1963. Pp. 15 + 205.

CHANDLER, B. J., LINDLEY J. STILES, and JOHN I. KITUSE. (eds.). *Education in Urban Society.* New York: Dodd, Mead, 1962. Pp. viii + 279.

C. E. D. *Distressed Areas in a Growing Economy.* New York: The Committee for Economic Development, 1961. Pp. 74.

CONANT, JAMES B. *Slums and Suburbs: A Commentary on Schools in Metropolitan Areas.* New York: McGraw-Hill, 1961. Pp. viii + 128.

CORWIN, RONALD G. *A Sociology of Education.* New York: Appleton-Century-Crofts, 1965. Pp. x + 454.

DUHL, L. J. (ed.). *The Urban Condition.* New York: Basic Books, 1963. Pp. xxi + 410.

DUNHAM, H. WARREN (ed.). *The City in Mid-Century: Prospects for Human Relations in the Urban Environment.* Detroit: Wayne State University Press, 1957. Pp. vii + 198.

DUNNE, GEORGE H. (ed.). *Poverty and Plenty.* New York: P. J. Kennedy, 1964. Pp. 142.

ECKARDT, WOLF VON. *The Challenge of Megalopolis: Based on the Original Study of Jean Gottman.* Twentieth Century Fund Report. New York: Macmillan, 1964. Pp. 126.

EDUCATION FOR SOCIALLY DISADVANTAGED CHILDREN. *Review of Educational Research,* **25** (December 1965). Entire issue contains a review of research on the topics.

EDUCATIONAL POLICIES COMMISSION. *Education and the Disadvantaged American.* Washington, D.C.: The Commission, 1962. Pp. 38.

ELIAS, C. E., JR., JAMES GILLIES, and SVEND RIEMER (eds.). *Metropolis: Values in Conflict.* Belmont, Calif.: Wadsworth Publishing, 1964. Pp. x + 326.

ELKIN, FREDERICK. *The Child and Society: The Process of Socialization.* New York: Random House, 1962. Pp. 121.

ERIKSON, E. H. (ed.). *Youth: Change and Challenge.* New York: Basic Books, 1963. Pp. xiv + 284.

EVANIER, DAVID, and STANLEY SIVERZWEIG, (eds.). *Nonconformers.* New York: Ballantine, 1961. Pp. viii + 284.

FERMAN, LOUIS A., JOYCE L. KORNBLUH, and ALAN HARBER, (eds.). *Poverty in America.* Ann Arbor: University of Michigan Press, 1965. Pp. 530.

FYREL, T. R. *Troublemakers: Rebellious Youth in an Affluent Society.* New York: Schocken Books, 1962. Pp. 347.

Ginzberg, Eli, and others. *The Negro Potential.* New York: Columbia University Press, 1956. Pp. xvi + 144.

Goodman, Paul. *Growing Up Absurd.* New York: Random House, 1960, Pp. xvi + 296.

Gottman, Jean. *Megalopolis: The Urbanized North-Eastern Seaboard of the United States.* Cambridge, Mass.: M.I.T. Press, 1964. Pp. 810.

Grambs, Jean D. "The Culturally Deprived Child." *The Education Digest,* **30** (January 1965), No. 5, pp. 1–4.

Gruen, Victor. *The Heart of Our Cities: The Urban Crisis: Diagnosis and Cure.* New York: Simon & Schuster, 1964. Pp. 368.

Harrington, Michael. *The Other America: Poverty in the United States.*

Havighurst, Robert J., and others. *Growing Up in River City.* New York: Wiley, 1962. Pp. xiii + 189.

————, and Bernice L. Neugarten. *Society and Education.* (New Edition) Boston: Allyn & Bacon, 1961. Pp. xv + 465.

Herber, Lewis. *Crisis in Our Cities.* Englewood Cliffs, N.J.: Prentice-Hall, 1965. Pp. xii + 239.

Hickerson, Nathaniel. *Education for Alienation.* Englewood Cliffs, N.J.: Prentice-Hall, 1966. Pp. 128.

Holstein, Ralph, Gerard Piel, and Robert Theobald. *Jobs, Machines, and People.* Santa Barbara, Calif.: Center for the Study of Democratic Institutions, 1964. Pp. 23.

Josephson, Eric, and Mary Josephson (eds.). *Man Alone: Alienation in Modern Society.* New York: Dell, 1962. Pp. 592.

Kaplan, Bernard A. "Issues in Educating the Culturally Disadvantaged," *The Phi Delta Kappan,* **40** (November 1963), No. 2, pp. 70–76.

Keeble, R. *A Life Full of Meaning.* New York: Pergamon, 1965. Pp. 226. Deals with the treatment of delinquents in England.

Kerber, August and Barbara Bommarito, (eds.). *The Schools and the Urban Crisis: A Book of Readings.* New York: Holt, Rinehart & Winston, 1965. Pp. xiv + 367.

Klopf, Gordon J., and Israel Lester, (eds.). *Integrating the Urban School.* New York: Teachers College, Columbia, 1963. Pp. viii + 126.

Lichter, Solomon O., and others. *The Dropouts.* New York: Free Press of Glencoe, 1962. Pp. xiii + 302.

Lohman, Joseph D. *Cultural Patterns of Differentiated Youth: A Manual for Teachers in Marginal Schools.* U.S. Department of Health, Education and Welfare, 1965.

Long, Nicholas J., William C. Morse, and Ruth G. Newman, (eds.). *Conflict in the Classroom: The Education of Emotionally Disturbed Children.* Belmont, Calif.: Wadsworth Publishing, 1965. Pp. xi + 515.

Morgan, James N., and others. *Income and Welfare in the United States.* New York: McGraw-Hill, 1962. Pp. x + 531.

Mumford, Lewis. *The City in History: Its Origins, Its Transformations and Its Prospects.* New York: Harcourt, Brace & World, 1961. Pp. xi + 657.

Murphy, Gardner. *Freeing Intelligence Through Teaching.* New York: Harper & Row, 1961. Pp. 64.

Myrdal, Gunnar. *Challenge to Affluence.* New York: Pantheon, 1963. Pp. viii + 172.

N.E.A. *No Room at the Bottom: Automation and the Reluctant Learner.* Washington, D.C.: National Education Association, 1963. Pp. 120.

N.E.A., A.S.C.D. *Nurturing Individual Potential.* Washington, D.C.: The Association, 1964. Pp. 91.

N.S.S.E. *Individual Instruction.* N.S.S.E. Sixty-first Yearbook, Part I. Chicago: University of Chicago Press, 1962. Pp. xii + 337.

Neisser, Ruth G. *School Failures and Dropouts.* Public Affairs Pamphlet No. 346. New York: Public Affairs Committee, 1963. Pp. 28.

Oeser, O. A., and S. B. Hammond, (eds.). *Social Structure and Personality in a City.* New York: Macmillan, 1954. Pp. v + 344.

Olson, Philip (ed.). *America as a Mass Society.* New York: Free Press of Glencoe, 1963. Pp. xii + 576.

Parker, Don H. *Schooling for Individual Excellence.* New York: Thomas Nelson, 1963. Pp. 285.

Passow, A. Harry (ed.). *Education in Depressed Areas.* New York: Bureau of Publications, Teachers College, Columbia University Press, 1963. Pp. xiv + 369.

Peet, Harriet E. *The Creative Individual: A Study of New Perspectives in American Education.* New York: Ronald Press, 1960. Pp. xi + 188.

Pomfret, John D. *New Opportunities for Depressed Areas.* Public Affairs Pamphlet No. 351, October 1963. New York: Public Affairs Pamphlets, 1963. Pp. 27.

"Poverty and the School," *Educational Leadership,* **22**, No. 7 (May 1965). Entire issue.

Riesman, David, and others. *The Lonely Crowd: A Study of the Changing American Character.* New Haven: Yale University Press, 1950. Pp. xvii + 386.

Reissman, Leonard. *The Urban Process: Cities in Industrial Societies.* New York: Free Press of Glencoe, 1964.

Riessman, Frank. *The Culturally Deprived Child.* New York: Harper & Row, 1962. Pp. xv + 140.

Sexton, Patricia Cayo. *Education and Income: Inequalities in Our Public Schools.* New York: Viking Press, 1961. Pp. xxi + 298.

Sheviakov, George V., and Fritz Redl. *Discipline for Today's Children and Youth.* New Revision by Sybil Richardson. Washington, D.C.: NEA Association for Supervision and Curriculum Development, 1956. Pp. iv + 66 (Pamphlet).

Silberman, Charles E. "Give Slum Children a Chance," *Harper's Magazine,* **228,** No. 1368. (May 1964), 37–42.

———, *Crisis in Black and White.* New York: Random House, 1964. Pp. xii + 370.

Stein, Maurice R., and Arthur J. Vidich, (eds.). *Identity and Anxiety: Survival of the Person in Mass Society.* New York: Free Press of Glencoe, 1960.

Strom, Robert D. *Teaching in the Slum School.* Columbus, Ohio: Merrill, 1965. Pp. x + 116.

Sykes, George (ed.). *Alienation: The Cultural Climate of Modern Man, I.* New York: Braziller, 1964. Pp. vi + 1237.

————. *Alienation: The Cultural Climate of Modern Man, II.* New York: Braziller, 1964. Pp. vi + 641.

TAYLOR, CALVIN W. (ed.). *Creativity: Progress and Potential.* New York: McGraw-Hill, 1964. Pp. xi + 241.

VERNON, RAYMOND. *The Changing Economic Function of the Central City.* New York: Committee on Economic Development, 1959.

WARNER, W. LLOYD. *American Life: Dream and Reality.* Revised edition. Chicago: University of Chicago Press, 1962. Pp. x + 291.

WEBER, MAX. *The City.* New York: Free Press of Glencoe, 1958. Pp. ix + 242.

WIRTZ, WILLARD W. (Chairman). *The Challenge of Jobless Youth.* Washington, D.C.: Government Printing Office, 1963. Pp. iv + 20.

WOOD, ROBERT C. *Metropolis Against Itself.* New York: Committee on Economic Development, 1959.

SELECTED FILMS

A Chance to Learn. (NEA) 30 min

Chance at the Beginning. 29 min

Children Without. (American Association of School Administrators) 55 min

The Dropout. (NEA) 29 min

Elementary School Teacher Education Series: Elementary School Children, Part I, Each Child Is Different. (McGraw-Hill) 16 min

Elementary School Teacher Education Series: Elementary School Children, Part II, Discovering Individual Differences. (McGraw-Hill) 25 min

Incident on Wilson Street (NET) 15 min
> An incident in a school in a depressed section of a large city.

Individual Differences. (McGraw-Hill) 20 min

The Newcomers. (Board of Missions, Methodist Church)

Knowledge and Skills. (Association) 21 min

Lewis Mumford on the City: (Contemporary) 28 min ea.
> The City—Heaven or Hell
> The City—Cars or People
> The City and Its Region
> The Heart of the City
> The City as Man's Home
> The City and the Future

Marked for Failure (NET) 59 min

A Place to Live. (Brandon) 18 min

Portrait of a Disadvantaged Child: Tommy Knight. (McGraw-Hill) 16 min
> Documentary film, highlighting a day in the life of a slum child—introducing special problems, needs, and strengths of the inner city child.

Portrait of the Inner City. (McGraw-Hill) 17 min
> Viewing the streets, the schools and the living quarters in the inner city of a large urban community in the U.S., giving the viewer some idea of what life is like in the inner city, reflecting its uplifting as well as degrading aspects. You see the inhabitants who serve as models for young Tommy Knight: the shoeshine man, junkman, porter, car-wash man. Also the more positive model of Tommy's older brother who works as a salesman in a store after school.

Portrait of the Inner City School: A Place to Learn. (McGraw-Hill) 19 min
   Focusing on Tommy Knight, shows many teaching techniques—some
   good, some ineffective, some harmful—and illustrates how a teacher can
   unconsciously discriminate against the culturally disadvantaged pupil.
   Shows teachers discussing methods which have proved successful or harm-
   ful.
Role Playing in Guidance. (University of California) 14 min
Step by Step. (International Film Bureau) 20 min
Urban Sprawl. (Arthur Barr) 15 min

Chapter 11. *Problems Occasioned by Population Trends*

POPULATION TRENDS, both in America and in the world, have experienced extreme shifts in recent years. These population trends have had significant effects on our social life and hence on education and the schools. During the period prior to World War II, a decreasing birth rate had a profound effect upon our economy and on our schools. During World War II and immediately after, the increased birth rate in America and throughout the world has had enormous implications for population problems. The effect of this trend on education during the latter period has been particularly acute in America, where an effort is made to provide the opportunity for education for almost everyone in our society from age six to age eighteen. We provide higher education for a much larger percentage of our population than do many well-developed countries. In the sections that follow, the changing trends in population and some of the problems they entail are discussed in more detail, with the implications for education set forth in the latter part of this chapter.

WORLD POPULATION TRENDS AND FOOD SUPPLY

Recent Changes in World Population

Man, being an adaptive animal, is found over the entire land mass of the globe, but his numbers are concentrated in those places most favorable for his existence. There is no exact count of his numbers, for census-taking is accurate only in the more progressive regions. A total of 2,913 million in 1960 appears to be a justified figure. It is expected to double by the year 2000. See Figure 11.

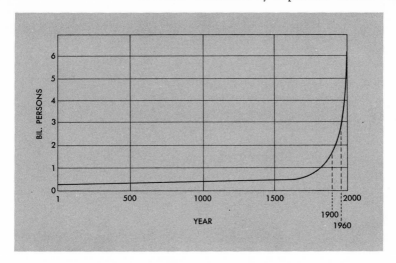

Figure 11. Twenty Centuries of World Population Growth.

Adapted from Leslie R. Brown, *Man, Land and Food* (U.S. Dept. of Agriculture, Foreign Economic Report No. 11, 1963).

Stamp quotes Julian Huxley as estimating roughly that at about 8000 B.C., the beginning of agriculture, the world held about 10 million people (probably not more than 20 million and not less than 5 million).[1] When the civilized era began—say, about 5000 B.C.—world population had increased to 20 million. There were perhaps 40 million when Egypt had its first dynasty, 100 million at the time of the Trojan War, and 175 million at the beginning of the Christian Era. By 1650 there were about 500 million, and since then the climb has been rapid. Another way of illustrating the tremendous upsurge is the statement that probably 2 to 3 per cent of all human beings (*Homo sapiens*) who ever lived are still alive.[2]

Estimates of human population by continents are helpful in interpreting these changes. In Table 11 will be found estimates of human population by continents from 1650 through 1960.

The large increase in population has been a direct result of many important changes in the ways of man's living. The two checks in the past on population growth have been the shortage of food and the widespread toll of disease, both of which have been intensified by war. One need only

[1] L. Dudley Stamp, *Land for Tomorrow* (Bloomington: Indiana University Press, 1952), p. 23.

[2] Authorities vary on this, some going as high as one person out of seven; others, more conservatively, one out of twenty (5 per cent). The writers are conservative, but even their figure is startling, since only two or three generations are alive at once (now) out of perhaps 30,000 generations since 8000 B.C. *Cf.* Annabelle Desmond, "How Many People Have Ever Lived on Earth?" in Stuart Mudd (ed.), *The Population Crises and the Use of World Resources* (Bloomington: Indiana University Press, 1964), pp. 27–616.

TABLE 11
POPULATION BY CONTINENTS AT SELECTED YEARS
(IN MILLIONS)

CONTINENT	1650	1700	1800	1850	1900	1940	1950	1960
North America	1	1	6	26	81	143	166	197
Middle America	6	6	10	13	25	42	51	66
South America	6	6	9	20	38	89	111	140
Europe	100	110	187	266	401	543	559	639
Asia	330	400	602	749	937	1186	1302	1636
Africa	100	98	90	95	120	157	198	235
World Total	545	623	906	1171	1608	2170	2400	2913

Source: Adapted from table in Leslie R. Brown, *Man, Land and Food* (U.S. Dept. of Agriculture, Foreign Economic Report No. 11, 1963).

think of the Black Death, the Thirty Years' War, and the modern famines of India and China to realize how millions of mankind have died in the past and are dying today. Better seeds and farming methods have resulted in more food; canning, freezing, and other means of preservation, together with better transportation, have made the food available. Better knowledge of health conditions and disease have allowed more to live—babies, mothers, and grandparents. Better means of production in factories have made men producers living in cities. With the possible exception of the Romans, it was not until about the middle of the eighteenth century that men had worked out satisfactory ways in which to supply any city, even a small one, with clean food and water, a minimal sanitary sewage disposal, moderately decent housing, and a small modern medical service. Wherever the benefits of the Industrial Revolution have spread, the people have been freed from a subsistence existence and their numbers have increased.

World Population and Food Supply

As soon as population and food supply are mentioned together, the name of Thomas Robert Malthus comes to mind. In 1791 Malthus presented the argument that population increases in a geometric ratio (1, 2, 4, 8, 16, 32, and so on) while food supply increases in an arithmetic ratio (1, 2, 3, 4, 5). Thus mankind must destroy himself through famine, pestilence, or war to maintain equality with his food! A review of history would, on the surface, apparently force one to agree with this. Even today, people frequently argue against aid to overpopulated countries by saying such aid will merely cause an increase in the birth rate and thus the problem will become worse instead of better.

An examination of the food supply of the more than 3 billion people in the world shows that most are underfed and undernourished. Two thirds of the people in the world have protein, vitamin, or mineral deficiencies in their diet (or deficiencies in all of these) that lead to slow starvation. This may be the result of poor soil, poor technology, poor land use, poor transportation, inability to afford better ways, lack of incentive, or religious and social taboos.

For conditions at almost their worst, one can examine south China, where it is estimated that 3,500 agricultural people live on each square mile of farm land. Twenty-three per cent of the farms are under one-half acre in size, and each farm must support an average of 4.4 people. These people get about 1,000 calories a day. In the United States, the average is about 3,400 calories. As would be expected, China has a death rate of 30 per 1,000 per year, an infant mortality rate of 160 per 1,000, and a life expectancy of 34 years. (Life expectancy in the United States is now over 70 years.)

Again, those who believe Malthus point to India, where population increased 18 per cent from 1932 to 1942, whereas cereal production increased only 6 per cent. This proportion is roughly true today. Accordingly, each person gets less cereal to eat—and cereal forms about 90 per cent of the diet. If reforms planned by the government are put into effect, India hopes merely to maintain the present level of food.

Further pessimism could come from an examination of probable populations in the future.

As Huxley says:[3]

Let me spell out quantitatively what this (population increase) means. Today, the annual net increase in the total of people of the world's surface is over fifty million. That means that the world's population grows by about 150,000 people every 24 hours, the equivalent of a medium-sized town every day, 365 of them every year. To bring the facts home to American audiences may I point out that this is the equivalent of ten baseball teams, complete with coach, every minute of every hour of every day. And yet there are people who seriously talk of exporting our surplus population to Mars or some other planet!

The single country, China, contains well over six hundred million people. A few months ago its net annual increase was stated to be over thirteen million—much larger than the *total* population of Australia and New Zealand combined—but the latest information indicates that it is really over fourteen million. This means that by the mid-1970's the *increase* in China's population will be greater than the present *total* population of the United States. . . . Clearly this business of doubling cannot go on indefinitely, or indeed for more than a few decades, without leading to disaster. This is especially clear when we consider the *differential* rate of increase in different countries. The very high rates of increase are found mostly in the countries of Asia and in the tropical regions of Latin America and parts of Africa. The population explosion in these areas is undoubtedly due primarily to the great advances in medical science and its application in better health services.

To sum up, the world's demographic situation is becoming impossible. Man, in the person of the present generation of human beings, is laying a burden on his own future. He is condemning his children's children to in-

[3] Julian Huxley, *The Human Crisis* (Seattle: University of Washington Press, 1963), pp. 50, 51, 52, 79, 80, 81, 83, 85, 86. Reprinted by permission of the publishers.

creased misery; he is making it harder to improve the general lot of mankind; he is making it more difficult to build a united world free of frustration and greed. More and more human beings will be competing for less and less, or at any rate each will have to be content with a lesser cut of the world's cake. If nothing is done about this problem by us who are now alive, the whole of mankind's future will suffer, including the future of our own children and grandchildren. . . .

We must take a new look at the problem. We must stop thinking in terms of a race between production and reproduction, a race that never can be won. We must realize that our aim is not mere quantity, whether of people or goods or anything else, but quality—quality of human beings and of the lives they lead. Once we have grasped this, things begin to fall into place. . . . Meanwhile, of course, we must do everything in our power to increase all types of production—production of food, production of machines, production of what I may call the infrastructure of modern life; but equally of course we must pay the maximum possible attention to the conservation of resources. . . . Another thing that the advanced and privileged nations should do is to set their economists and social scientists to thinking out ways and methods of providing economic and social incentives for promoting a lower rate of population increase. Whether by means of family allowances, differential taxation, or other measures, it would undoubtedly be possible to devise economic and social methods that would exert pressure in favor of population decrease. As complement to this, we should set our psychologists and sociologists to studying ways of providing psychological motivation for small families and a sane population policy. In India the authorities are already beginning to try to persuade people that the whole future of the country depends on reducing the birth rate, and consequently that it is unpatriotic to have too many children. This has already been achieved in Japan, with the result that the Japanese have been able to cut their birth rate in half within a generation.

We should support all legislation—state, national, and international—that makes birth control easier and more socially approved. We must start discussion groups and civic action groups and bring pressure to bear on our legislators and our governments.

Did Malthus figure correctly? He lived just as the Industrial Revolution was starting, and so he could not foresee the tremendous changes it wrought. People's mental attitudes changed also. One of the results was a different attitude toward family size, possibly because of the development of more rational approaches to human problems. In the countries most affected by the Revolution, a planned limitation on family size has been the result.

More positive hope for man's future comes from a revolution in his food supply. Through seed selection, better fertilizers, and more efficient use of land, the amount of food that can be grown on the present farms of the world could be greatly increased. But new developments are even more startling, for mankind is changing nature to suit his needs. Soil conditioners are changing soil texture; algae, containing trace elements, are being used for fertilizer; work is going on to purify sea water for desert irrigation;

hormones are changing plant growth; crops grown in solutions—hydro-ponics—eliminate the need for soil; algae, yeast, and seaweeds rich in food value are now just beginning to be used. Each new idea produces a crop of further ideas; by a change in education and food habits man can grow enough to feed many billions more than there are now. Some of the developments given above are now being used as economically feasible; others need more experimentation. However, they all show that starvation can be eliminated.

AMERICAN POPULATION TRENDS AND EFFECTS

Effect of Recent Birth Rate on American Population

As noted in previous sections, the world is in the midst of a long-range trend of decreasing birth rate. This trend seems to be temporarily reversed. However, in spite of the enormous increase in the number of births, the rate has not yet reached that of 1925. The increased birth rate, together with longer life expectancy and the recent post-World War II immigration, has resulted in a major spurt in American population trends.

The increase in birth rate in America has been due to several immediate causes. More persons have married than ever before. (There is currently the highest percentage of married persons in our population in the history of America.) More persons who have married have had at least one child. More families have consisted of more than one child. However, there are fewer families that have gone beyond three children. The differential in birth rate between the various classes has tended to decrease. This is accounted for by an increase in the number of persons born among middle-class families. All this has served to accentuate the rapid increase in population in the United States.

A study of the predictions that have been made by population experts in the past does not give us any great confidence concerning any prediction of future population trends. In the past, the experts have been unable to predict such trends as the amount of decline in birth rate or such spurts as that coming after a war. Practically all population experts predicted that, although there would be a short spurt following World War II, it would not be as high as it turned out to be, nor would it last as long.

The following appraisal of the population trends in the United States by the then president of the Population Reference Bureau may serve to set the problems:[4]

. . . The United States has a different kind of population crisis which in a number of ways poses serious problems for the future welfare of our country. We are in no danger of starving, as we well know, but the current rate of

---

[4] Robert C. Cook, "The Population Prospect: The Years Just Ahead," *Social Education*, **29**, No. 2 (February 1965), pp. 65–67 (Washington, D.C.: National Council for the Social Studies). Reprinted by permission of the publishers and the author.

increase of U.S. population is so rapid that it is generating extremely grave social, economic, and political problems. It may be noted that the U.S. population is increasing at least twice as fast as is the population of any other major industrial country of the Western world.

Because of the low birth rate of the 1920's and 1930's the number of women aged 20–29 in the United States has not changed materially for thirty years. There were 11 million in this age group in 1930, 12 million in 1940, 12 million in 1950, and 11 million in 1960. This will change rapidly in the years just ahead. By 1970, the number will rise to 15 million; by 1980, to 20 million; and by 1990, to 22 million. The number in these high-fertility years will double in just 30 years! This constitutes an enormous increase in fertility potential. If existing fashions in family size are continued, there is the prospect of a baby boom far exceeding that which we have just gone through.

At the present rate of increase of our population, the United States will reach 344 million by the year 2000—an increase of over 155 million in the next 35 years. This increase would be larger than the entire population of the United States in 1940! And after the year 2000, the acceleration would really get going. The Census Bureau has just predicted that a continuation of current marriage rates could give a growth in population in the first decade of the twenty-first century of 75 million!

If it is conceded that 155 million more people in the next 35 years represent a rate of increase beyond the optimum for effective adjustment, it may be emphasized that this very rapid rate of growth is not inevitable. It can be checked. In the United States today, the birth rate is under voluntary control to a remarkable extent. The evidence that this is so is conclusive.

By the mid-1920's, and during most of the 1930's, the United States birth rate was so low that, had it continued at those levels, population growth would have ceased by 1960 and a slow decline in population would have set in. For reasons that are not clearly understood, the birth rate began to go up well before the beginning of World War II. After 1945, as we know it, it went up astonishingly, to a point higher than at any time in the previous 30 years. This change in fertility was voluntary and due to a changing attitude regarding family size on the part of the majority of the American people.

That the current level of births is a matter of popular volition is proved by the birth pattern existing in the United States today. In recent years, the model age of mother at the birth of her last child has been under 30 years. The modern trend in reproduction is to have children close together and then to stop having them. A quarter of a century ago, when the average size of family was smaller than today, the reproductive pattern was quite different. A much larger proportion of children was born during the years between 30 and 40. There is no question, therefore, that fertility in this country is under effective voluntary control.

If fashions in family size were to change rather modestly, U.S. population by 2000 might be reduced by 50 to 75 million. During the past 15 years, reproduction in the United States has been at a level of about three children per woman. With current death rates, this degree of fertility means that the population increases by about a half in each generation. The replacement level, at the present time, is about 2.2 children per woman.

Differential Birth Rate by Socioeconomic Status and Geographic Area

One of the characteristics of birth-rate trends throughout the United States (or, for that matter, the world) has been the differential of birth rate among various socioeconomic classes and geographic areas. In general, in the United States the over-all decline in birth rate during the last twenty to twenty-five years has been more rapid in the cities than in rural areas and has tended to be at a relatively lower absolute rate. Also, the decline that occurred during the 1930's took place more rapidly among middle-class families than among lower- or higher-class families. This differential in birth rate coupled with a shift in the number of persons needed for agricultural purposes has caused a tremendous movement of population from rural to urban areas. This trend has continued since World War II.

There is some evidence that the differential birth rate has decreased somewhat since World War II. In general, studies indicate that although there is a decreasing size of the differential, there is still a differential among the various socioeconomic classes. The highest birth rate occurs among the low-income group, the second highest among the high-income group, with the middle class coming third. There is still a higher birth rate among rural groups than among those in the cities. The main trend has been a decrease in the amount of differential.

Part of the difference in birth rates in geographic areas is due to the differing socioeconomic status of those areas. For example, there is a heavy birth rate in the southeastern part of the United States as compared with other parts. This is due largely to the agricultural nature of this area, together with the fact of its relatively lower socioeconomic status. This differential in birth rate, which will probably continue and may even be accentuated if the birth rate tends to resume its long-term decline following the post-World War II period, does pose rather serious problems. Even if we ignore the genetic implications of possibilities of inheritance of poor mental and physical characteristics, the fact that a large part of our population must grow up under environmental conditions that are less conducive to all-around development certainly does lead to discouragement, as far as the improvement of our society is concerned. However, the fact that the general prosperity of the postwar period has caused a rise in the level of living—so that even the poorer groups live at a level higher than did the middle class, for example, in 1900—has led to some optimism in regard to the possibly improved cultural background of those persons born into the lower socioeconomic groups. Students of genetics do not seem to be completely agreed on the eventual effect upon the race of differential birth rates, as far as the type of physical and mental characteristics passed on to each new generation is concerned. At least at the moment, the increased cultural advantages apparently seem to cancel out or perhaps more than compensate for the disadvantages of the relatively lower environmental and, perhaps, inherited characteristics.

Mobility of American Population

The United States has always had a mobile population. It has been characterized for more than a century by a general westward movement and by a movement from the farms to the cities. Present major currents of population flow are (1) from the center of the country to the seacoasts, and (2) from the rural South to the industrial North. During the war periods and continuing during the postwar periods, there was a heavy mobility of our population due to the displacement caused by industrial expansion.

In recent years there has been a tendency toward moving from the centers of the cities to the suburbs and beyond. In many cases, this movement has been accentuated by urban renewal programs and by in-migration of racial or southern mountaineers into the central city itself. This has led to the formation of middle-class suburbs and middle- and upper-class "exurbs." This tendency for the population to move from the major city outward to the suburbs, coupled with the inability of cities to expand their legal limits to include the suburbs due to tradition and to legal restrictions, has helped to accentuate the urban problems. In the first place, it tends to cause people living in the suburbs—a different political subdivision in most cases—to feel a lack of responsibility for the problems of the inner city. This attitude occurs even though they may work in the central city, or at least are economically tied to it. Secondly, it leads to an accentuation of the tendency for persons of different social statuses to live in different sections of the metropolitan area and, therefore, to an increased lack of understanding and less opportunity for acquaintance with persons from different social statuses. These problems have been discussed more fully in Chapter 12 and also in Chapter 10 (Depressed Areas).

Changing Life Span and Effect on American Population

One of the factors that has led to the population increase has been the increased years of life expectancy. This is due to a decreasing death rate, particularly in the early years. For example, in 1900 the number of deaths per thousand for persons under one year was 162.4 as compared to 33 in 1950 (a decrease of about 80 per cent); whereas the number of deaths in the range from 65 years of age to 84 changed from 123 per thousand to 93 per thousand, a decrease of just 22 per cent.[5] This changing death rate has increased the proportion of persons of 65 years of age or over in our population from 2.6 per cent in 1850 to almost 10 per cent in 1965.[6]

The recent increase in birth rate has caused a temporary increase in the number of persons under 14 years of age. This factor, together with the one above, has caused a sizeable increase in the number of persons who

[5] J. Frederick Dewhurst and Associates, *America's Needs and Resources: A New Survey* (Twentieth Century Fund, 1955), p. 61.

[6] *World Almanac, 1965* (New York: New York World-Telegram and Sun, 1965), p. 286.

are dependent on those who are working. In 1953 there was a ratio of 1.7 persons of working age to each dependent (below 15 and above 64).[7] This ratio had decreased so that by 1960 it was approximately 1.5. This should mean a relatively high employment rate through 1960, since the working force is the lowest percentage of the total population in the history of America. What will happen when the flood of persons born in the past ten years enters the labor market?

One of the interesting concepts to conjecture about in the realm of changing life span is the concept of life expectancy. By 1962 it was 70.0 years for all persons, 66.8 years for males and 73.4 years for females.[8] The concept of life expectancy is, of course, a fictitious one. It represents the average age that a person of each sex would reach if born in a given year (for example, 1965) and living his entire life according to the survival rates of that particular year. Quite likely the persons born that year will live on an average much longer than that, because the life expectancy rate will be continually raised if present trends continue.

Problems Related to Increase in Percentage of Aged

Not all of the problems related to the increased numbers of aged have to do with dependency. The increase in social security programs, to be discussed in the next section, has helped to solve partially the problem of the support of the aged, although it in turn has led to some new problems. However, there are other problems that grow out of the increasing percentage of our population living to an older age than before. See Figure 12.

Part of the reason for the increasing longevity, of course, lies in the development of new medical techniques, including the use of antibiotics. This means that now death is seldom due to infectious diseases. Cancer, heart trouble, and other organic diseases of various kinds assume an increasing importance.

A whole new science of *geriatrics*, the medical treatment of the aged, has grown up. Another new term is *gerontology*. The difference between "gerontology" and "geriatrics" is that the former deals with methods of preventing the ailments that affect the aged, whereas "geriatrics" refers to the treatment of such ailments.

Perhaps even more important is the problem of the place of the aged in our population. No longer able to hold a useful position for pay, the aged find themselves in a "useless" place in society. Sometimes deteriorating in mental and physical strength and increasingly living in the past, they find it difficult to find something in life that can maintain and hold their interest. An increasing interest is being shown in this problem by the organizing of leisure-time activities for the aged, such as clubs for aged persons and special recreational facilities. The trend in America toward

[7] *World Almanac, 1965*, p. 286.
[8] *World Almanac, 1965*, p. 347.

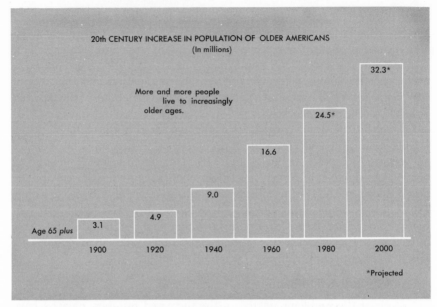

Figure 12. President's Council on Aging, *The Older American.* (Washington, D.C.: The Council, 1963), p. 4.

the family unit increasingly being the immediate family makes it difficult for another generation to live satisfactorily with the husband, wife, and children of the immediate family. Increasingly there is need for housing and for facilities, recreation and so on, for the aged among their kind. Some of these problems are receiving the attention of social workers and others in our society.

Effect on Socal Security and Welfare Programs of the Increased Life Span in America

The increased longevity has, of course, been beneficial to the life insurance companies, since the expectancy has been always higher than predicted. However, when we take into account the various social security annuity plans, the increasing longevity raises serious financial problems. With an increasing percentage of our population 65 and over, the problem of providing adequate pension plans and other social security welfare plans becomes an increasing drain on the working population. Money collected from a population with one type of life expectancy is needed for payments to a much higher percentage of people than anticipated. This problem has been accentuated by the inflation of the dollar, which has left many pension plans utterly inadequate to provide even a minimal existence for persons in retirement. Other kinds of social security programs, such as workmen's compensation and mothers' pensions, have also helped to mitigate some of the social ills of our society. With an increased portion of our population below the age of 18, there will be an increase in money needed for aid to dependent children as well. Since there are more homes, there are more homes broken by death. The mothers then will need to be given aid through mothers'-aid laws.

The fact that these welfare programs are a heavy drain upon the money of the persons who are in active work does not necessarily detract from their value. Both as a protection for those persons who are unfortunate or who are aged, and as a stabilizing economic influence in our society, social security programs are here to stay. The rapid increase in the extension of social security to new elements of our population by both Democratic and Republican administrations emphatically indicates this trend. The development of unemployment insurance, together with the encouragement of voluntary hospitalization plans, are all additional steps toward helping to stabilize our society and to protect the various individuals in it.

The development of systems of medical care, particularly of the aged, have been a recent concern (mid-sixties). The passage of the law establishing the Medicare program and the placing of it in operation in July, 1966, represented a step toward an attempt to improve the quality of medical care for the aged. Under Medicare any person under social security can be covered for hospital insurance and, voluntarily, for an additional charge shared by the federal government and the individual, may be covered for supplementary medical insurance. The supplementary insurance is voluntary even for those persons under social security. The hospital insurance is automatic for those under social security, but can be joined without additional charge by many others.

The problem of medical care is a difficult enough problem for the persons of normal age because of increasing cost of the services and the scarcity of doctors and nurses in our rapidly expanding society. But the population increase in the percentage of our groups in the aged and the necessity for a great deal more care for persons in that age span makes special consideration necessary. It is possible for a person to have his life savings wiped out through one illness. For this reason, Medicare has come into existence. It is really a federally financed payment of the premium for private hospital insurance, in many cases using the already available private insurance groups now used voluntarily by other persons in the various regions of the United States.

POPULATION TRENDS AND EDUCATION

Effect of Increased Birth Rate on American Schools

Changes in population will naturally change or influence the schools. The babies of yesterday become the pupils of today and tomorrow. Although the previous discussion was concerned with long-range changes in population, present-day schools are affected by current fluctuations. The lower birth rate during the 1930's produced smaller classes, just as the booming birth rate following World War II brought about a flood that engulfed the schools. The tidal wave hit the high schools in the early sixties; by 1965 it had pressed on the colleges. If we maintain the style of education to which we have become accustomed, we must provide more classrooms and more teachers, and we must consider greater possibilities in adult education.

Of great importance to educators and to all citizens is the number of children who are of school age. Figure 13 shows persons in the school population projected to 1973. (The children in school for this decade have

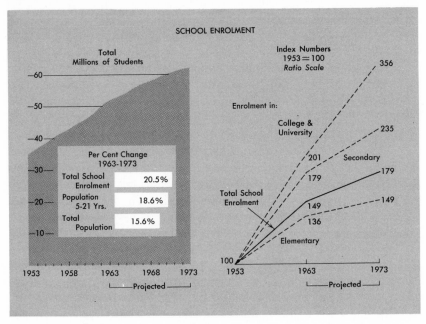

Figure 13. School Enrolment. *Road Maps of Industry,* No. 1516. February 16, 1965. Copyright, 1965. National Industrial Conference Board, Inc. Used by permission.

already been born.) Nonpublic institutions are quite sensitive to economic conditions, and so the continuing rise in their enrollments assume continuing prosperity.

By 1970, as compared to 1953, there will be 49 per cent more children in elementary school. By 1970, the high school enrolment will increase by 135 per cent more than that it 1953. Today (1965) over 90 per cent of the adolescents of high school age are actually in school, while about 75 per cent will graduate. It is estimated that college enrolment will be 256 per cent more in 1970 than in 1953!

All of these facts show clearly that the schools must provide more class-room space and more teachers, and this takes more tax money. The problem has been heightened by past troubles. From 1930 to 1940 the schools did not keep up their building pace because of economies needed during the depression; from 1940 to 1946 they fell behind because of World War II; and now they have fallen still farther behind because of the increased birth rate.

The problem is complex. With more people over 65 years of age, there may be competition for public support. As indicated earlier in this chapter, the population is highly mobile. The West Coast increased 49 per cent in one decade, from 1940 to 1950; many rural areas have gone down 12 per cent in the same length of time. This, of course, affects the school population directly. One fourth of all school children moved from at least one county to another, and besides the trend to the West, there is a strong one from the South to the North. Suburban industrial areas have grown greatly, with the result that schools in some sections are more hard pressed than those in others. With all of these changes, we can be certain that there will be more students—they will be more heterogeneous as to background and they will stay in school longer—there will be too few teachers, and classes will be larger.

Temporary solutions may be to extend the class day, with pupils coming at different times, or to increase class sizes and relieve the teachers of routine duties; but the only permanent solution will be to increase the size and number of schools. It then becomes necessary to increase the teacher supply as well as raise its standards. Enrolments are up 1 million per year in the elementary school alone, necessitating 30,000 additional teachers. In other words, the schools need at least many more qualified teachers than they are getting.

Implication of Population Problems for Education

The first and most obvious implication of the population problems for education grows out of the effect of the birth rate on the elementary and secondary schools. The problem of providing an adequate number of teachers from the young adult population, at low ebb due to the reduced birth rate of the 1930's, was extremely difficult during the late fifties and early sixties. By 1955 the increase in number of persons in college made it much more easy to solve this problem, but there were other factors that contributed to the lack of teachers in a great number of areas of teaching, such as elementary education and mathematics and science. One of these was the competition for the college graduates in areas that were more remunerative than that of teaching.

By far the most difficult implications for the period of the late sixties and on into the era of 1970's related to the problem of the expanding college. The amount of money necessary to build the buildings, to enlarge the campuses, to provide the additional equipment, and so forth, for the great hordes of people who were entering the college and university is enormous. The colleges and universities had expanded greatly between 1950 and 1965 due largely to an increased percentage of the population becoming interested in going to college. Then the population bulge which had been in the elementary and secondary schools hit the colleges, so that the estimate of the number going to college becomes quite great, as was indicated earlier in this chapter. The problem of how to get highly specialized and trained personnel to fill positions as college professors is an extremely difficult one that may be even more crucial than was the shortage of elementary and secondary teachers in the immediate post-World War II period. In the case of the elementary and secondary teachers, and in the case of the college professors, an improvement both in working conditions and salaries will have to be made in order to attract people into teaching against the competition with other professions requiring training and skill.

Another implication arises from the kind of education to be given in the world of the future. One of the things that makes the educational problem much more acute is the extent to which people desire more schooling. From less than 10 per cent of persons going to college before 1930, the figure had risen to more than 40 per cent in 1965 and may eventually go as high as 50 per cent of the population. Similarly the percentage going to high school may eventually rise to more than 90. This demand for education is proper in the light of the greater complexity of our world and the necessity of training to live in it and cope with its problems. The unbelievable expansion of human knowledge in the past few years and the inability of people to secure this knowledge merely from casual contacts with their culture present an unanswerable argument for the necessity for more education.

Still another implication arises from the necessity of providing schooling for a much longer period of time. The population trends point toward a need for additional educational or quasi-educational facilities for persons aged 65 or over. In many cases there may be a necessity for reeducating these people to live a different kind of life after their work period has passed, to help them face the many additional years of life in which, under our present family structure they must depend largely upon their own resources. The challenge for this kind of education for the aged is very great.

The challenges faced by the schools seem unsurmountable: rapidly swelling enrolments, limited teacher supply, inadequate numbers of classrooms, inadequate facilities in classrooms, the need for the extension of education, a challenge to improve education better to fit the conditions of the changing world, and an immediate need to improve the high school to meet the needs of the great heterogeneous mass of individuals now presenting themselves for education. The situation seems to be an almost impossible one to meet—even for a country as wealthy as the United

States. It certainly means that we must put an increasing amount of our energies, money, and time into the enterprise of education.

SUMMARY

In this chapter the details of the tremendous expansion of the world's population, frequently called the "population explosion," have been set forth. The possibilities of solution of this problem through the increase of the supplies of food and other necessities have been fully considered. The impact of the population changes both within America and throughout the world has been discussed in terms of the effect of these population changes upon such things as the care of the aged, social security and welfare programs, and the problems of getting schools ready to take care of the increased number of persons who desire more education because of a longer life span. There is both a longer period for formal education and a prolonged education in the form of adult education. Closely related to this is the increased demand for education at the college level, together with demands for additional schooling to upgrade skills made necessary by technological changes.

Implications in terms of the possibilities in population control and of the kind of life on this planet to expect if the population remains unchecked have been considered in this chapter.

SELECTED BIBLIOGRAPHY

BIRREN, JAMES E. *The Psychology of Aging*. Englewood Cliffs, N.J.: Prentice-Hall, 1964. Pp. ix + 303.

BORGSTROM, GEORGE. *The Hungry Planet: The Modern World at the Edge of Famine*. New York: Macmillan, 1965. Pp. xx + 786.

BROWN, LESTER R. *Man, Land and Food: Looking Ahead at World Food Needs*. Washington, D.C.: U.S. Department of Agriculture, Economics Research Service, Regional Analysis Division, November 1963.

BURGESS, ERNEST W. (ed.). *Aging in Western Societies*. Chicago: University of Chicago Press, 1960. Pp. xvi + 498. This volume is a survey of the problems of older persons and of the solutions for their welfare adopted by societies of western culture.

Committee for Medical Development. *A Forum on the Quality of Medical Care*. New York: Group Health Insurance, Inc., 1961. Pp. 24.

COOK, ROBERT C. "The Population Prospect: The Years Just Ahead," *Social Education*, **29** (February 1965), pp. 65–68, 73.

CROWTHER, BOSLEY. "Movies and Censorship." Public Affairs Pamphlet No. 332. New York: Public Affairs Committee, 1962.

DAY, LINCOLN H., and ALICE TAYLOR. *Too Many Americans*. New York: Macmillan, 1954. Pp. ix + 298.

DEWHURST, J. FREDERICK, and associates. *America's Needs and Resources: A New Survey*. New York: Twentieth Century Fund, 1955. Pp. xxix +1148.

DRUCKER, PETER F. *America's Next Twenty Years.* New York: Harper & Row, 1955. Pp. 114.

FAGLEY, RICHARD MARTIN. *The Population Explosion and Christian Responsibility.* New York: Oxford University Press, 1960. Pp. 260.

GUTTMACHER, ALLAN F. *Planned Parenthood: World Population,* Annual Report, 1963. New York: Planned Parenthood Federation of America, Inc.

HAUSER, PHILIP M. *Population Perspectives.* New Brunswick, N.J.: Rutgers University Press, 1960. Pp. 184.

HAVIGHURST, ROBERT, HERBERT GOLDHAMER, RUTH CAVEN, and ERNEST BURGESS. *Personal Adjustment in Old Age.* Chicago: Science Research Associates, 1949. Pp. 204.

The Health Care Issues of the 1960's. New York: Group Health Insurance, Inc., 1963. Pp. viii + 199.

HUXLEY, JULIAN. *The Human Crisis.* Seattle: Washington University Press, 1963. Pp. 88. Contains an essay on "The World Population Problem."

LEMICA, JAN, and ALFRED SAUVY. *Population Explosion: Abundance or Famine.* New York: Dell, 1962. Pp. 119.

MUDD, STUART (ed.). *The Population Crisis and the Use of World Resources.* Bloomington: Indiana University Press, 1964. Pp. xix + 562.

National Academy of Sciences, Committee on Science and Public Policy. *The Growth of World Population: Analysis of the Problems and Recommendations for Research and Science and Public Policy.* National Research Council, Publication 1091. Washington, D.C.: National Academy of Sciences, 1963. Pp. 38.

ORGANSKI, KATHERINE, and A. F. K. ORGANSKI. *Population and World Power.* New York: Knopf, 1961. Pp. 263 + ix.

OSBORN, FAIRFIELD (ed.). *Our Crowded Planet: Essays on the Pressures of Population.* Garden City, N.Y.: Doubleday, 1962. Pp. 240.

OSBORN, FREDERICK. *This Crowded World.* Public Affairs Pamphlet No. 307. New York: Public Affairs Committee, 1960. Pp. 28.

PETERSEN, WILLIAM. *The Politics of Population.* Garden City, N.Y.: Doubleday, 1964. Pp. x + 338.

Population Bulletin. (Published by the Population Reference Bureau.) All issues.

"President's Council on Aging," *The Older American.* Washington, D.C.: Government Printing Office, 1963. Pp. vii + 73.

SIMPSON, HOKE S. (ed.). *The Changing American Population.* New York: Institute of Life Insurance, 1962.

Social Security—What the New Law Holds for You. Chicago, Ill.: National Research Bureau, Inc., 1965. Pp. 31.

STAMP, L. DUDLEY. *Land for Tomorrow.* Bloomington: Indiana University Press, 1952. Pp. 230.

THOMPSON, WARREN S.; and DAVID T. LEWIS. *Population Problems.* New York: McGraw-Hill, 1965. Pp. xiv + 593.

United Nations, Department of Economic and Social Affairs. *The 1963 Demographic Yearbook.* New York: The United Nations, 1964.

VOGT, WILLIAM. *People: A Challenge to Survival.* New York: Sloane, 1960. Pp. xiv + 257.

WATTENBERG, BEN J. *This U.S.A.* Garden City, N.Y.: Doubleday, 1965. Pp. 520. "An Unexpected Family Portrait of 194, 067, 296 (March 31, 1965), Americans Drawn from the Census."

WOYTINSKY, W. S., and E. S. WOYTINSKY. *World Commerce and Government: Trends and Outlook.* New York: Twentieth Century Fund, 1955. Pp. 907.

————. *World Population and Production.* New York: Twentieth Century Fund, 1953. Pp. 1269. + xxii.

SELECTED FILMS

Aging—A Modern Achievement (University of Michigan) 30 min

Before the Day (Social Security Administration) 15 min

Gives an account of the founding of the several programs that make up social security and the story of what happened before the day social security started. Above all, it is the story of people who can face the future with greater confidence because they know the system they have built is working for them long before the day of need occurs.

Life with Grandpa. (March of Time Forum Films) 17 min

Portrays problems confronting older people in our society: disease, economic insecurity, emotional difficulties. Suggests several solutions.

The Population Explosion (CBS Reports Series) 43 min

A close and sobering look at the grave consequences of the abnormally high current rate of growth of the world's population, which may double in the next thirty years. India, the largest democracy in the world, is the locale of this film and is the most prominent example of a growing crisis that soon may become the world's number one problem—an excess of population over available food supplies.

Proud Years (Columbia University) 20 min

Film on the aged.

The Steps of Age. (International Film Bureau) 25 min

Portrays the confusion, fears, and far-from-easy struggle to understand herself that Mrs. Potter, 62, faced as she embarks on the last quarter of her life. The picture suggests that people need to begin early in life to handle well the situations that come with increasing age.

Chapter 12. *Problems Related to Representative Government and Public Opinion*

MANY OF THE PROBLEMS we face are those peculiarly related to the fact that we live under a representative type of government—one in which the people must ultimately make the decisions. This fact has certain implications for the structure of the government and also for the type of communication facilities. Especially pertinent are problems of the limitations of communication facilities, public sensitivity to propaganda, and the quality of communication.

COMMUNICATION FACILITIES

The availability and quality of the communications in a democracy, particularly a very large, complex, and intricately interrelated one, becomes of crucial importance to that society. Furthermore, it has enormous implications for the school in terms both of the availability of mass communication facilities for educational purposes and of the possibility of the schools' assistance in improving the communication facilities.

Modern Communication Facilities

Certainly there is no lack of opportunity for the citizens in America (as in many others of the highly industrialized nations) to gain access to any information that they may need, not only for understanding their roles in citizenship but also for their own cultural enlightenment and vocational improvement. The quantity of materials pouring off the presses—books, newspapers, and magazines—is increasing at a rate faster than that of our population. In spite of television, the circulation of books in libraries is increasing at least as fast as the population, if not faster. Radio and television, each with a very large mass audience, constitute two other important media of communication.

Technological improvements in the sending of reports from one point to another facilitate the almost immediate availability of news to all parts of the world. The greater ease of transportation and communication enables every corner of the world to be readily accessible to news-gathering agents and to persons trying to obtain information for educational purposes. The extent of communication facilities in the United States is truly amazing:

(1) NEWSPAPERS. In 1963, there were 1,754 English-language newspapers in the United States with a combined circulation of 58,905,251. There were 550 Sunday papers with 46,830,039 circulation. There were 8,151 newspapers with a circulation of 23,975,549.[1] Since it is estimated that there were around 50,000,000 families (households) in the United States in 1963, the extent of the circulation of the newspapers is readily apparent. In a later section we shall indicate the extent of increasing concentration of newspaper control and ownership.

(2) RADIO AND TELEVISION. It was estimated that in 1963 there were about 237 million radio and television sets in use in the United States out of about 482 million in the entire world. Of this number there were approximately 57 million homes with radios in the United States, 18 million in business places, institutions, and other such locations, 47 million automobile radios, and 61½ million television sets.[2] For comparison, it was estimated that there were in 1948 just 75 million radios in use in the United States and only 900,000 television sets (beginning of television broadcasting). The vast majority (over 90 per cent) of the population in the United States was within sufficient distance of transmitting stations to view television broadcasts.

(3) MAGAZINES AND BOOKS. In 1964 there were more than one hundred magazines in the United States that had over 350,000 circulation.[3] There was one magazine with over 10 million circulation, ten others with over 5 million circulation, and nine others with over 2 million circulation. In the case of books, in 1964 there were a total 13,968 new titles as against 11,901 in 1954.[4]

Advertising

One of the characteristics of America and of all other countries that have competitive economic systems is advertising. Advertising certainly is increasing in the United States. The public is bombarded with advertis-

---

[1] *World Almanac, 1965*, (New York: New York World-Telegram and Sun, 1965), p. 542.
[2] *World Almanac, 1965*, p. 768. This includes "homes" (or rooms) with single persons, not "households."
[3] *World Almanac, 1965*, p. 541.
[4] *World Almanac, 1965*, p. 56.

ing from billboards, radio programs, newspapers, and countless other sources.

Undoubtedly advertising has contributed greatly to the vaunted American standard of living. Through continual enticing of the buyer to spend his money as rapidly as possible for products, particularly for new types of products—the latest model—the economic system is stimulated to operate at a rapid rate. Money does not stay long in the pockets of the consumer. Some advertising, of course, does not contribute much to economic improvement, since it is competitive advertising for different brand-name products that are equivalent in quality. The tendency of such mass advertising is eventually to drive one or more of such competitive products out of business in favor of the ones that have better advertising campaigns, thus contributing to monopolistic or oligopolistic practices.

While the opinion of liberal economists and others is, in general, not so much opposed to excessive advertising as it was during the 1930's, there is a question as to whether or not all advertising can be justified as making a contribution toward the economic system. Certainly advertising responsibilities consume the energies of persons who might be better engaged in improving the product (or increasing the number of producers in our economic system—producers of actual products that can be consumed). One can well ask whether or not all advertising does contribute to the total economic betterment of our society. It does actually add to the cost of the article, unless the increased volume of sales contributes to lower unit costs in production. It is true that advertising does subsidize some of our communications, such as newspapers, magazines, radio, and television. It is also true that it partially controls what it subsidizes.

It is likely that advertising is with us to stay. Efforts should probably be made toward increasing the responsibility of advertisers for truthfulness. Legal action should probably be taken against advertisers who actually use false claims for their products, particularly in the field of food and drugs.

Readability

What about the problem of communicating ideas accurately and adequately? Many studies have been made concerning the readability of mass communications media. Such studies indicate that much of the material in the newspapers is not readable. This may be entirely due to the type of vocabulary used, but it also may be due to the wording of the material. The material needs to be supplemented with pictures, graphs, and other concrete illustrations. While it is beyond the scope of this book to indicate the suggestions for readability, certainly responsible publishers should be constantly alert to this problem. This does not necessarily mean bringing the contents down to the audience's alleged intelligence. What it does mean is presenting the ideas and facts in a context and in a manner that will be understood correctly.

PROPAGANDA AND PUBLIC OPINION

The problem of communication is not solved when mass media presents ideas effectively. The problems of the control of the opinion and of possible biases may exist. These will be explored in the next sections.

Growth of Newspaper Monopoly

For a considerable period in American history (since 1909), the number of separate English-language daily newspapers in the United States decreased at a fairly constant rate up to about 1949. After this point there has been a very slight increase. During this same period there has been a large increase of the population. The peak in the number of separate dailies was reached with about 2,600 in 1909.[5] In 1964 the number was 1,734.[6] Furthermore, the study from which the former figures were taken reports that only about one out of twelve of the cities in which daily newspapers are published had competing dailies in 1947. At that time there were ten states in which there were no cities with competing dailies and twenty-two states in which there no cities with competing Sunday newspapers. In this same study 40 per cent of the estimated total daily newspaper circulation at that time was judged to be noncompetitive.[7] It is true that nationally syndicated columnists and cartoons may be more influential than local editors in molding opinion on national and international issues. However, in cities with no competing papers, all these may be chosen with similar views.

There has also been a heavy concentration of mass circulation among a few very popular magazines. Of course, any study of the growth of monopoly among newspapers and magazines should always include the figures in the total increased circulation and the increased number of small magazines. However, the great mass of readers do read magazines published by a relatively few companies, and therefore the control that these companies potentially could exercise over the mass mind represents a possible threat. Advertisers (or the people who control the advertising budget) also can wield tremendous power over newspapers and magazines.

Possibilities of Bias in Communication

Rapidity of communication and massiveness of communication facilities may be utilized to disseminate accurate and unbiased information, or they may be used to propagandize a people—witness the silencing of *La Prensa* by Perón and the control of mass media for their own purposes by the Nazis, Fascists, and Communists. Even freedom of communication may

[5] Commission of Freedom of the Press, *A Free and Responsible Press: A General Report on Mass Communication; newspapers, radio, motion pictures, magazines, and books* (Chicago: University of Chicago Press, 1947), p. 37.
[6] *The World Almanac, 1965*, p. 542.
[7] Commission of Freedom of the Press, *op. cit.*, p. 38.

result in mass dissemination of false concepts. In the first place, in both magazines and newspapers there is a bias in favor of that which is interesting or which appeals. Sometimes a diet of the sensational aspects of the news or of developments in our country does not adequately portray what is really happening. There is also a bias in the mind of the reader toward the sensational as opposed to the humdrum. For examples, stories about juvenile delinquency that may involve only 4 to 5 per cent of our juvenile population may be given publicity that causes the public to feel that most young people are delinquent. Comparatively overlooked are the approximately 95 per cent who may be more ambitious, sober, and industrious than were young people of the same age fifty to seventy-five years ago. Reading the daily press and magazines would not give this impression to the reader. Yet this may not be deliberately done on the part of the magazine and newspaper editors or writers.

Other kinds of bias that may or may not be intentional arise out of the fact that newspaper publishing is "big business." As we have shown in the last section, the concentration of the newspaper and the publishing industry in ever larger companies is increasing. Since the persons who control newspaper policy are in big business, they themselves tend sometimes to favor attitudes of big business toward news. An unconscious, or sometimes conscious, bias appears in the selection of news items, in the writing of headlines, and in other aspects of the publication. This is especially evident on the editorial page, where the viewpoints, political philosophy, and so on, of the publisher of course are, and *should be*, expressed. Editorial viewpoints, however, may not adequately represent popular opinion.

Propaganda Analysis

In the preceding sections we have talked about possible biases of the press and other means of communication due to matters that were more or less unconscious. In America and elsewhere throughout the world there is also much deliberate attempt to influence public opinion. Where the attempt is deliberate through the manipulation of the means of communication and is for the purpose of influencing action on the part of the recipient, the term *propaganda* is applied to it. Although there may be an element of propaganda in education itself at times, ordinarily propaganda differs from education in that every attempt sould be made in the case of education to apprise the learner of many points of view other than that which the teacher or writer considers to be an appropriate one. In education none of the pertinent facts should be omitted.

Analyses have been made of propaganda in recent years, particularly by the Institute for Propaganda Analysis in New York City. The following are the seven types of propaganda that are commonly recognized.[8]

[8] For example, in Clyde R. Miller, "How to Detect and Analyze Propaganda" (New York: Town Hall, Inc., 1939).

1. The name-calling device.
2. The glittering generalities device.
3. The transferral device.
4. The testimonial device.
5. The plain-folks device.
6. The card-stacking device.
7. The band-wagon device.

We shall discuss each of these in turn.

Name-calling is used to prejudice the person against an idea by attributing it to a group that, for a variety of reasons, is considered to be bad. Once a name is applied to an idea, such as the adjectives "fascistic" or "communistic," it is condemned. Such use of names in a stereotyped manner is a short circuit to appropriate thinking and must be considered to be a propaganda-type technique. Yet it is used frequently, both in the totalitarian countries and in the democratic countries, to persuade persons to a point of view without having them consider at all the facts of the situation.

Glittering generalities is applied to the use of broad terms, sometimes called "virtue words," such as "love," "brotherhood," "Christianity," "religion," "democracy," or the "American way." Through the use of these terms a person can be persuaded to accept other ideas because they are part of a "total acceptance" pattern. Name-calling gets one to reject an idea, glittering generalities make one accept or approve it without completely examining the evidence one way or the other.

Transfer is the third device. In this case, a symbol such as the cross representing the Christian church or the flag representing America are used to stir up our emotions so that we will accept or reject an idea. Cartoonists use symbols such as "Uncle Sam" to cause people to accept an idea they are trying to portray.

The testimonial device is a technique of getting an outstanding person in some field to indicate that he is for an idea, thereby indicating that, since outstanding people are for it, the rest of us should be for it also. We quite often overlook the fact that sometimes the person to whom the testimonial is attributed may not be in position to judge with respect to this matter, even though he may be well qualified in certain other areas.

The plain-folks device is quite often used by a politician to indicate that he is a "man of the people." By using nicknames and folk terms, sometimes a person tries to appeal to other people by giving the impression that he is one of them and therefore would understand their problems. Advertising or political articles may be written in such a way as to appeal to the common man, who may sometimes have a feeling that he has been left out of representation when decisions are made.

The card-stacking device refers to a situation where evidence, which quite often is true, is quoted. However, what is quoted is not all the evidence, but only that part of it that supports the desired point of view. Evidence that does not support the point of view is suppressed or wrongly interpreted.

The band wagon is the final device listed above. This is quite often used in politics. "Everybody is doing it"; therefore, it must be good. "Let's get on the band wagon."

The above is only one of the many analyses of propaganda that could be made, but it should help teachers to get students interested in an analysis of propaganda. There is, of course, one danger in this proceeding —both the propaganda of our opponents *and that of our friends* may be recognized. There is no way of teaching the intelligent person to think critically without having him apply critical thinking to what the teacher may say as well as what the other person says. This is good, since the student who can recognize propaganda on whatever side should be able better to evaluate material pertinent to his needs.

Suggestions Toward the Improvement of Public Information Channels

By far the best study of the whole problem of communication in America, with particular emphasis upon the press, was made by the Commission of Freedom of the Press, which issued its general report in 1947.[9] The members of this body made certain recommendations after having studied carefully the status of communication facilities, including newspapers, radio, motion pictures, magazines, and books. They did not recommend a whole set of new laws controlling these facilities. They did recommend: (1) That the constitutional guarantees of the freedom of the press be extended and protected. (2) That governmental agencies continue to use their own communication facilities to supply the people with information concerning their activities both in this country and abroad. (3) That responsibility for maintaining standards of integrity and for the avoidance of either propaganda or bias with respect to its news items be placed on the communications industry as a quasi-public institution (perhaps the most important recommendation). This was not meant in any way to restrict the freedom of the newspaper to maintain positions in editorial columns or to restrict the freedom of other commentators within the paper. (4) That competence, independence, and effectiveness of the staffs of the newspapers be improved. (5) That the various nonprofit educational agencies accelerate the publishing of readable materials on a completely unbiased basis. This would include institutions such as libraries, educational radio, FM and TV stations. (6) That an annual survey be conducted on the performance of the press with respect to the problem of bias. With such a survey, cases might be spotted where newspapers had been notoriously biased with respect to important issues.

[9] Commission of Freedom of the Press, *op. cit.*

It should be remembered through all the discussions of this and the preceding sections that in spite of the shortcomings of communications facilities in America, the American people, relatively speaking, are very privileged in this respect. By and large, the American press is free. By and large, the American people have access to more facts and information untrammeled by censorship than any other people of the world. The suggestions that have been made are meant to improve and enlarge upon the free flow of information to the American people. However, the problem of adequate communication is not solved with getting the information to the people. There must also be consideration of the repsonsibility of education through other sources in preparing the people to utilize the information properly.

Public Forums, Community Discussion Groups, and Other Means of Stimulating Adult Thinking

Access to adequate information is of little avail if adults do not make sense out of the immense amount of information that is necessary to understand this rapidly changing world. This section is focused on the part-time education of adults, mostly post-school-age persons. In later sections we will talk of the role of the schools with full-time children and youth.

It is probable that if a person would read *and study carefully* all the material that is found in a good newspaper during a year's time, he would have the basis for a very good college education. It would require, however, that the person have learned how to read properly and how to evaluate information. It would also require that he be willing to look up and give further study to matters that were raised in newspaper articles and commentaries. Newspapers and magazines are trying to appeal to a wide variety of people; consequently they have all types of information. No one person ever reads carefully all the articles found in an ordinary newspaper.

Through adult education classes and classes in the public schools, people can be taught to evaluate information and to use the library and other resources for further study of the problems that are raised. In addition to formal and informal adult classes, communities should arrange for various kinds of community discussion groups in public forums. Some of these public forums can be on a national level and promulgated by means of radio and TV. There are some outstanding examples of the latter, such as CBS roundup of world news. Some of the group discussions, which are for the purposes of getting together all the facts on a given current problem, are excellent. Other types of discussion group have speakers—sometimes bitterly partisan—discuss differing viewpoints with respect to a problem. Sometimes such a debate or discussion becomes so heated as not to throw much light on the situation. Such discussions should use persons who are well informed and who are capable of bringing different viewpoints but have ability to see the viewpoint of others readily without emotion. There are, of course, times when the presentation of a point of view by a partisan is also educational in its nature.

DEVELOPMENT AND PRESENT NATURE OF REPRESENTATIVE GOVERNMENT

The exact nature of government is important as an aspect of the total culture of a society. Most Americans feel that they understand the general nature of our American governmental structure. However, it seems wise that a more careful analysis now be made in order to see ways in which the schools may play a part in preparing better citizens and in helping toward the solution of many of the political problems we face in the United States.

America, a Representative Form of Government with Checks and Balances

There is still some controversy within the American democratic culture concerning whether or not our form of government is a "republic" or a "democracy." As we shall show in the next section, there was some inclination among the founding fathers toward the setting up of a form of government that would not be completely amenable to the will of the popular majority. This means the trend was toward a "republic" form of government in which the powers of the people were somewhat limited. However, evolution made clear that we were establishing one in which the ultimate power lay in the hands of the people.

Our government today is a representative democracy with numerous types of checks and balances. In the first place, our national government is a federal-type government with limitations of sovereignty. Some of the sovereign powers have been allocated among the various states. Within the federal government itself, as well as in the various state governments, there has been division of power, with checks and balances. The division of power between the upper and the lower houses of the legislature is one of these. The independence of the executive, judicial, and legislative branches is another. The complex procedure through which the Constitution can be amended is a third. These checks and balances were obviously intended to give stability to the government and to prevent a wave of mass hysteria from causing steps to be taken foolishly without full realization of the consequences.

While it is obvious that the founding fathers had fundamental respect for the intelligence of man and felt that ultimately the citizen should make his own decisions in regard to problems, they feared that some wave of emotion or mass reaction might destroy important institutions or even democracy itself. Certainly some of the events in republics elsewhere in the world have indicated that this easily can occur.

Although ultimately the stability of any form of government depends on the character of the people making up the nation, it is probable that the form of government must be adapted to the particular state of the people at a given time. The evolving of the American government toward more democratic forms was in line with the increasing enlightenment of the American people and their ability to make political decisions.

We may summarize this section by saying that we do have a representative democracy, or a republic, in which certain powers have been allocated to the national or federal government, certain powers reserved to the states, and, in most cases, many powers in turn allocated to local governments within the states. The American people as a whole have thought the allocation of more powers to the central government to be dangerous, and sometimes they have held to that belief well beyond the period when it had become obvious that power had to be centralized to meet urgent social and economic needs. As such services as transportation and communication became more complete and rapid, as industry became more intricately tied in with all parts of the country, it became necessary to give the central government more powers in order to meet the problems with which the country was confronted.

Some of the problems that are faced in a period of adjustment to the new and intricate world in which we find ourselves are discussed in a later section.

Evolution of Governmental Form and Theory in America

Many of the men who were influential in writing such documents as the Declaration of Independence were strongly influenced by political theorists like Hobbes and Locke. Because of their experiences with an autocratic, oligarchic form of government, they feared a strong central government and a strong executive. They had great faith in the intelligence of the middle class but feared the concentration of power in the hands of a ruling group. Because of fear of the masses, the franchise was considerably limited during pre-Revolutionary days and in the immediate post-Revolutionary days. Various restrictions of property and rank made the suffrage available to only a minority of the community. Men of property and of standing were considered, however, to be capable of making decisions that were wise for their own self-government.

The influence of the frontier was very strong toward emphasis upon the individual and upon the extension of suffrage to a more complete democracy. Although the form still remains, the theory of selecting the President not directly by the voters but by a group of electors chosen by the voters was for all practical purposes done away with in the early years of the republic. This device was originally set up to guarantee the careful selection of an Executive in terms of his qualifications rather than on the basis of his popularity with the masses. It was one example of a lack of complete faith in ability of the masses to choose their leader. Another example was the special method of selection of the senators by the state legislatures;

this was not completely changed until the passing of the Seventeenth Amendment to the Constitution in 1913, which provided for universal popular election of the senators.

The elimination of laws in regard to the restricted inheritance of property and other such matters was also a move toward the democratization of American society. Along with these social developments, there were numerous others that led to the extension of democracy from a political concept to social concepts as well. The elimination of the class structure of early American society, discussed more fully in Chapters 4 and 9 was partly indicative of this change in ideas.

We have shown how the supposedly laissez-faire theory of government with respect to economic matters was gradually changed over a period of years, so that by 1930 the governments at both state and national levels were involved considerably in economic matters. As society became more complex and as new problems developed that needed solving, increasingly, men turned to government for action. All of this meant an increased amount of government and a strengthening of the government. Many of the decisions of the Supreme Court over a period of years strengthened the power of the central government by reinterpreting the Constitution. Quite early in the history of America a "loose" interpretation of the Constitution enabled the federal government to buy the Louisiana territory, to help in the development of canals, later to help in the development of railroads, and still later to participate in numerous projects leading more directly to the welfare of the individual.

The early theory held by most Americans, including the founding fathers, was that the "least" government governs best and that as much as possible should be left to the local government. As the problems became more intricate and complex, however, it was found that some matters that had been left with the local government must of necessity be turned over to higher levels. A lag in this respect constitutes one of the problems of American government that we shall discuss in a later section. By and large in this respect, the theory openly expressed by the American people is very similar to that of the earlier period. The type of problems we face already has required us in practice to change our institutions greatly. The "least" government at the present time is a great deal more government than in earlier times because of the complexity and intricacy of the problems we face.

Some of the trends toward further democratization are seen in the use of the *initiative,* the *referendum,* and the *recall*[10] in some of our state

[10] *Initiative:* the placing of a proposed law or constitutional amendment on the ballot by petition.

Referendum: the placing of an existing or proposed law on the ballot by petition or by action of the legislature.

Recall: a reconsideration by a special election through petition of the right of a person to hold his office. If he were turned down (or recalled), the position would be filled in accordance with regular procedures when a vacancy exists.

governments. We do not have any of these operating at the federal government level.

On the whole, the American people believe in the democratic form of government and the democratic way of life. There are many differences of opinion as to what this actually means. In Chapter 14 we shall indicate some of the values that can be considered to be fairly well accepted by all people in the American democratic society. There are, of course, a few persons on the extremes, both right and left, who do not really believe in democracy, however broadly it can be defined. Some, on the reactionary right, do not trust the people to make the correct decision, and quite often they argue that we have a republic rather than a democracy. By this they mean that through various kinds of control the people should be prevented from making decisions. They go on to point out that the check-and-balance ideas contained in our Constitution were in response to a realization that the upper classes—and by this they mean the "better" classes of people or the "elite"—should rule. On the other extreme we have "left-wing" persons who would like to do away with the freedom of our institutions in certain other respects through doctrinaire approaches to our economic problems, such as complete socialization or even communistic methods and a dictatorship of the proletariat—albeit a supposedly temporary one. Both of these extremes certainly lie beyond the pale of democratic thinking as ordinarily understood.

GOVERNMENTAL AND POLITICAL PROBLEMS IN AMERICA

It is important to go into some detail in regard to the political problems that we face in America, in order to get a better understanding of how we might go about strengthening our government through the schools.

Problems Inherent in the American Form of Government

There are problems inherent in the particular structure of any government. Other problems are inherent in the weaknesses of the people that make up the government. The problem of government is primarily that of getting a structure that will work best for the particular people, country and culture that are involved. There are, of course, certain difficulties inherent in the American governmental structure.

A first problem lies in the bicameral type of legislature. One state, Nebraska, has recognized this and has created a unicameral legislature. In many cases in the past, legislation has been prevented from going through because the measure had to pass two houses. This means duplication of effort on every bill. Furthermore, it increases the number of lawmakers, so that it is more difficult for the public to know a given lawmaker and to hold him responsible. A relatively small unicameral legislature fixes the responsibility more directly upon the members for their voting.

The bicameral legislature does have some advantages, for it sometimes prevents bad laws from slipping through and also provides for the correction of defects in laws that do not pass one house. Of course, if there is only one house, the bill might be checked more carefully before being permitted to pass.

A second inherent problem relates to the complete separation of the executive and legislative branches. Because the President is elected independently of the legislature and is not responsible to it, situations arise frequently in which the President and Congress are at odds with one another. This may be because they are of different political parties, or it may be that the President does not truly have the leadership as far as his fellow party members in the legislature are concerned. Many of the other democratic countries of the world have a responsible prime minister who serves at the pleasure of the majority of the legislature. This insures that he represents the will of the legislature, and at any time that he fails to do so his government falls and a new government is set up, or there is a new election. In England, and in several of the members of the British Commonwealth with what amounts to a two-party system, this has worked out fairly well. In France, which has a multiple-party system, it has led to a great deal of instability in government. France, of course, also has a president, corresponding to the monarch of England, to give some stability to the government. There is in all three countries—the United States, England, and France—a permanent government secretariat (or civil service) which gives stability to the ordinary running of government when there is a change of the administration.

A third basic problem arises from the division of powers between the federal and state governments. Many problems are broader than state lines, yet the Constitution is not always clear with regard to the jurisdiction of the federal government. An example in recent years was the control of the pollution of rivers. Although the federal government is clearly given by the Constitution the right to control commerce on rivers, it apparently is not given the right to control the dumping of sewage and other waste into them. Numerous makeshift devices, such as interstate or regional commissions, have to be set up to control the purity of rivers or to take care of the diversion of river water for irrigation, city water supply, and other purposes. Such a problem of jurisdiction would not arise in a country that had a unitary-type government as opposed to a federal-type government.

Another type of problem arises out of the practice of leaving a great deal of jurisdiction to the local governments and permitting the incorporation of villages. As cities grow and expand from their boundaries, quite often they are hemmed in by small cities and villages on their outskirts. Apparently there is no way under American jurisprudence for a village that has once been set up as a corporation to be merged later with a larger governmental unit except by the wishes and permission of that village. The problem of placing a contiguous industrial, metropolitan area under a single government for more efficient operation and for a unified attack on its problems exists not only in America but throughout the world. It has been an especially difficult matter in the United States, where there are constitutional precedents to prevent action on the annexation or consolidation of existing communities even when they border on each other and have common problems that they ought to face together. Toronto, Canada, is often cited as the only major city in the world that has been able to solve this problem. London, England, is a notorious example of a city that has not been able to do so satisfactorily.

Another set of problems in this general area of conflicting jurisdictions is the extreme chaos that exists in the marriage and divorce laws among the separate states. It is imperative that each state recognize the marriage and divorce laws of the other states, but so wide are the differences among the states that the problem becomes very complex and the validity of some divorces certainly is quite questionable.

A set of problems has also arisen out of police and judicial procedures in the United States. Due to recent judicial decisions relating to the treatment of prisoners or persons apprehended for investigation for criminal acts, there have been very strong restrictions placed upon police procedures. These procedures relate to such matters of informing the apprehended individual concerning his right to have counsel before he gives a confession, and to the use of force in the investigation or the obtaining of a confession. There is a fine line of distinction here between protecting the rights of the individual and making investigation by the police and other law officials so difficult as to make the apprehension of criminals almost impossible. The American Bar Association has this under investigation at the time of this writing.

Another problem of current significance that has arisen during the mid-sixties concerns the matter of equal representation in the lower house of the state legislatures. Many of these houses have indicated their representation on the basis of units or counties which, because of the rapid urbanization of certain counties, have caused the rural areas to be more highly represented than the city areas. The variation in ratio sometimes is quite high. The Supreme Court has ruled that there must be equal representation in the various states. A number of states are at this time in the process of passing legislation to conform to this Supreme Court rule.

Problems Resulting from Social and Economic Changes

In addition to problems of the type listed in the above section, there are others that could not possibly have been foreseen by the founding fathers. The development of the complex, interrelated, industrial world based upon mass production technology—let alone automation—could not have been envisioned by even the most prophetic of seers. The development of large corporations involving the lives of many people with resources exceeding those of many of our states could not have been foretold. Problems arose quite early in regard to interstate commerce, such as the regulation of railroad rates in the latter part of the nineteenth century, where it became obvious that the federal government would have to establish its power. By a series of interpretations of the Constitution and by certain amendments, such as the income tax amendment, the power of the federal government has been extended to meet many of these problems. There is, however, still considerable disagreement regarding the extent to which the federal government should increase its power beyond the point that is really necessary in order to meet the most urgent situations. There are still areas of debate, such as federal aid to education in the field of general instruction.

One of the problems that needed to be faced as a result of social and economic change was that of providing protection for the welfare of workers in our industrial society. Another problem was the prevention of certain companies from monopolizing a given industry and thereby hampering the economy by charging outrageous prices or holding down progress. The tremendous complexity of government needed to meet these problems, as well as to provide information and services of a wide variety such as weather bureau reports, aids to business and to farmers, and many others, necessitated the passing of laws that give wide discretion to elected officials in making decisions. Even in the case of laws and regulations themselves, there has been an increasing tendency at both federal and state levels to pass legislation that permits administrative regulations to be set up. Under appropriate safeguards these often have the force of law. This means, in effect, that the legislature delegates the details of many governmental policies to appointed or civil service officials. This is the field of the so-called administrative law. Many problems, however, develop in regard to providing necessary safeguards in this field, such as public hearings and provisions for repeal, changes, or revisions.

Because of the necessity for increasing regulations of various kinds related to the complexity of our social order, various kinds of safeguards are necessary; one of these is a safeguard against the bureaucracy itself. We have seen how democracy was protected by the advent of the initiative, the referendum, and the recall. We have seen that protection is given by legal aid societies, and in some states by the public defender, against the power and majesty of the law itself.

There has arisen in recent years in the Scandinavian countries a new government official called the *ombudsman*, which threatens to become an international word and can be best translated perhaps, as "commissioner of complaints and grievances." This office is now in operation in Sweden, Finland, Denmark, Norway, New Zealand, and West Germany. Great

Britain is considering instituting a similar plan.[11] The ombudsman in Finland is established by the legislature as a protection of the ordinary individual against bureaucracy. Quite often the persons who handle the application of administrative rules and regulations are insensitive to the problems of the person involved. The individual is not knowledgeable about the rules and regulations and how they can be applied, so he has no way of defending himself against a bureaucratic ruling. He knows that there is something wrong with the ruling, but he has no way to defend himself. This can be called to the attention of an ombudsman, who then investigates the complaint to see whether or not it is justified. In many cases it has been found that there was a misunderstanding on the part of the complainant. The reason for this misunderstanding, in a few cases, is because the complainant is not able to state his case properly in order to secure the justice due him. In still other cases, perhaps not more than 10 per cent, it has been necessary for the ombudsman to take some action in order to bring about justice. In some cases this has involved a legal mandamus suit through the courts in order to protect the individual. The possibility of an ombudsman is being investigated by political science in this country as well as the others that have been involved.

Problems Related to Political Indifference

One of the most important problems facing a democracy is the indifference or ignorance of the voting public. The small percentage of the citizens in America who exercise their voting rights and privileges is appalling. At best, only slightly over 50 per cent of the eligible population vote at any given election, including presidential elections. This means that most issues are decided by a plurality rather than by a majority of those persons eligible to vote. Of course, the effect that a higher percentage of voting would have on the ultimate issue is not known. Many other or more enlightened countries of the world have a much higher percentage of voting. Some of the free countries, such as the Scandinavian, may have as high as 80 or 85 per cent. Totalitarian countries sometimes have claimed percentages such as 98 or 99. However, in those cases voters usually have no real choice, and penalties are often placed upon those who do not vote.

An analysis was made by Elmo Roper and reported in the *Saturday Review*, March 18, 1961, of the reasons that such a large percentage of our population usually do not vote. In the 1960 election, out of 104 million citizens of voting age, less than 69 million actually voted. The magazine estimated the following number who did not vote for the reasons given:[12]

---

[11] Quentin L. Quade and Thomas J. Bennett, "Are Traditional Methods Adequate?" *Current* (March 1965), pp. 19–26.

[12] Adapted from Elmo Roper, "How to Lose Your Vote," *Saturday Review*, March 18, 1961. Used by permission.

1. Mobile adults unable to meet state, county, or precinct residence requirements 8,000,000
2. Adults kept from polls by illness at homes, hospitals, nusing homes, homes for aged, etc. 5,000,000
3. Adults traveling for business, health, vocation, and other reasons, unable to obtain absentee ballots 2,600,000
4. Adult Negroes in eleven southern states kept from polls by rigged literacy tests, poll taxes, various social pressures, etc. 1,750,000
5. Adult illiterates in twenty-five literacy-test states 800,000
6. Citizens of voting age in District of Columbia 500,000
7. U.S. citizens living abroad 500,000
8. Adult prison population 215,000
9. Adult preachers of Jehovah Witnesses who face a religious disability to voting 225,000

This would leave a total of about 16 million not voting because of indifference or inconvenience.

It has been suggested by some that there be compulsory voting, with fines or other penalties assessed against those people who do not exercise their rights. Some of the democratic countries of the world, such as Australia and Belgium, have compulsory voting statutes and do attempt to enforce them. Most of the penalties are monetary fines rather than imprisonment. Some of the penalties are merely publication of names.[13] There are some persons in the United States who have advocated compulsory voting. Abraham, after a very careful study of the problem and the difficulties of enforcement even in smaller countries, decides that such a law would be unwise, unconstitutional, and probably unenforceable under the conditions of American democracy.[14]

This means that the problems of increasing the number of voters and the enlightenment of those who do vote demand the attention of educators and the development of public opinion toward that end. Several suggestions that have been made in other sections of this chapter and throughout the book should be helpful.

Suggestions for the Alleviation of Governmental Problems

Numerous suggestions have been made from time to time as to how our government might be modified to better meet the problems we face. However, it should be pointed out that, with some exceptions where the rigid and fixed structure of our government built for one period handicaps us in the present age, the basic task is to get the people to understand our

[13] Henry J. Abraham, *Compulsory Voting* (Washington, D.C.: Annals of American Government, Public Affairs Press, 1955), pp. 16–20.
[14] Henry J. Abraham, *op. cit.*, pp. 30–33.

problems and then to be willing to work with their officials toward their solution.

Attempts to solve such problems as river pollution, garbage collection systems in metropolitan areas, traffic, and so forth, face almost insurmountable difficulties because of the many conflicting local subdivisions. Such barriers just do not make sense in the present age. Provisions should be made that areas that are joined together as to economic institutions (banks, industries, and stores), sewage, garbage collection, and other facilities should also be one political subdivision. This may cause a loss of some of the feeling of local autonomy that people have enjoyed heretofore. Consequently, some new scheme probably should be worked out whereby problems involving the entire community would be solved on a higher level, but where the city would be divided into smaller communities to solve local, neighborhood, and community problems on a basis entirely different from the township or small-town governments of an earlier era. The writers can point to no place where this has been done at present.

For the solution of problems that are too big for the state but not quite at the national level, the use of regional-type bodies has been suggested. The Ohio River compact for the control of pollution by the states bordering on the river is one example of a voluntary association to solve a problem that had been unsolvable on the basis of the present division of powers between state and federal government. In an entirely different type of venture, the Tennessee Valley Authority attempts to solve the problems of conservation, flood control, and power production in a valley covering parts of seven states. Recent attempts to do the same thing in certain other areas have not met with approval as far as public opinion is concerned. It is difficult to see where the Tennessee Valley Authority approach to the problem has in any way been detrimental, even to the welfare of established private businesses. The number of private industries and businesses coming into the Tennessee valley since the development of public power has been enormous.

The federal government's power to levy taxes where the money is and to distribute it where it is needed already has been put to use in numerous areas, such as unemployment compensation, aid to mothers and handicapped children, vocational education, and so on. In such cases money is granted to the states on a matching basis or on a basis of a formula, leaving the states to distribute the money and to administer its expenditure under their constitutional prerogative.

This combination of federal and state action seems to be a good compromise in a situation of divided sovereignty, such as our federal-state type of government. This same approach has been used with respect to federal aid to general education in the Elementary-Secondary Education Act of 1965. The reason for the development of federal financing is that quite often the areas that have the greatest needs have also the least resources with which to meet them. The head offices of corporations tend to be concentrated largely in New York and New Jersey; consequently, income and other tax sources are heavily concentrated in those areas, even though the money may originally come from all parts of the United States. Moreover, the greater need may exist in such states as Alabama, Mississippi, and Georgia, for example, where there are very few sources to be taxed. Yet the welfare of the people of Georgia, Mississippi, and Alabama is important to the welfare of the entire country. It is as much to the interest of New York State that the people of Georgia, Mississippi, and Alabama be well educated as it is that the people of New York should be. This is due not only to the very great mobility of our population, but also to the fact that our country is an economic unit and the prosperity of all parts contribute to the prosperity of the whole.

EDUCATIONAL IMPLICATIONS

The implications of this chapter for educational curriculum should be fairly obvious. The student must be made aware of the historic concept of our American democratic representative government as well as the ways in which it has changed in recent times through gradual evolution. He should also be aware of the many problems that are faced. Being made aware of the problems does not necessarily mean that the student is taught any one method of solving them. Perhaps, in some cases, it is better not to change the structure but to work on the problems on an intelligent basis within the present structure (which it may be important to safeguard for other reasons). The fact that there are serious problems needing solution should be made clear. Important suggestions that have been made by various groups for the alleviation of problems through changes of structure or other means should be discussed fully so that the student will have these ideas clearly in mind when problems arise and he must make some type of a decision as a citizen. Many solutions that forty or fifty years ago were not considered possible in a democracy are now not only accepted but considered to be an integral part of American democratic society.

Throughout all of the school curriculum should be found materials related to problems covered in this chapter. The student should be made clearly aware of what the problems are and also of alternatives in their solution. He should also be helped to develop a sense of dedication, to attempt to improve his country by thinking through the problems, proposing solutions, and bringing about whatever changes may be necessary to build a political structure that can face its problems adequately.

Use of Current History in the Schools

One of the problems of the schools is that of providing a background for understandings of current history. One of the improvements in recent years is the increased availability of materials in current trends written especially for use in our schools. Carefully edited and unbiased materials of this kind are now available at different maturity levels.[15] Writers of such materials usually expend greater effort to secure proper balance of material on both sides than do those of our ordinary newspapers and magazines. These materials should be used, particularly at the beginning of consideration of these problems. Emphases upon such current materials in the schools will certainly not eliminate the history, literature, and other courses already offered. In most cases these publications tie in with much of the current curricular materials and serve to enrich their study.

The use of current materials should not be limited to those specially prepared for the schools themselves. If it were, the students then would not get experience in evaluating the kind of materials they will read as adults. Consequently, current magazine articles and newspaper materials should be brought into class and read and evaluated. Examples of bias and propaganda techniques such as are indicated earlier in this chapter should be pointed out by the teacher and identified by the students.

Education for Discrimination and Critical Thinking

Very little has been said so far in this chapter concerning the educational values of those media that are primarily concerned with entertainment—plays, movies, and others. However, these do have an educational value. It is important that the school prepare people to appraise such media adequately. One of the jobs of a school is to broaden the student's taste and interests so that he will appreciate some of the things he has not previously met in his environment. Interest in such cultural matters as the legitimate stage, symphony, and ballet can be fostered by the school. The improvement of taste will insure that the students will choose more carefully the materials they read and the entertainments they enjoy. This is an important part of the problem of communication. A student or adult who reads little but comic books and "cheap" novels is losing a lot of the pleasure and satisfaction he should get out of life.

Another important thing, of course, is education for critical thinking. An aspect of this has already been covered in the discussion of propaganda analysis. The school should stress continuously the use of the scientific method of arriving at conclusions.

It is this problem of critical thinking that is the key to America's future. It has been referred to in Chapter 8 as a problem-solving approach to life. The difficulty lies in that professional educators do not know how to endow the youth of the nation with critical thinking. Problem-solving as a learning technique has been advocated for some years. The theory is beautiful. If all graduates of our schools possessed a high degree of

[15] Three of the most widely used sets of materials of this kind are published by the following companies: American Education Press, Civic Education Service, and Scholastic Magazines.

problem-solving ability and the attitude of using this rational approach to attack our social problems, the cultural lag between our technological inventions and our social inventions would be reduced rapidly. The fly in the ointment is that we do not as yet understand the mental processes involved in the construction of relevant hypotheses—what some psychologists refer to as the "ah-hah" phenomenon. This step is the heart of the technique.

The basic schemeta of the technique of the scientific process have been developed by Thorndike, Francis Bacon, Dewey, and many others. The best statement has perhaps been made by Dewey.[16] A workable sequence of steps consolidated from several sources is as follows:

1. An awareness of the problem.
2. Clarification of the problem.
3. Definition of needed data—construction of a "search model."
4. Collection and organization of data.
5. Formulation of tentative hypotheses.
6. Logical testing of hypotheses.
7. Drawing of conclusions.
8. Testing of conclusions.
   a. Logically.
   b. Empirically.

The major difficulties involved in teaching critical thinking as a method of attack are the psychological (and emotional) nature of many of life's problems, the need for extensive experiential bases, and the lack of understanding of how to develop generalizing ability in students. Each difficulty will be briefly summarized below.

Critical thinking is a logical procedure, not a psychological one. We are creatures of reason only to a degree. Logical reasoning breaks down in prejudicial areas—and those are the areas in which lie our major social problems. The propaganda techniques described in an earlier section of this chapter capitalize on that fact.

A broad base of experiences is necessary before one can become aware of a problem, clarify it, construct a search model, know where to search for data, or scientifically test the conclusion. This does not mean that teaching for critical thinking should be deferred. It means, rather, that problems posed to students at all ages should be appropriate to their mental maturity and experiential background.

The ability to generalize is necessary for the construction of hypotheses (the "ah-hah" phenomenon) and their logical testing ("if-then" thinking). We do not fully understand how to teach for generalizing ability. We do know that it is limited by native intelligence. This psychological fact has been capitalized upon by those who attempt to discredit democracy and

---

[16] John Dewey, *How We Think* (New York: Heath, 1937).

who plead for a government by the elite. We know from experience, however, that the average person has enough native ability to generalize on most of life's problems. Our dilemma, as professional educators, is that we know too little about how to capitalize on this native ability in teaching for generalization.

Some things we do know. We know that mere possession of all the data does not ensure intelligent decisions. We know, further, that the emotional attitude of consistently applying critical thinking to life's problems significantly increases the ratio of intelligent decisions. Pending further research into generalizing ability per se, the best available procedures for all teachers to follow are these:

1. Help the pupil become aware of the process (schema) he is using.
2. Provide the class with many problems appropriate to their mental maturity and experiential base.
3. Assist the class in applying the schema to the solution of their problems.
4. At the all-important step of formulating hypotheses, give many hints toward possible solutions. This has been proved to be our most effective technique in developing generalizing abilities.
5. Insist upon scientific testing of conclusions. It is at this point that most classroom teachers fail in the social subjects. Mathematics teachers insist that solutions be proved; social studies teachers tend to accept results of class discussions as final.

SUMMARY

We have indicated that our complex, industrialized modern life poses many problems that could not have been foreseen by our founding fathers. It pays tribute to their wisdom that our form of government, with minor revisions, has proved so nearly adequate to the solution of our modern problems.

The crux to the solution of these problems lies not in the basic structure of our government but in the wisdom of man. We have indicated the importance of our modern communications system in providing basic data. We have delineated the destructive forces of bias and propaganda. The final solution of these problems, however, rests upon the ability of the common man to utilize the basic data effectively and to recognize and combat the forces of bias and of propaganda.

Educators bear a major responsibility to increase these abilities in the common man. We have referred to this complex of abilities as critical thinking. In Chapter 14 we will set forth a possible list of basic values on which such thinking might be based. The degree of success with which educators can implant high ideals and skills of critical thinking in our youth will determine to what degree the social and governmental problems of America will be solved.

424   *The School in American Society*

SELECTED BIBLIOGRAPHY

ABRAHAM, HENRY J. *Compulsory Voting*. Washington, D.C.: Annals of American Government, Public Affairs Press, 1955. Pp. 38. An investigation into the feasibility of requiring all citizens to vote. Concludes that it is not constitutional, feasible, nor helpful.

ALLPORT, GORDON W., and LEO POTMAN. *The Psychology of Rumor*. New York: Holt, Rinehart & Winston, 1947. Pp. 247. A basic text that explains how rumors start and travel, and how to recognize them for what they are.

BLANCHARD, PAUL. *The Right to Read: The Battle Against Censorship*. Boston: Beacon Press, 1955. Pp. 339.

BRYCE, JAMES. *The American Commonwealth* (abridged edition). New York: Macmillan, 1934. Pp. xiii + 555.

CAMIEN, LAITEN LESTER. *Education: The Process and Social Institution*. New York: Vantage, 1964. Pp. 165.

Center for the Study of Democratic Institutions. *The Elite and the Electorate. Is Government by the People Possible?* Santa Barbara, Calif.: The Center and the Fund for the Republic, 1963. Pp. 22.

————. *The Mazes of Modern Government: The States, the Legislature, the Bureaucracy, the Courts*. Santa Barbara, Calif.: The Center and the Fund for the Republic, 1964. Pp. 38.

Commission of Freedom of the Press. *A Free and Responsible Press: A General Report on Mass Communications, Newspapers, Radio, Motion Pictures, Magazines, and Books*. Chicago: University of Chicago Press, 1947. Pp. xii + 138.

COWEN, ZELMAN, and others. *Fair Trial vs. A Free Press*. New York: The Center For the Study of Democratic Institutions, 1965. Pp. 37.

CROWTHER, BOSLEY. "Movies and Censorship." Public Affairs Pamphlet No. 332. New York: Public Affairs Committee, 1962.

DEWEY, JOHN. *How We Think*. Boston: Heath, 1933. Pp. x + 301.

ERNST, MORRIS L., and ALAN U. SCHWARTZ. *Censorship: The Search for the Obscene*. New York: Macmillan, 1964. Pp. vi + 288.

FORSTER, ARNOLD, and BENJAMIN R. EPSTEIN. *Danger on the Right*. New York: Random House, 1964. Pp. xviii + 294. The attitudes, personnel and influence of the radical right and extreme conservatives.

HARDLIN, OSCAR, and MARY HANDLIN. *The Dimensions of Liberty*. Cambridge, Mass.: Harvard University Press, 1961. Pp. 204.

KATZ, DANIEL, DORWIN CARTWRIGHT, SAMUEL ELDERSVELD, and ALFRED McCLUNG LEE (eds.). *Public Opinion and Propaganda*. New York: Holt, Rinehart & Winston, 1954. Pp. xx +779.

LIPSET, SEYMOUR MARTIN. *Political Man: The Social Bases of Politics*. Garden City, N.Y.: Doubleday and Doubleday Anchor Books, 1960. Pp. 432.

McDONALD, DONALD, with WILLIAM H. PARKER, Chief of Police of Los Angeles. *The Police* (One of a series of interviews on the American Character). Santa Barbara, Calif.: The Center and the Fund for the Republic, 1962. Pp. 30.

MacIVER, ROBERT M. *Academic Freedom in Our Times*. New York: Columbia University Press, 1955. Pp. xiv + 329.

MACKINNON, FRANK. *The Politics of Education: A Study of the Political Administration of the Public Schools. Toronto: University of Toronto Press, 1960. Pp. viii + 187.

MacNeil, Neil. *Forge of Democracy: The House of Representatives.* New York: David McKay, 1963. Pp. xi + 496.

Mason, A. Thomas. *Security Through Freedom: American Political Thought and Practice.* Ithaca, N.Y.: Cornell University Press, 1955. Pp. xi + 232.

Miller, Arthur S. *Private Governments and the Constitution.* Santa Barbara, Calif.: The Center and the Fund for the Republic, 1959. Pp. 16.

Miller, Clyde R. *How to Detect and Analyze Propaganda.* New York: The Town Hall, 1939. Pp. 36.

Nelson, Jack, and Gene Roberts, Jr. *The Censors and the Schools.* Boston: Little, Brown, 1963. Pp. ix + 208.

O'Brian, John Lord. *National Security and Individual Freedom.* Cambridge, Mass.: Harvard University Press, 1955. Pp. 84. An excellent appraisal of American "loyalty" progress and of the present condition of American liberties.

One-Man—One Vote. New York: The Twentieth Century Fund, 1962. Pp. 19. A statement of basic principles of legislative apportionment as agreed upon at a conference of research scholars and political scientists held by the Twentieth Century Fund.

Packard, Vance. *Hidden Persuaders.* New York: David McKay, 1957. Pp. viii + 275.

Quade, Quentin L., and Thomas J. Bennett. "Coping with Bureaucracy." *Current* (March 1965), No. 57, 19–26.

Rowat, Donald C. "Redress from Administrative Tyranny." *Current* (February 1963), No. 34, pp. 60–64.

Schramm, Wilber. *Responsibility in Mass Communication.* New York: Harper & Row, 1957. Pp. xxiii + 391.

Seldin, Joseph. *The Golden Fleece: Advertising in American Life.* New York: Harmon Associates. Pp. 305.

Tocqueville, Alexis de. *Democracy in America.* Two vols. New York: Knopf, 1945. Vol. I, pp. 434. Vol. II, pp. xiii + 401. A well-printed, intelligently edited new edition of "the greatest study of one country by a citizen of another," one of the earliest works to sense the critical implications of the American experiment in self-government.

Wanamaker, Temple. *American Foreign Policy Today.* New York: Bantam Books, 1964. Pp. vi + 250.

Wheeler, Harvey. *The Restoration of Politics.* New York: The Center for the Study of Democratic Institutions, 1965. Pp. 32.

White, Winston. *Beyond Conformity.* New York: Free Press of Glencoe, 1961. Pp. 230.

Worldwide Opinion Research Documentation. *Polls,* I, No. 1 (Spring, 1965).

Selected Films

China Under Communism (Indiana) 22 min

This documentary is an uncensored, eye-witness report by an authorized U.S. newsman permitted to travel in Red China. The film shows Communist methods of forcing radical and sweeping changes in traditional patterns of living: describes China's most critical social and economic problems, and considers the possible effects of Communist success in China on world security.

Communism (Indiana) 32 min

The film discusses the worldwide history and organization of the Communist Party; how its members operate in the United States to try to weaken and gain control of our political, social, and economic structure.

Communist Blueprint for Conquest (U.S. Army) 28 min

Mr. Boris H. Klosson, Department of State, explains the methods and techniques used by the Communists to seize power in a country. He describes the weapons of the Communist Party, discusses Communist tactics and attitude toward the individual in relation to the state.

Decision at Laurel Falls (Pennsylvania Department of Internal Affairs) 28 min

Demonstrates that good government is the result of a vital and continuing partnership between the elected and the elector.

Does It Matter What You Think? (British Information Service) 15 min

Discusses the factors that help to form public opinion, including mass media of communication and exchange of opinions with other individuals. Illustrates how public opinion is formed in groups, such as trade unions, charitable activities, etc.

Due Process of Law Denied (Teaching Film Custodians) 20 min

Excerpted from the feature-length motion picture, *The Ox-Bow Incident.*

Freedom to Read (Columbia University) 15 min

How a library can best serve freedom. Stresses the place of competing philosophies in a democratic society.

Great Lessons in American Politics: The State and the Nation (McGraw-Hill and Omnibus) 25 min

How to Judge Facts (Coronet Films) 10 min

How to separate facts from assumptions and faulty reasoning. Using a case study of a false story, the film points out the common errors of reasoning. Helps to be on guard against assumptions, false analogies, irrelevant facts, and double-meaning words.

Pressure Groups (EBF) 20 min

Explains what pressure groups are and reveals that, when democratically used, they are a necessary instrument for decision-making in a democracy. Illustrates methods used by a representative democratic pressure group to bring about legislation for a desirable civic project. Contrasts these methods with the underhanded and behind-the-scenes manipulation employed by a group attempting to prevent the passage of a bill.

Propaganda Techniques (Coronet Films) 10 min

Public Opinion (EBF) 10 min

Sets up criteria by which public opinion may be judged and measured, illustrating through development of public opinion that produced a waterworks project in a small community. An enlightened public opinion must have access to the facts; press and radio must be balanced in their presentation of the facts; competent witnesses or experts are needed; and the public must overcome prejudice and think objectively. In short, an analysis of public opinion—what it is, how it is formed, and what it can accomplish.

Chapter 13. *Problems of the United States in an Interdependent World*

SUFFICIENT DOCUMENTATION is found in the previous chapters to establish thoroughly that we do live in an interdependent world. The typical "100 per cent American" each day utilizes ideas and material products that have been incorporated into the American culture from sources all over the world; in some cases, the products are imported in the final manufactured or refined form.[1] This interdependent nature of the world, however, does not automatically lead to increasing understanding and cooperation. The realities of the present world center around the nation-states that evolved in the late medieval period. Man's loyalties, once centered within the tribe and later in his religion, are now focused rather definitely upon the nation-state. By and large, now it is only treason to one's nation, not to one's religion, that is punishable by death. Those who wish to help work toward an improvement in the solution of problems in the world must take into account this all-important fact of *nationalism* as a force in the present-day world.

Theoretically, nation-states are sovereign; that is, there is no power that can dictate to them what they should do. This means that, theoretically, we live in a state of international anarchy. Actually, it is only a state of relative anarchy, ameliorated by voluntary international agreements regulating such major matters as communications, transportation, commerce, tourist and commercial travel, and the rules of war. Departments of foreign affairs of each nation facilitate and regulate these international agreements through elaborate diplomatic protocol, including foreign embassy and consular posts. As individuals, we have long since realized that

[1] For example, see a list of examples of both types in Ralph Linton, *The Study of Man* (New York: Appleton, 1936), p. 32.

427

one's freedom and rights must end at the point where they conflict with the common concerns of the group. This principle is generally recognized among the free nations, but it can operate only on the basis of an agreed-upon cooperation. There is little disposition at present to solve international problems through an all-encompassing group, such as a world government, that would define the areas of freedom and responsibilities for each of the nations. It is within a framework of a group of nation-states, still free and independent, and not in the area of a possible immediate world government, that we apparently must explore the problems of the interdependent world.

The dominant fact in the field of international relations in the post-World War II period was the bipolarization of world power. One section of the world, under the hegemony or domination of the Soviet Union (Russia) has been opposed by another, under the somewhat reluctant leadership of America. By and large, this bipolarization of power represented a totalitarian group of countries with almost completely socialized economics and little internal freedom opposed by a group of free nations with a variety of economies and a variety of conditions of internal freedom. The second group has been composed mainly of democratic nations. In the sections to follow, we shall first analyze some of the potential and actual problem areas and summarize important developments on the world scene. Then we shall look at the major conflict (the Communist world, versus U.S.A. as leader of the "free" or Western world). Finally, we shall point out some educational implications.

SOURCES OF STRESS BETWEEN NATIONS

An analysis of the problems that cause difficulty among nations is necessary to determine ways in which these groups can work together and set up machinery for resolving their conflicts in some positive way.

Wide Range of Ideologies in the World

Just as there is a wide range of cultural patterns within the American scene, similarly there is a much wider range of cultural patterns throughout the world. Many examples may be cited—the attitudes toward the sacred cow in India, toward polygamous marriage in Africa, toward "Western-style" progress in many countries such as—let us say—Tibet. This wide range of ideologies poses a challenge as to how to enable the differing groups to get along together. Just as it is necessary for those of us in the United States to study and understand persons within the American democratic framework who are different from ourselves, so it is necessary for world understanding to study the cultural backgrounds of other persons in the world.

Population Variability

There are extreme differences in the number of people living upon the land in various areas because of the differences in the ability of the soil and its accompanying resources to support a population. There are also differences in the number of persons on the different lands that have the same potentiality for supporting a population. This is due to the technological stage at which the people find themselves or to the slowness of population growth in some lands that have been newly discovered.

The average population per square mile of the world at present is approximately 50 persons. It ranges from about 3 per square mile in semiarid areas or in tropical forest areas, through over 40 in the central part of the United States and in Russia, to 180 in the northeastern part of the United States, 310 in western Central Europe, 410 in India and Ceylon, and up to 500 in Korea and Japan.

Variability of Resources, Utilized and Unutilized

There is also tremendous variability in the amounts of the natural resources existing in different places on the earth's surface. The fertility of the land, the extent of forest, the amounts and kinds of minerals and oil, and the coal and water-power resources vary greatly. The most important economic differential among nations, however, seems to be the state of technology. For example, Great Britain has a high level of prosperity but has low potentiality in forest and water power and in petroleum and natural gas. At the same time, such places as the highlands of Eastern Africa, where a low level of living exists, have great potentiality in terms of water power, all kinds of minerals, and rich soil.

It can help to visualize the present world situation if we can consider, as an illustration, the present population consisting of over 3 billion to be compressed into a single town of 1,000 people.[2] In this imaginary town, the following picture of contrast can be presented. Sixty persons would represent the Americans in the town while 940 would represent all the other countries. These 60 Americans would receive one half of the total income of the town while the remaining 940 persons would share the other half.

Just 300 of the total population would be Christians, leaving the remaining 700 for all of the other beliefs. The next largest would be Moslems numbering approximately 150. Approximately 80 of the town's population would actually be card-carrying Communists. Three-hundred seventy of the town's population would be in countries which are Communist-dominated. Approximately 303 of the town's population would be white or Caucasian while the remaining 697 would be nonwhite.

[2] These comparisons have been developed from recent figures that can be found widely scattered throughout the literature. They have been quoted many times in the public press and in magazine articles.

The 60 Americans would have a life expectancy of slightly over 70 years. The life expectancy of all others would average below 40 years. The Americans would produce about one-sixth (16⅔ per cent) of the town's food. Most of the 940 others would be hungry most of the time. The Americans would use 15 per cent of the food supply and would store the remainder.

Each of the 60 Americans would have 12 times as much electricity, 22 times as much coal, 21 times as much oil, 50 times as much steel, and 50 times as much general manufactured equipment as each of the 940 remaining in the town.

The *lowest* income group of Americans would be better off than the *average* of the other 940.

Efforts Towards Earlier World Association and Cooperation

Ever since early times there have been conflict and warfare when men of different groups have come in contact; but there has also been cooperation on the basis of mutual advantage, usually through trade, which has helped bring about the diffusion of culture. In the recent years, with the development of the nation-states, mankind has attempted to set up a system of diplomacy to enable the peoples of the world to get along with each other. However, the world has been subjected to a series of wars, which have been growing in their intensity. There has apparently been no direct relationship between the enlightenment of the nations in respect to education, religion, or other such cultural advancement, and their ability to get along without resort to war. Consequently, man from time to time has sought to develop better methods of world association and cooperation through direct diplomacy. After the devastating World War I, an attempt was made to work out such an association in the League of Nations. There were several reasons why the League of Nations did not prove to be successful. One was that several of the powerful nations, including the United States, did not join it. Another was weakness of the structure of the League of Nations, arising as a result of the power conflict following World War I and from its consequent close tie-in with the Versailles Treaty, which was an outgrowth of the animosities of World War I. In the midst of World War II, the United States with its allies attempted to work out a system of world cooperation in the United Nations. This is not a world government but is an attempt to set up a systematic method of world consultation and joint action based upon a rational way of solving the problems that the nations face.

The United Nations

The present United Nations organization started as a development among those nations that were associated in the fight against the Axis powers. In San Francisco on July 26, 1945, these nations adopted the

United Nations Charter. This was later ratified by the respective governments of the countries concerned. About 120 nations are now members
of the United Nations proper.

Structure

Basically the United Nations consists of the Security Council composed
of eleven representatives of which five are permanent—namely Nationalist
China, France, the U.S.S.R., the United Kingdom (Great Britain), and the
United States—and the General Assembly, composed of the delegations
from each member nation, each with one vote. Closely associated with
the United Nations is the International Court of Justice, which was in
existence prior to the United Nations but has now become an integral
part of it. (See Figure 14.)[3]

The idea back of the Security Council was that the major nations would
agree on cooperative efforts to prevent war. The five permanent members
have a veto power over any actions of the Security Council. This was
deemed necessary, since the actions of the Security Council amounted to a
commitment of the nations concerned to take military action of necessary. Neither the United States nor the U.S.S.R. would have joined without it. However, this power has been one of the stumbling blocks in the
way of decisive action in the Security Council. The U.S.S.R. has used its
veto in a number of issues, thus blocking some of the important actions
of the Council. This problem has been partially alleviated after the Korean
episode by a provision whereby the General Assembly can be called into
action very quickly in case of a crisis to take action on any matter on
which the Security Council may be deadlocked. This has tended to reduce
somewhat the importance of the Security Council.

Under the General Assembly there are three main groups: the Trusteeship Council, the Economic and Social Council, and the Secretariat (the
permanent staff).

Under the Economic and Social Council there are many other commis-
sions as well as certain specialized agencies that have a link with the United
Nations but actually are separate groups. Nations belonging to the United
Nations may or may not belong to a specialized agency, and nations not
belonging to the United Nations may affiliate with the specialized agencies.
Some of these agencies will be discussed in a later section.

Successes and Failures

Since the United Nations was formed, it has undertaken numerous
problems. Many of these have been handled quite successfully. However,
these have not made the headlines as often as the basic conflict between
Russia and Red China on the one hand and the United States on the

---

[3] Proposals are now (1966) pending to raise the membership of the Security
Council to 15.

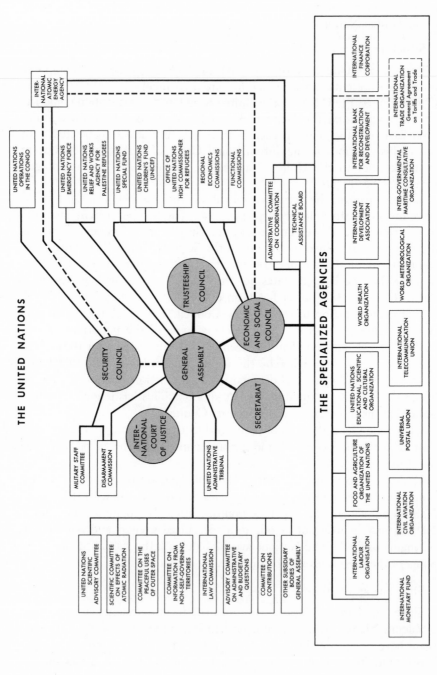

Figure 14. Structure of the United Nations and Related Agencies (Office of Education, "Teaching About the United Nations.")

other. Numerous clashes that might have led to war in Syria, Lebanon, Iran, Indonesia, Greece, Palestine, Kashmir, and elsewhere, all were given careful attention by United Nations staff members, and in many cases satisfactory solutions were worked out.

The crucial conflict in Korea, of course, developed into a small-size war and entailed considerable loss of life. This issue has not yet been decided, and it constitutes one of the failures of the United Nations to discover a peaceable method for the solution of international conflicts. The Arab-Israeli situation has certainly not yet been clarified either. The United Nations failed again on the matter of the control of atomic energy and weapons, because of the basic opposition of Russia to an inspection system.

In areas other than military, the United Nations has done a good job in sponsoring technical aid (including medical aid) to various "have-not" countries. The Commission on Human Rights has drafted the Universal Declaration of Human Rights, which was adopted in the Assembly on December 10, 1948. Many of the specialized agencies of the United Nations to be discussed later have also been quite successful in their programs.

Weaknesses

The weaknesses of the United Nations can be appraised from two viewpoints. One of these is held by those who desire a much stronger international structure bordering on, or going over completely to, a form of world government. The United Nations is not at present a world government. It has very little power unless its actions are backed by the moral and military forces of the nations that make it up. On the other hand, criticism also comes from those persons who think that participation in the United Nations constitutes an unwarranted weakening of the freedom of action of the individual nations concerned. These people are prone to "point with alarm" at such things as the Declaration of Human Rights, claiming that they abridge some of the rights of each nation to determine such matters internally.

Careful study of the UN does uncover certain basic weaknesses, which stem from certain inherent weaknesses of structure on the one hand and from public opinions and attitudes on the other. Both types of weaknesses are difficult to remedy. The veto power of the five major nations constitutes a definite weakness that can stymie action. The inability of the United Nations to enforce its decisions because it lacks a sufficient permanent military force also causes it to be somewhat weak. Another basic weakness lies in the fact that the United Nations is not wholeheartedly supported by the peoples of the world. Its successes and failures in the future will certainly be measured in terms of the support that it has from the peoples of the earth in demanding that their governmental representatives act in accordance with the welfare of the globe as a whole. The world is apparently not yet ready for world government. We still live in a real world of independent nation-states. People still feel their security lies in their own nation-states and not in a world organization.

The crucial problem, of course, is not whether world government is imminent but whether world destruction impends. A nuclear war could destroy modern civilization. The after-effects of such a war, including "fallout" of atomic dust on the areas of human habitation, conceivably could destroy the human race. Human energies must be directed in massive proportions toward peaceful coexistence between the free world and the slave. A legitimate part of this effort is the tremendous expenditure for nuclear and other devices for military preparedness, and for the exploration of the military potential of space. Much greater efforts must be expended, however, toward economic and diplomatic means of maintaining and stabilizing the present uneasy peace. The present structure of the UN provides only a limited avenue for the accomplishment of permanent peace. Upon the efforts of the independent nation-states, such as the United States, depends the question of peace or war—and possible extermination.

UNESCO

A section is devoted to a discussion of UNESCO because it is the organization affiliated with the UN that is most closely related to education. The letters stand for the United Nations Educational, Scientific, and Cultural Organization. The purpose of UNESCO "is to contribute to peace and security by promoting collaboration among the nations through education, science, and culture in order to further universal respect for justice, for the rule of law, and for human rights and fundamental freedoms which are affirmed for the people of the world, without distinction of race, sex, language, or religion, by the charter of the United Nations."[4]

Thirty-one nations made up the original list of members (now approximately 100) in this organization. It has a regular secretariat, which has been located in Paris. Most of its work is related to such things as the improvement of educational facilities, the promotion of international educational understanding, and the fight against illiteracy. It also promotes international scientific cooperation and the exchange of cultural activities in the various arts. It tries to assist in the free flow of information between the various member countries, particularly information that will be of help to the less advanced countries. UNESCO provides experts for technical assistance in various areas.

The United States became an original member of UNESCO by an overwhelming majority of the House of Representatives and by unanimous action of the Senate. The United States (as have other of the nations represented) has developed a national commission, which prepares policies

[4] UNESCO Constitution. Text taken from a leaflet, "The Specialized Agencies of the United Nations," p. 5 (New York: United Nations Department of Public Information, 1953).

that its representatives carry out in the general conferences of UNESCO. Important elements in our society, such as the Federal Council of Churches, Catholic and Jewish organizations, labor organizations, and scholarly organizations, all have representatives appointed to the commission of UNESCO.

In the United States, UNESCO has proved to be the most controversial of all the agencies of the United Nations. Some school systems have prohibited the use of UNESCO materials. The American Legion has been particularly vigorous in its condemnation of this agency. It has accused it of being Communistic and atheistic, and of promoting the ideals of world government as opposed to nationalism. A committee of the American Legion, composed among others of two former Legion presidents, made a careful study and declared that UNESCO was completely free of all these criticisms and recommended that the American Legion support it wholeheartedly.[5] At its convention in 1955, the American Legion refused to accept the recommendation of its committee and went on record again as condemning UNESCO. It did, however, approve the United Nations.

Important groups in the United States, including both political parties, have repeatedly endorsed the aims of UNESCO. Many school systems are utilizing its materials in the same fashion that other materials are utilized in the school curriculum.

Other UN Agencies

In addition to UNESCO, there are other specialized agencies that have done important work in developing international relations:

1. International Labor Organization (ILO). This is an organization with a delegation from each of the countries, composed of two members representing the government and one each representing management and labor. This agency works on such problems as labor conditions in the various countries of the world.
2. Food and Agricultural Organization of the United Nations (FAO). This agency deals with basic food problems of the countries. It collects information and distributes it in relation to developing better facilities for the production of food.
3. International Civil Aviation Organization (ICAO). This takes care of all matters related to nonmilitary aviation arrangements between the various countries.
4. International Bank for Reconstruction and Development (BANK). This agency helps to facilitate the interchange of credit facilities among the various countries.

[5] *Defense Bulletin*, N.E.A., **62**, September 1955, p. 5. Conclusions reported in entirety. See also U.S. National Commission for UNESCO *Newsletter* **4**, No. 14, July 26, 1957, for report of (U.S.) House Subcommittee on UNESCO. The conclusions were the same.

5. International Monetary Fund (FUND). This is a fund to facilitate the exchange of currencies between the various countries.
6. World Health Organization (WHO). This is an organization concerned with distributing information and technical assistance in regard to health matters in the various countries of the world.
7. Universal Postal Union (UPUN). The early machinery of this organization existed long before the United Nations. The Universal Postal Convention, which has been in effect for a great many years, is now organized through the Universal Postal Union. Practically all of the countries of the world are members of this organization.
8. International Telecommunication Union (ITU). This is an organization that correlates problems related to telegraph and radiotelegraph.
9. World Meteorological Organization (WMO). This is a matter of correlating information in regard to weather.

There are other organizations that were in existence but have now ceased to operate, as well as some that have not yet been put into existence but are planned.

The World in "Blocs"

Political life within a free country is usually organized into various political parties. This is to be expected in a country where there is freedom for opinion. People do not agree, and, not agreeing, they tend to organize in groups. In the case of the nations making up the United Nations and of those outside that body, the world has tended to organize around certain major power blocs. Nations within these blocs tend to vote together in the UN and to pursue policies somewhat in common.

The Communist Bloc

This bloc, which has developed rapidly after World War II, is composed mainly of the Union of Socialist Soviet Republics (Russia) and the so-called People's Republic of China. These two countries are quite independent and in the sixties have drawn rather steadily apart.[6] Closely associated with them are the so-called "satellite" countries, such as Poland, Hungary, Rumania, North Korea, and North Vietnam. One of the countries that is avowedly Communistic, Yugoslavia, *apparently* is independent of Russia and tends to go along, partially at least, with the democratic bloc.

The Moslem Bloc

There is some tendency toward the development of a so-called "Moslem" bloc. This could include all of the nations that are officially or nominally of the Moslem faith: Iran, Iraq, Lebanon, Egypt, and Syria (now the United Arab Republic), Pakistan, Indonesia, Yemen, Turkey, and others.

[6] Cf. Edward Crankshaw, *The New Cold War: Moscow vs. Peking* (Baltimore: Penguin, 1963).

These nations, however, all pursue a partially independent policy. Some are antagonistic to each other. Pakistan is strongly pro-American, while some of the other Mohammedan countries tend to lean more toward being anti-West. There was some evidence after the mid-1950's of the formation of an Afro-Asian bloc in the UN, including the Arab and other Asian countries, but this has not materialized.

South American Problems

To the south of the United States lie a group of countries, which, because of geographical position and other reasons, should have interests aligned closely with the United States and Canada. Because of a relatively retarded economic development, a large lower class, and poor development of some of their resources, these countries tend to be somewhat erratic in their governments and thus run a danger of swinging over to the Communist orbit. The predominant religion of South America (Roman Catholic), however, tends to be a stabilizing influence against Communist leanings. Very few of the South American countries have a stable government. They are subject to quite frequent revolutions. Although they are generally considered to be democratic nations, they are certainly not democratic in the sense of the United States or the members of the British Commonwealth of Nations.

India and Other "Neutrals"

There are other countries of the world that tend to consider themselves as neutrals. The most prominent of these, of course, is India. India, being antagonistic to the West because of her colonial experience with Great Britain, tends at times to be closely sympathetic with the Communist bloc. The Indians claim, however, that they do not have any predilection toward either side. This frees them to accept economic assistance from all sources. The Russians currently are financing the building of huge steel mills in India. The U.S. recently sent vast quantities of surplus grain to India. The Indians claim that they are in favor of peace. They *have* dealt strenuously with any Communist terrorists who have attempted to destroy the internal well-being of India. "Peaceful" India is very belligerent when her own border security is immediately threatened, as witness her disputes with Pakistan and with China. It remains to be seen what this vast country and the other neutral countries like her would do if a general conflict should arise.

The "Democratic" Nations

At the opposite pole from the Communist bloc there is the so-called bloc of the democratic nations. This surely includes the United States, the Philippines, and most of the British Commonwealth of Nations (the United Kingdom, Canada, the Union of South Africa, Australia, New Zealand, and possibly Ceylon). Almost all these nations can certainly be called democratic in the Western meaning of the term. However, the Union of South Africa is developing rapidly into an oligarchic state where a minority group, the European whites, are tending to pursue a policy of domination. The South American countries, before mentioned, tend to go along with the democratic bloc of nations on most issues. Spain also seems to pursue a foreign policy that is closely related to that of the democratic bloc. Spain, in its internal policies, is probably the nearest example of a Fascist state at present among those being discussed.

WORLD CONFLICTS

There are many conflicts between the two major powers that emerged from World War II, namely the United States of America and the Union of Socialist Soviet Republics (Russia); some of these are important issues but minor in nature as causes of a possible future world war, others are major in nature. There are also conflicts between nations that have similar cultures and governmental structures.

Conflicts Among Democratic Nations

Not all of the conflicts that afflict the world are between countries that differ in regard to their political ideology. There are numerous conflicts among the so-called democratic nations. They are in trade competition with each other. In some cases this is a matter of being in competition to sell to a third country. In other cases the competition exists between companies in the various countries to sell to customers within one or both of the countries concerned. For example, England and the United States, both being industrial countries, are in conflict in regard to the sale of manufactured goods of various kinds.

Sometimes there are conflicts between "democratic" countries over territories. Some of the boundary lines in South America are still not fully settled. There are also differences in regard to the ways to solve economic problems. The difference in the approaches of England and America to the solution of some of their economic problems is a source of friction, England tending more toward a socialist and welfare state, America tending to be somewhat more conservative in this matter. Some of the democratic nations are "have" nations and some are "have-not." This leads to conflicts of interest and attitude. Some of the democratic countries of the world were formerly colonies of other democratic countries. They may tend to be antagonistic toward the former "imperialistic" overlords and toward countries friendly to the latter. An example of this kind is India in relationship to England and her friends. Other areas of the world, not yet nations, are striving for autonomy in government. This leads to friction and serves as a possible source of war. The differences in the way in which the Union of South Africa is handling its race problems and the way in which some other countries in Africa and Europe are handling theirs, or as the United States seems to be evolving in its solution, are also sources of possible conflict.

Minor Conflicts Between Russia and the United States

There are some issues between the general ideologies and policies of the United States and those of Russia that are sources of conflict but that, in the view of many thinking persons (including the authors of this book), should not be considered by America to be causes for war. These can be summarized under forms of government, economic system, and religious policies.

The American people, believing as thoroughly as they do in democracy as a political form and as a way of life (see Chapter 14), are very much upset when a country fails to practice even the semblance of democracy as they see it. Even though the Russian constitution on paper apparently has democratic forms, in some respects more so than the United States, in practice, Russia constitutes a dictatorship by an oligarchy. All elections are controlled by the Communist Party, which, in turn, is controlled by a relatively few persons who hold high positions. The people have no real choice in their elections. Furthermore, in the state of terrorism maintained by the secret police, very little opportunity is given for the criticism of the basic premises of political ideas or economic practices in Russia. While we, the American people, would prefer to see a different governmental policy in Russia, we certainly are committed to the self-determination of peoples in regard to their government and certainly could not go to war to change the methods that are now being used in Russia for the political operation of their government. If we did this, we would also have to do the same thing in other countries that are not democratic, such as Spain.

The second minor conflict relates to the type of economic system in Russia. Our American Constitution does not commit us to any single way of solving our economic problems. We have, in fact, solved different economic problems within our country in diverse ways. In some cases this has involved private ownership with governmental control; in other cases it has involved public ownership.[7] Certainly we would not deny the right of another country to solve its internal economic problems as it pleases; however, most Americans would think that Russia has been unwise in the way in which it has done so, even though they would not wish to go to war on that particular issue.

The religious issue is the one of the three discussed here about which many persons would feel most strongly. Most Americans are quite religious and most Americans believe in religious freedom. Although, theoretically, the Russian state is supposed to practice religious freedom, it is doubtful if there is very much freedom of religion there. For a great number of years, the Russian state has propagated an atheistic point of view and substituted

[7] See Chapter 6.

a philosophy of Marxian materialism for religion. Although in recent years there has been some freedom of worship, there is certainly not any encouragement, or even a completely neutral position, with respect to religion. It is quite likely that no prominent position in government or in other aspects of life in the U.S.S.R. can be held by a person too closely identified with a religious point of view, whether Christian or Mohammedan. Certainly, however, the experience that the Western world has had with religious wars should discourage us from ever making war over a problem of religion. The question of religious freedom is one that any people will have to work out internally within their own country.

Major Conflicts Between Russia and the United States

This brings us to the problem of the basic conflicts between the two countries that have involved us in the cold war. It appears to the writers that these are two in number and that they do constitute not only a serious threat to America but also the other democratic nations of the world.

The first of these conflicts has been the tendency of the Russian nation to follow an expansionist policy, a continuation of trends under the old Czarist regime. This expansion has recently come about through taking over countries lying at its border under one pretext or another, dominating them either actually or behind the scenes, and making them a part of the so-called Communist bloc of nations. This factor, in the range of history, is not unique to the Russians, but the Russian Policy has been to continue the expansionist program in the democratic era. The present Communists have added to the age-old Russian expansionist policy the drive of propagandizing and spreading the Russian philosophy of its economic system. This goes far outside the nature of being an internal problem of Russia. It involves all of us. There can be no freedom of nations as long as one nation, however small or insignificant, is threatened by another that violates international law and order. Russian (or Communist Chinese) expansionism presents a threat to freedom-loving countries and consequently a threat to the entire world. The preservation of world peace and order depends upon the security of any nation against being forced to join other nations against its desire. The Russian system of supposedly independent but affiliated Communist states (satellites) is a thinly disguised use of force. The revolts of the mid-1950's in Poland, Hungary, and East Germany indicate considerable nationalist feeling even among Communists in these countries.

The other major conflict between the two nations is the policy of propagandizing for communism by means of activities within the various nations of the world. It has been definitely a policy of the Communists to set up organizations within all the countries of the world to propagandize and to work by devious means to bring about their philosophy in those countries. These political groups have also been used as part of the overseas apparatus of Russia and have engaged in espionage and other related activities. The official policy of these political parties or groups in the other countries has borne little relationship to the problems within these countries but has followed very closely striking shifts in the foreign policy of Russia. This was particularly noticed as Russia changed her attitude toward Hitler at least twice during the period from 1939 on. The policy of trying to put over a philosophy within another country by subversive means through agents in the pay of the first country and by other similar methods that are fundamentally clandestine is one that freedom-loving nations cannot tolerate. So long as such tactics are used, they will be a source of antagonism between the U.S.S.R. and the United States and could lead to war.

In the late 1950's there was considerable talk on the part of the Russian leaders, and also the Americans' emphasizing a state of competition between the two nations with respect to their economic and military systems *without resort to war*. An apparently sizable improvement in productivity in the U.S.S.R., the success of the Russians in sending up the first satellites, information reaching this country concerning the enormous expansion of the Russian educational system, all serve to point up the fact that Russian society has been making some progress in many fields. It would seem that peaceful competition of this kind, as long as it involves real progress, would be helpful rather than harmful. This policy, seemingly pursued by both countries in the sixties, should be stimulating and rewarding to both of them as long as it does not lead to war.

MILITARY PREPAREDNESS

The state of tension and the condition of cold war with which the world is confronted have led to frantic efforts to maintain the United States and other countries in a state of military preparedness. It becomes necessary to assess some of the problems that the terrific costs of military preparedness, in both money and effort, lay upon the country.

Economic Costs

One approach to the problem of maintaining world peace through military preparedness is a consideration of its tremendous costs to the world. The United States alone spends approximately $50 billion annually for defense. The total cost figures are not readily available, nor are they easily ascertainable. Moreover, numerous problems arise in connection with the classification and interpretation of such figures. For example, an expenditure may be classified by the Bureau of the Budget as military in one annual report, but it may not be so listed in a later annual report. Also, most sources do not include the cost of interest on this portion of the national debt. Other complications arise when some appropriations are carried over from one fiscal period to another, so that spending in any one year may be far greater than the appropriation for that particular year.

Few people are aware of the large percentage of our national budget that is set aside for military preparedness. The Federal Internal Revenue Service has estimated that at least sixty cents of every tax dollar are spent for military purposes, but this figure does not include benefits to veterans nor interest on the indebtedness. Another aspect of military preparedness is its increasingly higher costs. It has been estimated that in Caesar's time it cost seventy-five cents to kill a man, as compared to $50,000 in World War II.

A series of hemisphere and regional defense pacts created and sponsored by the United States during the past eight or ten years are adding millions of dollars annually to the foregoing figures. These pacts definitely commit us to a program of global proportions. Thus we see that any future war will involve more people, more resources, and far greater costs.

Economic and Other Effects of Military Preparedness

Budgetary expenditures, defense pacts, and such do not nearly approach the "real" or total cost of military preparedness. Other economic factors of startling proportions must be included, factors on which it is almost impossible to place a price tag. In reviewing the total situation, some economists have been concerned about the many dangers of prolonged military spending and its impact upon the long-range economy of our country. They are well aware of the displacement of industries and personnel. They realize the implications of the great diversion of human effort and strategic materials from consumer channels. They see personnel being trained for highly specialized military jobs for which there is little or no counterpart in normal consumer production. They see the civilian market being stripped of doctors, dentists, nurses, technicians, and other professional people who are sorely needed by their own communities. They see the shifts of population toward industrial centers, with the resultant overcrowding of those communities. Finally, the economists see the great readjustment that is needed when cutbacks in the military spending program are made. These economic costs of military preparedness cannot be clearly estimated or shown on graphs.

The Social-Psychological Costs of Military Preparedness

We cannot deal with the cost of military preparedness only in terms of money, since the "real" cost includes the human cost that a military atmosphere levies upon the social-psychological health of our nation. Social scientists are aware of the dangers of a prolonged state of military domination and emphasis in any culture or society. Continued military programs can cause strong government controls and bring about centralization to a dangerous degree, as has been demonstrated in Germany and Russia.

One of the costs of military preparedness is its effect upon attitudes of our civilian population. There is a danger that even a democratic people may become militaristic in its outlook on life in a world in which militarism becomes increasingly dominant. There is a genuine conflict between democratic ways and "military" ways of operating. A completely militarized state would seem, of necessity, to become a Fascist state.

The effect of military preparedness on the democratic countries would include uneasiness and tensions toward each other as well as toward those who are opposed to democracy. It is difficult to relieve tensions in a world of nations armed to the teeth, just as it would be difficult to do the same in a group of civilians all armed to the teeth. The real solution to our international problems must come when there is some way of putting down disturbers of the peace by means of an international police force. This course lies well in the future.

Other social-psychological disturbances caused by continued mobilization might be:

1. Migration of great numbers of people to areas ill equipped for such influx of population. (Included in this would be housing shortages, water shortages, traffic problems, and the like.)
2. Hasty marriages, broken homes, numerous divorces, juvenile delinquency.
3. General unrest, mentally disturbed men and women.
4. Increase in crime, breakdown in morals, and increase in alcoholism and drug addiction.

There is little doubt that "brink of war" conditions have far-reaching effects on the nation's leaders as well as on the population as a whole. These social-psychological disturbances are extremely dangerous in our society, and we as educators must be concerned about them. What, then, is the total cost? It is far too great, yet it is a problem that requires long-range planning and some intense soul-searching.

Necessity for Military Preparedness

The realities of the present world indicate that free nations must prepare themselves for any kind of eventuality. We do not now have guaranteed or enforced international law and order. We do not have a world government that can enforce the decisions of a world council on the member nations or upon the member citizens. The situation is something similar to that of vigilante days in the western part of the United States. There and then, raw force tended to prevail. Persons sought protection by allying themselves with neighbors of like mind. Finally order came about through the establishment of strong local governmental units. Similarly, for the moment, in today's world, military preparedness of the most technologically efficient kind possibly is a necessity for survival on the part of the larger nations of the world. Strangely enough, the smaller nations—being pawns among the great powers—do not have the same necessity for military preparedness that the larger nations have.

With such vast sums of money being allocated for the military, other much needed federal aid programs are being sacrificed or bypassed in attempts to keep down governmental spending. Education, health, and welfare must compete with the military for public funds. If only a fraction of the nearly two trillion dollars spent on World War II had been allocated to education, many of the critical school building and classroom shortages could have been prevented and the substandard teacher salaries could have been raised to attract better people to the teaching profession. Yet the military draws heavily upon the products of our educational system for personnel for their further specialized training and service. It would seem that increasing the support of the schools through larger federal appropriations would be of benefit to the national defense effort.

Positive and Negative Effects of Military Preparedness on Education

Military policy since World War II has permitted many thousands of service men the opportunity to continue their education or to learn new skills upon discharge through the now famous G. I. Bill of Rights. While serving in the armed forces, men were subjected to almost continuous training programs in military schools throughout the nation and operational areas. Thus the Army became a giant education system in itself. Nearly all armed forces personnel were permitted to take college extension courses through the United States Armed Forces Institute (USAFI).

In many instances, colleges and universities throughout the nation were encouraged to set up courses for military personnel as well as to participate in laboratory experimentation and projects. It was at the University of Chicago that Fermi, Compton, and others built the first "atom-smasher."

Military preparedness has resulted in some hardships on education through the drafting of young teachers, and, as stated above, through competition with education for public funds. In addition, large defense industries have located in sparsely settled unincorporated areas near cities and towns where tax assessments are quite low. These industrial plants draw upon the labor market for miles around, an area that may encompass many small school districts. Eventually, these plants attract additional families into the general region, thereby causing the overcrowding of the surrounding school districts, which receive no increase in their tax allotment. Thus a large industry that could support adequate schools avoids its share of responsibility.

ALLEVIATION OF CAUSES OF CONFLICT

We discussed earlier in this chapter some of the reasons that lead to conflict among nations. One of the potential dangers is that involved in the underdeveloped nations becoming restive and seeking short cuts in order to arrive at the same economic level of the more developed nations. It is on this basis and as a bulwark against the possibility of communism that the United States has engaged in a program of economic and technical aid to other countries. This may, of course, also involve at times military aid to certain countries threatened by neighboring countries. However, in this chapter we wish to discuss the giving of aid to countries that is not on a military basis.

Aid to Foreign Countries

Economic aid itself may mean the loaning of money or the sending of food or other raw or manufactured materials to the country in order to help out when there is a lack. This, in effect, is an aid that is emergency in nature and short in time. It is obvious that countries cannot live forever upon some kind of aid from countries from the outside. Thus it becomes more and more important to consider the next form of aid, namely technical aid.

In the latter part of the Truman administration, President Truman proposed to develop a program of technical aid to countries—"Point Four" in his address to Congress at that time. In other words, he proposed to teach them to help themselves. On this basis an enormous program of aid was developed. In some cases this means some giving of technical equipment to countries and teaching them how to use it; in other cases it is merely a matter of helping them to develop better methods as far as their country's resources are concerned. Technical aid has far-reaching, long-range effects and does not cost nearly as much as short-range economic aid. In the end, the country should be enabled to become self-sufficient because of the improved level of technology brought about by the technical aid. In the long run, this program is much less costly than direct economic or monetary aid.

A more recent version of technical aid that is perhaps even more successful and promising is the Peace Corps. This program was proposed by the United States first as a nation-state venture, although similar programs had long existed in church and in private philanthropic bases before this governmental venture. Since that time, other countries have also developed some kind of an aid program similar to our Peace Corps. Under the Peace Corps program, well-trained individuals are given special instruction, including a knowledge of the language and culture of the country, and are then sent to work side by side with the persons in that country on some enterprise, such as teaching, farming, engineering, health, and so on. The Peace Corps aid has advantages over the technical aid under the "Point Four" Program in general because members of the Peace Corps actually demonstrate how things should be done. In many cases under the earlier Technical Aid Programs, the cooperative effort is entirely at the upper levels; Americans work with and train the people who supervise and not those who actually do the work. The Peace Corps has been quite successful and there has recently been less criticism of it on the part of foreign countries; in fact, the demand for Peace Corps applicants is currently much greater than can be supplied at the rate of persons seeking admission to the program.

EDUCATION FOR WORLD UNDERSTANDING

It seems that the biggest contribution that education might make to world understanding would be the education of the generation now in school to the realities of the world situation. This means assessing realistically the nature of the world in which we live. It also means a positive effort toward international understanding. This is not necessarily in conflict with the ideal of loyalty to or pride in our own country. In the present world, the best interests of our country demand not only that we understand and faithfully adhere to our values, but also that we learn to work with others in developing, if possible, a world in which all can cooperate. The following are some of the elements that could be involved in the teaching of international or world understanding. These have been adapted with some variation from an address given by Dr. Walter H. Laves before the American Association of Colleges for Teacher Education, on February 18, 1956.[8]

1. Understanding of the basic characteristics of our own society; how the United States developed economically, politically, and socially; the nature of our representative system of government; the changing nature of free enterprise; the importance of voluntary associations; the changing functions of various levels of government in the United States; the role of the individual in the making of governmental policies; and the overwhelming significance of the recognition and observance of fundamental freedom, political, economic, and social, as conditions for the successful operation of our democratic form of government.

2. Understanding of the need for an individual sense of reponsibility as a prerequisite for national and international policy and action today.

3. Understanding of the nature of the problems affecting our national welfare that are no longer purely national in their character and the reasons why they must be handled cooperatively with other nations and with consideration for the welfare of others. Illustrations are numerous in the fields of trade, health, industrial and agricultural production, labor standards, etc. Without such an understanding on the part of the people, the adoption of sensible foreign trade policies, for example, becomes almost impossible.

4. Understanding of the time and space relationship that exists today among the peoples of the world. Changes in the time required for normal means of traveling the same distance at selected dates over the last century serve dramatically to show the true nature of our modern world. They show, for example, that Hong Kong is closer to Chicago today than Boston was to New York in colonial times. The implications of this greater proximity for defense, com-

---

[8] Walter H. C. Laves, "International Understanding and Our Schools." Address before the American Association of Colleges for Teacher Education, February 18, 1956. Used with some adaptations by permission of Dr. Laves.

merce, cultural impact, travel, sanitary controls, news reporting, etc. need considerable emphasis in classroom instruction.

5. Understanding that the United States of America and its people constitutes but one national group among many in the world, and that therefore our foreign policies must always take into account the interests and the views of others. Only with this understanding on the part of the citizen can our government move on a foundation of desired cooperation rather than that of arrogance and short-sighted nationalism. Emphasis upon the history of other countries individually and the nature of their problems and interests is one approach to achieving this understanding. In addition to a good map of the United States of America, every classroom should have a world map, preferably one not centered upon the United States.

6. Understanding of the world's institutions for international cooperation on common problems and the requirements that the cooperative method places upon the manner of conducting our relations with other countries. A host of international organizations, including the United Nations and the specialized agencies, today constitute necessary parts of intergovernmental machinery to deal with world-wide problems of health, agriculture, education, labor standards, capital investment, and economic development. Today's citizens must know the role and the work of these intergovernmental agencies as well as they do purely national governmental agencies.

7. Understanding of the significance of atomic energy in terms of human welfare and human relations both in time and peace and in time of war.

8. Understanding of the essential characteristics of the principal beliefs and faiths, such as Christianity, Mohammedanism, Buddhism, by which different people live and the effects that these have upon their relations to each other and upon their ways of life. It is important to know the relative strength of the principal religions and the countries that currently follow each. Special attention is needed as to the place of the individual in each system and the varying concepts of justice and human rights. Such an understanding is needed as a foundation for mutual confidence and for long-term cooperation.

9. Understanding of the necessity of consistency, continuity, and predictability in all our governmental policies that affect the welfare of friendly nations. A totalitarian regime like that of the Soviet Union can switch its policies arbitrarily without regard to the wishes of its people, and with the purpose of confusing any and every peace-loving country.

10. Understanding of the nature of Communism in theory and in practice and of the way in which it threatens free institutions. Understanding is also needed of the means by which free people can today reduce the prospect of Communist aggression in each country and in international relations.

SUMMARY

In this chapter a description has been given of the problems of the United States in the contemporary, complex, interdependent world. First, the necessity for solving these problems in the near future within the context of a group of sovereign nations—i.e., within a concept of nationalism—is set forth. The efforts of the United Nations and associated groups to work with some kind of cooperative relationship among the nations of the world and the problems involved thereby are described. The conflicts between the Soviet Union and the United States are discussed, and the possibility of a competitive economic race between the two countries without resort to war is presented. The effect of military preparedness on education and on attitudes in general is discussed. Some suggestions are made for better education for world understanding, which, if carried out by all countries, might eventually eliminate the necessity for war.

SELECTED BIBLIOGRAPHY

ALBERTSON, MAURICE L., and others. *New Frontiers for American Youth: Perspectives on the Peace Corps.* Washington, D.C.: Public Affairs Press, 1961. Pp. viii + 212.

ALT, HERSCHEL and EDITH. *The New Soviet Man.* New York: Bookman Associates, 1964. Pp. 304.

BOORSTIN, DANIEL J. *America an Image of Europe: Reflections on American Thought.* New York: Meridian Books, 1960. Pp. 192.

BORGESE, ELIZABETH MANN. *A Constitution for the World.* Santa Barbara, Calif., and New York: Center for the Study of Democratic Institutions, 1965. Pp. 110.

BRINTON, CRANE. *From Many, One: The Process of Political Integration; The Problem of World Government.* Cambridge, Mass.: Harvard University Press, 1948. Pp. vi + 126.

BROGAN, D. W. *America in the Modern World.* New Brunswick, N.J.: Rutgers University Press, 1960. Pp. 47.

CAMIEN, LAITEN LESTER. *Education: The Process and Social Institution.* New York: Vantage, 1964. Pp. 165.

Challenge to Americans: The Struggle We Face and How to Help Win It. New York: The Advertising Council, 1962. Pp. 27.

CRANKSHAW, EDWARD. *The New Cold War: Moscow vs. Peking.* Baltimore: Penguin, 1963. Pp. 167.

DANIELS, ROBERT V. *The Nature of Communism.* New York: Random House, 1962. Pp. xvi + 398.

Escalona, Sibylle. *Children and the Threat of Nuclear War.* New York: Child Study Association of America, 1962. Pp. 20.

First Annual Report to Congress. *Peace Corps.* For the Fiscal Year Ended June 30, 1962. Pp. 83.

Foreign Affairs Outline. *The United Nations in Transition.* Bureau of Public Affairs, Department of State, May, 1965. No. 12. Pp. 15.

GARDNER, RICHARD N. *United Nations Procedures and Power Realities: The International Apportionment Problem.* Reprinted from the Department of State Bulletin, May 10, 1965. Pp. 25.

HANSEN, JOHN W., and COLE S. BREMBECK (eds.). *Education and the Development of Nations.* New York: Holt, Rinehart & Winston, 1966. Pp. 544.

HOOK, SIDNEY. *World Communism: Key Documentary Material.* Princeton, N.J.: Van Nostrand, 1962. Pp. 255.

INKELES, ALEX, and KENT GEIGER (eds.). *Soviet Society: A Book of Readings.* Boston: Houghton Mifflin, 1961. Pp. xii + 703.

LAVES, WALTER H. C., and CHARLES A. THOMSON. *UNESCO: Purpose, Progress, Prospects.* Bloomington: Indiana University Press, 1957. Pp. xxiii + 469.

LIE, TRYGVE. *In the Cause of Peace: Seven Years with the United Nations.* New York: Macmillan, 1954. Pp. viii + 473.

McKEON, RICHARD (ed.). *Democracy in a World of Tensions: A Symposium by UNESCO.* Chicago: University of Chicago Press, 1951. Pp. xviii +540.

MEHNERT, KLAUS. *Peking and Moscow.* New York: Putnam, 1963. Pp. xiv + 522.

NEA, Educational Policies Commission. *The Contemporary Challenge to American Education.* Washington, D.C.: National Education Association, 1958. Pp. 31.

———. *The United Nations, UNESCO, and American Schools.* Washington, D.C.: National Education Association, 1952. Pp. 8.

Office of Education Committee. *Teaching About the United Nations.* Washington, D.C.: U.S. Department of Health, Education and Welfare, 1964. Pp. vi + 110.

On Coexistence. New York: The Center and the Fund for the Republic, 1965. Pp. 44.

On the Developed and the Developing. New York: The Center and the Fund for the Republic, 1965. Pp. 22.

On the World Community. New York: The Center and the Fund for the Republic, 1965. Pp. 33.

ORATA, PEDRO T. *Education for a World Community.* Columbus, Ohio: College of Education, The Ohio State University, 1965. Pp. 24.

PAULING, LINUS (ed.). *On the Developed and the Developing.* New York: The Center for the Study of Democratic Institutions, 1965. Pp. 24.

PRESTON, RALPH C. (ed.). *Teaching World Understanding.* Englewood Cliffs, N.J.: Prentice-Hall, 1955. Pp. x + 207.

ROSTOW, W. W., and others. *The Dynamics of Soviet Society.* New York: Norton, 1953. Pp. xvi + 282.

RUSK, DEAN (Secretary of State). *Guidelines of U.S. Foreign Policy.* Washington, D.C.: Superintendent of Documents, 1965. Pp. 16.

SALISBURY, HARRISON E. *A New Russia.* New York: Harper & Row, 1962. Pp. 143.

STALEY, EUGENE. *The Future of Undeveloped Countries.* New York: Harper & Row, 1954. Pp. 410.

STREIT, CLARENCE. *Freedom's Frontier: Atlantic Union Now.* Washington, D.C.: Freedom and Union Press, 1962. Pp. 308.

STROUT, CUSHING. *The American Image of the Old World.* New York: Harper & Row, 1963. Pp. xiv + 288.

The United Nations: What You Should Know About It. United Nations Office of Public Information, 1963. Pp. 52.

The United Nations: Who Needs It? Dodds Ferry, N.Y.: Oceana Publications, 1964. Pp. 60.

Toynbee, Arnold J. *America and the World Revolution and Other Essays.* New York: Oxford University Press, 1962. Pp. 231. Excellent presentation of the thesis that America did represent a truly revolutionary development and that her present challenge is to continue her revolution.

"Universal Declaration of Human Rights." United Nations, Office of Public Information.

UREY, HAROLD C. "The Case for World Government," *The Christian Century* (June 29, 1949), pp. 785–786.

VAN SLYCK, PHILIP. *Peace: The Control of National Power.* Boston: Beacon Press, 1963. Pp. xvi + 186.

WARD, BARBARA. *The Rich Nations and the Poor Nations.* New York: Norton, 1962. Pp. 159.

SELECTED FILMS

America and the European Common Market (Indiana University) 31 min
This film reveals the role of America in world trade and its relation to the national economy.

Americans All (UW—Govt.) 25 min
Film on South America. Published during the war by the U.S. government.

Atomic Power (McGraw-Hill) 19 min
A basic film on atomic power and on the bomb. Produced by March of Time.

Born Equal (Library Films) 10 min
Interprets the United Nations Declaration of Human Rights, with special emphasis on rights for children.

The Children (UN) 10 min
This film describes UNICEF's attack on the problems of the children of the world. We see the food production, the health programs, and the educational activities that are carried out in many areas to make a happier, healthier, and more hopeful world for tomorrow's citizens.

Communism (UWF) 32 min
Documentary film on communism and its history, contrast between communism and the American system, and a warning to avoid labeling as Communists all who disagree with the majority.

Crossroads of Life (UN) 35 min
This film highlights several cases of children with serious problems who are helped to understand their needs and become healthier people. There are scenes showing therapeutic work with children, which helps them relieve their aggressive feelings.

Defense of the Peace (UN) 12 min
Animated charts and maps, together with live-action scenes, show how the UN machinery provides a realistic way to deal with political and economic problems. The functions and structure of the General Assembly, Security Council, International Court of Justice, Economic and Social Council, and Trusteeship Council are described. The film ends with an appeal for citizen cooperation in action for peace.

Earth and Its Peoples Series (Louis de Rochemont Assoc.) 20 min ea.
Includes the titles: Malaya—*Nomads of the Jungle*; Norway—*Farmer-*

Fisherman; Java—*Tropical Mountain Land*; Guatemala—*Cross Section of Central America*; South Africa—*Riches of the Veldt*; and Argentina—*Horsemen of the Pampas*. The Malaya film is particularly recommended.

Expanding World Relationships (U.S. State Dept.) 11 min
   Contrasts the slow transportation and communication of Thomas Jefferson's day with the machine age, in which technological advances have lightened men's work and brought all the countries of the world into close contact and interdependence on raw materials and manufactured goods; emphasizes the necessity for world-wide cooperation.

India: Asia's New Voice (McGraw-Hill) 17 min

I.L.O. (NFB) 11 min
   International Labor Organization, an agency that survived the League of Nations and as part of the United Nations is active today in meeting workers' needs throughout the world.

Introduction to Foreign Trade (Coronet) 10 min
   First establishes the importance of foreign trade to our economy and then presents a general picture of the mechanics of international commerce. The role of monetary standards and control, national policies in reference to those controls, distribution of raw materials and markets are shown. Then, in an actual exchange of goods, the detailed domestic and foreign operations involved in the sale, shipment, and payment are portrayed.

The Land and Its People (UN) 23 min
   This film sets the stage for its sequel *New Horizons* (listed below). It is a description of the Patzcuaro district, the home of the Tarascán Indians. It tells something of the history, geography, and culture of these Mexican people and of their modern daily life before the UNESCO Fundamental Education Centre was established. The history and source of current problems are outlined and the need for the UNESCO project is defined. This film is most significant when shown as a prelude to *New Horizons*.

Mission of Discovery (Peace Corps) 15 min

New Horizons (UN) 26 min
   This film brings you an actual account of the work of the United Nations Educational, Scientific, and Cultural Organization in Patzcuaro, Mexico, where teachers from twenty Latin-American countries are being trained for an organized attack on illiteracy. Dominant throughout the film is the emphasis UNESCO places on creating a desire for knowledge and a realization that through their own efforts the people can create a better life for their entire community.

Of Human Rights (UN) 20 min
   An incident involving economic and racial prejudice among children is used to dramatize the importance of bringing to the attention of the peoples of the world their rights as human beings, as set forth in the Universal Declaration of Human Rights, proclaimed by the UN General Assembly in December, 1948.

One World—or None (Film Publishers) 9 min
   Federation of American (Atomic) Scientists assisted technically with this film. Chiefly through animation, the international aspect of atomic research is emphasized; control of mass-destruction weapons by the UN and measures to outlaw wars are advocated.

Patterns for Peace—Charter of the UN (BIS) 15 min
> Film on the beginnings of the UN.

The People's Charter (UN) 17 min
> Authentic documentary material shows the conception and beginnings of the United Nations organization. Scenes of wartime destruction illustrate needs of freedom-loving peoples. Fighting against aggression is not enough; a long-term goal has to be defined. At a meeting at sea the Atlantic Charter was born, and Dumbarton Oaks was followed by the historic San Francisco Conference. At last the UN Charter was "signed, sealed, approved—delivered to the free peoples of the world." This film closes with the words of the late President Roosevelt, urging the people to seek a peace both "durable and secure."

Pressure Groups (EBF) 20 min
> Explains what pressure groups are and reveals that, when democratically used, they are a necessary instrument for decision-making in a democracy. Illustrates methods used by a representative democratic pressure group to bring about legislation for a desirable civil project. Contrasts these methods with the underhanded and behind-the-scenes manipulation employed by a group attempting to prevent the passage of a bill.

Public Opinion (EBF) 10 min
> Sets up criteria by which public opinion may be judged and measured, illustrating through development of public opinion that produced a waterworks project in a small community. An enlightened public opinion must have access to the facts; press and radio must be balanced in their presentation of the facts; competent witnesses or experts are needed; and the public must overcome prejudice and think objectively. In short, an analysis of public opinion—what it is, how it is formed, and what it can accomplish.

Russian Life Today (Bailey Films) 21 min
> The modern story of people behind the iron curtain—how they earn their livings in cities and farm communities; their surroundings, their daily activities, their recreation. This film is designed to present an interesting, revealing and objective picture of the present-day life of the average Russian.

Searchlight on the Nation (UN) 17 min
> Modern methods of communication will help spread the big story of our times, the story of the United Nations. We go behind the scenes as the General Assembly prepares to meet. The different forms of communication are shown: radio, cables, newsreels, and television. The film interweaves the development of the UN meetings and the speeches of delegates with the ways in which the news reaches the public. But there are barriers to spreading the news. In large areas of the world, communication systems are not yet highly developed. "Half the human race has not yet the ears to hear." The UN considers new ways of sending news while it itself is making a new kind of news.

Somewhere in India (UN) 15 min
> A film on the work of the WHO (World Health Organization) and other allied agencies of the UN.

The Task Ahead (UN) 20 min

Getting the needs of all the people of the world for food, for literacy, for technical and scientific skills, and above all for peace is the mission of UNESCO. Among these are educational reconstruction; international exchange of literature, art, and science; the UNESCO coupon system for books, films, and technical equipment for soft-currency countries; studies of technical needs in press, film, and radio; fundamental education; draft agreements for free flow of education material.

This Is the Challenge (UN) 10 min

This film has been designed not only to remind us of some of the peacemaking achievements of these first years but to throw into dramatic perspective the determined attack launched by the United Nations and its member states upon the basic causes underlying dispute and war, causes that have remained obdurate and unchanging throughout man's troubled history. Overshadowed by wars and rumors of wars, the work of United Nations experts goes too often unnoticed.

This Is the United Nations (UN) 30 min

Series starting with Screen Magazine #1 and continually being added to, giving current developments.

United Nations 30 min

Check additional films by writing for latest list to Department of Public Information, United Nations, New York, N.Y.

United Nations in Korea (UN) 30 min

This authentic, accurate, and objective film is a unique record of how the United Nations Unified Command with troops from sixteen member states repulsed aggression and gained a truce through international cooperation, thus reaffirming in practice the concept of collective security.

Part IV. *The Role of the School in Modern America*

P ART IV ORGANIZES the implications of the materials presented earlier in this book. First comes a clarification of democratic values, based on some of the concepts sets forth earlier but also on some new materials —particularly the results of recent research in the fields of group dynamics and group relations. Second, a careful philosophical analysis is made of the contemporary conflicting viewpoints as to the role of the school. In Chapter 15 the writers do not themselves indicate that one of these views is clearly preferable to another. In the third place, the final chapter (16) presents a summary of the main findings from the entire book. This consists of the ideas concerning man and society that have been developing from research in the social sciences within recent years and the clarification of democratic values from man's experience over his history. It includes the kind of problems our culture faces as a result of social changes and some of the implications of these problems for schools. There is then presented a view of the "foreseeable future." Finally, the authors have sent forth some of their recommendations for the school in American society.

Chapter 14. *The Nature of Democratic Values and Processes*

IN THIS CHAPTER we shall explore the nature of democratic values. We shall try to indicate the sources of such values, the relationship between democracy and freedom, the problems of authority in democracy, and some of the conflicts concerning democratic values. We also shall attempt to indicate some consensus concerning them. In the latter part of the chapter we shall discuss processes that are related to democracy, including the whole new area of developments in group action and group dynamics.

DEMOCRATIC IDEAS: PRODUCT OF LONG PERIODS OF HUMAN EXPERIENCE

Students of history no longer think of democracy as being of ancient origin. Although there were cases among primitive men (including the Germanic tribes of Europe) in which there was some voting to select chieftains, this was a very crude form of democracy if it was democracy at all. Such a chieftain had enormous powers after his election. There were, however, cases in which decisions were made by consultations among the leading persons—elders—of the tribe. Democratic values have emerged quite recently, even though they are a result of the application of ethical principles that developed over a long period of years.

Democratic ideas, insofar as they are actually practiced, are by and large a product of the Western world after the medieval period. Their roots do, of course, go back into the medieval period and into the time of the Greeks. Among the Greeks, for example, there was a great deal of freedom of thinking and action. There was a strong emphasis upon individual rights. There was an almost pure democracy at times with respect to the formation of laws. The citizenry met as a group to propose and to adopt laws. However, Greek democracy was extended to only a very small group. It did not include the "noncitizens," nor the slaves; hence it excluded the great mass of the Greek people.

There was also a kind of democracy among the primitive Christians. This far exceeded that of the Greeks. In some cases they completely shared all their property, thus forming a type of communal democracy. This was of limited duration and did not constitute a political government.

There were at least two important factors that brought about a new emphasis upon the common man. One was the technological development resulting in such changes as the invention of gunpowder, which made one man with a gun the equal of several knights without firearms. Another was the commercial revolution, which gave prosperity to the middle class and made it reasonably free of the feudalistic rule of the barons. In this struggle the bourgeoisie (or middle class) appealed to the kings, as opposed to the barons, and were able to wrest certain freedoms for their commercial city-states. This struggle for freedom gave rise to the development of thoughts about the fundamental nature of such freedom. Such philosophers as Rousseau, Locke, and others began to write about the natural rights of men. These writings strongly influenced American thinking before, during, and after the Revolutionary period.

From the long struggle for freedom emerged certain important documents. The Magna Carta is generally considered to be one of the first of these. It concerned mainly the freedom of the barons in their struggle against the king. Town charters secured from the king by commercial groups constitute another type of written affirmation of freedom. Many of these rights were won first in England and then in other parts of the world. After the Glorious Revolution of 1688, the English Bill of Rights of 1689 was passed. This was a forerunner to the American Constitution.

It should be noticed, however, that the early bills of rights were for the bourgeoisie or wealthy middle- and upper-merchant classes, rather than for all the people. Over a period of years, in America as well as in England, the rights of suffrage and certain other freedoms were extended to all people. As these freedoms were won, various theories of freedom for all commenced to appear in written documents and gradually began to win widespread support. Such documents as our Constitution and Declaration of Independence are good examples. The development of workmen's compensation and other kinds of social insurance, from 1900 on, were a further extension of democracy and freedom. These are only a few of the major steps toward the development of democratic ideas. At each stage our democratic ideas and the application of them were quite incomplete. Democracy itself is continually growing. It may mean quite different things in different periods—or in different countries during the same historical period.

DEMOCRACY MORE A SET OF VALUES THAN A POLITICAL STRUCTURE

Some students of society have noted that democracy may exist under many forms of political structure. These are as different as the constitutional monarchies of Great Britain and The Netherlands, which have ministries responsible to the people, and the American system with its President and bicameral legislature. To the scholar, this indicates that, after all, democracy is basically a set of values held by the people rather than any particular form of political structure. This is borne out by the experiences of the South American countries, which indicate that political form and structure do not necessarily guarantee freedom nor democratic procedures. Basically, then, a free people has a set of verbalized values concerning freedom. They continually talk about and strive for these values. The accomplishment of these values is facilitated but not guaranteed by an appropriate type of political structure. Furthermore, since these sets of values change from time to time as new problems arise, the specific values in any of the democratic countries vary from time to time. Later in this chapter we shall indicate a set of values that are fairly well agreed upon by various groups in our American democratic culture at the present time.

DEMOCRACY AND FREEDOM

Ask anyone in the Western culture to define democracy and he will invariably use the word "freedom" or "liberty." Yet the extreme of freedom or liberty is not democracy, but anarchy. Democracy is a social order in which we have freedom on the one hand but responsibilities—duty, group action—on the other.

The concept of freedom in a democratic culture has to be defined more explicitly than the freedom to "do as you please as long as you do not interfere with anyone else's freedom." That would be a negative approach that would hinder *group* action. In this modern, interdependent world, where people must act conjointly, it is necessary at times to restrict freedoms in certain areas in order to increase the total amount of freedom. A simple concrete example of this is the ordinary traffic light. By restricting the freedom of a person to enter an intersection at any time that he pleases, we increase total freedom, since we prevent traffic jams and allow for the better flow of the total traffic. Another example is the compulsory-education law. By withholding from the child or his parents the right to decide whether or not he shall go to school, in the long run we increase the child's freedom of choice because we assure him an opportunity for a better background of education. Restriction for the sake of freedom may also be characteristic of many of the other regulations and rules that are found in a democratic society. We restrict the immediate freedom of an individual in order to insure the larger freedom.

There are several reasons why freedom must be given such a prominent place in democratic culture. First, there is no final authority to which we can turn in a democracy to find the answer to a problem. Consequently the minority must be free at any time to speak and to agitate for changes in the ideas and procedures of a democratic culture. Democracy itself, and the framework in which democratic principles may operate at any given time, must be subject to continual scrutiny. There can be no closed areas. The minority of one generation may well become the majority of the next. If there were not freedom of the minority (actually of any of the *many* minorities) to agitate for change, change would be prevented. Second, society grows only through the possible change that comes about as someone becomes dissatisfied with conditions the way they are. This means not only that a democracy *should permit* freedom of speech and of criticism but that this freedom *must be encouraged*. Third, although the fundamental unity of the people must be encouraged, we must also encourage diversity and a maximum of local and individual freedom. This diversity gives richness to the culture and permits things to be tried out in small areas that may be later adopted in the larger unit.

It was out of experiences where the minority, denied their rights, eventually became the "majority" by force, that the Bill of Rights and other freedoms were eventually hammered out in the Anglo-Saxon tradition of liberty and in Western culture as a whole. Certainly, in the extremely complex, interdependent society that is now emerging and that in the future probably will become more complex, there must always be a place for freedom of inquiry and agitation and for just plain freedom of choice among diverse ways of life.

THE NATURE OF AUTHORITY IN A DEMOCRACY

Although democracy is centered upon the theme of freedom, it does represent a kind of social order. Consequently there must be inherent in it some kind of authority to give it structure. It is important for those helping children and youth develop into effective citizens in a democracy, as well as for all citizens as they exercise their freedom, to understand the nature of authority in society.

In societies other than democracy or anarchy, final authority always is vested in some kind of fixed system—an absolute, hereditary, or constitutionally limited monarchy; an oligarchy of a small ruling class; a party (as in Russia); or, in the case of a theocratic state, religious leaders or a sacred set of books or teachings. In a complete democracy there is no such authority. In most democracies there is a written constitution that theoretically has transferred certain rights and responsibilities of government from the people to the political structure. These constitutions serve to define the limits of authority for a period of time. However, all constitutions are subject to continual scrutiny and possible change, and do not thus constitute any kind of sacrosanct document that cannot be continually re-examined.

The analysis in this section is not based primarily on government but on the authority that is inherent in any situation where a group of free people associate together to take action. This may be a democratic government, or it may be just a group of people who meet to accomplish certain things on an informal basis. The writers are indebted, in this analysis, to a very important study by Benne.[1] In this analysis of authority, Benne identifies the natural kinds of authority inherent in any situation where people associate together in some form of common action. He identifies these as of three kinds: the authority of the "expert"; the authority of the "rules of the game"; and the authority of the community. The following analysis, while developed around Benne's three types of authority, does not follow completely his discussion of them.

The Authority of the "Rules of the Game"

Whenever people are associated together, whether in playing a game or in any other kind of enterprise, they are unable to work together at all unless there is some agreement as to the "rules of the game." This can be readily observed if one watches young children attempting to play a game before they understand the importance of rules. The young children, quite often, wish to change the rules according to their own individual interpretation. The game is able to progress only after they learn that there must be a common agreement upon rules before the game is any fun. This represents a stage of maturity in the young child. Rules of the game primarily concern matters in which the decisions in and of themselves are not important. No group of people can work together—whether in an informal game, a committee meeting, a legislature, or a prisoners' enterprise—unless there is some agreement as to how they will work together and on the importance of having rules. Actually, just what rules are finally established does not matter much as long as rules exist. In football or basketball the rules could be quite different and the game could still go on. However, there *must be* rules; otherwise there can be no game. Similar is the authority of the "rules of the game" found throughout all of our society. One example of such rules of the game in America would be that of driving on the right side of the road rather than on the left. It is not particularly important which side is decided upon, but there must be agreement. In informal groups such rules often do not assume legal status, although the rules of parliamentary order frequently do. In governments such agreements are usually enforced by law. Unless the people by and large agree upon the rules of the game, society lacks any kind of coherency to make life worth living.

[1] Kenneth D. Benne, *A Conception of Authority: An Introductory Study* (New York: Bureau of Publications, Teachers College, Columbia University, 1943).

462 *The School in American Society*

The Authority of the "Expert"

A second type of authority in any group is that of the "expert." An accident occurs, a crowd gathers, there is uncertainty as to what to do. Finally a man steps up and says, "I am a doctor." Automatically the crowd adjusts itself to the authority of the expert in this situation. He is the natural leader, and, because of a peculiar background of training and experience, he *is* best able to cope with this problem. In other kinds of emergencies other persons would be the expert, for example a plumber, a minister, a lawyer, or a sailor. There are some areas in which we do not as yet recognize the authority of the expert as readily as we do that of the medical doctor in case of illness or accident. In problems involving economics, education, or other social issues, for example, every one considers himself to be an expert.

There are, of course, problems arising even within a field of expertness where the decision cannot be made wholly by the expert alone. Faced with such problems, society as a whole must make the decision after full utilization of the experience of the expert. Thus, in certain matters related to the social aspects of medicine, the final decision must be made by the public as a whole rather than by the medical profession. In problems involving such fields as economics, the same is true. However, the expertness of the economists and others ought to be recognized as contributing in a special way to such problems and to proposed decisions for the public welfare. This has been increasingly the case in recent years, when such events have occurred as the appointment of special economic advisors to the President of the United States or the employment of economic advisors on the staffs of most business corporations and other large groups, including labor unions.

In the school situation the teacher is the expert because of his special knowledge. He also has the "authority of the community," which is to be discussed in the next section. There is also, in the classroom situation, the authority of the rules of the game. Certain understood rules there must be in order that a group of people may be able to carry on successfully in the school situation or in any situation.

The Authority of the Community

The third kind of authority is the authority of the community. Whatever the use of expertness and the means of establishing the rules of the game, there must also be some procedures worked out to enable the community (whether local, regional, state, national, or international) to come to some conclusions with respect to the certain important problems that it faces. These are problems that *really* make a difference. Decisions *must* be made. After full discussion and full representative action, usually the community does make a decision. Whatever the decision may be, the minority must conform to that decision whether or not it agrees. The minority may wish to agitate for a change, but it must conform temporarily in order that societal operations may go on. In a democratic society it is assured that only when the action of the community is such as to cause excessive violation of the individual's rights would he ever rebel against the authority of the community. A democratic society ought not, of course, to take action that unnecessarily restricts the rights of individuals. However, there are cases in which such action might rightly be taken. A person following some type of religious cult in which harm was being done to his children or to others might expect the authority of the community to be visited upon him, at least with respect to this aspect of his behavior. Such procedures are illustrated in the cases of the "snake" religious cults of the Appalachian Mountains and the practice of polygamy among the Mormons in the latter part of the nineteenth century. In most cases the authority of the community is expressed in some kind of law or regulation. However, in some instances it is enforced only by general agreement. These informal (extralegal) regulations may not be necessarily merely rules of the game. They may be basic rules that have not been given the force of law but that are still of crucial importance in the community.

CONFLICTING VALUES WITHIN AMERICAN DEMOCRATIC SOCIETY

Persons who live in a society where the right of the minority to agitate for change is recognized and where diversity is encouraged can expect numerous conflicts concerning any ideas that may be expressed. This is certainly true of the concept of democracy. Democracy is a growing concept. At any time there is considerable difference of opinion as to what it means in action. Although there is a wide area of agreement within the American culture, there are also areas of conflict. In some cases where there is agreement as to wording, there are major disagreements as to what it means in action.

In the famous study of Middletown the Lynds discovered conflicting ideas about the American value system, and Robert S. Lynd expressed them succinctly in a later publication:[2]

Individualism, "the survival of the fittest," is the law of nature and the secret of America's greatness; and restrictions on individual freedom are un-American and kill initiative.

BUT: No man should live for himself alone; for people ought to be loyal and stand together and work for common purposes.

Democracy, as discovered and perfected by the American people, is the

[2] Adapted from Robert S. Lynd, *Knowledge for What?: The Place of Social Science in American Culture*, pp. 60–62. Copyright, 1939, Princeton University Press. Used by permission.

The examples given are selected from a list in this book on the pages noted above.

ultimate form of living together. All men are created free and equal, and the United States has made this fact a living reality.

BUT: You would never get anywhere, of course, if you constantly left things to popular vote. No business could be run that way, and no businessman would tolerate it.

The family is our basic institution and the sacred core of our national life.

BUT: Business is our most important institution and, since national welfare depends upon it, other institutions must conform to its needs.

Religion and "the finer things of life" are our ultimate values and the things all of us are really working for.

BUT: A man owes it to himself and his family to make as much money as he can.

Honesty is the best policy.

BUT: Business is business, and a businessman would be a fool if he didn't cover his hand.

Education is a fine thing.

BUT: It is the practical men who get things done.

Children are a blessing.

BUT: You should not have more children than you can afford.

Patriotism and public service are fine things.

BUT: Of course, a man has to look out for himself.

The American judicial system insures justice to every man, rich or poor.

BUT: A man is a fool not to hire the best lawyer he can afford.

While these conflicts are real and do serve to cause uncertainty about human action, they do not represent fundamental weaknesses in our society. While it is important for people to clarify their values and for our society to eliminate conflicts, it is true that the growing edge of a culture may reveal conflicts at a given time. If an entire culture agrees upon a value, the result is monolithic, like the oriental type of society described in Chapter 2, with very little chance of growth.

As we shall indicate in the next section, there are wide areas in which the American people do, by and large, agree on a basic set of values in the American democracy.

THE BASIC PREMISES OF AMERICAN LIBERTY

There have been many efforts to set forth the basic values inherent in American culture. Some of these have been made in connection with education. In the presentation of the Seven Cardinal Principles there was an excellent discussion of the nature of democracy.[3] In 1932 a committee on socioeconomic goals in America proposed a list of ten goals as a basis for educational and social development in our country.

There have also been statements of goals consistent with democracy from persons not in the field of education. President Roosevelt, during

---

[3] N.E.A., Commission of the Reorganization of Secondary Education, *Cardinal Principles of Education* (Washington, D.C.: Govt. Printing Office, 1918).

wartime, defined the goals of democracy in terms of the four freedoms: freedom from fear, freedom from want, freedom of speech, and freedom of religion. Attention should also be drawn to the Universal Declaration of Human Rights proclaimed by the United Nations on December 10, 1948.[4] This set of principles, developed by a joint group of the United Nations not all from countries called democratic, actually contains many of the values inherent in democracy. While this list is not as extensive as the one below, it is another example of a wide range of agreement among the nations of the world. Certainly, there is a disagreement among the various countries as to what these values mean. Also, there is considerable difference within any country, including the United States, concerning the extent to which the basic values are realized.

At the close of World War II a venture called the "Citizenship Education Project" was set up by Teachers College, Columbia University. This was to some extent encouraged by Dwight D. Eisenhower, who was at that time president of Columbia University. Among other things, this project developed a statement of the "Premises of American Liberty." The following is the list of such premises.[5]

The Free Individual

Basic Social Beliefs

Every person is of importance as an individual; his well-being is vital in itself.

All persons should have maximum freedom, consistent with the general welfare, to develop as they desire.

All persons should be considered as individuals and judged on their merit; their differences should be respected, their rights safeguarded.

All persons should possess equal rights and liberties.

The rights of any person should not be exercised so as to interfere with the rights of others.

The action of any individual or group must not endanger the welfare of the people or threaten the security of the nation.

Both competition and cooperation among individuals and groups are indispensable to the process of democracy.

Basic Social Guarantees

Freedom of religion.

Freedom of inquiry and criticism.

Freedom of speech.

Freedom of press.

The privilege of a public education.

---

[4] *"Your Human Rights"*: *The Universal Declaration of Human Rights Proclaimed by the United Nations, December 10, 1948* (New York: Ellner, 1950), p. 71.

[5] Reproduced from *When Men Are Free: Premises of American Liberty* by special arrangement with the Citizenship Education Project. Copyright 1955, Teachers College, Columbia University, and Houghton Mifflin Company. This particular version is in a book prepared for use in elementary schools.

Rights to Life and Liberty
> The right to life.
> The right to liberty of person.
> Freedom from slavery and involuntary servitude.

Rights of a Fair Trial
> The privilege of the writ of habeas corpus.
> The right to bail.
> The right to indictment by grand jury.
> The right to a speedy, public, and fair trial.
> Freedom from cruel and unusual punishment and from excessive fines.

Freedom from Unjust Laws
> The right to equal protection of the laws.
> No law may abridge the constitutional rights and guarantees of persons.
> No law may deprive any of life, liberty, or property without due process of law.
> No ex post facto law may be passed.
> No bills of attainder may be passed.
> Treason is specifically defined in the Constitution.

Social Responsibilities of the Individual
> Develop personal integrity and act with moral courage.
> Develop his talents and his skills in the fields of his interest.
> Restrain the exercise of his rights so as not to harm the general welfare or violate the lawful rights of others.
> In time of national emergency, accept the restriction or even the suspension of some of his rights and privileges in the interest of public security.
> Give direct, unselfish service to his family, his community, and his nation.
> If need be, take up arms in defense of his country.

THE FREE GOVERNMENT

Basic Political Beliefs
> Men have the ability to govern themselves.
> All power belongs to and comes from the people.
> Public officials are responsible to the people.
> The people have the right to reform, alter, or totally change their government by lawful means when they so desire.
> Government has a responsibility to promote the general welfare.
> Government should be by law duly adopted, and not by the whim of any man.
> The church and the state should be separate.

Constitutional Checks on Governmental Power
> The powers of government are distributed among the federal, state, and local governments.
> The executive, legislative, and judicial branches of government are separate, each exercising its own powers.
> These powers are so granted that certain powers of each branch act as checks on those of the other two branches.
> The military forces are under civilian control of the executive branch and dependent upon the legislature for appropriations and man power.

The terms of elective officers expire at regular times fixed by law; re-election to office, when permitted, is left to the discretion of the voters.

The Right to Influence Government

The right to select representatives in government in frequent and regular elections.

The right to run for public office.

The freedom of assembly.

The right to petition government.

Political Responsibilities

The people have the responsibility to keep informed about public problems and the action taken on them by those in public office.

Vote in elections.

Accept public office when public interest requires it.

Voice opinions and demands directly to representatives in government.

In time of public emergency, serve as the government may direct.

Use democratic methods to achieve group agreement—conference, debate, compromise—and abide by the will of the majority; the majority should respect the rights and opinions of the minority.

Consider the common good before group and class loyalties.

Obey the law and use only lawful means to correct injustices.

THE FREE ECONOMY

Basic Economic Goals

An increasing national productivity, made possible by technological development, that will lower the cost of goods and raise the standard of living.

The elimination of deep and prolonged depression.

The freest possible economic competition consistent with the general welfare.

Opportunity for full development.

Full employment under safe and healthful working conditions.

Fair pay.

Sufficient food, clothing, housing, and medical care.

Social security—protection against the basic hazards of existence such as old age, sickness, accident, and unemployment.

The opportunity to enjoy life—no one should be so hard-pressed to earn the necessities of life that he cannot take part in "the pursuit of happiness."

The Economic Guarantees of the Constitution

No one can be deprived of his property without due process of law.

No one can be enslaved or forced to labor involuntarily except as punishment for a crime.

No property can be seized for public use without giving the owner just compensation.

No tax can be imposed without the consent of the people, expressed through a majority of their representatives in government.

The Rights of Property

The individual may own and use land, houses, personal property, and money.

The individual may own natural resources and the means of production.

The individual may pass his property on to others of his own choosing.

No one may use his property in such a way as to conflict with the public health, safety, order, or interest.

The Privileges of Individual Enterprise

The individual may start his own business and profit financially from its operations.

The individual may employ, discharge, and direct his employees, providing he does not violate the law.

The individual may save, spend, or invest his money as he may desire.

The individual may make contracts with the assurance that they will be legally binding on all parties.

The individual may profit from his ideas and inventions, protected by patent and copyright laws.

The Privileges of Individual Labor

The individual may work at any job he can obtain and keep.

The individual may leave his job whenever he so desires.

The individual may join a labor union.

The Privileges and Responsibilities of Economic Organizations—Corporate Enterprise and Organized Labor

Both may organize—business in association and in corporations under state charters, labor in free and uncoerced unions.

Both may acquire financial power—corporations through profits and the sale of securities, unions by assessing members.

Unions, as the representatives of all or a specified group of workers in an industry or plant, may bargain with management.

Union members may strike and picket peacefully.

Neither business nor labor may use its organized power in restraint of trade.

Neither business nor labor may imperil the health or safety of the nation.

THE FREE WORLD

Premises Guiding Foreign Relations

The people influence the making and carrying out of foreign policy.

We are a politically independent nation, and we want to remain independent.

We are a nation in which the individual is allowed a large degree of freedom; we desire to retain unimpaired our individual rights and liberties; we believe that a large degree of individual freedom everywhere in the world offers the best hope of lasting peace.

We are a peaceful people, and we work to rid the world of war and the threat of war.

We are a friendly people with no traditional enemies, and we want to have friendly relations with all people.

We believe that all of the peoples of the world are entitled to freedom to develop in their own way.

Through the United Nations we hope to play an active and constructive part in the world community.

We favor the free and uncensored flow of ideas and information throughout the world.

It will be noted that some of the values in this list are of recent origin. There certainly will be some disagreement as to whether this list contains all of the items that should be basic premises of our American liberty.[6] There will also be some disagreement as to whether or not some of the above list should be eliminated. Certainly there would be even more controversy concerning what they mean. However, by and large, these are fairly well established as values to be strived for in our culture and as values toward which we have already made some progress by law and through practice. On the other hand, in almost every case instances can be cited where they have been violated. There are even some cases in our country where people are in violent opposition to some of the values stated here and are making no effort to carry them out. This is notable, of course, in the area of minority rights.

Democracy as a Way of Life

Democracy has been defined in this chapter as a set of values, not merely as a set of procedures or a kind of structure. An increasing number of students have indicated that democracy *really* involves a complete way of life. That is, it permeates all aspects of American culture. There are, of course, groups in our society that would object to this concept, even some who deny that our government is a democracy. For instance, they insist that it is a republic, not a democracy in a strict sense. By and large, events in our culture indicate that democracy is far more than a purely political or governmental concept. It is a way of life, and as such it defines relationships between persons in many areas. We have mentioned in Chapter 7 that family life is becoming democratized. This is not a matter of government but the result of a change in the climate of social opinion. The patriarchal or matriarchal family is no longer consistent with American culture.

The fact that democracy has become a way of life that permeates our culture does not mean that there is no place for individual sets of values. A majority of the persons in American culture adhere to a set of values that have been derived in part from a religious authority or tradition. Because of our policy diversity within unity, these values do not, in most cases, conflict with our democratic values. In many cases, such persons can adhere to the entire set of basic premises of American liberty just quoted and also to their religious ideas. As a matter of fact, many of these persons would insist that their religious ideas give a solid foundation to the democratic values. This is not to deny that at times there are serious

[6] See a similar list but with a different wording, although fundamentally the same, "Primer for Americans," conceived and developed by Sigmund S. Larson. Printed in *Look*, September 17, 1950. Another type of list is found in President's Commission on National Goals, *Goal for Americans* (New York: Columbia University, the American Assembly, 1960), p. 372.

conflicts between a point of view that is primary authoritarian and un-changing in nature (such as is typical of some religions) and the non-authoritarian concepts of American democracy. These conflicts, of course, will have to be worked out in the same way that other conflicts are. In some cases, the minority religious group may have to forego, in practice, the achievement of what they consider the implications of their belief be-cause of the lack of acceptance by the majority group. Wherever possible, however, in American culture these minorities are permitted to pursue their own ways of life within the general framework of the democratic society.

There needs to be an effort on the part of all persons in our society, in-cluding educators, to try to develop the distinctive nature of the values of our democratic culture. This is important if these values are to be more fully understood, in contradistinction from those of the nondemocratic areas of our world, and if their practice is to be most fully realized. The later sections of this chapter indicate ways in which groups can operate on the more democratic basis—the whole science of group dynamics and group action.

TEACHING MORAL AND SPIRITUAL VALUES

We have traced earlier the changing relationships between the church and the state and the relation of both to education (Chapter 3 and Chap-ter 4. Although the school has always placed some emphasis on moral and spiritual values, recent events have caused the attention of the people to be directed more closely to them. Some have felt the problem was so acute that it might be necessary to change the policy of the separation of church and state sufficiently to enable public schools to teach religious ideas as a base for moral and spiritual values. The increase in crime and juvenile delinquency and the general world conditions resulting from the cold war between American capitalistic democracy and Russian com-munism have caused a new interest in the basic values of our culture.

The school had always taught and was continuing to teach spiritual values. However, it was believed that a better job could be done. Discus-sion of this topic continued during the postwar period. Finally, the Educational Policies Commission, after careful consideration of a policy, issued a statement in 1951.[7] This commission of outstanding professional leaders followed a point of view similar to that of the committee of the John Dewey Society. They presented a careful study of the place of moral and spiritual values in the public schools. They reaffirmed a central place for such values in the school program. They reviewed the problem of the separation of church and state and reaffirmed the necessity for the

---

[7] N.E.A., Educational Policies Commission, *Moral and Spiritual Values in the Public Schools* (Washington, D.C.: National Education Association, 1951).

public school to refrain from the teaching of sectarian doctrines.[8] The Commission further explored some of the common values of American culture, irrespective of any theological background upon which they might have been based. They listed a total of ten values (actually cores of values). These are as follows:[9]

1. Human Personality—The Basic Value
Among the values here proposed, the *first* is fundamental to all that follow. The basic moral and spiritual value in American life is *the supreme importance of the individual personality.*

2. Moral Responsibility
If the individual personality is supreme, *each person should feel responsible for the consequences of his own conduct.*

3. Institutions as the Servants of Men
If individual personality is supreme, *institutional arrangements are the servants of mankind.*

4. Common Consent
If the individual personality is supreme, *mutual consent is better than violence.*

5. Devotion to Truth
If the individual personality is supreme, *the human mind should be liberated by access to information and opinion.*

6. Respect for Excellence
If the individual personality is supreme, *excellence in mind, character, and creative ability should be fostered.*

7. Moral Equality
If the individual personality is supreme, *all persons should be judged by the same moral standards.*

8. Brotherhood.
If the individual personality is supreme, *the concept of brotherhood should take precedence over selfish interests.*

9. The Pursuit of Happiness
If the individual personality is supreme, *each person should have the greatest possible opportunity for the pursuit of happiness, provided only that such activities do not substantially interfere with the similar opportunities of others.*

10. Spiritual Enrichment
If the individual personality is supreme, *each person should be offered the emotional and spiritual experiences which transcend the materialistic aspects of life.*

The Educational Policies Commission further implies that there are no sectarian disputes concerning the existence of these values and the necessity for them. In a footnote, they point out five religious versions of moral equality:

[8] N.E.A., *ibid.*, p. 6.
[9] From N.E.A., Educational Policies Commission, *Moral and Spiritual Values in the Public Schools*, pp. 18–30. Copyright, 1951, National Education Association. Used by permission (Italics added.)

Christianity—"Thou shalt love thy neighbor as thyself." Buddhism—"Minister to friends and families by treating them as one treats himself." Confucianism—"What you do not like done to yourself, do not do to others." Hinduism—"Let no man do to another what would be repugnant to himself." Judaism—"And what thou thyself hatest, do to no man."[10]

The Commission goes on to say that since life is a continuing series of moral decisions, the schools should help the students by teaching them how to make choices. There are two kinds of moral decisions that we face in life. One involves the decision as to whether or not to act in accordance with a value that we acknowledge and have agreed to follow. The second is one where certain of one's values are in conflict. Examples of such conflict of values might be (1) loyalty to our family as opposed to loyalty to our country; (2) a conflict between the values of equality and of respect for excellence; (3) a conflict between the value of brotherhood and the value of common consent. The book also illustrates the problem of moral choices with samples of different kinds of sanctions, such as justice, the law, property rights, and so on. Throughout this volume the whole intent is toward making the *study of values* the central core of the school. There is no suggestion that a set of values be imposed on the pupils. The Commission saw the job of the teacher as being one of helping each boy and girl to clarify his values and to apply them to life decisions.

The ideas expressed in this volume have gained wide acceptance. However, there is a group of persons of many differing points of view who feel that spiritual values cannot be taught apart from theology. These persons have advocated the teaching of theology by various kinds of proposals. One would be the increase of released time, which is still legal under Supreme Court decisions if conducted off the school premises. Another advocates a change, if necessary through amendments of our constitutions, to permit sectarian doctrines to be taught as electives in public schools.[11]

Recently there has been a proposal to solve the problem of teaching religious ideas through *shared time* and still possibly avoid constitutional questions. According to this proposal a student would be permitted to attend two accredited and recognized high schools at the same time. He might be a regular student at a public high school and go to a private, sectarian high school for some instruction. Or he might be a regular

[10] N.E.A., *ibid.*, p. 26.
See also Hanna's Chapter II, "Generalizations and Universal Values" in Ralph C. Preston (Chairman), *Social Studies in the Elementary School* (Chicago: University of Chicago Press, 1957), pp. 41–44. Also, the reader is referred to Virginia Newhall Woods, "Spiritual and Moral education in the Public School Curriculum" (unpublished thesis, Stanford University, 1950). Woods has identified nine lists of items—each from the Christian religion but supported in meaning by five other religions and approved unanimously by forty-seven representatives of major denominations in the United States.
[11] Tunis Romein, *Education and Responsibility* (Lexington: University of Kentucky Press, 1955).

student at a sectarian high school and attend the public school for certain classes. It is argued that at the present time a student may freely move from one high school to another at the end of each year and transfer his credits. It is argued that all shared time would be the transfer of credits simultaneously to one or two high schools the pupil attends. It can be seen that the administrative complexities involved would be quite great. Moreover, there have been questions raised concerning the constitutionality of shared time in some states.

Other points of view emphasize the teaching *about* religion as an adjunct of the curriculum, rather than the direct teaching of sectarian doctrines. This point of view holds that since religion is a part of our culture, the school's curriculum should be as much concerned with it as with other aspects of the culture. It contemplates an objective study of the different religions just as we study other aspects of the culture.

Without a doubt an increased emphasis upon moral and ethical values is good for education, and it is certain that the efforts of the schools will be improved as we know and understand more about helping boys and girls to clarify their values and to act in accordance with them.

UNDERLYING ALL SOCIAL PROBLEMS ARE PROBLEMS OF HUMAN RELATIONS

It has become increasingly evident to students of our culture that the problems we face are now predominantly problems of our own making. Furthermore, they are now more predominantly problems of persons lacking the desire and knowledge of how to act together on common needs than they are of those lacking the know-how to tackle the source of the problems. Increasingly, then, students and others have come to the position that most of our problems are basically problems of human relations.

At one time, when man knew little about the world in which he lived, he was ill equipped to solve his problems even with the best of cooperative effort. As we have developed technical competence in one physical area after another, it has become increasingly important that we develop appropriate value standards and the disposition to apply them to the solution of our problem. The ability of the individual to forget his own selfish interest in terms of a cooperative effort toward the common good, and in the long run for his own individual good as well, becomes of increasingly urgent importance.

We still have not been able to control the path of the hurricane; we still have not been able to conquer the scourge of cancer completely; we still have some technological problems to solve with respect to the automatic factory; and we still have not solved the problem of photosynthesis. But at least partial control of the environment may be effected even in the case by some of the problems that may be insoluble, such as the hurricane, through the cooperative effort of all persons. Warning systems, preparation for the storm, damage-control installations, fire-and-rescue parties, and salvage squads may mitigate the severity of damage.

As to most of our problems, including practically all of those discussed in this book, it becomes increasingly apparent that since man has created the conditions that have caused them to exist—at least in their present form—it is up to man to solve them through some sort of cooperative action. To summarize: It is the belief of the present authors that man must be made aware that he is in charge of his own destiny; that he must use all of his powers and all of his increasing knowledge of the world; and that he must bring this knowledge to bear upon his problems without prejudice with respect to past solutions and existing institutions.

In the area of human relations, one of the historic difficulties has been a lack of knowledge of the ways in which groups function and of appropriate means to increase their efficiency. Quite often one has heard persons say, "I suppose we ought to do it the democratic way, but if we do, we will get nothing but a lot of talk. Nothing will get done." This, of course, means that the person does not understand the "democratic way" or that techniques have not been developed to do it the "democratic way." In recent years there has been considerable research into the ways in which groups work, in which leaders can work with groups, and in which individuals within groups should work within the democratic framework. This growing area is the field of group dynamics.

THE DEVELOPMENT OF GROUP DYNAMICS

We have seen (in Chapter 2) that mankind apparently always has lived in groups. We have seen the important part that culture plays in the lives of humans, with the very quality of "humanness" arising from the transmission of culture within the group. Moreover, as we have indicated in Trend IV, Chapter 4, group activity and cooperation have become more important with increased specialization and the complexity of the various social and technological processes. At one time most achievements and advances were made by individuals, although certainly they were influenced by what the individual had learned from others. At the present time many of our most important advances are the result of the work of teams of individuals in research laboratories, in social organizations, and so on. It becomes of increasing importance, then, to understand more about group activity and about how members of groups function. The name that has been applied to the field of study concerned with how groups work and function and ways in which they can do so more effectively is *group dynamics*. Research workers in the field of group dynamics have been interested in helping the members of groups better to understand the forces operating in situations that tend to help or to hinder group action. They have also attempted to develop instruments and skills to facilitate the diagnosis of cases in which groups do not function properly. They have attempted to clarify the various aspects of group leadership and the role of the members necessary to the successful action of the group. They also have attempted to devise techniques of training individuals for better group membership and for the various leadership roles. Furthermore, they have tried to help members of the group bring about improvements in the group situation and to develop techniques and procedures for evaluating group relationships. An example of one of the bodies in this field is the National Training Laboratory in Group Development, which has done considerable research in group dynamics in the postwar period at summer workshops at Bethel, Maine.

A new field that has been closely related to group dynamics and actually draws its materials partially from the same areas of study is the field of *action research*. This is defined as research where the individuals are as much interested in putting the research into action and feeding back the results in further research as they are in the "pure" results of the research itself. It includes the involvement in the research of many persons who will be in a position to put the results into operation.

The Function of the Leadership in Groups

Even though the emphasis in group dynamics turns the attention from the leader to the group, it is essential that a group have a good leader if it is to function effectively. One common weakness of group action in America is the lack of leaders skilled in techniques for keeping groups working in democratic fashion. Good leadership has been commonly thought to be the ability of a person to get other persons to "go along" in accomplishing the purposes of the leader. This, of course, is an authoritarian concept and arises out of the fact that democracy is relatively a latecomer on the scene. There have been, in general, two types of leaders prior to democracy. One was the leader who had prestige because of the respect and affection in which he was held by the group. He was able to exercise leadership because the group felt that he had the answers to all the problems it faced. The other type of leader achieved results because he was feared, the group not daring to go contrary to his will. Neither of these types produces effective democratic processes.

The democratic leader succeeds by helping the group solve its problems through cooperative action. The assumptions for this kind of leadership are the same as the assumptions of democracy and are based on faith that human beings are capable of making their own decisions and of controlling the processes necessary to make changes in their own activities. This type of leadership is not the laissez-faire type where the leader merely tells the group to go ahead and do as it wishes and that he as a leader will help them to accomplish whatever they desire. It is apparent from the research done at Bethel and elsewhere that the leader must take a much more active role in helping the group to define what it wishes to accomplish. In laissez-faire leadership, usually someone else in the group becomes the aggressive leader if the leader himself does not effectively help the group accomplish its purposes.

The following are some of the positive things that leaders should do in order to help the group operate effectively:

1. The leader must help the group to clarify completely its purposes and to determine the scope and limits of the particular problem at hand.
2. The leader must see to it that all members of the group clearly understand the group's purposes and are involved in the process.
3. The leader must see to it that the group members are sensitized to the need for getting facts and evidence and for going far beyond the "talk stage" in attacking the problem.
4. He must help the group organize itself for specialized work in seeking information that will be helpful in making group decisions, and in having this information brought back to the group and used in deliberation.
5. From time to time he must help the group keep from straying from its purposes, either through one individual attempting to dominate or sway the group by monopolizing its time or other means, or by the group straying from its purposes by taking up extraneous matters.
6. He must help the group from time to time to realize that the final goal is action and decision rather than the process of deliberation.

The Roles of Individuals Within the Group

The individuals of the group have as important roles to play as the leader. One of the jobs of the leader is to help the individual to find himself in one or more of these roles and to help him in playing it. In the analysis given below, we have followed the materials common to much of the literature on group dynamics.

1. Types of group task roles. The following are some of the group task roles that have been listed by students of group dynamics as being possible roles that the members might take with respect to their group:
    a. The Initiator-contributor. This is the one who suggests new ideas and ways of working to the group. These suggestions may be related to a new interpretation of the problem, a new procedure, or some possible new solution that the group has not hitherto thought of.
    b. The Information-seeker. This is the person who asks for clarification of the facts or for more authoritative information or makes suggestions for additional research to get more facts pertinent to the problem under study.
    c. The Opinion-seeker. This is a person who not only searches for facts but also tries to get an interpretation of the attitudes and values that are shared by the members of the group.

d. The Information- or Opinion-giver. This is a person who gives "authoritative" facts and personal opinions relative to the problem for discussion by the group.

e. The Elaborator. This person makes suggestions in terms of examples and tries to predict what the results of other persons' suggestions might be.

f. The Coordinator. This is a person who tries to show the relationships between the various ideas and suggestions and tries to find some common points among them in order to clarify and simplify the matters under discussion.

g. The Orienter. This is the person who from time to time reviews what the group has done and tries to define the position of the group with respect to the purpose that has been agreed upon earlier, and who raises questions as to whether or not the group is moving in the direction in which it had planned to go.

h. The Evaluator-critic. This is a person who from time to time subjects the accomplishment of the group to some set of standards and raises questions about the practicality, usefulness, or logic of whatever may be the course of discussion.

i. The Energizer. This is a person who prods the group from time to time for decisions.

It will be noted that different individuals at different times will occupy different group task roles. It is not intended that the above list should be more than suggestive or that it be used as any kind of stereotype.

2. Group building and maintenance roles. These are some of the roles that may be taken by members of the group in order to extend group-centered attitudes and prevent the body from falling apart:

a. The Encourager. This is the one who accepts the contributions of others, offers praise and commendation, and provides the attitude of better understanding toward the ideas and suggestions that have been presented.

b. The Harmonizer. This is the person who takes up some of the differences that have been found within the group and tries to reconcile the conflicting views in order to relieve tension either through jest, a harmonious attitude, or a congenial approach.

c. The Compromiser. This person differs from the harmonizer and attempts to operate from within the conflict in which his own ideas or position are involved. He may offer a compromise to someone with a different position in order to maintain group harmony.

d. The Communication-facilitator. This person likes the participation of others and tries to keep the communication lines open among members and to limit the time that all may have an opportunity to speak.

e. The Standard-setter or the Ego ideal. This is a person who proposes the standards that the group ought to achieve, with respect to both group action and the quality of the group process.

f. The Group-observer. This is a person who keeps a record of the various aspects of the group process and from time to time reports his findings and interpretations during the periods for group evaluation.

3. Destructive roles within the group. Many groups contain individuals who are not oriented to group processes or who constitute themselves as a handicap to group action. The following is a suggested list of negative roles in group participation:

a. The Aggressor. This is a person who tries to inflate his own ego by deflating the status of others, by expressing disapproval of group procedures, by attacking members of the group, or by making light of certain conscientious contributions by other members.

b. The Blocker. This person tends to be negativistic and very resistant, disagreeing and opposing beyond reason, attempting to maintain and keep an issue before the group after it has been rejected by the other members.

c. The Recognition-seeker. This is a person who tries to call attention to himself in many ways by acting unusual or by using physical or facial antics.

d. The Self-confessor. This is a person who tries to take advantage of the group situation to express personal feelings irrelevant to the situation at hand.

e. The Playboy. This is a person who tries to be cynical or nonchalant or to exhibit horseplay.

f. The Dominator. This is a person who tries to assert his authority or superiority by manipulating the group or at least by manipulating certain members of the group.

g. The Help-seeker. This is a person who tries to gain sympathy by expression of personal confusion or self-depreciation beyond reason.

h. The Special Interest-pleader. This is a person who plans to promote the welfare of a group to which he belongs other than the one which he is operating, such as "small businessman," "laborer," "common man," "classroom teacher," and so on. In some cases personal prejudices and biases are hidden in the stereotype that best fits his desires.

4. Techniques to be used to help groups in action. Much experience in group work has suggested techniques that will help the groups to produce changes:

a. Reality practice or role-playing. Role-playing is a technique where the group arranges to have parts of the group dramatize a situation, problem, procedure, or type of group structure. By use of this technique it is possible to sensitize members of the group to operational problems, emotional factors, and other blocks. An important part of role-playing is the analysis by the spectators of what has been taking place.

b. The "Buzz" session. This turns the larger group into smaller groups for talking more freely, each taking up some aspect of the problem or all the subgroups attacking the same problem. After discussion, the groups then report back to the main group.

c. Brainstorming. This is a method that has been developed in industrial and other research groups in order to get hypotheses or ideas for investigation. In this procedure the group of persons concerned are brought together, and, after the problem has been stated, suggestions are secured as rapidly as they can be given, and without criticism. This is to avoid any inhibition to the thinking process. After the group has exhausted the possibilities of suggestions, and only then, does it begin to analyze and pick out the more promising ones for further investigation.[12]

d. The Sociodrama. This is the case where a situation is set up deliberately, in order to have persons express their feelings with regard to something. This is a method of catharsis—the release of pent-up feelings and tensions. In the sociodrama and other methods of catharsis (which include, in addition to sociodrama, letting each person "speak their piece," insuring full individual participation), members of the group are enabled to rid themselves of some of the feelings that may block group action.

e. Group discussion. The group-discussion technique is a very common one. Here the group as a whole tries to work out proposed actions appropriate to a democratic society.

Other techniques, such as demonstration, decision-making practice with respect to some smaller problem that can be demonstrated, or group recreational experiences so that the group can meet each other in matters not related to their work, are also helpful. Bringing in experts for panel discussions, reports, field trips, utilization of special member talents—these are all familiar procedures sometimes used in the group process.

THE AMELIORATION OF CONFLICTS BETWEEN GROUPS

One of the trends in our society (compare Trend X, Chapter 4) has been the increasing division of our society into groups that are antagonistic toward one another. Therefore one of our central problems in attempting to solve the situations in which we find ourselves is to develop some way

---

[12] See Alex F. Osborn, *Applied Imagination* (New York: Scribner, 1957).

for these groups to learn to get along better with each other. In other words, we must apply what we know about human relations and group dynamics in helping groups better to know and to understand *each other* as well as in helping group members to work well *within their own groups*.

Whenever two groups have a problem concerning the solution of which they do not agree, it usually means that they have that problem in common because they have common, overlapping interests. Quite often when they meet to take up a particular problem, they immediately begin to emphasize their differences. In almost all cases where the groups live in the same culture or similar cultures, they have more points in common with respect to the problem than they have differences. Consequently, the first step should be to clarify the problem to see whether or not the nature of the problem itself and at least part of the facts can be agreed upon. Second, they should set forth the areas of agreement with respect to the solution of the problem. There will then be left an area or areas within which are found their differences. Before any attempt is made to resolve or compromise these differences, every effort should be made to get at the facts to see whether or not there can be a decision based solely upon the agreed-upon facts and the common values. They should look at the problem from the point of view of the welfare of both groups and particularly of the long-range welfare of their society. If a common decision that embraces the welfare of both groups and of society cannot be reached, then compromises must be made. Each group must sacrifice something to the common welfare.

Even in a democracy, where the individual is supreme, some decisions must of necessity impair the immediate welfare of some groups. The adoption of labor-saving devices is a case in point. In such cases, the contribution to the welfare of the total society is such that common decency demands that the total society assume the responsibility for assisting the displaced persons in orienting themselves to new ways of living. Thus the dignity of the individual is maintained, even though his old ways of living have become obsolete.

Summary

In this chapter the nature of our American democracy is described. It is indicated that American democracy is more a set of values than it is a political structure. The nature of the authority in our democratic social order is elaborated, and some of the main values that have been formulated as the basis for American democracy are clarified. The problem of people in groups, the field of "group dynamics," is discussed and the possibility of the elimination of the difficulties between conflict groups within our culture by some kind of effective, peaceful method of obtaining intergroup agreement is suggested.

SELECTED BIBLIOGRAPHY

BARRETT, DONALD N. (ed.). *Values in America*. Notre Dame: University of Notre Dame Press, 1961. Pp. viii + 182.

BENNE, KENNETH D. *A Conception of Authority*. New York: Bureau of Publications, Teachers College, Columbia University, 1943. Pp. v + 277.

———, and BOZIDAR MUNTYAN. *Human Relations in Curriculum Change*. New York: Dryden Press, 1951. Pp. xiii + 363. A discussion of group dynamics in relation to the curriculum.

BLANCHARD, PAUL. *Religion and the Schools: The Great Controversy*. Boston: Beacon Press, 1963. Pp. 275.

BLAU, JOSEPH L. (ed.). *Cornerstones of Religious Freedom in America*. Boston: Beacon Press, 1949. Pp. viii + 250.

BODE, B. H. *Democracy as a Way of Life*. New York: Macmillan, 1937. Pp. xiv + 114.

BOLES, DONALD E. *The Bible, Religion, and the Public Schools*. Ames, Iowa: Iowa State University Press, 1961. Pp. ix + 308.

BOWER, WILLIAM CLAYTON. *Moral and Spiritual Values in Education*. Lexington: University of Kentucky Press, 1952. Pp. vii + 214.

BRUBACHER, JOHN S. (ed.). *The Public Schools and Spiritual Values*. A Seventh Yearbook of the John Dewey Society. New York: Harper & Row, 1944. Pp. x + 22.

BUTTS, ROBERT FREEMAN. *The American Tradition in Religion and Education*. Boston: Beacon Press, 1950. Pp. xiv + 230. The most authoritative source on the history of the separation of church and state in American history, particularly as it relates to education.

Citizenship Education Project. *When Men Are Free: Premises of American Liberty*. Boston: Houghton Mifflin, 1955. Pp. 167. Developed by this project set up by Teachers College, Columbia University, for use with junior and senior high schools. Contains a listing of the "basic premises" of American liberty together with a description of their meaning.

LYND, ROBERT S. *Knowledge for What? The Place of Social Science in American Culture*. Princeton, N.J.: Princeton University Press, 1939. Pp. x + 268.

———, and HELEN M. LYND. *Middletown: A Study in Contemporary American Culture*. New York: Harcourt, Brace & World, 1937. Pp. xviii + 604.

MANNHEIM, KARL. *Ideology and Utopia: An Introduction to the Sociology of Knowledge*. New York: Harcourt, Brace & World, 1936. Pp. xxxi + 318.

MASON, ROBERT E. *Moral Values and Secular Education*. New York: Columbia University Press, 1950. Pp. viii + 155.

MULLER, HERBERT J. *Issues of Freedom: Paradoxes and Promises*. New York: Harper & Row, 1959. Pp. xv + 170.

N.E.A., Educational Policies Commission. *The Education of Free Men in a Democracy*. Washington, D.C.: National Education Association, 1941. Pp. 115.

———. *Moral and Spiritual Values in the Public Schools*. Washington, D.C.: National Education Association, 1951. Pp. ix + 157.

———. *Policies for Education in American Democracy*. Washington, D.C.:

National Education Association and the American Association of School Administrators, 1946. Pp. 277.

NOTTINGHAM, ELIZABETH D. *Religion and Society: Studies in Sociology.* New York: Random House, 1954. Pp. x + 84. An excellent, scholarly, short introductory sociologist's study of religion.

OSBORN, ALEX F. *Applied Imagination: Principles and Procedures of Creative Thinking,* Revised Edition. New York: Scribner, 1957. Pp. xvi + 379. A book describing the process used by industry to develop new ideas—sometimes called "brainstorming."

President's Commission on National Goals. *Goals for Americans.* Columbia University, The American Assembly, 1960. Pp. 372.

PRESTON, RALPH (Chairman). *Social Studies in the Elementary School.* The Fifty-sixth Yearbook of the National Society for the Study of Education, Part II. Chicago: University of Chicago Press, 1957. Pp. xi + 320 + lxxxvii.

Rockefeller Brothers Fund. "The Power of the Democratic Idea." America at Mid-Century Series. VI Report of the Rockefeller Brothers Fund Special Studies Project. Garden City, N. Y.: Doubleday, 1960. Pp. 74.

STAHMER, HAROLD (ed.). *Religion and Contemporary Society.* New York: Macmillan, 1963. Pp xii + 282.

WALKER, EDWARD L., and ROGER W. HEYNES. *Anatomy for Conformity.* Englewood Cliffs, N.J.: Prentice-Hall, 1962. Pp. xiv + 103.

YOUNG, MICHAEL. *The Rise of the Meritocracy, 1870–2033.* Baltimore: Penguin, 1958. Pp. 190.

Your Human Rights: The Universal Declaration of Human Rights Proclaimed by the United Nations, December 10, 1948. New York: Ellner, 1950. Pp. 71.

WILLIAMS, DANIEL DAY. *What Present-Day Theologians are Thinking.* New York: Harper & Row, 1952. Pp. 158.

WILLIAM, J. PAUL. *What Americans Believe and How They Worship.* New York: Harper & Row, 1952. Pp. 400 + x.

SELECTED FILMS

Almanac of Liberty (Anti-Defamation League) 48 min
A film on Supreme Court Justice Douglas's book by the same name is a drama highlighting Bill of Rights Day. Justice Douglas' book, published in late 1954 by Doubleday, is a group of 366 short essays dealing with landmarks in America's struggle for freedom.

Belonging to the Group (EBF) 16 min
Examines the meaning of the idea of respect and explains its essential relation to living in a democracy. Illustrates the origin and the development of some of the barriers to respect, and suggests ways for eliminating them. Indicates how respect must be exchanged among all members of society.

Born Equal (MP, UN Film Board) 11 min
Uses specific examples to interpret the Declaration of Human Rights as it emerges out of the United Nations Charter. Stresses the acceptance of individual responsibilities as well as rights, and emphasizes the necessity for nations to support the provisions of the Declaration.

Defining Democracy (EBF) 18 min
> A combined version of the films *Democracy* and *Despotism*. Illustrates the conditions that lead toward democracy or despotism.

Discussion Technique (United World Films) 28 min
> Various methods used in conducting a discussion hour: Forum symposium, debate, panel, conference, committee, and informal techniques. Stresses importance of trained discussion leaders.

Due Process of Law Denied (Teaching Film Custodians) 30 min
> Excerpted from the feature-length motion picture, *The Ox-Bow Incident*.

Education for Democracy (Missouri State Teachers Assn.) 22 min
> Depicts with actual classroom scenes the manner in which Missouri schools achieve the purposes of education in our American democracy as outlined by the Educational Policies Commission of the N.E.A.

Four Religions (Ind.) 60 min
> This film examines four of the higher religions of mankind: Hinduism, Buddhism, Islam, and Christianity.

Heritage (McGraw-Hill) 10 min
> A short film of clever cartoon animation that defines the natural rights of man and indicates how those rights can be maintained by any individual. Produced by Anti-Defamation League, Catholic Youth Organization, and Christian Youth Movement.

Learning Democracy (Ed. Film Service) 20 min
> How young people can gain experience in the democratic process through participation in school-community projects. Filmed in sixteen Michigan communities. The cast is made up of the actual participants in the projects shown.

Of Human Rights (UN) 21 min
> On December 10, 1948, the Universal Declaration of Human Rights was proclaimed by the General Assembly of the United Nations. The importance of the fundamental human rights set forth in this declaration and the necessity of bringing these articles again to the attention of the peoples of the world are portrayed through a discussion between the editor of a small-town newspaper and his two employees.

Practicing Democracy in the Classroom (EBF) 25 min
> A high school social studies class exploring techniques of planning, sharing, gaining, and giving information, evaluating, and deciding. Shows group dynamics in action. Emphasizes democratic methods as adaptable to any subject and age level. Provides interpretation of schools' purposes and methods related directly to community needs. Helpful to adult groups.

Production 5118 (MOT) 30 min
> A dramatic story of understanding one another—communication.

Role Playing in Human Relations Training (N.E.A.) 25 min
> Demonstrates the role-playing of human-relations situations as an educational method. A training film on use of role-playing and how to do it, gaining insight into human relations problems by demonstrating and analyzing effects of different behavior, uncovering interpersonal relationships that are hindering group progress, practicing new behavior before trying it out in real-life situation, communicating human-relations skills.

Also develops skills required to use role-playing—how to take an inventory of problems, how to select one problem upon which the group agrees to work, how to find a real-life example of the problem, how to set up, get under way, and stop role-playing scene demonstrating the problem, how to lead the discussion after the role-playing. *Note:* Role-playing is a discussion technique and a complicated and interesting one, not a gimmick.

Secure the Blessings (N.E.A.) 27 min

In school the children of America learn the ways of liberty that they must practice tomorrow to keep America free. Typical adults are faced with decisions that involve the democratic way of living.

Chapter 15. *Contrasting Viewpoints as to the School's Role*

IN SPITE OF SOME fundamental agreements, there are in our democratic society numerous and conflicting points of view as to how the school should operate in a period of social change. In the next section we shall present an overview of the more important of these, and in the following sections we shall describe each one in more detail.

There is a sense in which *all* of these alternative points of view tend partially to reflect the fundamentally democratic nature of our culture. As a matter of fact, the authors present in this chapter only those ideas that are in general harmony with the democratic point of view as it is found in our American society. For example, we do not present the point of view of the American Communists, which represents a kind of extreme totalitarianism of the Left; neither do we present the point of view of the extreme Rightists in American society, who believe that there is only the "American way." According to the latter, there should be no unsettled issues. They define the "American way" strictly in terms of their own narrowly conservative point of view; there is no respect for persons who hold conflicting opinions. The American principles, handed down to us by tradition, are to be passed on unchanged and unquestioned to the next generation. Only the principles selected and defined by the extreme Rightists are accepted by them as being "American"—all other positions are "communistic." In the opinion of the authors, these extreme Rightists violate a basic principle of the American way of life in thus ignoring respect for the individual.

485

CONTEMPORARY CONFLICTING VIEWS ON THE NATURE OF THE SCHOOL
AS RELATED TO SOCIAL CHANGE

The accompanying table (Table 12) is a schematic attempt to set forth the conflicting viewpoints present in American democratic society with respect particularly to the role of the school in a period of social change.

TABLE 12
CONTEMPORARY CONFLICTING PHILOSOPHIES COMPARED

Points of Comparison	(Neo-) Humanism (Perennialism)	Social Evolutionism (Essentialism)	Realism (Social)
Leading Proponents	Mortimer Adler Norman Foerster Robert Hutchins Jacques Maritain Mark Van Doren	W. C. Bagley C. H. Judd H. C. Morrison	F. S. Breed T. H. Briggs Harl Douglass F. T. Spaulding
Central Ideas Related to the Nature of Education	Prime purpose of education is the development of intellect. The best method of developing intellect is contact with the product of great minds, the classics (great books), or with subject disciplines.	Main function of education is the passing on of the time-tested elements of our social heritage —those essential to social advance: primarily, language (reading and writing), computation, and essential character traits.	Schools exist to help develop individuals for effective social living—to teach people to do better what they would do anyway.
Basic Philosophical Assumptions	Reality dualistic; composed of two essences, matter and ideas (or spirit and form). Knowledge secured by scientific method for matter; ideas and values by reason, intuition, revelation, or faith.	A real knowable universe which is in a state of evolving. Scientific method paramount in getting of knowledge. Social progress result of man's social inventions.	Social progress result of utilization of scientific method by man to accomplish his goals.
Ideas on the School in Relation to Social Change; Other Suggestions as to Curriculum and Method	Social changes are surface phenomena; pose problems, do not change basic truths. Basic values, basic principles and assumptions unchange. Job of school to help student to find basic truths, which can then be applied to current problems.	The subject-matter curriculum of the past is satisfactory to the extent that it represents real aids to man's successful adaptation to his social and physical environment. Methods and adaptions of curriculum to individual differences need improvement.	Schools must quickly change; pupils must be taught to live in present society.

Points of Comparison	Experimentalism	Reconstructionism	Laissez-Faire (Educational)
Leading Proponents	Boyde H. Bode John L. Childs John Dewey W. H. Kilpatrick George Counts	T. Brameld Harold Rugg B. O. Smith Kenneth Benne	Probably does not exist in pure form; may be traced historically to Rousseau
Central Ideas Related to the Nature of Education	Main purpose of education is to develop critically minded individuals capable of living creatively in their society and of improving society in line with their clarified values.	Main purpose of education is to develop individuals with the ability and desire to create a better social order along the lines dictated by social knowledge.	Main purpose of education is to encourage the fullest development of the individual. Stress on individuality in the handling of students.
Basic Philosophical Assumptions	Reality is that of human experience. The world is dynamic, changing, parts in interaction. Knowledge is tested human experience. Values arise out of experiences and are tested in experience. Both knowledge and values must be continually retested.	Similar to Experimentalism—greater emphasis on hypothesis as predeterminant to the solution of the problem.	Similar to Experimentalism—greater emphasis on physical environment and on the individual's creative expression.
Ideas on the School in Relation to Social Change; Other Suggestions as to Curriculum and Method	School's job is to help individuals develop, to become creative in problem-solving in line with scientific ideas. Curriculum is selected experiences under guidance of the teacher.	Schools should find out the kind of society needed as a result of social change, prepare individuals to create that society.	Very little emphasis on society.

Source: Adapted from Justman, *Theories of Secondary Education in the United States;* Wynne, *Philosophies of Education;* and Brameld, *Patterns of Educational Philosophy.*

Any attempt to delineate the various points of view on any issue in American society will have numerous weaknesses, of which two are particularly significant for this discussion. In the first place, the very way in which the various opinions are classified will be affected somewhat by the position of the person making the classification. Secondly, since any creative thinker will diverge somewhat from all other persons, even those who are close to him in their points of view, any attempt to group persons under a small number of classifications will tend to do some injustice to the unique positions of individuals.

Every philosopher tends to be somewhat individualistic. He has specific points at which he is not in agreement with other persons who, in general, *do* agree with him. In spite of weaknesses and shortcomings, a classification system has merits. It serves to give the student an overview, simplified to be sure, of the range of possibilities. It also gives points of reference when more detailed discussions as to specific points may cause him to lose sight of the larger issues.

The classification system used in the charts and presented in this chapter has been taken from three main sources. Basically, it follows from the system developed by Justman.[1] To this have been added two points of view; namely reconstructionism and educational laissez-faire, suggested respectively by Brameld[2] and Wynne.[3] The final wording of the chart and explanation of it is, however, the responsibility of the writers.

The first point of view is what the authors have called *humanism*. This point of view is also called *neo-humanism* by some of its progenitors. One of several views under this general heading has been called *neo-Thomism*. This view is also sometimes termed *perennialism*. There are many different positions, based on somewhat differing philosophical assumptions, that have been lumped together under the term "neo-humanism" as used here; for example, it includes both those persons who are religious humanists and those whose views are not primarily based upon any sectarian religious point of view. In general, the various schools of thought included by the authors under "humanism" tend to have the following views in common: They believe that there are certain basic unchanging truths that exist in what is fundamentally an unchanging universe; that the main job of education is the passing on of these truths; and furthermore, that the prime function of education is the cultivation of the intellect.

Robert M. Hutchins, formerly chancellor of the University of Chicago, is probably the leading proponent of neo-humanism, even though he may not be quite as explicit in the underlying philosophical assumptions as some of the less well-known progenitors. Mortimer Adler, professor of Philosophy at the University of Chicago, has stated this point of view very clearly in numerous sources.[4]

The next point of view (Table 12), which is called by Justman *social evolutionism*, roughly corresponds to what has been called by some *essentialism*. (See Essentialist Manifesto discussed later in this chapter.) This point of view represents, by and large, the positions of Henry C. Mor-

[1] Joseph P. Justman, *Theories of Secondary Education in the United States* (New York: Bureau of Publications, Teachers College, Columbia University, 1940).
[2] Theodore Brameld, *Education for the Emerging Age: Newer Ends and Stronger Means* (New York: Harper, 1965).
[3] John P. Wynne, *Philosophies of Education* (Englewood Cliffs, N.J.: Prentice-Hall, Inc., 1947).
[4] For example, Mortimer Adler, "In Defense of the Philosophy of Education," Chapter V in John Brubacher (Chairman), *Philosophies of Education*, pp. 197–249. "Forty-first Yearbook, N.S.S.E." (Chicago: The Society, 1942).

rison, Charles H. Judd, and William C. Bagley. It differs markedly in its basic assumptions from humanism in that it does include the belief in a fundamentally changing, evolving world—one that, however, changes gradually. It holds that the main job of education is the transmitting of only those elements from the culture that have become thoroughly established in the onward evolution of man's society. This means that man looks back in his history to discover those essential things that have been helpful in promoting his onward and upward development. The job of the school is, then, to help insure the continuance of these things by passing them on to the young. These elements constitute the essentials of our civilization. Although there may be certain more or less permanent changes coming about at present, one will never know the exact nature or degree of permanence of these current problems, which may represent merely ebbs and flow in our culture. The main job of the school is, then, to pass on those essentials that can be recognized as thoroughly established by man's previous history.

The next point of view (Table 12) is that of which Justman speaks as *social realism*. There are many kinds of realism, including, of course, the realism of Judd and Morrison found under the previous point of view. Philosophically, realism takes many forms. This particular form of realism, social realism, is more of a social philosophy than it is a metaphysical one. Persons of this school of thought, who constitute a sizeable majority among the school administrators and others who make up such organizations as the American Association of School Administrators and the National Association of Secondary School Principals, believe that it is the job of the school to keep up with social change and to see to it that the currently prevailing values and ideas of our society are made clear to each generation. It is primarily the job of the school to fit each individual to meet the demands that his society places upon him. We look, therefore, to contemporary society for our values and for the subject matter for the curriculum for our schools. As society changes, so should the school. It should take on the general tenor of the society at any given time.

Another point of view (Table 12) which has been called *pragmatism* by the general philosophers and *experimentalism* in its educational version, tends to place the emphasis upon the development of critically minded, intelligent individuals to live and operate in a changing society. This group believes that one of the most significant features of our culture, or any culture, is the possibility (yes, the certainty) of change. Therefore it emphasizes provisions for experiences in problem-solving situations, and thus in making decisions that are in accordance with scientific methods and with conditions present in a given period of change. Its main goal is to develop critically minded individuals who seek to operate in accordance with the main values that have emerged and have been found important in our democratic culture.

The next point of view (Table 12) is called *reconstructionism* and is an offshoot of experimentalism. The reconstructionists believe as do the experimentalists with respect to most of the latter's interpretations of the nature of social change and also with respect to most of their metaphysical assumptions. They differ largely in their conception of the place of the school with respect to social change. They believe it is the main job of the school to help society make the necessary changes in its institutions in order to meet the demands created by the rapid changes in society. Indeed, it is held that such a reconstruction of our society is so urgent that the school *must* play this part if civilization is to be preserved. Therefore, according to the reconstructionist, the teachers and leaders of our schools must clearly think through what should be the nature of the future society, using the knowledge made available through the progress that has been made in the social sciences. We should then prepare the individuals in our schools to live and operate in such a way as to bring about the new society as quickly as possible.

There is one other point of view (Table 12) which does not have any well-identified proponents at present in our culture but which does represent a point of view sometimes erroneously identified with "modern education." This is the view Wynne calls *educational laissez-faire*. Its proponents hold that the main job of the school is to study the child and to develop an educational program or curriculum based upon the *felt* needs and desires of each child (as opposed to adult-recognized present and future needs of the child) and in accord with his particular stage of development. There is no social philosophy[5] inherent in this view except that of an extreme laissez-faire (in a broader-than-economic sense). It is doubtful that there are very many individuals who hold strictly to this philosophy or practice it completely, but it does represent a point of view that many people incorrectly ascribe to the so-called progressive educators. It has also been wrongly ascribed to John Dewey. The members of the Progressive Education Association (from which the term "progressive education" originated) represented many points of view having only one common central idea, namely to try to bring about an improvement of education away from what is termed the "traditional" school. A more complete explanation of the laissez-faire view, as related to so-called progressive education, will be found later in this chapter.

In addition to the systematic points of view that we have already indicated, two others have gained prominence in the United States in recent years. One of these is existentialism. This will be discussed more fully later, but at this time suffice it to say that existentialism is a philosophical approach that places great emphasis on individual choice and on individual responsibility for that choice. The other point of view is called philosophical analysis or, sometimes in a narrower version, logical positivism. This is rapidly gain-

[5] It extends through the so-called Romantic philosophers at least as far back as Jean-Jacques Rousseau. See his *Emile*.

ing adherents in the general philosophy departments of the United States. This view holds that the primary role of philosophy is to explore the meaning of statements people make. It is closely related to linguistics. It is concerned with the analysis of what is meant when a statement is made. Most of the statements of traditional philosophy are meaningless to this group, because they hold that there is no way of verifying whether or not the statements are true and hence the statements have no real meaning for human existence. These points of view will also be discussed more fully later in the chapter.

We are now ready to discuss each of the points of view in some detail. Under each, we shall present the material under four headings as in the tables, namely:

Central Ideas Related to the Nature of Education
Leading Proponents
Basic Philosophical Assumptions
Ideas on the School in Relationship to Social Change; Other Suggestions
    as to Curriculum and Methods

Schools for the Development of the Intellect—Humanism, Religious and Classical

Of the several points of view that are to be discussed in detail in this and the following sections, humanism is the one whose history goes back the farthest in an unbroken line. The continuity between classical humanism, which developed during the Renaissance period at the end of the Middle Ages, and modern "neo"-humanism is almost unbroken.

Central Ideas Related to the Nature of Education

Most of the persons we are here classifying as humanists hold that the universe is organized on a relatively few changeless principles. It is assumed that these principles can be ascertained by an intellectual-rational process by those persons who have minds capable of grasping such principles. The central purpose of education is thought to be the development of the intellect—that capacity of mind that is necessary for the grasping of these unchanging principles.

According to this position, the great classics that have come down to us from the past are examples in print of the efforts of great minds. One of the best ways to develop intellect is to come into contact with a great mind. The great minds are so few that the contact with the written result of a great mind (a great book) becomes the best way of touching the mind itself. Some of the humanists are not so much interested in teaching by means of the great classics as are others. These latter are usually interested in the organization of subject matter of the great subject disciplines, which have been produced by the great minds just as the classics have been.

The way in which the school can best serve present society, according to the humanist position, is in concentrating its efforts on the mental development of outstanding individuals who can become the leaders of our present society. It is the job of the schools carefully to select the best thoughts of the past, representative of the best minds, and transmit them to the present—at least to those persons who are capable of understanding and utilizing these thoughts in the solution of our pressing problems.

Leading Proponents

Two general types of individuals adhere to this point of view: the ones whose ideas are derived primarily from our intellectual heritage, and those whose concepts are derived primarily from a basis of revealed authoritarian religion. Among the first group, Robert Hutchins,[6] mentioned earlier, and Mortimer Adler, his onetime associate at the University of Chicago and professor of philosophy at that institution, are to be found. Other persons prominent in holding to these ideas are Norman Foerster and Mark Van Doren. All of the above persons and many others who have this general point of view, the "so-called liberal arts tradition," while not agreeing entirely among themselves, in general hold to the ideas that have been set forth earlier and will be set forth more fully in the remaining paragraphs of this section.

Basic Philosophical Assumptions

Certain main metaphysical assumptions are for the most part held in common by persons having this point of view, whether they are classical or religious humanists.

By and large this group adheres to the concept of a dualistic world composed of two substances or essences, the one of matter and the other of ideas (or spirit or form). The student of philosophy will recognize this concept as going back historically as far as the ancient Greek controversies on the nature of matter. It includes both the Platonic and the Aristotelian concepts. The student of philosophy will also recognize that there is a wide variety of viewpoints that may be taken with respect to the nature of these two types of essences and also with respect to the relationships between them. Also, it will be recognized that some individuals holding the other points of view may be dualists to a greater or less extent.

In general, the theory of knowledge that is adhered to by those in the humanist tradition places less emphasis upon the scientific development of knowledge in the modern connotation of the word "science" as necessarily involving careful experimentation, and more upon the securing of knowledge through the use of reason or the rational process. In some cases, of course, faith, intuition, or revelation is added to other methods for arriving

---

[6] Robert M. Hutchins, *The Conflict in Education* (New York: Harper, 1953).

at ideas of values. The scientific method in general *is* accepted by this group only as a method of securing knowledge concerning the material world. For more basic knowledge, including that of the metaphysical principles and certainly for the realm of values, we must go to other processes. These are held to lie in the realm of ideas where the scientific method is not applicable.

Man himself is considered to differ from animals because he possesses mind. Mind is the "quality of rationality" that makes man different from animals. In general, the chief values for this group are those that are in harmony with the unchanging values that have been accredited by the great figures and writers of the past.

While the American adherents to the humanist view are for the most part enthusiastic supporters of our democratic society, there certainly is a difference between their point of view toward democracy and some of the points of view to be described later. In general, those in the humanist position accept only the political definition of democracy: namely that it is a form of government in which the main officers or representatives are chosen by the people. Political equality is not held to mean social or intellectual equality. This group emphasizes quite strongly that everyone should recognize that there is a difference in the kind of contribution different individuals can make to our society. The humanists advocate improvement of the ability of the masses to select as their leaders members of the intellectual elite who can make the proper decisions for the rest of us. The humanists, for the most part, believe very strongly in the individual's civil liberties and think that we should protect them because individuals must be free to make decisions they wish to make.

Ideas on the School in Relationship to Social Change; Other Suggestions as to Curriculum and Methods

In general, those matters that we have usually termed social change, such as those described earlier in this book, are held by those in the humanist position not to be changes in the basic ideas underlying the universe. Consequently, although these changes pose problems, it becomes all the more important that we should not lose sight of the unchanging principles. The main job of the school, therefore, in times of slow change as well as in times of rapid change, is to see to it that methods of rational thinking are used in facing our problems. Thinking through to the basic principles that underlie solution of the problems we face is held central and paramount in the educational process.

One of the implications of this, of course, is that the school should not be basically concerned with current events. By being too much taken up with current problems, we lose perspective and sometimes do not get at the basic principles in the crosscurrents of our political and other problems. Once our minds have been trained to think rationally by coming in con-

tact with the great minds through study of the great books or of the subject disciplines, we shall then be able to use our trained intellects in the
solution of the present problems with which we are faced.

This apparent lack of interest by formal education in our present social
problems does not mean that none of the persons adhering to this philosophy is concerned about them. Many of them are. Robert Hutchins, for
example, tends to be a social liberal, even though, in his educational philosophy, he harks back to an earlier form of education, which he thinks
will enable us to develop leaders to help us solve the social problems we
face.

In the humanist point of view, the best form of education, at least the
education of the intellectual elite, is that which was used in our schools
in an earlier period: namely contact with the great classics and the lecture
method, perhaps supplemented by discussion in seminars with professors
familiar with the classics. The student will thereby be stimulated to think,
through contact with the ideas that are being promulgated in the great
books curriculum or in the subject disciplines. Contact with a great mind
that uses rational thinking is more important than practice in the utilization of proper procedures in the actual solving of concrete problems.[7]
After it has been ascertained in elementary school or early in high school
that certain individuals cannot attain any very great intellectual accomplishment, they should be given vocational training and training for citizenship so that they will be able to make wise decisions in choosing their
political leaders. Such training should not be called "education," because
real education is the development of the intellect.

Some of the statements contained in above paragraphs are too extreme
for some of the persons who would adhere at least partially to the ideas
expressed. There are many differences, for example as to the number of
persons who can be trained intellectually, among those people who
basically adhere to this point of view.[8] There is also a difference of opinion
as to the kind of education for other persons. We have already seen that
only a few humanists would strictly follow the great books curriculum.
There are also some individuals, particularly those adhering to a traditional
religion, who would accept the basic *philosophical assumptions* set forth
in this view but would accept in part *educational ideas* similar to those
to be described later.[9]

---

[7] The philosopher's contempt for the scientific method (in the realm of ideas)
apparently blinds him to the psychological research on processes designed to "stimulate
man to think." He offers no evidence to support his continued championship of an
educational methodology that has been prevalent throughout the period of the rapidly
increasing lag between material inventions and social inventions. The research proves
that he is wrong—so he dismisses the research!

[8] The psychological data on differences in ability in unselected populations is dis-
regarded. The philosopher prefers to depend on his opinion.

[9] These persons tend to base their philosophy on faith, their educational practices
on the scientific findings of educational psychology and educational sociology.

Schools to Pass on the Tested Heritage from Man's Historical Development—Social Evolutionism

Again, as in the case of the humanists, what we have called *social evolutionism* represents a number of related points of view. In this case the points of view probably are more similar in their basic philosophical assumptions. This general point of view differs markedly from that of the humanists with respect to its naturalistic approach to the universe and to man. This point of view, and the others of the series to follow, date (in their more mature forms) from the period after man had discovered the scientific method. What is here called social evolutionism probably can be traced at least as far back as Spencer, the scientist who first applied the Darwinian point of view to the field of social evolution. It is most definitely found within the scientific-evolutionary view as to the nature of man and of the universe.

In contrast to this emphasis on change, the conclusions for education tend to be of a conservative nature. Whereas the humanists tend to go back to an earlier period both for the subject matter of the schools and for the methods, the social evolutionists for the most part are satisfied with the present curriculum of the school, although some of them may have suggestions for the improvement of methods of teaching. In this group there are wide differences of opinion with respect to certain matters. For example, there is a difference of opinion as to the validity of intelligence tests. William C. Bagley was very critical of the use that was being made of their results in his time. There are also differences as to emphases. Bagley emphasized adaptability of methods to the individual, Morrison carefully worked out detailed units of study for the various subjects, and Judd emphasized the cultivation of the higher mental processes.

As indicated earlier, another name sometimes applied to this group is *essentialists*. This word is derived from the so-called Essentialist Manifesto, which was issued by the Essentialist Committee for the Advancement of American Education and which included among its sponsors William C. Bagley and Henry C. Morrison, who are both listed among the social evolutionists in our classification. This committee also included some persons who might better be classified as humanists or as social realists. This Essentialist Manifesto called for more emphasis upon the essential knowledges and skills to be passed on by the school and less emphasis upon "interest, freedom, immediate needs, personal experience, psychological organization and pupil initiative."[10] The Council for Basic Education would also, in general, be in agreement with this position.

In the discussion of social evolutionism to follow, under the same four

[10] William C. Bagley, "An Essentialist Platform for the Advancement of American Education," *Educational Administration and Supervision*, **24**, April 1938, pp. 241–256; quoted in John P. Wahlquist, *The Philosophy of American Education* (New York: Ronald Press, 1942).

subheadings under which we discussed neo-humanism, we shall limit ourselves to those positions that for the most part are held in common by the
persons to be indicated later as the proponents of this general point of
view.

Central Ideas Related to the Nature of Education

The social evolutionists look to man's evolutionary development in order
to get a basis for their ideas about the specific purposes of the school.
They note that a study of man's social development indicates that man
has been enabled to make progress because of specific adaptations or inventions he has made. Man learned to associate with his fellows for improved ability to secure food and to protect himself from danger. Later,
speech developed and still later, the art of writing. Various forms of organization that enabled man more effectively to carry on his group
organization were developed. Many kinds of adaptation of technology and
food-getting were discovered and then passed on culturally.

The net result of all this is that man owes his very quality of "humanness" to the social environment in which he is found. Society is pre-
eminent. Man gets his individuality from his contact with the society in
which he is found.

Education, according to the social evolutionist view, develops as a separate institution when its functions become so important or so complex that
they must be performed by specialists. The main function of education
is to see to it that those great inventions of the past that have enabled
man to make such progress are passed on to the young. The school acts
as a preserver of the cultural heritage. The school as an institution must
carefully study the past, determine those aspects of the past that are
worthy of being passed on, and see to it that the new generation is then
given the necessary skills, attitudes, and character traits that have been
validated by societies of the past. By and large, the traditional curriculum,
consisting of the subjects that incorporated the past successful discoveries
of mankind, did contain those elements that needed to be passed on to
the new generation. The school must do the most effective job possible in
seeing to it that these essentials of our time-tested cultural heritage are
passed on.

There is implicit in this point of view the assumption that the direction
of social evolution is inevitably upward and onward and that the direction
is good. Holders of other points of view are not so sanguine in their opinion that the evolution of mankind will necessarily continue in a direction
that can be called good. The social evolutionists do recognize that the
course of evolution has not always been upward. There have been dips
downward. In general, however, they believe mankind will continue in
the onward and upward evolutionary progress. In contrast, we will find
that the experimentalists, and reconstructionists in particular, believe that

man must consciously seek and work for good social progress rather than leave matters to "blind" social evolution.

Leading Proponents

There are three persons who have done most of the writing that would fall fairly close to this point of view as we have described it. Those men are William C. Bagley, Charles H. Judd, and Henry C. Morrison. Certainly there are many others who have similar viewpoints but who are not such prolific writers. Many persons who believe in the same general point of view with respect to the curriculum have not worked out its underlying assumptions so carefully. We have mentioned earlier that there are some points on which the above-named men differ, but the emphasis upon validation of objectives through an appraisal of factors necessary to the onward and upward societal evolution of man is found in common in the writings of all three men.[11]

Basic Philosophical Assumptions

In examining the basic philosophical assumptions of this point of view, we run into some fundamental problems, because some of these persons cannot be clearly classified in any of the "standard" general philosophical fields. Judd and Morrison are definitely realists in their basic metaphysical assumptions and could be classified on this aspect very similarly to the persons with the next point of view, social realism. Bagley tends to be more of an idealist, although his writings are not entirely clear in this respect. Many of the lesser-known persons holding this view could certainly be classified as having a dualistic interpretation of the nature of the universe and of man (similar to that of the humanists, involving matter and ideas).

To those of this group who base their concept of man on biological evolution, mind is a function of the organism that arose as a part of man's physical evolution. The mind, to this group, is that function of the organism that enables it to solve its problems and to adapt itself in other ways to the various environmental conditions it faces.

For most of the persons in this school of thought, the approach to the problem of knowledge, of course, comes largely through the scientific method. (The historical method is one aspect of the scientific.) Certainly the scientific method should be used to verify facts concerning the nature of the world and of man. The scientific method can also be used in establishing the facts of history. It is from history that, according to this point of view, the values for the use of the school are obtained. The values lie in the preservation of those things that have been validated through their success in man's previous history. The purpose of life therefore seems to be to build a society that would operate in terms of those values that have been fully established in man's previous social history.

[11] W. C. Bagley, *Education and Emergent Man* (New York: Nelson, 1934); C. H. Judd, *Education and Social Progress* (New York: Harcourt, 1934); H. C. Morrison, *Basic Principles of Education* (Boston: Houghton, 1934).

Ideas on the School in Relationship to Social Change; Suggestions as to Curriculum and Methods

Since the school is to validate its curriculum and its values by a study of the history of the race, educators need not be concerned about the events that are happening contemporaneously in the society. Indeed at this very point, when society is in a state of crisis, the school is needed most to act as a conservator or "balance wheel" to support basic social values. This does not mean that there is no change (over a long period of time) in certain basic values as man goes onward in his societal evolution and has new insights. For example, the development of democracy was a new insight that arose out of man's experience and was gradually proved to be helpful for his onward and upward evolution. The school plays no part, however, in these advances of society. It is enough that the school's program assures that the time-tested values and essentials of our culture are passed on, once they are established. By so doing, it will prevent the various societies from moving rather hastily in unknown directions. Any lack of attention to essential values and to man's past heritage may cause a society to deteriorate. As a matter of fact, they note, a study of history indicates this. In many cases a more gradual, and therefore a better, evolution of society would have occurred had the school done a more effective job of passing on the time-tested values of a culture.

For the social evolutionist, the curriculum of the school should consist of those essentials of subject matter, skills, attitudes, and character traits that have been time-tested and therefore have proved to be good in terms of man's past history. These essentials, for the most part, have traditionally (at least in the recent past) been held to be of most importance in the curriculum of the school. The present school subjects are satisfactory as far as they contain the essentials (knowledge and skills).

On the question of school methods, several social evolutionists have had suggestions to make. Morrison, for example, proposed the Morrison unit. For this type of unit (which is still widely used, sometimes with modifications) he listed in detail plans for teaching adapted to the different kinds of subject matter. William C. Bagley was also a specialist on methods. In each case, they believed that the *real essentials* could be taught to practically all persons regardless of their reputed slowness in learning ability. Bagley particularly decried the undue emphasis on the intelligence test and the implied notion that some people could not learn. He also opposed the separation of students by homogeneous grouping. He and Morrison both believed that methods could be adapted to the learning level of the various students involved. Morrison in particular stressed the mastery of the essentials. If certain items had been proved essential in the onward development of civilization, it was mandatory that the schools teach *for mastery* and *continue to teach* until there *was* mastery. He was very much opposed to the idea of developing a quite extensive curriculum that could not be fully taught. Some of the items that had at times been included in the curriculum were considered to be definitely unnecessary.

The central idea of this point of view can be summarized in the statement, "It is the school's job to pass on the essentials as effectively as possible to the greatest number of persons in our culture in order to insure the optimum conditions necessary for the further onward development of our society." To this group the main function of the school is to facilitate the onward development of our civilization by seeing to it that the essentials of our cultural heritage are passed on as unimpaired as possible to the next generation. Emphasis was upon mastery of essentials by all; no provision was made for leadership training for the gifted few.

Schools to Adjust Individuals to Present Society— Social Realism

The point of view here called *social realism* tends to represent more of a social philosophy than a general metaphysical point of view. For the most part, however, its proponents do adhere to a general philosophical point of view—that of realism. There are many kinds of realism, so we have attempted to differentiate them by calling this one *social realism*. The precise nature of the metaphysical assumptions will be set forth in a later section. As has already been noted, this point of view is a currently prevailing one among school administrators.

Central Ideas Related to the Nature of Education

In general, this point of view arose (as did social evolutionism) in response to the scientific movement, which came about in the Western world in the latter part of the seventeenth century. The scientific movement did not affect seriously the study of psychology until late in the nineteenth century with the work of Wundt and others in Europe and the group in America under the stimulation of William James. The point of view underlying almost all of science of that time was a strongly realistic one, philosophically speaking. It was felt that by a careful use of the scientific method we could amass a whole set of facts, each one established in an isolated investigation. These individual facts could then be added together until man could establish all knowledge, and on the basis of this knowledge he could develop the kind of world he wanted. In the field of science and in the scientific study of man, there was little place for values. As a matter of fact, in the early part of this period it was felt that, in order to be scientific, it was necessary to lay aside for the moment all questions of values. Consequently this group was very little interested in the problem of values as such. Indeed some of this group were, and are, quite antagonistic toward philosophy. In the period of the 1920's, when certain extreme aspects of this point of view were quite evident, in the movement of education called *scientism*, there was very little interest in a philosophical approach to the problems of education.

The social realists felt that the job of education is to insure that individuals are prepared to adjust to the present society. The emphasis was upon the preparing of individuals to *live in our present society*. Consequently one of the main procedures to be used in the selection of a curriculum was to conduct a careful study of the present society, in order to determine just what would be demanded of the students when they got out of school.

Another aspect of the problem was the desirability of helping the individual to fit into his proper place in society. This necessitated a careful study of the individual. It was found that individuals varied greatly with respect to their abilities. Each person probably had a definite place in society, which could be ascertained by a careful study of his abilities. It was then necessary to assist in fitting him into his niche.

Leading Proponents

Probably the person who has most clearly expressed the viewpoint of social realism is Frederick S. Breed[12] of the University of Chicago. Other persons who have been very explicit in this point of view in their writings have been Thomas H. Briggs,[13] Harl R. Douglass,[14] and Francis T. Spaulding.[15] With the exception of Breed there is very little evidence in the writings of these men to indicate an effort to probe the basic philosophical assumptions underlying their points of view. With a "scientific approach" to the problem, they have tended to go ahead with the procedural activities that are a necessary result of the point of view without fully clarifying the underlying assumptions. While the basic underlying ideas are derived from a view of the universe and of man arising out of the scientific age, they are just as much philosophic assumptions as are, for example, those of the humanists. Many realists appear not to be cognizant of this point. Since, in the early developments of the scientific movement, the "professional philosophers" were in opposition, the realists have often felt that theirs was a nonphilosophical or even an antiphilosophical approach. Some apparently feel that, by using the scientific method, they have avoided the endless disputes for which traditional philosophers have been noted.

Basic Philosophical Assumptions

The basic philosophical assumptions of the social realists are similar in some respects to those of the social evolutionists. The social realists believe very definitely in a real, knowable world that can be known apart from

---

[12] Frederick S. Breed, *Education and the New Realism* (New York: Macmillan, 1939).

[13] Thomas H. Briggs, *Pragmatism and Pedagogy* (New York: Macmillan, 1940).

[14] Harl R. Douglass, *Organization and Administration of Secondary Schools* (New York: Ginn, 1945).

[15] Francis T. Spaulding, *High School and Life: Report of the Regents Inquiry* (New York: McGraw-Hill, 1938).

the particular knower. In other words, this is not a subjective world. It can be known objectively. The means of knowing the world is through the scientific method, whereby knowledge can be validated. Most of the realists formerly thought that knowledge could be obtained by careful isolation of a phenomenon and by examining it in piecemeal fashion in accordance with the Newtonian scientific tradition. The newer point of view of Einsteinian science indicates that phenomena must always be studied in the total field of interrelationships. The realists hold that, when mankind has determined the facts concerning the world in which he lives, the problem remaining is to use them in accordance with the prevailing purposes and values of his culture. For the most part the implication is that as teachers and educators we may arrive at these values by a careful study of our culture. For example, as school administrators, we must objectively study our culture to determine its prevailing values and then we must proceed to develop the practices of the institution called the school so that it operates in such a way as to achieve those prevailing values.

The realists recognize that we live in a changing world. Consequently the school as an institution must change, both to keep up with the world and to be in touch with whatever values may become predominant at different times in our culture. The realists would agree with those points of view that hold that the values predominant in a democratic culture are different from those in, let us say, a feudalistic culture, and that the school at present must reflect in its practices the democratic nature of our culture.

Ideas on the School in Relationship to Social Change; Other Suggestions as to Curriculum and Methods

We have seen that the proponents of the social-realist point of view by and large desire that the school keep up with the changes in our society. A special problem arises when we recall that, if in an era of social change we are preparing people for the now-present society, the society to which they will have to adjust will be a different one within the next few years. Some of the social realists have recognized this problem and have arrived at answers similar to those of the experimentalists. They have become more concerned about the development of adaptable individuals because of the changing nature of our society. Another point that many of this group apparently have neglected is the existence of many conflicts in our society. It is difficult to find out what values are predominant. At any given time a whole series of values is in conflict. Sometimes sudden changes are made, perhaps reversions to previous ideas or values. Do we get our values merely by "counting noses" at a particular time? Does the school follow every change in the political and social weather vane? This issue appears to be faced in two different ways by different groups of realists. One approach is to ignore for the most part these values that are in serious conflict. Instead we may look at the fundamental activities in which man engages and attempt to duplicate them in the school, so that a man can learn as a child or youth to make proper adjustments in his social activities. Another approach among the realists is to handle this problem in a fashion similar to that of the experimentalists. The school would teach the student to handle problems of a controversial nature in a scientific manner and attempt to help him to arrive at satisfactory answers to the problems with which individuals and groups in our society are faced. In this latter process, an attempt is made to help the student to clarify his own values among the varieties of multiconflicting values found in our society. This latter approach would differ very little in operation from the methods usually used by the experimentalists. Only the underlying philosophical assumptions would be somewhat different.

To return now to the discussion of social realism in general, the curriculum of the school should be made up of those activities and selected subject matter that would be of direct, functional, practical value to the persons who are going to live and operate in our culture. The learning situation should be such as to secure maximum learning of facts and skills.

The emphasis on the part of some realists on the wide differences among individuals in regard to capabilities and the activities they will pursue later in life leads them to set up a number of differentiated curricula, particularly in the secondary school, according to the kind of life the individual plans to pursue later. Of course there will be a core of common studies, but there will also be curricula of many kinds, differentiated for persons of differing abilities and with respect to the quite different vocations into which they will enter. Some of the realists advocate plans that use homogeneous grouping of the students with respect to their abilities, so that both curriculum and methods can be more readily adapted to students of similar ability. This point of view has been manifest, of course, in some contemporary secondary schools. While there is still emphasis on special classes for those people requiring special help, such as the slow learner and the gifted, the general trend today is away from such a heavy emphasis on homogeneous grouping, even among some of the realists.

The realists in general advocate that the methods of teaching should be discovered through scientific research to determine the most effective way of accomplishing whatever purposes or values can be arrived at by the methods described above.

SCHOOLS TO DEVELOP INDIVIDUALS WITH ABILITY TO REFINE CRITICALLY THE SOCIAL HERITAGE AND TO IMPROVE SOCIETY—EXPERIMENTALISM

Experimentalism is the point of view that has been ascribed to John Dewey and others of his school of philosophy. In the field of general philosophy, it is based on what is called the pragmatic viewpoint. It is more commonly known as experimentalism as far as the implications for education are concerned. The word *instrumentalism* has sometimes been applied to it because of the stress upon the instrumental nature of the hypothesis or idea in assisting the human organism in solving its problems. This point of view has developed primarily within the American democratic culture, and it stems from democratic values coupled with the scientific method of getting at knowledge and with the general "practical" realistic point of view found in American society. John Dewey assimilated these elements into an integrated point of view to form his pragmatic philosophy.

Central Ideas Related to the Nature of Education

Most of the persons adhering to the experimentalist position place emphasis on the process of getting at knowledge through the method of tested human experience. Education as the construction and progressive "reconstruction of experience" is John Dewey's way of stating the relation of the educational process to ongoing activity.

The main purpose of education, then, is to develop critically minded individuals who are capable of seeking and finding (at least tentatively) creative answers to the problems they face in their society. Not only should they develop capabilities of finding answers to their own personal problems, but also abilities of being able to work well with others in a group solution to common problems. There is emphasis among the experimentalists on the clarification of the values of the students as a part of the educational process.

The above concepts mean that the curriculum is primarily to be thought of in terms of carefully selected experiences under the guidance of the teacher, in order to develop the kind of individuals who will be capable of the solution of their own problems and of common problems in conjunction with fellow students and later with fellow men.

Leading Proponents

John Dewey[16] is considered by almost all experimentalists as being their outstanding progenitor. Although his ideas go back to those of William James and thence to Charles S. Peirce, as far as general pragmatic philosophy is concerned, there are important differences in fundamental assumptions and emphases between the philosophy of John Dewey and that of these other two.

Dewey has had several rather outstanding followers who have served to carry his philosophy much further and to sharpen and clarify it: William H. Kilpatrick and John L. Childs,[17] both of Teachers College, Columbia University, and the late Boyd H. Bode[18] of the Ohio State University. This point of view, by and large, has been accepted, at least to a verbalistic

[16] John Dewey, *Democracy and Education* (New York: Macmillan, 1931). John Dewey, *Reconstruction in Philosophy* (New York: New American Library, 1953).

[17] John L. Childs, *Education and the Philosophy of Experimentalism* (New York: Appleton, 1931).

[18] Boyd H. Bode, *Democracy as a Way of Life* (New York: Macmillan, 1937).

extent, by a sizeable number of the persons who are now teaching courses in various teacher-education institutions in the United States. It is interesting to contemplate the amount of influence that John Dewey has had on educational philosophy and teaching method as taught in teacher-education institutions. John Dewey was not a very dynamic teacher himself, rather soft-spoken and fairly easygoing. He was actually in the Department of Philosophy at Columbia University and was not on the staff of a teachers college. His writings are not particularly easy to read nor particularly clear. Once a person is able to read through the difficult style, the ideas are found to be quite revolutionary in terms of the deep philosophical assumptions involved.

It has remained primarily for some of his followers to spell out in more concrete terms some of the implications for the schools.

Basic Philosophical Assumptions

John Dewey held that there are some metaphysical problems the solution of which we can never hope to find. Consequently we should begin to work on our practical problems without trying to settle in advance the answers to all those that are metaphysical. There is, however, a necessary set of assumptions under which the experimentalist operates. The earlier idealistic philosophy held that there were two basic essences of the universe, matter and spirit. The experimentalist tries to resolve this dualism, and along with it many other types of dualisms, by holding that reality is one, the reality of human experience. It is within this reality of human experience that mankind must seek the answers to its problems. This world of human experience in which we find ourselves and in which we attempt to solve our problems is a dynamic, changing world, the parts of which are in constant interaction with each other. All knowledge in that universe is tentative and is based upon tested human experience. Each new hypothesis for human action must be tested in terms of consequences for further human action. Hypotheses as to values arise out of human experiences in the same way that hypotheses as to facts do, and they are tested in that human experience. Both knowledge and values are tentative and must be continually retested.

Almost all experimentalists find three values emerging out of their experience that seem to be fairly universal. These values, also central to our democracy (see Chapter 14), can be summarized as follows: (1) respect for individual personality; (2) use of the reflective-scientific method as a basis for the solution of human problems; and (3) widening of the area of common concern through the increasing participation of all in the solution of problems.

These basic principles, which are much simpler than those of most of the other philosophies, are held by the experimentalists to be sufficient to define a point of view, but they are broad enough to be susceptible to a variety of meanings related to human experience as such experiences change through enrichment and through contact with a changing world. These assumptions are not held to be absolute but are subject to scrutiny and possible change from time to time.

Ideas on the School in Relationship to Social Change; Other Suggestions as to Curriculum and Methods

In general, the experimentalists hold it to be the school's job to help individuals to develop so as to become creative in problem-solving in line with the scientific method. The curriculum is to be selected experiences under the guidance of the teacher. The following principles of procedure in teaching, generally characteristic of experimentalists, can be listed: (1) experiential learning; (2) student participation in the selection and development of learning experiences; (3) integrated learnings; (4) individualization of the study of the child; (5) emphasis on intrinsic motivation; (6) continuous evaluation by group and self; (7) emphasis on social adjustment; (8) teaching as guidance; (9) emphasis on cultivation of problem-solving abilities; and (10) emphasis on refinement of the cultural heritage.[19]

Some of these principles are accepted also by persons holding other points of view, and, of course, individual experimentalists may well interpret them quite differently in light of their own individual experiential background. In general, these points of view do serve to define a pragmatic approach to the problems of the curriculum and methods of the school.

SCHOOLS TO DEVELOP INDIVIDUALS FOR A NEW SOCIETY BASED ON BEST SOLUTIONS TO PRESENT CONDITIONS AND TRENDS—RECONSTRUCTIONISM

The point of view called *reconstructionism* has become clearly defined only in quite recent years. Theodore Brameld, now at Boston University, has played a prominent part in its inception. Reconstructionism has stemmed from the experimentalist point of view and agrees with it in many of the basic philosophical assumptions. The reconstructionists however, have become quite impatient with the experimentalist teacher, who, they say, hesitates to take a position as a teacher with respect to a definite answer to the problems that the student faces, holding that the student must be "free" to make his own decisions.

Central Ideas Related to the Nature of Education

To the reconstructionists, the main purpose of education is to develop individuals with the ability and the desire to create the new social order now possible. The method to be used in discovering and developing the new social order is the scientific method. The school, however, must have examined available knowledge and must have arrived in advance at a pos-

---

[19] See also Ernest E. Bayles, *Pragmatism in Education* (New York: Harper, 1965).

sible solution as to the kind of society that we need in light of our present knowledge and of problems with which we are faced. The teacher then presents this solution to the student, with the evidence pro and con. The student, of course, is permitted to make his own decision with respect to whether or not he accepts or rejects the kind of society that the reconstructionist, in light of his interpretation of the evidence, has found that we need in order to deal effectively with the very crucial problems that we face.

Leading Proponents

Reconstructionism is a relatively new school of educational philosophy, and the persons who, in general, adhere to this point of view are not entirely agreed upon what should be the exact nature of the new society. Many of those listed below have not directly indicated in writing or otherwise (as far as is known) their particular adherence to it. The following people are here listed in the basis of an examination of their writings as being in general accord with this point of view: Theodore Brameld,[20] Harold Rugg, B. Othaniel Smith, Kenneth Benne, and William O. Stanley.[21] While these persons would not entirely agree on all aspects of the kind of school needed, they do agree in general that the nature of the school is determined by the urgency and the kinds of problems that we face. We must, because of the critical times in which we live, rapidly produce a new generation that will have the disposition to create the better society that our scientific knowledge indicates is needed in order to solve the problems we face.

Basic Philosophical Assumptions

The assumptions of the reconstructionist as to the nature of the world and their answers to other metaphysical problems are similar to those of the experimentalists. At times, some of them do stress the greater emphasis upon the hypothesis as a necessary determinant of the way in which we approach the solution of a problem. There is also on the part of those named, such as Harold Rugg, a greater emphasis on the esthetic and on other aspects related to the validating of knowledge or values than that of the tested experience emphasized by the experimentalists. For example, Rugg holds that an esthetic experience is intrinsically good in and of itself, rather than because it has been validated by testing its consequences for further human action.

Ideas on the School in Relationship to Social Change; Other Suggestions as to Curriculum and Method

In determining the curriculum of the school, the reconstructionists feel that teachers and others concerned with education must first examine the

[20] Theodore Brameld, *Education for the Emerging Age* (New York: Harper, 1965).
[21] William O. Stanley, *Education and Social Integration* (New York: Bureau of Publications, Teachers College, Columbia University, 1953).

facts and principles of knowledge that have been discovered by the social sciences and from them determine the kind of society we need. Then they should set up the school's curriculum in such a way as to present these facts and principles, including the "blueprint of the new society," so that the student may know what is needed to solve the social problems we face. Although the individual would be given arguments on other sides and would be permitted to choose whether or not he wanted to accept the new society, it is felt that in general he would accept the new society because it would be based upon scientific knowledge and principles. The nature of the new society is held to be readily apparent, given the facts of the situation and the facts and principles developed by the social sciences. It will be acceptable to the student if it is presented fairly to him along with the evidence. The main job of the school, then, is to prepare individuals to have the various skills needed and to know how to use the various procedures needed to bring about the new society.

Schools with Emphasis on Self-creativity and Individual Growth—Educational Laissez-faire

The point of view with emphasis on "self-creativity and individual growth" is the one labeled *educational laissez-faire* in Table 12. On the contemporary scene, this point of view does not exist in any sharply defined form. Sometimes we find it approximated among some persons who lay extreme emphasis on the child-study approach, or sometimes among those who have an extremist approach stemming originally from psychiatry (or at least from a smattering of psychology). In this point of view, there is very little emphasis upon society itself as a basis for determining the nature of the curriculum of the school. The emphasis is upon the individual child and his developmental trends. The main purpose of education is to encourage the fullest development of the individual. The stress of educational method is on individuality in the handling of pupils. There is great emphasis upon the individual's physical environment (to be sure that we have an environment that is conducive to his good development), and there is an emphasis upon trying to bring out the individual's creative expression. Particularly, there is an emphasis in opposition to positive efforts that might serve to thwart the individual's creative expression and his direction of wholesome development.

Some of the persons holding this point of view realize that the pupil does live in and grow with a dynamic, pervasive society, and do help him to understand his society and to learn to live within it. In this case, the point of view does not differ too greatly from that of experimentalists. The extreme point of view that some popular writers erroneously associate with the term "progressive education," that of "permitting a child to do as he pleases," stems philosophically from the laissez-faire point of view. This extreme point of view has been erroneously ascribed to John Dewey, even though Dewey in *Experience and Education*,[22] and Boyd Bode in *Progressive Education at the Crossroads*,[23] have clearly set forth the differences between their point of view, experimentalism, and an extreme point of view among some "progressive" educators of that time, similar to educational laissez-faire.

Experimentalism does have a very definite social philosophy in order to give it a definite direction, which Bode described as "democracy." The Progressive Education Association was organized originally by persons whose only common philosophy was a desire to move away from traditional practices. Some of them perhaps did go to extremes. In 1941, however, the society did officially adopt a philosophic point of view within the experimentalist position.[24]

EXISTENTIALISM

Existentialism as a point of view and as a well-defined system of thinking goes back to at least the nineteenth century. Some persons have held that it goes back to some aspects of Thomas Aquinas' thinking or even to Socrates and the ancient Greeks. In its more modern version, it has a great deal of acceptance among French intellectuals. It arose largely in the nineteenth century as a theological point of view in order to explain the nature of religion in a world in which scientific explanation seemed to do away with any logical basis. However, in the modern form it has two branches—a theistic and a nontheistic, or atheistic branch. John Paul Sartre is the most prominent proponent of the nontheistic branch. There are many prominent representatives of the theistic point of view. Examples are Martin Buber, Jacques Maritain, Paul Tillich, representing as they do respectively three different theological traditions, Jewish, Catholic, and Protestant.

Basically the existentialists hold that man lives in a world of despair that is bound to end up in an absurd, tragic finish. In this world in which there is no meaning to be found outside a man's own efforts to find or determine a meaning for himself, the most important thing is for man to recognize the necessity for choosing, and to accept his responsibility to live in accord with his particular choice. One cannot get the answer to one's existence from science or any other study discipline. Certainly the extent to which man has attempted to probe the meaning of existence in literature and the arts may help other persons to some extent, but basically the question comes back to one's own self, and each must finally make his own choice. What is the nature of my existence and what do I wish to become? "Existence precedes essence." We first recognize we exist; we then choose;

[22] John Dewey, *Experience and Education* (New York: Macmillan, 1938).
[23] Boyd H. Bode, *Progressive Education at the Crossroads* (New York: Newson and Co., 1938).
[24] See "Progressive Education: Its Philosophy and Challenge," *Progressive Education*, 8, No. 5 (May 1941), pp. 241–264. (Yearbook issue with special supplement.)

and then we develop into the "essence" (or nature) of our choice. This point of view has implications for education in terms of getting youngsters ready to recognize the necessity for choice and to prevent them from being pushed into conformity and standardization without facing up to the necessity for their own choice. This whole point of view is an anti-system. Consequently, there is *no* well-defined program of action for education. It is more of an attitude or temper than a programmatic point of view.[25]

PHILOSOPHICAL ANALYSIS

Philosophical analysts have some difficulty with the problem of values. For some of them, such as Ayer,[26] most value statements are nothing but expressions of the emotive feelings of the speaker. There are others, however, particularly the so-called "ordinary language" philosophical analysts, who follow the "later" Wittgenstein.[27] Wittgenstein in late life took the approach of trying to analyze what is the meaning of the speaker when he makes a "value" statement. The former attitude toward value problems makes it difficult for these analysts to determine purposes for education and, therefore, the implications of their philosophy for education. However, it can be assumed that there should be great emphasis upon the study of language, particularly on linguistics, and upon the careful use of logical analysis in exploring the subject disciplines as far as the schools are concerned. The point of view is a very rigorous, highly intellectual one, and certainly it has important implications for the school in terms of kind of subjects that would be emphasized and the approach to be used in teaching them.

It can be recognized that neither existentialism nor philosophical analysts fit into a system. Consequently they can be considered as "mavericks" as far as a systematic analysis of points of view is concerned. We will continue now with the presentation of a point of view that crosses over the lines of points of view within classifications systems, viz., the eclectic position.

ECLECTIC POINT OF VIEW

There are many persons who work in the field of education, including indeed some who are definitely students of philosophy of education, who have points of view that do not fit into the classification structure used in

25 See Van Cleve Morris, *Existentialism in Education* (New York: Harper, 1965).
26 For example, see A. J. Ayer, *Language, Truth, and Logic* (New York: Dover, n.d.), Chapter VI, p. 160.
27 George Pitcher, *The Philosophy of Wittgenstein* (Englewood Cliffs, N.J.: Prentice-Hall, 1964). Also, David Pole, *The Later Philosophy of Wittgenstein: A Short Introduction with an Epilogue by John Wisdom* (New York: Oxford University Press, 1963).

this chapter. The word *eclectic* has been frequently applied to those whose point of view does not fit into a standard philosophical position. In the first place, it should be noted that many eclectics are so classified only because they do not happen to fit into a particular structure as it has been set up by someone else. Were the structure different, they might well fit. Second, there is a sense in which all persons who have thought clearly and creatively develop ideas somewhat different from others whose general points of view are similar. This, of course, means they quite often have ideas that are also found in some other point of view. This would automatically make them "eclectics" by definition. Their particular combination of ideas may be very consistent (according to their assumptions) and may fit together into a well-coordinated point of view even though it does not fit into a "standard" classification.[28]

In a sense, each of the philosophical positions discussed in preceding sections may be "eclectic" according to one of the other points of view. If, for example, we were to ask an experimentalist how he would handle the problems of passing on the cultural heritage (in which we might be somewhat critical of his apparent lack of emphasis upon past tradition), the experimentalist would probably indicate that he had taken care of the matter because of his emphasis upon the "clarification or refinement of the cultural heritage." In other words, he would not ignore some of the things that are emphasized in other points of view; he would merely stress them in other ways. Similar questions directed at other groups, such as the place of scientific thinking for the humanist or of the importance of cultural change for the essentialist, would be answered in ways to indicate that they had taken into account that particular point but had answered it in a different way. All of them would deny that they were overlooking the emphasis of the other points of view.

All of this discussion on eclecticism indicates that each individual in a democratic society must work out his own point of view for himself in light of whatever criteria or assumptions he considers essential. In general, the point of view that the person may take will depend somewhat upon his own background of experiences. In continuously clarifying and examining his particular point of view, he will have to make his own decisions as to what *his assumptions* are. As a matter of fact, in our democratic society we stress the richness of our culture because we do have the diversity possible when each person is free to think for himself. It is not likely that in a democratic society we will ever have complete uniformity of point of view among thinking persons, unless someone enforces a single point of view from a single position of authority. The existence of such an authority is not consistent with the basic assumptions of a democratic society as seen by the authors.

[28] A third possibility, particularly for the less advanced students, is that their everyday operations are based upon conflicting philosophic assumptions not clearly revealed in the writings of the "authorities" nor clearly known to them.

SUMMARY

In this chapter there is a discussion of some of the viewpoints on what the school's role in a society in a period of rapid social change should be. Six different viewpoints were described in some detail. Some would stick to the classical tradition; some would stick to the conservation of those important elements established in the past by man's societal evolution; some would prepare students to live in current society; some would develop critically minded individuals capable of solving their own problems in a changing society; some would emphasize the schools' participation in the development of the new social order; some would limit themselves to helping individuals grow in ways in line with his own inner tendencies. Also, certain other groups would completely break with all of the above approaches. The analytical philosophers, for example, hold that the whole problem of philosophy is one of language. The existentialists, on the other hand, place the emphasis upon the necessity for each individual making his own nonrational value choice. Many persons of our society have developed some type of eclectic point of view in regard to philosophy and also to what they conceive to be the role of the school in a period of rapid social change.

SELECTED BIBLIOGRAPHY

ADLER, MORTIMER J. *The Conditions of Philosophy: Its Checkered Past, Its Present Disorder, and Its Future Promise.* New York: Atheneum, 1965. Pp. xi + 302.

AYER, ALFRED J. *Language, Truth and Logic.* New York: Dover, 1946. Pp. 160.

———. *The Problem of Knowledge.* Baltimore: Penguin, 1956. Pp. 224.

BAGLEY, WILLIAM C. *Education and Emergent Man.* New York: Nelson, 1934. Pp. xiv + 238. Bagley's best statement of his point of view. Has been discussed under "social evolutionism" in this chapter.

BAYLES, ERNEST E. *Pragmatism in Education.* New York: Harper & Row, 1965. Pp. x + 146.

BLACK, MAX (ed.). *Philosophical Analysis: A Collection of Essays.* Ithaca: Cornell University Press, 1950. Pp. 429.

BODE, BOYD H. *Democracy as a Way of Life.* New York: Macmillan, 1937. Pp. xiv + 114. A short statement on a modern view of the nature of democracy.

———. *Progressive Education at the Crossroads.* New York: Newsom, 1938. Pp. vii + 128.

BRAMELD, THEODORE. *Education as Power.* New York: Holt, Rinehart & Winston, Pp. 160. 1965.

———. *Philosophies of Education in Cultural Perspective.* New York: Holt, Rinehart & Winston. Pp. xvii + 446.

———. *Toward a Reconstructed Philosophy of Education.* New York: Holt, Rinehart & Winston. Pp. xiv + 417.

BREED, FREDERICK S. *Education and the New Realism.* New York: Macmillan, 1939. Pp. xx + 237. A clear statement of the view called "social realism" in this chapter.

BRIGGS, THOMAS HENRY. *Pragmatism and Pedagogy.* New York: Macmillan, 1940. Pp. xi + 124. A presentation of Briggs' conception of what is called "social realism" in this chapter—Briggs' concept is *not* "pragmatism" nor "experimentalism" as used in this chapter.

BROUDY, HARRY SAMUEL. *Building a Philosophy of Education,* Second Edition. Englewood Cliffs, N.J.: Prentice-Hall, 1961.

BRUBACHER, JOHN S. (ed.). *Eclectic Philosophy of Education: A Book of Readings,* Second Edition. Englewood Cliffs, N.J.: Prentice-Hall, 1962. Pp. viii + 560.

————. *Modern Philosophies of Education,* Third Edition. New York: McGraw-Hill, 1962. Pp. ix + 373. A presentation of contemporary concepts in American educational philosophy.

BURNS, HOBERT W., and CHARLES J. BRAUNER, (ed.). *Philosophy of Education Essays and Commentaries.* New York: Ronald Press, 1962. Pp. xiii + 442.

————. *Problems in Education and Philosophy.* Englewood Cliffs, N.J.: Prentice-Hall, 1965. Pp. 160.

BUTLER, J. DONALD. *Four Philosophies and Their Practice in Education and Religion,* Revised Edition. New York: Harper & Row, 1957. Pp. xvii + 618.

BUTLER, R. J. (ed.). *Analytical Philosophy.* New York: Barnes & Noble, 1962. Pp. vi + 235.

BUTTS, R. FREEMAN. *A Cultural History of Western Education: Its Social and Intellectual Foundations,* Second Edition. New York: McGraw-Hill, 1955. Pp. xii + 645.

————, and LAURENCE A. CREMIN. *A History of Education in American Culture.* New York: Holt, Rinehart & Winston, 1953. Pp. xii + 628.

CHILDS, JOHN L. *American Pragmatism and Education: An Interpretation and Criticism.* New York: Holt, Rinehart & Winston, 1956. Pp. x + 373. A comprehensive survey of pragmatism and its implications for education.

————. *Education and Morals.* New York: Appleton-Century-Crofts, 1950. Pp. xiv + 287. One of the most recent and the clearest, especially as related to the problems of morals, presentation of the experimentalist view.

————. *Education and Philosophy of Experimentalism.* New York: Appleton-Century-Crofts, 1931. Pp. xix + 264. A careful examination of the assumptions underlying experimentalism.

DEWEY, JOHN, *Democracy and Education.* New York: Macmillan, 1931. Pp. xiii + 434. A reprint of Dewey's famous classic—originally published in 1916.

————. *Experience and Education.* New York: Macmillan, 1938. Pp. xii + 116. A philosophic statement of the nature of experience as related to the means and the goals of education. A criticism of certain extremes in progressivism.

————. *Reconstruction in Philosophy.* New York: New American Library, 1953. Pp. 168. One of Dewey's clearest presentations of his philosophy.

GALLAGHER, DONALD, and IDELLA GALLAGHER, (eds.). *The Education of Man: The Educational Philosophy of Jacques Maritain.* Garden City, N.Y.: Doubleday, 1962. Pp. 191.

GRENE, MARJORIE. *Introduction to Existentialism.* Chicago: University of Chicago Press, 1962. Pp. viii + 149.

HOOK, SIDNEY. *Education for Modern Man: A New Perspective.* New York: Knopf, 1963. Pp. 235.

JUDD, CHARLES H. *Education and Social Progress.* New York: Harcourt, Brace & World, 1934. Pp. xii + 285. Judd's best statement of the point of view of what has been called "social evolutionism" in this chapter.

JUSTMAN, JOSEPH. *Theories of Secondary Education in the United States.* New York: Teachers College, Columbia University, 1940. Pp. viii + 481. The original piece of research used as a primary basis for the classification system of this chapter.

KELLY, EARL C., and MARIE I. RASEY. *Education and the Nature of Man.* New York: Harper & Row, 1952. Pp. xi + 209. Builds a philosophy of education on the nature of man as revealed by the biological and social sciences. Basically realist but ends with concepts very similar to experimentalism.

KIMBALL, SOLON T., and JAMES E. MCCLELLAN. *Education and the New America.* New York: Random House and Knopf, 1962. Pp. xiv + 44.

KNELLER, GEORGE F. *Existentialism and Education.* New York: Philosophical Library, 1958. Pp. x + 170.

————. *Introduction to the Philosophy of Education.* New York: Wiley, 1964. Pp. viii + 137.

LERNER, MAX. *Education and a Radical Humanism.* (Kappa Delta Pi Lecture Series, Vol. xxxiii.) Columbus, Ohio: Ohio State University Press, 1962. Pp. 63. Notes toward a theory of the educational crisis.

MARCEL, GABRIEL. *The Philosophy of Existentialism.* Second edition. New York: Citadel, 1962. Pp. 128.

MARITAIN, JACQUES. *Education at the Crossroads.* New Haven: Yale University Press, 1943. Pp. x + 120. The point of view of a lay religious humanist— a brilliant Catholic existentialist.

MEAD, MARGARET. *The School in American Culture.* Cambridge, Mass.: Harvard University Press, 1951. Pp. 48.

MORRIS, VAN CLEVE. *Existentialism in Education: What It Means.* New York: Harper & Row, 1966. Pp. x + 163.

————. *Philosophy and the American School.* Boston: Houghton Mifflin, 1961. Pp. xix + 492. An introduction to the philosophy of education.

N.E.A., EDUCATIONAL POLICIES COMMISSION. *The Central Purpose of American Education.* Washington, D.C.: National Education Association, 1961. Pp. 21.

————. *Moral and Spiritual Values in the Public Schools.* Washington, D.C.: National Education Association, 1951. Pp. xi + 100. Defines commonly agreed-upon values of American democracy as a way of life. Stresses the role of the school in transmitting to youth an intelligent and fervent loyalty to those moral and ethical principles that have made America great.

PHENIX, PHILIP H. (ed.). *Philosophies of Education.* New York: Wiley, 1961. Pp. vi + 137.

PITCHER, GEORGE. *The Philosophy of Wittgenstein.* Englewood Cliffs, N.J.: Prentice-Hall, 1964. Pp. xi + 340.

POLE, DAVID. *The Later Philosophy of Wittgenstein: A Short Introduction with an Epilogue by John Wisdom.* New York: Oxford University Press, 1963. Pp. 132.

REID, LOUIS ARNAUD. *Philosophy and Education: An Introduction.* New York: Random House, 1965. Pp. xv + 203.

SCHEFFLER, ISRAEL (ed.). *Philosophy and Education: Modern Readings.* Boston: Allyn & Bacon, 1958. Pp. ix + 311. Selection of readings tends toward analytical philosophy.

SMITH, PHILIP G. *Philosophy of Education: Introductory Studies.* New York: Harper & Row, 1965. Pp. x + 276.

SODERQUIST, HAROLD O. *The Person and Education: A New Approach to Philosophy of Education for Democracy.* Columbus, Ohio: Merrill, 1964. Pp. vii + 200.

SPAULDING, FRANCIS T. *High School and Life: Report of the Regents Inquiry.* New York: McGraw-Hill, 1938. Pp. xvii + 377.

STANLEY, WILLIAM O. *Education and Social Integration.* New York: Bureau of Publications, Teachers College, Columbia University, 1953. Pp. xi + 290. An excellent presentation of the implications of our society and societal problems and the type of education needed—from a point of view closely akin to reconstructionism.

THUT, I. N. *The Story of Education: Philosophical and Historical Foundations.* New York: McGraw-Hill, 1957. Pp. x + 410.

WAHLQUIST, JOHN T. *The Philosophy of American Education.* New York: Ronald Press, 1942. Pp. xiv + 407. A very readable presentation of the efforts in American Educational philosophy; uses the idealist, realist, pragmatic classification. Has some very well-chosen quotes.

WHITE, WINSTON. *Beyond Conformity.* New York: Free Press of Glencoe, 1961. Pp. 230.

WINGO, G. MAX. *The Philosophy of American Education.* Boston: Heath, 1965. Pp. 438.

WYNNE, JOHN PETER. *Theories of Education: An Introduction to the Foundations of Education.* New York: Harper & Row, 1963. Pp. xiii + 521.

SELECTED FILMS

Philosophies of Education Series (NET) 29 min ea.
  An Experimentalist Approach to Education
  The Classical Realist Approach to Education
  Education for Life Adjustment
  Education as Intellectual Discipline
  Education for Psychological Maturity
  Education for Moral Character
  Protestant Philosophy of Education
  A Roman Catholic View of Education

A Jewish View of Education
Education for Cultural Conservation
Education for Cultural Reconstruction
Education for National Survival
Education for a Free Society

Chapter 16. *The School's Role in Social Change*

In this final chapter, the authors draw together the ideas that have been brought out throughout the book into an over-all conception of the role of the school in an era of social change. The authors realize that many times their conclusion with respect to an issue is only one of several possible conclusions. It is also their contention that the contrasting philosophical conceptions that have been set up in Chapter 15 constitute only one aspect of the problem of choice. This book has been written primarily in the field of educational sociology and social foundations of education. It has therefore stressed material drawn largely from the social sciences. Decision-making with respect to the program of the school, as far as it is based upon sound scholarship, may be founded upon three bases:

1. Philosophy, the scholarly area, to assist in the clarification of the values that must be used by any institution in designing its program.
2. Sociology and the other social sciences, to give an understanding of our culture and of the nature of human civilization in order to help in the appropriate selection of pertinent subject matter.
3. Psychology, to provide better understanding of the learner and the learning process.

The suggestions that the authors make in this chapter are based on all three of these foundational fields.

Schools as Related to Their Societies

We have noted in Chapter 3 that the institution called the school tends to reflect the type of society in which it is found. There were times in the history of education when the school tended to reflect merely one of many

516

prevalent points of view in its culture. As a matter of fact, it did so more frequently than not in the period prior to the development of the common school. In pre-Christian societies, when the school was largely in the hands of the priestly class, it tended to reflect the point of view of that class. This was also true during the Middle Ages, the period of the dominance of institutional Christianity. Later, the humanistic ideas of the Renaissance and of the periods immediately following tended to reflect the social points of view of the ruling class—the intellectual or other forms of an elite class. This limitation of the extent to which all of society was represented in the school's purposes were primarily due to the fact that the privilege of education was limited to a small segment of persons of the culture, rather than to any deliberate attempt to indoctrinate all persons of the culture with a particular restricted point of view.

It is important to note that the methodology of the school, in contrast with the restrictive nature of its curriculum and its population, tended to reflect the prevailing point of view in society toward children and toward learning. Examples of issues: whether or not the society in general encouraged creativity, and whether or not there was rigid discipline. For example, in the early period of the Renaissance, with its general concern for man and emphasis on this world, there tended to be a greater trend toward creativity and toward gentleness in discipline than there was in the period of the Protestant Reformation. In the latter period there was a very rigid attitude toward the child, which reflected the strict moral point of view of the Protestant culture in which the school was found.

The Lag of the School Behind Society

We have already pointed out in Chapter 2 and 3 the nature of the lag of the school behind society. As soon as the school became institutionalized, it was inevitable that a lag would appear. There is, moreover, an additional factor toward producing a lag in the case of the school, as compared with other institutions, for the school has always had a "conservator" function—that of preserving the ideals of a culture, particularly in periods of stress. This means that, by and large, the school is fearful of experimentation and the public is afraid to have it experiment. Because the school is dealing with the youthful and the immature, society is very careful to have it teach only the tested and tried. There is a fear, culturally originating when society was prone to instability and new ideas tended to upset the stability, that the young might take up the new ideas too quickly or go off on some tangent that would be detrimental to society.

This fear has a very real basis in fact today. Our technological and economic progress has far outstripped our philosophic and governmental progress. Physical inventions have revolutionized modern life. Social inventions are few in number and slow of acceptance. Many people justly feel that some educators, impatient with the rapidly growing lag between social and material progress, may indoctrinate the young with hastily formed panaceas for our social ills.

As a matter of fact, according to almost all points of view, the school *does have* a conservator function. Any society that develops an institution such as the school would require that it transmit the universals of the culture; that is, those elements that various groups within the culture agree upon at any given time. If the school did not have such a function, the society would disintegrate rapidly and a new and perhaps drastically different society would develop. Most points of view (except a most revolutionary one, such as anarchism) would certainly agree that the stability of a society is at least partially assured when the various agencies of the society assist it in passing on the important elements of its cultural heritage. Many of the items listed in Chapter 14 are matters of agreement in our culture, and one of the important jobs of the school should be to help the boys and girls of our schools to understand clearly the nature of these ideas. There are many aspects of our culture that are not ideological in nature but that do represent the best of the past in terms of skilled ways of solving certain problems. An example of this might be the use of the Arabic number system in preference to the Roman number system. A negative example, in Western culture, is the preference not to use the abacus in actual computation. Other examples in all literate cultures would be grammatical usage and spelling. There are few or no questions about these particular points, and it is obvious that the school should play an important part in the transmission of these knowledges and skills.

On the other hand, there is certainly no well-developed point of view that would have the school teach patterns of behavior found in a society but generally recognized as deteriorative, even though such may be known to exist and even though they may be somewhat apologetically tolerated by the society. An example would be the institution of gambling. It is not likely that the adherents of any of the philosophic points of view would advocate that the school deliberately teach youngsters better ways of gambling. There are other aspects of our culture that, although tolerated by the society, are not usually recognized as falling within the scope of the school. The school has, in other words, a selective function in transmitting only the best elements of our culture to the young and immature.

Because of its institutional nature, then, and also because persons of many points of view explicitly hold the primary role of the school to be the preservation and passing on of the social heritage, the school has always tended to lag behind society in periods of change. This lag is not only in the facts, skills, values, and ideas taught but also in the methods of working with boys and girls. It has already been pointed out that in the early period of American history, when ideas of democracy were prevalent on the frontier (such as, "one man is as good as another," in the Jacksonian epoch), the schools were still operating on a highly autocratic basis. The schoolmaster was to be carefully checked before employment to see whether his ideas were in accord with the prevailing mores of the community. In the strict discipline of the schools of that day, the schoolmaster's word was law, and he was never expected to brook any questioning, in any way, of what he said, not only with respect to discipline but also with respect to what he taught. As the predetermined spokesman for the community, then, his word was to be respected as authority by the child.

The Role of the School in a Democratic (Nonauthoritarian) Society

Before we can discuss what the nature of the school ought to be in a democratic (nonauthoritarian) society, we have to be clear as to the nature of such a society. As shown in Chapter 14, there are many differences in points of view as to what constitutes democracy. Perhaps this is rightly so. One of the characteristics of a democractic society is that there apparently is no authoritative source other than the universals of the culture itself that can set forth a single, unchallengeable, definite point of view. There should be a wide range of ideas competing for attention at any time in the democratic society, even ideas about the fundamental nature of democracy itself, in order for the term to have real meaning. However, so that there can be communication among the different groups, those ideas should center around some agreed-upon key concepts. We have pointed out in Chapter 14 what some of those concepts might well be. Central among them are (1) the respect for the personality of the individual; (2) the use of the scientific method in solving a problem; (3) the widening of the areas of common concern.[1]

At this time we shall discuss fully only the first of these points, because it is most pertinent to the topic at hand. The respect for the individual personality in the democratic society means that each person has a right to propose ideas in accordance with his own thinking. At any given time, however, the majority point of view does prevail as far as action is concerned. This means that the overt actions of the individual must be in accord with the majority point of view, to learn how to think constructively, to obtain necessary data, and to be able to handle other points of view. If the school is to be thought of as an institution to aid the society in perpetuating itself, and if one of the characteristics of a democratic society is its ability to change peacefully, then the school might have some part to play in enabling people to bring about necessary changes in an intelligent fashion. This would definitely mean that the role of the school in a democratic (or nonauthoritarian) society would be quite different

[1] Cf. Chapter 14, pp. 465–469.

from that in an authoritarian society, where only one official point of view could be promulgated by any of the existing institutions.

The Meaning of the School as an "Agent of Society"

Ever since the school has existed as a separate institution in any culture, it has been an agent of that culture in order to carry out its values. In the days when the schools were either private enterprises charging tuition, or philanthropic enterprises, they existed almost as much in the capacity of agents of their society as in the present day when the public schools are legally authorized and established as a function of government. The various agencies of government have developed in society as devices for carrying out many activities beyond the scope of the individual or even of the large corporation or labor union. The decision as to whether to make the school a public institution offering education free to all persons was debated over a considerable period of time, and many points were not immediately clarified. Eventually it became clear that the decision for the free public school *definitely* made the school *an agent of society*. When education became compulsory, even more did the school become an agent of its society for the carrying out of certain ideas and principles that that particular society had established for itself.

Once having established the proposition that the school is an agent of society, we must then define its meaning. Certainly there are very few persons who would conceive the meaning of that proposition to be that the school must do the exact bidding of society only in those specific terms in which society itself can see the job to be done. It would be difficult to justify the use of specialized professional people with skilled backgrounds, or even the necessity for a separate institution such as a school, if it were not to offer some kind of leadership as the agent of society in doing the job that society wants done. We might present here an analogy from the field of law. If it were the job of a lawyer employed by, let us say, a businessman merely to carry out the purposes and the conception of the law as seen by the businessman (in other words, to operate purely as a technician, a hireling employed by the businessman), it is difficult to see what his special function as an agent would be. Lawyers are to interpret the law as it is and to advise the businessmen on the results of proposed future courses. We employ persons with professional abilities to help us so that we can take advantage of the special training, experiences, and other types of background they may have, in order to lead or guide us in the solution of our problems.

If we examine the various points of view described in Chapter 15, we can see that each interpretation of the role of the school is quite different. The neo-humanist (or perennialist) conceives of the main job of education as the development of the intellect and the transmission of the great ideas (unchanging ideas) of the past, so that they will be thoroughly understood by at least the elite of the present generation; he could not conceive of the school being limited by the vision of the present state of knowledge of the society in which it is found. The school must stand as a beacon light guiding and leading the society toward new goals, even those that the society may not conceive. The basic principles that are envisioned by the neo-humanists are not necessarily those that are customarily found among the prevailing ideas in our body politic.

The social evolutionists (or essentialists), with their emphasis upon the job of the school as the passing on of those things that have been found essential in the past, do not think their job is limited to passing on those things that are necessarily prevailing in the culture at any given time. As a matter of fact, they emphasize the importance of the school as an agency to preserve the culture against some of its own defects—such as forgetfulness of the essentials of the past and the tendency to be carried away by the exigencies of the moment.

The social realists would perhaps come closest to considering the school as an agent of society in the simpler sense. Certainly, to most social realists, the values that the school should be teaching are those that are prevailing in the culture. However, scientific research, which is not always available to the culture itself, may be needed to determine the best methods to carry out these values. Sometimes the body politic does not know the best method of carrying out the values that it does express. However, it is difficult to find social realists who envision any kind of a concept of the school as the agent of society in the sense of helping to achieve new social values, or to clarify present values at least in terms of the means of arriving at those values.

The experimentalists, of course, do conceive of the job of the school quite definitely as being one of developing critical-minded thinkers and thereby persons who will exercise creative leadership at all levels. The school in this sense is definitely an agency of society. It is an agent of society in its own development, for example, by improving the methods and procedures that are used by the individuals of that society in clarifying their values and in carrying out those values. Sometimes, when individuals are helped to clarify their values and are encouraged to carry them out, they may arrive at values that are not those commonly accepted by our population. Most new ideas originate as minority ideas, and sometimes they are vigorously challenged by the majority point of view, which quite often wishes to oppose the new ideas that arise. Even though the experimentalist may thus be in the position of trying to lead society in a direction in which it does not wish to go, the experimentalist would deny that he has any kind of fixed values (preconceived notions) in mind to which he is trying to lead society against its will. In the first place, he conceives of the values he holds as subject constantly to further critical study, not as absolutes—

as many other views do. Second, he thinks that the central values that he holds are those that have clearly emerged in our democratic culture. Furthermore, he thinks the school that will produce the intelligent, critically minded individual is the school that exemplifies best the values held dear in our democratic culture. Consequently, as long as the school is helping people to clarify their values and to develop scientific-reflective ways to achieve them, without furnishing any preconceived answers to the problems that we face as individuals, as small groups, or as a total society, it would not be in conflict with a democratic conception of the school as an agent of our society.

The reconstructionists are most concerned about a new interpretation of the proposition that the school is an agent of society. We are living, say the reconstructionists, in an age of crisis. As a matter of fact, the crisis is so acute that, unless we quickly bring to bear upon the solution of our problems the knowledge and understanding we already possess, we are in danger of losing our civilization. One of the ways in which society organizes itself, in order to be able to utilize the new data arising from the social sciences and other sources and bring them to bear upon a solution of our problems, is through the creation of the institution called the school. In this institution the young can be brought face to face with facts from the social sciences. These facts, say the reconstructionists, indicate very definitely certain positive solutions to the problems we face. These solutions should be clarified and presented by the teachers, together with the supporting facts and arguments as the answers to the problems we face; and the students should be guided in their study of the proposed solutions to recognize them as the best-supported alternatives. This position does not call for blind indoctrination. We live in a democratic society, and the students should study the existing or possible alternative points of view to the solutions proposed. However, it is the view of the reconstructionists that the teacher should take a position as to the answers that, they say, the facts quite definitely indicate. To summarize, the reconstructionist point of view is that the school as an agent of society should help society to accomplish that thing that it is not able to do by itself—namely its own reconstruction. The school guides the growth of society in the light of the most advanced knowledge we have and helps the new generation to understand and interpret that knowledge in the light of certain rather definite answers as to the solution of the problems that our society faces.

Persons holding the laissez-faire view are usually not too much concerned about the school as an agent of society, save perhaps in the sense in which the school is trying to help each individual to his own best self-realization. The existentialists are not so much concerned with social philosophy as they are with the individual and the necessity for choice. Neither are the writings of philosophical analysts greatly concerned with social philosophy.

THE SCHOOLS AND CONTROVERSIAL ISSUES

One of the questions faced by the school is the extent to which there should be discussion of controversial issues—issues such as those discussed earlier in this book. No major philosophical point of view would deny the place of controversial issues in the school upon the basis of any kind of restriction of the teacher's academic freedom. If there are differences of opinion among American philosophies of education, they follow from differences in their premises as to the function of the school and from differences in their relative emphases. All of these philosophical points of view would accord to the teacher the same right as that of any citizen in stating his viewpoint, both in the classroom and out. But certainly several of them would think it educationally undesirable for the teacher to use his classroom for the promotion of a partisan point of view with respect to some of the major controversial issues in our society.

In the case of the humanists, since the emphasis is upon either the great ideas that have come down to us from the past or on the content and organization of the subject-matter disciplines, there is no immediate critical need to look at the problem of controversial issues, unless we begin to suggest or talk about some of the implications of these ideas toward the solution of the problems we face. Robert Hutchins, the leading proponent of neo-humanism at the college level, has been outspoken in regard to many issues we have faced, in some cases taking what would be a minority and unpopular view. However, this is his right as a citizen, not merely his right as an educator. Hutchins' statements on academic freedom are among the strongest that have been made by anyone in the profession.[2] However, the main emphasis in the school curriculum, as Hutchins and others of his point of view would maintain, should not be upon the clarification of controversial issues as such, but upon the development of the intellect and the training in rational methods of thought that would enable at least the leaders of our country to think through clearly the basic nature of issues involved in our controversies. Emphasis upon the controversial issues themselves might cause us to overlook the more basic ideas—the principles and values—that lie behind them.

The emphasis of the social evolutionists on passing on the essentials of our social heritage causes them to have little concern with current events or with controversial issues in our society.

As we have seen, the realists differ among themselves with respect to the importance of controversial issues. Some tend to ignore them and to emphasize cultural agreements without too much attention to the problems within our society. Particularly do they emphasize those things established

---

[2] Statements by Hutchins can be found in many references. E.g., see Robert M. Hutchins, "Are Our Teachers Afraid to Teach?" *Bulletin, American Association of University Professors*, **40**, No. 2, Summer, 1954, pp. 202–208. This was written after he became associated with the Ford Foundation.

by means of the scientific method, conceived in its more rigid sense. Others of the realists, however, have felt that one of the things demanded of us in our present society is to handle the many controversies that rage at any given time; therefore, we must have instruction in our schools on the handling of controversial issues. This includes the development of skills in the collection and verification of data, in the utilization of data in the development of hypotheses, in the testing of hypotheses, and in the application of tentative conclusions. The persons who hold this latter point of view among the realists would advocate practices and experiences in the schools that would not differ greatly from those of the experimentalists.

The experimentalists feel that helping the student in the solution of his problems is the main purpose of the school. Consequently, the school must help him tackle all kinds of issues and problems, both those that he faces as an individual and those that society as a whole faces. The freedom to consider and to tackle controversial issues is essential to that type of school. The school itself does not take any particular side with respect to these controversial matters, but helps the child (as in the case of the second form of realism just discussed) to formulate his ideas, to test them, and to apply them.

The reconstructionists believe that controversial issues should be carefully discussed, and that the answers determined by the facts and understandings given to us by the social sciences should be set before the child, so he can see what the possibilities are in terms of the new society thus indicated.

If we are going to teach controversial issues in our schools, there are questions that may arise as to the ways in which the teaching should be handled. One of the questions is: What constitutes a controversial issue? Some things are controversial in some communities, whereas they are not in some others. Some things are controversial to some persons, whereas they are not to others. An example of the first is certain facets of the theory of biological evolution. An example of the second is the bacterial theory of disease, which is not accepted by Christian Scientists (perhaps among others). What constitutes a controversial issue? A rough working definition might well be: A controversial issue is one on which sizeable groups of a given community have taken different sides. There should be added to this, of course, cases where an entire community may take one side, but where the issue is still controversial in our society; this may occur where another view toward which the evidence may strongly point is not even considered by anyone in that particular community as a conceivably correct answer to the problem. Such an issue would be controversial, even though not so recognized in a particular community.

Another question is: What shall the teacher do in respect to revealing his own particular point of view on a controversial issue? If we are going to teach controversial issues in a democratic society, we should without question present all sides of the problem fairly. The reconstructionists, who believe that the teacher must have and present a point of view of his own, agree also to this. If the teacher must have a point of view, do the pupils have a right to know at some time during the discussion of an issue what his point of view is, or should he conceal it from them? If the teacher does give the student his point of view, at what point in the educational process should he do so—at the beginning, somewhere along the line of discussion, or at the end? Quite often, if the teacher gives his answer too early, it tends to stifle the thinking process. On the other hand, if he never reveals his viewpoint he has abdicated his position of leadership. Very few teachers do so; either consciously or otherwise, their own professional judgment as to the "correct" answers channel the thinking of the group into the "desired" directions.

Questions such as these have either not been fully and clearly answered by the philosophies discussed in this chapter, or are matters concerning which there is no agreement within any particular school of philosophy. Some of the points raised here are susceptible to research, and they call for it. The question for research might well be stated: What are the best ways of teaching controversial issues for the most effective development of clear thinking and critical-minded individuals with a will to action based upon sound moral and ethical principles as well as a will to think and to talk about the problems they are facing?

The Freedom of the Teacher—Limits and Responsibility

One of the implications that flow from the fact that we live in a free, democratic society is the right of the teacher, both as a citizen and as a professionally trained person, to be as free as possible with respect to what he teaches and the method he uses in teaching. Of course, on the other hand, when an individual accepts responsibility as a teacher, he assumes certain obligations and responsibilities and certain limits must be placed upon his freedom because of the nature of his position. However, let us first discuss his right to freedom as a citizen and as a professional leader. The following quotation, taken from a statement prepared by a committee of the Philosophy of Education Society, is only one of many in this issue that are consistent with the nature of our democratic society and its best traditions:[3]

Consequently, the freedom to inquire is a public necessity. Our society will be renewed not by those who know no other way to live, but only by those who, knowing others, prefer the democratic way. Thus the rights to inquire,

[3] A. Stafford Clayton, Chairman, and others, "A Statement by the Philosophy of Education Society" (pamphlet). Printed for the Society by the Journal Press, Columbia, Mo., n.d. Used by permission.

to hear, to speak, are not rights we hold privately, but rights we share in common through our citizenship. . . .

A democratic people puts its trust in procedures that provide a hearing for contending beliefs and the weighing of different ideas. Anything which prevents or restricts the process of public inquiry and free communications of ideas interferes with the process by which the people decide what is good in every aspect of their life. In this manner, they seek to improve the institutions which serve them. . . .

It is the obligation of a democratic community to provide the maximum opportunity for the full, free, and responsible exchange of ideas on matters of public concern.

There are, of course, limitations even to the freedom of speech of the citizen. The citizen is not free to make slanderous statements with respect to other persons in our society, statements that would be damaging to his character or reputation, unless they are true. A person is not permitted to make obscene or degrading remarks in an excessive manner that would tend to endanger public morals. A person may not use his freedom of speech to make threats against the lives of public officials or others in our democracy. All of these restrictions, which apply to citizens in general, apply also to teachers in their lives as citizens.

When a teacher accepts a position in a school, he has become in effect an official for the carrying out of certain obligations that government has assumed. This being the case, there are certain limitations on the freedom of the teacher in the classroom that do not apply to him outside the classroom. First and foremost, the teacher must not use his classroom for the promulgation of a partisan point of view. The school must belong to all the people and must be an open forum for ideas. Second, in the discussion of controversial issues, the teacher must also take into account the maturity level of the pupils with whom he works. Although there are many matters of controversy that can be taken up as early as the preschool or kindergarten age (such as how we get along with each other, how we treat persons who serve us, such as the mailman, the policeman, and the fireman), some of the issues that we face are of such complex nature that they have little meaning for young children or involve emotions that would be somewhat disturbing to them. The teacher must use his professional knowledge and wisdom in choosing the topics and the methods under which he discusses topics of a controversial nature within the particular community.

The question as to the rights and responsibilities of the teacher in the classroom immediately gives rise to a further question as to the selection of the kind of person who can adequately teach in the public school in a changing social order. The immediate question might well be: What shall we do about teachers who are not sympathetic to our democratic social order? An immediate case in point in our society is that of the Communist teacher. One of the prerequisites for a teacher given academic freedom in the classroom is the provision that he be free to examine all the evidence and draw his own conclusions, whatever they may be. If it can be ascertained that the teacher is sworn in advance to arrive at only certain predetermined conclusions, then one may seriously question his competence as a teacher leading a group in the consideration of all sides of controversial issues. Increasingly in our society, it is becoming recognized that a person who is a member of the American Communist Party is not for the most part free, under his obligations to the party, to pursue each problem wherever it may lead. As has been pointed out by many, including Sidney Hook, persons who are members of the Communist Party are members of a conspiracy that is committed to bringing about a change of government, not by persuasive democratic action but by overthrowing the existing government by whatever techniques or methods are necessary.

There are others in our society who are blinded by prejudice or some other type of preconceived notion toward certain definite conclusions on some controversial issues. Unless it can be proved that this is part of a conspiracy in order to change our way of life, the evidence of such prejudice per se should not disqualify the person from teaching. But it is obvious from our discussion that persons not able to examine all of the data and to look at them without prejudice do not make the kind of teachers we need in a changing society. It should be equally obvious that the teacher, as an agent of society, is responsible for loyalty to those basic principles upon which the society is founded.

THE PROCESS OF DETERMINING EDUCATIONAL OBJECTIVES

Although the local boards of education throughout the United States have been given the legal responsibility for determining the policies of the school, in a democratic society this means that the policies should be broad enough to permit discretion on the part of the professional staff, in order to develop a school program consistent with its educational philosophy, with the particular problems in the community, and with the group of children in the particular school. The fact that we live in a democratic society means that we should give as much freedom as possible to the individual teacher to carry out, according to his best thinking in the light of the values that he has clarified according to his educational philosophy, what seems best to do for the boys and girls in his particular room, within the framework of those cultural values consistent with the American democratic social order.

Educational groups at all levels, including official and nonofficial groups, have set up statements of purposes, or goals, for education. The authors hold, however, that such statements are of little value unless the persons most concerned in the educative process, the teachers, accept these goals and carry them out. The only point where learning takes place in the school is the point where teacher and child meet. Any statements promulgated from a central source without being wholly accepted in all their implications are of very little value.

Statements concerning educational values usually are not accepted unless the persons who are going to use them—in this case, the teachers—have participated in developing them. This seems to imply that those teachers who work together in a face-to-face situation in a building should work together in setting up their educational objectives and policies, within limitations posed by the general policies of their particular school district. Since we have already noted that persons (teachers and laymen alike) differ widely with respect to their conceptions of the school's purposes and of the curriculum, and with respect to some of their basic philosophical assumptions, how then can teachers get together on a set of objectives?

Since all the teachers live and work in a democratic society, it is assumed that on the operational level there will be many more points on which they agree than on which they disagree. It is also assumed that, when the group members think through their problems together, there may be sizeable areas of agreement at the operational level, even though the various group members may be drawing their implications from differing philosophical assumptions. Now if there are some areas of school policy within the building on which a decision has to be made but on which no unanimous opinion appears possible, it may be necessary to operate on administrative edict based on a consensus of opinion.[4] The settling of matters by the faculty of a school, of course, is to be done only with respect to problems that have been left to its discretion by its board of education.[5] Boards of education by and large should leave as much discretion as possible to the teachers working in a face-to-face situation in a local school building.

After common agreement on some problems has been reached and certain other matters settled by a majority vote, areas of disagreement or differing preferences may still remain. The authors envision a school where a teacher would be free to operate (within the limits indicated earlier in this section) to work with his children in accordance with his own values. Authority to define these areas of freedom is vested in the school administration, through policy statements of the board of education. In

[4] Most school administrators recognize that not all teachers are equally capable, but that "weighting" of votes is unfeasible; therefore, consensus of professional opinion may be the preferred basis for operation, rather than the formal vote. Such tentative decisions on the operational basis may provide time for further educational leadership by the administration in terms of in-service training of the staff.

[5] In such matters, responsibility for the decision is vested in the individual school administrator. He should encourage staff participation in decision-making—but be prepared to accept sole responsibility for the consequences of the decisions.

working with his children, the teacher should seek to get all information possible from all the sources available, including his administrators, fellow teachers, board of education, state department of education, and professional organizations. The important point to stress here is the final responsibility of the teacher for putting into action the values to which he has tentatively agreed on the basis of his understanding of the nature of our culture. A good teacher should continue the clarification and reclarification of those values in the light of any changes that may come about in our culture, and of new research in child growth and development and in the psychology of learning. This position is predicated upon the development of a teaching staff with training and abilities more nearly comparable with the training and abilities of the other professions. Among other things, this implies improvement in both the quantity and the quality of teacher training offered in our teachers' colleges and universities. It implies also an upgrading of selective teacher-recruitment policies and increased emphasis upon in-service training of our present teachers. Professional teachers will demonstrate by their abilities the right to ever-increasing freedom in working with children in accordance with values dynamically derived and modified by the teacher.

A Summary of Social Facts, Trends, and Problems

The authors now draw together some of the important information and data that have been collected in this book and indicate some of the possible future actions that seem to be indicated for the school by these data. First, let us summarize some of the important facts, trends, and problems found in Chapters 1 through 13.

Information that has been rapidly accumulating from the social sciences, particularly sociology, social anthropology, and psychology, have indicated the all-important place of culture in the formation of the characteristics of a human being. There have been no important changes in the biological nature of man for some 20,000 to 25,000 years. The changes are primarily those of culture. Man, born with a plastic nervous system, is able to absorb the changing aspects of his culture and thus keep up with whatever advances have been made in previous years.

A study of man's social evolution from the first development of simple societies reveals several distinct stages: (1) the stage of the nonliterate man, where only such culture as could be passed on directly could be sustained; (2) the stage of the Oriental-type culture, where a relatively high degree of civilization had been reached, bulwarked by opposition to change or progress; (3) the stage of Western civilization, with its central theme of progress, the latter stages of which have been centered on concepts of democracy, the use of the scientific method, and the application of improved technology; and (4) the possibility of a new stage of modern man, which would be based completely upon man's use of his own intelligence through the scientific method toward the solution of the problems he faces.

The school, however, did not exist as an institution among many of the nonliterate peoples; the function of education was performed by the tribe as a whole. The school eventually developed as a separate institution to do certain things that the tribe could not do. As an institution, it has reflected the fundamental nature of the culture in which it is found. However, it has typically lagged behind the culture and has not often provided leadership toward the improvement of that culture. It has acted primarily as a conservative factor in the culture, preserving those things that might otherwise be lost and doing certain specialized jobs, such as the teaching of literary skills.

An analysis of the cultural characteristics of America in recent times has revealed twelve rather outstanding characteristics which can be summarized concisely under twelve headings:

1. Development of Atomic Energy and Automation.
2. Increased Leisure Time Made Possible by Technological Efficiency.
3. Social Lag of Institutions Behind Material Changes.
4. Increased Necessity for Cooperative Action.
5. Increased Necessity for Long-range Planning.
6. Increased Social Control and Increasing Remoteness of Social Control.
7. Increased Need for Specialization.
8. Increasing Differentiation in Providing for Individuals.
9. Weakening of Traditional Controls over Human Conduct.
10. Increased Strains and Tensions.
11. Population Explosion.
12. America in a Position of World Leadership.

In spite of these enormous changes taking place in American culture, there are certain persistent values that are characteristic of our culture and that serve to distinguish it from other cultures and also to give it a certain stability. One of the jobs of the school certainly ought to be to help boys and girls to understand the nature of these accepted values and to apply them to problems they face.

Among the serious social problems we are facing are those related to the economic factors of our society. Spurred on by the use of the scientific method, one of the over-all impelling factors in American social change is the rapid advance in technology. This technology, coupled with changes in the structure of American industry, is bringing about enormous changes in our economic life. We have undergone basic changes from a theoretically laissez-faire society to a complex mixture of corporation capitalism, state capitalism, socialism, and cooperatives. We still face many serious problems of an economic nature. We have not yet solved the problems of the business cycle. The American people, as a whole, are not well informed on economic matters. The scientific study of economics in its modern form is quite young. Enormous implications for the school flow from the challenge of bringing the vast majority of the population up to a minimum level of economic understanding so that they can participate in policy-making in regard to economic problems.

The most important basic institution in all cultures, including the present, is the family. There are some factors in the present culture that make the family of crucial importance now. It is structuring the basic personalities of the future citizens of an uncertain world. Mutual respect and adaptability seem to be desirable personality characteristics in an America that is becoming increasingly dependent upon the rest of the world at a time when the very nature of that world is rapidly changing. The family, like other institutions, is also in a process of change; it is probable that there will emerge a type of family based on mutual respect and companionship, better suited to the uncertain future than the authoritarian family of pioneer America.

The age of anxiety in which we live now has given rise to an enormous increase of problems in the area of mental health. The extreme complexity of our culture and the rapidity of change have confronted many individuals with conditions that undermine their basic emotional security. Frustrations and anxieties beset many people. An increasing number of persons in our culture are being hospitalized for mental illness. Surely the school bears a responsibility to prepare individuals to be better equipped to deal with the problems of modern life. Other social institutions must cooperate in alleviating these problems that are related to mental hygiene.

Emotional problems relate not only to the personality disorganization that results in damage to the affected individual, but also to those persons who become antisocial and seek their security and recognition through committing acts that are contrary to the law of the land. Among these is the special and rapidly growing group, the juvenile delinquents. Both juvenile and adult crime is increasing. The disorganization of the home, the emphasis upon materialism in our culture, and the uncertainty about values—all are factors contributing to juvenile delinquency. Increased personal and social guidance of youth is a necessity. Home, school, church, and other social agencies must cooperate in this task.

Population pressures are very heavy in some parts of the world, where the number of persons far exceeds the presently developed resources to house, clothe, and feed them. It is also a problem in America, where the development of adequate schools, housing, and so forth has become important, even in a country as wealthy and as technologically advanced as the United States. There is, in the United States, no immediate danger of a scarcity of food and other resources, considering the country as a whole. Eventually, the problem of what is the maximum population the world can support will have to be faced on the world level. The time when this problem must be seriously considered depends upon future trends in birth and death rates and in advances in food technology.

Among the other problems that the world faces are those related to differing groups and their ability to live and work together. This is a world-wide problem as well as one within nations. We have primarily considered this problem within the American scene. The goal that is to be reached is found in the ideals of American democracy and of all the major religions. However, the immediate next steps and the processes by which we arrive at those goals are not so clear. Research in human dynamics has developed new and promising techniques in recent years. It then becomes a matter of education and cooperative endeavor to enable these techniques to be put into operation for the gradual improvement of the relationship between differing groups in our culture.

We live in a democracy characterized by a responsible, representative government. Many problems have arisen in this democracy: (1) problems of communication in an extremely complex culture; (2) problems of keeping communication free and untrammeled; (3) problems of the appropriate interpretation of the information received and the ability of the masses to arrive at appropriate decisions with respect to the information; (4) some problems of governmental structure, rising out of situations in which the governmental machinery set up for one age with one type of transportation (horse and buggy) cannot meet the problems of an age of jet propulsion. Among these problems are those of the conflicting political jurisdictions of metropolitan areas in which a growing percentage of our people do and will live.

Another of the big problems that we now face is that of living together with many other sovereign, independent nation-states in the world. This problem is aggravated because of a bipolarization of power between two nations, the United States and Soviet Russia, and their immediate friends and affiliates. The ability of these nations to work together to resolve differences and to operate through the United Nations and other international organizations must be improved in order to assure even the continued existence of the world. We have the possibility now that a worldwide war might result in the destruction of civilization as we know it. The threat of war, and arming as a deterrent to possible aggression, have vital implications for the internal policies of all countries, including the United States, where a large proportion of our energies are devoted to paying for past wars and preparing for another possible war.

We have now traced some of the outstanding facts, problems, and trends that have been set forth in the Chapters 1 through 13. In the next section we shall draw together some of the trends of the foreseeable future as these have been recently outlined by numerous experts.

THE FORESEEABLE FUTURE

Numerous scientists and other writers in recent years have freely predicted the future on the basis of what we now know.[6] This is referred to as the "foreseeable future," in contrast to some of the wild guesses often found in science fiction.

It appears to be agreed by scientists that the rate of technological change for the next twenty-five years, and most likely to the year 2000 A.D., will be at an ever-increasing pace. In the first place, the use of nuclear energy and the better use of other energy sources will enable us to increase our gross national product, so that by the year 2000, the 200 million or more people in the United States will have an average income of $5,125 per person, or $25,000 for a family of four persons (1965 dollars). This is approximately four times the average income at the present time.

Furthermore, the use of electronic and other automatic devices will enable the work of the factory and office to be more efficiently done so that the work week undoubtedly can be reduced to twenty-four hours.

Furthermore, the strides that have been made in medical science, increasing the span of life from 50 to 70 years in the past century, will certainly continue. A life span of at least 80 years will be attained within the next ten years. Any child born today might then be expected to live to the middle of the twenty-first century.

There will be a rapid increase in transportation and communication. With the use of commercial jets for long trips and the helicopter for short trips, the remote parts of the earth will be next door. We will soon have worldwide telephone service to *all* parts of the world. Worldwide TV programs have been made possible by Telstar satellite.

Advances in agriculture and in food preservation will probably enable man to feed the population of the world, which will be at least 6 billion by the year 2000 (present population over 3 billion). However, beyond that date or figure the remaining resources would likely be inadequate. Soon space would become a serious problem.

There will be great advances in the science of understanding human behavior and in the ability to use chemicals to control behavior and to alter personality patterns in some cases (tranquilizer pills are a current example). It is not likely that we will have completely solved all the problems in the field of anxieties, neuroses, and psychoses by the end of the twentieth century, but it is likely that we will be much nearer to a solution than we are at the present time.

---

[6] Among the better sources are Peter F. Drucker, *America's Next Twenty Years* (New York: Harper, 1957); Harrison Brown and others, *The Next Hundred Years: A Discussion Prepared for Leaders of American Industry* (New York: Viking, 1957); Sir George Thomson, *The Foreseeable Future* (Cambridge, England: University Press, 1955); Nigel Calder (ed.), *The World in 1984* (Baltimore, Md.: Penguin, 1965). Also see additional sources in the bibliography at the end of this chapter.

There are numerous consequences of these enormous scientific and technical advances. One is that we will have to teach respect for new ideas. This must include both the acceptance of technological changes themselves and the acceptance of the new patterns of living and institutions these changes make necessary. One of the characteristics of life in the future will be an enormous increase in the amount of leisure time. That leisure might mean that we could have a new renaissance of culture in America. The part that the school can play in this is, of course, quite basic. One of the main educational jobs of society and of the school, society's institution for doing that job, would be to teach for "adjustability," not for "adjustment" only. "Adjustment" implies education for a static society, whereas "adjustability" implies that the student can adjust himself and his institutions to changes that come about after his education has been completed.

EDUCATION FOR THE FORESEEABLE FUTURE

The authors believe that the information obtained from the social sciences, from the past history of man's social trends, and from these forecasts of the future, has certain definite implications for education. They have drawn specific implications in each of the chapters as the data has been presented. On the basis of their understanding of the nature of our culture and its recent changes as developed from data from the social sciences and psychology, and on the basis of a set of values they consider appropriate to education in a democratic society, they set forth the following as over-all suggestions for persons responsible for decision-making for education. Many of these are related to the basic questions raised in Chapter 1 as part of their purposes in writing a book presenting this analysis of society.

The authors believe that the schools have a very definite responsibility for providing a curriculum that will keep boys and girls apprised of the changes occurring in our society, the nature of the emerging society, and the trends in that society. Because the amount of knowledge is so great and being added to so rapidly, it is impossible ever to teach boys and girls all of the information they will need. It therefore becomes important that we teach boys and girls the process of seeking knowledge when needed—the scientific method and how to use the resources from the social and other sciences. This means that to the fundamental processes—important as they may be—must be added the basic job of teaching boys and girls to locate, verify, interpret, and apply knowledge (in short, research skills).

The fact that we live in a changing world means further that we must help boys and girls to develop a quality of adjustability. To be educated for adjustability means that the child must develop the ability to change as conditions warrant, must be able to recognize his own limitations and adjust to them, and must learn not only to operate within those limitations but also to grow within them. The youngster must develop a frame of mind that will enable him to see that new conditions require new remedies. The idea of adjustability and more is found in all of these concepts. We are educating children now who will live a great part of their lives in the twenty-first century under conditions different in many ways from those we have at present.

The increased amount of leisure time means that we must educate the youngsters for creative use of leisure. This does not mean a purely passive use of leisure or a routine whiling away of time. It means teaching for the creative use of talents, perhaps in a new intellectual renaissance. Creativity can be encouraged in all fields. The amount of wealth we have and the amount of time now available should enable us, with an appropriate background from our educational system, to forge ahead in the field of the creative arts.

The fact that our boys and girls must have a readiness to use unknown ways to solve problems that are not known means that we must teach problem-solving—the scientific method. About the only way to teach the problem-solving procedure is to give youngsters practice in solving problems while they are in school. An important part of problem-solving is, of course, the getting of the facts and information necessary for such solutions. But facts and information are not enough. Boys and girls must have practice in the actual solving of problems that are important to them.

The recent developments of the social sciences that indicate the fact that we as human beings are a product of our culture have many implications for the quality of the experiences we have in school. We are a product of our experiences. To the extent to which we adopt democratic methods in our schools, are taught how to solve our problems, and are helped to clarify our values—to that extent we will be better able to operate as adults in this very complex democratic social order.

The breakdown of values due to the rapidly changing society, and the urbanization of our culture with the consequent juxtaposition of differing and conflicting value systems, have led to confusion in values on the part of many individuals. The school must place more emphasis upon helping each boy and girl to arrive at a set of values he can live by.

Educators need to become greatly concerned with education in the area of values.[7]

Any idea that the thinker's job is to teach only his subject matter, his discipline, and not values is a major crime.

It is not enough to help children know their values. We must also assist children in their ability to collect evidence, compare, and select the priority value when they are confronted with conflicting values.

Further, teachers can be a "significant other" if they are not hollow men.

[7] Dr. Kimball Wiles in *ASCD News Exchange* (April 1964), p. 15. By permission.

Teachers should stand for the basic American values that enable a person to live effectively in plural cultures.

They should stand for the continuation of the human race. If human life is blotted from the face of the earth, there is no point in discussing other values.

They should be for the development of the potential of each human being. Simply maintaining mankind is not enough.

They should make the inclusive approach, which accepts all men as being important.

They should not want all people to accept the American culture, but work to develop a single moral community where all possess the same fundamental rights and obligations.

They should value an inclusive approach that will assign all men the same rights without insisting that they live by the same light.

They should stand for freedom of thought, worship, press and speech.

They should see differences and the exploration of it as the doorway to new insight, not as a threat to our cherished values.

They should see the interaction of peoples as the mutual seeking of more insight.

They should become more open rather than more protective.

They should be optimistic. They should believe that the future can be better.

They should see change as progress because they can make intelligent choices and [use] each action as a move in the direction of our destiny. Unless a given step is final, each advance can increase our vision and make possible more intelligent planning of our future.

Just what the affect of automation will be upon the nature of the school's job in the area of vocational and general education is not fully known at this time. However, it probably means that we ought to have a good general-education program for all of our students and postpone specific vocational education to nearer the time when the person is certain about the occupation he will follow. Very likely this specific training for the highly technical jobs of the period of automation ought to be given in institutions that are post-high school as high schools are now understood —two more years for boys and girls of ages 18 or 19. There is much evidence (in the mid-1960's) that the post-high school vocational institute or junior college is entering a period of rapid expansion. For the more highly complex jobs, the technical, professional, and engineering schools would be more appropriate institutions.

In this emerging educational system—based upon the educational implications of the findings of the social sciences, particularly philosophy, sociology, and psychology—the authors envision the schools and the teachers as being leaders of our cultural life and playing an important part in the communities in which they are located. Their leadership would operate not only among the children and youth but also among the adults. The authors do not envision the school as determining the direction or the nature of society, but as stimulating thinking and helping all the people to use the problem-solving methods learned in school to develop appropriate institutions and appropriate behavior for the kind of world that is emerging. The center of study of this school of the future would be man himself and his relations with other men—the new "humanities."

As a concluding section of this book we present a quotation, which, perhaps, succinctly expresses some of the propositions to which the writers subscribe. George Counts, after a masterly analysis of our present industrial age and of its conflicting social and technological trends, lists the following as needs for the "emerging industrial age."[8] This is a statement of goals for education on which it is possible that most would agree *as goals*, even though they might disagree sharply about how we should accomplish these goals.

EDUCATION FOR INDIVIDUAL EXCELLENCE

We need an education dedicated to the achievement of individual excellence of the highest order.

EDUCATION FOR A SOCIETY OF EQUALS

We need an education that will preserve, vitalize, and strengthen the principle of equality in our country.

We need an education that will make clear the meaning and worth of the principle of equality.

We need an education that will reveal the deficiencies in our heritage and the dangers threatening the principle of equality in the contemporary world.

We need an education that will cultivate in the young the spirit and practice, the attitudes and loyalties of equality.

EDUCATION FOR A GOVERNMENT OF FREE MEN

We need an education that will preserve, vitalize, and strengthen the principle of political liberty in our country.

We need an education that will make clear the meaning of political liberty.

We need an education that will give understanding of our American heritage of political liberty.

We need an education that will reveal the dangers threatening the life of political liberty today.

We need an education that will cultivate in the young a deep sense of worth ... and practice of political liberty.

EDUCATION FOR AN ECONOMY OF SECURITY AND PLENTY

We need an education that will be directed toward the achievement of an economy of security and plenty.

[8] From George S. Counts, *Education and American Civilization*, pp. 311–430, *passim*. Copyright, 1952, Teachers College, Columbia University. Used by permission of the publisher. Cf. to a list of challenges the school must face, found in Ralph L. Pounds and Robert L. Garretson, *Principles of Modern Education* (New York: Macmillan, 1962), pp. 428–437.

We need an education that will make clear the full nature of the task of developing an economy of security and plenty.

We need an education that will provide occupational guidance and training of the highest order.

We need an education that will insure general economic understanding.

We need an education that will develop the moral foundations of an economy of security and plenty.

EDUCATION FOR A CIVILIZATION OF BEAUTY AND GRANDEUR

We need an education that will prepare the young to build a civilization of beauty and grandeur.

We need an education in the arts that will make full use of our resources.

We need an education that will foster a broad and catholic artistic tradition.

We need an education that will discover and encourage the development of creative talents in all the arts.

EDUCATION FOR AN ENDURING CIVILIZATION

We need an education that will be dedicated to the building of an enduring civilization.

We need an education that will stress the critical nature of the present age.

We need an education that will instruct the young in the sources of civilizational decay and death.

We need an education that will stress the study of the future.

We need an education that will foster in the young a deep and enlightened love of country.

EDUCATION FOR A WORLD COMMUNITY

We need an education dedicated to the building of a world community.

We need an education that will foster a sustained sense of urgency and responsibility.

We need an education that will give a sense of the magnitude of the task of building a tolerable world order.

We need an education that will convey to the young an informed understanding of the Soviet Union and world Communism.

We need an education that will prepare positively for world citizenship.

We need an education that will keep America strong in every way.

The challenge to education from a set of objectives such as those listed by Counts is very great. The demands made on the teacher are heavy. By and large, teachers are at present inadequately equipped to discharge the duties necessitated by the problems posed by the changing society. There are many communities in our society that at present are not prepared to support the teacher adequately, either financially, socially, or with sympathetic approval as to the difficulty of his task. The status of the teacher of America must be greatly improved. He must be given compensation adequate for living a greatly enriched life. Efforts must be made to help him gain a comprehensive and profound understanding of the nature of the society in which we live and of the implications of that society for education. The net result of all this will be to develop a school system that will help the American people to achieve more fully the greatness inherent in the American democratic society, and to achieve it while maintaining a *free* democratic society.

Selected Bibliography

Baade, Fritz. *The Race to the Year 2000: Our Future a Paradise or the Suicide of Mankind.* Garden City, N.Y.: Doubleday, 1962. Pp. xix + 246.

Barnett, Lincoln. *The Universe and Dr. Einstein.* New York: New American Library, 1957. Pp. 128. Probably the most readable of the lay books on the implications of Einsteinian science.

Boulding, Kenneth E. *The Meaning of the Twentieth Century.* New York: Harper & Row, 1964. Pp. xvi + 199.

Boyke, Huge (ed.). *Science and the Future of Mankind.* Bloomington: Indiana University Press, 1961. Pp. vii + 380.

Brinkman, William W., and Stanley Lehrer, (eds.). *Automation, Education, and Human Values.* New York: School and Society Books, 1966. Pp. 419.

Brown, Harrison, James Bonner, and John Weir. *The Next Hundred Years: A Discussion Prepared for Leaders of American Industry.* New York: Viking Press, 1957. Pp. 193.

Calder, Nigel (ed.). *The World in 1984.* Baltimore: Penguin, 1965. Two volumes. Pp. 205.

Clark, Arthur C. *Profiles of the Future: An Inquiry into the Limits of the Possible.* London: Victor Gollancz Limited, 1962. Pp. 220.

Clark, Burton R. *Educating the Expert Society.* San Francisco: Chandler, 1962. Pp. xi + 320.

Counts, George S. *Education and American Civilization.* New York: Bureau of Publications, Teachers College, Columbia University, 1952. Pp. xiv + 491. A careful examination of the implications of the American way of life for education.

————. *Education and the Foundations of Human Freedom.* Pittsburgh: University of Pittsburgh Press, 1962. Pp. 104.

Drucker, Peter F. *America's Next Twenty Years.* New York: Harper & Row, 1957. Pp. 114.

Ernst, Morris L. *Utopia 1976.* New York: Holt, Rinehart & Winston, 1955. Pp. 305. Interesting nontechnical appraisal of the near future.

Fischer, Louis and Donald R. Thomas. *Social Foundations of Educational Decisions.* Belmont, Calif.: Wadsworth, 1965. Pp. 371.

Foley, John J. (ed.). *Human History: A Race Between Education and Catastrophe.* Philadelphia: Duquesne University Press, 1963. Pp. v + 119.

Fortune Editors. *The Fabulous Future: America in 1980.* New York: Dutton, 1956. Pp. 206. Symposium.

Frank, Lawrence K. *Nature and Human Nature.* New Brunswick, N.J.: Rutgers University Press, 1951. Pp. ix + 175. An excellent summary of modern knowledge about man.

FRANKEL, CHARLES. *The Case for Modern Man.* New York: Harper & Row, 1956. Pp. 240. An excellent survey and appraisal of man's cultural development, with a look to the future.

GEEN, ELIZABETH, and others (eds.). *Man and the Modern City.* Pittsburgh: University of Pittsburgh Press, 1963. Pp. 13.

HANNA, PAUL R. (ed.). *Education: An Instrument of National Goals.* New York: McGraw-Hill Book Co., 1962. Pp. viii + 210.

HARRISON, GEORGE RUSSELL. *What Man May Be: The Human Side of Science.* New York: Morrow, 1956. Pp. 278.

HUNNICUTT, CLARENCE W. (ed.). *Education A.D. 2000.* Syracuse, N.Y.: Syracuse University Press, 1956. Pp. 321.

HUXLEY, JULIAN. *Man in the Modern World.* New York: New American Library, 1952. Pp. 191.

LUNDBERG, FERDINAND. *The Coming World Transformation.* Garden City, N.Y.: Doubleday, 1963. Pp. 395.

LUNDSBERG, HANS H., LEONARD L. FISCHMAN, and JOSEPH L. FISHER. *Resources in America's Future: Pattern of Requirements and Availabilities, 1960–2000.* Baltimore: Johns Hopkins Press, 1963. Pp. xx + 1017.

MacIVER, ROBERT M. *Academic Freedom in Our Time.* New York: Columbia University Press, 1955. Pp. xiv + 329.

MEDAWAR, P. B. *The Future of Man.* New York: Mentor Books, 1959. Pp. xi + 125.

MICHAEL, DONALD N. *The Next Generation: The Prospects Ahead for the Youth Today and Tomorrow.* New York: Random House, 1965. Pp. xxvi + 218.

MONTAGUE, M. F. ASHLEY. *The Direction of Human Development: Biological and Social Bases.* New York: Harper & Row, 1955. Pp. ix + 404. An excellent summary of what is now known about man—a set of facts and understanding quite in contrast with nineteenth-century and earlier knowledge.

———. *Education and Human Relations.* New York: Grove Press, 1958. Pp. 191.

———. *Modern Man.* Chicago: Science Research Associates, 1956. Pp. 48. "The story of his present development and future possibilities."

MUMFORD, LEWIS. *The Transformation of Man.* New York: Harper & Row, 1956. Pp. xviii + 249. A well-written essay on the development of modern man and an outlook for the future.

N.E.A., Educational Policies Commission. *Universal Opportunity for Education Beyond the High School.* Washington, D.C.: The Commission, 1964. Pp. 36.

———, Project on Instruction. *Education in a Changing Society.* Washington, D.C.: National Education Association, 1963. Pp. 166.

THOMSON, GEORGE. *The Foreseeable Future.* Cambridge, Eng.: University Press, 1955. Pp. vii + 166. An excellent nontechnical discussion of the technical problems and possibilities of future advance in world technology.

TOYNBEE, ARNOLD J. *America and the World Revolution and Other Essays.* New York: Oxford University Press, 1962. Pp. 231. Excellent presentation of the thesis that America did represent a truly revolutionary development and that her present challenge is to continue her revolution.

Wagar, Warren W. *The City of Man: Prophecies of a World Civilization in Twentieth Century Thought.* Boston: Houghton Mifflin, 1963. Pp. x + 310.

Wilson, Logan. "Higher Education and 1984," *School and Society,* **93** (October 2, 1965), 343–346.

Selected Films

Assignment: Tomorrow (N.E.A.) 32 min

Deals with the vital role of the teacher in our culture; points out importance of the teacher as a teacher, as a community member, as a professional person, indicating roles played and contributions made in each. Also shows the activities in a modern schoolroom that help students to develop the ability to think for themselves, to be conscious of community needs, and to participate and cooperate with others. Contrasts this type of school with that in which adequate support is not supplied by the community.

Bertrand Russell Discusses Mankind's Future (Chantern) 13½ min

In speaking of his fears and hopes for the future, Lord Russell sees the possibility of a world so organized and static that "there will be no fun to be had anywhere." On the positive side, he feels that with education and the realization that many of the world's troubles lie in individual psychology, we could abolish war, poverty, and disease.

Better Tomorrow (Overseas Branch of OWI) 20 min

Shows progressive-education systems in three New York schools, demonstrating how learning is connected with everyday experiences in children's lives on the preschool, junior high, and senior high school levels.

Broader Concept of Method (McGraw-Hill) Two reels. 32 min

First reel: "Developing Pupil Interest" (13 min)

Presents the conventional, teacher-dominated, lesson-hearing type of school, followed by some alternative techniques designed to achieve broader educational objectives. Shows effects of methods on attitudes, response, and learning.

Second reel: "Teacher and Pupils Planning Together" (19 min)

Students learning to work together. They organize into functional groups, plan and carry out an investigation, prepare and present their findings, evaluate what they have learned.

Community Resources in Teaching (Iowa State University) 19 min

Explains how the schools can profitably use the community as a laboratory; follows a social-studies class as it visits a newspaper plant during a study of communications. Also points out the value of having resource people from the community come into the classroom.

Design of American Public Education (McGraw-Hill) 16 min

Compares and contrasts the operation of the "assembly line" kind of educational process with one that is tailored to meet the needs of today's young people and the needs of the community. Typical state, county, and local situations are presented.

Education for Democracy (Missouri State Teachers Assn.) 22 min
  Depicts with actual classroom scenes the manner in which Missouri schools achieve the purposes of education in our American democracy as outlined by the Educational Policies Commission of the N.E.A.

Learning Democracy Through School-Community Projects (University of Michigan & D.A.R.) 21 min
  Depicts experiences in democratic learning that are provided in Michigan schools; includes student councils, student elections, Junior Red Cross, youth centers, a community conference, a school safety patrol, an audio-visual service club, and a rural field day.

Learning for Life (N.E.A.) 28 min
  Gives the view of adult education as a new force in public schools through which people can learn to live for themselves and their communities.

New Schools for Old (MMA) 10 min
  Contrasts little red school house, its methods and results with modern classrooms and up-to-date techniques.

Preparation of Teachers (U.S. State Dept.) 20 min
  Uses the experiences of two prospective teachers during their training period to show that teaching is not just the business of getting information across but, includes sharing children's excitement and experiences; emphasizes the fact that a teacher must have a well-rounded background in order to help children to become useful and responsible citizens.

Satellites, Schools, and Survival (N.E.A.) 30 min
  A pictorial history of education in the United States during the last half century. Points up the challenge of present problems.

School (Ind.) 24 min
  Shows a progressive-education school in action. The dialogue is by fifth grade children in the classroom. Indicates that intelligent citizenship in a democracy is best achieved by permitting children at school to develop their own aptitudes and interests according to their individual abilities.

School in Centerville (N.E.A.) 20 min
  Depicts a life-centered program in a rural community setting. Has the character of a documentary report.

School and Community (McGraw-Hill) 13 min
  Animated film. Shows a school isolated from community neither benefiting its community nor being benefited by it; then describes the advantages to be derived from school and community cooperation.

Schoolhouse in the Red (Kellog) 42 min
  Describes a typical rural community debating whether to change from a system of individual small rural schools to a larger school-district system; discusses the sociological and psychological factors involved and pictures the facial expressions, actions, and opinions of the local citizens; shows how the little school district has become outmoded and emphasizes the considerations involved in the change of an educational system.

We Plan Together (Teachers College, Columbia University) 20 min
  An eleventh grade core class illustrates its ways of working, showing how needs and abilities are used in relation to problems, interests, and fields of knowledge.

Wilson Dam School (TVA and Alabama State Dept. of Ed.) 22 min

Depicts daily activities at the Wilson Dam School in Alabama. From the time the elementary pupils arrive in school buses until they leave, they are seen engaging in functional learning experiences, including such activities as taking care of pets and chickens, group singing, gardening, and games that require coordination and imagination. A medical examination given at the beginning of each year and parent cooperation and visitation are also shown.

Index